2000

Directory of American Poetry Books

Third Edition

Volume III

2000

Directory of American Poetry Books

Third Edition, Volume III

Compiled by Poets House through the Poetry Publication Showcase

POETS HOUSE

NEW YORK

Published by Poets House

copyright © 2000 by Poets House

Third Edition, Volume III

**LIBRARY OF CONGRESS
CATALOGING-IN-PUBLICATION DATA**

Directory of American Poetry Books/
[edited by] Poets House. — 3rd ed., vol III

p.   cm.
Includes Index
I.   American   poetry — Bibliography.   2.   Literature publishing — United States — Directories. I. Poets House (Firm)
Z1231.P7D57 2000
{PS303}   00-17778
016.811008 — dc20   CIP
ISBN 1-890695-02-5 (pb.)

Printed in the United States of America
Distributed by Poets House
72 Spring St., New York, NY 10012
212-431-7920
http://www.poetshouse.org

Contents

Acknowledgments

We wish to thank Deborah Pease and the Middlecott Foundation, Mary Kaplan and the J.M. Kaplan Fund, without whose help this volume of the Directory would not have been published. We acknowledge with gratitude the help of the National Endowment for the Arts and The Greenwall Foundation.

We thank all of those whose work on the Poetry Publication Showcase helped to gather the information reflected here, as well as those who assisted in the preparation of this volume, including: Suzanne Axtell, Carmen Britez, Dayna Crozier, Eileen Cuascut, Molly Desjardins, Molly Dempsey, Carolina Ebeid, Ellen Ivey, Dave Johnson, Kasey Jueds, Jeanne Lambert, Laura Minor, Bob Swiggert, Sylvia Williams, and Anne Wright. Special thanks to Chermayeff & Geismar Inc., especially Ivan Chermayeff and Chuck Rudy, for the cover design.

We thank the poets and publishers who continue to advise us on these projects, and all of those who contribute their books to the Showcase exhibit, whose enthusiasm encourages and supports us.

About Poets House

Poets House is a comfortable, accessible place for poetry — a 35,000 volume poetry library and meeting place that invites poets and the public to step into the living tradition of poetry. Its resources and literary events document the wealth and diversity of modern poetry and stimulate dialogue on issues of poetry in culture.

Founded in 1985 by Stanley Kunitz and the late Elizabeth Kray, Poets House is one of the only independent literary centers in the nation devoted to poetry. Through programs such as the annual Poetry Publication Showcase and Poetry in The Branches, Poets House is building a national archive of poetry while seeking to encourage broader readership and better representation of poetry in bookstores and libraries around the country.

Poets House is located at 72 Spring street, New York, NY 10012 and welcomes visitors between the hours of 11:00 am and 7:00 pm, Tuesday through Friday, and 11:00 am and 4:00 pm on Saturday. A non-profit organization, Poets House depends on donations for its support. For information about making a donation or becoming a member of Poets House, or for information about our programs and services, please write, call 212-431-7920, or visit our website at http://www.poetshouse.org.

About This Directory

The *Directory of American Poetry Books* is a buyer's guide for poetry readers, a publishing guide for poets, and a chart of the current status of the poetic voice in America. The only bibliographic resource that attempts to reflect the incredible diversity of poetry publishing at the turn of this century, the three volumes of the Directory provide information about all books published since the fall of 1991 by publishers of every kind from all parts of the United States.

This volume (III) includes comprehensive listings for books published from the fall of 1996 to the spring of 1999. The prior volume (II) covers the period between fall, 1994, and spring, 1996. The first volume (I) includes books published between June, 1991, and November, 1994. More current listings (including the rest of 1999 and many from the spring of 2000) are available on the *Online Directory* at http://www.poetshouse.org.

The Directory grows out of the Poetry Publication Showcase, inaugurated by Poets House in June, 1992. An annual exhibit and festival of events celebrating the year's new books, the Showcase was established by Executive Director Lee Briccetti to reflect Poets House's mission to make the range of modern poetry available to the public and to stimulate public dialogue on issues of poetry in culture.

Each year approximately 1,300 new books from publishers of all kinds — including commercial, university, independent and micro presses — are exhibited at Poets House. In tandem with the exhibit, readings and panel discussions bring poets together with publishers, reviewers and booksellers to explore issues in poetry publishing. The entire exhibit is then brought to the American Library Association's annual conference, a gathering of over 20,000 librarians.

The *Directory of American Poetry Books,* in print and on the web, extends the reach of the Showcase, providing bibliographic detail for all of the books displayed since the start of the project. As an inclusive rather than a selective listing, the *Directory* lists all books of poetry sent to us except those intended for children and those published outside the United States. While we make every effort to insure that these listings are complete, Poets House depends on the active participation of publishers for the information included in the *Directory*.

We include information about books from commercial, university, and independent presses. In addition, due to the long literary tradition of self-publishing, self-published books are included if they find their way into our hands. Further, we believe that no bibliographic reference could adequately reflect the range of the current poetic voice of America if it excluded author subsidized works. Our goal in editing this volume has been to draw a distinction between subsidized and vanity presses, excluding the latter.

These are difficult distinctions to draw and complete information is often difficult to obtain. Therefore, inclusion in these pages should not be interpreted as an endorsement by Poets House of any publishing enterprise.

Organized by author, each main entry also provides the editor (anthologies and posthumous publications only), translator, title, number of pages, ISBN, city and state of publication, publisher, and publication date, as well as a brief description of each book. If both paper and hardcover editions are available, both are described. For a paper edition, the abbreviation "pap." precedes the price. The descriptions provided for each book are excerpts from published reviews, recommendations provided by other poets or descriptive prose written by the publisher. In each case, the source of the quotation is identified.

A complete index of publishers begins on page 480. For each publisher we provide an office address, and, when it differs, an ordering address, as well as phone, fax, e-mail and website information. Wherever addresses provided in Volumes I or II differ from those provided here, these are the more recent. Names listed beneath the address are publishing staff members, ideally members of both the editorial and the publicity departments. Distributors and wholesalers are indicated next. For a list of frequently used abbreviations and for phone numbers of those distributors and wholesalers who appear most often, see the Key to the Index by Publisher on page 571.

New this year, the *Online Directory* provides information for over 3200 titles, including those featured in the 2000 Poetry Publication Showcase. The *Online Directory* is fully searchable by title, author, publisher, publication date, book type (i.e. chapbook, anthology, full length collection) and by any word in the description. It provides detailed publisher contact information, and will eventually provide links to publishers and to distributors. The *Online Directory* is free to anyone who wishes to use it at http://www.poetshouse.org.

If used properly, the *Directory* is an excellent source of information for poets seeking a publisher. When submitting your work, look first to see who publishes work aesthetically or thematically similar to your own. Then consider the track record of those poets already on their list. If, for instance, yours will be a first book, look for publishers of other first books. Examine the main entry for each of the books listed in the index for that publisher. Read at least some of the books themselves. Confirm that the publisher accepts unsolicited manuscripts by consulting *Poets Market*, or one of the other resources available. Remember the "tao" of poetry publishing: poets must support the all too often fragile literary journals and presses if they want their own work to be supported by them.

As a reader and/or buyer of poetry, you can use the *Directory* in much the same way, profiting from the editorial choices of the publishers as well as from the recommendations of reviewers or other poets provided in the main entries. We urge readers seeking to buy poetry books to visit their local bookstores. Many bookstores participate in STOP (Single Title Order Plan) and will be able to place a special order for you. You can also contact the publisher directly. However, we suggest that you call or write to the publisher before ordering by mail, as shipping and handling charges are not included in the prices listed here and most publishers can only fill pre-paid orders.

Remember that placing orders through your local bookstore supports the art of poetry both by supporting the bookseller and by demonstrating publicly your demand for poetry. Remember too that urging the acquisitions librarian at your local library to order poetry books for the collection ensures better access to poetry for everyone in your community.

Marni Ludwig, Showcase Coordinator
Jane Preston, Series Editor
Lee Briccetti, Executive Director

Abbott, Steve. *A Short History of the Word.* 32p. pap. $7.95 (0-944-754-341). Johnstown, OH: Pudding House Publications, Spring 1996; Spring 1999 (new edition). Poems that illustrate the individual's journey in the city and popular culture. — Pudding House Publications

Abee, Steve. *King Planet.* 143p. pap. $12.00 (1-884615-14-7). San Diego, CA: Incommunicado Press, 1997. Abee has a ringside seat at the circus. He lives in the city's bright orange heart. He is amazed by its streets, by its life, its death, by everything. In pursuit of prophetic agency he grabs at each thought as it is presented to him and squeezes it until it glows like a cultured pearl. —Lewis MacAdams

Aberg, William. *The Listening Chamber.* 57p. $18.00 (1-55728-464-4). pap. $12.00 (1-55728-463-6). Fayetteville, AR: University of Arkansas Press, 1997. These poems are the product of intolerable agony, misfortune, and despair, miraculously redeemed by eloquent conversation into acts of art. This book is frightening, forbidding, and inspiring. — Anthony Hecht. Few contemporary poets can manipulate light with the care and effectiveness of this one. These poems glow from within, although that light often comes from a tiny flicker or a drug-induced warmth. His surfaces come to life with texture and color from the play of light upon them, and the dreadful becomes even more dreadful in such a rich, luminous world. —Richard Shelton

Ablon, Steven Luria. *Flying Over Tasmania.* 63p. pap. $10.00 (1-56474-227-X). Santa Barbara, CA: Fithian Press, Fall 1997. Ablon brings to his poetry an admirable openness to diverse experience. His emotional accessibility makes us feel he is speaking directly to us of the mysteries of the human heart. It is the human warmth, the feeling for people, that one carries away from time spent with this fine book of poetry. —Richard Tillinghast

Ackerman, Al. *Meetings With Improbable Danglers: The Poets Meet John M. Bennett.* 28p. pap. $5.00 (0-9353-5099-3). Columbus, OH: Luna Bisonte Prods, Spring 1998. Startling, recombinant poems in which the poetry of John M. Bennett is blended with that of Whitman, Paz, Simic,

Catullus, and others. —Luna Bisonte Prods

Ackerman, Diane. *I Praise My Destroyer.* 128p. $18.50 (0-679-44878-0). New York, NY: Random House, Spring 1998. Vivid, playful, abundant, these poems constitute a directory of colors, an assembly of weathers, waters, creatures, and a bold, brash, invincible vote of confidence. — Anthony Hecht. In I Praise My Destroyer, Ackerman demonstrates once again her love for the specific language that rises from the juncture of self and the natural world, and her skillful use of that language. Whether she turns her attention to the act of eating an apricot "the color of shame and dawn," or to "the omnipotence of light," or to grief when "All the greens of summer have blown apart," her linking of unique images, her energetic wit and whimsy, her compassionate investment in life, always bring new pleasures and perceptions to the reader. —Pattiann Rogers

Ackerman, Diane, and Jeanne Mackin, eds. *The Book of Love.* 827p. $29.95 (0-393-04589-7). New York, NY: Norton, W.W., and Company, Fall 1997. Culled from love letters, poetry, fiction, personal essays, and memories, this lavish anthology celebrates love's many moods and majesties, from flirtation, seduction, and marriage to the tempests of suspicions, jealousy, and heartache. Included are poems ranging from Marvell to Ashbery, Browning to Graham, and letters from Baudelaire, George Eliot and Henry Miller. — W.W. Norton

Adair, Virginia Hamilton. *Ants on the Melon.* 160p. pap. $12.95 (0-375-75229-3). New York, NY: Random House, Spring 1996; Spring 1999 (new paper). Adair speaks directly and unaffectedly, in an accent stripped of mannerism and allusion. Ants on the Melon exhibits enough formal variety, freshness, and intelligence to confirm, at one stroke, that Adair is a poet of accomplishment and originality. —New York Times Book Review. Extraordinarily moving. Her voice is clear, assured, varied, and utterly her own. —New York Review of Books. She is very, very, very good, the fine, agile turn like an arabesque on ice that blasts, lightning-like, into a ghastly abyss. —E. Annie Proulx. How bright and unmuddled and unaffected and unswerving these poems are. There's such aplomb, no faking, such a hard true edge.

They never miss. —Alice Munro

Adair, Virginia Hamilton. *Beliefs and Blasphemies.* 109p. $22.00 (0-375-50017-0). New York, NY: Random House, Fall 1998. Adair treats religious themes with passion, wit, technical skill and accessibility. —Random House. She blends the surprise and precision of Sylvia Plath's poetry with the comforts of traditional form and feeling. Her work is both old-fashioned and contemporary, sophisticated and innocent. —San Francisco Chronicle. This collection points the way back to an American tradition of religious poetry understood and cherished by the likes of Elizabeth Bishop and Louise Bogan. —Publishers Weekly. Adair's poems are startling, funny, erotic, tragic, wise, sometimes all these at once. With what wit and intelligence she awakens the ordinary world. —Galway Kinnell

Adam, Cornel. *A Lookout's Letter.* 32p. pap. $7.00 (83-904541-5-7). Larkspur, CA: Mandrake Press, Fall 1997. Powerful poems, they are refreshing in every sense of the word — in the mastery displayed by their craftsmanship, in their simplicity of language and in the depth of their

philosophy. —John Waddington-Feather

Adams. *Conversations With Keith.* 96p. pap. $9.95 (1-882897-11-0). Fort Bragg, CA: Lost Coast Press, Fall 1997. This is a smart, beautiful and compassionate book of poems; the finest book of Adams' yet. —David St. John

Addiss, Stephen, with Fumiko and Akira Yamamoto. *Haiku People: Big and Small, in Poems and Prints.* 112p. $16.95 (0-8348-0417-4). New York, NY: Weatherhill, Spring 1998. One hundred forty-three haiku and over forty-six paintings and drawings, displaying the delicacy, charm, and wisdom of the best Japanese literature and art. —Weatherhill

Adnan, Etel. *There: In the Light and the Darkness of the Self and the Other.* 70p. pap. $13.00 (0-942996-28-3). Sausalito, CA: Post-Apollo Press, Spring 1997. There pursues questions that are at once ancient and modern, united in their urgency and difficulty. The "there" and "here" of Adnan's thought seek to engage the absences and presences of history and its processes, from the personal to the global and back again. In its investigations of the ways in which such apparent oppositions as self and other, "metropolis" and "periphery" are constructed, understood and, often, violently maintained, There asks that we turn with renewed attention to some of the most important matters before us. —Robert Kaufman. [Adnan's is] a committed social and political vision, a passionate and engaged post-modernism. —Michael Beard

Adoff, Arnold, ed. Drawings by Benny Andrews. *I Am the Darker Brother: An Anthology of Modern Poems by African Americans, Revised Edition.* 208p. $16.00 (0-689-81241-8). Simon & Schuster Books for Young Readers, Fall 1997. Simple, spare, and revealing, this new edition of a superb collection of poetry leads the reader into the heart of the African American experience. Included are, among others, Langston Hughes, James Weldon Johnson, Maya Angelou, Lucille Clifton, Amiri Baraka, Gwendolyn Brooks, and Paul Laurence Dunbar, and, in a foreword that is an original poem written for this new edition, Nikki Giovanni. —Simon & Schuster

Adolphe, Bruce. *What To Listen For in the World.* 104p.

$17.95 (0-87910-085-0). New York, NY: Limelight Editions, Fall 1996. With disciplined lyricism and entirely devoid of technical jargon, Adolphe's book probes into the heart of such matters as the role of memory and imagination in creative expression, the meaning of inspiration, spirituality in music, the challenge of arts education and how music communicates. The author, acclaimed for his pre-concert lectures for The Chamber Music Society of Lincoln Center since 1992, also considers the work of composers such as Bach, Mozart, Beethoven, Schumann and Ravel. —Limelight Editions. Adolphe is an inspired teacher and a wonderful musician with an unusual ability to translate complex musical concepts into words that any musician or music lover will appreciate. —Itzhak Perlman. What a great book! And what a great idea — to explain music via poetry. —Lukas Foss

Agoos, Julie. *Calendar Year.* 142p. $19.95 (1-878818-56-2). Riverdale-on-Hudson, NY: Sheep Meadow Press, Fall 1996; Spring 1999 (new paper). This title is currently on display at Poets House as part of the 2000 Poetry Publication Showcase.

Complete bibliographic information will be available soon.

Agosín, Marjorie. Translated by Celeste Kostopulos-Cooperman, Cola Franzen and Mary G. Berg. *An Absence of Shadows.* 209p. pap. $15.00 (1-877727-92-X). Buffalo, NY: White Pine Press, Fall 1998. Published to celebrate the 50th Anniversary of the United Nations Declaration of Human Rights, this book joins two of Agosin's most acclaimed books with new work. Zones of Pain and Circles of Madness, both now out of print, give voice to the victims of the corrupt dictatorships that existed in Latin America during the past three decades; they insist that we remember what happened and refuse to let it happen again. —White Pine Press

Agosín, Marjorie. Translated by Richard Schaaf with Cola Franzen and Mónica Bruno. *Dear Anne Frank.* 144p. pap. $10.95 (0-87451-857-1). University Press of New England/Brandeis University Press, Spring 1998. With transparency and authenticity, Agosín leads us through the universe of Anne Frank. With her poems as our guide, we traverse history's darkest corridors, yet are reminded of the endurance of the human spirit.

This is a poetry that is both memorable and haunting. — Isabel Allende. Agosín, one of the most lyrical and refined voices in Latin America, offers us in this book about Anne Frank further proof of her depth and sensibility. It is a book that must be read, illuminating poems that unveil the spirit of two extraordinary women. —Claribel Alegría

Agosín, Marjorie. Translated by Monica Galmozzi Bruno. *Melodious Women.* 160p. pap. $13.95 (0-935480-91-9). Pittsburgh, PA: Latin American Literary Review Press, Fall 1997. A celebration of individuality, beauty and courage, Melodious Women is a collection of more than eighty-five poems in tribute to women in history. From the mythical Ariadne and the literary genius Rosario Castellanos to the passionate conviction of Rachel Carson, Agosín's verses honor these accomplished, ground-breaking figures, as well as the universal roles women play. —Latin American Literary Review Press

Agosín, Marjorie. Translated by Mary G. Berg. *Starry Night.* 103p. pap. $12.00 (1-877727-66-0). Buffalo, NY: White Pine Press, Fall 1996. First published in Spanish in

1995, Starry Night won the coveted Letras de Oro Award. Agosín creates a sensual portrait of Vincent Van Gogh and his world using a vivid lexicon to recreate the artistry of Van Gogh's great works. —White Pine Press

Agran, Rick. *Crow Milk.* 80p. pap. $10.95 (1-882291-55-7). Durham, NH: Oyster River Press, Spring 1998. In Crow Milk you will find the unloved things, forgotten or unseen, returned to life, and celebrated in Agran's clear vision: crows, abandoned children, people with AIDS, the tattooed and marked ones, even famous writers playing basketball in dreamtime. In this vision, the children have seen far too much but survive into artful singing. Often, it's the adults who choose not to see and suffer the consequences. Agran cherishes all that his eye beholds. He holds it all up for us to see, with the same humor and sass as his crows, as if to say, Don't you see how it all shines? —Mekeel McBride

Aho, Margaret. *The Only Light We Read By.* 32p. pap. $15.00 (0-931659-37-X). Boise, ID: Limberlost Press, Fall 1998. Poems about growing up near Los Alamos, New Mexico during the 1950s Cold War era. —Limberlost Press

Aizenberg, Susan, Suzanne Qualls, and Mark Turpin. Edited by Askold Melnyczuk. *Take Three: AGNI New Poets Series: 2.* 96p. pap. $12.95 (1-55597-254-3). St. Paul, MN: Graywolf Press, Spring 1997. Featured in this welcome second volume in the series are collections by three poets who have contributed to AGNI's biannual journal. Internal and external sight lines unite this sampler, which delivers further on the promise of the Take Three series. —Publishers Weekly

Akhmatova, Anna. Translated by Stanley Kunitz with Max Hayward. *Poems of Akhmatova.* 173p. pap. $13.00 (0-395-86003-2). Boston, MA: Houghton Mifflin Company, Spring 1997 (paper). The acclaimed bilingual edition of verse by "an extraordinary woman, the history of an epoch mirrored in her life." —New York Times Book Review

Akiko, Yosano. Translated by Sam Hamill and Keiko Matsui Gibson. *River of Stars: Selected Poems of Yosano Akiko.* 135p. pap. $11.00 (1-57062-146-2). Boston, MA: Shambhala Publications,

Spring 1997. Akiko is one of the most famous Japanese writers of the twentieth century. Although probably best known for her exquisite erotic poetry, Akiko's work also championed the causes of feminism, pacifism, and social reform. River of Stars is the first book presenting the full breadth of her poetic vision. Included are ninety-one of Akiko's tanka (a traditional five-line form of verse) and a dozen of her longer poems written in the modern style. —Shambhala Publications

Akmakjian, Alan P. *California Picnic and Other Poems.* 71p. $29.95 (0-89002-333-6). pap. $9.95 (0-89002-330-1). Thomaston, ME: Northwoods Press, Fall 1997. Akmakjian's celebration of family traditions and high school picnics and the landscapes of Edward Hopper shows what can still be done in free verse. The tiny, intense poems of this sequence are like snapshots, absolutely accurate. —Northwoods Press

Alberti, Raphael. Translated by Carolyn L. Tipton. *To Painting.* 251p. $29.95 (0-8101-1351-1). Northwestern University Press/Hydra Books, Fall 1997. The only surviving member of the Generation of '27 — a group of poets includ-

ing Federico García Lorca, Jorge Guillén, and Vicente Aleixandre, whose work brought about a literary renaissance in Spain — Alberti is one of the great poets of the twentieth century. To Painting is the collection many critics consider his best. Each of the poems is inspired by one of three different elements of painting: the painter, the colors, or the instruments used in creating the painting. A work of grand design and noble vision, To Painting is a book not to be missed. — Northwestern University Press

Albiach, Anne-Marie. Translated by Keith and Rosmarie Waldrop. *A Geometry.* 26p. pap. $5.00 (1-886224-31-5). Providence, RI: Burning Deck, Spring 1998.

Albon, George. *Empire Life.* 72p. (1-55713-376-X). Los Angeles, CA: Littoral Books, Fall 1998. This is the first, full-length edition of Albon's work. Empire Life brings together two long pieces: the title poem is a workaday fleshing out of time spent under inner and outer American weathers; while "Cosmophagy" marks a daring incursion into the heart of the sentence, serving as both guide and treacherous ground. —Littoral Books

Albrizio, Eileen. *Messy on the Inside.* 90p. pap. $12.00 (1-889289-32-9). New Haven, CT: Ye Olde Font Shoppe, Fall 1998. Albrizio writes of ancient anguish, today's torment, and impending iniquity in both classical and modern forms and meter. —Priscilla Herrington. Sensitive topics, contemporary ones, handled expertly within the formal style. —Suzy Lamson

Alcosser, Sandra. *Except by Nature.* 82p. pap. $12.95 (1-55597-273-X). St. Paul, MN: Graywolf Press, Fall 1998. National Poetry Series winner and winner of the 1998 James Laughlin Award of The Academy of American Poets. Alcosser describes an American South that is ripe to the point of decay, where the ooze of Louisiana's swampland insinuates itself into every corner of human life, sugary, erotic, and oppressive. This is a rich, well-worked book. —Library Journal. The stitching that binds the elements within each of her poems is sure and subtle, as invisible and perfect as the stitching that creates a forest or the threads that link the stars. The poems in Except by Nature are full of the riches and the risks, the words and the contemplations of the earth, and the place of the human within those realms. —Pattiann Rogers. Except by Nature is an exceptional collection: feisty, accomplished, and mature, its poems brim with serious delights. —Eamon Grennan. Alcosser's superbly sure-voiced poems possess intelligence and passion in equal measure. Here is a poet who knows the fine-grained textures of thought, the precise distinctions of feeling, and the lush wisdom of language itself. Specific and grounded in the things of the world, yet winged with imaginative mind, Except by Nature is an extraordinary work. —Jane Hirshfield

Alegría, Claribel. Translated by Darwin Flakoll. *Thresholds / Umbrales.* 80p. pap. $10.95 (1-880684-36-5). Willimantic, CT: Curbstone Press, Fall 1996. Thresholds/Umbrales distills the life and thought of El Salvador's most beloved poet in a triumph of lyricism. —Curbstone Press. The nine parts of this long poem are rich with symbolism and acknowledge the dualities of life as we move from youth to age. —Multicultural Review

Aleshire, Joan. *The Yellow Transparents.* 97p. pap. $12.95 (1-884800-13-0). Marshfield, MA: Four Way Books, Spring 1997. These story-telling poems meditate in brilliant particulars and subtle turns of language on landscape, art, friendship, childhood memories, the nature of risk and political resistance. Aleshire's reflective turn of mind, her profound engagement with nature, coupled with her gifts of music and insight, mark her as a poet to cherish and applaud. — Colette Inez

Alexander, Elizabeth. *Body of Life.* 85p. pap. $10.95 (1-882688-12-0). Chicago, IL: Tia Chucha Press, Fall 1996. A work of uncommon skill, intelligence and beauty. It demands to be read through as a book, while individual poems blaze out from the whole. —Adrienne Rich. Wide-ranging and yet quite personal in its tender coverage of post-desegregation black experience, Body of Life is a book of learning, lust, sorrow, and, above all, song. It might as reasonably be called "Diva Studies" (one of its finest pieces) for all it reveals about an earnest woman's twofold apprenticeship to black glamour and black grief. The result is a joy to read. —Garrett Hongo

Alexander, Pamela. *Inland.* 82p. pap. $10.95 (0-87745-582-1). Iowa City, IA:

University of Iowa Press, Spring 1997. Winner of the 1996 Iowa Poetry Prize. Alexander's poetry is characterized by inventive language, scrupulous accuracy of imagery, and a winning fusion of the comic and the deeply serious. Her subjects vary as widely as her settings, which range from the New Hampshire woods to the Arizona desert. —University of Iowa Press. Alexander's Inland is quietly acute, witty, and lovely to read. Her poems embrace the outdoors; her poems are giant houses that have beds for foxes, spiders, and tender people. —Alan Lightman

Alexander, Robert; Mark Vinz, and C.W. Truesdale, eds. *The Talking of Hands: Unpublished Writing by New Rivers Press Authors.* 304p. pap. $19.95 (0-89823-199-X). Minneapolis, MN: New Rivers Press, Fall 1998.

Alexander, Will. *Towards the Primeval Lightning Field.* 120p. pap. $10.50 (1-882022-30-0). O Books, Spring 1998. I love the way that reading [Alexander] is like looking into Cornell's boxes: personal and isolate spaces evolve into a silvery science — and plunge through the eye of eternity. Cold black. —Fanny

Howe. [Alexander's] work resembles no one's, and is instantly recognizable. In part, he is an ecstatic surrealist on imaginal hyperdrive. He is probably the only African-American poet to take Aimé Césaire as a spiritual father. [Alexander is] a poet whose ecstasy derives from the scientific description of the stuff and the workings of the world. —Eliot Weinberger

Alexie, Sherman. *The Summer of Black Widows.* 144p. $22.00 (1-882413-35-0). pap. $13.50 (1-882413-34-2). Brooklyn, NY: Hanging Loose Press, Fall 1996. Alexie is one of the best young poets writing in America today. [He] brings a fresh approach to Native American writing. — Ray González, The Bloomsbury Review. The legacy of American history is difficult. This worthy poetry makes an important contribution to coming to terms with it. —Library Journal. Alexie opens to us the complexity and contradiction of a contemporary multicultural identity. —Publishers Weekly

Algarín, Miguel. *Love Is Hard Work: Memorias de Loisaida.* 155p. pap. $13.00 (0-684-82517-1). New York, NY: Simon & Schuster/Scribner, Fall 1997.

At once a moving personal memoir and a colorful portrait of life in New York's Lower East Side (Loisaida), this masterly collection of poems brings to life his private loves and the turbulent excitement of the Nuyorican Poets Cafe, and offers a searing, unsentimental look at himself and his life. —Simon & Schuster/Scribner. Algarín's Love Is Hard Work is another unique statement, an important work by one of the most significant poets and cultural workers in the U.S. today. — Amiri Baraka

Ali, Agha Shahid. *The Country Without a Post Office.* 96p. $19.00 (0-393-04057-7). pap. $11.00 (0-393-31761-7). New York, NY: Norton, W.W., and Company, Spring 1997; Spring 1998 (new paper). Combining humane elegance and moral passion, Ali speaks for Kashmir in a large, generous, compassionate, powerful, and urgent voice that cuts through everything else. Few poems in this country have such a voice or such a topic. —Hayden Carruth. Ali's Kashmir, in his poems, is our own lost but inalienable homeland. He makes it clear to us in what we think of as our own language, the words we have in common. But the grace and wit, the perceptions and illuminations they serve, their accent, are his own. — W.S. Merwin. [Ali is] one of America's finest younger poets. —John Ashbery

Ali, Quraysh, ed. *I Represent: A Collection of Literary Works From Gallery 37.* 110p. pap. $11.95 (0-938903-21-7). Chicago, IL: Tia Chucha Press, Fall 1996. Gallery 37, Chicago's award-winning arts education program, provides youth, ages 14-21, with job training in the arts. This is a collection of screams, prayers and insights made manifest through searing, introspective poetry, beguiling prose and thought-provoking playwriting. —Tia Chucha Press

Allardt, Linda. *River Effect.* 56p. pap. $12.00. Brockport, NY: State Street Press, Fall 1998. Allardt is one of the "bred listeners" whose rhythms and sounds are so sure that she finds for us the underground river of language, the source. —Judith Kitchen

Allen, Dick. *Ode to the Cold War: Poems New and Selected.* 160p. $25.00 (0-9641151-9-0). pap. $14.95 (1-889330-00-0). Louisville, KY: Sarabande Books, Spring 1997. Known both for his poetry and for his innovative writing on poetics, Allen has

long promoted the idea that our art must move away from narrow self-concern and include the worlds of contemporary events, science, and religion. Allen's poems, wide-ranging, visionary, and unique, powerfully engage the intellectual and moral questions of our time. Ode to the Cold War is a showcase for over thirty years of work by this increasingly celebrated master of American verse. Whether his focus is historical, scientific, or intimate, he is unfailingly empathic. —Booklist

Allen, Paul. *American Crawl.* 73p. pap. $10.95 (1-57441-027-X). Denton, TX: University of North Texas Press, Spring 1997. Winner of the Vassar Miller Prize in Poetry. Allen's American Crawl is as exciting a first book as I have seen in years. In a time of much inconsequential verse a book of such singularity and originality, not to mention quality, poem by poem, is exciting and welcome. American Crawl is a work by which we can all set our moral and emotional — and yes, our intellectual — compasses. —Sydney Lea

Allen, Paula Gunn. *Life Is a Fatal Disease: Selected Poems 1962-1995.* 224p. pap. $16.95 (0-931122-85-6).

Albuquerque, NM: West End Press, Spring 1997. Allen works in a great tradition of storytelling and education, delightmaking and argument. Particularly compelling is the variety of her poetic skills: her rich references, her lyrical flights, and — always — her earnest and compassionate voice. —West End Press

Allen, Robert H. *Simple Annals: 200 Years of an American Family.* 208p. $22.00 (1-56858-090-8). New York, NY: Four Walls Eight Windows, Spring 1997. Simple Annals draws the dead out of country obscurity, and forces them back into the stories of their lives. These talking ghosts, Allen's rural Tennessean ancestors (distant Southern cousins of the Spoon River haunts), bristle with particularity in a collection of poems and short prose pieces that is at once a memoir, family history and folkloric conjuration. —Publishers Weekly

Allen, William. *Sevastopol: On Photographs of War.* 90p. (1-879378-30-2). pap. $13.00 (1-879378-29-9). Riverside, CA: Xenos Books, Fall 1997. Allen's book of poems, based on photographs of war and its aftermath, is a book of profound conscience.Sevastopol is the work of an outraged

heart wrought with emotive power — an important book. —Daniela Gioseffi. Allen has created a unique body of work over the past two decades. At times lyrical, poignant, hilarious, and relentlessly moral, his is a poetry of history, investigation and justice. History is in the closed eyes, the massed skulls, the sites where men studied war too well. Sevastopol is an amazing achievement by a late twentieth century poet, a volume endowed with moral courage, keen humor, and a willingness to seek hope. —Patricia Spears Jones

Allen, William M. *Old New Borrowed Blue.* 70p. pap. $11.95. Louisville, KY: Allen, William, 1997.

Allen, William M. *The Irish Had a Word For It: Limerick.* 50p. pap. $3.95. Louisville, KY: Old Wine Press, 1994. Allen's limericks are witty and full of surprises. By turns his verses make you laugh out loud; groan over some horrible but delightful pun; see something about yourself; or expose a delicious bit of truth. —Jim Erskine

Alley, Rick. *The Talking Book of July.* 64p. $23.00 (0-910055-34-3). pap. $12.50 (0-910055-35-1). Cheney, WA:

Eastern Washington University Press, Fall 1997. Alley is an original, true poet, one we need, one to cherish. These crisp poems whisk the elusive essence of desire. — James Tate. Like the ancient oracles, Alley watches for omens: "If this is a sign, let it be urgent and true." Sensual as "three hornets / sipping a pear's soft wound," Alley's stunning language shows us how to "go on being more than one thing." This is a book to savor. —Peggy Shumaker

Almquist, Norma. *Traveling Light.* 62p. pap. $9.00 (1-56474-192-3). Santa Barbara, CA: Fithian Press, Spring 1997. A critic has said that if enough good poetry were written, we could each of us become another, and that is exactly what the precise and intimate poetry of Almquist does — transforms us into another, each of us through the alchemy of her poetry refined into more than we were. — John Hermann

Alschuler, Mari. *The Nightmare of Falling Teeth.* 20p. pap. $7.95. Johnstown, OH: Pudding House Publications, Spring 1998. Poems from a clinical social worker and hypnotherapist specializing in poetry therapy and stress management. — Pudding House Publications

Alson, Sheila; Cheryl Boyce Taylor, Zephryn Conte, Patricia Landrum, Kathy Price, and Clara Sala. *Cayenne.* 100p. pap. $10.00 (0-9639585-2-6). New York, NY: Fly by Night Press/A Gathering of the Tribes, Spring 1994. This collection in five parts features poems, incantations, radical blues and red-hot passion from six New York City-based performance poets. Cayenne takes on such eternal themes as strength, anger, and the Goddess and makes them new again. These six unique voices play against each other in unexpected and exciting ways: there's no shortage of sparks here. The poems rise up with dramatic power and perform as exquis-itely on the page as on the stage. —Gerry Gomez Pearlberg

Amichai, Yehuda. Translated by Glenda Abramson and Tudor Parfitt. *The Great Tranquility: Questions and Answers.* pap. $12.95 (1-878818-68-6). Riverdale-on-Hudson, NY: Sheep Meadow Press, Fall 1997. Amichai begins to look more and more like a truly major poet — in the strict sense of the term. That is, there's a depth, breadth and weighty momentum in these subtle and intricate poems of his, even in the slightest, that sounds more and more like the undersong of a people. Who else is dipping his bucket into such a full river of experience and paid-for feelings? —Ted Hughes. Amichai has entered that small, accidental, permanent company of poets — Hikmet, Milosz, Vallejo — who speak for each of us and all of us by redefining our nobility, by speaking to us in his voice of many selves. In a time of vile politics and lost gods, Amichai continues to struggle with both in the midst of everyday life. —Stephen Berg

Ammons, A. R. *Glare.* 294p. $25.00 (0-393-04096-8). pap. $15.00 (0-393-31779-X). New York, NY: Norton, W.W., and Company, Spring 1997; Fall 1998 (new paper). Glare delivers a bawdy and brave meditation on a variety of issues: poetry, God, sex, popular culture and death, in a playful, recursive rant. Ammons may have written the long poem of the latter half of the century. —Michael Graber, Memphis Commercial Appeal. Glare is Ammons at his most original and unrestrained — it leaps from shock to shock, and from radiant epiphany to yet more radiance. Ammons at seventy is totally audacious: his bones make no awful noise against the light, and he is now freed into as much light as he can take, which is enormous. Glare is high testimony. — Harold Bloom

Anderson, Daniel. *January Rain.* 71p. pap. $11.00 (1-885266-54-5). Ashland, OR: Story Line Press, Fall 1997. Anderson's American scenes— rural, suburban, urban — promise a world as lush and precise as a Hudson River School painting. But enter this richly rendered realm at your peril. At once rueful and stiletto-sharp, the elegant poems in January Rain are packed, line by authoritative line, with observation, wit, and a kind of lacrimae rerum ache. — Rachel Hadas. There is a refined angularity in Anderson's poetry that I find nowhere else. These soft-spoken poems are remarkable for the care they demonstrate. No one is more precise with the imprecisions of our daily getting about. This is a first book you do not want to miss. — Wyatt Prunty

Anderson, J.J., ed. *Sir Gawain and the Green Knight, Pearl, Cleanness, Patience.* 319p. pap. $6.95 (0-460-87510-8). Boston, MA: Tuttle, Charles E./Everyman, Fall

1996. A comprehensive edition, with introduction and appendices. —Charles E. Tuttle/Everyman

Anderson, Jack. *Traffic: New and Selected Prose Poems.* 76p. pap. $14.95 (0-89823-191-4). Minneapolis, MN: New Rivers Press, Fall 1998. Anderson is one of our great tightrope dancers. His balance is exquisite, even when he's holding a chair, an umbrella, and an elephant. Perhaps his most amazing trick is that the tightrope doesn't always lead to the same destination, sometimes reaching high hilarity, sometimes utmost seriousness, frequently both at once. —Robert Hershon. Anderson's prodigious imagination creates alternate realities as easily as if they were prefabricated worlds, but so close to our own are they in every wickedly funny and poignant detail that we soon realize we've not been looking out a window but at a mirror. —Mort Marcus

Anderson, Sandy. *Jeanne Was Once a Player of Pianos.* 36p. pap. $15.00 (0-931659-45-0). Boise, ID: Limberlost Press, Fall 1998. These poems explore the dark side of the psyche in which the frailty of both the mind and the human heart are traced. This is a com-pelling book, an integrated series of poems linked by a common voice which reads as a continuous narrative. The poems are sharply focused and uniformly powerful. —David Lee

Andonov, Nicole. *Accent.* 28p. pap. $3.00. New York, NY: New School Chapbook Series, Fall 1996. There is something quick, agile and light at the center of Andonov's poems. What happens, happens fast. But the pleasure of her surprising insights lingers. With a style that is both lush and spare, Accent proves just how distinctive and accomplished this poet's voice really is. — Elaine Equi

Andrews, Claudia Emerson. *Pharaoh, Pharaoh.* 58p. $19.95 (0-8071-2158-4). pap. $11.95 (0-8071-2159-2). Baton Rouge, LA: Louisiana State University Press, Spring 1997. Pharaoh, Pharaoh is one of the strongest poetry books I have ever read. —Fred Chappell. In a style that is both allusive and evocative, Andrews paints images of her home in Chatham, Virginia, that reach deeply into the personal sense of "home" that dwells in us all. —Richmond Times Dispatch

Andrews, Nin. *Spontaneous Breasts.* 36p. pap. $6.00 (1-88219-08-4). Long Beach, CA: Pearl Editions, Spring 1998. Winner of the 1997 Pearl Poetry Prize.

Angeleri, Carl, ed. *Fire Island Poetry Festival: 20th Anniversary Reading of the Fire Island Poets.* 31p. Ocean Beach, NY: Ocean Beach Boat House, Fall 1997. In this small volume are the voices of Fire Island, those of the people who walk its beaches, swim in its waters, and watch the summer sunset. —Ruth Reichbart

Angelou, Maya. *I Shall Not Be Moved.* 48p. $15.00 (0-679-45708-9). New York, NY: Random House, Spring 1997. Angelou's poems are like her shadow — painfully revealing, honestly enraged and hurting with the pain of being a woman. —Louise Meriwether

Angelou, Maya. *Just Give Me a Cool Drink of Water 'fore I Diiie.* 48p. $15.00 (0-679-45709-7). New York, NY: Random House, Spring 1997. Just Give Me a Cool Drink of Water 'fore I Diiie, the first collection of poetry by Angelou, reflects the remarkable sense of life and love and loneliness of one of America's most beloved authors. — Random House. You will hear the regal woman, the mischievous street girl, you will hear the price of a black woman's survival and you will hear of her generosity rooted in specific experience. Black, bitter and beautiful, [Angelou] speaks of our survival. — James Baldwin

Angelou, Maya. *Oh Pray My Wings Are Gonna Fit Me Well.* 66p. $15.00 (0-679-45707-0). New York, NY: Random House, Spring 1997. The thirty-six poems in this second volume of Angelou's poetry are eloquent evidence of the poet's continuing celebration of life. Here are poems of love and memory, poems of racial confrontation, poems of misplaced patriotism, songs of the street and songs of the heart. —Random House. It gives me heart, to hear so clearly the caged bird singing. It is true poetry. —M.F.K. Fisher

Anglund, Joan Walsh. *Love Always Remembers.* 55p. $13.00 (0-679-40903-3). New York, NY: Random House, Fall 1997. Anglund, the beloved author/illustrator. . . returns to the theme of love for her thirteenth book of illustrated poetry, Love Always Remembers. — Random House

Ansel, Talvikki. *My Shining Archipelago.* 64p. $18.00 (0-300-07031-4). pap. $11.00 (0-300-07032-2). New Haven, CT: Yale University Press, 1996. Winner of the 1996 Yale Series of Younger Poets Competition. Ansel's poetry is refreshingly original. She renders the heat, the closeness, the mystery, and the terrible fear of the undisclosed, the lurking, the waiting to happen. This is true imagination, true craft. —James Dickey

Anstett, Aaron. *Sustenance.* 89p. pap. $12.95 (0-89823-173-6). Minneapolis, MN: New Rivers Press, Fall 1997. Opening Anstett's Sustenance is like switching on cable TV: no telling what'll be on. Perhaps the great bluesman Robert Johnson; or a back-stage glimpse of a lyrical stuntwoman; or a brief, loopy lecture on the three hearts of the octopus. It might be the kitsch genius of pro-wrestling's Baron von Claw or the title poem's strange, unforgettable prayer. Anstett proves the adage: you can indeed write a poems about "anything." But few can match his buoyant music, witty intelligence, sinewy syntax and wicked eye for detail. —David Graham

Anyidoho, Kofi, ed. *The Word Behind Bars and the Paradox of Exile.* 248p. pap. $17.95 (0-8101-1393-7). Northwestern University Press/TriQuarterly Books, Fall 1997. Assessments in prose, poetry, and drama of the many facets of the exile experience. The value of this collection lies not only in the expressiveness of the works, but also in the varied terms the authors employ to narrate and contextualize their personal experiences and their visions for the future. A powerful fusion of the personal and the political, this book offers a timely perspective on conditions of literary production in many parts of Africa today. —Northwestern University Press

Aplon, Roger. *It's Mother's Day: Poems 1990-1995.* 99p. pap. $12.95 (0-9651329-0-0). Escondido, CA: Barracuda Press, Fall 1996. Includes a studio produced CD of Aplon reading 28 selections with musical punctuation by John Logan. —Barracuda Press

Appelbaum, Samuel. *Chtcheglov.* 66p. pap. $10.00 (1-878580-62-0). Paradise, CA: Asylum Arts Publishing, Fall 1998. The life and work of Ivan Chtcheglov have been sequestered together in the obscurity of apparently permanent institutionalization, drugs and shock therapy. This is a text that can never conclude, that will always want to suppress itself. A provisional, reflexive text, evoking the unrehabilitated subject: the perpetually disquieting dematerialization, nearly fifty years ago, of Ivan Chtcheglov. — Asylum Arts

Applewhite, James. *Daytime and Starlight.* 64p. $19.95 (0-8071-2149-5). pap. $11.95 (0-8071-2150-9). Baton Rouge, LA: Louisiana State University Press, Spring 1997. Daytime and Starlight is a lyrical dream of home places, parents, solitude, and ease, a pastoral walk through a very personal history. But it's also a poetry of all our histories if we have the wit and the will to see through the clouding shadows. Eloquent, elegiac, electric as the single naked light bulb in a farmhouse where once we thrilled to the old stories, Daytime and Starlight is Applewhite's best poetry. It turns and returns us until we find ourselves in those rooms we thought consigned to history, those contingencies of the heart we thought resolved. — Dave Smith

Arbolay, Dominick. *The Phantoms.* 39p. pap. $6.00. Hourglass Press, Fall 1997.

Argüelles, Ivan, and Jack Foley. *New Poetry From California: Dead/Requiem.* 127p. pap. $9.95 (1-880766-16-7). Berkeley, CA: Pantograph Press, Spring 1998. [This collaboration is] experimental, yes, but steeped in the traditions of glorifying them. —Neeli Cherkovski

Argüelles, Ivan, and Jake Berry. *Purisima Sex Addict II.* 23p. pap. $7.00 (0935350640). Columbus, OH: Luna Bisonte Prods, Spring 1997. A long collaborative poem, in a visionary and surrealist style. —Luna Bisonte Prods

Armalinsky, Mikhail. *Zhizneopisaniye Mgnovenia (The Chronicle of a Moment): Poems 1994-1997.* 92p. pap. $8.00 (0-916201-21-X). Minneapolis, MN: M.I.P. Company, Fall 1997. Armalinsky became well-known all over the world for his publication in the US of the Secret Journal 1836-1837 by A.S. Pushkin. The only emigre author whose works are still banned in Russia, [Armalinsky} reveals not only new facets of talent but the reasons why such a ban is imposed. —M.I.P. Company

Armantrout, Rae. *True.* 63p. pap. $12.95 (1-891190-03-2).

Berkely, CA: Atelos, Fall 1998.

Armantrout, Rae. *Writing the Plot About Sets.* 14p. pap. $6.00. Tucson, AZ: Chax Press, Spring 1998. Letterpress edition.

Armitage, Simon, and Robert Crawford, eds. *The Penguin Book of Poetry From Britain and Ireland Since 1945.* 443p. (0-670-86829-9). (0-670-88325-5). New York, NY: Penguin Books/Viking Penguin, Fall 1998. The first major anthology to survey the poetry from Britain and Ireland published in the half-century after the Second World War, a period whose immense political, social and scientific changes have altered both poetry and its readership. The earlier-twentieth-century rhetorical, aristocratic stance of Yeats in Ireland, and the brilliant, highly educated poetry of Eliot and the young Auden in Britain, have given way gradually to a sense of burgeoning poetic pluralism. Wider in its franchise, sometimes less formal in structure and often more attuned to vernacular cultures, here is some of the best poetry written by men and women in the postwar era. —Penguin Books

Arroyo, Rane. *Pale Ramón.* 96p. pap. $13.00 (0-944072-94-1). Cambridge, MA: Zoland Books, Fall 1998. Truly absorbing. An original new voice in American poetry. —Richard Katrovas. The poems in Pale Ramon are poems of reclamation and therefore of discovery. Arroyo is one of our most valuable cultural workers, and this book is a beautiful work of art. —Maggie Anderson. The vibrancy and energy of Arroyo's language and imagery are truly dazzling, whether he's writing about Puerto Rico or Pittsburgh. — Jim Daniels

Arteaga, Alfred. *Love in the Time of Aftershocks.* 46p. pap. $5.00 (1-891823-00-0). Moving Parts Press/Chusma House Publications, Spring 1998.

Arthur, Ross G., trans. *Three Arthurian Romances: Poems From Medieval France.* 216p. pap. $7.50 (0-460-87577-9). Boston, MA: Tuttle, Charles E./Everyman, Fall 1996. A unique selection of new prose translations, with introduction, notes and bibliography. — Charles E. Tuttle/Everyman

Arthur-Simons, David. *Hairven in the Line Profiles of New York 1997.* 24p. New York,

NY: Dasling Publications, Spring 1997. A collection of 20 sonnets, paired with 20 drawings executed in human hair. The drawings were exhibited at the Australian Consulate General in New York in February, 1997. — Dasling Publications

Asekoff, L. S. *North Star.* 93p. $20.00 (0-914061-57-7). Alexandria, VA: Orchises Press, Spring 1997. In Asekoff's field of vision, stars, roses, swans, and mirrors have left the walled garden of Symbolisme, ventured into contemporary sites of upheaval, and put on the black leather of Surrealism — without, I think, ever relinquishing a fundamental cultivation and refinement. Reading these poems, you'll be briefly reminded of Asekoff's exacting precursors — Kafka, Desnos, Celan, Joseph Cornell, Plath, Jabés — but finally these are only assistants in an interior cinema of which Asekoff is the indisputable auteur. —Alfred Corn

Ashbery, John. *A Wave.* 89p. pap. $12.00 (0-374-52547-1). Farrar, Straus and Giroux/Noonday, Spring 1998 (new paper). The charm of Ashbery's urbane style — so various, so beautiful, so new — persists throughout A

Wave, and will induce the rereadings the poem demands. It is a style that resists, in its glowing reflectiveness, the approaching darkness of the cimmerian moment. —Helen Vendler, The New York Review of Books. No book by Ashbery is ever quite like the one that came before it. If he sometimes seems to be a figure out of the recent future, that is because Ashbery has the true innovator's desire not to repeat himself. —J.D. McClatchy, Poetry

Ashbery, John. *Can You Hear, Bird.* 175p. $20.00 (0-374-11831-0). pap. $12.00 (0-374-52501-3). Farrar, Straus and Giroux/Noonday, Fall 1995; April 1997 (paper). Whitman argued that the new American poet was to be"indirect and not direct or descriptive or epic." Ashbery's indirectness takes many forms_slippery syntax, elusive personae, narrative uncertainty, the blending of incongruous dictions—yet like Whitman's, it is essentially a means of involving the reader in the poem on what Whitman calls "equal terms" . . . Ashbery is poised, like Tennyson's Ulysses, for departure, at once peering into the abyss and rallying the crew. —Mark Ford, The Times Literary Supplement.

Ashbery's best, liveliest, and most various collection since A Wave. There are more things in Ashbery's corner of heaven and earth than are dreamed in anyone's philosophy. —David Lehman, The Washington Post BookWorld

Ashbery, John. *Flow Chart: A Poem.* 216p. pap. $15.00 (0-374-52549-8). Farrar, Straus and Giroux/Noonday, Spring 1998 (new paper). Flow Chart, Ashbery's magnum opus, is the fullest demonstration to date of this poet's fascination with what Pater described as "that strange, perpetual weaving and unweaving of ourselves." [Ashbery] is likely to be seen as the defining voice of his nation and time. —Robert Crawford, Poetry Review. Ashbery has produced a remarkable series of longer poems. But perhaps none is quite so various, so beautiful and so new as Flow Chart. —Marjorie Perloff, The New York Times Book Review

Ashbery, John. *The Mooring of Starting Out: The First Five Books of Poetry.* 389p. $25.00 (0-8800-1-527-6). pap. $18.00 (0-88001-547-0). Hopewell, NJ: Ecco Press, Spring 1997; Fall 1998 (new paper). Ashbery's poetry appeals not because it offers wisdom in a packaged form, but because

the elusiveness and mysterious promise of his lines remind us that we always have a future and a condition of meaningfulness to start out toward. This book of beginnings takes us back to the mooring of Ashbery's starting out. It contains a poetry whose beauties are endless. —New York Times Book Review. This is the best possible introduction to the brilliant, difficult, and beautiful work of this poet. —Publishers Weekly. Stemming in part from Mallarmé and in part from Whitman, Ashbery's work creates a tension in which the fine networks of linguistic reverie are balanced by the strong sense of an American tradition. —Peter Ackroyd, Times Literary Supplement

Ashbery, John. *Wakefulness.* 80p. $20.00 (0-374-28598-5). New York, NY: Farrar, Straus and Giroux, Spring 1998. Even the as-yet-unconverted will find delight in watching Ashbery record, with fresh verve and subtlety, the motion and sway of the mind's wanderings. At once feisty, diverting and wistful, this is Ashbery at his most inexhaustible. —Publishers Weekly. Ashbery is a tireless recorder of atmospheric disturbances, a suave riddler, and a clever dramatist, spinning long-breathed poems that occupy the page like surreal collages. His graceful, sly, and tender poems glimmer and shift like aurora borealis in the mind's dark, making our synapses glow, not with reason and sense, but with impressions and sensibility. — Donna Seaman, Booklist. Ashbery's work — more dramatically than that of most other poets — allows us to see the purely figurative without reliance on the literal and to accept it as literal — which is of course the experience poetry itself was designed to embody. —Library Journal

Ashfield, Andrew, ed.
Romantic Women Poets 1770-1838. 327p. pap. $27.95 (0-7190-5308-0). New York, NY: Manchester University Press, 1997 (revised edition). Over one hundred and eighty poems from some forty women poets are collected together in this new anthology, edited and annotated for a student audience. From Anna Seward to Elizabeth Barrett, this volume provides a detailed picture of female poetic activity from the earliest developments of Romanticism up to the Victorian era. Many of the poets are reprinted here for the first time and several hitherto unknown figures have been discovered. —Manchester

University Press. Ashfield has brought us closer to the female voices of the period, voices too long left unheard and unanswered. His book provides both an important feminist document and a real means of unravelling Romanticism. —Times Literary Supplement

Asner, Marie A., and Rochelle Lynn Holt. *The Tree of Life.* 60p. pap. $10.00 (0-934536-61-9). Kindred Spirit Press, Fall 1996. This literary duet between women of opposing views blends centuries of women's voices into a choir of imagery and sensory perception. —Mary-Lane Kamberg

Athens Avenue Poetry Circle. *A Year on the Avenue: A Collection of Poems by the Athens Avenue Poetry Circle.* 160p. pap. $8.95 (1-891090-00-3). Dear Isle, ME: Two Dog Press, Fall 1997. The zenith of web-published poetry. —E.A. Fichtl, Anthem. A Year on the Avenue is alive with lush, vivid images, exquisite language and evocative tones. A grand trip through the human experience. —C.K. Tower, Conspire Poetry Journal

Atwan, Robert; George Dardess, and Peggy

Rosenthal, eds. *Divine Inspiration: The Life of Jesus in World Poetry.* 595p. $35.00 (0-19-509351-8). New York, NY: Oxford University Press, Spring 1998. Organized thematically around the life of Jesus, the book pairs passages from the Gospels with poems they inspired. The dual effect is rewarding: the collection boasts a strong sense of biblical narrative enlivened by moments of stirring lyrical beauty, allowing opportunities for devotional meditation as well as confrontation with the stark questions of faith and doubt. —Publishers Weekly

Atwood, Margaret. With Art by Charles Pachter. *The Journals of Susanna Moodie.* 90p. $30.00 (0-395-88043-2). Boston, MA: Houghton Mifflin Company, Fall 1997. Dazzlingly illustrated with Pachter's silkscreens, this is the early poem cycle that gave rise to Atwood's Alias Grace — the story of a Canadian woman in nature and in civilization. —Houghton Mifflin Company

Auster, Paul, trans. *Translations.* 407p. pap. $16.95 (1-56886-033-1). New York, NY: Marsilio Publishers, Fall 1997. Translations brings together in one volume four extraordinary and quite different works translated by Auster: The Notebooks by Joseph Joubert; A Tomb for Anatole by Stéphane Mallarmé; The Uninhabited by Andre Du Bouchet; and On the High Wire by Philippe Petit. Each of these works, like Auster's own fiction, conjures the complexities of language, art and the nature of human experience; taken together, they offer a vivid portrait of this important postmodern writer's sensibility. — Marsilio Publishers

Avara, Rosalie, ed. *Summer's Treasures VI.* 50p. pap. $4.95. Amarillo, TX: Rio Grande Press, Spring 1997.

Avara, Rosalie, ed. *Summer's Treasures VII.* 36p. pap. $4.95. Amarillo, TX: Rio Grande Press, Fall 1998.

Avara, Rosalie, ed. *Winter's Gems VI.* 50p. pap. $4.95. Amarillo, TX: Rio Grande Press, Fall 1996.

Avara, Rosalie, ed. *Winter's Gems VII.* 50p. pap. $4.95. Amarillo, TX: Rio Grande Press, Fall 1997.

Avara, Rosalie, ed. *Winter's Gems VIII.* 48p. pap. $4.95. Amarillo, TX: Rio Grande Press, Fall 1998.

Avena, Thomas. *Dream of Order.* 114p. pap. $14.00 (1-56279-102-8). San Francisco, CA: Mercury House, Fall 1997. Cool, hot, relentlessly clear, Avena's poems take on the age of AIDS and paradoxically draw strength from it. This is a lean and passionate performance: poetry for our time, alas. —John Ashbery. Elegiac, tragic, hopeful, fragile, and very very tough, these remarkable poems struggle with and against their own considerable elegance and beauty in a courageous search for wisdom. Here are poems in which some of life's harshest extremes — oppression, illness, death — are made knowable, approachable without being domesticated, without losing their terror. Having said all that, so solemnly, I should mention that these poems are also precise, erudite pocket-biographies, mappings and gleanings of the lives of remarkable people — and a great joy and pleasure to read. —Tony Kushner

Axel, Brett. *The Spastic Grandson.* 40p. pap. $5.50. Chester, NY: Heaven Bone Press, Spring 1998. Axel is a talent to watch. —Chris Farlekas, Times Herald Record

Ayala, Naomi. *Wild Animals on the Moon.* 70p. pap. $10.95 (1-880684-44-6). Willimantic, CT: Curbstone Press, Fall 1997. In lyrical, original language expressing anger, hope, optimism and a fierce independence, Ayala explores being Puerto Rican on the mainland — displaying pride in her culture coupled with the pain of exclusion, vividly describing her encounters with racism and poverty, and the power of love in these difficult circumstances. —Curbstone Press. Ayala writes poems like water, a clear, strong current, sometimes tranquil, sometimes furious, but always swirling with life. —Martín Espada

Aygi, Gennady. Translated by Peter France. *Selected Poems 1954-94.* 238p. pap. $14.95 (0-8101-1540-9). Northwestern University Press/Hydra Books, Spring 1997. Aygi forces the Russian language to do things it has never done before. The language of his free verse is disjunctive, subconscious, antirational. His poetry is at the confluence of avant-garde European modernism and the traditional culture of his near-Asiatic homeland. His themes — stillness, communion between human and non-human worlds, memory, birth, sleep — provide room for deeply felt responses to both private and public events. This is the first substantial presentation of Aygi's poetry to the English-speaking world, with original texts and facing translations, the translator's critical introduction, and end notes. —Northwestern University Press. The most original voice in contemporary Russian poetry, and one of the most unusual voices in the world. —Jacques Roubaud, Times Literary Supplement

Ayhan, Ece. Translated by Murat Nemet-Nejat. *A Blind Cat Black and Orthodoxies.* 81p. pap. $10.95 (1-55713-102-3). Los Angeles, CA: Sun & Moon Press, Fall 1997. Ayhan takes the reader through the dark streets of the Galata district of Istanbul, an area where European minorities lived historically side by side with red light sexual activities. Like a modern-day Rimbaud, Ayhan, in this amazing translation, explores linguistically and thematically what Turkish culture and authorities have forbidden. — Sun & Moon Press

Azzopardi, Maria. Translated by Grazio Falzon. *Naked As Water.* 178p. (1-879378-12-4). (1-879378-11-6). Riverside, CA: Xenos Books, Fall 1996.

Azzopardi is the enfant terrible of contemporary Maltese poetry. There is no right way for him: he breaks all the rules. He is fearless in his attempts to mock tradition or to push it to the limits of his passion for life and for words. His poetry is a verbal pyrotechnics sprawling in a phantasmagoria of sounds, images and rhythms. —Grazio Falzon

B., Cheryl. *Motor Oil Queen.* 20p. pap. $3.00. New York, NY: By the Seat of Your Pants Press, Spring 1998. Motor Oil Queen is a poetic journey through a young woman's psyche with pit stops for love, sex, jealousy, violence, ignorance and life-altering revelations. —By the Seat of Your Pants Press

B., Cheryl. *Ripe.* 24p. pap. $3.00. New York, NY: Dr. Ducky Doolittle, Fall 1996. Ripe exposes the oppressive confines of adolescence and the experience of social exclusion and self disgust determined by negative body image. —Dr. Ducky Doolittle

Baal-i-Jibreel. Translated by Naim Siddiqui. *Iqbal: A Verse Translation.* 156p. pap. $12.00 (0-9652293-1-9). Fremont, CA: Alhamra Publications, 1996. Siddiqui has made this first English verse translation of Baal-i-Jibreel in the hopes that it will be helpful in a correct evaluation of Iqbal's impact on modern Islamic thought. —Alhamra Publications

Babb, Sanora. *Told in the Seed.* 65p. pap. $8.95 (0-931122-90-2). Albuquerque, NM: West End Press, Fall 1998. Babb is a writer of great skill and humanity. She is a clear-eyed observer of human behavior, a lyric poet of great sensitivity, and a gentle satirist of human folly. It is a treat to now have a selection of her poems. —Douglas Wixson

Baer, William. *The Unfortunates.* 65p. $25.00 (0-943549-46-9). pap. $15.00 (0-943549-47-7). Kirksville, MO: Thomas Jefferson University Press/New Odyssey Press, Fall 1997. The subjects of this astonishing portrait gallery of poems are profoundly unnerving, alarming, haunting, touching and distressing. This is one of the most deeply unsettling books of poetry I have read in a very long time. —Anthony Hecht. Baer is drawn to compulsions. My favorite of his poetic portraits is the pair of lovers who climb over the airport fence to lie in a ditch by an active runway. But there is also the unregenerate cultist, a

roller-coaster addict, a housebreaker, a baby snatcher, and many others to choose from. This is a highly original first book. —Maxine Kumin. Above all, these poems feed the reader's primary addiction: watching in his own mind, after each last line, as the large explodes out of the small. —Mona Van Duyn

Baeyvsky, David. *Parapushkinistika.* 194p. pap. $12.00 (0-91620-1228). Minneapolis, MN: M.I.P. Company, Spring 1999.

Bahu, Sultan. Translated by Jamal J. Elias. *Death Before Dying: The Sufi Poems of Sultan Bahu.* 145p. (0-520-21135-9). (0-520-21242-8). Berkeley, CA: University of California Press, Fall 1998. Sultan Bahu is one of India's enduringly beloved and influential Sufi poets. Death Before Dying offers a window into the Sufi mystical tradition, providing a rare glimpse into the religious lives of rural Muslims during the days of the Mughal Empire. — University of California Press. Elias's delightfully readable rendering of Sultan Bahu's short poems offers a fine introduction to an important figure in South Asian Islamic vernacular literature. With their earthy charm and engaging simplicity, these Punjabi verses convey the immediacy of the spiritual quest as expressed in the popular idiom and imagery of the country-side. —John Renard

Baker, David. *The Truth About Small Towns.* 79p. pap. $16.00 (1-55728-517-9). Fayetteville, AR: University of Arkansas Press, Spring 1998. These poems measure the distances between memory and reality, between the living and the dead, in beautiful cadences and gritty detail. But the real achievement here is that we are invited to stand on the boundary between the lived world and the lost one and, as we read on, it is hard to distinguish between them. Baker has an unswerving purpose in these poems. And he draws us into it. —Eavan Boland. The Truth About Small Towns is first and foremost a book about love — lost love and abiding love, the joys of love and the sacrifices. Baker deftly traces the ways love for those who are absent, threads through love for those who are still here, and makes it stronger. This [is] his finest book yet. —Andrew Hudgins

Baker, Donald W. *Search Patterns.* 44p. pap. $5.95 (1-884482-08-2). Brewster, MA: Steppingstone/Sugar Creek,

Fall 1996. Baker is a wonderful poet. His poems are deceptively simple and colloquial, but very powerful. — Elizabeth Spires. In every poem there is an isolated, abstract, unique, elusive insight the reader can not pin down: the music of poetry. — Simon Perchik

Baker, Donald W. *The Readiness: Poems From the Cape.* 20p. pap. $7.95 (1-884482-06-0). Brewster, MA: Steppingstone/Sugar Creek, Fall 1996.

Balaban, John. *Locusts at the Edge of Summer: New & Selected Poems.* 154p. pap. $15.00 (1-55659-123-3). Port Townsend, WA: Copper Canyon Press, Spring 1997. It's wonderful to have this integrated New & Selected Poems at hand. Balaban seems to me to be our moral spokesperson, our lyricist, polemicist, exhorter, anti-consoler: in short, the poet we need. —Maxine Kumin. A witness to war's savageries and the brutalities of life, [Balaban] yet feels the possibilities of redemption in the natural world, and in the power of poetry: "Crossing the moonlit fields / stippled bright with human bones, / Tu Fu wrote that poetry is useless, /

in a poem alive these thousand years." —Daniel Hoffman

Balbo, Ned. *Galileo's Banquet.* 68p. pap. $12.00 (0-931846-52-8). Washington, DC: Washington Writers' Publishing House, Spring 1998. Balbo investigates a cosmology of human aspirations that is deeply intimate and openly public. Wherever Balbo trains his lens, we discover a poetry that both historically wise and psychologically complex. His supremely lyrical narrative pulsars will be with us, I'm confident, for many, many years to come. —David St. John. Galileo's Banquet marks the elegant debut of a writer whose poems link the history of the galaxy to a family burdened with secrets. His images and his mastery of meter and form will take your breath away. — Nancy Willard

Ballard, Charles G. *Winter Count Poems.* 64p. pap. $12.95 (0-912678-96-8). Greenfield Center, NY: Greenfield Review Press, Fall 1997. Winner of the 1996 North American Native Authors First Book Award for Poetry. Ballard is an enrolled member of the Quapaw tribe and also of Cherokee descent. Whether chronicling journeys to Europe, describing the flag

carrier at a pow wow or viewing a Picasso painting, his vision is as clear as the shapes drawn on a buffalo robe. — Greenfield Review Press

Balter, Frances. *The River's Bend.* 59p. pap. $12.95 (0-941895-15-7). Amherst, MA: Amherst Writers & Artists Press, Spring 1998. Certain sections of [Balter's] poetry rival the painted image in immediacy. She renders emotion through visual imagery with a precision that makes us participate in the moment as if we stood beside her and saw the scene and felt it as she felt it. These works refresh the senses. —Philip Pearlstein

bandele, ashe. *Absence in the Palms of My Hands and Other Poems.* 128p. pap. $12.00 (0-86316-013-1). New York, NY: Writers and Readers Publishing/Harlem River Press, Fall 1996. Confronting truth fearlessly — [bandele's] rhythmic use of language sets every page on fire. —Jessica Care Moore. If you didn't know where poetry was going after Audre Lorde, June Jordan, Jayne Cortez, or Sapphire, then let this book knock you upside your head. bandele's words fall like hard rain. —E. Ethelbert Miller. Hear bandele, whose raw words whip and whose uncompromising analysis makes literature a force for activation. In the tradition of Lorde and Brooks, here is a single voice that becomes a rousing chorus, a song familiar and new. Here bandele delivers a wake-up call to our dreams. —Bob Holman

Bang, Mary Jo. *Apology for Want.* 80p. $25.00 (0-87451-821-0). pap. $11.95 (0-87451-822-9). University Press of New England/Middlebury College Press, Fall 1997. Winner of the 1996 Bakeless Prize for Poetry. Enjoyable [for the] nice tension between the clarity of form and the open-endedness of Bang's articulated emotion. — Publishers Weekly. How purely defined the deciderative heart is here. This is a consuming poetry — full of will and curiosity and hankering. Bang is a poet of exquisite distillation, of lavish distances, of comb and control, unwanting and wish. Apology for Want is a consummate book. —Lucie Brock-Broido. Intent on what remains when "loss is what you live with," Bang's poems are fastidious exorcisms, though their message is stringent: "to grasp with wet hands the cold / metal of life, then find a way to let go." This is a new resonance, tough, wounded, vigilant, and

I am enthralled by its powers. —Richard Howard

Baraka, Amiri. *Eulogies.* 228p. $26.95 (1-568886-007-2). New York, NY: Marsilio Publishers, Fall 1996.

Baraka, Amiri. Edited by Paul Vangelisti. *Funk Lore: New Poems (1984-1995).* 119p. pap. $11.95 (1-55713-296-8). Los Angeles, CA: Littoral Books, Fall 1997. This new book of previously uncollected poetry (1984-1995) demonstrates Baraka's gift for the music of thought, and reveals his continued mastery of tone and performance. Engaging in the primary issues of African-American music and contemporary politics, and imbuing his homages to such grand figures of America as Duke Ellington, Thelonious Monk, Sarah Vaughn, Albert Ayler, and John Coltrane with a passion that has not abated over the years, Baraka glories in his own virtuosity. — Littoral Books

Barber, Jennifer; Mark Bibbins, and Maggie Nelson. *Take Three 3: AGNI New Poets Series.* 134p. pap. $12.95 (1-55597-282-9). St. Paul, MN: Graywolf Press, Fall 1998. Selected by Askold Melnyczuk and the poetry panel of AGNI magazine,

Take Three: 3 is the third in an important annual series designed to launch the work of new poets. —Graywolf Press. Barber's poems are sensual, attentive lyrics which move with a growing necessity and insight and surprise. I am grateful for this fine book. — Jean Valentine. [Bibbins's] Swerve announce[s] the arrival of a brilliant young poet. —John Ashbery. Do you wonder what the 21st century will bring to the poetic voice? Look to [Nelson's] alluring combination of deftness and vulnerability. —Molly Peacock

Bargen, Walter. *At the Dead Center of Day.* 36p. pap. $6.00 (1-886157-08-1). Kansas City, MO: BkMk Press of the University of Missouri-Kansas City, Fall 1997. What sets this collection apart is its steadfast refusal to acquiesce, to give up that act of sympathy and compassion by which we will, if indeed we will, outlive this difficult century. —Sherod Santos. Bargen's poems answer our time's varied, terrifying belligerence with an insistence on knowing each end, the trajectory of each jawbone. The poems demand we not turn back, we not be too busy hiding another breath. They dare us to share this difficult undertaking, to

discover not only these anguishing ends but to what hopefully countering grace the imagination and language can be put. —Dennis Finnell

Barkan, Stanley H. Translated by Adam Szyper. *Under the Apple Tree.* 73p. (83-86900-64-4). Cross-Cultural Communications/Oficyna Konfraterni Poetów, Fall 1998.

Barnes, Jim. *Paris.* 101p. pap. $16.95 (0-252-06622-7). Champaign, IL: University of Illinois Press, Spring 1997. The people and places of Paris come alive in this eighth volume of poetry by Barnes, in poems at once formal, allusive, quickening, and completely accessible. From Stein on rue de Fleurus to de Beauvoir and Sartre in Café de Flore to the death of Yves Montand, the writing here exudes both the aura and the tone that are the quintessence of contemporary poetry. — University of Illinois Press

Barnstone, Willis, trans. *To Touch the Sky: Poems of Mystical, Spiritual and Metaphysical Light.* 224p. pap. $15.95 (0-8112-1396-X). New York, NY: New Directions, Spring 1998. To Touch the Sky contains Barnstone's translations of some of the most profound and inspiring writing of world literature: ten mystical and spiritual poets spanning three thousand years. As Barnstone says in his introduction, "There is a moment of vision, otherness, apparent timelessness, erotic sublimity, where the ordinary becomes extraordinary, for which there is no easy verbal equivalent except in the metaphors of poetry. In the instance of these authors, the unsayable has been refashioned into the precision of poetry." —New Directions. Willis Barnstone has a problem: he's too good. Everything he writes is a breathtaking achievement. —Carolyn Kizer. I think Barnstone has been appointed a special angel to bring the "other" to our attention, to show how it is done. He illuminates the spirit for us and he clarifies the unclarifiable. I think he does it by beating his wings. —Gerald Stern

Barone, Dennis. *Wag, Bound.* 24p. pap. $4.00 (1-893032-06-X). Talisman House, Publishers / Jensen/Daniels, Fall 1998.

Barr, John. *The Hundred Fathom Curve.* 88p. $20.00 (1-885266-43-X). pap. $10.00 (1-885266-38-3). Ashland, OR: Story Line Press, Spring 1997. Published over 25 years and collected in complete form here, these poems tell of journeys shared by many Americans. Here are voyages from youth to responsibility, from the midwestern hills of his boyhood to Vietnam, from the self alone to the self in nature. —Story Line Press. Barr is a poet of elegant saying rather than singing, and his subjects are the familiar guiding stars of our common life: love, its presence or absence; war; the physical world and, especially, as in the quiet but profound requiem "The Dial Painters," the investigative empathy toward others that keeps us civilized. — Mary Oliver

Barr, Tina. *The Fugitive Eye.* 43p. Philadelphia, PA: Painted Bride Quarterly, 1996. Barr traverses a substantial psychological and emotional tableau. Here's poetry that entertains and challenges. Through mythology, pragmatic psychology, and a near-blues insinuation, The Fugitive Eye coaxes us to see ourselves in truth-seeking reflections. This collection works because each poem dares the reader. — Yusef Komunyakaa

Barrax, Gerald. *From a Person Sitting in Darkness: New and Selected Poems.*

201p. $24.95 (0-8071-2313-7). pap. $17.95 (0-8071-2314-5). Baton Rouge, LA: Louisiana State University Press, Fall 1998. Gracefully brought to light in these poems are an African American man's struggle to justify the wrenchingly apparent injustice of the ways of God to man, a bold and honest witness, and a language so clear sometimes, you can see clear through to deep truth. —Marilyn Nelson. Every poem in this book took [Barrax] an entire lifetime to write in the sense that he is totally in every word. There is real bravery here — poetic bravery. From a Person Sitting in Darkness is not simply a collection. It is a consummation. —Samuel Hazo. Across the four decades in which he has been making poetry, Barrax has time and again both acknowledged and advanced the soul-creating power of art. Silence and song, he loves them both. What a pleasure it is — how important it is! — to have together in one volume Barrax's life work. —Andrew Hudgins

Barrows, Anita. *A Record.* 48p. pap. $5.00 (1-890044-08-3). Scottsdale, AZ: Riverstone Press, Fall 1998. Winner of the 1998 Riverstone Poetry Chapbook Award.

Bartley, Jackie. *The Terrible Boundaries of the Body.* 24p. pap. $5.95. Fox River Grove, IL: White Eagle Coffee Store Press, Fall 1997. The poet's originality of perception infuses ordinary experience with new meaning, linking the minute with the gargantuan and seconds of time with eternity. Hers is the eye of the scientist, finding life and death in a drop of blood, marveling over the terrible beauty of illness, confronting all of history in a chip of rock. —Jill Peláez Baumgaertner

Bascove, ed. *Stone and Steel: Paintings & Writings Celebrating the Bridges of New York City.* 96p. $30.00 (1-56792-081-0). Boston, MA: Godine, David R., Publisher, Spring 1998. This book is a celebration of New York City's bridges, their architects and designers, their builders and their advocates. In it, readers will find prose and poetry, from the classics by Hart Crane and William Carlos Williams, to lesser known, but no less resonant work. Bascove's 14 resplendent paintings form the cornerstone of the book. This is not a book of architectural paintings, but a book of art — graced by some of the best writing of the past two centuries. —David R. Godine, Publisher

Basso, Eric. *Accidental Monsters: Poems and Texts 1976.* 166p. pap. $14.00 (1-878580-81-7). Paradise, CA: Asylum Arts Publishing, Fall 1998. [Basso] carries us through a world where landscapes and interiors merge, a terrain vague of fleeting visions, gnomic adventures, enigmas, grotesque creatures and bizarre mechanisms. This is a poetry of convergences, set in the time-warp which traps that disquieting moment between the dream and the awakening. —Asylum Arts Publishing

Bateman, Claire. *At the Funeral of the Ether.* 64p. pap. $10.00. Greenville, SC: Ninety-Six Press, Fall 1998.

Bates, Jennifer. *The First Night Out of Eden.* 96p. $19.95 (0-8130-1596-0). pap. $10.95 (0-8130-1597-9). Gainesville, FL: University Press of Florida, Spring 1998. Bates's inaugural book of poems introduces a skillful young poet who already possesses a distinctive style and a wide range of themes and concerns. These poems are deeply felt and speak to everyone. — Robert Pack. Bates writes in a fresh, young voice about the old, post-Eden country of pain. Her poems are at once tough, vulnerable, and brave.

Whether she speaks as a contemporary woman or as Eve, Persephone, or Saint Teresa, she is convincing and moving in her honesty and clear-sightedness. —Linda Pastan

Bates, Julia. *Vernissage.* 80p. pap. $10.00 (1-56474-266-0). Santa Barbara, CA: Fithian Press, Fall 1998. I found the poems to be diverse and wise; rich with elegant phrasing, compassion, reflection. They speak to all of us and cut to the heart of things. —Steven Gilbar. In this courageous book, Bates faces the subject few poets dare — her end. She weaves moments together that give comfort, showing us how to transcend with grace. — Perie Longo

Battaglia, Carol. *Jagged Rhythms.* 89p. pap. $12.95 (1-880254-45-X). Long Branch, NJ: Vista Publishing, Spring 1997. [Battaglia] eloquently illustrates the mutual traits of innocence, frustration, vulnerability, care and compassion that bond nurse and patient in a special union. —Judith A. Bejna

Battin, Wendy. *Little Apocalypse.* 74p. pap. $10.00 (0-912592-40-0). Ashland, OH: Ashland Poetry Press, Spring 1997. Winner of the 1997 Richard Snyder

Memorial Publication Prize. Amid the incoherence of things, between the coarse lines of dissolution, after our last photogenic war, the "fever-vivid" language of Battin's Little Apocalypse threads between lucidity and lyricism, surface and depth to the very fovea of song. An exquisite collection. —C.D. Wright. Battin doesn't look to nature for metaphors; she looks to it as metaphor. I would say she has a deeply religious imagination, if that adjective weren't now suspect. —J.D. McClatchy, The Hudson Review

Baudelaire, Charles. Edited by Carol Clark and Robert Sykes. *Baudelaire in English.* 257p. pap. $14.95 (0-14-044644-3). New York, NY: Penguin Books/Viking Penguin, Fall 1997. This superb anthology brings together the translations of his poetry and prose poems which best reveal the different facets of Baudelaire's personality: the haughtily defiant artist, the tormented bohemian, the savage yet tender lover, the celebrant of strange, haunted cityscapes. —Penguin Books/Viking Penguin

Baudelaire, Charles. Translated by Norman Shapiro. *Selected Poems From Les Fleurs du Mal.* 248p. $25.00 (0-226-03925-0). Chicago, IL: University of Chicago Press, Fall 1998. Shapiro translates over seventy poems from the complete Flowers of Evil, the masterwork of the nineteenth-century dark poet, whose influence pervades subsequent Western poetry, and whose structured verse Shapiro smartly recreates in these formal renderings. —Kirkus Reviews. In these translations [Shapiro shows] a scholar's accuracy and a poet's formal exactitude. He captures that tension between lapidary form and romantic emotion which is Baudelaire's signature. — Richard Wilbur. Shapiro has found here in splendid translation what is most often lost. —John Hollander

Bauer, Bill. *Last Lambs: New and Selected Poems of Vietnam.* 64p. pap. $11.95 (1-886157-12-X). Kansas City, MO: BkMk Press of the University of Missouri-Kansas City, Spring 1997. Bauer avoids the verbiage of diatribe and makes the war real by paying close attention to detail, allowing the war's natural language and vivid imagery to evoke its own terrible legacy. The book gives us insight into the moral ambivalence and personal frustration of the American soldier and why so many continue to struggle long after the war is officially over. —BkMk Press

Bauer, Grace. *The Woman at the Well: Poems and a Revelation.* 102p. pap. $15.00 (0-916620-33-6). New Orleans, LA: Portals Press, Fall 1996. "And I know what courage it takes / to tell it right," says Lilith in Bauer's feisty retelling of stories based on the Old and New Testaments. Funny, wry, always surprising and smart. Bauer's women get it right and speak for us in the tradition of revisionist mythmaking we cherish these last days of the twentieth century. —Hilda Raz

Beam, Jeffery. *Little.* 30p. pap. $out of print.00. Hillsborough, NC: Diminishing Books/Green Finch Press, Fall 1997. This little book of one line poems was published in a dinky edition of 300 copies for exhibition and distribution at the First International Think Dinky Invitational (an exhibition of miniature art), September 1997. — Diminishing Books. Trying to become invisible, unlearning all that impairs one's ability to see, concentrating you feel you've left your bones behind.

—Reuben Cox. Less is not always more, but little is definitely BIG! —James McGarrell

Beam, Jeffery. *Submergences.* 70p. pap. $6.00. Carrboro, NC: Off the Cuff Books, Spring 1997. Submergences narrates the story of an unfolding, youthful, love relationship using dreamlike, surreal sequences, achieving a bleakness and wild, strange beauty. —Off the Cuff Books

Beasley, Bruce. *Summer Mystagogia.* 102p. $25.00. pap. $11.95 (0-87081-438-9). University Press of Colorado/Center for Literary Publishing, Fall 1996. Winner of the Colorado Prize. Beasley's wonderful third book of poems is a sly and forceful combination of Georgia drawl and the mythic language of the world. He builds a voice and a way of seeing that is truly his own and that we recognize as ours to boot. There are moving narratives of childhood family functions and disfunctions, everything emotionally resonant and linguistically crystallized under the white light of memory and desire, the little spiritual and familial Armageddons all our lives live through and eventually harbor in. —Charles Wright

Beaumont, Jeanne Marie.
Placebo Effects. 86p. $21.00
(0-393-04128-X). New York,
NY: Norton, W.W., and
Company, Fall 1997; Fall
1999 (new paper). Winner of
the National Poetry Series.
Beaumont's poems are smart
and full of feeling, heart-bro-
kenly in love with the snares
and clarities of the language
she writes in, and lit throughout by a kind of wry wonder.
Here's a first volume to celebrate. —William Matthews.
All of the high spirits, deep
feeling, and wide wordwitch-
ery that we expect from poetry
are here in Beaumont's book
— but a strict (and eccentric)
formal consciousness fixes
this dazzlement in place with
pins of exactitude. One
poem's speaker says "there is
no danger / of running out of
material." That's good news
for the fans Placebo Effects
will create. —Albert
Goldbarth

Beck, Al. *Songs From the
Rainbow Worm: Poems,
Drawings, Photographs and
Ceremonial Masks.* 86p. pap.
$9.50 (0-934852-65-0). Black
Mountain, NC: Lorien House,
Fall 1997. Beck's poetry tick-
les the fancy and stirs the
libido, bringing a refreshingly
different perspective to dialec-
tic designs in this old world of
ours. —Lorien House

Beckman, Joshua. *Things Are
Happening.* 74p. $23.00 (0-
9663395-0-9). (0-9663395-1-
7). Philadelphia, PA:
American Poetry Review, Fall
1998. Winner of the APR /
Honickman First Book Prize. I
think [Beckman] is a visionary
poet, by which I mean he is in
touch with something tenuous,
and that he feels the other
voice or the other thing inside
him. There is form, diction,
subject matter, language, and
music, but it is this imprint,
this print, that captures us. If I
had to give a name to it — for
Beckman — I would call it
affection. —Gerald Stern. This
book seduced me on the spot.
I instantly started longing to
become friends with the world
in it. It's fresh, it's new, its
fairness makes me grateful for
reading it. —Tomaz Salamun

Beckman, Madeleine. *Dead
Boyfriends.* 68p. pap. $8.95
(1-891219-68-5). Siasconset,
MA: Linear Arts, Fall 1998.
What if an Impressionist nude
leapt from her gold frame to
become the quintessential millennium woman? Surely it
would be Beckman who
would give her voice. Dead
Boyfriends anatomizes
romance in the luxurious, but
changing, details of moonlight
and daylight. Wryly resigned,
experienced but undaunted —
and always irrepressible —

Beckman is the direct inheritor of a grand female sensualist tradition. —Molly Peacock

Bedient, Cal. *Candy Necklace.* 96p. $25.00 (0-8195-2234-1). pap. $11.95 (0-8195-1221-4). University Press of New England/Wesleyan University Press, Spring 1997. Alive in every direction. . . an altogether unexpected and brilliant poetic debut. —Robert Hass, Boston Review. There is a truly original and powerful mind at work in this collection. It reflects one of the most sophisticated understandings of poetic voice in contemporary poetry. —David St. John. Poems with an edge that makes them truly vivid and literally astonishing. —Donald Revell

Bednarik, Joseph, ed. *The Sumac Reader.* 238p. (0-87013-427-2). pap. $17.95 (0-87013-462-0). Michigan State University Press, Spring 1997. Remaining true to Sumac's expressed mission — to publish "all sides of the geographical rifts" in American writing — The Sumac Reader gathers together a range of poetry, experimental fiction, and translations which originally appeared in the magazine. — Michigan State University Press. This collection func-tions as a cultural time capsule, putting the work of poets who are now widely recognized, such as Adrienne Rich, Louis Simpson and Gary Snyder, in context. It allows us to read them in the company they kept twenty-five years ago and also provides a snapshot of poetry's attempts to assimilate the era's turbulence. —Publishers Weekly. Refreshingly unpredictable and remarkably undated. — Sunday Oregonian

Beeaff, Dianne Ebertt. *Homecoming.* 65p. pap. $10.95 (0-9656188-0-3). Tucson, AZ: Hawkmoon Publications, Spring 1997. With a life-long affinity for most things related to the British Isles, [Beeaff's] first visit was "a sort of homecoming". This collection is based on that experience. — Hawkmoon Publications

Behar, Diane. *Collected Poems.* New York, NY: Stinehour Press, Fall 1998. Behar's poetry confronts the vital core of our very existence: the wish not to give in. It is suffused with the tone of human courage. —Ulla Hahn

Behrendt, Stephen C. *A Step in the Dark.* 69p. pap. $11.00 (0-922811-27-X). Minneapolis, MN: Mid-List Press, Fall 1996. A Step in the Dark has the rich savor of work aged in the heart and mind. Behrendt sees and hears keenly, testifies, and presents to us the roiling universe of nature and culture. These poems are brilliant and wise, deeply satisfying and compassionate. I can't imagine having lived without them. — Hilda Raz. Whether he writes of humans or animals, Behrendt feels the Other as an extension of himself, and his empathy makes his work profoundly moving. The poems in A Step in the Dark are not afraid to be gorgeous, yet Behrendt's eloquence is free of preening and preciousness. — Alice Fulton

Bein, Sarah. *Instead of Indonesia.* 64p. pap. $9.95 (1-888996-10-2). Palmdale, CA: Red Hen Press, Fall 1998. This is a powerful book of poetry, a significant female voice and a clear re-entry into the mythology of Woman's mystery. The poems are full of joy, yet lead deep into pain with a courage older than time. Her voice is altogether accessible, enjoyable and useful; I honor Bein's poetry. Men and women will draw strength from this poet. — Kurt Kristensen

Belitt, Ben. *This Scribe, My Hand: The Complete Poems.* 222p. $26.95 (0-8071-2323-4). pap. $19.95 (0-8071-2324-2). Baton Rouge, LA: Louisiana State University Press, Fall 1998. Bringing together almost 50 years of poetry by this famous translator of Lorca, Neruda, and Borges, this volume showcases Belitt's never-tiring devotion to baroque vocabulary, sound-play, and the loftiest poetic meters and sentiments. — Publishers Weekly. I have enjoyed and admired Belitt's poems for half a century, and am moved and delighted to have them brought together in This Scribe, My Hand, a Keatsian title that Belitt has earned. Belitt has been an authentic poet visionary. His achievement is finely wrought, and the best of his poems ought to endure. —Harold Bloom. [Belitt] writes by a kind of radar — a characteristic combination of great elaboration with great intensity. A neglected master. —Howard Nemerov. Over the course of his long career, Belitt has built a body of work to last. He has used autobiography to make myth, he has used art to fashion soul, he has used the green world to reveal a heartscape.

This Scribe, My Hand is a crucial collection, and a stirring, resplendent reminder that Belitt is a major figure in the American visionary company that stretches back to Hart Crane and Walt Whitman. — J.D. McClatchy

Bell, Marvin. *Ardor: The Book of the Dead Man, Volume 2.* 76p. pap. $14.00 (1-55659-081-4). Port Townsend, WA: Copper Canyon Press, Fall 1997. I find Bell's Dead Man to be a vast companion, enormous in spirit, an archive as well as an immediate presence. This book may actually be used for consultation when one needs wisdom or heart. Bell is David the Psalmist's Beat brother. A supremely accomplished work. —Sandra McPherson. The Dead Man knows Blake's Marriage of Heaven and Hell and Bierce's Devil's Dictionary, And Beckett. He's a standup tragic, a wise guy. "Why so whale of a jolly?" Bell's extraordinary new book asks about the Dead Man. Because laughter like this is spiritual. —William Matthews

Belli, Angela, and Jack Coulehan, eds. *Blood and Bone: Poems by Physicians.* 224p. $29.95 (0-87745-637-2). pap. $17.95 (0-87745-638-0). Iowa City, IA: University of

Iowa Press, Fall 1998. I admire this brave and accessible anthology. The drama is immediate. The effects are visceral. There are stories and facts in this collection that will knock you off your pins. Worthy of the classroom, but worthy too of a private chair by a window. It has a strength that can't be faked. —Marvin Bell

Ben-Lev, Dina. *Broken Helix.* 70p. pap. $11.00 (0-922811-31-8). Minneapolis, MN: Mid-List Press, Spring 1997. These poems are radiant with wit, energy and tough-minded grace. They announce in their unflinching, sure-handed way a poet of tremendous promise. —Linda Bierds. Broken Helix is a deeply conceived first book, a rare achievement for such a young poet. All her poems exhibit an integrity and honesty that are stunning, and her finest take us to places no one's been before. —Stuart Friebert. These poems are wide-eyed and wise, playful and fragile. —Denise Duhamel

Benbow, Margaret. *Stalking Joy.* 76p. $17.95 (0-89672-375-5). Lubbock, TX: Texas Tech University Press, Spring 1997. These tough, tender, often comic lyrics crackle with energy and a distinctive vitality. [Benbow] bears witness to the ways in which even the tiniest of the world's happy accidents can flare into radiance. —Ronald A. Sharp. These poems are a wild, wild ride. Fierce and chancy, passionate and bawdy, Benbow's exuberant first book is nothing short of rapturous, enrapturing. In language that flashes and dazzles, exfoliating through its Anglo-Saxon sinewy roots, these poems. . . "aim for the heart, make things jump." —Ronald Wallace

Bender, Thomas, Dir. *New York: A Divided City.* 63p. Project on Cities and Urban Knowledges International Center for Advanced Studies, Fall 1998.

Benedict, Elinor. *The Tree Between Us.* 23p. pap. $6.00 (1-882983-36-X). Greensboro, NC: March Street Press, Fall 1997. I was mesmerized by the surefooted, indirect strategies Benedict calls upon to drive the reader into a galvanizing moment, a moment where the intersection between a hard-sought revelation and a beautifully rendered landscape detail ignites. I'm looking forward to rereading The Tree Between Us for the rest of my life. —Roger Weingarten

Benedict, James S. *The Phoebe's Nest: An Illustrated Collection of Poems and Stories.* 179p. $15.00 (1-892015-00-5). pap. $10.00 (1-892015-01-3). San Pedro, CA: JB Press, Spring 1998. The latest collection of poems and short stories by Dr. Benedict, a retired thoracic and cardiac sugeon, which explores the natural world, France, and unique portraits of people. — JB Press

Bennett, Guy. *Last Words.* 88p. pap. $9.95 (1-55713-336-0). Los Angeles, CA: Sun & Moon Press, Fall 1998. A collection of brief, densely metaphorical lyrics characterized by a tension of form, syntax and meaning. Bennett fuses together a variety of poetic timbres and stylistic registers into a single lyric voice. The result here is a suite of humorous, often enigmatic poems whose potential meanings lie somewhere in the linguistic, yet in inevitably human space that separates the reader from the work. —Sun & Moon Press

Bennett, John M. *Know Other.* 65p. pap. $10.00 (1-89228-000-0). Columbus, OH: Luna Bisonte Prods, Fall 1998. Large-format collection of poetry and visual poetry in one of Bennett's unique Avant styles. —Luna Bisonte Prods

Bennett, Paul. *Appalachian Mettle.* 191p. pap. $15.95 (1-886028-27-3). Superior, WI: Savage Press, Fall 1998 (second edition). I challenge first time Bennet readers NOT to be totally captive by the end of the first few pages. — Michael D. Eisner. This book is a luscious surprise, a great harvest, a feast served by a master. —Clark Blaise. I rely on [Bennett's] poetry as a constant reminder that a clear language bespeaks a clear heart. —Molly O'Neill

Bennett, Saul. *Jesus Matinees and Other Poems.* 30p. pap. $7.95. Johnstown, OH: Pudding House Publications, Spring 1998. Bennett, after a lengthy career in public relations, began writing poetry upon the sudden death of his eldest daughter, Sara, at the age of 24. A full length collection, New Fields and Other Stones was published by Archer Books in 1998. — Pudding House Publications

Bennett, Saul. *New Fields and Other Stones: On a Child's Death.* 111p. $19.95 (0-9662299-0-8). Santa Monica, CA: Archer Books, Fall 1998. As a poet who also has lost a child, and written

about it, I have great admiration for the courage, grace, and voice of memory/experience that Bennett shares in this moving, redemptive collection. This is as strong a debut as any poet has made into the world of letters. — Michael Bugeja. Poetry written with a sword of sorrow, emanating tortured confusion, yet exploding with love. Bennett's lines sear you with an Old Testament quiet fury. . . ultimately, they astound you for their soul-wrenching imagery. How grateful I am to Saul for exposing his heart and putting out his hands to embrace all of us who have been reshaped by grief. — Antoinette Bosco

Bentley, Beth. *Little Fires.* 144p. pap. $15.95 (1-885942-04-4). Seattle, WA: Cune, Spring 1998. Bentley's poems range the geographies of our culture. The poems about her own life are travels to the interior. As a "ghost, traversing a dim gallery, sleep-walking in time's museum" she searches for an éclaircie, that rare moment of illumination, found in language and memory. — Cune. How wonderfully spare and full these poems are and how true to consciousness. [Bentley writes] poems which are alive in a dull and noisy time. —Richard Wilbur

Berg, Stephen. *Shaving.* 109p. pap. $12.95 (1-884800-14-9). Marshfield, MA: Four Way Books, Fall 1998. Berg's work is meditative, "metaphysical": it presents profound psychic knots and tries to untie them or at least show us their shape. There is an amazing variety in this work, of tone, of movement, of narrative, of anecdote, of subject. Something absolutely new is being done in this book. — Four Way Books. A book of strenuous and often dangerous self-witness; an astounding overview of American urban life at the apex and turning point of a major civilization; a probing into memory — both of the individual and of the race — at the moment when memory might be the medium that both saves us and finally condemns us; most importantly, it is brilliantly written, brilliantly perceived — the kind of book you simply can't stop reading once you've started it. In reading Berg you will be reading the master of the prose poem. —Jorie Graham

Berg, Stephen. *The Steel Cricket: Versions: 1958-1997.* 255p. pap. $16.00 (1-55659-075-X). Port Townsend, WA: Copper Canyon Press, Spring 1997. For nearly 40 years, Berg has sought inspiration in the work of scholars whose translations range from ancient Nahuatl religious chants, to twentieth century Hungarian and Latin American poets; from ageless Eskimo songs, to turn-of-the-century Russian poets, as well as poems from the Classical Zen tradition. The result is an exploration of the vision of other poets from other cultures presented in a unifying and unique context. —Copper Canyon Press. It is astonishing how the voice in these versions is simultaneously that of the poets being translated and the poet doing the translating. I hear the separate music of Radnoti, Mayakovsky, and Leopardi, yet it is Berg's music, lucid, pleading, observant, wise, that I am listening to. —Gerald Stern

Berger, Jacqueline. *The Mythologies of Danger.* 85p. $24.00. pap. $11.00. Emporia, KS: Bluestem Press, Spring 1998. Winner of the 1997 Bluestem Poetry Award. Berger explores the vagaries of desire, the entanglements of the self and the dangerous process of knowing and being known. "I am trying to isolate the present / as dancers locate a particular muscle / and work it," she writes. Her poems "work" the present with passion and a lively curiosity. This is an impressive debut.

—Chana Bloch. These are poems of immediate human energy and willful edge, whose voice stays with us even after the book is closed. —Alberto Alvaro Rios

Berger, Terry Wapner. *Haunted by 13 Places.* 37p. pap. $5.95. New Haven, CT: Berger, Terry Wapner, Fall 1998.

Berger, Terry Wapner. *Lives: Plucked From a Discarded Address Book 1965-1995.* 188p. (0-9652366-0-9). New Haven, CT: Berger, Terry Wapner, 1996.

Bergman, David. *Heroic Measures.* 85p. $19.95 (0-8142-0783-9). pap. $10.95 (0-8142-0784-7). Columbus, OH: Ohio State University Press, Fall 1998. Some of the best AIDS literature of any kind, [Bergman's poems] introduce characters who come alive and tell stories, not all directly about AIDS, that bring the poet and his anxieties to life, too. Poem after poem is fluent, intelligent, well shaped, and memorable. —Booklist. Here are poems of friendship and travel, the ravages of an epidemic, love and fear for aging parents, an elegy for the handsomest of hairdressers. Bergman's compassionate

book gives shape to the occasions of life. —Mark Doty

Berkowitz, James. *Canteen Trumpets at Noon.* 20p. los angeles, ca: Berkowitz, James, Spring 1998.

Bernard, Pam. *My Own Hundred Doors.* 68p. (0-9646844-4-6). Treadwell, NY: Bright Hill Press, Fall 1996. Winner of the 1996 Bright Hill Press Poetry Book Award. As a painter, Bernard has an eye for the pathos of disproportion, asymmetry and saturation of color. This same eye gives to her poetry a painterly fullness and a special emotional intensity. This is a very welcome first book. —Reginald Gibbons, TriQuarterly Magazine. Bernard's poems seem natural to the core. They are simultaneously passionate and coolly observed, as though she had just left the room where the event occurred, sat down, and — with the door still open — recorded all there was of importance to say. —Carol Frost

Bernstein, Carole. *Familiar.* 80p. $20.00 (1-882413-37-7). pap. $12.00 (1-882413-36-9). Brooklyn, NY: Hanging Loose Press, Spring 1997. Bernstein's poems are raw — as a wound is, or a flower.

They are also canny and compelling. Familiar is an exhilarating book, quickened by blood-bright longings and a restless intelligence. —J.D. McClatchy. Narrative momentum, intensity of feeling, accuracy of observation, and impassioned honesty mark these poems. Familiar is a memorable first book. — Daniel Hoffman

Berrigan, Anselm. *They Beat Me Over the Head With a Sack.* 14p. (1-890311-03-0). Washington, DC: Edge Books, Fall 1998.

Berrigan, Daniel. Edited by John Dear. *And the Risen Bread: Selected Poems, 1957-1997.* 300p. $37.50 (0-8232-1822-X). pap. $17.95 (0-8232-18221-8). Bronx, NY: Fordham University Press, Spring 1998. Forty years of poetry by Berrigan. Beginning with poems written largely on biblical themes, the book moves on to reflect the increasingly experiential inspiration of Berrigan's poetry — poems written from the front lines of the struggle for peace and justice, poems from the courtroom and the prison cell, and finally, poems of harsh but hopeful reflection. — Fordham University Press. The range of these poems may surprise, going well beyond politics and religion. It is [Berrigan's] engagement with the world that makes him a poet worth our attention. Highly recommended. — Library Journal

Berry, D.C. *Divorce Boxing.* 79p. pap. $14.00 (0-910055-44-0). Cheney, WA: Eastern Washington University Press, Fall 1998. At once lyric and satiric, this always delightful and occasionally scary book not only documents "the woe that is in marriage," but it also reveals the surreal goofiness of being single again. Berry has not just written a compelling book; he has also crafted a deeply humane one. — Dana Gioia

Berry, Jake. *Brambu Drezi: Book Two.* 63p. pap. $9.95 (1-880766-18-3). Berkeley, CA: Pantograph Press, Fall 1998. Berry places language under a tremendous pressure, opening up the mythic realm of the gods driven out of our technological culture. Here the author's mastery of the materials of his craft is completely subsumed in the service of this unusual vocation, to allow the world's divinites to resume their central place on the impoverished stage of our denatured and deadened existence. This book is simultaneously utterly unique and full of ancient familiar beings. — Harry Polkinhorn. Not to know Berry's work is to miss something essential and stunningly beautiful about the late twentieth century. —Jack Foley

Berry, Jake. *Drafts of the Sorcery.* 36p. pap. $7.00 (0-937013-81-1). Elmwood, CT: Potes & Poets Press, Fall 1998.

Berry, James. Illustrations by Reynold Ruffins. *Everywhere Faces Everywhere.* 80p. $15.00 (0-689-80996-4). Simon & Schuster Books for Young Readers, Spring 1997. Drawn from Berry's experiences in the Caribbean and the United Kingdom, these poems are windows into different cultures, yet are remarkable for their universality. This masterful poet has created a richly seasoned work that will astonish readers with its beauty, its lyricism, and its clarity. — Simon & Schuster

Berry, Wendell. *A Timbered Choir: The Sabbath Poems 1979-1997.* 216p. $22.00 (1-887178-68-6). Spring, TX: Counterpoint Publishing, Fall 1998. For more than two decades, Berry has spent his Sunday mornings in a kind of walking meditation, observing the world and writing poems.

A Timbered Choir gathers all of these singular poems written to date. Berry's voice is quiet, meditative, and wholehearted. [His] evocation of the natural world shows us time and again the exquisite beauty of the commonplace. — Counterpoint Publishing. Berry's poems shine with the gentle wisdom of a craftsman who has thought deeply about the paradoxical strangeness and wonder of life. —The Christian Science Monitor. A major poet of our time. —The Baltimore Sun

Berry, Wendell. *The Selected Poems of Wendell Berry.* 178p. $20.00 (1-887178-84-8). Spring, TX: Counterpoint Publishing, Fall 1998. In elegy, subsersive call, song or meditation, Berry's clear yet complex vision of what it means to be human is rare in American poetry. In these one hundred poems, drawn from nine previous collections, Berry's play of sound and syntax moves in our minds like something just remembered, and remains with us like an afterimage on the eye. — Counterpoint Publishing

Berssenbrugge, Mei-mei. With Artist Kiki Smith. *Endocrinology.* 32p. pap. $17.00 (0-932716-41-5). Berkeley, CA: Kelsey Street

Press, Fall 1997. In this collaborative work, the immaterial is examined in physical and mental sensations taken back to their material source in the endocrine system. These poems continue Berssenbrugge's brilliant explorations of language and perception in the light of changes in the body's chemistry. —Kelsey Street Press. An intense, vibrant communication, a modern anatomy. Here the body's porous system is turned inside out like a glove. —Chris Tysh, Metro Times Literary Quarterly

Berssenbrugge, Mei-mei. *Four Year Old Girl.* 77p. pap. $12.00 (0-932716-46-6). Berkeley, CA: Kelsey Street Press, Fall 1998. This volume of poems represents the most comprehensive collection of new work by Berssenbrugge to date. The greater length encompasses new breadth, in which the reader is drawn into a profound act of rearrangement of human presence in the phenomenal world. —Kelsey Street Press

Bezner, Kevin. *The Tools of Ignorance.* 62p. pap. $10.00 (0-9633551-3-9). Cincinnati, OH: Cincinnati Writers' Project, Spring 1997. In his first full-length collection, Bezner examines baseball,

childhood and family, nature in his backyard and in the wild, work, and the story of Lizzie Borden. His poems cut across all regions of the country. . . With an unusual vision and outlook, Bezner's poems put into essential language one poet's view of the United States at the end of the century. —Cincinnati Writers' Project

Bialosky, Jill. *The End of Desire.* 78p. $21.00 (0-679-45455-1). pap. $13.00 (0-679-76606-5). New York, NY: Knopf, Alfred A., Fall 1997; Fall 1998 (new paper). Quiet poems. Like whispers in a fierce forest. Bialosky has given us things we shall never be able to forget. —Hayden Carruth. This haunting, deliberative, hard-won sequence is made as much from legacy as memory. Bialosky's first book of poems is really one poem, one elegy, beautifully focused. The unique empathic power of the writing comes from the fact that the losses belong to a family, to four women, and not simply to the poet. Bialosky's genius as a witness is that she has created, with graphic precision, a community for her grief. —Stanley Plumly

Bidart, Frank. *Desire.* 61p. $20.00 (0-374-13824-9). New

York, NY: Farrar, Straus and Giroux, Fall 1997. Nominated for a National Book Award and National Book Critics Circle Award. In can be said of Bidart as of no other poet now writing in English that he truly expresses the civilization of which he is a part; not merely a witness or memoirist, he accumulates and broods over the collective experience of Western culture and deepens that culture with his own response.Desire exhibits Bidart's trademark idiosyncrasies of expressive punctuation and capitalization and like his earlier volumes is distinguished by a complex and multivoiced long poem. This collection should appeal strongly to serious readers. Highly recommended. — Library Journal

Biderman, Stan. *Everything Changes: A Spiritual Journey.* 100p. pap. $14.95 (0-911051-87-2). Austin, TX: Plain View Press, Fall 1997. With skill, style and sensitivity, Biderman sets words to the pathos of his people's traumatic past. I highly recommend this book to people of all faiths who struggle with the concept of: God, justice, truth, beauty or goodness. —Alice Holden

Biel, Steven, ed. *Titanica: The Disaster of the Century in Poetry, Song, and Prose.* 20p. pap. $11.00 (0-393-31873-7). New York, NY: Norton, W.W., and Company, Fall 1998. In the eighty-six years since the Titanic sank, socialists and chauvinists, Christians and reformers, anarchists, conservatives, and pitchmen have all drawn on the power of the century's worst disaster to move their audiences, in sermons, editorials, poems, songs, and ads. Now Steven Biel has gathered some of the most telling of our culture's responses to create an invaluable sourcebook for anyone who wants to discover firsthand what people then and now have made of this unforgettable tragedy. —W.W. Norton

Bierds, Linda. *The Profile Makers.* 64p. $23.00 (0-8050-5535-5). pap. $12.95 (0-8050-5536-3). New York, NY: Holt, Henry, and Company, Fall 1997. Bierds' poems, with their constantly surprising delicacy and their language rich with insight and a sensuous music, radiate real power and authority and animal presence. Her true originality has no need of quirkiness to emphasize it, and the range of her interests, empathy, knowledge, and imagination is imposing. —W.S. Merwin. Her sureness of hand and emotional range get even greater with each book. —William Matthews

Bird, Gloria. *The River of History: Prose Poems.* 36p. pap. $7.00 (0-932264-13-1). Portland, OR: Trask House Books, 1997. Bird's poems are brilliant as they arise from the blood river of history. They are sharp, penetrating illuminations of the heart, so startling as they emerge from the War Zone. —Joy Harjo

Bishop, Michael, trans. *Women's Poetry in France, 1965-1995: A Bilingual Anthology.* 392p. pap. $17.95 (0-916390-79-9). Winston-Salem, NC: Wake Forest University Press, Fall 1997. Women's Poetry in France, 1965-1995 is the first bilingual anthology of modern French women poets yet published. Bishop's translations are true to each of the twenty-eight distinctive voices in this volume. This anthology could reshuffle canons, alter the international perception of French poetry, and bring pleasure to many individual readers. —Wake Forest University Press

Bishop, Suzette. *Cold Knife Surgery.* 32p. pap. $5.00 (1-891387-00-6). Alexandria, VA: Red Dragon Press, Fall 1998. In this poem based on her own experience surviving cervical cancer, Bishop has created a powerful book of healing. Cold Knife Surgery reads as real and surreal introspective deliberations as she sorts out medical and financial obstacles, fear and frustration. —Red Dragon Press

Bishop, Wendy. *Mid-Passage.* 48p. pap. $9.95 (1-879205-77-7). Troy, ME: Nightshade Press, Fall 1998. Winner of the 1997 William and Kingman Page Chapbook Award. A tightly written clutch of compelling narratives that get right to the bone of everyday life in the late 20th century. —Nightshade Press

Bisso, Ray. *Buddy Bolden of New Orleans: A Jazz Poem.* 80p. pap. $10.00 (1-56474-268-7). Santa Barbara, CA: Fithian Press, Fall 1998. The first important name in jazz history is that of Buddy Bolden, who formed his first band eleven years before Jelly Roll Morton claimed to have invented jazz. The legend of this coronetist who rose from nobody to Kid to King, defined the music of his time, and then slowly and quietly went insane, is documented here in Bisso's biography in verse. —Fithian Press

Black, Star. *October for Idas.* 75p. pap. $12.00 (0-9651-5581-1). New York, NY: Painted Leaf Press, Fall 1997. Language here is a swarming and continually metamorphosing presence — "Too many photosats gag the oracle" — through which the poet navigates a course measured by what is displaced. The most unaccountable juxtapositions, of trance and gruel, telecast and musk, are drawn into quick and startling harmonies, and a book made in part through collage techniques achieves a remarkable unity of feeling and texture. — Geoffrey O'Brien

Blackhawk, Terry. *Trio: Voices From the Myths.* 36p. pap. $10.00 (1-56439-074-8). Detroit, MI: Ridgeway Press, Fall 1998. Myths of long ago rewritten from a strong feminist point of view. This volume contains wonderful original artwork to complement poems by one of Detroit's best poets. —Ridgeway Press

Blackshear, Helen F. *Alabama Album: Collected Poems.* 144p. $20.00 (1-881320-85-5). Montgomery, AL: Black Belt Press, Fall 1996. Alabama's poet laureate reaches new heights in giving the reader simple but strong images from her 85 years in Alabama. —Black Belt Press. Her poetry is deeply moving and evocative. She writes of daily life, of everyday happenings. There is a connection here that only gardeners know, lovers of plants and the earth. —Reese Kilgo. In the 14 lines of "Beauty Shop" she covered everything it took Steel Magnolias two hours to say, a splendid collection of poems. —Tom Fitzpatrick, Jr.

Blanchot, Maurice. Translated by John Gregg. *Awaiting Oblivion.* 85p. $26.00 (0-8032-1257-7). Lincoln, NE: University of Nebraska Press, Spring 1997. Awaiting Oblivion is one of the crowning works by the French philosopher and novelist Blanchot. Located at the crossroads of fiction and philosophy, it is a daring, innovative, and strikingly original experiment in literary form. —University of Nebraska Press. The distinction between "novels," "narratives,' and "criticism" is progressively weakened in Blanchot until, in [Awaiting Oblivion], language alone is allowed to speak. — Michel Foucault

Blanco, Richard. *City of a Hundred Fires.* 74p. (0-8229-56837). Pittsburgh, PA: University of Pittsburgh Press, Fall 1998. Winner of the 1997

Agnes Lynch Starrett Poetry Prize. These poems are more than gems, they are the truth not only about the Cuban-American experience, but of our collective experience in the United States, a beautiful land of gypsies. —Virgil Suarez. City of a Hundred Fires is vibrant and diverse, infused with energy and formal dexterity, equally at ease in Spanish and English. As if that weren't enough, it feels like an important cultural document as well — a bicultural document, testimony to the dualities of identity central not only to Cubans but to all "hyphenated Americans" — exile and citizen, emigrant and immigrant, elegist and celebrant. Blanco is a poet of remarkable talents — in any language. —Campbell McGrath

Blaski, Steven. *Keep the Killer Asleep.* 84p. pap. $9.95 (0-932112-34-X). Durham, NC: Carolina Wren Press, 1994. Blaski writes gay history poem. [He has discovered] a way to talk about the world in certain lush and terror-stricken notes. The chilling announcement here is that persecution, AIDS and the collective will have changed the world in which we live by relocating the witnesses. In no other book of poems in recent memory have I felt the experience of one of those witnesses so eloquently expressed. — Michael Klein

Blehert, Dean. *I Swear He Was Laughing: Poems About Dogs (Mostly) Who Only Think They Are People, But Aren't, So Can't Read This Book, So Will You Please Read It for Them.* 84p. pap. $8.95 (0-9644857-4-5). Santa Ana, CA: Words & Pictures Press, Fall 1996. To an amazing degree Blehert succeeds in writing poetry designed for, and deserving of, a wide general audience. —Miles David Moore

Blehert, Dean. *No Cats Have Been Maimed or Mutilated During the Making of This Book: But Some of Them Are Disappointed--Deeply Disappointed--in Me.* 84p. pap. $8.95 (0-9644857-5-3). Santa Ana, CA: Words & Pictures Press, Fall 1996. Blehert manages to be witty, ribticklingly funny, unabashedly sentimental and honestly realistic all at the same time. He brings sanity and perspective to our love / annoyance relationship with our four-legged friends. — Hilary Tham. [Blehert's] ramblings offer outrageous puns and language tricks that send you off in one direction so that his sneaky insights into being human can snatch you back the other. —Larry Gross

Bloch, Ariel, and Chana Bloch, trans. *The Song of Songs: A New Translation.* 253p. (0-520-21330-0). Berkeley, CA: University of California Press, Fall 1998. Next to Genesis, no book in the Hebrew Bible has had a stronger influence on Western literature than the Song of Songs. This attractive and exuberant edition helps to explain much of its power, while leaving its mystery intact. —Alicia Ostriker, The New York Review of Books. Quite simply the best version in the English language. Its poetic voice, intimate, dignified, and informed by meticulous scholarship, carries us into the Eden of the original Hebrew text: a world in which the sexual awakening of two unmarried lovers is celebrated with a sensuality and a richness of music that are thrilling beyond words. —Stephen Mitchell

Bloch, Chana. *Mrs. Dumpty.* 68p. $17.95 (0-299-16000-9). pap. $10.95 (0-299-16004-1). Madison, WI: University of Wisconsin Press, Fall 1998. Winner of the 1998 Felix Pollack Prize in Poetry. The supply of forceful metaphor seems inexhaustible, the lan-

guage sounds like a living voice. This is a stunning collection. —X.J. Kennedy. A woman who knows her own strength, and the strength of the beautiful and suffering world, tells the story of the life and death of a marriage; this is a clear-eyed and heartbreaking sequence of poems. —Jean Valentine. An exceptionally strong book. Mrs. Dumpty succeeds in healing with words, making this life livable. —Yehuda Amichai

Bloom, Harold, ed. *The Best of the Best American Poetry: 1988-1997.* 383p. $30.00 (0-684-84279-3). New York, NY: Simon & Schuster/Scribner, Spring 1998; Fall 1998 (new paper). Bloom precedes his selections with a compelling and highly provocative essay on the state of American letters, in which he fiercely champions the endangered realm of the aesthetic over the politically correct, announcing his "obligation to help (if that I can) make it possible for another Bishop or Swenson or Merrill to develop without being impeded by ideological demands." The seventy-five poems Bloom has chosen go a long way toward defining a contemporary canon of American poetry. Included are unforgettable poems from the poets mentioned above and from A.R. Ammons, John Ashbery, Louise Glück, Jorie Graham, Mark Strand, and Richard Wilbur, among many others. Diverse in form, style, method, and metaphor, the poems are united in their power to move and enlighten readers. Here is American poetry at its most memorable. —Simon & Schuster/Scribner

Bloomfield, Maureen. *Error and Angels.* 90p. $15.95 (1-57003-193-2). pap. $9.95 (1-57003-194-0). Columbia, SC: University of South Carolina Press, Fall 1997. With mythic spiderlike precision Bloomfield casts stories of the heart's sore places — the ruin found there, the hidden paths out. —Maureen Seaton. Bloomfield's poems have the feverish acuity of paintings seen in dreams. Spylike, she slips back and forth across the psychic borderline between portent and plain common sense. —Tom Disch

Bly, Robert. *Holes the Crickets Have Eaten in Blankets: A Sequence of Poems.* 21p. pap. $7.50 (1-880238-58-6). Rochester, NY: BOA Editions, Fall 1997. Letterpress Edition. Poems that speak to family and relationships and to the grief that comes with the death of a family member. —BOA Editions

Bly, Robert. *Morning Poems.* $23.00 (0-06-018251-2). pap. $12.00 (0-06-092873-5). New York, NY: HarperCollins Publishers, Spring 1997; Fall 1997 (paper). There is a lot of human knowledge in this book, and at the same time it has the vigor of youth. How can that be? —Galway Kinnell. Morning Poems is a sensational collection — Bly's best in many years. Inspired by the example of William Stafford, Bly decided to embark on the project of writing a daily poem: every morning he would stay in bed until he had completed the day's work. These are morning poems, full of the delight and mystery of waking in a new day, and they also do their share of mourning, elegizing the deceased and capturing "the moment of sorrow before creation." The whole is a fascinating and original book from one of our most fascinating and original authors. —David Lehman

Bly, Robert, ed. *The Soul Is Here for Its Own Joy: Sacred Poems From Many Cultures.* 268p. pap. $15.00 (0-88001-475-X). Hopewell, NJ: Ecco Press, Fall 1995. Bly's groundbreaking anthology of spiritual poems, the result of over a decade of personal research, celebrates the ongoing role of the divine in literature. He gathers poems from a wide range of cultures and traditions: selections include the work of Dante, Dogen, Goethe, Hafez, Juan Ramón Jiménez, Kabir, Lalla, Li Po, Mirabai, Mary Oliver, Owl Woman, Rilke, and Rumi, in addition to Blake, Dickinson, Donne, Hopkins, Stevens, Yeats and other important English and American poets. —Ecco Press

Boccia, Edward. *No Matter How Good the Light Is: Poems by a Painter.* 77p. pap. $12.50 (1-56809-045-5). St. Louis, MO: Time Being Books, Spring 1998. Boccia's head has "fallen off and rolled among the leaves." How fortunate for us. Boccia is to Wallace Stevens AND Picasso what Wallace Stevens is to Picasso. This painterly poet helps me see things otherly. —Jennifer Bosveld, Pudding Magazine. [Boccia] suggests that "any man who hides under his bed / at night, cursing the darkness, / ought to buy a Renoir." I'm here to tell you that Boccia's book is a viable, and less expensive, alternative: you won't need track lighting, extra insurance, or security alarms — not to mention some impossible wall space — for these quirky figments of the painter's imagination; you'll have a hard time getting them out of your head. —David Clewell

Bogen, Don. *The Known World.* 72p. pap. $11.95 (0-8195-2237-6). University Press of New England/Wesleyan University Press, Spring 1997. Short poems in this collection cohere around the long title poem, which explores the nineteenth century through more than thirty sections in different voices and styles, including lists, mock letters, brief narratives, and lyric passages. The result is lively and illuminating. —University Press of New England / Wesleyan University Press. One of the most remarkable and unsettling aspects of The Known World is the way in which the wonderful and odd events Bogen describes about the nineteenth century, slowly, inevitably, begin to sound like events of the present century and how they echo the dark details of our particular lives. In The Known World Bogen has discovered the stories that will illuminate the threshold of the next millennium. — Michael Collier

Bogen, Laurel Ann. *The Last Girl in the Land of the Butterflies.* 59p. pap. $10.00 (1-889504-00-9). Los Angeles, CA: Red Wind Books, Fall 1996. Bogen talks to us through clenched teeth. Her poems are hard and sharp; thcy bitc; thcy draw blood and leave scars. —Bitterroot. Bogen deserves to be read for her "this-is-how-it-is-with-no-excuses" attitude and for her hard-won decisive language. —Holly Prado, Los Angeles Times

Bogomolny, Abby. *People Who Do Not Exist.* 64p. pap. $13.95 (0-934172-45-5). San Jose, CA: Woman in the Moon Publications, Fall 1997. People Who Do Not Exist needs to be taken seriously. Bogomolny's writing is brave, honest and compassionate. It is a breathing portrait. — Maria L. Masque. Bogomolny preserves the vital language and lifestyle, the Yiddishkeit, of her parents and grandpar-ents, with wit and heart. — Lesléa Newman

Bogue, Lois. *Where Pheasants and Meadowlarks Nest.* 58p. pap. $7.00 (1-877649-29-5). Canton, SD: Tesseract Publications, Spring 1997.

Boire, Jennifer. *Little Mother.* 82p. (0-9699349-1-2). Cross-Cultural Communications /Hochelaga Press, 1997. This book represents women's sto-ries, a woman's stories, the kind we tell and don't dare tell each other, in a language both quicksilver and quotidian. — Mary di Michele. A moving account of the author's redemptive journey from care-taker and troubled daughter to mother of her own children. Many readers will recognize their own experiences here. — Susan Glickman

Boland, Eavan. *An Origin Like Water: Collected Poems 1967-1987.* $25.00 (0-393-03852-1). pap. $12.00 (0-393-31601-7). New York, NY: Norton, W.W., and Company, Spring 1996; Fall 1997 (paper). Here is the collected early work, long unavailable in the United States, of one of our major poets. Comprising poems from Boland's five early volumes,An Origin Like Water demonstrates how Boland's mature voice has developed from the poetics of inner exile into a subtle, flexi-ble idiom uniquely her own. —W.W. Norton. Boland com-bines impeccable craft, resilient metaphors and, above all, moral authority to witness human difficulties. —Jan Garden Castro, Nation

Boland, Eavan. *The Lost Land.* 67p. $21.00 (0-393-04663-X). New York, NY: Norton, W.W., and Company, Fall 1998; Fall 1999 (new paper). Here the internationally acclaimed Irish poet continues to merge private and mythic history to interrogate our definitions of the historical, the political, and the national. —W.W. Norton. Boland is one of those rare figures who, like Adrienne Rich or W.B. Yeats, has influenced the course of poetry during her own lifetime. She is increasingly officialised as one of the more important poets to emerge internationally over the past thirty years. — Jody Allen Randolph, Irish Times. One of Ireland's finest contemporary writers, as passionate and ambitious as Kennelly, as classical and meticulous as Heaney. — Booklist

Bond, Bruce. *Radiography.* 79p. pap. $12.50 (1-880238-51-9). Rochester, NY: BOA Editions, Fall 1997. There is a genuine warmth, a real drama and imaginative wit in these accounts of the life of the mind, the senses and the body's mysterious ways. — Anthony Hecht. Reading these wise, mature poems we begin to feel that every gesture within them is inevitably a gesture of faith. Time and time again, Radiography accomplishes the nearly impossible — the world we believe we know becomes a world transformed by the clarity and simplicity of true vision. —David St. John

Bonnell, Paula. *Japan in Duxbury: A Series of Poems in Tribute to Japan's Living Treasures.* 20p. pap. $10.00 (1-928668-03-8). Mill Creek Press, Fall 1998. A tribute to the Living Treasures of Japan, practitioners of age-old arts and crafts which include Kabuki, the making of paper, dolls, and swords. —Mill Creek Press

Borczon, Mark. *Drinking From the Toilet.* 44p. pap. $4.50 (1-889289-07-8). New Haven, CT: Ye Olde Font Shoppe, Fall 1996.

Borteck, Benjamin. *Having Accomplished So Little.* 31p. pap. $5.00 (1-890887-00-5). Santa Barbara, CA: Mille Grazie Press, Fall 1997. In Having Accomplished So Little, we are invited to examine the shining surfaces that comprise a life in constant wonder at small moments, and to look just as clearly at the darker inner compartments that struggle with loss and uncertainty. —Mille Grazie Press

Boruch, Marianne. *A Stick That Breaks and Breaks.* 108p. $22.95 (0-932440-79-7). pap. $12.95 (0-932440-80-0). Oberlin, OH: Oberlin College Press, Fall 1997. These poems range widely, letting themselves be triggered, often, by quite ordinary events and people, in order to launch themselves into questions and considerations we could not have predicted. At their center, the poet — observant, reflective and usually solitary — meditates with the care of a scientist and the precision of a magician on the way our lives weave a pattern that is both comic and tragic. —Oberlin College Press

Bosselaar, Laure-Anne. *The Hour Between Dog and Wolf.* 95p. pap. $12.50 (1-880238-47-0). Rochester, NY: BOA Editions, Fall 1997. Bosselaar understands the complexities and the endless contradictions of our contemporary human predicament. Hers is an authentic poetic voice, one serious enough to be heard at the end of this long and brutal century. She writes wise poems about memory, poems whose art lies in their ability to make these memories ours too. What more could any one

of us ask of poetry? — Charles Simic

Bosveld, Jennifer, ed. *Prayers to Protest: Poems That Center and Bless Us.* 229p. pap. $19.95 (0-614-10187-6). Johnstown, OH: Pudding House Publications, Spring 1998. Here are a plethora of political-spiritual poems: Earth-centered, humanist, agnostic, Eastern, liberal Christian, and other viewpoints. Life passages, relationships, social justice, alternative worship, chants, newprayers, rants, more. — Pudding House Publications

Bowen, Kevin. *Forms of Prayer at the Hotel Edison.* 73p. pap. $12.95 (1-880684-55-1). Willimantic, CT: Curbstone Press, Fall 1998. Poems that record the experience of rural and urban isolation, of dislocation and violence, and the histories of war and reconciliation in our century. —Curbstone Press. This wonderful book of poems is made up of Bowen's love of the people and landscapes of Vietnam, Ireland and [Boston]. His voice, his language is true and there's a strong music from those far countries as well as ours that has been singing in his ear — and now in ours. —Grace Paley. These poems cut to a reader's heart.

They are prayers less for peace and love than for the truth — which is why they cut, and why they are so precious. —James Carroll

Bowen, Kevin; Nguyen Ba Chung, and Bruce Weigl, eds. *Mountain River: Vietnamese Poetry From the Wars, 1948-1993.* 266p. $40.00 (1-55849-140-6). pap. $15.95 (1-55849-141-4). Amherst, MA: University of Massachusetts Press, Fall 1998. This powerful and moving bilingual collection affirms the importance of poetry in the formation and perpetuation of Vietnamese national identity and testifies to the centrality of war in Vietnamese history and experience over the past fifty years. —University of Massachusetts Press. These translations are among the best I've ever seen. [Mountain River] could easily be used as a course text. A most useful and beautiful work. —Renny Christopher

Bowers, Edgar. *Collected Poems.* 168p. $25.00 (0-679-45456-X). pap. $15.00 (0-679-76607-3). New York, NY: Knopf, Alfred A., Spring 1997; Fall 1998 (new paper). Surety of rhythm, swiftness of thought, and deftness of phrase animate Bowers's triumphant poems about loss and the struggle to be whole. — The New Yorker. One of our very finest poets, Bowers has always represented that power, very rare in contemporary poetry, generated when epigram expands into meditation, and when restraint gains in force as well as elegance by the acknowledgment of passion. —John Hollander. Bowers's Collected Poems is the sort of victory that requires nothing less than a lifetime of writing patiently and well. His sometimes difficult poems consistently make the deeper choices, wait for the strangely right phrase, and reward attention with freshets of meaning. —Richard Wilbur. Bowers is a master. His Collected Poems are already, to my mind, a classic. —Donald Justice

Boyce Taylor, Cheryl. *Raw Air.* 98p. pap. $11.00 (0-9639585-7-7). New York, NY: Fly by Night Press/A Gathering of the Tribes, Spring 1998. Raw Air is required reading for anyone who is interested in learning how social and personal awareness can be integrated into a beautifully conceived and sensitively executed poetic structure. Boyce Taylor writes eloquently about relationships, race, alienation, and struggle. A woman who is not afraid to immerse herself in the difficult questions, she speaks — no, sings — from a conviction which flows naturally out of her uncompromising commitment. —Susan Sherman, IKON Magazine. Here is Boyce Taylor, "Poet Laureate" of Trinidad via Low East Side/Brooklyn, in full book regalia! Read silently, you become a part of family history — a family who lives in places where bodies connect and separate, where joy and pain are food. Open Raw Air and breathe deep! —Bob Holman

Boyd, Tammy. *To Walk in Rivers of Fire.* 38p. pap. $5.00 (0-940895-29-3). Chicago, IL: Cornerstone Press Chicago, Fall 1996.

Bozanic, Nick. *This Once: Poems 1976-1996.* 79p. pap. $10.00 (0-938078-49-6). Tallahassee, FL: Anhinga Press, Spring 1997. Bozanic has the ear of an angel, and he understands prosody as a range of musical options that will allow him to guide the reader through his poems in a way that enables us to feel as if we are inside the luminous moments he's captured as they happen. He writes easily and gracefully within a rigorous measure as well as within a free verse line, each charged and wisely informed by a

practiced knowledge of the other. —Bruce Weigl

Brackenbury, Rosalind. *The Butterfly.* 8p. pap. $7.00. Key West, FL: Interim Books, Spring 1997.

Bradley, George. *The Fire Fetched Down.* 72p. $21.00 (0-679-44620-6). pap. $13.00 (0-679-76602-2). New York, NY: Knopf, Alfred A., Spring 1996; Fall 1997 (paper). Bradley, now fully individuated, has the cognitive power, the rhetorical gifts, the primal exuberance of language, and the spiritual vision to develop into the Merrill or Ashbery of his own generation. —Harold Bloom

Bradley, George, ed. *The Yale Younger Poets Anthology.* 306p. $35.00 (0-300-07472-7). pap. $16.00 (0-300-07473-5). New Haven, CT: Yale University Press, Spring 1998. This anthology of the longest-running poetry series in the United States tells the story of American poetry in this century, and contains poems from the first book by each of the ninety-two winners of the annual Younger Poets contest. The anthology is divided into two sections: "The Early Years," which briefly presents the first thirty-one winners of the contest, and "The Modern

Series," which gives ample room to the early work of some of America's finest poets. All poets are introduced by a biographical note, and in the second section Bradley has added brief commentary directing the reader to the salient features of each poet's work. —Yale University Press. An important and elegant history of American poetry — how it has been written, received, and read over the course of the century. It's a fascinating survey of the shifting tides in this country's literary taste. —J.D. McClatchy

Bradley, Jane Buel. *Tree of Life.* 48p. pap. $8.00 (1-888219-11-4). Long Beach, CA: Pearl Editions, Fall 1998. The backyards, parks, lagoons, marshes and shorelines of Long Beach are as much the holy landscape of her poems as is the landscape of the human heart. —Donna Hilbert

Bradley, Jane Buel. *World Alive.* 40p. pap. $6.00 (1-888219-07-6). Long Beach, CA: Pearl Editions, Spring 1997. These poems chronicle a life of passionate engagement in the plural tasks of living: domesticity, friendship, political activism, bird watching, philanthropy and writing. — Donna Hilbert

Brady, Denise. *Proof.* 1p. pap. $15.00. Omaha, NE: Bradypress, Fall 1997. Letterpress Edition. A poem about observing and connecting with the "other side". — Bradypress

Brady, Philip. *Forged Correspondences.* 101p. pap. $10.00 (0-938621-03-3). Binghamton, NY: New Myths Press/SUNY Binghamton, Fall 1997. After spending time with Herb Score and Sandy Koufax, Heraclitus and the Queen of Sheba, the reader is escorted home again, breathless from Brady's singular, expansive talents for narrative and song. This book is a journey through glittering empires of the imagination. —David Citino. Brady takes us on a bitter pilgrimage to his past and the past of places where he has lived, a wary traveler who knows how hard it is to tell heartbreak from the absurd. He can say, as Marianne Moore did, "I am troubled, I'm dissatisfied. I'm Irish." —Elton Glaser

Braggs, Earl S. *Walking Back From Woodstock.* 114p. pap. $10.00 (0-938078-45-3). Tallahassee, FL: Anhinga Press. Spring 1997. Braggs's book is jaunty, heartbroken, fast-talking, and true. — William Matthews. Here is a direct and uncompromising look into the heart of the 1960's, no romanticism here, but a witnessing with wit and irony, with the subtle wisdom that rises only out of experience and passion, with imagery right out of the fire. —Christopher Buckley

Branch, Debby. *Snippets From Obtuse Bird Jonesing.* 23p. pap. $7.00. NEW YORK, NY: Between Rock and a Reading, Spring 1998.

Brannon, Jack. *Vigil.* 102p. pap. $12.00 (0-9660365-0-6). Austin, TX: Abbey Press, Fall 1997. "This is what my father did for me," says Brannon, in this testament to his father's care during a childhood illness. —Abbey Press

Braschi, Giannina. *Yo-Yo Boing!.* 205p. pap. $15.95 (0-935480-97-8). Pittsburgh, PA: Latin American Literary Review Press, Fall 1998. Braschi's melange of prose and poetry, English and Spanish, is admirable for its energy, its experimental format and its insistence on Spanglish as a literary language. —Publishers Weekly. It bristles with lively literary conversation. —Kirkus Reviews. Braschi's Yo-Yo Boing! is the best demonstration yet of her command of many different registers, her dizzying ability to switch between English and Spanish. —Jean Franco

Brass, Perry. *The Lover of My Soul: A Search for Ecstasy and Wisdom.* 97p. pap. $8.95 (0-9627123-8-8). Bronx, NY: Belhue Press, Fall 1997. Brass offers a biography of himself as well as a spiritual journey of nakedness, surrender, and transcendence. Witty, angry, sensuous work achieving finally both wisdom and ecstasy. —Belhue Press

Breedlove, Charlene, ed. *Uncharted Lines: Poems From the Journal of the American Medical Association.* 160p. $20.00 (0-9651879-4-2). Boaz, Fall 1998. JAMA led the way among medical journals in establishing a regular poetry and medicine column almost ten years ago. Selected poems from that remarkable series are now available in this handsome new collection. Great as a teaching resource, this volume should also be welcomed by all those who care about medicine and poetry. —Anne Hudson Jones. Let no one be surprised that the physicians in this book are such good poets. These intense, precise, moving poems tell us much about what it is to be a doctor—but they tell us most about being human. —John Timpane

Brennan, Liz. *Sewing Her Hand to the Face of the Fleeting.* 28p. pap. $4.00 (0-9656161-3-4). Haydenville, MA: Quale Press, Fall 1998. Using her observations on growing up, falling in love, visiting friends — even on the "discovery" of the New World and an invasion of bears, Brennan does some amazing things with language in this collection of 22 prose poems. No one pushes syntax to its limit better. —Quale Press

Breskin, David. *Fresh Kills.* 82p. $22.50 (1-880834-32-4). pap. $12.00 (1-880834-31-6). Cleveland, OH: Cleveland State University Poetry Center, Fall 1997. Breskin is a contemporary town crier, a businessman-bard, an ironic prophet who goes for the jugular in these canny and acute renderings of our American moment. —Edward Hirsch. Breskin informs the reader with a brash honesty hovering near eloquence, and still grounded in our world, sport, cyberspace, the off-tempos of family; and he has serious intentions to speak for most everybody, which is less a question of voice, and more a responsibility of humanity. This is not tokenism, or

hopfencing; it is artistry. — Michael S. Harper

Brewer, Kenneth W. *The Place In Between.* 38p. pap. $20.00 (0-936159-52-3). Boise, ID: Limberlost Press, Fall 1998. Poems written from the perspective of an elderly man. —Limberlost Press

Bricuth, John. *Just Let Me Say This About That: A Narrative Poem.* 124p. $22.95 (0-87951-902-4). Sewanee Writer's Series/Overlook Press, Co-publishers, Fall 1998. From the poetic alter ego of literary critic John T. Irwin, this hilarious and lyrical narrartive poem takes the form of a press conference, hosted by "Sir," who is either God, the President of the United States, everybody's father, or a combination of the three. — Sewanee Writer's Series / Overlook Press. Here is Frost on speed, Nabakov on rollerblades. Here is the long, astonishing, magnaminous poem we've been waiting for. —J.D. McClatchy. As strong and moving, funny and high-energetic and horrifically splendid a long poem as our language has been lately blessed with. —John Barth

Bright, Susan. *Trades and Evidence of Grace.* 158p. pap. $12.95 (0-911051-58-9). Austin, TX: Plain View Press, 1992.

Bright, Susan, and Margo LaGattuta, eds. *Everywhere Is Someplace Else: A Literary Anthology.* 256p. pap. $17.95 (1-891386-01-8). Austin, TX: Plain View Press, Fall 1998. A most unusual anthology. The poems were selected and ordered by the poets them- selves, working in close har- mony and communal spirit. Here are poems that focus on the most central human con- cerns, poems whose perspec- tives range from the veins in a hand to the pulsing heat of the stars. —Rick Lott. Drawn from lives as varied as a cab driver, college professor, letter carrier, community activist, pastor, scientist, business owner — these writers share with us their heartfelt concern for the individual and global communities in which we all strive to survive. —Larry Gross

Bright, Susan, and Margo LaGattuta, eds. *Wind Eyes: A Woman's Reader and Writing Source.* 200p. pap. $14.95 (0-911051-90-2). Austin, TX: Plain View Press, Fall 1997. This isn't simply an anthology — it is a body of work with all the essential parts in all the right places. Wind Eyes is truly a book that one can enter — like one enters a good novel or autobiography — and emerge from some 200 pages later utterly refreshed. —Herb Scott. There are many books on the market claiming to help the writer; few deliver the goods as this one does. — Jack Grapes

Brin, Herb. *Poems From the Rubio.* 109p. $18.00 (0-9645651-0-2). Los Angeles, CA: Heritage Publishing, 1995. This is a man who is not finished, who has not finished with his mission, with his work, with himself, and who will not let his measure be taken. Don't expect his poems to be finished, either. They are forever migrating to new lev- els of meaning. But read them on the wing. They will loft you into a perspective which is today all too rare for its innocence and integrity. — Heritage Publishing. These poems reverberate in the read- er's soul with nostalgia and tenderness. —Elie Wiesel

Brink, Leonard. *Ascended Distance.* 32p. pap. $4.00. Saratoga, ca: Instress, Fall 1998.

Brock-Broido, Lucie. *The Master Letters.* 83p. pap. $14.00 (0-679-76599-9). New York, NY: Knopf, Alfred A., Fall 1995; Spring 1997 (paper). Brock-Broido has imaginative finesse, chutzpah, swank, wit, humor, playfulness, and sheer brilliance to spare; . . . she's an utter original. —Calvin Bedient, Parnassus. Reading The Master Letters we feel we are in the presence of something entirely new. Not even Brock-Broido's wonderful first book, though set in the same general universe of metaphysical lyric, prepares us for this bold encounter. —Bonnie Costello, Boston Review

Brodsky, Joseph. *So Forth.* 132p. $18.00 (0-374-26641-7). pap. $12.00 (0-374-52553-6). New York, NY: Farrar, Straus and Giroux, Spring 1996; Fall 1996 (paper). Brodsky's final collection of poems, representing eight years of self-translation from the Russian, as well as a body of work written directly in English. —Farrar, Straus and Giroux. Brodsky developed a voice and a view that were deeply personal in their details and broadly human in their reach; he was, by the end, a truly international poet. Here, his flexible, distinctive style absorbs and celebrates language and experi-

ence that is sophisticated, coarse, and learned; the sly slant rhymes complete the effect of a beautiful strangeness, addressing the predicaments of human life in history. His epiphanies salvage a kind of gladness from the work of the poet. —Library Journal

Brodsky, Louis Daniel. *The Complete Poems of Louis Daniel Brodsky: Volume One, 1963-1967.* 633p. pap. $25.00 (1-56809-020-X). St. Louis, MO: Time Being Books, Fall 1996. The first volume of an impressive series comprising the full collection of Brodsky's verse captures the unloosing of a poet's voice. Beginning with Brodsky's first poem, written during his final months at Yale, in 1963, the book traces the maturation of the author during his apprentice years, when he was a graduate student at Washington University in St. Louis, and presents the hundreds of poems, prose poems, and short, autobiographical prose works he had composed by June of 1967, when he launched his professional writing career. —Time Being Books

Brodsky, Louis Daniel. *The Eleventh Lost Tribe: Poems of the Holocaust.* 105p. pap. $12.95 (1-56809-042-0). St.

Louis, MO: Time Being Books, Fall 1998. The Eleventh Lost Tribe is a thoughtful meditation on the post-Auschwitz human condition. The collection sensitively explores the limits of language and the enormity of loss for the generations who come after the Holocaust. —Alan L. Berger

Brodsky, Louis Daniel. Edited by Sheri L. Vandermolen. *Three Early Books of Poems: 1967-1969.* 205p. pap. $16.95 (1-56809-031-5). St. Louis, MO: Time Being Books, Spring 1997. Brodsky is a poet you read with all the pleasure of feeling your brains go up onto the tips of their toes, dancing. You know there's a high intelligence here. You feel the wit. —Charles Muñoz

Brodsky, Louis Daniel. *Toward the Torah, Soaring: Poems of the Renascence of Faith.* 81p. pap. $14.50 (1-56809-047-1). St. Louis, MO: Time Being Books, Fall 1998. For Brodsky, writing poems is prayer. These are poems of awe and gratitude, open and vulnerable. This book is an exploration of self, faith, and the religious imagination. — Dan Jaffe

Brodsky, Nicole. *Getting Word.* 62p. pap. $7.00 (1-889292-01-X). San Francisco State University Chapbook Series, Fall 1998. Winner of the 1998 Michael Rubin Award. For its grammar and usage, so playfully in hand. For the formal invention of the original and more difficult longer sequences. And for the poignant, fabulous "cow" series: "close your eyes and empty." Undeniable. This book. —Carol Snow

Bronk, William. *All of What We Loved.* 162p. pap. $13.95 (1-883689-65-1). Jersey City, NJ: Talisman House, Publishers, Fall 1998. Arguably the most metaphysical poet of his generation. — Hungry Mind Review. One of the most solid and unfrivolous contemporary poets. —Kirkus Reviews. He is brilliant. — Southwest Review. One of our modern masters. —Michael Heller

Bronk, William. *Life Supports: New and Collected Poems.* 241p. pap. $16.95 (1-883689-59-7). Jersey City, NJ: Talisman House, Publishers, 1997 (new edition). Winner of the American Book Award. Bronk's rare gift is the ability to float difficult truths on fleeting snatches of broken breath. —Voice Literary

Supplement. Bronk perceives lives as more than necessary fictions devised against the absurdity of eternity; belief reappears continually in his work as a salvation. — Publishers Weekly

Bronk, William. *Some Words.* 70p. pap. $9.95 (1-883689-73-2). Jersey City, NJ: Talisman House, Publishers, Spring 1999. Originally published in 1992, Some Words includes some of Bronk's most characteristic and insightful poems. —Talisman House, Publishers

Bronk, William. *The Cage of Age.* 102p. pap. $10.50 (1-883689-41-4). Jersey City, NJ: Talisman House, Publishers, Fall 1996. He is, at this moment, our most significant poet. —The Nation. One of our finest. . . poets. —The New York Times Book Review. One of the most solid and unfrivolous contemporary poets. —Kirkus Reviews

Brontë, Emily, Anne, and Charlotte. Edited by Susan L. Rattiner. *Best Poems of the Brontë Sisters.* 64p. pap. $1.00 (0-486-29529-X). Mineola, NY: Dover Publications, Spring 1997. Presents a careful selection of 47 poems by the talented Brontë sisters, including twenty-three poems by Emily, 14 poems by Anne,

10 poems by Charlotte. Reproduced from standard editions. —Dover Publications

Brooks, David. *Right Livelihood.* 30p. pap. $5.00 (1-886350-80-9). Scotia, nY: Pavement Saw Press, Fall 1998. Winner of the 1997-98 Pavement Saw Press Chapbook Award. Right Livelihood is full of both a hard-earned reverence and a refreshing irreverence. Brooks is not afraid to poke fun at himself — one man trying to cope with life's absurdities. These poems celebrate our continuing urge to dream; [they] are full of the kind of laughter that hurts just a little bit — laughter that sinks in, and stays with you for a long time. —Jim Daniels

Broughton, James. Edited by Jim Cory. *Packing Up for Paradise: Selected Poems 1946-1996.* 331p. $27.50 (1-57423-053-0). pap. $16.00 (1-57423-052-2). Santa Rosa, CA: Black Sparrow Press, Fall 1997. The theme of this fifty year selection of Broughton's poetry is Eros Ascendant and Transcendent. Deceptively simple, indecorous, irreverent, challenging of assumption, disturbing, Broughton's poetry is entirely affirmative. — Black Sparrow Press

Brouwer, Joel. *This Just In.* 41p. pap. $5.00 (1-892184-05-2). Venice, CA: Beyond Baroque Books, Spring 1998.

Brown, Dale S. *I Know I Can Climb the Mountain.* pap. $8.95 (1-881650-04-9). Columbus, OH: Mountain Books, 1995. A collection of poems and prose written while Brown was growing up, not knowing she had attention deficit disorder. —Mountain Books. [Brown's] story shows us that when you are made of the right stuff, years and years of pressure and tension result in a diamond. This diamond now reflects brilliant light onto others still struggling to climb their mountain. —Larry B. Silver

Brown, Dan. *Matter.* 53p. $14.00 (0-9647581-0-5). pap. $9.00 (0-9647581-1-3). New York, NY: Crosstown Books, Fall 1996. Brown's poems are splendid demonstrations of the power to be obtained from drawing the reins really tight. —X.J. Kennedy. Brown's laconic and supremely intelligent lyrics pulse with precision and wit. Matter is a rare and bracing pleasure to read. —Rachel Hadas

Brown, Kurt. *Recension of the Biblical Watchdog.* 32p. pap. $5.00. Palo Alto, CA: Anamnesis Press, Spring 1997. Winner of the 1996 Anamnesis Poetry Chapbook Award.

Brown, Kurt, and Laure-Anne Bosselaar, eds. *Night Out: Poems About Hotels, Motels, Restaurants, and Bars.* 378p. pap. $14.95 (1-57131-405-9). Minneapolis, MN: Milkweed Editions, Spring 1997. A night in a motel is like a night alone with your soul. It's best to either go to sleep, or write some poetry. — Tom Bodett. Included here is the work of 125 who wrote poetry, such as James Wright, Richad Hugo, W.S. Merwin, Susan Mitchell, and Joy Harjo. Together, they provide a look at ourselves in places where, as Gerald Stern says in his introduction, "ordinary events — ordering a meal, spilling a little wine — take on significance that can only be called mythical." —Milkweed Editions

Brown, Kurt, ed. *Verse and Universe: Poems about Science and Mathematics.* 339p. pap. $15.95 (1-57131-407-5). Minneapolis, MN: Milkweed Editions, Fall 1998. Science and art come together in Verse & Universe, a comprehensive selection of poetic voices revealing the beauty, the precision, the triumphs, and the destructive power inherent in science and technology. In sections such as "Space," "Matter," and "Heavenly Bodies," eighty contemporary poets contemplate the revolutions in physics, astronomy, mathematics, chemistry, geology, botany, biology, and medicine. Their words celebrate our curiosity and inventiveness, as well as our delight in the act of discovery, as they turn the revelations of science into poetry and capture the nature and spirit of modern scientific inquiry. Just a few of the outstanding poets included in this collection are Loren Eiseley, Jorie Graham, Howard Nemerov, Pattiann Rogers, and Charles Simic. — Milkweed Editions

Brown, Stephanie. *Allegory of the Supermarket.* 89p. pap. $15.95 (0-8203-2068-4). Athens, GA: University of Georgia Press, Fall 1998. Winner of the Contemporary Poetry Series Competition. There is a devastating playfulness at work in these poems. They are indeed allegorical, but this is a thoroughly modern allegory dealing with frighteningly up-to-date situations. —University of Georgia Press. Here's a poetic voice calling out from a postmodern arcade, where "each day the sun shines steadily, no more than is necessary," toward a post-California arcadia, where "sacrifice order and love" take on frightening proportions. — Jane Miller

Brown-Davidson, Terri. *The Doll Artist's Daughter.* 34p. pap. $5.00. Fox River Grove, IL: White Eagle Coffee Store Press, Fall 1996.

Browne, Laynie. *Lore.* 32p. pap. $4.00. Saratoga, ca: Instress, Fall 1998.

Browne, Laynie. *Rebecca Letters.* 78p. pap. $10.00 (0-932716-43-1). Berkeley, CA: Kelsey Street Press, Spring 1997. In these prose-poem sequences Browne makes structures that appear to be sentences caught just before their meanings become transparent. —Lisa Robertson, The Stranger. Browne's alchemically applied linguistics unfold the space between poem and prose, revealing a crepuscular zone "where it's warm enough to stop on the street." —Lee Ann Brown. "A mind with an eye" explores the phantoms of memory and dream as if we could "learn sleep through observation." It boldly skews the dimensions of our world. Breath is "relocated to another organ," and the ordinary tilts into strangeness. —Rosmarie Waldrop

Browne, Michael Dennis.
Selected Poems 1965-1995.
123p. $20.95 (0-88748-243-0).
pap. $11.95 (0-88748-244-9).
Pittsburgh, PA: Carnegie
Mellon University Press,
Spring 1997. As a librettist,
[Browne] has written many
texts for music. —Carnegie
Mellon University Press

Browning, Elizabeth Barrett.
Edited by Colin Graham.
Selected Poems. 392p. pap.
$7.50 (0-460-87425-X).
Boston, MA: Tuttle, Charles
E./Everyman, Fall 1996. The
most comprehensive paper-
back edition available, with
introduction, notes, selected
criticism and chronology of
Browning's life and times. —
Charles E. Tuttle/Everyman

Bruce, Debra. *What Wind
Will Do.* 62p. pap. $11.95 (1-
881163-19-9). Oxford, OH:
Miami University Press,
Spring 1997. I admire Bruce's
adroit use of form. Through
it, paradoxically, she has
acquired the freedom to con-
front subjects that range from
cancer to infertility and she
does so with considerable
grace. —Maxine Kumin.
What strikes me about What
Wind Will Do is Bruce's wonderful eye for the luminous

detail and the wrenching but
understated lyricism of immi-
nent loss. I admire how Bruce
combines an intimacy and
accuracy of feeling and diction
with the control and skill of
formal structures. —Julia
Alvarez

Brugnaro, Ferruccio.
Translated by Jack Hirschman.
Fist of Sun / Pugno di sole.
120p. pap. $10.95 (1-880684-
52-7). Willimantic, CT:
Curbstone Press, Spring 1998.
By turns tender, loving, angry,
satiric, these are passionate
poems by Italy's best-known
working-class poet — skillfully crafted, clear, and filled
with powerful images. —
Curbstone Press. Earthy,
direct and bone-deep honest,
Brugnaro's poetry lays to rest
any fear that communism or
proletarian culture is dead. —
Nelson Peery

Brukner, Ira Beryl.
*Questions, Short Poems,
Water & Air.* 80p. pap. $11.00
(1-881523-08-X). San Diego,
CA: Junction Press, Fall 1998.
These enigmatic, haiku-like
compressed poems have a
teasing mystery to them.
Wonderful. —John Francis
Haines, New Hope
International. These are poems
of disarming simplicity, whose
precisely-chosen detail sug-
gests landscapes and histories

beyond the words. And the good news here is that the language swings, swings in places hard as good jazz. — Quincy Troupe

Bryan, J.B. *How Can I Follow My Beautiful Dreams?*. 32p. pap. $7.00 (1-888809-05-1). Albuquerque, NM: La Alameda Press, Spring 1997. Sing praises, this stuff is the real, all-the-way, luscious thing. A wild bliss comes up reading these lines aloud to anyone near. This is a blast from our lingual future, fresh language like new cream, rico. Where have these poems been all my needy life? [I am] ecstatic to have them at last, in hand! —Judyth Hill

Bryant, Philip. *Sermon on a Perfect Spring Day.* 96p. pap. $12.95 (0-89823-185-X). Minneapolis, MN: New Rivers Press, Spring 1998. To be instructed by exhortation in scripture from a pulpit is a return to fundamentals; Bryant loves to riff in short exhortations, treatises, assays on the controversial, on the impolitic, and on the rare aesthetics of jazz musicians and the vocabulary of the blues. Bryant is at heart a teacher, he believes in daylight, so you can see the night. —Michael S. Harper

Buck, Paula Closson. *The Acquiescent Villa.* 51p. $19.95 (0-8071-2304-8). pap. $11.95 (0-8071-2305-6). Baton Rouge, LA: Louisiana State University Press, Fall 1998. The celebration in these poems is so probing and relentless it approaches an incandescence of mind itself. But it's never pure. The impure, that is, the world in its materiality, is always hugely present in Buck's lines. What a gift. —Li-Young Lee. These are powerful, daring poems, and a new voice is immediately audible in them. They are original in that they speak with authority out of one life, the light and hope and pain that play through it, the moments and singular details they touch upon. The Acquiescent Villa is a remarkable debut, and Buck, I believe, is already a poet to read with care, and to watch for. —W.S. Merwin. Gorgeous, impassioned, mysterious, inspiring. With her debut collection, it seems as though Buck has entered the skies from some hidden or obscure place to become one of the brightest lights around. —Kelly Cherry

Buckley, Christopher. *Fall From Grace.* 77p. pap. $11.95 (1-886157-18-9). Kansas City, MO: BkMk Press of the

University of Missouri-Kansas City, Fall 1998. He has an exquisite ear for language and a gutsy way of blending bravado with humility. No concept is overstated — it's all marvellously fresh. —Library Journal. Buckley's poems [are] full of the pain and pleasure of his relentless memory. His subject is radiance. So he hates fascism and believes we are more than dust. So I read him. —Gerald Stern

Buckley, Cicely, ed. *Thoughts for the Free Life: Lao Tsu to the Present.* 105p. pap. $12.95 (1-882291-56-5). Durham, NH: Oyster River Press, Fall 1997. Here are a plethora of ideas on free thought, the natural way and the art of living. Among the jewels: quotes from May Sarton, Cervantes, Tagore, Neruda, and Isaiah. —Margaret Grierson

Buckley, W.K. *81 Mygrations.* 80p. pap. $10.00 (1-56474-241-5). Santa Barbara, CA: Fithian Press, Fall 1998. Poems celebrating the American language, the American road, and the American imagination. — Fithian Press. This collection of poems really is a mygration through the geography of contemporary America. The poems are sign posts, pit stops along a dizzying spatial/tem-poral trip across the land-scape/mindscape of America. It is an insistent search for patterns of meaning, from primeval remnants to the insubstantial digital of now, by a writer whose eyes and mind absorb the many contradictory insensibilities of our times. An American road-movie in verse. —Csaba Polony

Bugeja, Michael. *Talk.* 60p. $18.00 (1-55728-471-7). pap. $12.00 (1-55728-472-5). Fayetteville, AR: University of Arkansas Press, Fall 1997. In Talk, Bugeja showcases those moments when words change people's lives. His poems feature an eclectic cast of characters: William Carlos Williams as Bugeja's neighbor; Lady Mary Wroth as a confessional poet; the Virgin Mary as an eyewitness new source, and more. —University of Arkansas Press. Girl talk, boy talk, woman talk, man talk — whatever the talk, Bugeja is a master of it. He is a formal wizard — his sestinas, sonnets, villanelles, ballades, and pantoums effortlessly levitating off the page. In this exuberant and unforgettable volume, mixing a lyrical sweetness with a tragic awareness of loss and death, he draws on cosmology, theology, biology, psychology, history, politics, pop and high culture to evoke the richness and variety of human experience. —Ronald Wallace

Bukowski, Charles. *Bone Palace Ballet: New Poems.* 363p. $27.50 (1-57423-029-8). pap. $15.00 (1-57423-028-X). Santa Rosa, CA: Black Sparrow Press, Spring 1997. The dance of death in Bukowski's bone palace takes shape as autobiography: yarns about his Depression child-hood and early literary pas-sions, his apprentice days as a hard-drinking, starving poetic aspirant, and finally the bitter-sweet later years when he looks back over his shoulder at fate with a measure of undefeatable defiance. — Black Sparrow Press

Burch, Claire. *Stranger on the Planet: The Small Book of Laurie.* 192p. pap. $10.00 (0-916147-67-3). Oakland, CA: Regent Press, Fall 1997. A scathing indictment of the state psychiatric labels and inadequate social policies that left her adoptive daughter dead. Through Laurie's aston-ishing and beautiful poetry and her mother's searching prose, this book provides a haunting image of a child's Coney Island ride into terrified womanhood. —Regent Press

Burdine, James M., ed. *Mountains to Motown: A Brief Anthology.* 55p. pap. $15.00 (1-56439-067-5). Detroit, MI: Ridgeway Press, Spring 1997. This limited edition anthology celebrates the many friend-ships between writers in Detroit and Woodstock, NY. The book features Edward Sanders, Mikhail Horowitz, Donald Lev, Enid Dame, M.L. Liebler, Barry Wallenstein, and many others. — Ridgeway Press

Burgess, Hugh. *Penny's Hill.* 28p. pap. $4.00. Baltimore, MD: Lite Circle Books, Spring 1998.

Burkard, Michael. *Entire Dilemma.* 87p. $20.95 (1-889330-17-5). pap. $12.95 (1-889330-18-3). Louisville, KY: Sarabande Books, Fall 1998. Inventive in terms of syntax, image, and flexibility of line, Burkhard's seventh collection delivers what human commu-nities have always asked of their poets and poems: wonder and song. —Sarabande Books. What a joy — and how hum-bling — to be confronted by an artist who has utterly aban-doned himself to beauty and truth. —Denis Johnson

Burns, Michael. *It Will Be All Right in the Morning.* 60p. pap. $15.00 (1-55728-516-0).

Fayetteville, AR: University of Arkansas Press, Fall 1998. Clarifying the language like so much butter, Burns provides a particular insight into national, local, masculine, and finally human concerns, all with a dry eye and a warm heart. It is the very best butter. —Richard Howard. I like the way Burns's quiet irony and a submerged ache work their way to the surface of the language in poems whose transparent simplicity proves deceptive. —Rachel Hadas

Burns, Robert. Edited by Donald A. Low. *Poems in Scots and English.* 206p. pap. $8.95 (0-460-87786-0). Boston, MA: Tuttle, Charles E./Everyman, 1996 (re-issued). A comprehensive paperback edition, with introduction, annotations, extensive glossary of Scots words, selected criticism, and chronology of Burns's life and times. This edition, published to commemorate the bicentenary of his death, conveys the range and excellence of Burns's poetic output. — Tuttle, Charles E./Everyman

Burrows, E.G. *The Birds Under the Earth.* 32p. pap. $7.00 (0-937669-60-1). Camano Island, WA: Owl Creek Press, Fall 1997.

Bursk, Christopher. *Cell Count.* 90p. $18.95 (0-89672-385-2). Lubbock, TX: Texas Tech University Press, Spring 1997. Bursk knows that injustice is a human and spiritual issue as much as a mere sociological one, and he reminds us of this distinction time and time again in Cell Count, which is a book of powerful lyrics and portraiture. . . gracefully structured of unusual depth and resonance. — David Wojahn

Buyer, Laurie Wagner. *Glass-eyed Paint in the Rain.* 80p. pap. $10.95 (0-931-271-40-1). Glendo, WY: High Plains Press, Fall 1996. Here is a poet who brings us the Rocky Mountain West, realistically and lyrically. Her deep-felt connections with nature grew from the hard physical work of a rugged homestead lifestyle in the Montana backcountry, 86 miles from the nearest town. Her poetry is a stunning and intimate revelation of landscapes, both external and internal. —High Plains Press. Buyer has brought the myth of the ranch woman home for supper. Her poetry makes sense of the struggle. While the soup stirs steam and the bread bends the toweling with a yeasty fragrance, Buyer tells

the story of her living. —
Linda Hussa

Byer, Kathryn Stripling.
Black Shawl. 53p. (0-8071-
2250-5). Baton Rouge, LA:
Louisiana State University
Press, Fall 1998. The poems
of Black Shawl, like migratory
birds, carry a legacy of
Highland ballads through the
New World Appalachians, to
startle and delight us with
their intensely lyrical mystery
of origins. Byer's haunting
wildness and sorrow become a
new, still ancient-seeming,
lonelier and lovelier voice in
the American mountains. —
James Applewhite. Byer's
poems are both explorations
and expositions of life made
by hand and heart displaying
an alert intelligence. They also
contain the enduring mysteries
of language and affirmations
of human survival that surface
in transient silences. This tender yet earnest (or fierce)
singing verse forms a mosaic
of compassion full of daring
intensity which reminds one of
the old Celtic bards needing to
sing the world alive. —Menna
Elfyn. Blending medieval
Celtic lyrics with Cherokee
myth, Old Europe with
Appalachia, Byer weaves a
wide net, a fabric of magic.
The poems shimmer and link
into purest song. —Betty
Adcock

Byrd, Bobby. *The Price of
Doing Business in Mexico and
Other Poems.* 132p. pap.
$12.95 (0-938317-40-7). El
Paso, TX: Cinco Puntos Press,
Fall 1998. [Byrd] is an emotional writer. He is often
haunted by personal tragedy,
his own and anyone else's.
Bad things happen in this
book. Existence verges on
becoming a joke — if not for
a sweetness that suffuses
Byrd's poems and says that a
life lived, part by part, is holy.
—Eileen Myles. If you
worked about fifty years, let's
say, at absorbing the essences
of the Border and making
music out of the food, speech,
good and bad habits, and sheer
surreal instances of the people
who live on both sides of it,
you still wouldn't be Bobby
Byrd. —Andrei Codrescu

Byrkit, Rebecca. *Zealand.*
76p. $25.00 (0-933313-27-6).
pap. $14.95 (0-933313-28-4).
Tucson, AZ: SUN/gemini
Press, 1995. This astonishing
debut book of poems resusci-
tates language in a phantas-
morgia of erotic encounters. In
so lively a theater, death also
has its way. There is genius
here, strobing the orgy and
elegy. —Jane Miller. If Dylan
Thomas had married Mae
West, these are the poems
their daughter would have
written. Like Thomas, she puts

language back in the mouth, where it belongs. Like West, she speaks with a voice simultaneously sassy, witty, and smart. Byrkit's poems cut deep into some very important places: where we hurt, and where we love. —Steve Orlen

Cabico, Regie. *I Saw Your Ex-Lover Behind the Starbucks Counter.* 53p. pap. $7.00. New York, NY: Big Fat Press, Spring 1997. Cabico's comic poems explore male celebrity worship, real life love, the despair of betrayal, and the "halo of calm" that follows permanent loss. —Big Fat Press

Caccia, Fulvio. Translated by Daniel Sloate. *Aknos and Other Poems.* 59p. pap. $10.00 (1-55071-048-6). Guernica Editions, Fall 1998. A first-time translation of Caccia's poetry which appeared in the original French-language Aknos, winner of the Governor General's Award. —Guernica Editions

Cadet, Guichard. *Lonewolf's Cry: Episodes of a Haimeri Poetic Lifetime, Volume 1.* 143p. pap. $8.00 (0-9647635-0-8). Riverdale, MD: La Caille Nous Publishing, ©1991. Haitian-born writer Guichard Cadet brings another dimension to the black looking-glass. In Lonewolf's Cry, he walks a bridge that is often travelled yet rarely described. —La Caille Nous

Cage, John. *I-VI.* 452p. pap. $24.95 (0-8195-6313-7). University Press of New England/Weslcyan University Press, Fall 1997. More like performances than lectures, these six mesostics — a complex horizontal arrangement of text to form vertical letter sequences that spell out key words — illustrate the concept of "nonintention," a kind of meticulously choreographed anarchy in which choice and chance join to redefine the concepts of meaning and meaningfulness. Drawing text from Thoreau, Wittgenstein, Joyce, McCluhan, and daily newspapers, Cage used a computer program to combine seemingly disparate lines into a whole that explored fifteen central aspects of his compositional credo. This edition includes the mesostics and a CD recording of Cage reading in a sonorous baritone that infuses the mesostic with life, depth and musicality. — University Press of New England/Wesleyan University Press

Cagnone, Nanni. Translated by Stephen Sartarelli. *The Book of Giving Back: A Poem.*

64p. pap. $10.00 (0-964-6466-4-1). New York, NY: Edgewise Press, Spring 1998. Cagnone writes of the gift of giving something back, of peering into the void, in an unrelenting act of restitution that restores the formlessness of the source of things. His is a poetry of spiritual restitution, a poetry of spiritual restitution, a non-religious poetry, in the great pagan narrative epic tradition of Homer or Whitman. —Edgewise Press

Cahill, Susan, ed. *Wise Women: Over Two Thousand Years of Spiritual Writing By Women.* 395p. pap. $15.00 (0-393-31679-3). New York, NY: Norton, W.W., and Company, Spring 1996; Fall 1997 (paper). Here are the voices of women ranging from Sappho to Joan of Arc to Marian Wright Edelman. Ancient goddesses and contemporary poets alike, these visionaries see justice and love, loss, aging, and freedom, and it inspires them to artistic expression and political action. This deeply moving collection of memoirs, stories, poetry, letters, prayers, and theologies is a source of empowering insight for women in any time, at any age. —W.W. Norton. A very satisfying anthology, illumi-

nating and useful. — Publishers Weekly

Caine, Shulamith Wechter. *Love Fugue.* pap. $10.00 (1-878851-10-1). Eugene, OR: Silverfish Review Press, Spring 1997. Winner of the 1995 Gerald Cable Book Award. The beautifully crafted lyric poems of Caine seem to reach out hands to touch what they tell, so affectionately do they hold the world in words. To a silken and sensual language of desire, she brings a wise restraint, a knowing eye, the composure of an achieved artistry and an uncorrupted heart. —Eleanor Wilner. In her moving, compassionate collection, Caine takes us from her grandmother's native Russia to Utamaro's Japan. Again and again, the oddities, the particulars of love are named and made vibrant. —Elaine Terranova

Cairns, Scott. *Recovered Body.* 74p. pap. $12.95 (0-8076-1437-8). New York, NY: Braziller, George, Fall 1998. The poet's richly cadenced style of storytelling offers theological poetry that leaves even the most cynical of readers nodding and grinning. — George Braziller. Cairns is one of the best poets alive. — Annie Dillard. Cairns has the imaginative power and verbal grace to resurrect a deadened world — relocating the sacred in the body, where it belongs. —Eleanor Wilner

Calbert, Cathleen. *Lessons in Space.* 60p. pap. $11.95 (0-8130-1503-0). Gainesville, FL: University Press of Florida, Fall 1997. For all the toughness, asperity, gall, in her exacting inspection of those circumstances we find so hard to make out — adolescence, marriage, love, la condition féminine — there is an abiding sweetness in Calbert's poems. Her poems are like pomes, indeed, delectable within the rind, but guarded, sly. —Richard Howard. Lessons in Space is a wonderful, truly distinctive debut. These poems are richly narrative in a way that has the formal and imaginative dash of real poetry, enlivened by a fresh, untamable spirit. — Robert Pinsky

Caldiero, Alex. *Various Atmospheres: Poems and Drawings.* 64p. pap. $10.95 (1-56085-101-5). Salt Lake City, UT: Signature Books, Fall 1997. Sometimes meditative, sometimes playful poems that celebrate both holiness and farce. —Signature Books

Califia, Pat. *Diesel Fuel: Passionate Poetry.* 336p. pap. $12.95 (1-56333-535-2). Masquerade Books/A Richard Kasak Book, Spring 1997. An extraordinary volume from this renowned sexual pioneer. The author of such bestselling — and infamous — volumes as Sensuous Magic and Macho Sluts, reveals herself to be a poet of unusual power and frankness in this first collection of verse. Not for the timid, Diesel Fuel is nonetheless one of this year's must-read explorations of underground culture. — Masquerade Books. Dead-on direct, these poems burn, pierce, penerate, soak, and sting. Not to mention cut. To the quick. Califia leaves no sexual stone unturned, clearing new ground for us all. — Gerry Gomez Pearlberg

Campana, Dino. Translated by I.L. Salomon. *Orphic Songs: Pocket Poets Series Number 54.* 179p. pap. $12.95 (0-87286-340-9). San Francisco, CA: City Lights Books, Fall 1998. A unique, visionary masterwork of Italian literature, written when Campana was still in his twenties. These poems and prose poems, ablaze with the fury of a poet crazed by life, "read as though they were thrown into the wind in an ecstasy of violence," writes the translator I.L. Salomon. The originality, rapturous language, and strange beauty of [Campana's] work make him as important to twentieth-century poetry as García Lorca or Mayakovsky. —City Lights Books

Campbell, Carolyn Evans. *Tattooed Woman.* 128p. pap. $11.95 (1-888219-05-X). Long Beach, CA: Pearl Editions, Spring 1997. The appeal of "Reflections of a White Bear," one of the long poems included in this collection, is in the compelling panorama Campbell chooses to draw. The overall effect is symphonic in the way disparate elements are brought together into a unified whole. "Reflections" has all the amazing life force of a courageous mother on her own in the world. —Ted Kooser, The Georgia Review

Canan, Janine. *Goddess Poems.* 12p. pap. $5.00. Port Townsend, WA: Sagittarius Press, Fall 1997. Handset, handsewn letterpress limited edition.

Capitol Hill Poetry Group. *The Other Side of the Hill, 1975-1995.* 95p. pap. $10.00 (0-938572-18-0). Hedgesville, WV: Bunny and the Crocodile Press/Forest Woods Media Productions, Fall 1996. A collection of verse by nine poets

who live near our Capitol and move — unlike more celebrated inhabitants of the Hill — from the tragic to the comic with wisdom and grace. — Reed Whittemore

Cardenal, Ernesto. *The Doubtful Strait/El estrecho dudoso.* (0-253-31318-X). pap. $14.95 (0-253-20903-X). Bloomington, IN: Indiana University Press, 1995. Constructed almost entirely from unaltered fragments of documents and histories from the colonial era, the poem opens with Columbus' fourth voyage and concludes with the apocalyptic destruction of León, Nicaragua, by the volcano Momotombo in 1609. A parallel plot tells the story of the political events and economic conditions of more recent Nicaraguan history. — Indiana University Press. A truly magnificent poem. The best history of Central America ever written. —Paul W. Borgeson, Jr.

Carey, Tom. *Desire.* 76p. pap. $12.00 (0-9651558-4-6). New York, NY: Painted Leaf Press, Fall 1997. These are strong poems, exceptional in their emotional honesty; their graven sureness has a luminous aura of shakiness. They embody a morally formidable conception of time: that the past is not memory but still occurring in the present. So you haven't gotten away with anything, and the texture of life — of these poems — is dense, painful, idiotic, and beautiful. —Alice Notley

Carlson, Lori M., ed. *Cool Salsa: Bilingual Poems on Growing Up Latino in the United States.* 123p. $15.95 (0-8050-3135-9). New York, NY: Holt, Henry, and Company, 1994. Growing up Latino in America means speaking two languages, living two lives, learning the rules of two cultures. Cool Salsa celebrates the tones, rhythms, sounds, and experiences of that double life with poets such as Sandra Cisneros, Martín Espada, Gary Soto and Ed Vega. By selecting poems about the experiences of teenagers, Carlson has given a focus to that rich diversity. — Henry Holt and Company

Carlson, Nancy Naomi. *Kings Highway.* 63p. pap. $10.00 (0-931846-50-1). Washington, DC: Washington Writers' Publishing House, Spring 1997. Kings Highway is freighted with loss, though loss is the poet's route to understanding and acceptance. At the center of these poems, literally and metaphorically, is breath, as in the acute atten-

tiveness to a newborn's giving breath up [or] to a violin's breath rising from the "rosined bow / against each string." These are poems attuned to the subtle motions of grief and love that give need to words in the first place. —Merrill Leffler

Carpenter, Jill, ed. *Of Frogs & Toads: Poems and Short Prose Featuring Amphibians.* 131p. pap. $10.95 (0-9666674-0-9). Sewanee, TN: Ione Press, Fall 1998. In a multiplicity of voices, the writers in Of Frogs and Toads address the range of human relations with amphibians — from their place in literature and folklore to their croaking in ponds and biology laboratories. —Ione Press. Poems and short prose featuring amphibians will delight natural history fans of the frog. This [book] will complement any collection on amphibians, providing an ode to toads and packing in enchanting and literary pieces. —Reviewer's Bookwatch

Carpenter, Leo. *The Altonberrys of Sandwich Bay.* 99p. pap. $14.95 (0-9653966-6-5). Port St. Joe, FL: Karmichael Press, Fall 1997.

Carravetta, Peter. *The Sun and Other Things.* 148p. pap.

$13.00 (1-55071-026-5). Guernica Editions, Spring 1998. Written over a period of twenty years, The Sun and Other Things is a metamorphic journey through language, history, styles, and particular events in the poet's mind and life. The poems gathered in this collection inscribe possibilities for uttering what in principle cannot be expressed. —Guernica Editions. The Sun and Other Things is an intriguing poetic journey through time and the Western psyche as manifested in both hemispheres. The trip is impressive in both scope and ambition. —Lawrence R. Smith

Carroll, Jim. *Void of Course: Poems 1994-1997.* 113p. pap. $12.95 (0-14-058909-0). New York, NY: Penguin Books/Viking Penguin, Fall 1998. Void of Course presents new work by diarist and rock musician Jim Carroll. Carroll's major themes — love, friendship, desire, time and memory, and above all, the ever-present city — emerge in an atmosphere where dream and reality mingle on equal terms. — Penguin Books

Carson, Anne. *Autobiography of Red.* 150p. $23.00 (0-375-40133-4). New York, NY: Knopf, Alfred A., Spring 1998. Carson is a daring, learned, unsettling writer. Autobiography of Red, which perhaps comes closest to representing the range of her voice and gifts, is a spellbinding achievement. —Susan Sontag. Carson, is, for me, the most exciting poet writing in English today. She is a rare talent — brilliant and full of wit, passionate and also deeply moving. Autobiography of Red is a wonderful, mongrel work, a strange and ambitious bridge between classical texts and contemporary autobiographical poetry. —Michael Ondaatje

Carson, Ciaran. *Opera Et Cetera.* 96p. $15.95 (0-916390-76-4). pap. $9.95 (0-916390-75-6). Winston-Salem, NC: Wake Forest University Press, Fall 1996. Torqueing and tuning his long lines in this new volume to the demands of rhyme, Carson skitters from Northern Ireland to Romania, from the Irish language to the Latin roots of English. Words and stories proliferate, exuberantly and often hilariously. —Wake Forest University Press. The gravitational field of wordplay, of allusions might be called scholarly except for their thoroughly irreverent tone. —Pamela Alexander, The Boston Book Review

Carson, Ciaran. *The Alexandrine Plan.* 88p. pap. $12.95 (0-916390-83-7). Winston-Salem, NC: Wake Forest University Press, Fall 1998. In these translations from the sonnets of the major nineteenth-century French poets — Rimbaud, Baudelaire, and Mallarmé — the relation of the poet to his world is adapted to the wild, fruitful imagination of Carson, while formally the poems hold to their "Alexandrine plan," twelve-syllable lines in the rhyme schemes of the original. As Carson carries these poems across into his own idiom and sensibility, he restores, with startling freshness, the essential joy and verve of the earlier poems. —Wake Forest University Press. By common consent, Carson is one of the most gifted poets now writing in England and Ireland. —Ben Howard, Shenandoah

Carson, Ciaran. *The Twelfth of Never.* 88p. $16.95 (0-916390-85-3). pap. $10.95 (0-916390-84-5). Winston-Salem, NC: Wake Forest University Press, Fall 1998. The Twelfth of Never — seventy-seven sonnets composed in alexandrines — floats on or submerges in the Otherworld

promised in fairy stories, lines of cocaine, revolutionary ideals and Utopia. —Wake Forest University Press. Carson continues to demonstrate what it means to have ears that truly work. He is one of the best poets we have on both sides of the Atlantic and the publication of every one of his books is a major event in our literatures. —Charles Simic

Carson, Meredith. *Infinite Morning.* 83p. $22.95 (0-8214-1211-6). pap. $12.95 (0-8214-1212-4). Ohio University Press, Fall 1997. Carson writes poems so well-controlled in tone that the language of conversation takes on an elegance rarely found in contemporary poetry, but emphatically contemporary. —Miller Williams. What we have in these poems is a lifetime of an intelligent and compassionate mind engaged in the only real work that allows us to rise above the human drift and toil — the act of thinking, observing, and distilling the phenomena of the world as it is in all its seemingly random peculiarities. Carson gives us hope — that we become forces of nature when our minds passionately, unrelentingly interact with the world around us. —Cathy Song

Carter, Anne Babson. *Strike Root.* 85p. pap. $12.95 (1-884800-21-1). Marshfield, MA: Four Way Books, Spring 1998. The music of Carter's poems is utterly new, yet as traditional as American hymns, striking for its emotional accuracy and compelling for its vivid landscapes. She is simultaneously innocent and worldly, her vision pure, her spirit adventurous. Hers is a fresh, original voice. —Grace Schulman

Carter, Michael. *Broken Noses and Metempsychoses.* 72p. pap. $10.00 (0-9639585-6-9). New York, NY: Fly by Night Press/A Gathering of the Tribes, Fall 1996. Carter writes moving, lyrical poems about love and survival in the East Village and in Prague. The neighborhoods in which he sets his poems may have changed, yet his voice remains constant. He's like a reflective Neil Young who has traded his guitar for a typewriter. —Hal Sirowitz

Carter, Patricia, and Nancy Adams. *So Close: Selected Poems.* 80p. pap. $10.00 (0-932616-55-0). New Poets Series/Chestnut Hills Press, Fall 1997. Carter and Adams are identical twins who have been calling one another on the phone for years to read the latest poem, sometimes between Tokyo and New York, sometimes between Frankfort and Washington. —New Poets Series/Chestnut Hills Press. These are astonishing new voices, tender and subdued. —Berry Morgan

Carver, Raymond. *All of Us: The Collected Poems.* 386p. $27.50 (0-375-40398-1). New York, NY: Knopf, Alfred A., Fall 1998. In what would have been his sixtieth year, and ten years after his death, Carver's poems — more than three hundred in all — are collected in this volume, allowing readers to experience their full range and overwhelming cumulative power. Hailed as our own Chekhov, Carver is revealed in All of Us as the "heir to that most appealing poetic voice, the lyricism of Theodore Roethke and James Wright,"(The New York Times). —Alfred A. Knopf. There is a severity of language, an understatement of emotion, that endows the poems with the feel of extraordinary experience. To read them is to have the sense this man has lived more than most of us. We trust him because of the plainly conversational diction and the lapel-grabbing rhythms. They are very moving, very memorable. —Dave Smith, Poetry

Cassells, Cyrus. *Beautiful Signor.* 120p. pap. $14.00 (1-55659-124-1). Port Townsend, WA: Copper Canyon Press, Fall 1997. Unabashedly passionate, feverishly baroque, these lyrics reach back to the Song of Songs and St. John of the Cross, claiming a place in that tradition in which the body of the beloved leads to the Divine Body. Divine seems precisely the adjective for these gorgeous, operatic poems, in which Cassells reinvents himself as troubadour and dervish, visionary and diva. —Mark Doty. With Beautiful Signor, Cassells confirms his reputation as a poet of exquisite skill. These love poems are resonant, even haunting, born of an acute sensual awareness, the images like "mosaics / clarified by rain." Cassells evokes ancient ruins and turquoise seas in a song of extraordinary tenderness. Beautiful, indeed. —Martín Espada

Cassian, Nina. *Take My Word For It.* 95p. $21.00 (0-393-04654-0). New York, NY: Norton, W.W., and Company, Fall 1998. Cassian has always been a miraculous poet, but her latest feat is the most amazing of all — she has reinvented herself in English. This new Cassian is a bit different from the Romanian classic many of us have long adored. She is now more spare and angular, but her genius for the harmonics of heartbreak and delight remains as seductive as ever. —Dana Gioia. Cassian is, as she says of herself, "no indexed bird"; she is highly personal, intimate, particular, and reading her work is a unique and wonderful experience. Her poems have wit and substance and are, quite simply, unforgettable. —William Jay Smith. Cassian's poems are emotionally clear, beautiful in their particulars, and profound. The mind in these pages fears pain and the abyss, but is still courageously and even ferociously alive to all of experience. [Her writing is] dense with feeling and intelligence. —Jane Kenyon

Cassity, Turner. *The Destructive Element: New and Selected Poems.* 246p. $29.95 (0-8214-1221-3). pap. $15.95 (0-8214-1222-1). Ohio University Press, Spring 1998. Cassity may be the most brilliantly eccentric poet in America. —Dana Gioia. If you require your poets to be politically correct, don't buy Cassity's book. Do buy it if you enjoy a highly original sensibility you're not quite sure you approve of, who has the sang froid to send up the accepted pieties of our time.

—The New York Times Book Review. Joseph Epstein has recently lamented the dearth of poems with single, memorable lines as once there were in the days of Yeats and Eliot. Let him read Turner Cassity, and begin to memorize again. —Poetry

Castleman, David. *The Wood and the Wilderness.* 98p. pap. $6.00 (83-904541-7-3). Larkspur, CA: Mandrake Press, Spring 1998. Poems, stories, and essays, frequently un-facetiously satirical, sometimes fabulous and/or fantastic. — Mandrake Press

Caston, Anne. *Flying Out With the Wounded.* 110p. $25.00 (0-8147-1561-3). pap. $12.95 (0-8147-1560-5). New York, NY: New York University Press, Spring 1997. It is with a surgeon's precision that Caston opens up a world of blood and stainless steel, of bodies and instruments, taking the reader on a tour of those working hours when most of us are asleep: the graveyard shift. Compassionate, but veering away from sentiment, she examines the horrors in this night world and offers up her own brand of intensive care. When [Caston] compresses an anecdote into verse, her poetry is as sharp and bright — and sometimes as

revealing — as a scalpel. — Publishers Weekly

Castro, Adrian. *Cantos to Blood & Honey.* 158p. pap. $12.95 (1-56689-067-5). Minneapolis, MN: Coffee House Press, Fall 1997. A rhythmic debut poetry collection powered by the pulse of the Caribbean, Cantos to Blood & Honey presents a synthesis of Afro-Caribbean, Hispanic, and North American mythology, language, and aesthetics. Castro creates a circular motion of theme, tone, subject matter, style, and cultural history, giving rise to a new illuminating archetypal poetry. —Coffee House Press. Castro has long been layering Spanish, English, and Yoruba dialects, musical sound, and drum rhythms, Cuba, Miami, Africa, and the Santeria religion. He seems well on the way to inventing a brand new Miami patois. —Jordan Levin, The Miami Herald

Castro, Guillermo. *Toy Storm.* 36p. pap. $7.00. New York, NY: Big Fat Press, Spring 1997. A native of Argentina, Castro fuses political upheaval and everyday domestic normalcy with a natural candor, grace, and humility. —Big Fat Press

Catlin, Alan. *Killer Cocktails.* 30p. pap. $4.00. Milwaukee, WI: Four Step Publications, Fall 1997. A never ending cast of characters; some dangerous, some pathetic, and some just plain loopy. One hell of a ride we got here, señor. —Four Step Publications

Catterson, Thomas M. *This Pot Has Pepper.* 32p. $15.00 (0-89304-084-3). Cross-Cultural Communications /Nightingale Editions, Fall 1998.

Cauthen, Carolyn Rebecca. *The Ties That Bind.* 30p. pap. $10.00. St. Louis, MO: DDDD Publications, Spring 1998.

Cavalieri, Grace. *Heart on a Leash.* 28p. pap. $5.00 (1-891387-01-4). Alexandria, VA: Red Dragon Press, Fall 1998. Cavalieri is best known as the host of the award-winning radio program, "The Poet and the Poem," which, for twenty years, featured readings and interviews with U.S. Poet Laureates and Pulitzer Prize winners, as well as less-celebrated poets. The deepest lights and darks of her own verses unite and intensify the tempers, tones and intents of the uncountable number of poems she has opened to the reader and listener. —Red Dragon Press

Cavalieri, Grace. *Pinecrest Rest Haven.* 57p. pap. $10.00 (0-915380-39-0). Washington, DC: Word Works, Fall 1998. Cavalieri's poems are offerings she serves up to the gods or muses, and if someone else happens to overhear, that is a gift in return. I love the wrestling in Pinecrest Rest Haven. It is Jacob and the Angel once more. —Merrill Leffler. How much these poems, written with agility, strength and wonder, honor the disenfranchised, the ghosts of ourselves among us. — Robin Holland

Cave Canem Workshop/Retreat. *Cave Canem II.* 72p. pap. $8.00. New York, NY: Cave Canem Workshop/Retreat, 1997. This anthology is the work of participants and faculty at Cave Canem's workshop/retreat for African American poets in 1997.

Celan, Paul. Translated by Muska Nagel. *A Voice. . . Translations of Selected Poems.* 238p. pap. $15.95 (0-913006-67-X). Orono, ME: Puckerbrush Press, Fall 1998.

Cepero, Nilda. *Sugar Cane Blues.* 50p. pap. $6.95 (1-890953-02-4). Miami, FL: LS Press, Fall 1997. Cepero shows us the path of Cuban exile, through separation, pain, death, salvation and transformation. —LS Press. Lyrical and wistful. No matter how mournful the subject, [Cepero] writes with irrepressible hope. —Margarita Engle

Cesereanu, Ruxandra. Translated by Claudia Litvinchievici. *Schizoid Ocean.* 95p. pap. $10.95 (1-883881-23-4). Binghamton, NY: ESF, Spring 1997.

Chace, Joel. *The Melancholy of Yorick.* 64p. pap. $12.50 (0-913559-44-X). Delhi, NY: Birch Brook Press, Fall 1998. Letterpress edition with wood engravings by Frank Eckmair. A selection of poems on lost love, youth, and life with classical overtones often in a bucolic setting. —Birch Brook Press

Chace, Joel. *Twentieth Century Deaths.* 64p. pap. $9.00 (1-880286-26-2). Canton, CT: Singular Speech Press, Spring 1997. Chace can be as direct as Jeffers, as delicately and as bluntly apt as Stevens. —Ronald Bayes. I admire the variety and honesty of Chace's poems. He takes

many different approaches to the matters that engage him, and makes each of them his own. —Henry Taylor

Chadbourne, Eugene. *Bye Bye DDR.* 120p. pap. $12.00 (1-56439-037-3). Detroit, MI: Ridgeway Press, Fall 1997. Experimental music icon Eugene Chadbourne combines humor with a twist of the weird as he recalls his many tours of East Germany as a rock style musician before the Berlin Wall fell. The book features original cartoons by German cartoonist Carsten Scheinplug. —Ridgeway Press

Chadwick, Cydney, ed. *An Avec Sampler, 1997.* 64p. pap. $8.50 (1-880713-10-1). Penngrove, CA: Avec Books, 1997. New writing by Laura Moriarty, Chris Stroffolino, Laynie Browne, George Albon, Stephen-Paul Martin, Lissa McLaughlin, and Susan Smith Nash. —Avec Books

Chaet, Eric. *Poems for Uprising Ypsilanti Marlon Gillespie.* 16p. pap. $5.00. DePere, WI: Chaet, Eric, Spring 1997.

Chandler, Janet Carncross. *Why Flowers Bloom.* 115p. $12.00 (0-918949-38-6). pap. $8.00 (0-918949-37-8).

Watsonville, CA: Papier-Mache Press, Spring 1994. Why Flowers Bloom is a triumph. The book is clearly her best — lively, perceptive, intense, wryly humorous, and brave. Old age and a consequent awareness of the coming of death are the themes, but the poet is a relentless exponent of life, of the adventure of sapient human awareness. —Bill Hotchkiss

Chang, Diana. *The Mind's Amazement: Poems Inspired by Paintings, Poetry, Music, Dance.* 68p. pap. $10.00. Islip, NY: Live Poets Society, Spring 1998. Chang writes from the inside out, in the way a mystic contemplates. She sees that one unrelenting inner force runs throughout art, poetry, music and dance. [Her] images unlock our emotions and abstractions excite our reason, making these poems mystical — not as prayers, but as revelations. — Edward Boccia. Chang is a poet who grants us extraordinary adventures through her lyric line, her refinement of phrase, her whole shaping of thought and language so that we may truly hear, see, feel, and know. The sublime presence of art arises out of these poems. — Georgette Preston

Chang, Juliana, ed. *Quiet Fire: A Historical Anthology of Asian American Poetry, 1892-1970.* 164p. pap. $14.95 (1-889876-02-X). New York, NY: Asian American Writers' Workshop, Fall 1996. Chang breaks new ground by providing the first historical survey of any branch of Asian American poetry. —Choice. The poems were selected to reflect both the high quality and wide range of Asian American poetic discourse. An important sourcebook, Quiet Fire makes a significant contribution to the remapping of American poetry and Asian American literature. —Asian American Writers' Workshop

Chapman, Matthew. *Poem.* 8p. pap. $7.00. Key West, FL: Interim Books, Spring 1998.

Chase, Naomi Feigelson. *Stacked.* 16p. pap. $7.00 (1-882329-11-2). Truro, MA: Garden Street Press, Spring 1998. Naomi Chase's wise and witty Stacked should be read by every male on the planet and by every daughter. Does that include everybody? Clones and extraterrestrials would also enjoy and be enlightened by this book. — Bill Knott. I can't promise you'll be blond and thin after reading Chase's Stacked, but I can promise you'll have a healthy glow from laughing so hard. —Denise Duhamel

Chelnik, Peter. *Wildflower Serenade: Selected Poems.* 161p. pap. $10.00 (0-9642708-9-7). New York, NY: Little Sky Press, Fall 1997. Chelnik's poetry reflects the rhythms of urban American life, its frenetic pace, its roaring energy. This is a poet whose roots go back to Whitman and Ginsberg, a poetry crammed with specific details that sensually recreate the poet's life and places in which he lives it. Chelnik is a unique and often startling poet. —Maria Maziotti Gillan

Cherry, Kelly. *Death and Transfiguration.* 64p. $19.95 (0-8071-2211-4). pap. $11.95 (0-8071-2212-2). Baton Rouge, LA: Louisiana State University Press, Fall 1997. Cherry's poetry is marked by a firm intellectual passion, a reverent desire to possess the genuine thought of our century — historical, philosophical, and scientific — and a species of powerful ironic wit that is allied to rare good humor. — From the citation naming Cherry the recipient of the first James G. Hanes Poetry Prize of the Fellowship of Southern Writers. For years I have admired Cherry's poems. They are always so direct and

movingly humane. Death and Transfiguration is surely her most powerful collection. It is a book of ghosts — her parents, her first husband, her unborn child. And yet Cherry bears the burden of her grief and terror without ever becoming imprisoned by it. Boldly her poems conclude not in elegy but vision. — Dana Gioia

Chichetto, James Wm. *Homage to Father Edward Sorin.* 52p. pap. $11.95 (0-9618657-4-1). New Haven, CT: Connecticut Poetry Review Press, Fall 1998 (revised edition). Chichetto has given us a book rich in the experience of his religious community, the Congregation of the Holy Cross. His poetry is vital, often formal, and always vivid. —R.A. Speers. Chichetto's book is mature, deft, and moving, an important contribution to the "voice portrait" genre. —The Small Press Review

Chin, Justin. *Bite Hard.* 124p. pap. $11.95 (0-916397-47-5). San Francisco, CA: Manic D Press, 1997. With scathing humor, brutal honesty, and unflinching detail, award-winning spoken-word / performance artist Chin chews through society's limitations and stereotypes of race, desire and loss. —Manic D Press. Chin embodies the pan-cultural strains that run rampant through the current San Francisco literary scene. — San Francisco Focus. He plugs the stage microphone into the page and lyrically blasts the heart out of our fears, rage, and import-export nightmarish dreams. —R. Zamora Linmark

Chitwood, Michael. *The Weave Room.* 96p. $21.00 (0-226-10397-8). pap. $11.00 (0-226-10398-6). Chicago, IL: University of Chicago Press, Spring 1998. Chitwood is one of our most interesting younger poets. His focus on the work lives of ordinary people and his feel for the rhythms of vernacular speech, together with his tremendous lyrical gift, make him eminently pleasurable to read. — Wendy Lesser, The Threepenny Review. This is a tremendously attractive book, an authentic addition to the line in American poetry that runs through Masters and William Carlos Williams. The Weave Room as a whole has a buoyancy and verve that are rare at all times. It's a breath of fresh air. —Frank Bidart

Chock, Eric; James R. Harstad, Darrell H.Y. Lum, and Bill Teter, eds. *Growing Up Local: An Anthology of Poetry and Prose From Hawai'i.* 382p. pap. $15.00 (0-910043-53-1). Bamboo Ridge, Fall 1998.

Cholst, Sheldon. *The Psychology of the Artist.* 336p. pap. $14.95 (0-931174-05-8). New York, NY: Beau Rivage Press, Spring 1997. A book of poetry and prose by a psychiatrist exploring why artists create. —Beau Rivage Press. A book on psychology that artists can really enjoy. Pleasant, humorous, artistic. —Kenneth Rapp. This is an amazing book full of insight, wit, and Cholst's absolutely unique approach to questions about life, language, evolution and sexuality. —J.K. Canepa

Chorlton, David. *Country of Two Seasons.* 28p. pap. $6.95 (0-614-24053-0). Johnstown, OH: Pudding House Publications, Spring 1997. Chorlton is a poet of borders and margins, exile and invisibility, the bard of the stranger, the outsider. His poems resonate with the echo of many voices condemned to oblivion, voices which would dissolve in the air were it not for the ear of the poet, from refugees crossing the desert to indigenous people buried in the ground stolen from them long ago. The poems never yield to abstract rhetoric; rather, they are moored in the concrete foundation of the image, vividly, memorably. —Martín Espada

Christie, A.V. *Nine Skies.* 57p. pap. $11.95 (0-252-06644-8). Champaign, IL: University of Illinois Press, Fall 1997. It is easy enough to say that Christie's Nine Skies is a remarkable first book of poems — it is, in fact, remarkable regardless. Only the best poetry is written this well, with this much craft and conviction. Of course the poems are meditative and elegiac, brilliant and finely detailed, but they are also thought through and wholly felt, so that even in their small moments they celebrate. — Stanley Plumly. These poems are a reminder that where there is beauty there is often carnage. In art, as in life, they must coexist. Christie writes with a Romantic's eye and a Realist's heart, so there is no sentimentality, that sickness afflicting our age. The voice on these pages is hard-bitten, luxuriant and true. —Henri Cole

Christo, Cyril. *The Twilight Language.* 56p. pap. $12.00 (1-886435-05-7). Sag Harbor, NY: Canio's Editions, Fall 1996. Christo writes with the fire of youthful imagination.

He has escaped from the prison of the studious and the adept. You see in his first book the same impulse you find in the first books of Hart Crane and Wallace Stevens. — Hayden Carruth

Christopher, Nicholas. *The Creation of the Night Sky.* 99p. $22.00 (0-15-100344-0). pap. $13.00 (0-15-600565-4). San Diego, CA: Harcourt Brace/Harvest Books, Spring 1998; Spring 1999 (new paper). One of the five most important "magic realist" poets writing today displays both his trademark mastery of language and astonishing range. —Harcourt Brace. A haunting, multifaceted work filled with astonishing, surreal images. —The New York Times Book Review. Essential reading, these poems are a spiritual awakening. —Library Journal. He must now rank among the very best poets of his generation. —Anthony Hecht

Christopher, Renny. *Longing Fervently for Revolution: Upward Mobility and Its Discontents.* 48p. pap. $6.00. Niagara Falls, NY: Slipstream Publications, Spring 1998. Winner of the 1998 Annual Slipstream Poetry Chapbook Competition.

Chute, Robert M.
*Androscoggin Too: The
Pejepscot Poems.* 30p. pap.
$9.95 (1-879205-71-8). Troy,
ME: Nightshade Press, Fall
1997.

Cinader, Martha. *When the
Body Calls: Selected Writings.*
127p. pap. $12.00 (0-86316-
279-7). New York, NY:
Writers and Readers
Publishing/Harlem River
Press, Spring 1998. [Cinader]
is like a female Sun Ra who
can coax words out of her saxophone. She never omits any
detail even when she's taking
us to another stratosphere.
This book is daring and
unflinching. An important
body of work. —Hal Sirowitz.
This book contains multitudes.
Cinader enters the realm of
bookography with a slingshot
satellite launch of new groove.
Genre-busting from perfpo to
presepo, I tell you this —
Martha C. meshes body organs
and imagination in an arena of
politics from the inside out.
Hail, Poet of the Future! —
Bob Holman. In style and substance both provocative and
original, When the Body Calls
is a challenge and a pleasure
to read. Cinader is a poet
whose sensual prose takes us
into a world full of complex
questions. —Len Cao

Ciscel, Dennis. *Tiny Stories.*
43p. pap. $12.95 (0-911051-
62-7). Austin, TX: Plain View
Press, 1992. Ciscel has made
the generally unimaginable
scale of the now fifteen-year
old AIDS epidemic potently
comprehensible. He imbues
his Tiny Stories with the sim-
plest compassion and tenderness, again and again showing
us the blank face of denial,
and ultimately supplanting it
with the face of God. —
Georgia Cotrell

Citino, David. *Broken
Symmetry.* 92p. $27.50 (0-
8142-0730-8). pap. $14.95 (0-
8142-0731-6). Columbus, OH:
Ohio State University Press,
Spring 1997. A poet approaching the end of the 20th century
takes stock of a life: of its
family and culture, history,
and beliefs; of the contemporary forces that shape it; of the
land — and even the body —
it calls home. Employing
"broken symmetry" as a
description of the contemporary fractured world and his
own fitfully declining health,
Citino seeks to know whether
an unbroken symmetry ever
existed, or whether it is human
nature to believe fervently in
some lost golden age. —Ohio
State University Press

Citino, David. *The Book of
Appassionata: Collected*

Poems. 178p. $35.00 (0-8142-0773-1). pap. $18.95 (0-8142-0774-X). Columbus, OH: Ohio State University Press, Fall 1998. Sister Mary Appassionata has been talking herself into Citino's poetry collections for many years. Charming when she wants to be, pushy by nature and by vocation, determined to say what she has to say, Sister Mary has evolved into a recognized literary personality. She has now persuaded both poet and press that she is ready for her own breakthrough book. —Ohio State University Press. Ever since reading The Appassionata Doctrines I've looked to Citino to give me poems I really want to read. He can be funny, passionate, lyrical, and not infrequently wise as well. Often (which is exceptional) he can be all of these things at once. —Denise Levertov. Citino is a much better than average poet, possibly a great one. What stands out in his Appassionata poems — aside from their beauty — is their learnedness and their humor. —Jonathan Holden

Claman, Elizabeth, ed. *Hard Love: Writings on Violence and Intimacy.* 315p. pap. $17.50 (0-9638992-3-6). Berkeley, CA: Queen of Swords Press, Spring 1997.

Hard Love gathers together poetry, essays and fiction by 78 women and men from across the U.S. on the subject of intimate violence, including its broader cultural context and strategies for healing. — Queen of Swords Press. Divided into four sections Hard Love begins with various aspects of violence, explores issues of intimacy, moves through trust, betrayal and the struggle to heal and finally arrives at a celebration of intimacy. —Kimber Williams, Register Guard

Claman, Elizabeth, ed. *Passionate Lives: Eight Autobiographical Poem Cycles.* 204p. pap. $12.99 (0-9638992-4-4). Berkeley, CA: Queen of Swords Press, Fall 1998. This anthology grew organically from the work of eight poets who represent in passionately charged language lives lived with intensity, whether they write as lovers, social activists, political observers, or chroniclers of family history. —Queen of Swords Press

Clampitt, Amy. *The Collected Poems of Amy Clampitt.* 471p. $30.00 (0-375-40008-7). New York, NY: Knopf, Alfred A., Fall 1997. Here, for the first time in a single volume, are Clampitt's five books of poems, from the first, published at the age of 63, to the last, published the year she died. The subjects of the poems were the interests of Clampitt's life: the natural world of her Iowa childhood and Maine summers, her travels in England, Greek art and mythology, the poet Keats, the Wordsworths, New York's village life. A brilliant poet of place, she also wrote passionately of displacement, in rich allusive language, with rhythms and patterns entirely her own. —Alfred A. Knopf

Clark, Emilie, and Lytle Shaw. *The Rough Voice.* 45p. pap. $40.00. Berkeley, ca: Idiom, Fall 1998.

Clark, Jeff. *The Little Door Slides Back.* 105p. pap. $10.95 (1-55713-314-X). Los Angeles, CA: Sun & Moon Press, Fall 1997. Winner of the 1996 National Poetry Series.The wide-ranging and imaginatively animated expressions of self-revelation at work in these texts establish an original and confident presence, that takes its step, in part, from the visionary writing of such poets has Trakl, Desnos and Michaux. This is a book that, at its core, asks subtle questions about the self-reflective aspect of poetry — the very nature of whose

answers offers a further sense of the perplexing consolations that bring us, in our flight from platitudes and tethered monodies, to seek out the poem in the first place. A rare achievement. —Ray DiPalma

Clark, Tom. *Empire of Skin.* 232p. $27.50 (1-57423-051-4). pap. $15.00 (1-57423-049-2). Santa Rosa, CA: Black Sparrow Press, Fall 1997. From the moment survivors of Captain Cook's third voyage of discovery found that sea otter skins procured from Northwest Coast Indians would bring $100 apiece on the Chinese market, the future of the coast, the Indians, and the sea otters was irrevocably altered. Clark's serial poetic history of the maritime fur trade (1785-1810) documents and elaborates that change, linking white world fur traders with indigenes in extended metaphors of contact and confrontation. —Black Sparrow Press

Clark, Tom. *White Thought.* 64p. pap. $10.00 (1-889097-20-9). West Stockbridge, MA: Hard Press, Fall 1997. Meditations on death and mourning. Brilliant, lyrical, rhapsodic, these poems are raised as a bulwark against despair. —Hard Press

Clark, William Lewis. *Gardens of the Streets: Poetry and Pictures of Urban Rescue Missions and the People They Serve.* 95p. pap. $12.95 (1-878044-40-0). Mahomet, IL: Mayhaven Publishing, 1995.

Clausen, Andy. *40th Century Man: Selected Verse 1996-1966.* 190p. pap. $8.00 (1-57027-064-3). Brooklyn, NY: Autonomedia, 1997. Clausen's character voice is heroic, a vox populi of the democratic unconscious, a "divine aver-age' thinking workman per-sona. As "one of the roughs," a Whitmanic laborer, his bardic populism's grounded on long years' painful sturdy experience earning family bread by the sweat of his brow. The expensive bullshit of Government TV poetics suffers diminution of credibili-ty placed side by side with Clausen's direct information and sad raw insight. —Allen Ginsberg

Clay, Steven, and Rodney Phillips. *A Secret Location on the Lower East Side: Adventures in Writing 1960-1980.* 342p. pap. $27.95 (1887123202). New York Public Library/Granary Books, Fall 1998.

Clinefelter, Jim. *A Throw of the Snore Will Surge the Potatoes: John M. Bennett meets Stéphane Mallarmé.* 12p. pap. $7.00. Columbus, OH: Luna Bisonte Prods, Fall 1998. Large-format collection of illustrated surrealist poems using poetry by John M. Bennett and Mallarmé as sources. —Luna Bisonte Prods

Clinton, James Harmon. *What Is Fair.* 54p. $19.95 (0-8071-2195-9). pap. $11.95 (0-8071-2196-7). Baton Rouge, LA: Louisiana State University Press, Fall 1997. Literate and resourceful, Clinton's poetry is subtle and at the same time very clear. He is not afraid to explore human situations that are painful and sometimes inca-pable of solution. Among the many first books published in the last few years, his is out-standing. —James Dickey. In this important first book, Clinton creates the language of "echo" and "wing" to ana-lyze the vectors of his life and describes his early memories with such verve that he bril-liantly recaptures the "shim-mer" of the past. Like a home run in flight out of the park, What Is Fair is a powerful book. —Sue Owen

Clinton, Robert. *Taking Eden.* 80p. $20.95 (1-889330-09-4). pap. $12.95 (1-889330-10-8). Louisville, KY:

Sarabande Books, Spring 1998. Clinton's Taking Eden is a brilliant first book. Powerful, imaginative, grounded in the first premises of earth and Earth (Eden indeed), these poems / prose poems are "randomness acknowledged" and fate celebrated. —Bill Knott. A knotty intensity and sly, Frostian intelligence inform these poems, each "a structure of reflections." Always surprising, richly mordant, Clinton's work questions its own process of becoming, its "greenest melancholy," as language quickens toward meaning. Taking Eden dazzles with its freshness and complexity. —Michael Waters

Clocys, Ed. *Sad Angel Smile: Poems and. . ..* 51p. pap. $8.00 (1-887012-04-4). Newtown, CT: Hanover Press, Spring 1998. These poems delight, surprise, and ultimately pierce the reader's heart. — Terryl Paiste. [Clocys] knows all the rules and takes great pleasure in breaking them. His writing ranges from Beat to the off-beat. The writings here are fast paced, thought provoking, and very original. [Clocys's] work will stick to you, it's unavoidable. —Faith Vicinanza

Clover, Joshua. *Madonna anno domini.* 68p. $19.95 (0-8071-2147-9). pap. $11.95 (0-8071-2148-7). Baton Rouge, LA: Louisiana State University Press, Spring 1997. Winner of the 1996 Walt Whitman Award from the Academy of American Poets. Something unique and transformational is going on with this collection. Reading it is akin to channel-surfing a possessed television on which CNN shows horror movies and Court TV embraces magic realism. —Publishers Weekly. With this extraordinary first collection, Clover has written a poetic manifesto — as well as a prayer book — for the millennial generation. Part metrical magician, part avant-gardist mathematician, the speaker of this book searches out the avenues of belief through a vertigo-ridden array of technical, moral, aesthetic, and imaginative means. — Jorie Graham

Cobden, Lynda. *A Date With Destiny.* 21p. Concord, CA: Small Poetry Press, 1996.

Codrescu, Andrei. *Alien Candor: Selected Poems 1970-1995.* 303p. $27.50 (1-57423-014-X). pap. $15.00 (1-57423-013-1). Santa Rosa, CA: Black Sparrow Press, Fall 1996. Surrealist reporter, revolutionary speculator, partisan of poetics, intellectual provocateur, Romanian emigré, Codrescu has ingrained his trenchant, idiosyncratic critical view, his nimble wit and sparkling ironic intelligence into the weave of our national text. —Black Sparrow Press

Cofer, Judith Ortiz. *The Latin Deli: Prose and Poetry.* 170p. pap. $11.00 (0-393-31313-1). New York, NY: Norton, W.W., and Company, ©1993. The stories and poems in The Latin Deli depict the author's coming of age with the sensitivity and verisimilitude of a James Agee, a Carson McCullers, or a Harper Lee. —R. Baird Shannon, Magill's Literary Annual. This powerful collection of stories, essays, and poems shows a remarkable range. Like a great singer, Cofer knows how to hit all the notes. —Larry Brown

Coffman, Lisa. *Likely.* 62p. pap. $9.50 (0-87338-555-1). Kent, OH: Kent State University Press, 1996. Winner of the 1995 Stan and Tom Wick Poetry Prize. Coffman is a major poet in the making. Imagine a voice that combines heart-of-America brooding like James Wright's with a shaded elegance like Elizabeth Bishop's. Imagine Whitman's spirit somewhere

in the vicinity. Imagine a love of small towns ringed by mountains, a shrewd ear for lonely folk's dialogue, and a music that seems to pour out of your own life as you read these poems. Likely is a book brimming with surprises and beauty. —Alicia Ostriker

Cofrancesco, Joan. *Cat Bones in the Tree.* 72p. pap. $10.00 (0-9643477-4-1). Syracuse, NY: Hale Mary Press, Fall 1998. Cofrancesco's poems have excellent sharp detail, her own tone, real feeling, great timing, and a good spare sense of form. Out of her loves and loneliness she carves fine, modest, passionate poems. Reading them is a pleasure. — Howard Nelson. Though set in her own sometimes grungy or fragmented darkness, Cat Bones in the Tree is a visionary book. —William Heyen

Cohen, Marc. *Mecox Road.* 80p. pap. $12.00 (1-877593-02-8). Port Washington, NY: Groundwater Press, Spring 1997. Cohen's poetry is a kind of highly polished metaphysical poetry. His poetry hungers after the sublime in the same way Hart Crane's does, without making any concessions to the ancillary graces and seductions of poetic language, yet achieving them almost fortuitously, through his intense concentration on the task at hand — the making of the poem. —John Ashbery

Cohen, Michael. *In This Sea.* 29p. pap. $6.00. New York, NY: New School Chapbook Series, Spring 1997. In This Sea is a 24 poem cycle on love, memory and the creation of the self through poetry. —David Shirley

Cohen, Michael. *One-Eyed Cat Takes Flight: Selected Poems.* 56p. pap. $10.00. Red Balloon collective, Fall 1996. These poems have been shown to be effective decay-preventative artifices that can be of significant value when used in a conscientiously applied program of creative hygiene and regular metaphorical care. — American Association of Dental Poets. Extraordinary, superior, wonderful. —Roget's Thesaurus. There is no copyright here, but a copyleft: No borders, no prisons, no human being is illegal. —Red Balloon Collective

Cohen, Rob, ed. *Scream When You Burn: A Pound of Seared Flesh From the Lap of Coffee Culture.* 248p. pap. $14.00 (1-888277-00-9). San Diego, CA: Incommunicado Press, Spring 1998. Over 80 writers from the West Coast

and beyond, featuring five previously unpublished poems by Charles Bukowski, plus work from Michelle T. Clinton, Dave Alvin, Allen Ginsberg, and dozens more. —Incommunicado Press

Cohn, Jim. *The Dance of Yellow Lightning Over the Ridge.* 160p. pap. $12.00 (0-9618487-4-X). Rochester, NY: Writers & Books, Spring 1998. A new collection of poems from the author of Prairie Falcon and Grasslands. Cohn is the voice of the post-Beat generation. —Writers & Books

Cole, Barbara. *Little Wives.* 28p. pap. $7.00 (0-937017-82-X). Elmwood, CT: Potes & Poets Press, Fall 1998.

Cole, Barbara. *Postcards.* 24p. (0-9667655-1-6). Wayne, PA: Beautiful Swimmer Press, Fall 1998.

Cole, Henri. *The Visible Man.* 67p. $22.00 (0-375-40396-5). New York, NY: Knopf, Alfred A., Fall 1998. In a poetry nervously alive to the maladies of the contemporary, yet suffused by a rare apprehension of the delights of the senses, Cole has relished the world while being unafraid to satirize it. In poems that are both decorative and plain-spoken he permits his readers to share a keen and unsentimental view of the oddities, horrors, and solaces surrounding them at the end of the twentieth century. —The American Academy of Arts and Letters. The Visible Man persuades me that Cole will be a central poet of his generation. Keats and Hart Crane are presences here, and Cole invokes them with true aesthetic dignity, which is the mark of nearly every poem in The Visible Man. —Harold Bloom

Cole, Norma. *Desire & Its Double.* 40p. pap. $4.00. Saratoga, ca: Instress, Fall 1998.

Cole, Peter. *Hymns & Qualms.* 109p. pap. $12.95 (1-878818-64-3). Riverdale-on-Hudson, NY: Sheep Meadow Press, Spring 1998. Cole is our most vital translator of medieval and contemporary Hebrew poetry; in these new poems he invents his own modern medievalism — a playful sensuality implicating always the persistent tradition of law and legend. He has mastered a clear line but can also give us a ferocious deposition against fanaticism ("I sing a doubled song"). With Hymns & Qualms he introduces to American poetry a startling synthesis of the poet-

ry-of-wisdom and the freshest music. —David Shapiro. The keenness of his mind and the moral seriousness of his work astonish. Backed a screw's turn from sweetness, his poems retain the stink of sun-warmed earth, the "ground-slug and smear of existence." —Forrest Gander

Cole, Susan. *Passion for Apocalypse.* 36p. pap. $5.00 (0-9637704-7-0). Alexandria, VA: Red Dragon Press, Spring 1997. Contrary to its title, the poems in this book are not about a cosmic cataclysm, but about the little events in the lives of ordinary people, the decisions that must be made over and over in every life, the individual choices that, one upon another, shape a society. Cole asks, can we make these decisions differently, and how then will the large events of our times be formed? —Red Dragon Press

Coleman, Ralph S. *A Skiff of Snow.* 32p. pap. $6.00 (1-885912-16-1). Abingdon, VA: Sow's Ear Press, Fall 1997. Poems of rural life, work, and death. —Sow's Ear Press

Coleman, Wanda. *Bathwater Wine.* 288p. $27.50 (1-57423-065-4). pap. $15.00 (1-57423-064-6). Santa Rosa, CA: Black Sparrow Press, Fall 1998. Los

Angeles poet Coleman charges all of her writing with high-voltage confrontational energy, and Bathwater Wine is no exception. These poems demonstrate once again a controlled outrage, as well as wry political awareness, dark humor, and heady sensuality. —Black Sparrow Press

Coleridge, Samuel Taylor. *Poems and Prose.* $12.50 (0-375-40072-9). Knopf/Everyman's Library Pocket Poets, Fall 1997. A generous selection from the work of the Romantic poet whose exotic images, from albatross to pleasure dome, are wonderfully alive in our language today. —Knopf

Coles, Katharine. *A History of the Garden.* 71p. pap. $10.00 (0-87417-298-5). Reno, NV: University of Nevada Press, Spring 1997. The poems in A History of the Garden — their discursive agility, their clarity, their poised and authoritative intelligence, their insightfulness, and finally, their beautiful and seductive music — are unmatched by any young poet now writing. Coles is quite simply a superb poet, one whose apprenticeship has ended and whose mature work has triumphantly begun. — Mark Strand

Collier, John. *Save Our Covered Bridges.* 26p. Tiverton, RI: Collier, John, Fall 1998.

Collins, Billy. *Picnic, Lightning.* 103p. (0-8229-5670-5). Pittsburgh, PA: University of Pittsburgh Press, Fall 1998. I have never before felt possessive about a poet, but I am fiercely glad that Collins is ours — smart, his strings tuned and resonant, his wonderful eye looping over the things, events, and ideas of the world, rueful, playful, warm-voiced, easy to love. — Annie Proulx. Collins writes lovely poems. Limpid, gently and consistently startling, more serious than they seem, they describe all the worlds that are and some others besides. —John Updike. Collins's poetry is heartbreakingly beautiful. It is also wise, funny, and brilliant. My ten favorites keep shifting all the time. Ovid is in again; so is Billy Collins. —Gerald Stern

Collins, Martha. *Some Things Words Can Do.* 120p. pap. $12.95 (1-878818-74-0). Riverdale-on-Hudson, NY: Sheep Meadow Press, Fall 1998. The idiosyncratic territory of Collins's work lies south of Emily Dickinson, west of H.D., a little to the left of Louise Bogan, and within easy commuting distance of Gertrude Stein. While her poems deal with war and oppression, contemporary relationships, civil rights and censorship and homelessness, she is fluid, musical, full of wit and wordplay and suggestiveness. —Boston Book Review

Collins, Robert. *The Glass Blower.* 18p. pap. $6.95. Johnstown, OH: Pudding House Publications, Fall 1997.

Collom, Jack. *Dog Sonnets.* 28p. pap. $4.00 (1-893032-05-1). Talisman House, Publishers / Jensen/Daniels, Fall 1998.

Colquitt, Betsy. *Eve From the Autobiography and Other Poems.* 260p. $24.95 (0-87565-174-7). Fort Worth, TX: Texas Christian University Press, Fall 1997. This exciting sequence traces the life of the first woman from her creation by the "Great Mother," through the years in the Garden of Eden, where Eve helps bring Adam out of the mud of Mother Earth, down to the present, as Eve looks at life and comments from the perspective of wise and eternal Woman. — Texas Christian University Press

Congdon, Kirby. *A Century of Progress.* 16p. pap. $6.00 (0-914320-02-5). Key West, FL: Cycle Press, Fall 1997.

Congdon, Kirby. *Birds.* 12p. pap. $3.00. Key West, FL: Cycle Press, Fall 1998.

Congdon, Kirby. *Discus Thrower.* 12p. pap. $6.00. Key West, FL: Cycle Press, Spring 1997.

Congdon, Kirby. *Fundamentals.* 8p. pap. $6.00. Key West, FL: Cycle Press, Spring 1997.

Congdon, Kirby. *In Key West.* 20p. pap. $3.00. Key West, FL: Cycle Press, Spring 1998.

Conkling, Helen. *Red Peony Night.* 80p. $25.00 (0-8229-4042-6). pap. $12.95 (0-8229-5647-0). Pittsburgh, PA: University of Pittsburgh Press, Fall 1997. Winner of the 1996 Agnes Lynch Starrett Poetry Prize. These are poems that have been blessed by compassion, keen memory, and a passionate belief in the transformative value of the imagination. Conkling's voice remembers music and makes her own. —Margaret Gibson. Red Peony Night is a book of voices. Warmed, like instruments, by the touch of this entranced musician, they find, like

Conkling's "Chiaretti" the violinist, "the heart of every note." —Irving Feldman

Connaroe, Joel, ed. *Eight American Poets: An Anthology.* 306p. pap. $13.00 (0-679-77643-5). Vintage Books, Fall 1997. In this generous anthology, Conarroe has assembled the work of eight poets who have shaped — and to some extent defined — American verse since 1940. The 164 selections in Eight American Poets include widely anthologized works like Roethke's "My Papa's Waltz," several of Berryman's "Dream Songs," Merrill's "Lost in Translation," and Sexton's "Ringing the Bells," as well as poems that are less familiar but just as haunting. These poems are crystalline in their lucidity, harrowing in their emotional rawness, and always sensuous and surprising in their use of language. The result is a collection that will prove indispensable to new and veteran readers of American poetry alike. — Vintage Books

Connellan, Leo. *Short Poems, City Poems 1944-1998.* 56p. pap. $10.00 (1-887012-16-8). Newtown, CT: Hanover Press, Fall 1998. Connellan's integrity has been a measure for his fellow poets for years and

years now. This present collection is a solid demonstration of why his work stays a benchmark for poetry of common terms, of unobtrusive art, of the enduring facts of our daily lives. His perception and care are unique — his heart a persistent refuge for any one of us, in any time, in any place. —Robert Creeley. Connellan's poems are vivid, harsh, spare, surely cadenced and colloquially eloquent. — Richard Wilbur

Connolly, Geraldine. *Province of Fire.* 82p. pap. $12.00 (0-916078-46-9). Oak Ridge, TN: Iris Press, Fall 1998. Connolly is an intelligent writer, restrained, yet bold and capable of embodying her landscapes with complexity and resonance. —Tony Hoagland, Cimarron Review. Connolly is a "soaring beast with smoking hair," a poet who has not turned sheepish or haggard, not been swallowed, as her ancestors were, by harsh lives in the mine and factory. She has survived her childhood with a springing energy that gives lilt to her lines. In these poems she draws crisp and keenly felt portraits of her family and claims herself as a powerful woman come into her active and sexual own. —Stephanie Strickland. In these avid, joyous, and sorrowful autobiographical poems, an irrepressible female spirit rises to the surface across the generations, and she is after nothing less than "the true wildness/within her." To read Province of Fire is to feel its radiating heat. — Edward Hirsch

Conte, Giuseppe. Translated by Laura Stortoni. *The Ocean and the Boy.* 177p. pap. $15.00 (0-9641003-0-4). Berkeley, CA: Hesperia Press, 1997. For us today, what are the gods? For Conte, they are the presence of prehistory, or pre-human history rather, in the landscape, the beginnings of plants and animals, and still farther back, the formation of the structure of the earth; they are the enduring astonishment of origins, the quivering eagerness of the first human look, distinguishing and naming plants, animals, constellations. —Italo Calvino

Contogenis, Constantine, and Wolhee Choe, trans. *Songs of the Kisaeng: Courtesan Poetry of the Last Korean Dynasty.* 80p. pap. $11.50 (1-880238-53-5). Rochester, NY: BOA Editions, Fall 1997. These poems are deceptively simple, thwarted love remaining their paradigm. But they also represent what we might, with historical hind

sight, call "feminist" views since they depict rare instances in which Korean women were permitted to address their own emotions. Call them courtesan blues from the Chosun Dynasty, and read them for both pleasure and edification. —Sam Hamill

Cook-Lynn, Elizabeth. *I Remember the Fallen Trees: New and Selected Poems.* 128p. pap. $15.95 (0-91005545-9). Cheney, WA: Eastern Washington University Press, Fall 1998. Cook-Lynn, a member of the Crow Creek Sioux Tribe, is a foremost scholar of Indian history. In this work, without casting aside that mantle, Cook-Lynn joyfully embraces the people and the world she knows and loves. She scolds their detractors, scarifies their enemies, sings and dances with them, loves them as much for their sins as for their virtues; venerates them. Thus through her sorrowful, mocking, searing indignation, we participate in her celebration of the indestructible human spirit. —Eastern Washington University Press

Cooley, Peter. *Sacred Conversations.* 99p. $20.95 (0-88748-255-4). pap. $11.95 (0-88748-256-2). Pittsburgh,

PA: Carnegie Mellon University Press, Spring 1998. With his stunning eye for detail, with his ability to manipulate voice for dramatic expressiveness, with his skill in weaving in and out of a range of styles from the subtly impressionistic to the overly dramatic, Cooley is one of our most distinctive American poets. —Prairie Schooner. Cooley finds occasion for celebration in the minute and circumstantial events of day-to-day living. . . [his] obsession with interpreting each aspect of the "miraculous ordinary" forms the most distinctive feature of his verse. —The Gettysburg Review

Cooper, Dennis. *The Dream Police: Selected Poems, 1969-1993.* 134p. $16.00 (0-8021-1569-1). New York, NY: Grove Press, 1995. In another century or era, Cooper's books would be circulated in secret, explosive samizdat editions that friends and fans would pass around and savor like forbidden absinthe. He would risk his life for them, or maybe he'd just be sent to a mental asylum, like the Marquis de Sade, to whom he has been compared. This is high risk literature. It takes enormous courage for a writer to explore, as Cooper does, the extreme boundaries of human behavior and amorality, right to the abyss where desire and lust topple into death. Catherine Texier, The New York Times Book Review

Cooper, Lisa. *& Calling It Home.* 99p. (0-925904-17-1). Tucson, AZ: Chax Press, Fall 1998. [Cooper] investigates the binding power of literary tradition and the poem's legacy of music. In response to her artful ruses and rousing intelligence, the powers of language, poetry and music come when she calls. —Mary Margaret Sloan. [& Calling It Home]seems to me a kind of complex and various daybook, a constantly shifting brilliance that suffers itself with an exquisite sense of music and measure. This is a deeply felt and painfully accurate journey; I read it at one sitting and was transformed by it. —Jon Anderson

Corazzini, Sergio. Translated by Michael Palma. *Sunday Evening: Selected Poems.* 67p. pap. $13.00. Stony Brook, NY: Gradiva Publications, 1997. The first English translation of Corazzini, whose high reputation as a poet has not diminished in the nine decades since his death. Focusing upon Corazzini as a free-verse pioneer, this volume contains all of his poetry not in traditional forms, from his earliest experiments to the haunting and enigmatic "The Death of Tantalus," written only eight days before Corazzini's own death from tuberculosis. It also contains the complete text of Book for Sunday Evening, the last and best of his six booklets of verse. —Gradiva Publications

Corazzini, Sergio. Translated and edited by Michael Palma. *Sunday Evening: Selected Poems.* 68p. pap. $10.00. Stony Brook, NY: Gradiva Publications, Spring 1998. The first English translation of Corazzini, whose high reputation as a poet has not diminished in the nine decades since his death. Focusing upon Corazzini as a free-verse pioneer, this volume contains all of his poetry not in traditional forms. —Gravida Publications

Corey, Del. *Pardon My Allusions.* 64p. pap. $10.00 (1-56439-064-0). Detroit, MI: Ridgeway Press, Spring 1997.

Corless-Smith, Martin. *Of Piscator.* 96p. pap. $15.95 (0-8203-1947-3). Athens, GA: University of Georgia Press, Fall 1997. As an alien in several senses of the word, the mind behind these poems looks at the world from a dizzying but also dazzling per-

spective. Populated by snakes, birds, vines, insects, and mysterious lovers, Of Piscator is a dreamscape of natural and manmade jungles. — University of Georgia Press

Corless-Smith, Martin. *The Garden at Theophany or Eccohome a Dialectical Lyric.* 32p. pap. $6.00 (0-9666303-2-7). New York, NY: Spectacular Books, Fall 1998.

Corman, Cid. Edited by Philippe Briet. *Tributary.* 62p. pap. $10.00 (0-9646466-2-5). New York, NY: Edgewise Press, Fall 1998. Corman's series of sustained lyrical poems, each seven lines long in a 1-2-1-2-1 disciplined format, focuses on "color" as simultaneously a race and aesthetic issue. Includes color reproductions of five paintings by Beauford Delaney. — Edgewise Press

Corn, Alfred. *Present.* 112p. $22.00 (1-887178-31-7). pap. $13.50 (1-887178-69-4). Washington, DC: Counterpoint, Spring 1997. In Present, his seventh collection of poetry, Corn draws with impressive skill on narrative, figurative, and metrical resources to frame challenging contemporary issues, autobiographical themes, and vivid observations of both the extra-

ordinary and the everyday. —
Counterpoint. Corn's work
shimmers with a mastery of
styles, from rhymed stanzaic
forms to verses with
unmetered lines to prose. —
Grace Shulman, The Nation

Cornford, Adam. *Decision
Forest.* 86p. pap. $8.95 (1-
880766-15-9). Berkeley, CA:
Pantograph Press, 1997.
Cornford's third collection
scans the ongoing three-way
collision between science,
class society and the self. The
book is a struggle for imaginative vision adequate to challenge our accelerating,
increasingly exploited reality
— and to reveal "the infinite
which was hid." —
Pantograph Press. These
poems fill a page with clarity
after clarity, satisfying the eye
and ear as well as the mind.
That tool of the new age, the
computer, has found, at last,
its poet. —Ronald Johnson

Cornish, Sam. *Cross a Parted
Sea.* 128p. pap. $11.95 (0-
944072-71-2). Cambridge,
MA: Zoland Books, Fall 1996.
Cornish has a direct and insistent commitment to statement
understood by feeling, experience, history, memory. He is a
sharpener and a sander and a
honer. —Amiri Baraka. In
Cross A Parted Sea Cornish
continues to turn plain speech

into song. His poetry informs
and illuminates and we are
fortunate to have him/it. —
Lucille Clifton. In this piano-
tickling ramble through the
sawdust and gumbo back
streets of America, the poet
renders a vision that is more
song than poem and more
moan than melody, but it's all
vintage Cornish, and should
be read by anyone interested
in African-American history.
—Gerald Hausman

Cortázar, Julio. Translated by
Stephen Kessler. *Save
Twilight: Selected Poems.*
160p. pap. $12.95 (0-87286-
333-6). San Francisco, CA:
City Lights Books, Fall 1997.
The landmark publication of
Cortázar's poetry, available for
the first time in English translation. World-renowned as a
master of modern fiction,
Cortázar was also a prolific
poet who, in the final months
of his life, assembled what he
wanted saved of his life's work
in verse. Informed by his
immersion in world literature,
music, art, and history, and
most of all his own emotional
geography, Cortázar's poetry
traces his paradoxical evolution from provincial
Argentinean sophisticate to
cosmopolitan Parisian
Romantic, always maintaining
the sense of astonishment of

an artist surprised by life. —
City Lights Books

Corwin, Phillip. *Binoculars:
New and Selected Poems.*
128p. pap. $10.00 (0-
9615475-1-0). New York, NY:
Catnip Press, Spring 1997.
Several poems are drawn from
recent experiences in the former Yugoslavia. —Catnip
Press

Cory, Jim. *The Redheads.*
35p. pap. $8.00 (1-882827-07-
4). Philadelphia, PA: Insight
To Riot Press, Spring 1997.
One of America's best-kept
secrets. —Los Angeles
Weekly

Costanzo, Gerald, ed. *The
Devins Award Poetry
Anthology.* 242p. pap. $16.95
(0-8262-1161-5). Columbia,
MO: University of Missouri
Press, Spring 1998. The
Devins Award Poetry
Anthology, is at once a recog-
nition and a celebration of this
important American poetry
series. [including] from four to
nine of the most representative
poems by each of the twenty-
nine award winners, notably
Nancy Willard, Jonathan
Holden, Diana O'Hehir, C.G.
Hanzlicek, Mary Kinzie, and
Wesley McNair. —University
of Missouri Press

Coursen, H.R. *History
Lessons: New Poems.* 74p.
pap. $12.00 (1-891979-00-0).
Randolph Center, VT: Mad
River Poetry, Spring 1998.
What a pleasure to read a poet
who is clean as a new knife!
—Bart Giamatti

Coursen, H.R. *Poems From
"The Metamorphoses".* 60p.
pap. $11.00 (1-891979-11-6).
Randolph Center, VT: Mad
River Poetry, Fall 1998. He
should be America's most
famous poet. —Grace
Cavalieri

Coursen, H.R. *The Green of
Spring and Other Poems.* 54p.
pap. $10.00 (1-880664-16-7).
Randolph Center, VT: Mad
River Poetry, 1997. Coursen
writes quiet, serene landscapes
of woods, coast, fields, cutting
firewood with nipped ears,
birds, clammers — they are all
here in his abundant, observant view. —Alan Lockwood

Cox, Mark. *Thirty-Seven
Years From the Stone.* 105p.
(0-8229-5669-1). Pittsburgh,
PA: University of Pittsburgh
Press, Fall 1998. In this confident, large-hearted, and enor-
mously readable book, Cox
demonstrates what might seem
to be impossible: how a voice
can be at once tender and
toughminded, passionate and
casually down-to-earth, disil-

lusioned and thoroughly glad to be alive. —Mark Doty. Cox has a wry, deadpan humor, a piercing wit, and a keen knowledge of the contradictions of the human heart. These poems transcend their own ironies to sing with a moving simplicity, with an open and vulnerable voice. —Edward Hirsch. A splendid book, a book so rich and human and original it will help you remember why you love poetry. —Thomas Lux

Crabtree, Lou V. *The River Hills and Beyond.* 64p. pap. $12.00 (1-885912-19-6). Abingdon, VA: Sow's Ear Press, Fall 1998. The River Hills will strengthen as well as broaden Crabtree's reputation. —Raliegh News & Observer

Cramer, Steven. *Dialogue for the Left and Right Hand.* 57p. pap. $13.95 (1-57129-033-8). Cambridge, MA: Lumen Editions/Brookline Books, Fall 1997. This poet's made a pact with emotional life that goes like this: Nothing here will be inflated, everything here will be confronted, and whatever music feeling will yield will be tuned to the heart's true pitch. Thus, full as they are with the difficult stuff of the real, these poems also startle us with their plain and

daily beauties. —Mark Doty. Passionate, self-aware, lucidly intelligent, Cramer's poems achieve an ideal synthesis between naturalness of expression and musical pleasure. His voice is beautifully embodied by his verse, and his direct, fearless engagement with his subjects verifies his formal virtuosity. He achieves a rare balance between perceptions elegantly recorded and the power of art to scour and clean. —Tom Sleigh

Crane, Stephen. *War Is Kind and Other Poems.* 64p. pap. $1.00 (0-486-40424-2). Mineola, NY: Dover Publications, Fall 1998. War Is Kind and Other Poems offers new insight into the mind and genius of an author primarily known for his fiction. Includes The Black Riders, War Is Kind, and a selection from Crane's uncollected poetic works. —Dover Publications

Creeley, Robert. *Life & Death.* 85p. $19.95 (0-8112-1384-6). New York, NY: New Directions, Spring 1998. If youth asks the mirror, "Am I the fairest?" then age, in Creeley's skillful, ironic, and tender voice asks, "Do you remember me?" And the poems of Life & Death are the mirror's answers: a collage of recollection and salvage, a gathering-in before winter's night. —New Directions. There is [in Creeley's work] precisely a soulful tenacity, a hybrid between devotion and obsession, that keeps him a major poet. —Richard Silberg, Poetry Flash

Creeley, Robert. *So There: Poems 1976-83.* 248p. pap. $14.95 (0-8112-1397-8). New York, NY: New Directions, Fall 1998. So There combines three earlier collections of Creeley's work: Hello (1976); Later (1979); and Mirrors (1983). In 1976, Creeley set off to visit nine countries in the Far East, to explore his sense of self in a foreign land-scape. That trip transformed his life and work. He sees today that these three books in a single volume emphasize the "determined change in my life they are the issue of." —New Directions. His influence on contemporary American poet-ry has probably been more deeply felt than that of any other writer of his generation. —Terry Southern, The New York Times Book Review. [Creeley] is on anyone's short list of the best working American poets. —The Washington Post Book World

Cregg, Magda, ed. *Hey Lew: Homage to Lew Welch.* 101p. pap. $12.00. Hey Lew Books, 1997.

Crist, Robert, trans. *Grind the Big Tooth: A Collection of Contemporary Greek Poetry.* 61p. pap. $7.95 (1-56315-075-1). Pittsburgh, PA: Sterling House, Fall 1997. Rich in imagery, texture and insight, this astonishing collection of poems represents the finest works of fourteen of the most renowned contemporary Greek poets. —Sterling House

Crocker, Daniel. *People Everyday and Other Poems.* 92p. pap. $12.00 (1-891408-06-2). New York, NY: Green Bean Press, Spring 1998. Daniel Crocker has "it." A young writer with something special, he defines what "Post-Beat Independent" is all about. Clarity, strength, passion, vision, and wisdom all come to mind when I think of his writing. —Dave Christy. Crocker is one of a lively band of modern poets who write not from the ivory tower of acade-mic indulgence, but from the heartland of the people, and I stress heart, because Crocker's poetry comes from deep inside him. He brings a fresh breath of vitality to an all too often stale small press poetry scene. This is a powerful collection of poems. —A.D. Winans

Crockett-Smith, D.L. *Civil Rites: New and Selected Poems.* 62p. pap. $5.95 (0-933296-17-7). Oakland, CA: Black Scholar Press, Fall 1996. Civil Rites is propelled by a fresh, cutting edge modernism and a relentless social conscience. Autobiographical in thrust, Civil Rites dazzles with its keen intelligence and sudden explosions of lyricism. Few poets of his generation have Crockett-Smith's command of metric and his unfailing sense of the music of black life, whether he sings of Alabama or Chicago, Nicaragua or Hamburg. — Black Scholar Press. Deriving power from the African-American idiom, the poetry of Crockett-Smith is direct in its language, and powerful and timely in its message. — Quincy Troupe

Crooker, Barbara. *In the Late Summer Garden.* 23p. $5.00 (0962079030). H & H Press, Fall 1998.

Crowe, Thomas Rain, ed. *Writing the Wind: A Celtic Resurgence, The New Celtic Poetry.* 335p. pap. $14.50 (1-883197-12-0). Cullowhee, NC: New Native Press, Fall 1997. Here is a first comprehensive look at poets from Wales, Brittany, Scotland, Ireland, Cornwall and Isle of Man writing in Welsh, Breton, Scottish Gaelic, Irish Gaelic, Cornish and Manx. Along with poets who are household names in their native countries, such as Sorley MacLean, Bobi Jones and Anjela Duval, are more than fifty of the new young voices of modern Celtic literature, the progeny of hundreds of years of ancient cultural tradition, yet as modern as anything being written anywhere in the world today. — New Native Press

Crowe, Thomas Rain, trans. *In Wineseller's Street: Renderings of Háfez.* 86p. pap. $12.95 (0-936347-67-8). Ibex Publishers, Spring 1998. [Crowe] hears the rambunctious lilt in Háfez and brings that across with a rather eloquent, yet sensitive modernism of his own making — making it his own, and therefore unique. —Coleman Barks

Cruz, Victor Hernández. *Panoramas.* 190p. pap. $12.95 (1-56689-066-7). Minneapolis, MN: Coffee House Press, Fall 1997. Cruz seeks out the most disparate images, ideas, people, and finds in them confluence, rather than conflict. Utilizing a system of Caribbean syntheses, he meditates on his native soil and its diaspora. Inspired by Latin

American oral traditions and literature and diverse northern poetics, he melts these influences into a tapestry, creating a unique North American contemporary style truly his own. —Coffee House Press. In these new poems and essays, colorful, percussive, erudite, and innovative as ever, Cruz once again shares a world of generosity and live tradition. Wit, insight, and faith in the survival of a human universe combine to make this book a tonic and a gift. Arriba Victor! Arriba Puerto Rico! —Anselm Hollo

Cruz-Bernal, Mairym. *On Her Face the Light of La Luna.* 87p. $35.00 (0-944854-23-0). pap. $10.00 (0-944854-22-2). Provincetown, MA: Provincetown Arts Press, Spring 1997. I am grateful to Cruz-Bernal, whose magical lyric opens, full faced, on a life entire. Her authority lives in passionate disclosure, vulnerability, rebellion, lives in an outrageous insistence on parting company with her readers in order to make art. —Deborah Digges, Boston Review. These are poems that dare, challenge, burn, thrill and terrify: are you equal to them, reader? They are what life would be if one lived fully open and had the intelligence, the honesty, and the poetic tal-

ent of Cruz-Bernal. —Susan Mitchell

Csoóri, Sándor. Translated by Len Roberts. *Selected Poems of Sándor Csoóri.* 113p. pap. $11.00 (1-55659-047-4). Port Townsend, WA: Copper Canyon Press, 1992. Csoóri is the leading Hungarian poet of the post-World War II generation. Memories of war intrude at unexpected intervals throughout his work to punctuate his existential sense of moral responsibility, creating a strongly ambivalent note regarding the society he surveys. Never reluctant to examine greed or hypocrisy, his poems seek a sense of moral equilibrium in the midst of social chaos. Csoóri also writes love poems of remarkable tenderness and vulnerability as well as poems of deep introspection. Roberts's translation captures the poignant, direct, uncluttered style of the original, poems that embody a sweeping sense of history at the personal scale, and Csoóri's extraordinary gift for locating the telling image. — Copper Canyon Press

Cully, Barbara. *The New Intimacy.* 52p. pap. $14.95 (0-14-026480-9). New York, NY: Penguin Books/Viking Penguin, Spring 1997. Winner of the 1996 National Poetry

Series. [Cully's] post-apoca-
lyptic, fin de millénaire poems
reach us as cracked code or
canary song, should the canary
have survived its flight from
the mine shaft. She is a poet
reading the world for the brutality of its inequities, aware
of the flattening compression
of historical memory and the
dissolution of the body. She is,
in her transgressive, ruptural,
and disjunctive poetics, seeking a language for the
unspeakable shame of the
world. . [Finally she] locates
her hope in a present glimmer-
ing with futurity. —Carolyn
Forché

Cummings, E.E. Edited by
Richard Kostelanetz with John
Rocco. *AnOther E.E.
Cummings.* 310p. $25.00 (0-
87140-157-6). New York, NY:
Liveright Publishing, Spring
1998. Here is an eye-opening
selection of Cummings's most
avant-garde poetry and prose.
Cummings was a pioneer in
sound and concrete poetry. He
worked with the traditional
form of the sonnet until he
made it all his own through
linguistic and typographic
inventions that have never
been properly recognized. To
read the avant-garde
Cummings is to read a writer
who wrote in many genres,
who consistently broke with
establishment norms, as he

once put it, "never to rest and
never to have: only to grow."
—Liveright Publishing

Cummings, E. E. Edited by
George James Firmage. *No
Thanks.* 88p. pap. $12.00 (0-
87140-172-X). New York, NY:
Liveright Publishing, Fall
1998. No Thanks contains
some of Cummings's most
daring literary experiments,
and it represents most fully his
view of romantic individual-
ism. The poems celebrate an
openly felt response to the
beauties of the natural world,
and they give first place to
love, especially sexual love, in
all its manifestations. The title
refers ironically to rejections
he received from fourteen
publishers: although
Cummings was in mid-career
by 1935, his recognition was
still in the future. —Liveright
Publishing

Cummings, E. E. *ViVa.* 87p.
pap. $12.00 (0-87140-169-X).
New York, NY: Liveright
Publishing, Fall 1997. First
published in 1931, ViVa contains some of Cummings' most
experimental poems as well as
some of his most memorable.
Fresh and candid, by turns
earthy, tender, defiant, and
romantic, Cummings' poems
celebrate the uniqueness of
each individual, the need to
protest the dehumanizing force

of organizations, and the exuberant power of love. — Liveright Publications. He is a wit; this much is apparent in all his work, and one finishes ViVa with the conviction that he is one of the wittiest poets in the English language. — Malcolm Cowley

Cummings, E. E. *Xaipe.* 78p. pap. $12.00 (0-87140-168-1). New York, NY: Liveright Publishing, Fall 1997. Cummings, along with Pound, Eliot and Williams, helped bring about the twentieth-century revolution in literary expression. XAIPE (Greek for "rejoice"), which first appeared in 1950, contains some of Cummings' finest work. —Liveright Publications

Cummins, James. *Portrait in a Spoon.* 79p. $15.95 (1-57003-191-6). pap. $9.95 (1-57003-192-4). Columbia, SC: University of South Carolina Press, Fall 1997. Cummins's new sestinas reveal the master sestina-maker at work, turning the intricate form into a vehicle for a subtle exploration of the erotic life. Portrait in a Spoon includes non-sestinas as well, and these poems, too, are possessed of the joy and sadness and humor that makes Cummins's work such a rare treat. —David Lehman. As

always, Cummins's poems are dazzlingly inventive, but these new poems are something more as well — they are deeply felt and deeply moving. —Susan Wood

Cunningham, J.V. Edited by Timothy Steele. *The Poems of J.V. Cunningham.* 253p. $28.95 (0-8040-0997-X). pap. $16.95 (0-8040-0998-8). Athens, OH: Ohio University Press/Swallow Press, Fall 1997. The lifework in verse of one of the first and liveliest American poets of the twentieth century, this collection of the poems of Cunningham (1911-1985) documents the poet's development from his early days as an experimental modernist during the Depression to his later emergence as a master of the classical "plain style," distinguished by its wit, feeling, and subtlety. —Ohio University Press / Swallow Press. It is time to say that Cunningham is one of the best poets in America. —David Donoghue, The New York Times

Curbelo, Sylvia. *The Secret History of Water.* 75p. $18.95 (0-938078-53-4). pap. $10.95 (0-938078-52-6). Tallahassee, FL: Anhinga Press, Fall 1997. Curbelo's poetry is accomplished, daring, full of energy and intelligence; it is the generous first manifestation of an authentic and original gift. — W.S. Merwin. Curbelo's poetry conjures ghosts—not only of family and former selves, but of acts and gestures whose "secret history" surrounds an archipelago of human lives. Her cadences are marked by the urgency of smuggled testimony. In Curbelo's intimate telling, even water in a drinking glass is "a river begging to be named." —Carolyn Forché

Cushman, Stephen. *Blue Pajamas.* 55p. $19.95 (0-8071-2302-1). pap. $11.95 (0-8071-2303-X). Baton Rouge, LA: Louisiana State University Press, Fall 1998. Poetry may be more philosophical than history, but when the events of war or peace become poetry, as in Cushman's poems, the impact doubles, the poems both generally and incidently true. Blue Pajamas brings us a major new voice and a major new range. —A.R. Ammons. Cushman has learned his craft and its refinements, and he has developed his intellect so as to be able to call upon them whenever the poetic occasion requires him to do so. This is a splendid book, one of the best I've seen in years. —David R. Slavitt

Cutler, Bruce. *Seeing the Darkness: Naples, 1943-1945.* 77p. pap. $11.95 (1-886157-16-2). Kansas City, MO: BkMk Press of the University of Missouri-Kansas City, Spring 1998. Sweeping narrative power, gorgeous visual detail, and varied and surprising music. —Amy Clampitt. The lines of these poems are as unique as the old tragic city they remember. Together [these poems] become a Twentieth Century tale. You will smell the smoke and hear the clamor of the multitudes. —Bill Bauer

Cypser, Cora E. *Think on These Things.* 102p. pap. $8.00 (1-892063-01-8). Katonah, NY: Kim Pathways, Fall 1998.

D., Ramola. *Invisible Season.* 64p. pap. $12.00 (0-931846-51-X). Washington, DC: Washington Writers' Publishing House, Spring 1998. In these lyrical and inward poems, Ramola D. constructs a personal but deeply interactive poetics of self and culture, self and object, self and world. Her gift for the beautiful is singularly impressive, though the beautiful remains as much a barrier as an end to desire. This is a signal of the poet's insight, which seems to originate in the moment of pure sensual awareness, but climbs quickly back toward mind and identity, where the beautiful alone cannot endure. —Susan Tichy

Dahl, David. *Bright Garden at World's End.* 32p. pap. $7.00 (0-9623693-8-1). Chester, NY: Heaven Bone Press, Fall 1996.

Daldorph, Brian. *The Holocaust and Hiroshima.* 70p. pap. $10.00 (0-910479-00-3). Warrensburg, MO: Mid-America Press, Fall 1997. The one brave thing that Daldorph has done is to give us all a little peek into the hearts of such monsters as Mengele, Himmler, Bormann, among others. The morally easy choice would be to write a book strictly from the victim's point of view. In The Holocaust and Hiroshima, Daldorph has gone back and forth from monster to victim. —Todd Moore

Dalton, Roque. Translated by Jonathan Cohen, et al.; Edited by Hardie St. Martin. *Small Hours of the Night: Selected Poems of Roque Dalton.* 243p. pap. $14.95 (1-880684-35-7). Willimantic, CT: Curbstone Press, Fall 1996. Named one of the outstanding translations of 1996 by the American Literary Translators

Association. One of the greatest figures in Central American letters of this century. His genius is transcendent. —Arturo Arias. [Dalton's poetry illustrates] his profound conviction that the poet can and must, in his life as in his work, serve as the finely-honed scalpel of change, both in word and deed. —Claribel Alegría. This man's work hits me harder than springtime. — E. Ethelbert Miller. A great gift to American poetry. — The Boston Globe

Daniel, John, ed. *Wild Song: Poems of the Natural World.* 144p. pap. $14.95 (0-8203-2011-0). Athens, GA: University of Georgia Press, Spring 1998. The diverse poems in this collection, most of them first published in Wilderness magazine, offer visions of the wildness within and around us all the time, even in the places we have altered most. Gathered here are eighty-three poems by eminent poets and emerging talents, including Wendell Berry, Jane Hirshfield, W.S. Merwin, Naomi Shihab Nye, Pattiann Rogers, and William Stafford, among many others. These poems decry ecological injuries, celebrate nature's beauties, point to its many mysteries, and bear witness to our ever-available opportunity to recognize ourselves as rightful members of the evolutionary flow of earthly life. —University of Georgia Press

Daniels, Jim. *Blessing the House.* 80p. $25.00 (0-8229-3988-6). pap. $12.95 (0-8229-5636-5). Pittsburgh, PA: University of Pittsburgh Press, Spring 1997. These are tender, moving and nostalgic poems about an American life, beautifully wrought and vividly close to the experience of all of us born in small towns — close to parents and siblings we loved, providing a foundation for a decent mature life on which love and faith are founded. Reading these poems will make you feel better about who you are and where you are. —Carolyn Kizer

Daniels, Kate. *Four Testimonies.* 100p. $19.95 (0-8071-2259-9). pap. $12.95 (0-8071-2260-2). Baton Rouge, LA: Louisiana State University Press, Spring 1998. Daniels's third collection ambitiously links the joys of her own domesticity to the testimonies of others less fortunate. —Kirkus Reviews. The poems in Daniels's extraordinary new collection are set on the threshold of the tragic and the everyday. Whether her subject is man-made or natural catastrophe, the terrors of his-

tory or the struggles of private life, Daniels irradiates with hard-won, often unbearable, but always artful clarity, the horrible contingencies of human life. This is a beautiful, heart-wrenching book whose beauty is part and parcel of its ferocious power. —Alan Shapiro

Daniels, Keith Allen. *Satan Is a Mathematician: Poems of the Weird, Surreal and Fantastic.* 168p. pap. $12.95 (0-9631203-6-0). Palo Alto, CA: Anamnesis Press, Fall 1998. A haunting masterpiece — a fusion of poetry and science and a flight into an exotic universe of dream and desire. —Clifford Pickover. Daniels's poems are characterized by breadth of vocabulary, by the straddling of lexicons, and by an inventive attraction to the uncanny. —Richard Wilbur. Daniels ranges far and wide, high and low, from ghostly neutrinos swifting at the speed of light to the slow fornication of tortoises. There is something here to delight any lover of poetry or fantastic literature. —Joe Haldeman

Danly, Susan, ed. *Language as Object: Emily Dickinson and Contemporary Art.* 103p. pap. $13.95 (1-55849-066-3). University of Massachusetts Press/Mead Art Museum at

Amherst College, Spring 1997. Produced in conjunction with an exhibition organized by the Mead Art Museum at Amherst College, this handsome volume explores the impact of Dickinson's persona and poetry on contemporary art in America. Spurred by feminism and recent critical writings, many visual artists have turned to the poet's life and literary images for inspiration. They have engaged the issues raised by her poetry and the particular circumstances of her life and have attempted to transform her oblique language into tangible objects. Presenting the work of thirteen artists, as well as ten poets, this book showcases a wide range of responses to Dickinson's poetry. — University of Massachusetts Press/Mead Art Museum at Amherst College

Dante, Alighieri. Translated by Robert Pinsky. *The Inferno of Dante.* $35.00 (0-374-17674-4). pap. $18.00 (0-374-52531-5). New York, NY: Farrar, Straus and Giroux, Spring 1995; Fall 1997 (paper). Winner of the L.A. Times Book Prize and the Harold Morton Landon Translation Award given by the Academy of American Poets. The primary strength of this translation is the way it maintains the original's episodic and narrative velocity while mirroring its formal shape and character. It is no small achievement to reproduce Dante's rhyme scheme and at the same time sound fresh and natural in English, and Pinsky succeeds in creating a supple American equivalent for Dante's vernacular music where many others have failed. —Edward Hirsch, The New Yorker

Dauer, Lesley. *The Fragile City.* 59p. pap. $11.00 (1-878325-16-7). Emporia, KS: Bluestem Press, Fall 1996. The surreal poems of Lesley Dauer comprise a kind of Spoon River Anthology of the mid-nineties as filmed by Roman Polanski or David Lynch. But the vision of this poet is interested neither in violence nor in the perverse. It is interested in love. The tentative inhabitants of her city are rendered with such compelling tenderness and empathy that they become versions of all of us. — Johnathan Holden. The book's great achievement is that it can do what its characters find so difficult: understand the sadness of others. —William Matthews

David, Almitra. *Impulse To Fly.* 77p. pap. $10.95 (0-

9660459-1-2). Shutesbury, MA: Perugia Press, Spring 1998. A cogent collection of unsentimental portraits of ordinary people constrained by society, poverty, or their own personal circumstances. From urban Philadelphia to sixteenth century Italy to the shores of Chesapeake Bay, David evokes a tone both ancient and contemporary. —Perugia Press. Purity of feeling and clarity of vision literally shine through these poems: how David can remain so uncorrupted by the evil her unflinching truthfulness confronts is one of the wonders of this collection. These poems alter the very air we breathe with their recovery of the unheard, the dignity of their restraint, and the sweetness of their sorrowing compassion for us all. —Eleanor Wilner

Davidson, Michael. *The Arcades.* 93p. pap. $10.00 (1-882022-35-1). O Books, Fall 1998. Davidson has fashioned a work of extraordinary wit, human insight and verbal invention. —Michael Palmer. An often intensely autobiographical series of poems, Davidson's most recent collection represents a stunning exploration of the uneasy relation between public and private, pain and pleasure, in our puzzled and puzzling end of the millennium culture. — Susan Howe

Davis, Christopher. *The Patriot.* 104p. pap. $14.95 (0-8203-1991-0). Athens, GA: University of Georgia Press, Spring 1998. Winner of the Contemporary Poetry Series Competition. This splendidly outrageous book is a visionary delight. —Donald Revell. The Patriot is an antidote to all those shimmering surfaces parading around as if poetry were merely a decorous masquerade rather than the hot hard flesh that the imagination lusts for ever after. These poems will knock you between the eyes before getting down on hands and knees to beg your forgiveness (and maybe more). So crack it open and weep. —Timothy Liu

Davis, Cortney. *Details of Flesh.* 71p. $23.95 (0-934971-58-7). pap. $11.95 (0-934971-57-9). Corvallis, OR: Calyx Books, Spring 1997. These poems jolted me. They're like bulletins from the nursing front, only they slipped by the official censor. Crafted with a shrewd and penetrating tenderness, they awaken us to a world of flesh imbued with a transcendent spirit. —Belle Waring. Davis is a revelation. A practicing nurse, Davis creates indelibly vivid portraits of patients and healers. This book offers us a new vocabulary for agony and tenderness, mortality and the transcendence of mortality. —Martín Espada

Davis, Dick, trans. *Borrowed Ware: Medieval Persian Epigrams.* 206p. $24.95 (0-934211-52-3). Washington, DC: Mage Publishers, Spring 1998. Davis's translation of the best of Persia's medieval short poetry, Borrowed Ware, is a wonderful book, suffused with love, beautifully produced and with a comprehensive introduction to Persian courtly poetry. —The Independent. Many of the best poems in Borrowed Ware are mystical, and Davis is probably the first translator to have succeeded in conveying their intensity of focus. — Times Literary Supplement

Davis, Jordan. *Poem on a Train.* 40p. pap. $5.95. Barque Books, Fall 1998.

Davis, Meg. *Avidly Perplexed.* 44p. pap. $9.95 (0-933313-22-5). Tucson, AZ: SUN/gemini Press, 1994.

Davis, Olena Kalytiak. *And Her Soul Out of Nothing.* 84p. $17.95 (0-299-15714-8). pap. $10.95 (0-299-15710-5). Madison, WI: University of Wisconsin Press, Fall 1997.

Winner of the 1997 Brittingham Prize in Poetry. And Her Soul Out of Nothing is, quite simply, unlike any other collection I can remember reading in recent literature. There is an eerie precision to Davis's work — like the delicate discernment of a brain surgeon's scalpel — that renders each moment in both its absolute clarity and ultimate transitory fragility. Her language is quirky in the very best sense of that word; her use of syntax is brilliant. — Rita Dove. I respond to the deep undercurrents of feeling in this ironic, lyrical, and elusive book of soul-making, this astonishing debut volume. What an abiding pleasure to discover an initial — and initiating — book that renders an inner world, an interior life, the arc of a soul emergent, a soul in action. —Edward Hirsch

Davison, Peter. *The Poems of Peter Davison, 1957-1995.* pap. $17.50 (0-679-76589-1). New York, NY: Knopf, Alfred A., Spring 1995; Fall 1997 (paper). The Poems of Peter Davison comprises eight previous books, and adds a final section of new poems. The new poems are his best yet. This collection is a literary event of the first order. Davison revives sources of freshening truth, of purity, that make a mockery of all our efforts to create a new horizon for poetry, and just in time. —Tom D'Evelyn, The Boston Book Review

Day, Jean. *The Literal World.* 112p. pap. $12.95 (1-891190-01-6). Berkely, CA: Atelos, Spring 1998. Day's book was commissioned as the first of the Atelos project, the publication of 50 volumes of writing which challenge conventional definitions of poetry by crossing traditional genre boundaries. —Atelos Press

Day, Lucille Lang. *Fire in the Garden.* 63p. pap. $9.95 (0-914370-72-3). Berkeley, CA: Mother's Hen, Spring 1997. Fire in the Garden is a book of beauties and mutilations, erotic intimacies, distances and mysteries, seductive dreams and sardonic deflations of our common dreamlife. It runs hot, cold and shivery, and will keep surprising you with the "taste of ash" on its lips. — Alicia Suskin Ostriker

de Andrade, Eugénio. Translated by Alexis Levitin. *Another Name for Earth / O Outro Nome da Terra.* 105p. pap. $12.95 (0-936609-37-0). Fort Bragg, CA: QED Press, Fall 1997. The great little country that is Portugal turns

out great big poets like Camóes, Pessoa and, more recently, de Andrade. His verses are not prosaic like so much that is being written now, but rather they have the succinct lyricism that [sums] things up in a moment, much like haiku. But, then, Portugal is a succinct country. Levitin's version are right to that exact point. Enjoy! —Gregory Rabassa. De Andrade writes the sort of poetry that leaves after-images flickering in the mind. There is much pleasure to be derived from his poetry, a kind of pleasure hard to find outside of the best Japanese haiku. —Carlos Cunha

De Burgos, Julia. Translated by Jack Agüeros. *Song of the Simple Truth: The Complete Poems.* 523p. pap. $21.95 (1-880684-24-1). Willimantic, CT: Curbstone Press, Fall 1997. De Burgos looms larger than life in the literary psyche of Puerto Rico. —Publishers Weekly. This first bilingual edition of de Burgos' complete poems, more than 200 of them, is a literary landmark — the first time her poems have appeared in a complete edition in either English or Spanish. [De Burgos] broke new ground in her poetry by fusing a romantic temperament with keen political insights. This book will be essential reading for lovers of poetry and for feminists. —Curbstone Press

de Cristoforo, Violet Kazue, trans. *May Sky: There Is Always Tomorrow: An Anthology of Japanese American Concentration Camp Kaiko Haiku.* 287p. $29.95 (1-55713-253-4). Los Angeles, CA: Sun & Moon Press, Fall 1997. May Sky: There Is Always Tomorrow is an account of the significant contribution made by the haiku writers to wartime literature. Through years of research and study, de Cristoforo has tracked down most of the haiku members of the different camps and documented their activities. Equally importantly, she has chosen a large selection of haiku written in the camps and translated them into English. This significant collection presents a large selection of these works in the original nihongo (Japanese) and romaji (Japanese written in the Latin alphabet) in addition to the English. —Sun & Moon Press

de la O, Marsha. *Black Hope.* 86p. $22.00 (0-932826-50-4). pap. $12.00 (0-932826-51-2). Kalamazoo, MI: New Issues Press, 1997. Black Hope is a book that takes us deep into the unparaphrasable regions of human consciousness, and it goes there not to mystify but to clarify, to drag back out into the light our cruelty and brutality as well as our moments of joy and delight. —Chase Twichell. Whatever it is that "darkens in us every day," this is just what de la O has willed into the light in these gorgeous, harrowing poems. I don't know what I admire most, her merciless intelligence or her merciful spirit. I know we are luckier for having these fresh and remarkable poems. —Nancy Eimers

de Palchi, Alfredo. Translated by Sonia Raiziss. *Anonymous Constellation.* 96p. $23.00 (1-879378-24-8). pap. $13.00 (1-879378-23-X). Riverside, CA: Xenos Books, Spring 1997. Here de Palchi defies the idea of evolutionary progress, asserting that violence levels all creatures and brings them back to their primeval state. The cycle of poems presents a view of history turned upside down: history does not instruct, does not help, but only repeats the great struggle, pitting human beings against other humans beings, human beings against animals, animals against other animals. —Xenos Books. De Palchi is both tough and imaginative. He is absolutely uncompromising, and his poems are painful and exalting to read. One does not come away from his stark and terrible and hilarious work untouched. — James Dickey

Debeljak, Ales, ed. *The Imagination of Terra Incognita: Slovenian Writing 1945-1995.* 468p. pap. $20.00 (1-877727-77-6). Buffalo, NY: White Pine Press, Fall 1997. The Imagination of Terra Incognita presents the rich literary tradition of Slovenia, the first of the newly independent former Yugoslavian republics. Taking its title from the series that celebrates the unknown literature of Central Europe, this anthology presents Slovenian writers as the driving force of resistance to oppression in their land — oppression both from within and without. Spanning the latter part of this century, this anthology gathers together some of the best writing in the post-war era, capturing the voices of those who wrote against the current of their day. —White Pine Press

Delgado, Juan. *Working on It.* 9p. Berkeley, CA: Chicano Chapbook Series, Fall 1997. The Chicano Chapbook Series, edited by Gary Soto, issued twelve title in the late 1970's and early 1980's, including works by Sandra Cisneros, Alberto Ríos, Jimmy Santiago Baca and others. The chapbooks are distributed free of charge to selected libraries with Chicano collections. Working on It is #14.

Delp, Michael. *The Coast of Nowhere: Meditations on Rivers, Lakes, and Streams.* 120p. pap. $14.95 (0-8143-2711-7). Detroit, MI: Wayne State University Press, Fall 1997. Delp is a writer of exquisite tenderness and wild imagination, and this is his best book yet. —Jack Driscoll. In The Coast of Nowhere Delp has fashioned a series of lyrical meditations from a prose as limpid and flowing as his subject: rivers. Delp has created a paradox — he captures the movement of water, which is by its very nature elusive. It's a gift. — Stuart Dybek

Deming, Alison Hawthorne. *The Monarchs: A Poem Sequence.* 88p. $19.95 (0-8071-2230-0). pap. $12.95 (0-8071-2231-9). Baton Rouge, LA: Louisiana State University Press, Fall 1997. Deming has done for monarch butterflies what Ted Hughes did for crows; she has found in them modes of expression for myriad facets of existence. This is one of the finest and truest fusions of ecological thought and precise, evocative poetics to emerge in the history of American arts and letters. —Gary Paul Nabhan. I greatly admire Deming's lucid and precise language, her stunning metaphors, her passion, her wild and generous spirit, her humor, her formal cunning. I am taken, as all readers will be, by the knowledge she displays and how she puts this knowledge to a poetic use; but I am equally taken — I am more taken — by the wisdom that lies behind the knowledge. —Gerald Stern

Deming, Alison Hawthorne, ed. *Poetry of the American West.* 328p. $24.95 (0-231-10386-7). Irvington, NY: Columbia University Press, Fall 1996. Spanning five hundred years, from the fifteenth-century flower songs of the Nahuatl Indians to contemporary verse about urban Los Angeles, Poetry of the American West features over 150 selections by more than seventy poets, along with forty arresting photographs of this landscape so central to the American psyche. Cowboy songs mingle with protest poems of the Chicano farmworkers' movement, the early epic poems of Gaspar Pérez de Villagrá appear alongside those of Allen Ginsberg. This is the first major collection to cover the broad spectrum of Western poetry. —Columbia University Press

Dennis, Carl. *Ranking the Wishes.* 71p. pap. $14.95 (0-14-058779-9). New York, NY: Penguin Books/Viking Penguin, Spring 1997. With a minimum of strain and rarely raising his voice, Dennis disrupts the temporal ground beneath us. He confidently questions, discusses, commands, conjectures, and turns directly to the audience, breaking the fourth wall, and gathers us into his wanderings and musings with a candor so engaging we can't but follow. —David Yezzi, Parnassus

Dépas, Albert. *Metamorphosis of Joy.* pap. $8.95 (0-9651473-0-4). New York, NY: Mega Press, 1996. Dépas here metamorphoses his voice from talker to singer as his diction transforms from commonplace expression to the highly charged forms of poetic speech. One of the many pleasures of this book is the way his poetry records shifting perspectives, from joy to the expression of loss or doubt, from the dogged optimism of the title poem to those less certain poems which engage us in darker moods. Changing joy into other states of awareness, the poet provides us with the real world, maybe less easily sung about, but convincing when deeply felt. —Mega Press

Der-Hovanessian, Diana. *The Circle Dancers.* 112p. pap. $12.95 (1-878818-55-4). Riverdale-on-Hudson, NY: Sheep Meadow Press, Fall 1996. I feel her poems in me, the sense of destruction and unquenchable life, of creativity and genocide, fragmentation and connectedness. They are profoundly touching, heart reaching. I feel admitted in some way to her Armenian culture and experience through a kind of generosity and openness in the poems. — Adrienne Rich. Der-Hovanessian's poems are a kind of miracle in the extraordinary way they keep alive and fresh the diaspora of a vanished Armenia and knit it quite simply into ordinary life. When I came upon these poems first I was bowled over. —May Sarton

Derricotte, Toi. *Tender.* 80p. $25.00 (0-8229-3993-2). pap. $12.95 (0-8229-5640-3). Pittsburgh, PA: University of Pittsburgh Press, Spring 1997. Derricotte's poems show us our underlife, tender and dreadful. And they are vibrant poems, poems in the voice of the living creature, the one

who escaped — and paused, and turned back, and saw, and cried out. This is one of the most beautiful and necessary voices in American poetry today. —Sharon Olds. The poems that radiate from the centerpoint of Tender strike the reader at the core of being. This is bold, courageous work of exceptional beauty. The poet guides us into the interior of herself, ourselves. — Michelle Cliff

Derry, Alice. *Clearwater.* 87p. pap. $11.00 (0-911287-23-X). Yakima, WA: Blue Begonia Press, Fall 1997. This is a rare and astonishing book and its publication is cause for rejoicing. I know of no one else who writes like Alice Derry. The impact of these unsparingly honest and intimate poems is overwhelming, as they take us inside the poet's actual and felt life as a mother, wife and teacher, a life that is as rich as it is contradictory and uncontrollable. As readers, we are not so much addressed as included and embraced. All of us are enlarged by the empathy and candor of this extraordinary poet. —Lisel Mueller

Derry, Alice. *Not As You Once Imagined.* 33p. pap. $7.00 (93-2264-00-X). Portland, OR: Trask House Books, 1993.

Derry loves the real work so intensely that she trusts and delights in the authenticity of its smallest gesture. In these intimate poems she focuses on the fine threads and tiny knots that make up the evolving tapestry of family relationships, as interdependent, though never as perfect, as the plant life that surrounds and sustains her. She has made her peace with imperfection. These poems are acts of praise, not highly won, arising from a truthful and noble spirit. —Lisel Mueller

Di Biasio, Rodolfo. Edited by Barbara Carle. *Patmos.* 53p. pap. $10.00 (1-892021-01-3). Stony Brook, NY: Gradiva Publications, Fall 1998. Di Biasio's language possesses an austere grace and, at the same time, an incisive capacity of recreating the sensation of trauma. His poetry retains a fresh voice which expresses an acute sense of time and the nothingness it brings. — Barbara Carle

Di Blasi, Debra. *Drought & Say What You Like.* 39p. pap. $10.95 (0-8112-1332-3). New York, NY: New Directions, Spring 1997. Di Blasi writes from the heart of the Postmodern American Gothic. A native Missourian, she plumbs the depths of psycho-sexual repercussion and searing sentiment behind the region's parched, pitchfork-bearing facade. —New Directions. People content to name the will's inevitable defeat "God" or "History" will not long endure these restless stories. Di Blasi writes for the rest of us, the comfortless unconfessed of us. —H.L. Hix

Di Prima, Diane. *Dinners & Nightmares.* 160p. pap. $14.95 (0-86719-395-6). San Francisco, ca: Last Gasp Press, Fall 1998.

Di Prima, Diane. *Loba.* 314p. pap. $14.95 (0-140-587-52-7). New York, NY: Penguin Books/Viking Penguin, Fall 1998. A visionary epic quest for the reintegration of the feminine, hailed by many when it first appeared in 1978 as the great female counterpart to Ginsberg's Howl. Now published for the first time in its expanded and revised form, Loba explores the wilderness at the heart of experience through the archetype of the wolf goddess. —Penguin Books. Loba is a mysterious compelling poem or series of poems whose vision of the female godhead is precise, ever changing, ever deepening. It incorporates ecstasy and rot, all the forms of the female experience from birth through death. Di Prima has borrowed from many mythologies to create her own numinous myth. —Marge Piercy. Blood-drenched and liberating, this is a poem for the ages. —Robert Hunter

Diamond, Red. *R.I.P. Muthafucker: Poems and Stuff.* 87p. pap. $7.95. Olympia, WA: NoNo Publications, Fall 1995.

Dickey, James. Edited by Robert Kirschten. *The Selected Poems.* 183p. pap. $15.00 (0-8195-2260-0). University Press of New England/Wesleyan University Press, Fall 1998. For years we have needed a judicious selection from the poems of James Dickey, a book that would bring new readers to the best of his work. With generosity and tact, Robert Kirschten has given us that book. —David Mason

Dickinson, Emily. Chosen by the The New York Public Library. *Selected Poetry of Emily Dickinson.* 299p. $15.00 (1-385-48718-5). New York, NY: Doubleday/Anchor Books, 1997. Gathers a rich harvest of the finest of [Dickinson's] poems, each carefully selected by the staff of the New York Public

Library. Arranged chronologically, they chart the development of a poetic sensibility fired by immediacy of perception and a magnificent grasp of language. Dickinson and her world are further evoked with rare manuscripts and prints drawn from the Library's special collections, including a selection of the poet's handwritten letters. — Doubleday/Anchor Books. No lyric poet before or since has written of human emotions with Dickinson's blazing exactness. She was one of the most intelligent of poets and one of the most fearless. If fearlessness ran out, she had courage, and after that she had her recklessness. —Galway Kinnell

Digges, Deborah. *Rough Music.* 54p. pap. $15.00 (0-679-76597-2). New York, NY: Knopf, Alfred A., Fall 1995; Spring 1997 (paper). Digges's new verse is at times rowdy and elemental — its music is that of Bruegelesque romp, open to ecstasy and wild surrender. —The New Yorker. Digges's new book is exacting and forceful; its demands on itself are severe and its rewards are the kind won from the ordeals of difficult fate. Digges writes without self-pity or blame, reaching for self-understanding, for discipline, strength. —David Baker, The Kenyon Review

Dinh, Linh. *Drunkard Boxing.* 36p. pap. $8.00 (0-935162-18-6). Philadelphia, PA: Singing Horse Press, Fall 1998. Vietnamese-born Dinh's first book of poetry is also the first book from the Philadelphia Publishing Project, which responds to the need for national exposure for emerging writers living in the Philadelphia area. —Singing Horse Press. Simply fabulous. The book is like discovering a world you never knew existed and which makes absolute sense. —Ron Silliman

DiPalma, Ray. *Letters.* 63p. pap. $10.95 (1-5571337-4-3). Los Angeles, CA: Littoral Books, Fall 1998.

Disch, Tom. *The Dark Old House.* 24p. pap. $7.50. Edgewood, KY: Barth, Robert L. (R.L.B.), Fall 1996.

Divakaruni, Chitra Banerjee. *Leaving Yuba City: New and Selected Poems.* 114p. pap. $12.95 (0-385-48854-8). New York, NY: Doubleday/Anchor Books, 1997. Divakaruni's poetry carries a wisdom rarely seen in contemporary poetry, run through the reader like a cool drink of water on a hot day.

Leaving Yuba City is a magical, mysterious, beautiful book of poetry, strong, passionate, lyrical. —Quincy Troupe. Leaving Yuba City weaves a rich fabric of women's lives. Divakaruni's word-threads are gold, black, red, and green, and a faint scent clings to the cloth. But let no one think these poems exotic. In their very particularity, they hold a universal tale of community and individuation, of the hunger for a larger life that remains connected. —Jane Hirshfield

Dobie, Ann Brewster, ed. *Uncommonplace: An Anthology of Contemporary Louisiana Poets.* 256p. $32.50 (0-8071-2254-8). pap. $19.95 (0-8071-2255-6). Baton Rouge, LA: Louisiana State University Press, Fall 1998. Dobie has dropped her trawl into Louisiana's waters and brought up a rare catch of poets. Here are fine works that spring from love of a piquant, stormy piece of the map where food, family, waterscape, and spirit bloom into music and pictures — a net full of meaning found nowhere else. — Tim Gautreaux. These poems haunt me, humble me, sometimes scare me like good jazz for all their ambidextrous reach to the local and cosmopolitan in one breath.

Reading, I feel a sizzling urge to sit down and write my family portrait, my own stunned account of my childhood, my own spell for the lost good thing. —Kim Stafford

Dodd, Wayne. *The Blue Salvages.* 92p. $20.95 (0-88748-290-1). pap. $11.95 (0-88748-259-7). Pittsburgh, PA: Carnegie Mellon University Press, Spring 1998. Dodd is making poems of consequence—eloquent, deeply felt, vital—that testify to the survival of an intelligent and personal poetics in a time of frivolity and imitation. His significance should not be underestimated as we look toward the future of American poetry. He has given us an impressive body of work. —Michael Waters

Donoghue, Emma, ed. *Poems Between Women: Four Centuries of Love, Romantic Friendship, and Desire.* 209p. $24.95 (0-231-10924-5). Irvington, NY: Columbia University Press, Fall 1997. With poems in English by more than one hundred female poets spanning 400 years, this anthology reflects the historical development of women's attitudes toward intimacy between women and the changing mores of society. Included are poets from Aphra Behn to Dorothy Wordsworth; Margaret Fuller to Audre Lorde. —Columbia University Press

Dorn, Edward. Edited by Burton Hatlen. *Sagetrieb: Edward Dorn.* 272p. pap. $8.95 (0-943373-52-2). Orono, ME: National Poetry Foundation, Spring 1998. This special issue of the journal devoted to poets in the Imagist / Objectivist tradition includes fifty pages of recent poems by Dorn and two hundred pages of critical essays on his work, as well as a facsimile of Bean News, Dorn's newspaper. — National Poetry Foundation

Doty, Mark. *An Island Sheaf.* 28p. $175.00 (1-891472-14-3). New York, NY: Dim Gray Bar Press, Fall 1998. Letterpress limited edition of 125 copies, each signed by the author. — Dim Gray Bar Press

Doty, Mark. *Farrile.* 12p. pap. $35.00 (1-891472-13-5). New York, NY: Dim Gray Bar Press, Fall 1997. Letterpress edition of 65 copies, printed on handmade Kitakata paper. Each copy is handsewn in wrappers of a different marbled paper. —Dim Gray Bar Press

Doty, Mark. *Sweet Machine.* 118p. $22.00 (0-06-055370-7).

pap. $12.00 (0-06-095256-3). HarperCollins/HarperFlamingo, Spring 1998. In fits of glorious mimesis, Doty lavishes adjectival cascades on the fantastic objects of his inclination, reflecting their glamour and allure. Crafting sharp-eyed celebration from "ash and attitude, scorch and glory," this now very arrived poet gathers enough force to render "the world / that's on everyone's lips. —Publishers Weekly. Nothing escapes [Doty's] gaze and nothing — death, devastation, the ghost of a gesture — escapes its sheer insistence on beauty, the world "lustered by the veil." Doty is a master, repainting our sad daily canvas, heightening the gold light, the diffusion, the shocked shattered glass and the artificial bath of attitude, letting us see it all arrayed, as he says, under the un-compromising vault of heaven. —Carol Muske

Doubiago, Sharon; Devreaux Baker, and Susan Maeder, eds. *Wood, Water, Air and Fire: The Anthology of Mendocino Women Poets.* 330p. pap. $22.95 (0-9656052-3-X). Camptche, CA: Pot Shard Press, Fall 1998. Wood, Water, Air and Fire presents sixty-three distinctive voices from an area of northern California known for the austere beauty of its redwood trees and rugged Pacific coastline. The poets here range in age from fourteen to eighty-eight, and often paint a vivid picture of rural life. But if the context of these poems is elemental, the emotional tone is rich and varied. Sometimes subtle, often surprising, even startling, these poems arising from spirit of place go on to explore intimate personal experience. The result is a fascinating tapestry of lives. — Pot Shard Press

Dowell, Karen. *Cooking With Dogs.* 64p. $19.95 (1-891090-01-1). Dear Isle, ME: Two Dog Press, Fall 1998. In Cooking With Dogs, Dowell explores the special bond between dogs and the people who love them in a series of delightful, beautifully illustrated vignettes that speak to and about dogs. —Two Dog Press. This playful and attractive book reveals a true celebration of our friendship with dogs. —The Bark

Driscoll, Frances. *The Rape Poems.* 80p. pap. $12.95 (0-9651413-1-4). Port Angeles, WA: Pleasure Boat Studio, Spring 1997. It is impossible to praise this book too much — its power, maturity, sorrow, and fierce resistance. This book should be required reading in America. —Lynn Emanuel. A deeply disturbing, compelling and somehow beautifully rendered sequence of poems, in which a terrible wounding has been transformed by long meditation, careful attention to detail, and superb artistry. Though hers is a landscape one would think would be strewn with the landmines of sentimentality and self-pity, there is never a false step here. Of how many books of poetry can one truly say, "I could not put this book down until I'd read it through to the end? This is one of those rare books. —Paul Mariani. In this psychologically searing collection of poems, Driscoll is wise, clear-eyed and unrelenting. As her readers, we're asked to attempt a reckoning with an act and experience of violence so intimate it rips the fabric of an entire life. The poet asks not only if one can ever triumph over the pain and psychic debris of such an event, but also if this isn't perhaps, what it can truly mean — the terror, the misappraisals of family and friends — to be a woman in American today. —David St. John

Duba, Ursula. *Tales From a Child of the Enemy.* 153p. pap. $8.95 (0-14-058787-X). New York, NY: Penguin

Books/Viking Penguin, Spring 1997. In these deceptively simple, evocative, and unforgettable narrative poems, Duba tells of a child subjected to nonstop bombings, hunger, and family turmoil; of a girl who grows up hearing the constant lament of the suffering inflicted on Germany; and of a young woman who, thirteen years after the end of the war, learns of the Holocaust, of her country's complicity in it and denial of responsibility for it. —Penguin Books/Viking Penguin. A beautiful, truthful collection of poem-stories. The language is simple, direct — the feelings complex and strong. —Grace Paley

Dubris, Maggie. *WillieWorld.* 59p. pap. $6.95 (0-9666328-2-6). New York, NY: CUZ Editions, Fall 1998. A 59 page prose poem largely drawn from the author's ten years of experience as a 911 paramedic in New York City. —CUZ Editions

Duddy, Thomas. *On Boca Ciega Bay.* 42p. pap. $7.50 (0-935252-54-1). Sound Beach, NY: Street Press, Fall 1997.

Dudley, Ellen. *Slow Burn.* 65p. $35.00 (0-944854-25-7). pap. $10.00 (0-944854-24-9). Provincetown, MA:

Provincetown Arts Press, Fall 1997. Dudley's poems are powerful and real, visceral, so alive that some of them might frighten the faint of heart. That's good. But Slow Burn is better than good — it's a brilliant and unforgettable debut. —Thomas Lux. Dudley's poems come by their sex and violence quite naturally — survival is strenuous. And death, too, when survival can't be had. But she's not only a Tough Gal poet (Bette Noire?); grace and tenderness, too, drench these clear and lovely poems. —William Matthews

Dufault, Peter Kane. *New Things Come Into the World: Poems and Verse-Logues.* 184p. pap. $14.95 (0-940-262-62-2). Hudson, NY: Lindisfarne Press, 1993. To read Dufault is to enter a privileged suspension between the long-term and the evanescent. His work throughout is distinguished not only by largeness of theme but also by a precision and wit that are uniquely his own. —Amy Clampitt. Dufault has been at it for many years, writing poems full of vigor, knowledge, and felicity. They are the real thing, and this collection is welcome indeed. —Richard Wilbur. His brilliant metaphors transform ordinary events into miracles. —Nancy Willard

Duffy, Timothy J. *Poetic Praise: Jesus Christ Is Lord.* 75p. pap. $8.95 (1-880451-21-2). Baden, PA: Rainbow's End, Spring 1997.

Duhamel, Denise. *Kinky.* 96p. pap. $12.95 (0-914061-61-5). Alexandria, VA: Orchises Press, Spring 1997. If there is a better young poet than Duhamel in the USA, don't tell me. I can't take it, I can barely take her! Frank O'Hara said something about only 3 American poets being better than the movies, but I think Duhamel would make him add a 4th. —Bill Knott. She chose poetry but she could have chosen music videos or comic strips: Duhamel is wildly satiric, and we are blessed by this true & fierce mirror of our straight gate. —Jean Valentine

Duhamel, Denise, and Maureen Seaton. *Exquisite Politics.* 71p. pap. $10.95 (1-882688-15-5). Chicago, IL: Tia Chucha Press, Fall 1997. In poems that speak in a breezy, conversational style or with taut lyric intensity, these gifted writers probe the mysteries of relationships, personal histories, and issues of sexual and political identity. —

Tia Chucha Press. In this unique and successful collaboration, Duhamel and Seaton have created a powerful mix of provocative poetry. Exquisite Politics is wicked, insightful, bold and fun. — Jessica Hagedorn

Dukes, Jonnie. *The Lost Chronicles of Love.* 80p. pap. $6.95 (0-9641606-2-5). Cupertino, CA: Easy Break, First Time Publishing, Spring 1998. Unabashedly autobiographical, these poems tell the story of a lost love: romance in its blossoming and frank desire, betrayal, loss and death. —Easy Break, First Time Publishing

Dunbar, Paul Laurence. Edited by Glenn Mott. *Selected Poems.* 80p. pap. $1.00 (0-486-29980-5). Mineola, NY: Dover Publications, Fall 1997. Dubbed the "Poet Laureate of the Negro Race' by Booker T. Washington, Dunbar (1872-1906) wrote verses in dialect and in standard English that captured many elements of the black experience in America. This is a rich amalgam of lyrics encompassing patriotism, a celebration of rural life and homey pleasures, anger at the inequalities accorded his race, and faith in ultimate justice. —Dover Publications

Duncan, Robert. Edited by Robert J. Bertholf. *Selected Poems.* 171p. pap. $12.95 (0-8112-1345-5). New York, NY: New Directions, Spring 1997 (revised and englarged). Bertholf's selections are so attuned to the essentials of Duncan's writing that even those familiar with the whole body of Duncan's work will become more sensitized to his recurring imagery and consistency of thought pattern throughout this collection. — Publishers Weekly

Dunlop, William. *Caruso for the Children & Other Poems.* 96p. pap. $9.95 (0-9651210-2-X). Seattle, WA: Rose Alley Press, Spring 1997. Since the early 1960s, Dunlop has had a coterie reputation as one of the finest poets of his generation, notorious for his reluctance to allow his work to be published. Now, at last, we can read the poems that have so long been a matter of rumor among his friends and students. He is a brilliant metrical technician. No one alive handles the classic iambic line of English verse with greater subtlety and unexpectedness. His poems have stings in their tails, and they make the reader laugh. One rejoices with them at the simple pleasure of finding darkness made so wittily

palpable in rhyme and meter.
—Jonathan Raban

Dunn, Robert. *Zen Yentas in Bondage.* 64p. $20.00 (0-89304-082-7). pap. $10.00 (0-89304-083-5). Cross-Cultural Communications/Ostrich Editions, Spring 1997. Dunn has taken his considerable skill as a poet, satirist, and parodist, and blended them with care, fashioning a superb collection of 41 poems, [like] a sandwich of scattered puns and scathing witticisms pressed between observations as sharp as aged cheddar, layered with laughter on wry. — Leigh Harrison, Small Press Review

Dunn, Stephen. *Loosestrife.* 96p. $19.00 (0-393-03982-X). pap. $11.00 (0-393-31683-1). New York, NY: Norton, W.W., and Company, Fall 1996; Spring 1997 (paper). Finalist for the National Book Critics Circle Award. To read a few lines of a Dunn poems is to feel suddenly in touch with the way things are, and the way we really feel about them. — Richard Wilbur

DuPlessis, Rachel Blau. *Drafts15-XXX, The Fold.* 91p. pap. $12.00 (0-937013-65-X). Elmwood, CT: Potes & Poets Press, 1997. Writing in a form that supersedes the poets she

has admired — Oppen, Zukofsky —, DuPlessis, hanging on to that "golden twist," the poet's survival kit, continues a golden pursuit. Drafts 15-XXX, The Fold gives rare evidence of a record of time. In her exploration of poetics, a rare cerebral intimacy forms as we are drawn into her schemata. She creates a dynamics that causes regret on leaving each Draft. Yet Time, in DuPlessis's increasingly expressive hands, is busy with new upheavals, new "tests" of poetic survival. Mindful, as she says, of "Writing being mired forever / in its own inky letters. . . placement / gap, and spell." —Barbara Guest

DuPlessis, Rachel Blau. *Renga: Draft 32.* 48p. pap. $9.00 (0-9667655-0-8). Wayne, PA: Beautiful Swimmer Press, Fall 1998.

Durham, Flora. *Baby Lady.* 26p. pap. $5.00. Portland, OR: 26 Books, Spring 1997. A long prose poem exploring the identity and experience of mother and baby. This is the fourteenth of 26 books of contemporary poetry from the Pacific Northwest. —26 Books

Eady, Cornelius. *The Autobiography of a Jukebox.*

75p. $20.95 (0-88748-211-2).
pap. $11.95 (0-88748-212-0).
Pittsburgh, PA: Carnegie
Mellon University Press,
Spring 1997.

Easley, Craig. *Deja' Voodoo.*
42p. pap. $5.00 (0-9653587-3-
9). San Francisco, CA:
Meridien PressWorks, Fall
1996.

Easter, Charles. *Spirit Dance.*
43p. pap. $7.00. Somerville,
NJ: Black Bough, Spring
1997. Haibun on family, childhood and the environment. —
Black Bough Press

Economou, George. *Century
Dead Center and Other
Poems.* 123p. pap. $15.00 (1-
880516-23-3). Barrytown, NY:
Left Hand Books, Fall 1997.
Century Dead Center contains
Economou's prose, poetry,
translations and visual art — a
selection of work spanning
eighteen years. —Left Hand
Books

Ehret, Terry. *Lost Body.* 77p.
pap. $11.00 (1-55659-057-1).
Port Townsend, WA: Copper
Canyon Press, 1992. Selected
for the National Poetry Series
by Carolyn Kizer. Ehret takes
the reader into myth, memory,
dream, sexual desire, and in
the final section, through an
imaginative interpretation of
ancient hieroglyphic text. If

H.D. had been a language
poet, she might have written
something like this. —Copper
Canyon Press. Ehret is a wonderfully various, resourceful
poet. Her play with forms
works always towards ease
and freedom. Her timing is
faultless, a joy in itself, and
her fearlessness is exhilarating. —Ursula Le Guin. To
read Ehret is to become
invested, repeatedly. . . at the
most serious and disquieting
level of song, where one
crosses over to the unfamiliar
and recognizes it and is
changed. —Kathleen Fraser

Ehrmann, Max. *The
Desiderata of Hope: A
Collection of Poems to Ease
Your Way in Life.* 79p. $14.00
(0-517-70887-6). New York,
NY: Crown Publishers, Spring
1997. The fifth book in the
highly successful series that
began with the legendary
Desiderata (more than 200,000
copies sold), this collection of
poems. . . on the theme of
hope will inspire courage in
even the most trying times.
—Crown Publishers

Eimers, Nancy. *No Moon.*
84p. (1-55753-099-8). West
Lafayette, IN: Purdue
University Press, Fall 1997.
Winner of the Verna Emery
Poetry Prize. The force and
allure of what's absent,

shrouded, invisible but palpable are what Eimers's No Moon propitiates. She navigates, then, by dead reckoning. And the book moves from accuracy to accuracy like a blind person in a familiar room. —William Matthews

Eliot, T.S. Edited by Christopher Ricks. *Inventions of the March Hare: Poems 1909-1917.* 428p. pap. $15.00 (1-15-600587-5). San Diego, CA: Harcourt Brace/Harvest Books, Spring 1998. Included here are early drafts of such important poems as "The Love Song of J. Alfred Prufrock" and "Portrait of a Lady," as well as pages of bawdy verse that Eliot never shared with his readers and that reveal a very different man from Eliot's public persona. This important volume finally reveals what inspired and influenced the early work of one of this century's most important men of letters. —Harcourt Brace. Surely one of the literary events of our era. Probably only the discovery of a cache of sonnets by a youthful Shakespeare could excite literary scholars more. —The Jerusalem Post

Eliot, T.S. *The Waste Land: 75th Anniversary Edition.* 64p. pap. $4.00 (0-15-600534-4). San Diego, CA: Harcourt Brace/Harvest Books, Spring 1997.

Eliot, T.S. *The Waste Land, Prufrock and Other Poems.* 64p. pap. $1.00 (0-486-40061-1). Mineola, NY: Dover Publications, Spring 1998. A rich collection of much of Eliot's greatest work, including the title poem and the complete contents of Prufrock. An indispensible resource for all poetry lovers, this modestly priced edition is also an ideal text for English literature courses from high school to college. —Dover Publications

Elmslie, Kenward. Edited by W.C. Bamberger. *Routine Disruptions: Selected Poems and Lyrics 1960-1998.* 256p. pap. $15.95 (1-56689-077-2). Minneapolis, MN: Coffee House Press, Fall 1998. Routine Disruptions gathers together a broad selection of Elmslie's work, including autobiography, visually-shaped performance pieces, confessional love poetry, lyrics from Elmslie's musical plays and opera librettos, along with his innovative poem songs. —Coffee House Press. A various, campy, never-tiring display of verbal skyrockets and sweet, soap-opera dilemmas, Elmslie's oeuvre makes for joyous readings. Few [poets] manage to sustain his excess, scale and abundance while remaining so thoroughly poised. — Publishers Weekly. Elmslie tells the insistent tales of our tribe with great humor and seemingly endless invention. —Robert Creeley

Elsberg, John. *A Week in the Lake District.* 72p. pap. $22.00. Winchester, VA: Red Moon Press, Fall 1998. Nominated for the Virginia State Library Poetry Book of 1998, this unusual book of haiku recollects, in diary fashion, the author's excursion through the Lake Country of England. —Red Moon Press

Elsberg, John. *Broken Poems for Evita.* 32p. pap. $5.00 (1-57141-041-4). Port Charlotte, FL: Runaway Spoon Press, Fall 1997. Poems that combine the visual with intraverbal deconstruction. — Runaway Spoon Press

Elsberg, John. *Family Values.* 20p. pap. $5.00 (1-57141-29-5). Port Charlotte, FL: Runaway Spoon Press, Fall 1996. Avant-garde poems featuring chant-like rolling block poems. —Small Press Review

Elsberg, John. *Offsets.* 72p. pap. $13.00 (1-888832-14-2). St. Augustine, FL: Kings Estate Press, Fall 1994; Spring 1998 (new edition).

Elytis, Odysseas. Translated by Olga Broumas. *Eros, Eros, Eros: Selected and Last Poems.* 171p. pap. $18.00 (1-55659-083-0). Port Townsend, WA: Copper Canyon Press, Fall 1998. In this definitive edition of the work of the Greek Nobel Laureate Elytis, poet and translator Broumas has chosen poems from the full range of his career: work written during his association with the surrealists, the long poem The Little Mariner, as well as a previously unavailable selection of his last poems. Passionately committed in equal parts to both justice and a life of imagination, Elytis is truly one of the world's great poets. —Copper Canyon Press. This is a poetry of luminosity and resonance, clarity of soul, and deep transformative power. Such work arises out of the language itself, and such a language out of the sea, the rocks, the history and light of Greece. — Carolyn Forché

Emerson, Jean. *Cycles of the Moon Vine.* 69p. pap. $10.00 (0-938572-17-2). Hedgesville, WV: Bunny and the Crocodile Press/Forest Woods Media Productions, Spring 1997. The writing is clear and careful, full of the gorgeous sensual images, hazy in retrospect, the emotional details exact. — Phyllis Koestenbaum. This captivating books of poems tackles family legends, distorted or crippling myths, and puritanical pride. Cycles of the Moon Vine holds some universal truths. —Gail Clark, Small Press Review

Emmons, Jeanne. *Rootbound.* 99p. pap. $12.95 (0-89823-184-1). Minneapolis, MN: New Rivers Press, Spring 1998. Whether it's piano practice, window washing, or a game of jacks, Emmons brings to her domestic poems a rich lyric awareness and a wise if wistful acceptance of human limitations. —Maxine Kumin. What exemplary poems these are! At once graceful and meticulous, articulate and intense — they seem not so much made as grown. —Phil Hey. Emmons's fine ear and delicate eye subtly untie knots of language so that each word lovingly illumines and clarifies the extraordinary in the unexamined clutter of our daily lives. —Michael Carey

Engels, John. *Sinking Creek.* 134p. $25.00 (1-55821-646-4). pap. $16.95 (1-55821-638-3). New York, NY: Lyons Press, Spring 1998. A finalist for the Pulitzer Prize for his previous collection, Weather-Fear, Engels gives us poems on the pleasures of life: country, sport, books and food. Engels is increasingly recognized as one of America's finest poets. —The Virginia Quarterly Review

Engler, Robert Klein. *Departures.* 70p. pap. $10.00 (0-944300-21-9). Chicago, IL: Alphabeta Press, Fall 1998. Engler is not only one of today's premier gay writers, but an inspiring wordsmith for all audiences. —J. Masiulewicz, U-Direct. A poet of the first rank. —Michael Morgan

Engler, Robert Klein. *Medicine Signs: Selected Poems.* 90p. pap. $10.00 (0-944300-18-9). Chicago, IL: Alphabeta Press, Spring 1997. This is the stuff poetry is made of. A contemporary voice offered to us with form and grace. —Hiruki Yamamoto. Engler delights in finding poems from the ordinary and not so ordinary events of gay life in America. This new book reaches beyond earlier ones to explore fresh areas of human experience. —Mary Stetson

Engman, John. *Temporary Help.* 105p. pap. $12.95 (0-930100-82-4). Duluth, MN:

Holy Cow! Press, Fall 1998. We would all rather have seen this wonderful book in print before Engman's unexpected death in 1996, but having it now we at least have something of him back: the sly wit, the self-deprecating sweetness of his voice. These poems are without pretense, casually but shrewdly crafted, often spiced with irony but never bitterness. —Jim Heynen. Engman is perhaps the most underestimated poet of his generation. —Mary Karr. Engman was the Kafka of Minneapolis, the Charlie Chaplin of Hennepin Avenue. Utterly devoted to poetry, he wrote wildly original poems about our bewildering condition here at the close of the century. The more time I spend with his work, the more I'm convinced that Engman is one of the essential poets of his generation. — Barton Sutter

Equi, Elaine. *Friendship With Things.* 40p. pap. $8.00 (0-935724-93-1). Great Barrington, MA: Figures, The, Fall 1998.

Equi, Elaine. *Voice-Over.* 96p. pap. $13.95 (1-56689-078-0). Minneapolis, MN: Coffee House Press, Fall 1998. Equi's new book is her best to date. She calibrates the nuances of voices in these poems until they ring like music, all the while giving us images and tableaux of sharp contrasts and the subtlest colorations. In poem after poem, Voice-Over unfolds as a wonderful assemblage, carefully constructed, infused with mystery and delight. —Nicholas Christopher. [Equi] is at once an entertainer and an oracle: a winning combination. — Wayne Koestenbaum. Equi finds in small things — gestures, moments, objects — a core simplicity, neither pious nor reductive, which recovers and redefines an essential American spirit. As lucid and welcome as dawn itself, these poems ride to us on spare lines. This is a collection to guide you safely into the next millenium. —Ann Lauterbach

Erba, Luciano. Edited by Alfedo de Palchi and Michael Palma. *The Metaphysical Streetcar Conductor: Sixty Poems.* 151p. pap. $13.00 (1-892021-00-5). Stony Brook, NY: Gradiva Publications, Spring 1998. This anthology brings together some of the most significant poems written by Erba over half a century, from about the mid-forties to the mid-nineties. [In this book] Erba confirms his gnomic-fantastic talent as a "domestic," definitely postmodern, profoundly antirhetorical, moody, and irreverent poet, which makes him all the more necessary in the landscape of these closing years of the twentieth century. —Luigi Fontanella, from the Introduction. In the panorama of contemporary Italian poets, [Erba] stands out more sharply than most for his natural originality, his irony and sarcasm, his dry humor and tight phrasing. The reader cannot confuse his work with that of anyone else. Just as with the poetry of Catullus, it is always green and belongs only to its author. —Alfredo de Palchi

Erdrich, Heid E. *Fishing for Myth.* 80p. pap. $12.95 (0-89823-174-4). Minneapolis, MN: New Rivers Press, Spring 1997. Erdrich's Fishing for Myth has the fresh astonishment of the violent change of weather. —Jim Harrison. In these poems Erdrich not only evokes the physical reality of places as unlike one another as Paris and the Dakota prairie, but she demonstrates the bound nature of land, history, and people, and recreates in her reader an intense, almost frightening sense of the emotional and spiritual heartbeat of place. — Kimberly M. Blaeser

Eshleman, Clayton. *From Scratch.* 190p. $27.50 (1-57423-071-9). pap. $15.00 (1-57423-070-0). Santa Rosa, CA: Black Sparrow Press, Fall 1998. Many of these poems reflect on the lives and works of creative artists such as William Blake and Francis Bacon. Others range through time and history from the mythic-Paleolithic to the topical present, from the caves of the Dordogne to the courtroom of O.J. Simpson, zooming in and out between the cosmic to the personal. —Black Sparrow Press

Espada, Martín. *Imagine the Angels of Bread.* 107p. $18.95 (0-393-03916-1). pap. $11.00 (0-393-31686-6). New York, NY: Norton, W.W., and Company, Spring 1996; Fall 1997 (paper). Espada continues doing what he does best: evoking the Hispanic experience in language at once brutal and luminescent. Don't let this book pass you by. — Library Journal. An extraordinary book. Here is the true poet laureate of this nation. In Espada, America has a poet equal to the demands of giving voice to its least-heard people. —Bloomsbury Review

Espada, Martín, ed. *El Coro: A Chorus of Latino and Latina Poetry.* 166p. $30.00 (1-55849-110-4). pap. $13.95 (1-55849-111-2). Amherst, MA:

University of Massachusetts Press, Fall 1997. The widest window on some of the liveliest poetry being written in this country today. Espada has chosen not just poets but individual poems that prove there is no such thing as a single Latino / a manner or outlook — poems that delight and bite and exhilarate from start to finish. —Paul Jenkins, Massachusetts Review

Espaillat, Rhina P. *Where Horizons Go.* 70p. $25.00 (0-943549-55-8). pap. $15. (0-943549-56-6). Kirksville, MO: Thomas Jefferson University Press/New Odyssey Press, Fall 1998. Winner of the 1998 T.S. Eliot Prize for Poetry. Has any Latina written more movingly of the rich and heavy inheritance of bilinguality? Where Horizons Go is a gift to the English language. —Dana Gioia. Poem after successful poem add up to an impressive total. Such developed skill and such mastery of rhyme and meter are certainly rare anymore; so is plainspeaking. All in all it's a collection likely to persuade readers who think they don't like poetry that they do, after all. —X.J. Kennedy

Essinger, Cathryn. *A Desk in the Elephant House.* 70p. $18.95 (0-89672-401-8). Lubbock, TX: Texas Tech University Press, Fall 1998. In a time when so many poets are out to unload the dead weight of their pasts on the reader, it is refreshing to read the work of Essinger who realizes that before it can do anything else, poetry must give pleasure. Smart, sweetly crafted, and open-voiced, her poems are propelled not only by memory but by thought and wit. — Billy Collins

Etter, Carrie. *Subterfuge for the Unrequitable.* 39p. pap. $6.00 (0-937013-79-X). Elmwood, CT: Potes & Poets Press, Fall 1998.

Eulert, Don. *Field: A Haiku Circle.* 90p. pap. $15.00 (0-944676-41-3). Gualala, CA: AHA Books, Spring 1998. A haiku-a-day by the founder of American Haiku, the first journal in English devoted to these Zen poems of Japanese tradition. —AHA Books. Eulert has a genuine feeling for haiku, and he is among the best of the Americans using the form. —Lucien Stryk

Everson, William (Brother Antoninus). *The Residual Years: Poems 1934-1948.* 382p. $27.50 (1-57423-056-5). pap. $17.50 (1-57423--055-7). Santa Rosa, CA: Black Sparrow Press, Fall 1997. This magisterial work collects the entirety of Everson's early poetry in a single volume allowing us a fascinating first look at this poet's beginnings and the development of his art. —Black Sparrow Press

Evetts, Dee. *endgrain: haiku and senryu 1988-1997.* 51p. pap. $10.00 (0-9657818-1-X). Winchester, VA: Red Moon Press, Fall 1997. In these haiku and senryu, Evetts brings a world's-eye-view to the great outdoors, the bedroom, and everything in between. Basho might have written these poems — had he settled in New York City toward the end of the twentieth century after traveling the globe for decades. Tenderness and wit run through endgrain; reading it we know the poet's days and hours, and our own. —William J. Higginson. With endgrain, Evetts enters haiku's front ranks. —Cor van den Heuval

Fairchild, B.H. *The Art of the Lathe.* 78p. pap. $9.95 (1-882295-16-1). Farmington, ME: Alice James Books, Spring 1998. The Art of the Lathe measures a world inhabited by those for whom life has made its meanings plain by constant subtraction, like the raw metal being hewn into shape by the lathes, both real and metaphorical, that figure

so prominently in this collection. James Joyce's Stephen Dedalus spoke of forging the conscience of his race in the smithy of his soul; in the dusty light of a Kansas machine shop, Fairchild has performed similar magic. —R.S. Gwynn. Fairchild brings sympathetic insight to the machinists, welders, and farmers he writes of. And like a fine novelist, he has a gift for focusing on those moments when lives constrained by psychological or economic circumstances are touched by beauty and significance. —Timothy Steele

Falconer, Sandra Evans. *Imagining the World.* 36p. pap. $10.00. Philadelphia, PA: Gateway Press, Spring 1998. Whatever world these poems walk, Falconer offers us a poetic geography that is at once landscape and psychescape. The poems gathered here underscore the poet's reverential sense of living and being fully alive. —Gary Blankenburg. Falconer writes poems that are at once poignant and disquieting. I invite the reader to feel a distinct heartpang, or gasp aloud, as I did. —Keith Parker. These poems are cat-like in their mystery and grace, magical, able to leap between worlds and still come for the morning

milk. The reader is riveted. —
Kendra Kopelke

Fallows, Cathey. *The Heart of
a Woman.* 51p. pap. $10.00 (1-
887905-11-1). Boone, NC:
Parkway Publishers, Fall
1998. Fallows's lines sing and
flash with honest, poetic
observations. —Marian Coe.
A poet of passionate conviction, startling insight and
extraordinary integrity,
Fallows is a voice to which we
can all respond with warmth
and gratitude. —Rachel
Rivers-Coffey

Fan Chengda. Translated by
Lois Baker. *Four Seasons of
Field and Garden: Sixty
Impromptu Poems.* 163p. pap.
$12.00 (1-57889-083-7).
Pueblo, CO: Passeggiata
Press, Spring 1997. These
translations describe [rural
Chinese life], marking not
only the changing seasons and
the play of yin and yang but
the work and rituals of the
family and village as well.
These poems were written, as
it were, on the wing. They
don't brood. They are the
world of human labor-in-
nature seen through Fan's
eyes. Four Season of Field
and Garden is one of the best
[West Coast translations of
Chinese poetry] to appear in a
long time. —Portland
Oregonian

Fay, Julie. *The Woman
Behind You.* 81p. (0-8229-
5682-9). Pittsburgh, PA:
University of Pittsburgh Press,
Fall 1998. Fay leads us inward
through the aqua lenses of our
senses, inward to knowledge
of the world as it is, moment
by exquisite moment. —Judith
Vollmer. A superb manifestation of the contemporary possibilities of lyric poetry and a
sustained and gripping narrative of a late-20th-century
woman's life, exemplary in its
specificities, picaresque in the
geographic and erotic vicissi-
tudes of its quest. —Marilyn
Hacker

Fay, Steve. *What Nature.* 69p.
$35.00 (0-8101-5078-6). pap.
$14.95 (0-8101-5079-4).
Northwestern University
Press/TriQuarterly Books, Fall
1998. As responsive to nature
as Gary Snyder or Mary
Oliver, Fay combines a command of the poetic craft with
rich descriptive exactness as
he describes physical and psychological landscapes, particularly of his native Midwest. —
Northwestern University
Press. The poems of Steve Fay
aren't like anyone else's; his
voice carries its own authority
— original in both senses of
the word, with a taproot deep
into origins, while arrestingly
fresh in language and vision.
—Eleanor Wilner

Fayth, Doc. Edited by Graham Everett. *The Doc Fayth Poems.* 16p. pap. $5.00 (0935252-58-4). Sound Beach, NY: Street Press, Fall 1998. Doc Fayth, ignored for years by the poetry community, sought a poetics that reflects reality yet also refines it when possible without creating further falsifications. This edition gathers the known bulk of Fayth's jottings regarding such poetic practice and provides a venue for his skewed view of existence, bookended as it appears by the unknown. — Street Press

Fein, Richard. *To Move Into the House.* 80p. pap. $10.00 (0-932616-56-9). New Poets Series/Chestnut Hills Press/Stonewall, Fall 1996. Fein can be funky, lusty, glitzily and cynically worldy-wise; but make no mistake, he's one of the Ancient Sages, allied with the voices of Sacred Mystery, and with a deep reverence for the past. What a lively mix! —Albert Goldbarth

Feinstein, Sascha, and Yusef Komunyakaa, eds. *The Second Set: The Jazz Poetry Anthology, Volume 2.* 250p. $35.00 (0-253-33053-X). pap. $15.95 (0-253-21068-2). Bloomington, IN: Indiana University Press, Fall 1996.

[Coupled] with The Jazz Poetry Anthology, this volume offers a comprehensive exploration of the history of jazz poetry. The Second Set fills out the history of jazz poetry with poems written before WWII, as well as works from the Black Arts Movement of the 1960's, and includes Ai, Rita Dove, Joy Harjo, Charles Simic, Derek Walcott, Yevgeny Yevtushenko, and others. —Indiana University Press

Feirstein, Frederick. *New and Selected Poems.* 188p. pap. $14.00 (1-885266-51-0). Ashland, OR: Story Line Press, Fall 1997. Twenty-five years and five books later, New and Selected Poems confirms Feirstein's reputation as a master of the narrative poem and the poetic sequence. As a central figure in "Expansive Poetry"—a movement dedicated to expanding the audience for poetry—Feirstein consistently combines meter and rhyme with a tough contemporary diction to create dramas of urban life. —Story Line Press. Feirstein. . . challenges the smug contemporary assumptions of what will or will not work in verse. — Dana Gioa, The Hudson Review. [He is an] odd blend of Woody Allen and T.S. Eliot. —American Book Review

Ferlinghetti, Lawrence. *A Far Rockaway of the Heart.* 124p. $21.95 (0-8112-1347-1). pap. $10.95 (0-8112-1398-6). New York, NY: New Directions, Spring 1997; Fall 1998 (new paper). In A Far Rockaway of the Heart, his newest collection of poetry, Ferlinghetti writes with the ecstatic energy that has made A Coney Island of the Mind an enduring 20th century poetic text. The themes of love, light, art, history, and landscape dance through this suite of 100 poems, as Ferlinghetti, a self-styled "stand-up tragedian," leaves no cultural stone unturned. —New Directions. One of our ageless radicals and true bards. —Booklist. [He has written] in ways that those who see poetry as the province of the few and educated had never imagined. That strength has turned out to be lasting. —Joel Oppenheimer, The New York Times Book Review

Ferlinghetti, Lawrence. *The Street's Kiss.* 14p. pap. $15.00 (0-931659-43-4). Boise, ID: Limberlost Press, Fall 1998. Aphorisms on poetry first read over Pacifica Radio KPFA-FM in the 1950s. [These poems have] only recently been recovered and transcribed to appear here in print for the first time. —Limberlost Press

Ferraris, Fred. *Older Than Rain: Early and Recent Poems1970-1997.* 128p. pap. $8.00 (1-882775-08-2). Selva Editions, 1997. There's a powerful and distinctive rhythm to this book; an admirably sane if bipolar dance between neighborly engagements with the so-called natural world and citizenly enragements at our collective presumptions upon it. It's a pleasure to welcome these poems into print. —Ted Pearson. Ferraris has a genuine poetic mind. His writing is notable for its intimate geological and ecological feel. The sense of foreboding in some of this work comes off as a very real, not alarmist or trendy, environmentalism. —Reed Bye

Ferry, David, trans. Translated by David Ferry. *The Odes of Horace.* 344p. $35.00 (0-374-22425-0). New York, NY: Farrar, Straus and Giroux, Fall 1997. Ferry is a poet with a sure and delicate ear, and a love for the original. He also clearly relays many of Horace's own abiding virtues: an assured quiet tone conveying complexities of feeling with unfailing proportion and grace. We are fortunate that he has devoted himself to Horace. —W.S. Merwin. Ferry's translations from Horace are wonderfully right as to spirit, movement, and tones of voice. I admire the way he finds what English meters will serve each poem, and weaves down through them with Horatian fluency and momentum. This is in every way a masterful performance. —Richard Wilbur

Field, Edward. *A Frieze for a Temple of Love.* 228p. $27.50 (1-57423-068-9). pap. $15.00 (1-57423-067-0). Santa Rosa, CA: Black Sparrow Press, Fall 1998. This new book confirms Field's reputation as one of our finest poets in the discursive narrative tradition. Field, a native New Yorker and long-time gay activist, writes poetry that is literate, immediate, funny and completely personal. These unforgettable poems are like small essays on the human condition, spoken by a friend we trust. —Black Sparrow Press

Field, Greg. *The Longest Breath.* 91p. pap. $10.00 (0-910479-01-1). Warrensburg, MO: Mid-America Press, Spring 1998. Winner of the 1997 Mid-America Press Writing Award. These poems dramatize a great love and the loss of that love, then a new beginning in which the poet's strength and faith are tested. The poems themselves function as vehicles of healing. —

David Ray. Field comes to grips with the limits that temper life, and with the insistence of life to go beyond apparent limits. His images are as tough-minded as they are elegant, celebrating all experience. These are, we might say, love poems for adults. —Robert Stewart. The poems, like breath itself, move between the interior experience of human consciousness, and the exterior world in which humans are placed. Each poem is a meditation, assembled from unforgettable images, and suspended within the rhythms of language. The book is a feast to feed the best parts of the soul. —Denise Low

Fike, Francis. *After the Serpent's Word.* 80p. pap. $10.00 (1-56474-217-2). Santa Barbara, CA: Fithian Press, Spring 1997. Fike is a serious poet of considerable accomplishment. He finds grace and ceremony in the ordinary. I admire his lyrics, his epigrams, his skilled translations from Old English, French, and Latin. Fike aims high: clearly he sets himself to write in the great tradition of those who insisted, like Hardy and the late master formalist Yvor Winters, on clear sense, moral insight, and tightly controlled craft. —X.J. Kennedy

Filkins, Peter. *What She Knew.* 62p. pap. $12.95 (0-914061-66-6). Alexandria, VA: Orchises Press, Spring 1998. One of the many pleasures of What She Knew is its consistency of tone, the way the poems add up to create a singular sensibility: a man who is humane but wary, alert to the deceptions of our world, yet drawn to praise, to celebrate renewal when renewal means "something that we make, then remake again." This is how it becomes possible for us to see the world and return "a little more amazed." —Lawrence Raab

Finch, Annie. *Eve.* 66p. $22.00 (1-885266-46-4). pap. $11.95 (1-885266-36-7). Ashland, OR: Story Line Press, Fall 1997. Women's experiences, past and present, real or invented, fill the pages of this engrossing debut. Nine sequences of lyric poems are organized around ancient goddesses, including "Brigid," the divine ancestor of the ancient Celts; "Coatlique," the oldest pre-Columbian deity; "Nut," a goddess of African, and later, Egyptian mythology; and "Aphrodite." In clear, modulated language, Finch deftly captures the immanence of these figures and their stories and compares them to particular experiences of modern women. —Publishers Weekly. Finch's brilliance as a young poet lies in her view of the world as complex: her passionate examinations of family relationships, of family history, of the search to understand one's place in the world are underpinned by a syntax and a poetic design equally passionate and complex. This is a formidable first volume of poetry. —Molly Peacock

Fink, Sid. *Taxi Poet.* 24p. pap. $5.00. Port Townsend, WA: Sagittarius Press, Spring 1996; Fall 1998 (new edition). The author explores his life as a taxi driver in this stream-of-consciousness rant. — Sagittarius Press

Finkel, Donald. *A Question of Seeing.* 96p. $22.00 (1-55728-501-2). pap. $14.00 (1-55728-502-0). Fayetteville, AR: University of Arkansas Press, Fall 1998. In lines electrified with lyricism and wit, Finkel carves a clearing out of the backyard brush and the intellectual brambles of existence. He delights in naming weeds and towering trees, cars and streets. Yet, in each poem, there is a constant tension between the actual wind and the words we must use to convey the wind's force. — University of Arkansas Press

Fishman, Charles. *An Aztec Memory.* 30p. pap. $3.50 (0-9625011-6-6). North Port, FL: Anabiosis Press, Spring 1997. Winner of the 1996 Anabiosis Press Chapbook Contest.

Fishman, Lisa. *The Deep Heart's Core Is a Suitcase.* 57p. pap. $12.00 (0-832826-47-4). Kalamazoo, MI: New Issues Press, Fall 1996. What great passions and tender illuminations fill Fishman's marvelous debut collection. These intimate unravelings and eloquent meditations are constantly reminding us of the harsh exigencies of experience and the fierce disquiet of desire. Graceful and gracious, these poems are often heartbreaking and always remarkably, truly wise. —David St. John

Fitzpatrick, Kevin. *Rush Hour.* 84p. pap. $9.00 (0-935697-08-X). St. Paul, MN: Midwest Villages and Voices, Fall 1996. In Rush Hour, FitzPatrick evokes the daily life of a city and its myriad people. Whether his vision is turned outward or inward, FitzPatrick is a master of shrewdly observed detail. His ability to elevate ordinary life resonates throughout Rush Hour, and his capacity for connecting with the dispossessed shows him to be, above

all, a poet with heart. —Ethna McKiernan

Fitzpatrick, Tony. *Dirty Boulevard.* 44p. pap. $10.00 (0-9638433-6-2). West Stockbridge, MA: Hard Press, Spring 1998.

Fletcher, Ralph. Drawings by Walter Lyon Krudop. *Ordinary Things: Poems From a Walk in Early Spring.* $15.00 (0-689-81035-0). Simon & Schuster/Atheneum, Spring 1997. Walking with Fletcher, one discovers the extraordinary in all the ordinary things we hardly notice: telephone poles, clotheslines, streams, litter, rocks, circles, leaves, mailboxes, daffodils, railroad tracks. "Each footstep is like a word," Fletcher says. It's worth it to take a step with him. —Simon & Schuster

Fletcher, Ralph. *Room Enough for Love: The Complete Poems From I Am Wings and Buried Alive.* pap. $4.99 (0-689-81976-5). Simon & Schuster/Aladdin Paperbacks, Spring 1998. Regarding I am Wings: Poems About Love: While this book tells a story that has been told before, it does so with fresh images and without clichés, — School Library Journal, starred review. Regarding Buried Alive: The Elements of

Love: Articulate, intense poems that treat the subject of love with dignity and compassion. —Kirkus, pointer review

Foerster, Richard. *Trillium.* 95p. pap. $12.50 (1-880238-61-6). Rochester, NY: BOA Editions, Spring 1998. Foerster is a poet of great patience, able to see into objects — be they tulips, fiddleheads, wood ducks — and capture their deeper, transparent energies. He offers poems that challenge the dogma of organized religion and help restore us to a sense that the sacred has always been here and now. —BOA Editions. With a gardener's faith in precision and abundance, Foerster applies his considerable knowledge and compassion to matters of politics, science, literary history, flora and fauna, exile, death, disease and survival, always bringing the marginal and eccentric to the center of our attention. His poems engage us with their beauty and call us back with the wisdom of their enthusiastic ceremonies. —R.T. Smith

Follett, C.B. *Visible Bones.* 130p. pap. $14.95 (1-891386-00-X). Austin, TX: Plain View Press, Spring 1998. Follett's wit and invention are delicious, and the emotional depth each poem possesses is often breathtaking. —Ruth Daigon. Follett is a poet of astonishing breadth who addresses both the life of the body and the life of the spirit. When she tackles universal truths, she expands our understanding of the world. —Susan Terris

Follett, CB, ed. *Beside the Sleeping Maiden: Poets of Marin.* pap. $22.00 (0-9657015-3-0). Sausalito, CA: Arctos Press, Spring 1997. Includes poems by Robert Hass, Brenda Hillman, Jane Hirshfield, and others. A majority of these poems use the landscape of Marin as either subject or setting. Because of that, there's an overlapping imagery — hawks and deer, hills and sea and fog—that gives the experience of reading the book the feel of turning a jewel in your hand to study the various facets. Sleeping Maiden celebrates the local; and implicit in that stance are both appreciation for, and responsibility towards, where one finds oneself on the earth. That's a sense of the world that's more and more in danger of becoming extinct, but it's still alive and kicking in this book. — Kim Addonizio, Poetry Flash

Forman, Ruth. *Renaissance.*
144p. $18.00 (0-8070-6840-3).
pap. $15.00 (08070-6841-1).
Boston, MA: Beacon Press,
Spring 1998; Spring 1999
(new paper). Stunning and
beautiful, Forman's poems use
incantatory language that
heals. The work builds a
bridge for a new generation.
—Library Journal. Forman has
a commitment to the possibilities of life. Joy. Beauty
(though terrible at times on
this earth). What an impressive, rich song she sings. —
Sonia Sanchez. Renaissance
marks the rebirth and reemer-
gence of one of America's
most gifted young poets.
Forman's lyricism dances on
and off the page, and her eye,
her ear, and her tongue allow
us to see, to hear and to taste
the intricate nuances of her
world. Indeed, like the great
Langston Hughes, it is
Forman's uncanny ability to
document the simplicity of life
which makes her work so
complex, so universal, and so
important to read. —Kevin
Powell

Foster, Edward. *Boy in the
Key of E.* 28p. Brownsville,
vt: Goats + Compasses, Spring
1998.

Foster, Linda Nemec. *Living
in the Fire Nest.* 140p. pap.
$15.00 (1-56439-060-8).

Detroit, MI: Ridgeway Press,
Fall 1996. Foster writes from
a place of deep passion —
vivid, vital, alive to the sizzle
of story and need. Her sounds
and images crackle and
explode. If these rich "History
of the Body" prose poems
don't ignite you, nothing will!
—Naomi Shihab Nye. In
poem after brilliant poem,
Foster presents us with the
balancing acts people perform
as they move between their
ordinary lives and the secret
lives they imagine. Even in
her most autobiographical
poems Foster finds the
strangeness that gives meaning
to everyday events. —Lisel
Mueller

Foust, Graham. *3 From
Scissors.* 20p. pap. $5.00.
Buffalo, NY: Meow Press, Fall
1998.

Fox, Hugh. *Strata.* 24p. pap.
$5.50 (0-932412-12-2).
Saginaw, MI: Mayapple Press,
Spring 1998. Fox is the Paul
Bunyan of American Letters,
part myth, part monster, and a
magnificent non-stop storyteller. —Bill Ryan. Fox is one
of the most interesting and
novel developments on the
alternative culture and
Littlemag scene. He is for real
but might better be explained
as a fictional creation. He has
become one of the foremost

(who knows, maybe the foremost) authorities on pre-Columbian American cultures. —Roger Sagehorn

Fox, Kirsten. *The Necessary Exile of Blackie Dammit.* 28p. pap. $8.00. Calhoun, GA: Sally Loves Sweet Baboo Press, Fall 1996.

Fox, William L. *One Wave Standing.* 64p. pap. $12.00 (1-888809-06-X). Albuquerque, NM: La Alameda Press, Fall 1998. One Wave Standing follows an extended metaphor as it passes through the literal geographies of ocean and desert, and the figurative one of love and family. A meditation on the nature and art of life and land, Fox alternates autobiography with the theoretical physics of growing up, marriage, and divorce. —La Alameda Press. Fox composes an elegant series of waves that explore dislocation and location, loss and recovery, memory and desire. —Arthur Sze

Franco, Michael. *How To Live as a Single Natural Being: The Dogmatic Nature of Experience.* 128p. pap. $14.00 (0-944072-95-X). Cambridge, MA: Zoland Books, Fall 1998. Franco's is the vision of the endless passage of any life and he records it here with a brilliant, particu-larizing insistence. —Robert Creeley. The poems of How to Live affirm the continuing vitality of the romantic-projective tradition (Whitman to Williams to Duncan and on) in American poetry. They constitute a lyric rite of participation in the brokenness of the actual. —Michael Palmer

Franking, Cecile M. *From Ink and Sandalwood.* 76p. pap. $10.00 (0-910479-03-8). Warrensburg, MO: Mid-America Press, Fall 1998. In this collection — a walk through the life of a woman caught between American and Chinese cultures — Franking explores her roots and family. She learns America's prejudices, but through finding a good home, family, and husband, she learns to bring together the yin and yang of life. When readers come away from this collection, they will find Franking "sticks like a shadow." —Maryfrances Wagner. [A] fascinating journey to self-discovery and reconciliation. Against a backdrop of wars, the poet's life unfolds, slowly, sweetly, sometimes with pathos, often with irony and humor. — Gloria Vando

Fraser, Kathleen. *il cuore: the heart: Selected Poems 1970-1995.* 198p. $35.00 (0-8195-2244-9). pap. $16.95 (0-8195-2245-7). University Press of New England/Wesleyan University Press, Fall 1997. Fraser's poems are exhilarating and daring, bringing her longtime love of words as objects into play with provocative ideas. —Carol Muske, New York Times Book Review. My respect for Fraser's work is elevated again. Her later poems retain an earlier hi-jinx and delight, while yearnings of technique are replenished by maturity. Fraser is reminding us she considers poetry to be a sublime progression. — Barbara Guest

Frech, Stephen. *Toward Evening and the Day Far Spent.* 13p. pap. $4.75 (0-87338-556-X). Kent, OH: Kent State University Press, 1996. Frech takes a time-honored, traditional subject, the life of Christ, and brings it to life again. At the same time he deftly explores the divided nature of human beings — what it means to be a spirit living in flesh, what it means to be incarnate. These fine, subtle, thoughtful poems again and again find the myth inside the real and the real inside the myth. —Andrew Hudgins

Freed, Ray. *All Horses Are Flowers.* 114p. pap. $10.00 (0-935252-56-8). Sound Beach, NY: Street Press, Fall 1998. Clear and resonant, Freed's voice is unmistakably his own. It sings with lyrical concision in a broad range of moods and images that celebrate the core of his experience. His tools are his perception, memory, and a transcendent sense of the natural world. Freed is a poet of no little strength and subtlety. —Jim Tyack

Freisinger, Randall R. *Plato's Breath.* 80p. pap. $9.95 (0-87421-236-7). Utah State University Press, Fall 1997. Plato's Breath renders — richly — three of art's highest pursuits: precision, human bafflement, and the desire to touch. Three cheers for Freisinger. —Gary Gildner. The poems in Plato's Breath combine powerful personal narratives with a rich sense of language. They are a pleasure to read — a mixture of drama and noise that gives them an almost three-dimensional palpability. In addition, Freisinger's attentiveness to the linguistic intricacies of English give testimony to his passion for poetry, both in its making and its celebration. —Stephen Dobyns

Fried, Michael. *To the Center of the Earth.* 68p. pap. $9.00 (0-374-52471-8). New York, NY: Farrar, Straus and Giroux, Fall 1994; Fall 1997 (paper). Fried's brilliant new poems locate infallibly the point at which sensation and intelligence intersect, and ignite.. [They] have no other purpose than the secular revelation of human being identified by love. In America today there is no lyric work more compelling and well made than To the Center of the Earth. — Allen Grossman. The striking classical severity and concision of Fried's poems convey something by turns histrionic, Romantic, vertiginous, savage. Clarity and maelstrom at the same moment. Or eerie poise. These wonderful, unique poems have long been the passion of an intense coterie; now, with much new work, they are gathered for all. — Frank Bidart

Fried, Philip. *Quantum Genesis and Other Poems.* 71p. pap. $12.00 (0-9655200-0-5). New York, NY: Zohar Press, Spring 1997. I find much to recommend in Quantum Genesis. Its language crackles with energy, its lines are lean and hard, and its tone is often wryly humorous, making serious subject matter more accessible and more palatable. There isn't a weak poem in the collection. — Robert Collins. Here in a major new testament the great questions are reconsidered, re-presented — how the large and small inhabit each other, how indifferences allow differences, how the palpable can be the residence of the widest spirit. The graphic and the philosophical, the human and the godly interplay in a quiet attentiveness explosive with realization and recognition. As in one of his lines, Fried "raises his hand like a conductor / assembling silence. " —A.R. Ammons

Fried, Philip, ed. Photographs by Lynn Saville. *Acquainted With the Night.* 160p. pap. $25.00 (0-8478-1979-5). New York, NY: Rizzoli/Universe Publishing, 1997. Acquainted With the Night contains phosphorescent shots of New York nightscapes (as well as scenes of such farflung locales as India, Portugal and Greece after dark) that strike with disarming simplicity at the heart of what is exhilarating about the midnight hour. Saville's photos are accompanied by the poetry of Frost, Rilke, Paz, Keats and others. If, lately, you haven't spent a contemplative wee hour observing the city's changed nocturnal face, this book will make you yearn

for a night on the town. —
Susan Kelly, Time Out New
York

Friedman, Jeff. *Scattering the*
Ashes. 87p. pap. $11.95 (0-
88748-257-0). Pittsburgh, PA:
Carnegie Mellon University
Press, Spring 1998.
Friedman's second book
places him among the most
talented younger poets writing. He is, in many of the
poems, a near master of the
ordinary event — plain, sharp,
and intense; his gift for
poignant music and fresh
description issues from a
respectful eye and ear held
powerfully close to his subjects. You will recognize
yourself in this book, and be
grateful. —Stephen Berg.
Friedman's are poems of
fusion: they mingle plain-song
diction with meditative intensity, anecdotal harmonics with
lyrical melodies, the manifold
motions of dispersion with the
solidifying integration of the
center, wit with soul. At the
end of a century of ideology
and diffraction, Scattering the
Ashes is a brilliantly gracious
and necessary book. —
Stephen Tapscott

Fries, Kenny. *Anesthesia.*
83p. pap. $14.95 (0-9627064-
6-9). Louisville, KY:
Advocado Press, Fall 1996.
1997 Lambda Literary Award

finalist. In a deftly orchestrat-
ed collection, Fries brings to
light a complex awareness of
his history as a Jew and as a
gay man physically disabled at
birth. Tough-minded and
sparely written. Fries is not
content with the merely personal; his work spins into
wider worlds. —Colette Inez

Friman, Alice. *Inverted Fire.*
76p. pap. $11.95 (1-886157-
07-3). Kansas City, MO:
BkMk Press of the University
of Missouri-Kansas City,
Spring 1997. Here is the
embodiment of "truth and
beauty" — form and content
melded in a "balance for
weighing the soul." Myth and
lyric married, all affectation
spurned, idiomatic speech
rides elegiac rhythms. For
those who love poetry, this is
home. —Marilyn Kallet.
Friman's sensuous poems
edify, surprise, and amuse.
She is a poet who can capture
the pain of loss and chart and
route recovery with equal
skill. Read. —Diana Der-
Hovanessian

Frisby, Cathy. *Shades of*
Light: A Poetic Look at a
Woman's Life. 84p. pap. $9.95
(1-880451-28-X). Baden, PA:
Rainbow's End, Fall 1997.
This book will challenge and
captivate those who are inter-
ested in reading words that

deal with the realities of life with passion and truth. — Rainbow's End

Frost, Celestine. *I Gathered My Ear From the Green Field.* 105p. pap. $8.00 (0-9651401-0-5). Harrisburg, PA: Logodaedalus Press, Fall 1996. Frost's "inquiry into the origins of lyric thought" arrays an impressive panoply of poetic forms; textual, verbo-visual and visual elements mix in a postmodern sublime. — Logocrit

Frost, Robert. Edited by John Hollander. *Poems.* 256p. $12.50 (0-679-45514-0). Knopf/Everyman's Library Pocket Poets, Spring 1997. From one of the most brilliant and widely read of all American poets, a generous selection of lyrics, dramatic monologues, and narrative poems — all of them steeped in the wayward and isolated beauty of Frost's native New England. —Knopf

Frumkin, Gene. *The Old Man Who Swam Away and Left Only His Wet Feet.* 144p. pap. $14.00 (1-888809-08-6). Albuquerque, NM: La Alameda Press, Spring 1998. This book brings together two previously released chapbooks of Frumkin's, along with new poems from the last decade —

thirty years of writing. — La Alameda Press. The range of Frumkin's writing shows his wit, his engagement with the written word, his interest in broad subjects, and his ability to distinguish between what is important and what is not. — John Jacob, American Book Review. Frumkin brilliantly and genuinely conceives work that invites repeated reading and deepens with each new exposure. To read Frumkin is to renew faith in the power of language to crystallize experience in a transformative way. This work is supremely satisfying, integrating genius and humility in writing and living. —Sheila E. Murphy

Fuller, Heather. *Perhaps This Is a Rescue Fantasy.* 72p. pap. $10.00 (1-890311-00-6). Washington, DC: Edge Books, 1997. Fuller's lines are "moves" being made, as if in her peripheral vision where everything's happening. The poems start out before we read them; or as if simultaneous, to one side of us. One has the sense of the reader being the speaker who at once does not know, hasn't pre-formed, what is being said. The writing is "the cut and joining when you are speaker and not knowing." —Leslie Scalapino

Fuller, William. *Aether.* 61p. GAZ, Fall 1998.

Funkhouser, Erica. *The Actual World.* 85p. $20.00 (0-395-87707-5). Boston, MA: Houghton Mifflin Company, Fall 1997. Funkhouser's poetry is as big and small as America itself. I hear a music I've known all my life and yet I don't know it; I can dance to it, but can't play it. I stand in awe of her gift. —Ken Burns. I can hardly put into words what I like so much about these poems, but it has a great deal to do with truthfulness: they have the feel of experience rescued from the conventional by a great steadiness of regard and clarity of naming. —Rosanna Warren

Futoransky, Luisa. Translated by Jason Weiss. *The Duration of the Voyage: Selected Poems.* 95p. pap. $11.00 (1-881523-07-1). San Diego, CA: Junction Press, 1997. [Futoransky's] major concern, never far beneath the surface of poems that are often wry and street-wise observations of her own and the lives around her, is the complex phenomenon of exile. With great clarity of language, and a subtle, discursive music, [Futoransky] navigates through poems that mirror the vagaries of her voyage. —

Junction Press. Exile and home, those who leave and those who weave: Futoransky's poetry, finally in translation, will touch those who are lucky enough to read her. —Ariel Dorfman

Gach, Gary, ed. *What Book!?: Buddha Poems From Beat to Hiphop.* 248p. pap. $15.00 (0-938077-92-9). Albany, CA: Parallax Press, Fall 1998. The "humor, quickness, diversity, and insistent, mundane humanness" so particular to where poetry intersects meditation are richly evident in this fine volume of poetry. From Suzuki to Kerouac, Gary Snyder to Susan Griffin, Thich Nhat Hanh to Peter Coyote, and Jane Hirshfield to Yoko Ono, just about everyone under the sun who's paid verbal homage to the Buddha spirit has at least one poem represented. This is "mindful poetry" at its best. —Napra Review. This enigmatically titled anthology offers numerous delights and valuable evidence that great poetic variety, from haiku and witty two-liners to page-long discourses, has by now given distinct expression to Western Buddhism. —Publishers Weekly. Each poem is a firecracker, a small chili pepper explosion in your mouth and mind and heart, an invitation to join in. Just bring your attention, your humor, your open and permeable life. — Jane Hirshfield

Gale, Kate. *Selling the Hammock.* 88p. pap. $10.95 (1-888996-06-4). Palmdale, CA: Red Hen Press, Fall 1998. Even in the most direct, narrative poems of Gale's there is a mysteriousness, something dark and glittery under the surface that makes the poems even more interesting and edgy. I like her gutsy sensuality and the way she deals with damage, separation, isolation, things blurring, what is just on the verge of, on the edge. Many of these poems have a dream-like quality, feel like dream walking, are rich with haunting images of women's lives. —Lyn Lifshin. Doubts, sensuality, and secret disappointments are the knots that secure this hammock; childhoods, past and present, are the trees it is stretched between. Selling the Hammock is a collection which will entice you to stretch out, to consider, to hang suspended in midair. But beware: do not, under any circumstances, relax. —Melody Stevenson

Gallagher, Tess. *Owl-Spirit Dwelling.* pap. $15.00 (0-93-

2264-01-8). Portland, OR: Trask House Books, 1995.

Galvin, Brendan. *Hotel Malabar: A Narrative Poem.* 50p. pap. $10.95 (0-87745-597-X). Iowa City, IA: University of Iowa Press, Spring 1998. Joseph Conrad or Graham Greene might have written something like Hotel Malabar as prose, but Galvin has made it genuine poetry as well as first-rate storytelling. —Fred Chappell. Hotel Malabar is a weird, gripping, and altogether remarkable poem about America's imperial excesses and the twilight world of espionage in which paranoia and manifest destiny jostle with the familiarity of burlesque comics doing their ancient routines. Galvin is one of our finest poets, [and preeminent] as a master of the long poem. —David Slavitt

Galvin, Brendan. *Sky and Island Light.* 47p. $22.95 (0-8071-2108-8). pap. $15.95 (0-8071-2109-6). Baton Rouge, LA: Louisiana State University Press, Fall 1996. Sky and Island Light is a resounding expression of joy by a remarkable poet, one who combines uncannily scrupulous habits of observation with astonishing stylistic grace. Here are locales ranging from Ireland to the Outer Hebrides, the Orkneys, the Shetland Islands, and the poet's native Cape Cod. Cemeteries, deserted villages, lost faces — such fragments Galvin transmutes into meditations on the blood-deep mysteries of death, desire, and the evolution of consciousness. —Louisiana State University Press

Galvin, James. *Resurrection Update: Collected Poems 1975-1997.* 277p. pap. $16.95 (1-55659-122-5). Port Townsend, WA: Copper Canyon Press, Spring 1997. For more than 20 years, Galvin has been crafting poems which are at once formally and metaphysically complex, yet are models of clarity, economy, and accessibility. Resurrection Update collects all of the poet's work from four previous hard-to-find books, as well as a generous selection of new poems, an ongoing exploration of postmodern aesthetics, institutional theologies, the uses of history and poetic traditions, and all the wonder and terror induced by spiritual solitude. —Copper Canyon Press

Gander, Forrest. *Science & Steepleflower.* 88p. pap. $12.95 (0-8112-1381-1). New York, NY: New Directions, Fall 1998. Science & Steepleflower is a break-through book for Gander, a poet whose richness of language and undaunted lyric passion land him in traditions running from Dickinson and Hopkins to Duncan and Ondaatje. His poetry has been called "desperately beautiful" by Thom Gunn, and "original and fascinating" by John Ashbery. Gander plumbs the erotic depth of human interaction with the land, bringing us to new vistas of linguistic and perceptive grace. —New Directions. A sound master. . . Eros presides over these generous poems that ring with the wondrous names of lowly things. —Voice Literary Supplement. His sharp sense of place has made him the most earthy of our avant-garde, the best geographer of fleshy sites since Olson. — Donald Revell, The Colorado Review

Ganick, Peter. *Ex-Finite: Danger's Dancer. . ..* 24p. pap. $4.00. Saratoga, ca: Instress, Fall 1998.

Ganick, Peter. *Next By Default Too.* 32p. pap. $7.00 (9035350977). Columbus, OH: Luna Bisonte Prods, Fall 1997. A sequence of innovative poems in a neo-language style. —Luna Bisonte Prods

García Lorca, Federico.
Translated by Greg Simon and
Steven F. White; Edited by
Christopher Maurer. *Poet in
New York, Revised Edition.*
303p. pap. $16.00 (0-374-
52540-4). Farrar, Straus and
Giroux/Noonday, Fall 1998.
Written while García Lorca
was a student at Columbia
University in 1929-30, Poet in
New York is one of those rare
books that have changed the
direction of poetry in both
Spain and the Americas.
Christopher Maurer has
revised this vital work, using
previously unavailable or
untranslated material. The
book includes a prose poem
missing from previous editions, as well as extensive
notes and letters, revised versions of all the poems, an
interpretive lecture by Lorca
himself. —Farrar, Straus and
Giroux. This symphonic narrative takes Lorca beyond the
gypsy-folk lyrics of his early
work, and surreally depicts the
spiritual emptiness of the
urban landscape and the existential loneliness of the poet
lost in the materialist city. —
Kirkus Reviews. This is a
superb translation. Simon and
White have succeeded so well
that I can't imagine anyone
trying to improve on what
they've done. —Mark Strand.
It does what one wants a
translation to do: make the

original really come alive in
the second language. —W.S.
Merwin

Gardner, Joann, ed.
*Runaway With Words: A
Collection of Poetry From
Florida's Youth Shelters.* 122p.
pap. $14.95 (0-938078-47-X).
Tallahassee, FL: Anhinga
Press, Spring 1997. Written by
participants in the Runaway
with Words program, these
poems take us into the domain
of runaway, abused, and aban-
doned teenagers. We emerge
from these pages with a new
understanding of their lives,
an appreciation for the
resiliency of the human spirit,
and a growing respect for the
creative abilities of these marginalized youth. —Anhinga
Press

Garrett, George. *Days of Our
Lives Lie in Fragments: New
and Old Poems 1957-1997.*
222p. $26.95 (0-8071-2283-1).
pap. $18.95 (0-8071-2284-X).
Baton Rouge, LA: Louisiana
State University Press, Spring
1998. Whether he's watching a
red-winged blackbird "rock
and roll" on a cattail, imagining Hitler as a boy carrying
beer to his father or giving
voice to biblical figures like
Jacob or Eve, Garrett brings
erudition and wit to this collection of poems, which spans
40 years in his career as a

poet, novelist, critic, and screenwriter. —The New York Times Book Review. With its wit, hilarity, energy, and profondeur, the poetry of George Garrett has been a demonstration of technical facility and spiritual poise that has been important in my work and my life for forty years now. He is one of the few contemporary poets from whom I have learned, and continue to learn, not only how to write but to what we may aspire. The publication of Days of Our Lives Lie in Fragments is an occasion for celebration. — David R. Slavitt. Perhaps the single best word to describe Garrett's poetry is "generous." It welcomes the reader and assumes a common humanity with the poet; there is no defensive elusiveness, but a striking duality of this religious poet who is also a satirist deeply acquainted with evil in every form. — Monroe K. Spears

Garrison, David Lee, and Terry Hermsen, eds. *Food Poems.* 48p. pap. $2.50 (0-933087-48-9). Huron, OH: Bottom Dog Press, Fall 1998. What does food tell us in these poems? It tells us our heritage, who we are, who we were, about love and our rituals: a mother's Sunday morning habit, standing "in a slip / lost in blues, / and those collards, /

wild-eared, / singing." — Bottom Dog Press

Garrison, Deborah. *A Working Girl Can't Win and Other Poems.* 80p. $15.00 (0-679-45145-5). New York, NY: Random House, Spring 1998. These brave, elegant, edgy poems are as up to the minute, and as classic, as a black dress and pearls. Garrison is a strong and witty observer of the way we live now, and also — which is much harder — of herself. —Katha Pollitt. These witty poems draw the reader in with their cadence, their flair, their look-at-me elegance and urbanity. Then comes the surprise. There is a darkness, a heartbroken charm here which keeps giving way to a beautiful undersong of contemporary life which is both winning and memorable. —Eavan Boland. What an abiding pleasure to have these clear-eyed charms against the darkness, these charmed poems of Love and Work (those two great mysteries) in Garrison's splendidly winning and long-awaited first volume of poems. —Edward Hirsch

Garrison, Peggy. *Charing Cross Bridge and Other Poems.* 20p. pap. $5.00 (1-893068-00-5). P&Q Press, Fall 1998. With astonishing, unflinching honesty, Garrison peers into herself and probes her world: childhood, family, love, art. She rides vectors of modern paintings into desperate harbors of sensuality and remembered losses. Seeing life as "a thin bridge / held up by flamingoes," her precise vision reveals that reverberating tonality of connections we call the present. —D.H. Melhem

Garrison, Peggy, and David Quintavalle. *With Candor: Related Poetry.* 26p. pap. $6.95 (1-893068-02-1). P&Q Press, Fall 1998.

Gates, Beatrix. *In the Open.* 96p. pap. $12.00 (0-9651558-7-0). New York, NY: Painted Leaf Press, Spring 1998. These are some of the strongest poems I know — tough without meanness or complaint, new knowledge and the language to carry it. —Grace Paley. Gates is a discoverer. Her poems of the lost and the found are transparently true to the time we live in. They move us because she has endured until she found words steady enough to present them. Her language is wonderfully lucid — modest and dazzling, so that we see our crimes and privileges in her view, rising out of her anguished love-affair with the real world. Her landscapes are intensely alive, peopled by those who are suffering and stricken by hope. Her discoveries allow us to imagine what else there is, once we refuse the dual anesthesia of shock and despair. —Marie Ponsot. Gates is out on the cutting edge. She writes with a rare combination of lush sensuality, fine intelligence, and honesty. Her language evokes the body's wisdom as it sinks a plumb line to deep feeling. — Joan Larkin

Gavronsky, Serge, trans. *Six Contemporary French Women Poets: Theory, Practice, and Pleasures.* 113p. pap. $14.95 (0-8093-2115-7). Carbondale, IL: Southern Illinois University Press, Fall 1997. Contemporary French women poets generally have been vastly underrepresented in American periodicals and anthologies. Here Gavronsky introduces six of the best to American readers: Leslie Kaplan, Michelle Grangaud, Anne Portugal, Josée Lapeyrère, Liliane Giraudon, and Jacqueline Risset. — Southern Illinois University Press

Gellis, Willard. *Bronco Junky.* 48p. pap. $6.00 (0-917455-22-3). Big Foot New York/Wild Strawberry Press, 1994.

Gellis, Willard. *Fire Rat: Part 2 of Namjam.* 33p. pap. $6.00 (0-917455-28-2). Big Foot New York / Orpheophrenia Series, Fall 1998. Carnage and metaphysics combine in this rapid-fire, hard-edged combat poetry. —Big Foot NY

Gellis, Willard. *Namjam.* 58p. pap. $5.00 (0-917455-27-4). Big Foot New York, Fall 1996.

Gellis, Willard. *Wayless Way.* 50p. pap. $5.00 (0-917455-29-0). Big Foot New York, Fall 1996.

Gelman, Juan. Translated by Jean Lindgren. *Unthinkable Tenderness: Selected Poems.* 191p. $45.00 (0-520-20586-3). pap. $16.95 (0-520-20587-1). Berkeley, CA: University of California Press, Fall 1997. At last, a marvelous translation into English of the soulful and celebratory and heartbreaking words of Gelman, one of Latin America's most extraordinary poets. —Ariel Dorfman. [Gelman] has committed the crime of marrying justice to beauty. From such a dangerous and fertile embrace, a general uneasiness must issue. I believe that this voice, voice of voices, at once so delicate and so powerful, sounds louder than any other in the pre-sent-day poetry of the Spanish language. —Eduardo Galeano

Gensler, Kinereth. *Journey Fruit: Poems and a Memoir.* 70p. pap. $9.95 (1-882295-13-7). Farmington, ME: Alice James Books, Spring 1997. Gensler has travelled far, moving freely across barriers, from Skowhegan to Jerusalem, from Hyderabad to Boston, and she brings everything she knows into the continuous present of poetry. Journey Fruit is a graceful, wise, and rewarding book. —Chana Bloch. In understated poems and brilliant short prose memoirs, Journey Fruit tells of a lifetime's travel ("an orange is the perfect journey fruit"). Alert to irony and at ease with sorrow, Gensler offers us a generous, exciting book. —Alice Mattison

George, Anthony. *Alternatives in Free Verse Form.* 36p. pap. $5.00 (1-877968-19-6). Manasquan, NJ: Iniquity Press/Vendetta Books, Spring 1998.

Gershenson, Bernard. *Between Ice Ages.* 85p. pap. $15.00 (0-940592-29-0). Woodside, CA: Heyeck Press, Spring 1997. Gershenson begins each poem with an epigraph regarding ancient times from Will and Ariel Durant's

The Story of Civilization; then he leaps several thousand years to particular lives in California of the 1990's. The juxtapositions are sometimes startling, sometimes funny, sometimes sobering, but always enlightening. — Heyeck Press

Gerstler, Amy. *Crown of Weeds.* 88p. pap. $14.95 (0-14-058778-0). New York, NY: Penguin Books/Viking Penguin, Spring 1997. The poems' exteriors are untranquil surfaces, edged with a wit that speaks to the benightedness of human existence, and their interiors are lined with something close to terror. Gerstler's imagery is incubated with a splendid strangeness. —Alice Fulton. Gerstler's poems are an instrument of perception in every sense of that word. They feel as improvisational as the best jazz. —Michael Ryan

Getty, Sarah. *The Land of Milk and Honey.* 89p. $15.95 (1-57003-158-4). pap. $9.95 (1-57003-159-2). Columbia, SC: University of South Carolina Press, Fall 1996. With a sure hand, she builds poetry which, quite unexpectedly, breaks from plain imagery and speech into narrative music of transfiguring, almost visionary, beauty. —

Honor Moore. Getty tells us in vivid sensuous detail how it was in the Illinois of her childhood, where corn fields were "our forest, our ocean." Her sense of family history illuminates the title poem and makes radiant the role of women over more than a century of physical and metaphysical voyaging. Here, poignantly, are "mortals telling their stories." —Maxine Kumin

Gewanter, David. *In the Belly.* 84p. $24.95 (0-226-28872-2). pap. $11.95 (0-226-28873-0). Chicago, IL: University of Chicago Press, Spring 1997. Gewanter's language offers us exactitude and surprise, but there's more here than freshness; In the Belly delivers a startling, unexpected emotional weight. These poems examine the body, the inescapable locus of desire and of loss, of persistence and of decay. Gewanter's careful ear and delicate eye are engaged in a sustained work of investigation: a struggle to find, in the difficult stuff of experience, what can be known, and said. —Mark Doty. The poems in Gewanter's first collection are spiked throughout with a surprising musicality and built with skilled formal elegance. —Boston Review

Giannini, David. *Fist.* 20p. pap. $6.00. Otis, MA: Trader Books, Fall 1997.

Giannini, David. *Others' Lines.* 36p. (1-885089-07-4). Seattle, WA: Cityful Press, Fall 1997. Others ' Lines uses a new, admittedly minor form, the "Collage Haiku," which utilizes first lines from poems by others, often in personal as well as collegial and historical juxtapositions. The feeling is always, as Levi-Strauss noted, the intuition that a woodpecker has kinship (mythship?) with a toothache. —Cityful Press

Giannini, David. *RIM.* 72p. $25.00 (0-9661239-0-5). New York, NY: Indian Mountain Press, Spring 1998. An extended narrative prose poem with several voices combined with 32 woodcuts. —Indian Mountain Press

Gibb, Robert. *The Origins of Evening.* 107p. $21.00 (0-393-04644-3). New York, NY: Norton, W.W., and Company, Spring 1998; Fall 1999 (new paper). Winner of the 1997 National Poetry Series. The deft language and lyric intent of these poems serve one purpose: slowly and exactly they expose the dark, silvery images of a lost world. There is no elegy here because not a single detail of this remarkable landscape has ceased to exist. It is all there, all alive, all available to language. This is a rare and forceful book of poems. —Eavan Boland. The Origins of Evening is a sequence of celebrations — of a natural, ritual world able to outlast the autumnal century fires of industry; and of a working people who have survived in Gibb's pure, clear words. This is a book of life, not nostalgia, and a lyricism of reinstatement. —Stanley Plumly. Through quietly intense, beautifully nuanced language, Gibb recovers and redeems a difficult past. Simultaneously direct and reflective, his narrative is infused, always, with a radiant lyricism. These are magnificent poems of survival, praise, and celebration. —Susan Ludvigson

Gibbons, Reginald. *Sparrow: New and Selected Poems.* 152p. $22.95 (0-8071-2232-7). pap. $15.95 (0-8071-2233-5). Baton Rouge, LA: Louisiana State University Press, Fall 1997. This selection confirms Gibbons as a master of the minor key — a poet who has made a supple, intimate blues instrument of the American vernacular, what he calls "the good-enough mother tongue." Gibbons's work is a memorable, sorrowing, and some- how consoling meditation on life's fragility and hope's end. —Eleanor Wilner

Gibson, Margaret. *Earth Elegy: New and Selected Poems.* 200p. $24.95 (0-8071-2145-2). pap. $17.95 (0-8071-2146-0). Baton Rouge, LA: Louisiana State University Press, Spring 1997. Wonderful strong lyric poems, veined with sharp and striking insights and sure continuities that ground us in the implaca- bility of earth and life, eros and spiritual longing. —Peter Matthiessen. These sensuous, transcendent poems explore how the concrete drama of nature's particulars can become the luminous medium through which earthly myster- ies are revealed. —Library Journal

Gifford, Barry. *Flaubert at Key West: New and Selected Poems.* 98p. pap. $12.00 (1-889960-03-9). Lawrence, KS: First Intensity Press, Fall 1997. [These are] spare, ellip- tical poems, formally "open" and underpunctuated but read- ily comprehensible. At his best [Gifford] recalls William Carlos Williams: particular, lyrical but laconic, compas- sionate but unsentimental. — Publishers Weekly. Gifford never fails to surprise. These

poems are like Zen dominoes: no matter how shuffled, they always seem to come out right. —Booklist

Gilbert, Celia. *An Ark of Sorts.* 31p. pap. $4.95 (1-882295-18-8). Farmington, ME: Alice James Books, Spring 1998. First in the new Jane Kenyon Chapbook Award Series. An Ark of Sorts chron- icles a mother's grief follow- ing the death of a child: "I go round the grindstone reducing grain/to something that could be bread." —Alice James Books. These poems, elo- quent, quiet, painfully clear, rise from a profound willing- ness to face the irremediable. This is a beautiful book—this ark built to carry survivors through the flood waters of grief and loss—this ark of covenants between the living and dead. —Richard McCann. These poems are transformed into literal neces- sities by the hand of a poet who writes from a time in her life when there was nothing but necessity. The poems themselves become indistin- guishable from bread, wine, stone, and staircase, and in this sense they are objects of force—contemplative issue— absolutely good. —Fanny Howe

Gildner, Gary. *The Bunker in the Parsley Fields.* 88p. pap. $10.95 (0-87745-587-2). Iowa City, IA: University of Iowa Press, Spring 1997. Winner of the 1996 Iowa Poetry Prize. There is a unique and unabashed sweetness to [these] stories, whether of an old grandfather or the young daughters who watch their parents play ball, "their shocked pigtails pointing out / the four known directions. Gildner cares deeply about the world he lives in, and this book is his unequivocal testament. —Robert Creeley

Gilfillan, Merrill. *Satin Street.* 71p. pap. $12.95 (1-55921-182-2). Wakefield, RI: Asphodel Press/Moyer Bell, Fall 1997. If John Clare had toured the United States with Oscar Wilde, their notebooks, twisted together in a tornado and edited by Audubon and Escoffier, might have read like these poems: evocative, sophisticated and as ever-in-the-present as memory must always be. —Tom Raworth. Language is all, a flow of fresh, rich phrases: a loose-jawed gate, a double yolk of a day, the towering American emptiness of an October day that leaves one vaguely happy. —Philadelphia Inquirer

Gillespie, Theresa Courtney. Edited by Anne Cheney. *Ophelia's Legs and Other Poems.* 133p. pap. $8.95 (0-936015-68-3). Blacksburg, VA: Pocahontas Press, Spring 1997. [Gillespie's] untimely death at the age of 26 left a void in the writing community of Blacksburg. This volume celebrates her memory through her poems and through the poems written for her, to her, about her, by the people she left behind. — Pocahontas Press

Gilroy, Tom; Anna Grace, Jim McKay, Douglas A. Martin, Grant Lee Phillips, Rick Roth, and Michael Stipe. *The Haiku Year.* 120p. pap. $11.00 (1-887128-25-5). New York, NY: Soft Skull Press, Spring 1998. In 1996, seven friends wrote one haiku a day which they then mailed to each other. The Haiku Year is the result. —Soft Skull Press. There are some pretty awesome haiku here. JANE Magazine. The real revolution will begin when we all start communicating with each other with love, honesty, and purity of heart — and this book is a three-line jump in that direction. These haiku remind us to look, listen, and feel what's right at the end of our noses. —Todd Colby

Gilson, Saul. *Basilisk.* 96p. $25.00 (0-89304-472-5). pap. $12.50 (0-89304-473-3). Cross-Cultural Communications/Nightingale Editions, Fall 1996. Gilson, an internist, merges his classical perceptions of literature with his daily struggle to keep his cancer patients alive, a little longer, with as little pain as possible. —J.C. Hand, Small Press Review

Giovacchini, Chris. *On Ivory Goose.* 40p. pap. $7.95. Giovacchini, Chris, Fall 1996.

Giovanni, Nikki. *Love Poems.* 96p. $12.00 (0-688-14989-8). New York, NY: Morrow, William, and Company, Spring 1997. Bold and erotic, articulating in sensuous verse what we normally know only instinctively, Giovanni's collection of love poems confirms her place as one of our nation's most powerful truth-tellers. —William Morrow and Company. For Giovanni, "love isn't just a mirror, it is also glass and sand and silicon." New Orleans Times Picayune

Giscombe, C.S. *Giscome Road.* 75p. pap. $10.95 (1-56478-184-4). Normal, IL: Dalkey Archive Press, Spring 1998. This is a work of great originality, authority and ver-

bal beauty, a book that will reward many readings. Giscombe has attempted much, and realized much, in this long, enthralling poem. —Adrienne Rich. Giscombe has opened up new territory where we've least expected it, seeking the roots of identity in a poetics that is literally projective: across cultures, centuries, races. Giscome Road is a remarkable and surprising book. —Ron Silliman

Gizzi, Michael. *No Both.* 120p. pap. $12.00 (1-889097-16-0). West Stockbridge, MA: Hard Press, Fall 1997. Razor sharp but also rich and generously compelling, Gizzi's poetry lambastes as it celebrates, bringing us finally to a place of poignant irresolution. —John Ashbery. Cross James Joyce and Jack Nicholson in a high energy construct machine and you have Gizzi's poems. He will tell you everything you knew was true but didn't have the guts to say. Physiologically, psychologically and geographically, Gizzi locates the voices of us, Olson's "last first people," with an element of quick surprise that is all his own. — Lisa Jarnot

Gizzi, Peter. *Artificial Heart.* 96p. pap. $10.00 (1-886224-21-8). Providence, RI:

Burning Deck, Spring 1998. As the title indicates, the collection tries to negotiate both artifice and the turbulent domain of feeling. Formally a sampling of lyric history from the troubadours to post-industrial punk, it has the haunting quality of a song heard from a distance, overlayed with playground noise, lovers' oaths and cries of loss. —Burning Deck

Gladstone-Gelman, Rachel. *Gentle on the Heart.* 32p. pap. $3.00 (0-9657408-0-3). Brooklyn, NY: Third Rail Press, Fall 1997.

Gladstone-Gelman, Rachel. *In Public.* 80p. pap. $8.95 (0-9657408-2-X). Brooklyn, NY: Third Rail Press, Fall 1997. Quirky, intelligent poems with an assured voice, pointing to unvarnished, homespun epiphanies. —Leigh Harrison, Medicinal Purposes Literary Review. An intriguing collection of poetry with the self-discovery necessary to the philosopher. —Laura Lonshein Ludwig

Gladstone-Gelman, Rachel. *Tear Here.* 36p. pap. $3.50 (0-9657-408-1-1). Brooklyn, NY: Third Rail Press, Fall 1997.

Glaze, Andrew. *Someone Will Go On Owing: Selected Poems 1966-1992.* 190p.

$25.00 (1-881320-91-X). pap. $16.00 (1-881320-93-6). Montgomery, AL: Black Belt Press, Spring 1998; Fall 1999 (new paper). Balance, born of conciliated tension and contradiction, characterizes Glaze's work collected here. Without conceit or embarrassment he purposefully inhabits the role of poet as bard and minor prophet. —Publishers Weekly. Glaze's work demands such honesty from the reader that despite thirty years of publishing some of the most exciting poetry of our time, Glaze remains relatively unknown. —William Doreski

Glazer, Michele. *It Is Hard to Look at What We Came to Think We'd Come to See.* 80p. $25.00 (0-8229-4047-7). pap. $12.95 (0-8229-5651-9). Pittsburgh, PA: University of Pittsburgh Press, Fall 1997. Winner of the 1996 Associated Writing Programs' Award Series in Poetry. [Glazer has] a capacity for seeing so profoundly accurate one feels the ghost of [Elizabeth] Bishop hovering, and an ear so finely tuned it cannot but register all the finest, filamentary truths the eye discerns and translate them for us into idea, gesture, turn of mind. It is an extraordinary experience to be the reader of this ethically awake, brilliantly stoical — and inci-

dentally very sexy — book.
—Jorie Graham. A work of
desperate, beautiful invention:
vision and fierce revision. —
Carole Maso

Glazner, Greg. *Singularity.*
92p. $19.00 (0-393-03992-7).
pap. $11.00 (0-393-31808-7).
New York, NY: Norton, W.W.,
and Company, Fall 1996. This
is a startling book. Beginning
with "I didn't know how to
live," Glazner creates a brilliant narrative of living at the
end of the millennium, bitter
and comic, and painfully wise.
—Shirley Kaufman. Glazner's
poems affirm the original
power of the imagination to
coalesce the disparate into a
singular, new whole. Against
a darkening backdrop, these
fine poems pulse and shine.
—Arthur Sze

Glover, Albert. *Relax Yr
Face.* 59p. Glover Publishing,
Fall 1998.

Glûck, Louise. *Meadowlands.*
61p. $22.00 (0-88001-452-0).
pap. $13.00 (0-88001-506-3).
Hopewell, NJ: Ecco Press,
Spring 1996; Spring 1997
(paper). Glück interweaves the
dissolution of a contemporary
marriage with the story of The
Odyssey. Here is Penelope
stubbornly weaving, elevating
the act of waiting into an act
of will; here, too, is a worldly
Circe, a divided Odysseus, and
a shrewd adolescent
Telemachus. Through these
classical figures,
Meadowlands explores such
timeless themes as the endless
negotiation of family life, the
cruelty that intimacy enables,
and the frustrating trivia of the
everyday. —Ecco Press.
Although Glück is still in the
middle of her career, it's clear
that she is one of those poets. .
. whose writing is provoked
their unfolding temporal life.
For more than a decade, Glück
has been writing books of
poems that are meant to be
encountered like novels, and
has been looking into the difficult problem of finding a
structure whereby an essentially lyric gift can be adapted to
epic and unifying ambitions.
Meadowlands gives us her
most elaborate and satisfying
solution. —The New Yorker

Glück, Louise. *The First Four
Books of Poems.* 216p. $22.00
(0-88001-421-0). pap. $15.00
(0-88001-477-6). Hopewell,
NJ: Ecco Press, Fall 1995;
Spring 1997 (paper). This collection shows Glück in con-
scious evolution. Readers will
hear the ferocious tension of
her first book, the lyricism of
her second, will note the use
of icons in her third book, and
the archtypal mythic scale of
her fourth. —Ecco Press

Goedicke, Patricia. *Invisible Horses.* 158p. pap. $12.95 (1-57131-403-2). Minneapolis, MN: Milkweed Editions, Fall 1996. This is a splendid book by a poet, always excellent, who manages to get better and better. —Carolyn Kizer. Not since I first read Roethke have I experienced the sense of powerful inner forces and movement working at the very edge of the words. Goedicke evokes a part of our physiology that I did not think accessible: touching primary consciousness without calling upon the devices of mysticism. This is a brave enterprise. —Gerald M. Edelman

Goethe. Translated by John Whaley. *Selected Poems.* 175p. pap. $17.95 (0-8101-1643-X). Northwestern University Press/TriQuarterly Books, Fall 1998. One of world literature's most towering figures, Goethe dominated two centuries of European writing. Now at last his work has been opened up to English readers. In this major new bilingual selection, Goethe's verse can at last be appreciated in the English it deserves, full of music, humanity and grace. —Northwestern University Press

Gold, Sid. *Working Vocabulary.* 67p. pap. $10.00 (0-931846-49-8). Washington, DC: Washington Writers' Publishing House, Spring 1997. These poems speak the honest language of everyday. Their distinctive energy derives from his gutsy approach and from his surprising images. Gold's poems have the dual good sense of lacking pretension and of carrying evocative pictures of the life energy in his city. —Martin Galvin

Goldbarth, Albert. *Adventures in Ancient Egypt.* 109p. $24.95 (0-8142-0714-6). pap. $14.95 (0-8142-0715-4). Columbus, OH: Ohio State University Press, Spring 1997. Adventures in Ancient Egypt is a brilliant, harrowing, abundant book of poems, and should serve as a landmark in the achievement of this truly original writer. —Kenyon Review. With their whirlwind energies and combustible enthusiasms, their zany encyclopedic lore, chromatic lingo, and sheer chutzpah, Goldbarth's poems are bravura extravaganzas. There's seemingly no field of knowledge so obscure nor slice of American life so cornball that it can't give rise to a Goldbarth tour de force. —David Barber, Poetry

Goldbarth, Albert. *Beyond.* 103p. pap. $13.95 (1-56792-087-X). Boston, MA: Godine, David R., Publisher, Fall 1998. Goldbarth is American poetry's consummate showman. With their whirlwind energies and combustible enthusiasms, their zany encyclopedic lore, chromatic lingo, and sheer chutzpah, Goldbarth's poems are bravura extravaganzas. Peerlessly irrepressible, he's the only poet going whose sensibility conceivably owes as much to Barnum as to Whitman. — Poetry. There is simply no poet like him. —Kenyon Review. Goldbarth is a poet of remarkable gifts — a dazzling virtuoso who can break your heart. —Joyce Carol Oates

Goldberg Barbara, ed. *The First Yes: Poems About Communicating.* 96p. (0-931-848-92). Takoma Park, MD: Dryad Press, Fall 1996. Published in Cooperation with the American Speech-Language-Hearing Foundation to mark over 50 years of funding, research, scholarships, and innovative projects on behalf of the 42 million Americans with hearing, speech, and language problems. I'm astounded that there are so many poems about stuttering or aphasia, or Alzheimer's disease, or tinni-tus, or what if feels like to be deaf. It proves that poetry is not merely elegant discourse, but the language of the essential world. —James Earl Jones

Goldensohn, Barry, and Lorrie Goldensohn. *East Long Pond.* 10p. pap. $35.00. Omaha, NE: Cummington Press, Fall 1997. Letterpress edition. This final publication from the Cummington Press consists of three poems set at a summer house on a lake. Publisher Harry Duncan designed the page, hand set the type, and selected the text paper in the months before his death in April, 1997. — Cummington Press

Goldsmith, Ellen. *No Pine Tree in This Forest Is Perfect.* 32p. pap. $8.00 (0-9624178-7-4). Sleepy Hollow, NY: Slapering Hol Press, Fall 1997. "If I lose a glove now, I become the glove," writes Goldsmith. Her incandescent collection explores a world of terrifying contingency, through the focus of breast cancer. The poet's task is breathtaking: to accept loss as an absolute, and then to build a language, line by line, that will transcend it. —Dennis Nurkse

Goldstein, Marion. *Blue Prints.* 28p. pap. $5.00. New York, NY: New School Chapbook Series, Spring 1997. In her brilliant atlas of the human condition Goldstein has mapped out entire territories of survival. She finds benediction in a leaf and solace in the habit of water-lilies. This is a talent that cannot be ignored. It is lyrical and compassionate. Goldstein has retrieved from the hive of experience the final honey of language and insight. —Pearl London

González, Ray, ed. *Touching the Fire: Fifteen Poets of Today's Latino Renaissance.* 304p. pap. $12.95 (0-385-47862-3). New York, NY: Doubleday/Anchor Books, Spring 1998. Bringing together the very best work of fifteen contemporary poets, Touching the Fire celebrates one of the most vital, exciting periods in the history of Latino poetry — the present. —Doubleday/Anchor Books

Goodell, Larry. *Here on Earth: 59 Sonnets.* 73p. pap. $12.00 (1-888809-00-0). Albuquerque, NM: La Alameda Press, Fall 1996. Here and now on Earth, Goodell's work is exemplary in its sharp wistful humorous attention to the phenomena of mind and matter. If and when the species gets around to terraforming other planets, Here on Earth will be required reading for the pioneers of that enterprise. In the meantime, the rest of us are privileged to walk our minds through his garden of free-form sonnets, marveling at a flowering (but never flowery) record of brave verbal consciousness devoted to "this extended sentence of life." —Anselm Hollo

Gordon, Helen Heightsman. *Age Is a Laughing Matter: How To Laugh Through the Second Half of Your Life: Humor and Light Verse.* 48p. pap. $4.95 (0-9666192-1-8). Santa Barbara, CA: Anacade International, Fall 1998. Limericks, parodies and playful light verse about birthdays, aging, Elderhostel trips, late-life romance, time's wisdom, and humor in a retirement community. —Anacade International

Gordon, Helen Heightsman. *Life, Love, and Laughter: Selections from the Poetry and Light Verse of Helen Heightsman Gordon.* 32p. pap. $3.00 (0-9666192-0-X). Santa Barbara, CA: Anacade International, Spring 1998. Gordon's most frequently requested poems, award winners, and personal favorites make her first chapbook varied, witty, playful and profound. —Anacade International

Gorham, Sarah and Jeffrey Skinner, eds. *Last Call: Poems on Alcoholism, Addiction & Deliverance.* 192p. pap. $14.95 (0-9641151-8-2). Louisville, KY: Sarabande Books, Spring 1997. Here is the poetry of affliction and addiction — wonderfully crafted, fierce, pure, sly, subtle, poignant and alarming. Here are the truths of desire, suffering, and possibility, a multitude of voices that reflect about the experience of the self's enslavement to that which is the most self-destructive. —Maggie Scarf. The poems in this anthology feel hard-won — as if the language had been hauled, chiseled, sieved, and saved to let the voice contain, express, and transform difficult experience. —Poetry Calendar

Gorlin, Deborah. *Bodily Course.* 84p. pap. $12.00 (1-877727-71-7). Buffalo, NY: White Pine Press, Fall 1997. 1996 White Pine Press Poetry Prize Winner. Gorlin's writing is richly musical, colloquial and smart. Her fresh sensibility sparkles and resonates. — Hungry Mind Review. InBodily Course, a complex

love affair occurs just at the juncture where language and the unsayable collide. These poems crackle with urgent verve. —Mekeel McBride. Gorlin is a poet of visceral wisdom. "You can't botch dying," she says in her poem "Graces." [She writes] as a scientist of the human condition, always observing what is or might be under the skin. — Diane Wakoski

Gould, Roberta. *Three Windows.* 38p. pap. $5.00 (0-960-8920-2-8). Kingston, NY: Reservoir Press, Fall 1997. A procession of gongs and silence, powerful and affecting. —Stanley Nelson. Gould is remarkably economical in technique, intense and highly disciplined, concise and communicative. And her subject matter varies greatly. This volume should be considered for any comprehensive collection of present day poets. — Choice

Gouri, Haim. Translated by Stanley F. Chyet. *Words in My Lovesick Blood.* 258p. pap. $19.95 (0-8143-2594-7). Detroit, MI: Wayne State University Press, Fall 1996. The inspiring consciousness formed by Gouri's generation poignantly resonates in this introductory collection. Gouri's humane body of crisp modernist verse mingles learned references, Mediterranean sensuousness, melancholy and mundane colloquialism with biblical allusions, Hebraic traditions and a defining sense of the solidarity of a people "born with a knife in their heart." —Publishers Weekly

Grabel, Leanne. *Flirtations.* 26p. pap. $5.00. Portland, OR: 26 Books, 1997. This is the sixteenth of 26 chapbooks to be published in a new series of poetry from the Pacific Northwest. —26 Books

Grabill, James. *Listening to the Leaves Form.* 88p. $24.00 (0-89924-097-6). pap. $12.00 (0-89924-096-8). Portland, OR: Lynx House Press, Fall 1997. Grabill is doing a theology of deep image, a surrealism of cosmogenesis and subatomic physics. The rollin' and tumblin' of associations (like blues and jazz) occur underground or within molecules, or between ideas and flesh, or among galaxies. Everything is connected and reflects in these poems. —John Benson

Grade V Classes of the Nightingale-Bamford School, eds. *Poems for Life: Famous People Select Their Favorite Poems and Say Why It Inspires Them.* 107p. pap.

$10.00 (0-684-82695-X). Simon & Schuster/Touchstone, Fall 1997. Poems for Life presents works selected by fifty well-known people, from Jane Alexander to Elie Wiesel to Tom Wolfe, from Peter Jennings to Isabella Rossellini to Wendy Wasserstein. The poetry is as diverse as the respondents, ranging from Shelley's classic "Ode to the West Wind" to Noël Coward's "I've Been to a Marvelous Party." Letters to the students from each contributor introduce each poem and describe why poetry has been a source of amusement, solace, or inspiration in their lives. Poems for Life is a heart-warming gift from old to young and from a group of American children to refugee children around the world. Proceeds from Poems for Life will be donated to the Women's Commission for Refugee Women and Children. —Simon & Schuster/Scribner

Graham, Jorie. *The Errancy.* 112p. $22.00 (0-88001-528-4). pap. $14.00 (0-88001-529-2). Hopewell, NJ: Ecco Press, Fall 1997; Spring 1998 (new paper). Few poets address the predicament of the postmodern soul as rigorously or intelligently as Graham. "An icy thing, even in its fluency," this masterful collection takes risks in naming "the small hole inside I'm supposed to love," and coldly, bleakly and dazzlingly succeeds. — Publishers Weekly. Graham stands among a small group of poets (Dickinson, Hopkins, Moore) whose styles are so personal that the poems seem to have no author at all: they exist as self-made things. Each of her books has interrogated the one preceding it, and The Errancy feels like a culmination. It is her most challenging, most rewarding book. —The Nation

Graham, Jorie, ed. *Earth Took of Earth: A Golden Ecco Anthology.* 283p. pap. $13.00 (0-88001-536-5). Hopewell, NJ: Ecco Press, Fall 1996. The poets here are rich and poor, they die young, they live to be old, they are gay, straight, married, consumptive, alcoholic, secular, religious — their fathers beat them, their mothers scare them, they are loved madly, they are raped and tortured, they live quiet domestic lives, they die in trenches, they live in exile, in jail, in pretty suburban houses — they teach, sell shoes, work in gas stations, in museums, in defense factories, in kitchens — they are explorers, seducers, upstanding citizens, fascists, Marxists, visionaries, lunatics. They live all this out in one beautiful everchanging language — of vocables, of forms, of assumptions, of beliefs, of idioms — all sinewed by depth of soul, love of words, and an extraordinary capacity for original honest emotion. —from the Introduction

Graham, Ruth Bell. *Ruth Bell Graham's Collected Poems.* 284p. $16.99 (0-8010-1138-8). Grand Rapids, MI: Baker Books, Fall 1997. The only comprehensive volume of Mrs. Graham's poems available, this fine collection spans more than sixty years of living. It reflects the personal trials and joys of a woman of steadfast faith and constant love. —Baker Books

Grapes, Jack,ed. *13 Los Angeles Poets: The ONTHE-BUS Poets Series Number One.* 160p. pap. $13.95 (0-941017-47-8). Los Angeles, CA: Bombshelter Press, Spring 1997. Poetry by Kathleen Zeisler Goldman, Stephanie Hager, Diana Jean, Mifanwy Kaiser, Stellasue Lee, Priscilla Lepera, Elaine Mintzer, Gilla Nissan, James O'Hern, Jan Ruckert, Patricia L. Scruggs, Terry Stevenson, and Jeremy Stuart.

Gray, Janet, ed. *She Wields a Pen: American Women Poets of the Nineteenth Century.* 420p. $29.95 (0-87745-574-0). pap. $15.95 (0-87745-575-9). Iowa City, IA: University of Iowa Press, Spring 1997. Gray's landmark anthology restores to a century's literature the feminist strand and with it the sense that poetry represents not merely the strivings of solitary genius but the collective concerns of human communities, not only the elaborate intellectual edifices of self-consciously literary writing but the speaking voices of real women in a multiracial America. — University of Iowa Press. Formidably comprehensive. Gray provides her readers with a timeline setting her poets' lives and careers against important social and cultural landmarks. —Women's Review of Books

Green, Daniel. *All Told.* 160p. pap. $9.95 (1-56474-225-3). Santa Barbara, CA: Fithian Press, Fall 1997. Poems by a nonagenarian about travel, people, the world, and aging. —Fithian Press

Green, Jaki Shelton. *conjure blues.* 93p. pap. $10.95 (0-932112-37-4). Durham, NC: Carolina Wren Press, Fall 1996. It's magic the way these poems lift off the page to your ear through your eye. The melody herein you hear in the meaning: language is breath's utterance. Relaxing into joy, all of a sudden it's a spell where life and Green walk hand in hand conjuring the blues. And that's what I call poetry! —Bob Holman. Green knows the incant for hurt foot, for sore hand, for aching heart. In conjure blues, words are spoken at the crossroads of poetry and social consciousness. The context here is sisterhood, racism, the South, the good dirt and the strength of kinship. These words document while they conjure. They hex, declare and insist. —Michael Chitwood

Green, Jaki Shelton. *Dead on Arrival.* pap. $9.95 (0-932112-38-2). Durham, NC: Carolina Wren Press, Spring 1997. When it first appeared, Dead on Arrival announced the emergence of a strong new voice in African-American verse. Fresh and unadorned, these poems were deeply rooted in Green's own life and family. Yet they were also magical, visionary, and often angry, moving beyond the local to encompass the tidal sweep of history and the struggles of a race. [We] are pleased to re-issue the second edition of Dead on Arrival . . .

so that readers may now see the development of Green's voice over two decades of poetic achievement. — Carolina Wren Press

Greene, Jeffrey. *American Spirituals.* 63p. pap. $10.95 (1-55553-378-7). Boston, MA: Northeastern University Press, Fall 1998. Winner of the 1998 Samuel French Morse Poetry Prize. Throughout the many poems about New Haven, his home, Greene contrasts the ordinary or sinister life of the city with the rarefied atmosphere of the university, to telling effect. His poetry is suffused with what used to be called "social conscience." This is lovely writing, precise observation, tender yet realistic. I admire these poems and recommend them. —Carolyn Kizer

Greene, Jonathan. *Inventions of Necessity: Selected Poems.* 96p. pap. $13.50 (0-917788-70-2). Frankfort, KY: Gnomon Press, Spring 1998. A selection from seven of the poet's previous books, some hard to find, and printed in only limited editions. —Gnomon Press. Greene's low-keyed objectivity lets him take on an impressive variety of subjects: nursing homes and cocktail parties, lovemaking and lectures, wedding albums, soap operas,

teenage gangs. He is haunted by oblivion, writes beautifully of dying generations, yet shows himself possessed of a delicate and benign wit. — Village Voice. Unlike most of the current poets who report what they feel, Greene gives the living experience to respond to. —Choice. When we say "dead serious" we mean what is most alive. These poems are mature and dead serious. Most poetry is neither. I like the difference. —William Bronk

Greene, Jonathan. *Of Moment.* 64p. pap. $10.50 (0-917788-68-0). Frankfort, KY: Gnomon Press, Spring 1998. A selection of short poems influenced by Asian poetries, but still the author's own succinct take. —Gnomon Press. These poems take the risk of brevity and survive. By their brevity they invite, and reward, the closest attention. —Wendell Berry. These brief poems give access to great spaces of the spirit. While Of Moment reminds us of the work of Han Shan and the Zen poets of Japan, the vision is distinctly of our time, of Kentucky, and the voice, the spark, the indirection, the vivid detail, are uniquely Greene's. —Robert Morgan

Gregerson, Linda. *The Woman Who Died in Her Sleep.* 80p. $19.95 (0-395-82290-4). pap. $13.00 (0-395-82289-0). Boston, MA: Houghton Mifflin Company, Fall 1996; Fall 1997 (paper). A rare blend of imaginative generosity, philosophical seriousness and lyrical power. It's a remarkable book. — Jonathan Aaron, Boston Globe. Wondrous and disturbing in its narratives of the corruptible and incorruptible body. She has achieved, by technical prowess, a line that sounds like personal prayer and can support such leaps of image and utterance as would frighten poets less skilled and daring. [This book] will win awards and establish this poet's place in the firmament. —Detroit Free Press, Best Books of 1996

Gregor, David. *Variations on All the Perfect Things.* 84p. pap. $10.95 (0-9631094-2-1). Seattle, WA: Alki Press, Fall 1997. We see the writer's mind at work as his poems move easily from subject to subject—observing and assessing, recalling and imagining, regretting and celebrating the world around us. From waiting in plastic chairs, to putting a brother in a clothes dryer; from blue Parisian rooms, to the sun shining on a Spanish onion field; and from the reflections of dying Emperor Tong, to a man in a Los Angeles coffee shop worried about his soul—David Gregor's poems are micro stories that illuminate the everyday world. —Alki Press

Grennan, Eamon. *Relations: New and Selected Poems.* 228p. pap. $16.00 (1-55597-280-2). St. Paul, MN: Graywolf Press, Fall 1998. This first major collection of Grennan's work ranges from delicate early lyrics to poems that explore in larger meditations the complex realms of family, the natural world, and love. These are poems that in the minute fidelity of their images and the refined mastery of their language prompt us to experience at a higher frequency the world we mostly take for granted. — Graywolf Press. [Grennan] is on one hand one of the legitimate heirs of the Irish poet-monks, with their fine attunement to natural phenomena, and on the other a contemporary writer, intent, in the contemporary manner, on themes of memory, darkness, and loss. —Library Journal. Few poets are as generous as Grennan in the sheer volume of delight his poems convey, and fewer still are as attentive to the available marvels of the earth. To read him is to be led on a walk through the natural world of clover and cricket and, most of all, light, and to face with an open heart the complexity of being human. —Billy Collins

Grey, John. Edited by Bobbi Sinha. *Poking the Gun: The Selected Poetry of John Grey.* 58p. pap. $4.95. Concord, CA: Dark Regions Press, Fall 1998. The literate yet never overbearing sophistication of both form and language, the sometimes nasty sense of humor. It's all in there, in [Grey's] poems, waiting to jump out and dazzle and enrich you. —Jim Lee, Scavenger's Newsletter

Gridley, Inez George. *Journey From Red Hill: Selected Poems 1931 to 1996 to. . ..* 450p. $32.95 (1-879969-07-6). pap. $24.95 (1-879969-05-X). Outloudbooks, Spring 1997. Insightful, literate, a farm wife, a school teacher, Gridley recalls a rural past in deft and musical poems. Hers is a clear and singular voice. This is an important book. —Colette Inez. Gridley sends us graceful poems from a rugged place, where even "the depth of mud is a gauge of worth." She has drawn an unsentimental history of the Catskills, in

lines that ring with hope and amusement and affirmation. —Paul Violi. These poems are profound whispers of celebration, of sorrow and of awareness. —Janice King, Woodstock Times

Griffin, Susan. *Bending Home: Selected and New Poems 1967-1998.* 249p. pap. $17.00 (1-55659-087-3). Port Townsend, WA: Copper Canyon Press, Fall 1998. A celebration not only of feminism and femininity but, more importantly, of human nature. Griffin combines eloquent rhythms, unique imagery, and internal rhymes to carry the speaker's voice from the page to the reader's ear. The talent displayed in the longer poems places Griffin among the best of her contemporaries. Highly recommended. —Library Journal. Griffin weaves webs of words that capture the complex interrelationships among the body, history, language, memory, and politics. [She] combines the personal and the political with a poet's eye for illuminating and unexpected juxtapositions, and a humanist's faith in the healing power of the word. —The Utne Reader

Griffith, Geraline M. *Heartbeat.* 48p. pap. $6.00 (0-929688-34-1). Eureka Springs,

AR: Bear House Publishing, Fall 1997. Griffith writes vibrantly of a couple's journey together through fifty years of life. —Bear House Publishing

Griffo, Cari. *Ripening.* 88p. pap. $12.00 (0-9656981-9-X). Santa Fe, NM: Molti Frutti Productions, Spring 1997. Made from the plump and ruddy fruits of her own life, Griffo's Ripening is a very rich literary liqueur. These are poems to savor and, like good brandy-wine, they will get you memorably drunk. Rare in a first book, these are poems with many layers. —Michael W. Eliseuson. Her poetry is truly exquisite. —Weekly Alibi

Grim, Jessica. *Fray.* 81p. pap. $10.00 (1-882022-34-3). O Books, Fall 1998. The poems here are generous, always complicated, at times quiet. —Juliana Spahr. Grim achieves an extraordinary subtle and varied movement of words and silences in her poems. Altogether a beautiful book. —Jackson MacLow

Grimm, Susan. *Almost Home.* 40p. pap. $6.00 (1-880834-35-9). Cleveland, OH: Cleveland State University Poetry Center, Fall 1997. Almost Home is a tightly weaved collection in celebration of the

doggedness of life. Again and again, these poems offer a hand, insisting on seasons, on fevers, on dentist appointments, on giddiness after love-making, ultimately on "the old names and their desires." With unabashed intimacy, her stunningly lyrical voice directs us away from the darkness, home. —Claudia Rankine

Grol, Regina, trans. *Ambers Aglow: An Anthology of Polish Women's Poetry (1981-1995).* 440p. $40.00 (0-924047-15-1). (0-924047-16-X). Austin, TX: Host Publications, 1996. As the recent award of the Nobel Prize to Wislawa Szymborska has shown, Polish women's poetry constitues a powerful body of literature, which deserves to be better known in the West. This judiciously chosen and excellently translated anthology illustrates the range of poetry, its stylistic variety and interest. A important and richly rewarding collection. —Eva Hoffman

Grosman, Ernesto Livon, ed. *The XUL Reader: An Anthology of Argentine Poetry 1980-1996.* 136p. pap. $15.95 (0-937804-67-3). New York, NY: Roof Books, 1997. During the dictatorship that started in Argentina in 1976 and ended in 1983, a small poetry magazine, XUL, published its first issue, poetry and writing in which politics and formal experimentation were no longer conceived as mutually exclusive. We have now, for the first time, a bilingual anthology that presents us with the unmapped territory of Argentina's poetry of the last 16 years. —Roof Books. The XUL Anthology brings into English a collection of poems and essays from Argentina's most formally and socially investigative poets, a group largely unfamiliar to North American readers. This book opens up a dialogue: it is to our great benefit to read it and respond. —Charles Bernstein

Groves, Maketa. *Red Hot on a Silver Note.* 67p. pap. $10.95 (1-880684-22-5). Willimantic, CT: Curbstone Press, Fall 1997. Groves has a strong, bright lyric gift. Her poems come out of music and are full of music. They bring us the sounds of the streets and the sounds of nature, and make us see once again that they are parts of the same song. Groves celebrates American lives as they are lived today. This is poetry that relentlessly shows us the beauty in the world, with all its struggles and complexity, and demands that we go out to

meet it with open hearts. — Diane di Prima

Gruswitz, Nik. *Red Bandanna.* 74p. pap. $10.00 (0-9668693-03). Newton, NJ: Dead Tree Press, Fall 1998.

Gudath, Lauren. *The Blonde.* 19p. Berkeley, ca: Idiom, Fall 1998.

Gurney, John. *The Voodoo of Doll Shoes.* 48p. Vacaville, CA: Delta Press, Fall 1996.

H.D. Reader's Notes by Aliki Barnstone. *Trilogy: The Walls Do Not Fall, Tribute to the Angels, and The Flowering of the Rod.* 206p. pap. $10.95 (0-8112-1399-4). New York, NY: New Directions, Fall 1998. This reissue of the classic Trilogy now includes a new introduction and a large section of referential notes for readers and students compiled by Aliki Barnstone. As civilian war poetry (written under the shattering impact of World War II), Trilogy's three long poems rank with Eliot's Four Quartets and Pound's Pisan Cantos. —New Directions. Ecstasy, ecstasy in language, in beautiful language, is what carries me through the entire trilogy, not only content with her tricks, but enchanted with her whole poem, not to say enraptured. —Hayden Carruth,

The Hudson Review. H.D. spoke of essentials. It is a simplicity not of reduction but of having gone further out of the circle of known light, further toward an unknown center. — Denise Levertov

Haag, John. *Stones Don't Float: Poems Selected and New.* 117p. $17.00 (0-8142-0716-2). pap. $11.95 (0-8142-0717-0). Columbus, OH: Ohio State University Press, Spring 1997. Not comfortable in the literary mainstream, Haag has created his own streams. He makes his art by taking to the grand expanse of the sea or by discovering that secret place "where only green light filters down." Haag's timely and timeless accounts of the lands and seas he explores are nothing less than a careful cataloging of the limitless varieties of human love and longing. —Ohio State University Press

Hadas, Pamela White. *Self-Evidence: A Selection of Verse 1977-1997.* 230p. $35.00 (0-8101-5073-5). pap. $14.95 (0-8101-5074-3). Northwestern University Press/TriQuarterly Books, Spring 1998. Hadas has selected the best of her published work and combined it with poems never before collected. Self-Evidence contains legendary, mythic, historical, and imaginary characters — Lilith, Pocahontas, Simone Weil, the wives of Watergate, a circus performer, and others. With playful originality and virtuoso voicing, Hadas weaves tapestries of women's lives and labors. Perhaps uniquely in our time, she contrasts a spareness of autobiographical detail with an unusual intimacy of tone. Hadas's literary inventiveness is far-ranging, entertaining, and eclectic — an artistic accomplishment Howard Nemerov called "odd, quirky, humorous and exact." —Northwestern University Press

Hadas, Rachel. *Halfway Down the Hall: New and Selected Poems.* 234p. pap. $17.00 (0-8195-2251-1). University Press of New England/Wesleyan University Press, Fall 1998. What a generous collection this is — a whole life, flesh and spirit, brought to light. Hadas has an uncanny eye, an unerring ear, urgent sympathies, and a rich imagination. This gathering is a book, not for the library but for the bedside table — to help explain the day and prepare for the night. —J.D. McClatchy. A remarkable achievement. The poems are urgent, contemplative, and finely wrought. In them, antiquity illuminates the present as Hadas finds in ordinary human acts "what never was and what is eternal." —Grace Schulman

Hafez. Translated by Gertrude Bell. *The Hafez Poems of Gertrude Bell.* 176p. (0-936347-39-2). Bethesda, MD: Iranbooks, 1995. The most popular poet of the Persian language, Hafez has challenged the translating abilities of Goethe, Emerson and Fitzgerald. Bell's renditions, done when she was in her twenties, are considered the best in the English language. —Iranbooks

Hahn, Susan. *Confession.* 82p. $24.95 (0-226-31273-9). pap. $11.95 (0-226-31274-7). Chicago, IL: University of Chicago Press, Spring 1997. Hahn's voice is unique and unforgettable. Hahn's self-revelation is so startling, and her details so extraordinary, that she virtually detonates her poems with energy. — Booklist. Like the artist Orlan, whose performances involve plastic surgery upon her own body, Hahn has created a disquieting work of memory and carnality. Confession encounters and exposes emotions considered too unseemly for poetry. How does one praise, in a sentence or two, a book so unremitting, even painful, in its engagements and revelations? To read it is

to participate in the excruciation and transgression as bandages are ripped off and secrets opened. It is impossible to read this book unfeelingly. —Alice Fulton

Haines, John. *At the End of This Summer: Poems, 1948-1954.* 80p. pap. $14.00 (1-55659-079-2). Port Townsend, WA: Copper Canyon Press, Fall 1997. In these previously unpublished poems, Haines exhibits the distinctive visionary and musical clarity and the intelligence that would inform his work over the following fifty years, setting the course for the poetry and prose for which he is justly famous. — Copper Canyon Press. It behooves us to listen to a poet who deepens the silence around us and touches upon an ancient environmental wisdom. —New York Times Book Review

Haldeman, Joe. *Saul's Death & Other Poems.* 80p. pap. $10.95 (0-9631203-4-4). Palo Alto, CA: Anamnesis Press, Spring 1997. The first collection of poetry by the well-known author of The Forever War and The Hemingway Hoax. —Anamnesis Press. Haldeman is one of the few contemporary writers who has successfully fused the medium of poetry with the genre of science fiction. And within the context of that fusion, what makes his poems even more distinguished is their overriding humanity. —Bruce Boston. Haldeman knows how to spin words so that the worlds they make acquire gravity, atomosphere and beauty. —Michael Bishop

Hall, Donald. *The Old Life: New Poems.* 144p. $19.95 (0-395-78841-2). pap. $13.00 (0-395-85600-0). Boston, MA: Houghton Mifflin Company, Spring 1996; Spring 1997 (paper). Here is an astonishing anecdotal autobiographical sequence that takes Hall from early childhood onward, through an "old life" that changed unalterably with the death of his wife. At times lighthearted, at times somber, the volume masterfully tells the truth about the challenges of one man's time on earth. —Houghton Mifflin. These autobiographical poems are free of self-pity, engagingly frank without being in any sense "confessional," and often wildly comic. All are first-rate. —Minneapolis Star-Tribune

Hall, Donald. *Without.* 96p. $22.00 (0-395-88408-X). pap. $13.00 (0-395-95765-6). Boston, MA: Houghton Mifflin Company, Spring

1998; Spring 1999 (new paper). Hall laments the death of his wife and fellow poet Jane Kenyon, who passed away from leukemia several years ago; he also delivers his crowning achievement. A companion volume to both The Old Life, the autobiographical volume of poetry which took Hall's life up to the threshold of Jane's death, as well as to the late Kenyon's Otherwise, this heartbreaking book of verse examines the grief and anger which are products of suffering such a tremendous loss. —Houghton Mifflin. A remarkably beautiful and generous book, beautiful in all its terrible specifics of the daily ordeal of death, and generous to the memory of the force of life his wife possessed. The result, I think, is his strongest book yet, a work of art, love, and generous genius. Without is not an easy testament, but a mighty one. —Liz Rosenberg, Boston Globe. This book stands as a poignant and powerful testimony to both love and loss, celebration and lament. —Ploughshares. The mosaic of a whole period, with all its inner moods and its physical accessories, is masterfully accomplished. —John Bayley, New York Review of Books

Hall, Floriana. *The Sands of Rhyme.* 106p. pap. $10.00 (1-885519-07-9). St. Louis, MO: DDDD Publications, Fall 1998. Hall's writing inspire[s] others [and] lift[s] spirits. Themes in her poetry [include] the joy of living and overcoming misfortune. —DDDD Publications

Hall, Judith. *Anatomy, Errata.* 59p. pap. $11.95 (0-8142-0765-0). Columbus, OH: Ohio State University Press, Spring 1998. Anatomy, Errata is a single, powerful song of resemblances and absences; a song of "ontogeny, // Ontology, oncology." Death, art, and a woman's beauty have come together before, but Hall's poems remake the controversial trio into a vivid music that is startling and intimate and sublime. —Ohio State University Press. A woman's body, luminous repository of soul, having triumphed or at least traveled so far as to be no longer a girl's, is still the heroine here, much beset by inner ills and outer inducements, temptations of High Capitalism which can turn a child into Shirley Temple, a daughter into her mother, and a lover into a lever whereby pleasure is prised free. Yet for all her fritillary unrest, a mystery abides: Hall's pervasive mastery of

form, "a secret-song," overheard and unforgettable. — Richard Howard

Hall, Thelma R. *Sunlight and Stones.* 96p. $15.95 (0-9662255-0-3). Rome, GA: Shorter College Press, Spring 1998. Whether set in China, New York, Hiroshima, Auschwitz, in graveyards or her own back yard, Hall's poems pay homage to the delicate powers of the natural world and to the powerful intimacies within the human one. —Andrea Hollander Budy

Hallerman, Victoria. *The Night Market.* 18p. pap. $7.00. New York, NY: Firm Ground Press, Spring 1998.

Halme, Kathleen. *Equipoise.* 72p. $20.95 (1-889330-19-1). pap. $12.95 (1-889330-20-5). Louisville, KY: Sarabande Books, Fall 1998. For readers eager to experience "the ache of paradise," these poems chart consciousness with obvious pleasure. But here is an intellect made lyrical. Despite contemporary trends of cynicism and despair, Halme braves happiness and discovers a refreshed version of mindfulness in daily life. — Sarabande Books. Here is a volcanically poised and deliciously balanced book of meditative graces, of provisional lyric holdings, of sumptuous meditations shored against the ruins. —Edward Hirsch

Halperin, Amor. Translated by Ida Halperin. *Along the Roads of the Universe/Por los caminos del universo.* 144p. pap. $12.95 (1-882291-57-3). Durham, NH: Oyster River Press, Spring 1998. Halperin aligns the innermost infrastructure of the human with the outermost cosmos. The voice of these poems resonates in the heart —Stephanie Marlis. [Halperin] observes the astonishing events and people of our times: Eva Perón, Bucky Fuller, the landing of the first space vehicle on Mars. In a nostalgic flow of memory he articulates the human experience of cosmic loneliness, the dehumanization of our cities — and his hope for that little happiness that is love. —Elias Ramos

Hamill, Sam. *Gratitude.* 134p. pap. $12.50 (1-880238-65-9). Rochester, NY: BOA Editions, Spring 1998. Raised in the West and influenced by the great Chinese and Japanese masters, Hamill's poems draw from both traditions, returning us "to that world beyond / words, which are only / a reflection of desire." —BOA Editions. A wonderful compendium of

good sense regarding human thought and conduct, presented in simple, natural images. The poems are beautifully written, prosodically and musically — a real pleasure to read. But over and over I've said to myself, "That's the truth, that's exactly what we need to do," recognized with all the shock of perennial originality. —Hayden Carruth

Hamill, Sam, trans. *Only Companion: Japanese Poems of Love and Longing.* 124p. pap. $10.00 (1-57062-300-7). Boston, MA: Shambhala Publications, March 1992; Spring 1997 (new edition). Written by court princesses, exiled officials, Zen priests, and recluses, the one hundred and fifty poems translated here represent the rich diversity of Japan's poetic tradition. Varying in tone from the sensuous and erotic to the profoundly spiritual, each poem captures a sense of the poignant beauty and longing known only in the fleeting experience of the moment. —Shambhala Publications. These poems come from one of the great treasure troves of world literature, the thousand year tradition of Japanese tanka. Like diamonds, or drops of dew, these highly compressed meditations on human existence gather and return light, illuminating our deepest emotional and spiritual concerns. In Hamill's translations — free, strong, and clear — the deep currents of the originals run true. —Jane Hirshfield

Hamilton, Colin. *The Memory Palace.* 17p. (0-87338-591-8). Kent, OH: Kent State University Press, Fall 1998. Hamilton has combined the visible and the invisible into a truly unusual first book. In three poetic sequences, The Memory Palace weaves layers of psychological narrative into separate versions of an inner biography. The writing is exquisite, the mysteries engaging, and the result original. — Marvin Bell. The poetry, page after page, is of the kind that keeps the reader on the critical edge, both ecstatic and lucid, both active and illumined. — Stavros Deligiorgis

Hammad, Suheir. *Born Palestinian, Born Black.* 97p. pap. $12.00 (0-86316-244-4). New York, NY: Writers and Readers Publishing/Harlem River Press, Spring 1997. The true "manifest destiny" of Hammad is to raise her searing vigorous voice, a brave flag over the dispossessed — to sing stories of indelible origin and linkage. —Naomi Shihab Nye. The poems are

political, but then we are in need of such things. I was born black, and Hammad has taught me what it means to be Palestinian. People must continue to learn from each other. This book opens a door. —E. Ethelbert Miller

Hammond, Ralph. *Vincent Van Gogh: A Narrative Journey.* 158p. $20.00 (0-942979-45-1). pap. $10.00 (0-942979-46-X). Livingston, AL: Livingston Press, Fall 1997. This unique book intertwines poetry and biography. As we follow Van Gogh from his childhood to his ecstatic periods of creation and final madness, we discern a parallel life: that of the author himself, who we meet first as a WWII correspondent pondering the rubble of the house where Van Gogh lived, then fifty years later tracking his life and paintings through contemporary Europe. —Livingston Press

HaNagid, Shmuel. Translated by Peter Cole. *Selected Poems.* 236p. $39.95 (0-691-01121-4). pap. $14.95 (0-691-01120-6). Princeton, NJ: Princeton University Press, Fall 1996. Cole's groundbreaking versions of HaNagid's poems capture the poet's combination of secular and religious passion, as well as his inspired linking of Hebrew and Arabic poetic practice. This annotated Selected Poems is the most comprehensive collection of HaNagid's work published to date in English. —Princeton University Press. These very fine translations of the work of a remarkable medieval poet gain their authority as much from the literary gifts of the poet-translator as from his linguistic and historical knowledge. —John Hollander

Hancock, Kate. *The Lazarus Method.* 24p. pap. $4.75 (0-87338-557-8). Kent, OH: Kent State University Press, 1996. Hancock's poems combine intellectual rigor with emotional recklessness like oil and water under special dispensation. This rare ability is a telltale sign of a true poet, and the reader who lets these poems have their sure way with him or her will not forget them. —William Matthews. Hancock's poetry is a soaring celebration of fallen angels, of language and insight as relentless and tender as her uncommon world. —June Berkley

Hankla, Cathryn. *Negative History.* 72p. $19.95 (0-8071-2153-3). pap. $12.95 (0-8071-2154-1). Baton Rouge, LA: Louisiana State University Press, Fall 1997. Imagine the

peculiar, unsettling effect on a viewer if a woman's personal history were to be presented as a series of photographic negatives. Hankla's poems work in just such a way, creating places where "scars begin to tell stories," where photographs become "tight frames of liberation." Hankla writes, "this camera's gaze means revelation," the poet herself the camera, able to achieve effects that are both passionate and dispassionate, skewed and perfectly lucid. Hankla's poems resonate with a disquieting, revelatory power that only grows stronger with each successive reading. —Elizabeth Spires

Hanley, Elizabeth Jones. *The Art of Making Tea: An Album of Recipes, Portraits and Other Rituals.* 41p. pap. $10.00 (0-910479-04-6). Warrensburg, MO: Mid-America Press, Fall 1998. Hanley's poems collect images, echoes, and memories of growing up in a small town in Missouri. —Mid-America Press

Hansen, Twyla. *In Our Very Bones.* 64p. pap. $12.95 (0-9635559-7-9). Lincoln, NE: Slow Tempo Press, Fall 1997. In Our Very Bones is a book of self-reflection and self-awareness in the best sense.

These poems are made of life's realities; carefully drawn; movingly portrayed; beautifully woven with dignity, humor, vibrance and joy in the act of living; yet wonderfully free of self-absorption. —David Lee

Harding, Jay. *Teardrops on the Counter.* 36p. pap. $5.00 (0-929688-96-1). Eureka Springs, AR: Bear House Publishing, Fall 1997. First place winner of the 1997 Lucidity Poetry Journal Chapbook Award sponsored by the Poetry Society of Texas. —Bear House Publishing

Harjo, Joy, and Gloria Bird, eds. *Reinventing the Enemy's Language: Contemporary Native Women's Writings.* 576p. $27.50 (0-393-04029-1). New York, NY: Norton, W.W., and Company, Spring 1997. These women writers stand on their own terms, unassimilated, speaking from the heart of many cultures. For the non-Indian reader, this is a chance to overhear what's not primarily addressed to us, truth-telling unsweetened by wishful thinking, histories we never learned, voices of unquenchable beauty and integrity. —Adrienne Rich. Clearly one of the most significant anthologies ever to be published in English,

Reinventing the Enemy's Language is a book I have been yearning for all my life. I sat before a blazing fire, reading this gift: enthralled, enchanted, in tears, in happiness and hope for four days. —Alice Walker

Harmon, William, ed. *The Classic Hundred Poems: All-Time Favorites, Second Edition.* 360p. pap. $18.95 (0-231-11259-9). Irvington, NY: Columbia University Press, Spring 1998. The Classic Hundred Poems presents the most anthologized poems in the English language in chronological order. — Columbia University Press. Why did no one think of this before? The 100 English and American poems in this juicy anthology were chosen not by the error-prone mind of some fastidious critic but by a simple, objective appeal to vox populi. —New York Times Book Review

Harms, James. *The Joy Addict.* 72p. $20.95 (0-88748-265-1). pap. $11.95 (0-88748-281-3). Pittsburgh, PA: Carnegie Mellon University Press, Spring 1998. Winner of the PEN/Revson Foundation Fellowship. Harms has a real gift for engaging his reader with the palpability of loss and what he terms "the stillness that follows loss." His eye and hand are brilliantly coordinated, as in his evocation of Los Angeles: "I drove today as if to somewhere. / I spun the dial left to find a song. / And the space between stations / was a thousand throats clearing. / It's in "the space between" that Harms clears his throat and so effectively finds his song. — Judges for the Pen/Revson Fellowship Paul Muldoon, Robert Pinsky, Ellen Bryant Voigt

Harper, Linda Lee. *The Wide View.* 27p. pap. $5.95. Fox River Grove, IL: White Eagle Coffee Store Press, Fall 1998. Winner of the White Eagle Coffee Store Press Fall 1997 Poetry Chapbook Contest. This book, with its evocative, sensual, Nabokovian language and creative humor, invites us to become another person for one week—a person of excess, richness, daring, and considerable spirit. In reading The Wide View, I found myself wishing I had the "daredevil, dirigible heart" of this book's subject, as well as the ability to write in a way that constantly surprises, as Harper does. —Kris Piepenberg

Harris, Bill. *Yardbird Suite Side One: 1920-1940.* 85p. pap. $12.95 (0-87013-435-3). Michigan State University

Press, Spring 1998. Winner of the 1997 Naomi Long Madgett Poetry Award. This collection of biopoems — fictionalized accounts of the life of Charlie "Yardbird" Parker — marvelously interprets instrumental music through poetry. — Michigan State University Press

Harris, Jana. *The Dust of Everyday Life: An Epic Poem of the Pacific Northwest.* 248p. $19.95 (1-57061-068-1). Seattle, WA: Sasquatch Books, Fall 1997. Harris has written an epic poem about Northwest pioneer life that's difficult to put down. Written in the form of diary entries or letters, the poems are dramatic monologues in which the characters recall the harsh, sometimes funny, sometimes compassionate, events that shape their fates. Harris's knack for plain speech, her historical accuracy and her use of metaphors drawn from physical details ("unspoken names, heavy as harnesses") lets us witness rather than romanticize pioneer life. —Emily Warn, The Seattle Times

Harris, Joseph. *Countries of the Mind.* 47p. pap. $10.00. Greenville, SC: Ninety-Six Press, Fall 1997. Frequently wrought as variations on traditional forms, Harris' poetry is often reminiscent of the tradition of Jonson, Herbert, and Marvell — at once passionate and lapidary. —Ninety-Six Press

Harrison, Jim. *The Shape of the Journey: New and Collected Poems.* 463p. $30.00 (1-55659-095-4). Port Townsend, WA: Copper Canyon Press, Fall 1998. Beginning with spare and lovely poems from Plain Song, Harrison offers the best of seven subsequent collections, followed by a set of new poems that go off, like fireworks, with a bang followed by a radiant bloom. [He] is drawn to the endlessly enlightening beauty of nature and sustained by the awareness of mind kindled by the practices of writing, Zen Buddhism, and walking the earth. Readers can wander the woods of this collection for a lifetime and still be amazed by what they find. —Donna Seaman, Booklist. Behind the words one always feels the presence of a passionate, exuberant man who is at the same time possessed of a quick, subtle intelligence and a deeply questioning attitude toward life. Harrison writes so winningly that one is simply content to be in the presence of a writer this vital, this large-spirited. —The New York Times Book Review. He

doesn't write like anyone else, relying entirely on the toughness of his vision and intensity of feeling to form the poem. Or, we should say, relying on the untrammeled renegade genius that has made him one of the most unappreciated writers in America. Harrison will shock and delight readers who think they already know what a poem is supposed to be. The experierience is something like coming across a Whitman or Dickinson, a Keats or Rimbaud after a long diet of formal and classical verse: here's a poet talking to you instead of around himself, while doing absolutely brilliant and outrageous things with language. —Publishers Weekly

Harrod, Lois Marie. *Part of the Deeper Sea.* 88p. pap. $12.00 (1-889806-15-3). Aiken, SC: Palanquin Press, Fall 1997. Harrod's poems are everything I need poetry to be: smart, sensual, risky, willing to tell the strange truths of the ordinary heart. Harrod knows how deceptive the bright surface of domestic life can be. Her poems are like sonar, sent down from a shimmering surface to sound the submerged terrain where we really live. Harrod has found all the right words in these remarkable, bracing poems. —Lynn Powell

Hart, Henry. *The Rooster Mask.* 87p. pap. $14.95 (0-252-06692-8). Champaign, IL: University of Illinois Press, Fall 1998. Hart's Puritan plainness and his love of simple things and chilly landscapes make for much welcome clarity. —Kirkus Reviews. Hart writes in a fine chiseled language through which he creates powerful surfaces and depths and a vision that oscillates between the creative potentials of nature and the haunting wounds of history. —Peter Balakian. Hart emerges here as one of the best poets of his generation. —Jay Parini

Hart, Melanie, and James Loader, eds. *Generations: Poems Between Fathers, Mothers, Daughters, Sons.* 350p. (0-14-058784-5). New York, NY: Penguin Books/Viking Penguin, Fall 1998. In this collection, men and women write of the mothers and fathers they worship or resent, love or mourn, and poets who are parents describe what it means to create life, bear and bring up children. Here are poems from down the centuries and across the world. Many are by established writers such as Ben Jonson, Pablo Neruda, Sylvia Plath, and Christina Rossetti, while others are by exciting contemporary voices, Simon Armitage, Les Murray and Sharon Olds among them. —Penguin Books

Harter, Penny. *Lizard Light: Poems From the Earth.* 96p. pap. $14.00 (1-890932-02-7). Santa Fe, NM: Sherman Asher Publishing, Spring 1998. A gifted poet of nature. —Bloomsbury Review. Minute observations of the natural world. Every word dances like a cobra to the mind's flute. —Inside/Outside Southwest

Hartman, Arleen. *What I'm Doing.* 18p. pap. $6.00 (0-945112-23-8). Cleveland, OH: Generator Press, Fall 1997.

Haskins, Lola. *Extranjera.* 69p. pap. $12.95 (1-885266-57-X). Ashland, OR: Story Line Press, Spring 1998. Haskins's poems are small vignettes and stories, brief glimpses into the lives of locals and travelers. Tightly worded, they snap with a mariachi's nimble feel for music. She understands Lorca's idea of duende, a passionate spirit, and evokes it naturally in her work. Her writing demonstrates an acuteness of perception and a maturity of restraint that are

refreshing because they pro-
duce subtle, thoughtful expres-
sions that stand out from
today's stream of in-your-face,
confessional and therapeutic
verse. —Booklist. Extranjera
offers us no wish-you-were-
here postcards, but plenty of
the rich and seductive darkness of a landscape of native
gods and Catholic apparitions
and heretics. I loved the book.
—Dionisio D. Martinez

Hass, Robert, ed. *Poet's
Choice: Poems for Everyday
Life.* 210p. $23.00 (0-88001-
566-7). Hopewell, NJ: Ecco
Press, Spring 1998. "There is
news in poems," argues Hass.
This collection gathers the full
two years' worth of Hass's
choices [for his nationally syn-
dicated "Poets Choice" news-
paper column], including
recently published poems as
well as older classics. With a
brief introduction to each poet
and poem, a note on the selection, and insights on how the
poem works, Hass acts as your
personal guide to the poetry
shelves at your local bookstores and to some of the best
poetry of all time. —Ecco
Press

Haug, James. *Fox Luck.* 23p.
pap. $25.00. New York, NY:
Center for Book Arts, Fall
1998. Winner of the 1998

Center for Book Arts Poetry
Chapbook Competition.

Haugen, Paal-Helge.
Translated by Roger
Greenwald. *Wintering With the
Light.* 96p. pap. $10.95 (1-
55713-273-9). Los Angeles,
CA: Sun & Moon Press, Fall
1997. Wintering With the
Light is a book of poems in
four parts, written in Haugen's
spare, honed style. Taking as
his motif the light that outlasts
winter, the poet explores sur-
vivals, moving among personal, historical, artistic, and
political dimensions. Haugen
is concerned not only with the
remnants of value we inherit
or seek out, but with what we
can make of them and how we
can maintain the meanings we
discover. —Sun & Moon
Press

Hawley, Ellen, ed. *One
Minute of Knowing.* 92p. pap.
$5.00. Minneapolis, MN: Loft,
The, Fall 1996. An anthology
of poetry and creative prose
by the winners of the 1996
Loft-McKnight Awards and
Awards of Distinction. —The
Loft

Haxton, Brooks. *The Sun at
Night.* pap. $14.00 (0-679-
76596-4). New York, NY:
Knopf, Alfred A., Spring
1995; Fall 1997 (paper). This
book clearly demonstrates that

Haxton is a poet of impressive technical and aesthetic sophistication. His poems have a shimmeringly lunar, susurrant beauty and an impressive range of literary and historical allusions. —Christine Stenstrom, Library Journal. Haxton has drawn together several styles of verse and several schools of thought. The result is a book that employs lyrical beauty, harsh realism, boyish romanticism and brushstrokes of regret in the service of a host of subjects, from flowers to love to the study of the planets. — Stan Friedman, The New York Times Book Review

Hayden, Dolores. *Playing House.* 24p. $25.00. pap. $7.50. Edgewood, KY: Barth, Robert L. (R.L.B.), Spring 1998. Hayden writes with poignancy and skill about pregnancy and childbirth. Rich in personal observation, these poems show an equally keen awareness of larger social worlds. —Timothy Steele

Hayes, Alice Ryerson. *Water: Sheba's Story.* 30p. pap. $24.95 (1-880404-17-6). Charlottesville, VA: Bookwrights Press, Fall 1997. In this exquisite poem the biblical Queen of Sheba tells the story of her visit to King Solomon. In language as evocative as it is economical Sheba simply recounts the facts of her extraordinary journey. The delicacy of the text is echoed in Jeffrey Abt's drawings, which illustrate this remarkably handsome book. —Lisel Mueller. This is stitch music. Hayes works language to its limits. —Gwendolyn Brooks

Headley, Robert, and Rafael Zepeda. *The Wichita Poems.* 44p. pap. $6.00 (1-888219-04-1). Long Beach, CA: Pearl Editions, Spring 1997. This travel collection recounts the experiences encountered by the authors (during the 1993 Western Literature Association annual conference). . . and speaks to all readers who enjoy being skillfully taken on a most interesting trip. — Ronald Moran, Northeast

Heaney, Seamus. *Opened Ground: Selected Poems 1966-1996.* 444p. $25.00 (0-374-23517-1). New York, NY: Farrar, Straus and Giroux, Fall 1998. The best of Nobel laureate Heaney's poems, gathered from 12 previous collections, create a substantial volume that charts the course of one man's thoroughly examined personal life and reflects a volatile era in the life of his troubled country, Northern

Ireland, though the particulars Heaney renders so vibrantly become archetypal and unbounded in their tragedy and bliss. His lyricism is glorious: his melodic lines are made of stone and water, iron and cloth, bread and prayer, flesh and dream. Heaney provides a glimpse into his writerly self in his Nobel lecture, which is included. — Booklist. Anyone who reads poetry has reason to rejoice at living in the age when Seamus Heaney is writing. —Richard Tillinghast, The New York Times Book Review

Heaney, Seamus. *The Spirit Level.* 82p. pap. $11.00 (0-374-52511-0). Farrar, Straus and Giroux/Noonday, Spring 1996/April 1997 (paper). [Heaney] has been and is here for good. His poems, resting at the balance ponts between what we see as opposites, can make us realize that at times our vision utterly deceives us. They will last. Anyone who reads poetry has reason to rejoice at living in the age when Heaney is writing. — Richard Tillinghast, The New York Times Book Review. [Heaney's] new collection keeps up the provision of pleasure. It's like watching the three-card trick in Oxford Street. Suddenly the table is folded up under the arm and the trickster vanishes into the crowd — excepting that, when you tap your pocket, you find you have something valuable you could have sworn wasn't there a moment ago. —James Fenton, The New York Review of Books

Hecht, Anthony. *Flight Among the Tombs.* 76p. pap. $15.00 (0-679-76592-1). New York, NY: Knopf, Alfred A., Fall 1996; Fall 1997 (paper). Hecht's majestic development into a great poet has progressed across half a century. Flight Among the Tombs is his poignant and ironic masterpiece. Few poets stand with Henry James and Marcel Proust; Ransom, Auden, Merrill, and Hecht are in that company. —Harold Bloom

Hedge Coke, Allison Adelle. *Dog Road Woman.* 97p. pap. $12.95 (1-56689-061-6). Minneapolis, MN: Coffee House Press, Spring 1997. Hedge Coke presents an autobiographical sketch of a contemporary mixed-blood native life. These poems recount surviving diaspora, domestic violence, racism, and an extraordinary number of challenges. —Coffee House Press. Hedge Coke's dense narrative poems are crowded with memorable characters and situations. . . she is a welcome new voice in

American poetry. —Jessica Hagedorn. Hedge Coke is a skilled, spirited, young poet who is transforming and honing her social and personal experience and reflection to speak with the voice of a whole people. —Amiri Baraka

Hedin, Robert. *The Old Liberators: New and Selected Poems and Translations.* 105p. pap. $12.95 (0-930100-80-8). Duluth, MN: Holy Cow! Press, Fall 1998. [Hedin] is an accomplished craftsman, using simple language to cast images of great resonance and beauty. His is a powerful voice that tells us what we did not know we knew. —Betty Adcock. A fine book, self-effacing and life-affirming, humble before the world, generous in its accessibility, and masterful in its artistry. —Ted Kooser. Hedin is one of the quietest, most spiritually sensate poets of our time. His syllables cherish time so precisely it yields its fury and lingers, dilating human dimension to that of the spirit. His lyrical conscience witnesses, with joy and humility, the slow mysteries of hope, home, justice. —Olga Broumas

Hedin, Robert, ed. *The Zeppelin Reader: Stories, Poems, and Songs From the Age of Airships.* 290p. (0-87745-629-1). Iowa City, IA: University of Iowa Press, Fall 1998. Tracing the history of the airship from its beginning in the nineteenth century to its fiery conclusion in 1937, Hedin has gathered the finest stories, descriptions, poems, music, and illustrations about what the era was like in fact and spirit. —University of Iowa Press. A remarkable achievement. The fascinating tales of these remarkable fliers has been long overdue. —John Toland

Heffley, Carole J., ed. *Womankind: The Poetry of Women, Volume 2.* 132p. pap. $23.95 (1-88331-24). Easton, PA: Anderie Poetry Press, Spring 1997. An annual compilation of poetry by women poets throughout the United States. —Anderie Poetry Press

Heinrich, Amy V., ed. *Seasons of Sacred Celebration; Flowers and Poetry From an Imperial Convent.* 113p. pap. $16.95 (0-8348-0464-6). Weatherhill/Institute for Medieval Japanese Studies, Fall 1998. Eighteen unusual paintings preserved at Daishoji Imperial Convent in Kyoto, Japan are presented here for the first time. They include

beautiful calligraphic renderings of classical poems and
delicate floral illustrations
linking each poem to the
appropriate season. —
Weatherhill

Hejduk, John. *Such Places as
Memory: Poems 1953-1996.*
128p. (0-262-58158-2). MIT
Press, Spring 1998. The
poems of John Hejduk are
almost nonpoetic: still lives of
memory, sites of possessed
places. They give a physical
existence to the words themselves and an autobiographical
dimension to the author, who
is Dean of the School of
Architecture of the Cooper
Union. This is the first comprehensive collection of
Hejduk's poems to be pub-
lished outside an architectural
setting. —MIT Press. The
uncanny lure of Hejduk's
voice, its demotic authority, is
something both inimitable and
infectious. Here, a native-born
architect speaks, be it about
seashells, disease, or
Delacroix, and Hejduk's
indelible writings have built
up a cinematic vertigo of these
voices, all his own. —David
Shapiro

Held, George. *Salamander
Love and Others.* 36p. pap.
$4.00. Talent, OR: Talent
House Press, Fall 1998.

Hell, Richard. *Weather.* 36p.
pap. $5.95 (0-9666328-0-X).
New York, NY: CUZ Editions,
Fall 1998.

Heller, Michael. *Wordflow:
New and Selected Poems.*
130p. pap. $10.50 (1-883689-
49-X). Jersey City, NJ:
Talisman House, Publishers,
1997. Heller's is a questing
intelligence, forever on the
trail of the epistemological,
the "flimsy beatitudes of
order." —The New York
Times Book Review. Heller's
poetry and prose are noble in
gesture and intent, superbly
rich and profoundly emotional. They should be considered
a unique and vital part of the
contemporary canon. —
Dictionary of Literary
Biography

Hellus, Al. *Alternative
Baseball and Other Poems.*
34p. pap. $8.00 (1-56439-066-
7). Detroit, MI: Ridgeway
Press, Spring 1997. This is
poetry with gusto, raw and full
of life. Hellus is a mid-
American urban poet who
knows his craft well and
relates to the community
around him. —Ridgeway
Press

Henderson, Bill, ed. *The
Pushcart Prize XXII: Best of
the Small Presses.* 651p.
$29.50 (1-888889-01-2). pap.

$15.00 (1-888889-07-1). Wainscott, NY: Pushcart Press, Fall 1997. Indispensable. . . . Get it, read it, lug it around with you; as always this book is essential. —Library Journal. A fascinating peek at the vast and largely hidden world of noncommercial publishing. —Time. There is nothing else quite like this labor of love. Long may it appear. —Choice

Henderson, David. *Neo-California.* 144p. $20.00 (1-55643-275-5). Berkeley, CA: North Atlantic Books, Fall 1998. Henderson's poetry is the world echo. —Amiri Baraka. [Henderson is] a poet whose sometimes rhapsodic voice brings off a sharp sense of place. Explosive, bitter, charged with outrage and spleen, Henderson's poems display a gift for social exposition. —Colette Inez

Henderson, E.A., and Ted O. Badger. *Intriguing Etheree.* 18p. pap. $2.50 (0-929688-84-8). Eureka Springs, AR: Bear House Publishing, Fall 1996. Devised about 20 years ago by an Arkansas poet named Etheree Taylor Armstrong, the Etheree consists of ten lines of unmetered and unrhymed verse, the first line having one syllable and each succeeding line adding a syllable, with the total syllable count adding up to fifty-five. Concise and focusing on one idea or subject, the Etheree usually takes on the quality of an epigram. —Bear House Publishing

Henriques, Anna Ruth. *The Book of Mechtilde.* 85p. $35.00 (0-375-40023-0). New York, NY: Knopf, Alfred A., Fall 1997. A ravishingly beautiful modern-day illuminated manuscript created by a brilliant young Jamaican artist who weaves together in words and paintings the story of her mother's life and death. Inspired by texts from the Book of Job, Henriques tells her mother's story in the form of a fable, sometimes in prose, sometimes in poetry. Each scene is illustrated with a painting encircled with calligraphy and set in a gold border of flowers, fruit, or symbolic creatures. —Alfred A. Knopf

Henson, Lance. *Strong Heart Song: Lines From a Revolutionary Text.* 72p. pap. $8.95 (0-931122-86-4). Albuquerque, NM: West End Press, Fall 1997. Stark, militant, and searching, bearing a fierce witness, [these poems] constitute [Henson's] mature view of the American experience. —West End Press

Herman, Corie. *Radishes Into Roses.* 52p. pap. $8.95 (1-891219-17-0). Siasconset, MA: Linear Arts, Fall 1997. Herman's poems involve us in compelling urban interiors that unfold before us visually and aurally through the emotions and mind of a city's "lover," "daughter," the one who gazes at the beauty and destruction with a sharp sensitivity for nuance, documentation, and song. —Judith Vollmer

Herman, William R. *Alone.* 96p. pap. $10.00 (0-9655245-0-7). Wrightsville Beach, NC: Arnold & Johnson, Publishers, Spring 1997. Herman believes the task of poetry is to tell stories about being a human being. He has many memorable stories to tell. —Arnold & Johnson, Publishers

Herndon, John. *Road Trip Through the Four Spheres.* 24p. San Francisco, CA: Mike & Dale's Press, Fall 1998.

Heyen, William. *Diana, Charles, & the Queen.* 124p. pap. $12.95 (1-880238-69-1). Rochester, NY: BOA Editions, Fall 1997. Diana, Charles, & the Queen is a multi-leveled literary work, stunning in its depth, and far removed from what has previously been offered the reading public on the subject of the royal family.

—BOA Editions. [Heyen] is a remarkable poet in whom the "visionary" and the unblinkingly "historical" are dramatically meshed. —Joyce Carol Oates

Hicok, Bob. *Plus Shipping.* 100p. pap. $12.50 (1-880238-67-5). Rochester, NY: BOA Editions, Fall 1998. Hicok's gift lies somewhere between those of the surgeon and the gods of the the foundry and convalescent home: seamlessly, miraculously, his judicious eye imbues even the dreadful with beauty and meaning. — The New York Times

Higman, Perry, trans. *Sueñan. Lloran. Cantan. They Dream. They Cry. They Sing: Poems for Children from Spain and Spanish America.* 104p. (0-910055-41-6). (0-910055-42-4). Cheney, WA: Eastern Washington University Press, Fall 1998. Higman has gathered an offering of poems from the Hispanic tradition which spans four centuries and two continents. Alberti, Lorca, Machado, Gabriela Mistral, and Neruda are among the fifteen poets represented in this edition meant for parents who wish to engage their children's senses and imaginations, and extend their understanding of both languages. —Eastern Washington University Press

Hill, Geoffrey. *Canaan.* 76p. $22.00 (0-395-87550-1). pap. $14.00 (0-395-92486-3). Boston, MA: Houghton Mifflin Company, Fall 1997; Fall 1998 (new paper). Hill's poems serve exalted artistic ends. They display burnish, sensuality and coiled force. —Michael Dirda, Washington Post Book World. Canaan is one of the few serious books we wil have to mark the millennium. —William Logan, The New Criterion. In an age of broadening secularity, Hill's is that rare achievement — a profoundly religious poetry. —David Yezzi, Commonweal

Hill, Geoffrey. *The Triumph of Love.* 80p. $22.00 (0-395-91235-0). Boston, MA: Houghton Mifflin Company, Fall 1998; Spring 2000 (new paper). Hill's poems demand and reward reading upon reading; the ascent is steep, the view austerely sublime. — Merle Rubin, The Wall Street Journal. His is, in every sense, a sacrificial art, tormented by Christian theology. It is an art of the highest lyric intensity. It stands with the work of Mandelstam and Montale. — Rosanna Warren, Boston Globe. Hill, always the heir of William Blake and D.H.

Lawrence, more than confirms his calling as poet-prophet in The Triumph of Love. The poem is a great and difficult moral, cognitive, and aesthetic achievement — "a sad and angry consolation" almost beyond measure. —Harold Bloom

Hill, Lindsay. *NdjenFerno.* 66p. pap. $8.95 (0-9654877-3-3). Vatic Hum, Fall 1998. It would seem appropriate for these murderous lyrics to be half-spoken, half-sung by a demonic rhythm-and-bluesman in some post-apocalyptic border town. This is a book about that ultimate border between violence and meaning, illuminating the truth of Benjamin's definition of history as an accumulation of wreckage. Hill talks a high-tension lingo stripped of tense and person, denuding and freshly wounding time and subjectivity. —Andrew Joron. Demolishing our preconceptions about language, cadence, and the way a poem can hold itself together, NdjenFerno is an astonishing book. The works in this collection offer us a dazzling vision: terrifying, apocalyptic, unforgettable. —Lawrence R. Smith

Hill, Nick. *Mundane Rites / Ritos Mundanos.* 26p. pap. $5.00. New York, NY: New

School Chapbook Series, Spring 1997. Mundane Rites transcends the protest to lift us to universal oneness. In this world where we all better become one or we are done, Hill reminds us, "The invisible aren't dead forever." These [are] important poems. —Leo Connellan

Hillman, Brenda. *Loose Sugar.* 116p. $25.00 (0-8195-2242-2). pap. $11.95 (0-8195-2243-0). University Press of New England/Wesleyan University Press, Spring 1997. Structurally virtuosic, elaborate without being ornate, Loose Sugar is spun into series within series: each of the five sections has a dual heading (such as "space / time" or "time / work") in which the terms are neither in collision or collusion, but in conversation. It's elemental sweet talk, and it's Hillman's most experimental work to date, culminating in a meditation on the possibility of a native — and feminine — language. —University Press of New England / Wesleyan University Press. Memories (real or imagined) are gathered into highly "scenic" poetics. I admire the way Hillman attaches a plumage (or energy) to her nude expressive details. I see Loose Sugar as part of the anatomy of the rare bird of "autobiographical" experimentation. —Barbara Guest

Hirsch, Edward. *On Love.* 86p. $22.00 (0-375-40253-5). New York, NY: Knopf, Alfred A., Fall 1998; Spring 2000 (new paper). On Love takes up the subjects of separateness and fusion, autonomy and blur. The initial progression of fifteen shapely and passionate lyircs opens out into a sequence of arresting love poems, spoken by a gallery of historical figures from Baudelaire and Emerson to Zora Neale Hurston and Colette. Personal, literary, On Love offers the most formally adept and moving poetry by the author Harold Bloom hails as utterly fresh, canonical, and necessary. —Alfred A. Knopf. Hirsch is one of the finest poets we have! He has wonderful gifts to offer us: a strong, touching narrative voice; an alert, mindful eye; the moral energy that informs his manner of writing and his choice of subjects; a desire to reach his readers, bring them into the world he observes, creates. —Robert Coles

Hirsch, Steve. *Ramapo 500 Affirmations and Other Poems.* 32p. pap. $8.00 (1-893411-00-1). Flower Thief Press, Spring 1999. Ride what's left of Whitman's and

Kerouac's road with this big-eared, heartsteering, motor-mouthing, Sutra-blowing poet, who won't surrender a single joy in all the beaten miles of be-all and end-all. —Mikhail Horowitz, Woodstock Times. Hirsch's poetry celebrates the pleasures of following a long ribbon of asphalt to the farthest horizon, and will be appreciated by even confirmed anti-poetry types. —Clement Salvadori, Rider Magazine. Top notch — among the best motorcycle-oriented poetry we have seen. —Dan Kennedy, Whitehorse Press. The music of this poetry is like nothing else. Hirsch's poems move, but speed is not their only quality. One senses here perhaps a new "New York School." Kerouac, Basho, Whitman, Ginsberg, and O'Hara are breathing in these lines. —Jack Foley

Hirshfield, Jane. *The Lives of the Heart.* 108p. pap. $13.00 (0-06-095-169-9). HarperCollins/HarperPerennial, Fall 1997. [Hirshfield] approaches the poem in a way that feels exactly right to me: plainly, reverently, intelligently. —Robert Pinsky

Hirshkowitz, Lois. *Pan's Daughters.* 74p. (1-879457-58-X). San Francisco, CA: Chi Chi Press, Fall 1998. The voice in Hirshkowitz's poems is an active one. Frenetic. Energetic. Rather than static words on a page, she creates typographical landscapes through which ideas and sounds can migrate and reverberate. Here is a poetics of transformational and musical grammar that invites the reader to compose these poems, anew and different each time, along with the author. — Elaine Equi. Tantalizingly inventive, funny and smart, Pan's Daughters is difficult in the most exciting sense — you may feel you are encountering this intriguing book as much as reading it. Fabulous resemblances and their equally fabulous disjunctions distinguish Hirshkowitz's work. Gutsy, quirky, and always shining, her poems are also whimsically wise. —Molly Peacock

Hirson, Denis, ed. *The Lava of This Land: South African Poetry 1960-1996.* pap. $17.95 (0-8101-5069-7). Northwestern University Press/TriQuarterly Books, Fall 1997. This anthology, containing more than two hundred poems by over fifty poets, spans five distinct historical periods in the contemporary development of South Africa, from the worker strikes in Durban in the late 1960's to the dismantling of the apartheid apparatus in the 1990's. Most of the poems have been written in English; others were translated from Afrikaans, Zulu, Xhosa and /Xam, a Bushman linguistic group. Together, they provide a fascinating and moving rendering of South Africa's hybrid landscape, and a unique and recognizably African worldview. —Northwestern University Press

Hix, H.L., ed. *Poets At Large: 25 Poets in 25 Homes.* 54p. pap. $12.95 (1-884235-19-0). Kansas City, MO: Helicon Nine Editions, Spring 1997. Poems by 25 poets who read in 25 unique and historic homes throughout Kansas City in an all day salute to National Poetry Month. —Helicon Nine Editions

Hoagland, Tony. *Donkey Gospel.* 71p. pap. $12.95 (1-55597-268-3). St. Paul, MN: Graywolf Press, Spring 1998. Winner of the 1997 James Laughlin Award of The Academy of American Poets. Hoagland's effervescence and a jujitsu cleverness sparkle thought poems about negotiation and compromise, gender and culture, sex and rock and roll. From the boy who speaks only in "Kung Fu" dialogue to the man visiting a lesbian bar, Hoagland gives a sense of

finally being able to tell the truth about the credentials of contemporary manhood. — Graywolf Press. In Donkey Gospel, there's an underlying sweetness to the poems, and a gratitude for having survived so much human fecklessnes (including, of course, one's own), and these complicate the poems' anger and puzzlement and rumple their severe surfaces. The resulting mixture has much of the complexity of a personality that willingly weathers its own perplexities and experience, rather than striking a pose of competence and trying to ride out the storm. —William Matthews

Hodge-Williams, Valerie A. *A Time for Healing.* 145p. pap. $19.95 (0-935273-10-7). Baltimore, MD: CHESS Publications, 1997. This moving prose and poetry history of Hodge-Williams' enounter with breast cancer fills the psychologic needs of not only patients, but also their loved ones. —CHESS Publications

Hoefer, David. *New, Improved Wilderness.* 62p. pap. $7.95 (0-9654877-1-7). Vatic Hum Press, 1997. Hoefer's nearly unique perspective as a poet-businessman creates a poetry which engages multiple inputs simultaneously. Its startling juxtapositions illustrate the distance between the cyber-adcopy construct and the human face upon which it is projected. The poems model profound displacement with intensity and precision. — Lindsay Hill. A post-apocalyptic work of strange realism, equal parts cynicism, despair, wonder and anger. [Hoefer's] book is a courageously millennial spectacle. —Hank Lazer

Hoffmann, Yoel, ed. *Japanese Death Poems: Written by Zen Monks and Haiku Poets on the Verge of Death.* 366p. pap. $16.95 (0-8048-3179-3). Tuttle, Charles E., Spring 1998. A wonderful introduction to the Japanese tradition of jisei, this volume is crammed with exquisite, spontaneous verse and pithy, often hilarious, descriptions of the eccentric and committed monastics who wrote the poems. —Tricycle: The Buddhist Review

Hogan, Wayne. *What on Earth Is.* 48p. pap. $6.00 (1-888832-10-X). St. Augustine, FL: Kings Estate Press, Spring 1998. Illustrations with humorous captions. —Kings Estate Press

Holahan, Susan. *Sister Betty Reads the Whole You.* 64p. pap. $10.95 (0-87905-758-0). Layton, UT: Smith, Gibbs,

Publishers/Peregrine Smith Books, Spring 1998. Sister Betty Reads the Whole You carries the fever of moments besieged by other moments. Intensely awake, quick as the neck of a bird looking from side to side, Holahan's poems have absorbed the emotional cast that things pick up from use and the emotions of people who are pulled a thousand ways at once. Her book is a true portrait — ardent, political and familial: the whole you. —Marvin Bell. Offbeat, probing, and "fast as Chinese takeout," Holahan's poetry takes in news from the air waves, the junk of yard sales, menus, kids, and mothers, and rivets them into a fierce but loving tableau of our lives and times. Her dazzling language and syntax mirror her quick intelligence. "I want the poem," she says, "more like a soup pot you just put on the stove and you / don't know what's going into it yet." Holahan's poems carry off that bold aesthetic with verve and a novel shapeliness. — Deborah Tall, Seneca Review

Holden, Karen. *Book of Changes.* 82p. pap. $11.95 (1-55643-263-1). Berkeley, CA: North Atlantic Books, Spring 1998. Mingling prose poems with metered verse, this luminous collection offers a personal rumination on the I Ching. Each of the poems connects with one of the 64 hexagrams in this ancient and popular Chinese oracular text, revealing how the author's emotions and experiences mirror, or complicate, the traditional meaning of each divination. —North Atlantic Books. The delicate yet strong weave of Holden's syntax; her subtle yet forceful ways with rhythm; and the spectrum of her perceptions, each shaded in a particular and unexpected hue — all this makes Holden's poetry a gentle but indelible voice among us, uncompromised and unafraid. —Michael Ventura

Hollander, Benjamin. *The Book of Who Are Was.* 109p. pap. $10.95 (1-55713-291-7). Los Angeles, CA: Sun & Moon Press, Fall 1997. Hollander explores, through a negotiation with poets of the past and present such as Paul Celan, Edmond Jabès, and Anne-Marie Albiach, how to "project memory on stage." Recognizing poetry as a theatrical field, a performance so to speak, The Book of Who Are Was contemplates the process of poetic creation in which it is actually the reader's or spectator's memory that is projected upon the stage or text. The result is a startlingly

original poetry, a series of mysterious, transformative encounters among figures, occasions, and voices of the past, of the poet, of the reader. —Sun & Moon Press

Hollander, John, ed. *Marriage Poems.* 256p. $12.50 (0-679-45515-9). Knopf/Everyman's Library Pocket Poets, Spring 1997. A collection of poems about virtually every aspect of matrimony: courtships and weddings, adulteries and separations, domestic harmony, wedded bliss. Here are marriages made in many cultures and eras, evoked by poets ranging from Ovid and Omar Khayam to D.H. Lawrence and Mona Van Duyn. —Knopf

Hollander, John, with David Lehman, eds. *The Best American Poetry 1998.* 332p. $30.00 (0-684-81453-6). pap. $14.00 (0-684-81450-1). New York, NY: Simon & Schuster/Scribner, Fall 1998. Diverse in form and method, the poems collected here help answer that perennial question, What is American about American poetry? Hollander has chosen work work from both eminences such as Richard Wilbur, Donald Justice, and Robert Pinsky, and newer talents including Annne Carson, Henri Cole,

and Brigit Pegeen Kelly. —
Simon & Schuster. This yearly
compendium is not to be
missed. —Publishers Weekly.
A truly memorable anthology.
—Chicago Tribune

Holley, Margaret. *Kore in
Bloom.* 64p. pap. $10.95 (0-
914278-74-6). Providence, RI:
Copper Beech Press, Fall
1998. Here is the physical
world with its own sometimes
ferocious, sometimes tender
artistry; here are family and
friends; and here is the poet
herself, who, in this intelligent
and magical book, is the best
company of all. Holley
deserves a wider audience
than she has had so far; Kore
in Bloom should bring her
many new readers. —Mary
Oliver. [Holley] has a capacity
for communicating pleasure
and even joy which sets her
apart from most of her contemporaries. —Michigan
Quarterly Review

**Hollo, Anselm; Anne
Waldman, and Jack Collom.**
Polemics. 203p. pap. $14.95
(1-57027-070-8). Brooklyn,
NY: Autonomedia, Fall 1998.
Poetry and polemics have typ-
ically gone in opposite directions — the fine flame of the
sonnet versus the raging
blazes of oratory. Now three
poets long associated with the
Jack Kerouac School of

Disembodied Poetics have
joined their linguistic bonfires
in a volume of polemical
poems. Put a dark glass over
your mind's eye and read. —
Autonomedia

Holman, Amy. *Dwelling With
Fire.* 26p. pap. $7.95 (1-
891219-02-2). Siasconset,
MA: Linear Arts, Spring 1997.
With a voice that is impecca-
bly formed and a measure that
takes its pace from deliberate
urgency and seamless ambigu-
ity, Holman has gathered in
these poems a study of experience and the memory of place
set between an horizon of catastrophe and the limit of its
foreknowledge. —Linear Arts

Holmes, Elizabeth. *The
Patience of the Cloud
Photographer.* 70p. pap.
$11.95 (0-88748-240-6).
Pittsburgh, PA: Carnegie
Mellon University Press,
Spring 1997.

Holmes, Janet. *The Green
Tuxedo.* 60p. pap. $12.00 (0-
268-01036-6). Notre Dame,
IN: University of Notre Dame
Press, Fall 1998. Winner of
the 1999 Ernest Sandeen Prize
in Poetry. Holmes's second
book of poems exhorts us to
look beyond the face value of
what presents itself, to resist
literal interpretations, and to
plumb the many depths afford-

ed by each encounter with the world outside ourselves. — University of Notre Dame Press. Holmes possesses an enviable virtuosity. Her subtle shifts of mind and canny juxtapositions delight the reader with digressions and returns, with perceptiveness and grace. —Susan Ludvigson. A wonderful book. Godspeed [its] light into the darkness that surrounds us all. —Thomas Lux

Holt, Rochelle L. *Bolts: Fractured Sonnets.* 60p. pap. $10.00 (0-934536-68-6). St. John, KS: Chiron Review Press, Fall 1998. Holt's imagery is vivid. She never falters. —Marie Aser, The Pilot. Bolts is the psychic equivalent of being struck by lightning. —Virginia Love Long

Holthaus, Gary. *An Archaeology of Home.* 36p. pap. $15.00 (0-931659-47-7). Boise, ID: Limberlost Press, Fall 1998. Poems about growing up on an Iowa farm. — Limberlost Press

Homer. Translated by Robert Fitzgerald. *The Odyssey.* 515p. $30.00 (0-374-22438-2). pap. $10.00 (0-374-52574-9). New York, NY: Farrar, Straus and Giroux, Fall 1998. Fitzgerald's modern translation of The Odyssey is the only one admired in its own right as a great poem in English. The classicist D.S. Carne-Ross explains the many aspects of the poem in his introduction, written especially for this edition, which also features a map, a glossary of names and places, a guide to critical writing on Homeric poetry, and Fitzgerald's own postscript. — Farrar, Straus and Giroux. A masterpiece . . . an Odyssey worthy of the original. — William Arrowsmith, The Nation. This is translation as interpretation, filtered through one of the finest poetic sensibilities of our time. —John Freccero, The Boston Book Review. Here there is no anxious straining after mighty effects, but rather a constant readiness for what the occasion demands, a kind of Odyssean adequacy to the task in hand. —Seamus Heaney

Hooper, Patricia. *At the Corner of the Eye.* 65p. pap. $13.95 (0-87013-467-1). East Lansing, MI: Michigan State University Press/Lotus Poetry Series, Fall 1997. Hooper's work is really extraordinary, almost Shaker in its clean lines. Her language has the simplicity of work that's been finely crafted — a fine showcase for the lightning-flash complexity of her subject matter. There is nothing artificial in the hard-earned wisdom that emanates from these poems. —Mekeel McBride

Hoover, Paul. *Viridian.* 86p. pap. $14.95 (0-8203-1895-7). Athens, GA: University of Georgia Press, Spring 1997. Hoover's concern with language's representational inadequacy is shared by the L=A=N=G=U=A=G=E poets he's championed for years. However his own poems are more direct, more lyrical, and sometimes seethingly and seductively melancholic. — Boston Review

Hopmans, Walt. *Some Possible Poets.* 76p. pap. $10.00 (1-885021-06-2). Long Beach, CA: Orange Ocean Press, Spring 1997. Cartoons, and a handful of poems, about all aspects of the life of a poet today, from inspiration through publication (and/or rejection) to "success." — Orange Ocean Press

Houghton, Timothy. *Riding Untouched.* 80p. $21.95 (0-914061-68-2). Alexandria, VA: Orchises Press, Spring 1998. In Riding Untouched, Houghton extends the reach of his previous work, adding to the fine discrimination of his previous work a bracing awareness of the scientific and geopolitical universe. — Orchises Press

Howe, Fanny. *One Crossed Out.* 64p. pap. $12.95 (1-55597-259-4). St. Paul, MN: Graywolf Press, Fall 1997. Howe's poems speak in the voice of May, the girl crossed out, the bad girl, the mad and drunk girl, the jailed and drugged girl. May is swirling in language, and the language convinces us that we really are deep in the core of human consciousness, near the foul rag-and-bone shop of the heart. May is a neo-nomad, bringing the world the opposite of worldliness, offering a glimpse of the invisible. — Graywolf Press. There is a dizzying wildness in Howe's work that draws the reader headlong across her page. In the unstoppable rush of that language she unites the dispersed elements of our tumbling humanness. O Guerilla poet! —Maureen Owen

Howe, Marie. *What the Living Do.* 91p. $21.00 (0-393-04560-9). New York, NY: Norton, W.W., and Company, Spring 1998; Spring 2000 (new paper). Howe has reinvented the elegy as a poem for the living, a poem of instruction, how we're educated by grief, brought to ourselves and our senses as we are "gripped by. . . cherishing." These conversational lyrics ring with the clarity of struck speech, and their astonishing intensity wakes us to our ordinary crisis: here we are now, in the plain everyday, which is where any sort of illumination, any possible transcendence will take place. Scrupulously attentive, rigorously self-questioning, What the Living Do is an achievement of remarkable power. —Mark Doty. The tentative transformation of agonizing loss into redemption is Howe's signal achievement in this wrenching second collection, which uncovers new potential for the personal poem. —Publishers Weekly

Howe, Susan Elizabeth. *Stone Spirits.* 88p. pap. $9.95 (1-56085-107-4). Provo, UT: Redd Center Publications, Fall 1997. Rocks are prominent elements in Howe's poetic landscape. But Howe's West is not limited to the arid canyon-lands; it also extends to the cow-casino-bordello town of Elko and to the urbanized valleys of the Wasatch Front. It is apparent from the broad topical and thematic range that her poetry is not limited by geography though it is defined by it. Even when the subject matter ranges most widely, there is always something Western in the perspective. —Redd Center Publications

Howell, Christopher. *Lady of the Fallen Air: Poems From the Chinese.* 85p. pap. $14.95 (0-932264-21-2). Portland, OR: Trask House Books, Fall 1998. Howell found himself writing for a short time in the persona of a 14th century Chinese scribe. To penetrate the psyche of this character, to more completely hear his tone, he set out to translate a group of poems from the Chinese. — Trask House Books

Howell, Christopher. *Memory and Heaven.* 79p. $24.50 (0-910055-27-0). pap. $14.00 (0-910055-28-9). Cheney, WA: Eastern Washington University Press, Spring 1997. There is an ease about Howell's ability to slip out into the amazing and return to the reader, smoking. It is as if the poem were the iridescent overflow of a profoundly abundant imagination. —Tim Barnes. Tangled, fertile, obsessed with time, elegiac, comic, shifty, and always sharply, freshly observant, each syllable carries on a running battle with those who would reduce life to mock-turtle simulations and virtual realities, and each word is stroked on the loom of gratitude for the power of the imagination we are given. — Bill Tremblay

Howley, Michael. *The Painter's Dream.* 51p. pap. $5.00 (1-886124-02-8). New York, NY: Three Mile Harbor, Spring 1998.

Hudgins, Andrew. *Babylon in a Jar: New Poems.* 80p. $22.00 (0-395-90994-5). Boston, MA: Houghton Mifflin Company, Fall 1998. In these poems, [Hudgins] probes the nature of Southern experience and the conflict between religion and worldliness, and searches out the origins of poetry and the joys and perils of family life. The breadth and sweep of this volume, in its involvements with experience, with mythology, and with chaos, surpass anything Hudgins has written before. —Houghton Mifflin. Hudgins has become a national treasure. —Richard Howard. Hudgins says the unsayable in his poetry and makes beauty often out of the unbeautiful. In cadences and phrasing that are like no other poet's, Hudgins expresses the passion for life, the drive to exist, shared by everything that breathes. His genius is undeniable. —Mark Jarman

Huggins, Peter. *Hard Facts.* 68p. $19.95 (0-942979-43-5).

pap. $9.95 (0-942979-44-3). Livingston, AL: Livingston Press, Fall 1998. In his deft, witty, learned poems, Huggins treats hard facts with a delightful, deceptive ease. Such clear language handled with such a light touch welcomes the reader into the world of the poem. —Thomas Rabbit. This first collection of poems by Huggins reveals a distinctive new Southern voice. His poems pass freely from registers of homegrown surrealistic wit to intensities of feeling, plainly expressed. This is a book to read and read again. —Charles Martin

Hughes, Frieda. *Wooroloo.* 64p. $20.00 (0-06019271-2). HarperCollins/HarperFlamingo, Fall 1998. Hughes's language is possessed of an almost painterly sensitivity and a sublime mastery of craft. The self she depicts is one who is tested by loss, danger, betrayal, and abandonment, yet one who is transformed through experience into a world beyond nihilism and despair: a place that makes possible truth, strength of character, and the redemptive powers of love. Wooroloo foretells what is certain to be an important body of work from this exquisite literary artist. —HarperCollins

Hughes, Ted. *Birthday Letters.* 198p. $20.00 (0-374-11296-7). New York, NY: Farrar, Straus and Giroux, Fall 1997; Fall 1998 (re-print). This volume of 88 poems tells one of the most powerful stories of postwar literary history: the romance of Ted Hughes and Sylvia Plath, from their first meeting in 1956 until her suicide in 1963. In the 35 years since her death, Hughes has never commented in public about Plath. The poems (with two exceptions) are written in the form of letters addressed to Plath — some love letters, others recollections, ruminations, animal poems, and ventures into myth. Birthday Letters is his artistic statement about their life together. —Farrar, Straus and Giroux

Hughes, Ted. *Tales From Ovid.* 257p. $25.00 (0-374-22841-8). New York, NY: Farrar, Straus and Giroux, Fall 1997. Winner of the Whitbread Prize in England for the best book of the year. There's a natural affinity between Ovid and [Hughes], a writer known for both his delightful bedtime stories and dark, earthy animal myths. —Publishers Weekly. Hughes seizes on Ovid's prime characteristic — fascination with extreme passions, especially lust — to spark his versions, but it is the muscularity of his language and rhythms that makes them ignite. He gives us a great way to reaquaint ourselves with these bloody, wonderful tales. —Booklist

Hummell, Austin. *The Fugitive Kind.* 45p. pap. $14.95 (0-8203-1885-X). Athens, GA: University of Georgia Press, Fall 1996. Much like the soliloquy of Aeneas at the center of the collection, the poems' many voices meditate on exile in both place and time, on belatedness, on memory made sacred, and on what Virgil called the poetry of lacrimae rerum. But no matter the doubt, suffering, homelessness, or confusion, the poems of The Fugitive Kind are animated with a transforming astonishment and humor that invariably turn from lamentation to praise. —University of Georgia Press

Humphrey, James. *Léf.* 77p. pap. $15.00 (0-936641-22-3). Yonkers, NY: Poets Alive! Press, Fall 1997. The power of Humphrey's writing, always bears exceptional witness and testament and makes a very dear pact with what it's all about. He tells it as best it can be ever. —Robert Creeley

Humphrey, James. *Mize & Kathy.* 86p. pap. $17.00 (0-936641-25-8). Yonkers, NY: Poets Alive! Press, Spring 1998. Mize & Kathy is a freeform improvisation within the narrow novella margins about a young couple discovering intimacy. —Poets Alive! Press

Humphrey, James. *Paying the Price.* 115p. pap. $17.00 (0-936641-23-1). Yonkers, NY: Poets Alive! Press, Fall 1998. The power of Humphrey's writing, always, bears exceptional witness and testament and makes a very dear pact with what it's all about. He tells it as best it can be ever. —Robert Creeley. Love, despite all, is primary, a heal-all. His poems pluck the flower and offer it. A moralist of the imagination. Redeeming the language. His poems: a lexicon of the heart's ecology. —Daniel Berrigan

Humphrey, James. *SIZ.* 83p. pap. $16.00 (0-936641-21-5). Yonkers, NY: Poets Alive! Press, Spring 1997. A novel as poetry? Poetry as novel? This much is certain: No American work of literature can rival Humphrey's SIZ for the depth of its roots in tragic farmland, nor for the sad beauty of its blossoms. An important book. —Kurt Vonnegut

Hunter, Robert. *Glass Lunch.* 100p. pap. $14.95 (0-14-058777-2). New York, NY: Penguin Books/Viking Penguin, Spring 1997. A new collection of poetry from the primary lyricist for The Grateful Dead. —Penguin Books/Viking Penguin

Hunting, Constance. *The Shape of Memory: New and Selected Poems.* 67p. pap. $9.95 (0-913006-68-8). Orono, ME: Puckerbrush Press, Fall 1998. Hunting is surely one of the distinguished poets of the twentieth century — a poet whose poems become myths as one reads them. —May Sarton. It comes as no surprise that William Carlos Williams with his well-tuned ear should have been drawn to her work, for Hunting's serious training in music is the Grundlage of her work. As for poetic schools, better leave it that she is her own poet, drawing from many traditions, yet claiming none. —David Gordon

Huntington, Cynthia. *We Have Gone to the Beach.* 80p. pap. $9.95 (1-882295-11-0). Farmington, ME: Alice James Books, Fall 1996. Winner of the 1996 Beatrice Hawley

Award. Huntington's poems do what the best poems do—they move us profoundly and stir our deepest longing for beauty. —Annie Dillard. Huntington's is a poetry of wit, surprise, observation, and exemplary intelligence. Reading her sentences, the leap from word to word provides a distance like turning the page. —Donald Hall, The Boston Review

Hussa, Linda. *Ride the Silence.* 90p. pap. $10.00. Reno, NV: Black Rock Press/Rainshadow Editions, 1995.

Ibáñez, Armando P. *Wrestling With the Angel.* 96p. pap. $11.95 (1-889848-08-5). Los Angeles, CA: Pluma Productions, Fall 1997. Roman Catholic priest and poet Ibáñez celebrates the spiritual bond between man and nature even while he laments the seaming absence of God amid the tortures of rape and AIDS. His cadences descend from the rituals of the church, his diction from the experience of the Chicano community. —Pluma Productions. Of particular interest to me is the way that he deftly uses Spanish, Spanish and English (what he calls Tex-Mex language), and English to express his feel-

ings, an important element in defining the triple sensitivity of a Chicano. —Jesús Rosales

Ignatow, David. Edited by Virginia R. Terris. *At My Ease: Uncollected Poems of the Fifties and Sixties.* 136p. pap. $13.50 (1-880238-55-1). Rochester, NY: BOA Editions, Spring 1998. Drawing from literary fathers Walt Whitman and William Carlos Williams, Ignatow writes poems that eschew ornamentation as they locate the fierce, uncompromising truths of the human spirit. These poems reflect city life weaving in and out of taxis, subways, and crowds, meditate on chance meetings and observe strangers at work. —BOA Editions

Ignatow, David. *I Have a Name.* 75p. pap. $11.95 (0-8195-2240-6). University Press of New England/Wesleyan University Press, Fall 1996; Spring 1997 (paper). [Ignatow's] language, which is without ornament and beautiful in its honesty, does not date. —Poetry. Ignatow is a superb, a major poet. What I like most about I Have a Name is what I have always liked most about his poems, the wisdom, and the humility. They are truly there. We are in the presence of an overwhelmingly important voice. It is eternity speaking. —Gerald Stern. Beautiful — very moving and individual. Ignatow is a true and honest poet whose engagement with life has been and is passionate. We are fortunate to have his unique distillation of a life. —Ruth Stone

Iino, Tomoyuki. *The History of Rain.* 24p. pap. $7.00 (1-877593-03-6). Port Washington, NY: Groundwater Press, Spring 1997. The first book of poems published by the Japanese translator of John Ashbery. —Groundwater Press

Inada, Lawson Fusao. *Drawing the Line.* 140p. pap. $12.95 (1-56689-060-8). Minneapolis, MN: Coffee House Press, Spring 1997. As World War II began, not only were Japanese Americans herded into internment camps, the young men were then drafted. But at Heart Mountain, a group of resisters drew the line—they refused to comply, on constitutional grounds—and wound up in federal prison. Inada revisits this moment of history with pain, pride, and thoughtful historical perspective. . . . This is a rich, varied collection of poems brimming with hope, nourished by the wisdom of the past, alive with the elec-

tricity of the moment. — Coffee House Press

Inez, Colette. *Clemency.* 92p. pap. $11.95 (0-88748-270-8). Pittsburgh, PA: Carnegie Mellon University Press, Spring 1998. Inez's work can be characterized as lively, literate, passionate and learned. . . every poem becomes a kind of mirror in which she contemplates the mysteries of her "demon mask." —Library Journal. Her curiosity is insatiable, her intuition is vibrant and somehow right. It is a joy to observe her vivid language at work. —Robert McDowell, Hudson Review

Inman, Sue Lile. *Voice Lessons.* 64p. pap. $10.00 (0-9645778-3-6). Greenville, SC: Emrys Press, Spring 1998. Though Voice Lessons shifts from a rendering of a young woman's life in the early pages to a more mature woman's take on the world, it feels all of a piece from beginning to end. —Frances Dowell, The Writers' Network News

Isaksson, Kimberly. *Judgment.* 24p. Good Poet Press, Fall 1998.

Iskrenko, Nina. Translated by John High, Patrick Henry and Katya Olmsted. *The Right to Err.* 108p. $15.00 (0-89410-

806-9). pap. $14.00 (0-89410-807-7). Pueblo, CO: Passeggiata Press, Fall 1995. The fundamental quality of Iskrenko's poetry is excess. Literary critics, perplexed by each new development, have enrolled the poet in the camp of Polystylistics. For Iskrenko, however, the constant running of one word into the next, the confusion of style and vocabulary, crossed-out words, slips of the tongue, word games, and idiosyncrasies are not an aesthetic platform. It is, rather, an agonizing and desperate attempt to adequately show to the world the human essence of the poet. —Evgenii Bunimovich

Issa, Kobayashi. Translated by Sam Hamill. *The Spring of My Life and Selected Haiku.* 184p. pap. $14.00 (1-57062-144-6). Boston, MA: Shambhala Publications, Fall 1997. Issa, along with Basho and Buson, is considered one of the three greatest haiku poets of Japan, known for his attention to poignant detail and his playful sense of humor. Issa's most-loved work, The Spring of My Life, is an autobiographical sketch of linked prose and haiku in the tradition of Basho's famous Narrow Road to the Interior. —Shambhala

Publications. Issa's renowned Spring of My Life has found a brilliant voice in Sam Hamill. These poems have the quiet dominance of the moon. — Jim Harrison

Ivry, Benjamin. *Paradise for the Portugese Queen.* 80p. pap. $12.95 (0-914061-69-0). Alexandria, VA: Orchises Press, Spring 1998. Deeply observant, Ivry is a lyrical intellectual. He experiences his reading and reads his experiences. At times he is reminiscent of Auden. The music of his verses is real and felt music. I wish Paradise for the Portugese Queen a substantial and well-deserved acclaim. —Muriel Spark. Not since Henry J.M. Levet (natch?) have Europe's cultural follies been so wildly, so wistfully, so wittily intoned. Immerse these pretty crystals in the water on your brain and presto! — or largo, perhaps — instant Untergang! —Richard Howard

Ivy, Evie. *Characters: I Like Myself the Way I Am.* 36p. pap. $6.00 (0-9622889-9-3). Bronx, nY: Something More Publications, Fall 1998.

Jackson, Angela. *And All These Roads Be Luminous: Poems Selected and New.* 197p. pap. $14.95 (0-8101-

5077-8). Northwestern University Press/TriQuarterly Books, Spring 1998. And All These Roads Be Luminous is filled with an impressive variety of characters engaged in compelling explorations of identity, creativity, spiritual experience, and the rites and rituals of race and sexuality. Jackson moves with ease from the personal to the historical. Filled alternately with wonder, righteous anger, tenderness, and a tangible intensity, Jackson's is a rich and passionate voice. — Northwestern University Press

Jackson, Gale P. *Bridge Suite.* 83p. pap. $15.00. Brooklyn, NY: Storm Imprints, Spring 1998. Narrative poems based on the the lives of African and African American women in the early history of these new black nations. —Storm Imprints

Jackson, Gale P. *Khoisan Tale: Of Beginnings and Ends.* 12p. pap. $10.00. Brooklyn, NY: Storm Imprints, Spring 1998. An adaptation of a Southern African folktale. — Storm Imprints

Jacobik, Gray. *The Double Task.* 75p. pap. $10.95 (1-55849-142-2). Amherst, MA: University of Massachusetts Press, Spring 1998. Winner of the 1997 Juniper Prize. The language of these poems is rich, sonorous, and precise. The intelligence is keen and never flagging. Add to this a sensuality that is occasionally sexy and always appealing. The combination of these qualities makes Jacobik a rare poet, one not to be missed. — James Tate. Her language is both lush and smart, rich and crafted. Jacobik's cultural scope allows her, like the English Metaphysicals, to use what she knows to discover and express what she feels. Open this book, and it will pull you in. —Billy Collins. There is a sensuousness of language married to unabashed passion and the richness of her mind. Jacobik captures female awareness in its physical magnitude and celebrates the larger, often ecstatic, victory beyond. — Linda Gregg

Jacobs, Alan, ed. *The Element Book of Mystical Verse.* 532p. $39.95 (1-85230-875-3). Boston, MA: Element Books, Fall 1997. The most comprehensive collection of mystical verse available today, it contains poems from writers as diverse as Donne, Dante, Rosetti, Whitman, Thoreau and Bly, poetic passages from the Bible, the Upanishads and the Bhagavad Gita and works by religious figures such as Teresa of Avila, Rumi and Ramana Maharishi. — Element Books

Jacobs, Bruce A. *Speaking Through My Skin.* 62p. pap. $10.95 (0-87013-455-8). East Lansing, MI: Michigan State University Press/Lotus Poetry Series, Spring 1997. Jacobs's poems feel direct, honest, a mix of the different worlds he's moved in, always observing, saying what he has to, incredibly aware of the ironies, the laughs on ourselves. I like the way his work shows me what I forgot I knew about some relationships as well as angles I haven't seen, don't know. —Lyn Lifshin

Jacobs, J.L. *The Leaves in Her Shoes.* 66p. pap. $12.00 (0-918786-49-5). Barrington, RI: Lost Roads Publishers, Fall 1998. The Leaves in Her Shoes blends aspects of the everyday and the spiritual, infusing simple domestic rituals with latent wonder. With a deft hand Jacobs mixes the "voice above," the voice of the spiritual and divine, and the "voice below," that of earth and life. —Lost Roads Publishers. I don't think I've ever read a first book of poems so haunted as The

Leaves in Her Shoes. Reading these poems is like listening to snatches of song or overhearing half-sentences, mutterings, broken chants of a lost tribe. Jacobs assembles these shards into a startling and unforgettable collage. —Carol Muske

Jacobson, Bonnie. *In Joanna's House.* 54p. pap. $12.00 (1-880834-42-1). Cleveland, OH: Cleveland State University Poetry Center, Fall 1998. In this brilliant sequence of forty-six 26-line poems, Jacobson has created a memorable character, whom we laugh at, but can't help loving. —Cleveland State University Poetry Center

Jacques, Geoffrey. *Suspended Knowledge.* 27p. pap. $8.00 (0-938566-77-6). Easthampton, MA: Adastra Press, Fall 1998. Ten poems in a breezy, jazz-riffing voice. — Adastra Press

Jaffe, Louise M. *The Great Horned Owl's Proclamation and Other Hoots.* 58p. $10.95 (0-944957-90-0). New York, NY: Rivercross Publishing, Fall 1997. These are poems that provide a refreshingly new approach to life in the natural world. At the same time, they satirize the limitations of egotistical human beings. Give a listen! Give a hoot! Enjoy! —Rivercross Publishing

Jaffe, Maggie. *How the West Was One.* 96p. pap. $12.00 (1-885215-19-3). Tucson, AZ: Viet Nam Generation/Burning Cities Press, Fall 1997. How the West Was One lifts the veil of history and reveals the corruption, greed, and arrogance that hide behind noble-sounding phrases. Jaffe's poignant poetry transcends propaganda and didacticism and shows the impossibility of separating the political from the personal. —Jon Forrest Glade

Janeczko, Paul B. Illustrated by Carole Katchen. *That Sweet Diamond: Baseball Poems.* 39p. $16.00 (0-689-80735-X). Simon & Schuster/Atheneum, Spring 1998. Whether offering a "Prayer for the Umpires" or "A Curse Upon the Pitcher," advice on "How to Spit" when at the plate, or "Things to Do During a Rain Delay," Janeczko's images are as sharp as the crack of a bat and as inspiring as a ball hit way over the fence. Here is a collection of poems for baseball fans of all ages. —Simon & Schuster

Jare, Karen. *The Third Day.* 104p. pap. $12.00 (1-879742-32-2). New York, NY: Jewish Women's Resource Center, Spring 1998. Jar's poems are remarkable. Intense, delicate, magical, Jare is a poet who knows what matters; her poems give us tenderness, wisdom, and heart. —Maria Mazziotti Gillan

Jarman, Mark. *Question for Ecclesiastes.* 100p. $22.00 (1-885266-42-1). pap. $10.00 (1-885266-41-3). Ashland, OR: Story Line Press, Spring 1997. Nominated for a National Book Critics Circle Award. In this deeply impressive collection, Jarman is concerned with God, His grace, and humans' relation with Him. In 20 "Unholy Sonnets," he takes up matters of theology directly and so appositely for these times that some of them may become pulpit as well as anthology staples. —Booklist. In his sixth collection, Jarman, a preacher's son, continues his impressive probe into the meaning and pretenses of holiness. With a biblical cadence, he devotes carefully articulated attention to the life around him. His forte lies in his ability to cherish things as minuscule as the buttonholes on a child's dress. —Library Journal

Jarnot, Lisa; Leonard Schwartz and Chris Stroffolino. *An Anthology of*

New (American) Poets. 352p. pap. $21.95 (1-883689-61-9). Jersey City, NJ: Talisman House, Publishers, Spring 1998. Brings together representative selections from thirty-five of the most promising young American poets at work today. —Talisman House. Read this book if you think nothing's happened in poetry since The Beats, Black Mountain, several generations of New York School, San Francisco Renaissance, Language Poetry & followers went historic. Read this book by a wild conglomeration of independents to keep faith in the scintillating rhizomatic dance of language. Read this book for challenge & pleasure. It's a welcome "thinking" compendium of the vital American — bigger than that, planetary — poetry scene. And a boon to the ongoing struggle to keep the world safe for poetry. A bow to the new generation. —Anne Waldman

Jarvenpa, Diane. *Divining the Landscape.* 59p. pap. $11.95 (0-89823-168-X). Minneapolis, MN: New Rivers Press, Fall 1996. Jarvenpa tells us there are things we cannot see: how flowers grow, what the prairie dreams, how summers come, where muskrats go. She honors too the complexities of the people closest to her, like her immigrant grandparents and her parents. She knows there are some things that can only be explained with poetry. That is why these poems begin with words but always end in music. —Jim Johnson

Jason, Philip K.; Barbara Goldberg, Geraldine Connolly, and Roland Flint, eds. *Open Door: A Poet Lore Anthology 1980-1996.* 98p. pap. $10.95 (0-9654010-0-6). Bethesda, MD: Writer's Center Editions, Spring 1997.

Jasson-Holt, Sophie. *Unfold the Chaparral.* 74p. pap. $10.95. San Francisco State University Chapbook Series, Fall 1996. Jasson-Holt manages to get inside language and make it work for her in original, striking ways. The world of these poems is erotically charged, and she not only sounds it out with skill and daring but explores the limits of the page itself. She is clearly a poet unafraid to take risks. —August Kleinzahler. Jasson-Holt breaks ground in her first collection. Her tilted language and her questioning, conditional approach to subject excite the lyric impulse at the core of each poem. Her minimalist instincts must yield over and over to the sensuous image. The result is a tense, lush poem. Unfold the Chaparral introduces a poet of fierce delicacy. —Frances Mayes

Jaycox, Faith, ed. *Ebony Angels: A Collection of African-American Poetry and Prose.* 96p. pap. $10.00 (0-517-88746-0). New York, NY: Crown Publishers, Fall 1996. The first collection of poetry and prose excerpts from the work of African-American literary figures, religious leaders, social commentators, and political activists, all rich in the imagery and spirituality of angels. Includes work by Martin Luther King Jr., Phyllis Wheatley, W.E.B. Du Bois, Langston Hughes, Bessie Smith, Countee Cullen, Amiri Baraka, Ntozake Shange, Toni Morrison, and many others. —Crown Publishers

Jayme, Michael. *Look Back and Laugh.* 10p. Berkeley, CA: Chicano Chapbook Series, Fall 1997. The Chicano Chapbook Series, edited by Gary Soto, issued twelve title in the late 1970's and early 1980's, including works by Sandra Cisneros, Alberto Ríos, Jimmy Santiago Baca and others. The chapbooks are distributed free of charge to selected libraries with Chicano collections. Look Back and Laugh is #16.

Jenkins, Jerry H. *Avian.* 36p. pap. $5.00. Palo Alto, CA: Anamnesis Press, Spring 1997. Second Prize winner in the 1996 Anamnesis Poetry Chapbook competition.

Jenkins, Louis. *Just Above Water: Prose Poems.* 73p. pap. $10.95 (0-930100-75-1). Duluth, MN: Holy Cow! Press, Fall 1997. It's a beautiful book, brilliant and stubborn, full of poems. . . that you read and then look for someone to read out loud to. I don't think they have poets like this outside of Minnesota. You have to go through a long winter to get this good. — Garrison Keillor. Most people writing prose poems now agree that Jenkins is the contemporary master. —Robert Bly

Jenkins, Paul. *Radio Tooth.* 51p. pap. $12.95 (1-884800-11-4). Marshfield, MA: Four Way Books, Spring 1997. Winner of the 1995 Four Way Books Award Series. These are bold poems, rugged and good, hard the way diamonds should be, but the way coconuts are as well. These works both sustain and delight, but what I'm saying most is that they crack open, and constantly. "Past the tired cemetery where the three year old / Asks what's that little city made of teeth," these poems surprise and push, line by line. —Alberto Ríos

Jobe, James Lee. *Red Skelton's Ghost.* 33p. pap. $4.00. Cold River Press, Fall 1998.

Johnson, Angela. *The Other Side: Shorter Poems.* 44p. $15.95 (0-531-30114-1). New York, NY: Orchard Books, Fall 1998. A Coretta Scott King Award Author Honor Book. On a journey back in time, a young woman recounts her thoughts about growing up in Shorter, Alabama — about the people and landscape of her childhood and adolescence. Johnson has created a narrator with a clear voice, rich in emotion, that young and old alike will understand. Her deceptively simple poems are focused, honest, and thoughtful. —Orchard Books

Johnson, Eric. *Buffalo, Rome.* 80p. pap. $8.00 (0-9655547-0-8). Santa Monica, CA: Split Shift, Spring 1997. An elegant book. I love Johnson's drawings. The visual delicacy of the graphics & verbal images makes a nice synergy with the content of the text. It is a very readable & engaging book. I

find myself going back repeatedly for another hit. —Shaun McNiff

Johnson, Jacqueline. *A Gathering of Mother Tongues.* 119p. pap. $12.00 (1-877727-79-2). Buffalo, NY: White Pine Press, Fall 1998. Here is the poetry of proclamation and purification. Johnson claims not only language but also the ground beneath her feet. She gives birth to herself and restores her own memory. I believe this poet comes out of the stars. She reminds us why the sky is so beautiful and African American literature so rich. Johnson asks a very important question which must be answered: "Where does a black woman go for freedom?" —E. Ethelbert Miller

Johnson, Margery A. *Celestial Dreamsongs.* 72p. pap. $12.00 (1-56474-218-0). Santa Barbara, CA: Fithian Press, Spring 1997. Johnson's verse has a simplicity and freshness that should appeal to many readers. —J.F. Webb

Johnson, Peter. *Love Poems for the Millennium.* 36p. pap. $5.00 (0-9656161-2-6). Haydenville, MA: Quale Press, Fall 1998. These prose poems are love poems — comic, sexual, and endlessly inventive. It may be only coincidental that the cities and places titling these poems find their namesakes in travel brochures. But maybe not. Reality is a strange place, in constant drift, like the very continents of this planet. Sometimes it is only coincidence that brings together the lost edges, so that chance becomes coincidence, and coincidence becomes fate. — Russell Edson

Johnson, Peter. *Pretty Happy!: Prose Poems.* 94p. pap. $12.00 (1-877727-75-X). Buffalo, NY: White Pine Press, Fall 1997. The excitement of prose poetry is that it transgresses the rules to let the reader catch a glimpse of what could be called the true life of the imagination. This is what Johnson gives us. What more could we ask of a book of poems? —Charles Simic. In these madcap works, the profane is what we know of glory. There is a dark beauty here and fearful edginess. —Jay Meek. Johnson is a champion of the prose poem and one of its most eminent practitioners. These poems send the reader spinning from one world to another. It's an exhilarating ride. —Louis Jenkins

Johnston-Rowbotham. *The Not-So-Perfect, Perfect Parent Bill of Rights.* 109p. pap.

$12.95 (1-880254-56-5). Long Branch, NJ: Vista Publishing, Fall 1998.

Jolliff, William. *Whatever Was Ripe.* 42p. pap. $6.00 (0-9646844-8-9). Treadwell, NY: Bright Hill Press, Fall 1998. Winner of the 1997 Bright Hill Press Poetry Chapbook Competition. These vigorous poems are packed with delights of the land and language, the joys and longings of the human heart. —Walt MacDonald. A hard-earned elegy of life on the farm in southern Ohio. [Jolliff's] poems are sturdy as burlap and true as a furrow left behind a careful plowman. — Paul Willis

Jonas, Ann Rae. *A Diamond Is Hard But Not Tough.* 64p. pap. $10.00 (0-915380-36-6). Washington, DC: Word Works, Spring 1998. 1997 Washington Prize Winner. Jonas's deceptively low-key poems offer a wealth of distilled information often pressed into service as metaphor; her imagery is drawn from disciplines as diverse as physics, geology, cartography, and archaeology. But Jonas also knows — or feels — a good deal of what it means to be human; this is her true subject, approached patiently and skillfully in laconic poems dense with hard-won wisdom. —Rachel Hadas

Jones, Dwyer. *Fabulous Meat City.* 64p. pap. $5.00 (1-877968-11-0). Manasquan, NJ: Iniquity Press/Vendetta Books, 1996.

Jones, Hettie. *Drive.* 120p. $21.00 (1-882413-51-2). pap. $12.00 (1-882413-50-4). Brooklyn, NY: Hanging Loose Press, Spring 1998. [Jones] knows where all the pedals are but hardly needs them. She flies with language, and there's an unleaded heart in her tank. —Lawrence Ferlinghetti. Jones is a bird, a strong singer, loud in the street-rooted honeysuckle, her joy unkillable. Right in the face of New York, she comes with her straight gaze, her hot wit, and her rich felt life. She sees more chances more sharply than most of us. And she takes them at top speed, riding the spin of her own verbal music. I love her display of what it is to be alive; I love her poems, because they are beautiful. — Marie Ponsot

Jones, Hettie, ed. *Aliens at the Border: The Writing Workshop, Bedford Hills Correctional Facility.* 68p. pap. $8.00 (0-937804-66-5). New York, NY: Segue Books, 1997. With this second collec-tion, Jones's group sings so tellingly, so irresistibly that we find the walls dissolving. These writers feel themselves to be aliens at the border. But if this candor and courage, this hard-won compassion, be alien, what is left for the rest of us? —Bell Chevigny. Time of the same old same old in late 20th Century American poetry? Try this book for an honest and humbling read. When poetry is good, it refreshes us. When it's great, it surprises, challenges and changes us. I suspect this book is the latter. —Cornelius Eady. To read Aliens at the Border is to attend a gathering of remarkable voices. This collection is a testament to the fact that the mind and the heart cannot be confined. — Chuck Wachtel

Jones, Jean. *I Have Seen the Mermaids Singing.* 36p. pap. $2.95 (0-9648133-1-9). Tulsa, OK: New Thought Journal Press, Fall 1997.

Jones, Richard. *48 Questions.* 64p. pap. $10.00 (0-941017-30-3). Huntington Beach, CA: Tebot Bach, Spring 1998. Jones is one of the most vital and compelling voices of his generation. His art is so skill-fully subtle as to become almost transparent, while his poetry opens a luminous world. —Sam Hamill

Jones, Rodney. *Things That Happen Once: New Poems.* 96p. $19.95 (0-395-77143-9). pap. $14.00 (0-395-85601-9). Boston, MA: Houghton Mifflin Company, Spring 1996; Spring 1997 (paper). Selected by Publishers Weekly as one of the Best Books of 1996. Jones' poems are blood-stirring, white-hot things. One can but marvel at this poet's demonic energy and demotic bravura. —Washington Post Book World

Jong, Erica. *Fruits & Vegetables.* 87p. $21.00 (0-88001-569-1). Hopewell, NJ: Ecco Press, Fall 1997. Here is the 25th anniversary edition of Erica Jong's first book: a sur-realistic, funny, gastronomic, erotic, serious look at being human and female and American. —Ecco Press. I read these poems the way you watch a trapeze act, with held breath, marveling at the agili-ty, the lightness of touch, the brilliant demonstration of the difficult made to look easy. —Margaret Atwood. Out of the commingled pleasure of the table and the bed, [Jong] makes a high, not frivolous, comedy. This is a reckless and shameless first book, and

it is a joy to read. —Stanley Kunitz

Jordan, Barbara. *Trace Elements.* 64p. pap. $14.95 (0-14-026531-7). New York, NY: Penguin Books/Viking Penguin, Spring 1998. Jordan's vision has always been twofold: that of the reli-gious contemplative and that of the more empirically-mind-ed Linnaean scientist. The poems here — bracing, often terrifying, all the more so for the grace and mind and lan-guage behind them — posit faith as something archaeolog-ically retrievable, and science not as a means of dismantling but of bringing us ever closer to the sacred. Trace Elements reads like a hymnal for the nuclear age — that elegiac, and that persuasive. —Carl Phillips

Jordan, June. *Kissing God Goodbye: Poems 1991-1997.* 100p. pap. $12.00 (0-385-49032-1). New York, NY: Doubleday/Anchor Books, Spring 1998. Jordan's work, at this point and for many years now, is perfect. She says exactly what she means to say, and says it so powerfully that the reader hears each phrase. She manages to tap into that place where race and sexuali-ty, class and justice, gender and memory come together.

She doesn't go with the cutting-edge idea but reaches for that difficult terrain where others may fear to tread. —American Book Review. She is among the bravest of us, the most outraged. She feels for all. She is the universal poet. —Alice Walker. Jordan is one of the most musically and lyrically gifted poets of the late twentieth century. —Adrienne Rich

Joseph, Allison. *In Every Seam.* 92p. $25.00 (0-8229-3994-0). pap. $12.95 (0-8229-5641-1). Pittsburgh, PA: University of Pittsburgh Press, Spring 1997. A wry and bittersweet narrative of the growth of the poet's mind, a coming of age account which is refreshing because it is shorn of easy and familiar visionary posturings in favor of a hard-bitten realism. An impressive achievement. —David Wojahn. In these powerful, lucid poems, Joseph looks unflinchingly at the chronic angers of an unromanticized urban childhood. The vividly rendered neighborhoods of In Every Seam unfold before us, showing us how the young are taught over and over that the glittering, sparkling, dazzling things of the world are beyond their grasp. But Joseph, a survivor of these neighborhoods, brilliantly disproves these

lessons. In Every Seam is literally a triumph. —Maura Stanton

Joseph, Allison. *Soul Train.* 83p. pap. $11.95 (0-88748-247-3). Pittsburgh, PA: Carnegie Mellon University Press, Spring 1997. Unabashedly jubilant, always direct in her manner, and possessed of an abundant relish of bodily life, [Joseph] has created a moving book by baring the anatomy of one of our poetry's most neglected subjects: fun. —Rodney Jones. Joseph's poems pulsate with nostalgic seventies' details—disco balls, pants suits, Shaft, and Chaka Khan—and resonate a deep understanding of those in-between times: puberty, the nomadic life of early marriage, the adjustment of her immigrant parents to life in the U.S. Full of glittering detail and rhythmic precocity, Joseph's Soul Train is indeed "the hippest trip in America." —Denise Duhamel

József, Attila. Translated by John Bátki. *Winter Night: Selected Poems.* 127p. pap. $14.95 (0-932440-78-9). Oberlin, OH: Oberlin College Press, Fall 1997. In pure song-like lyrics and longer elegiac poems József inscribed not ' only his own sad fate but that of millions in an East Europe that was only nominally "between the wars" during the '20's and '30's of our century. His poetics informed by Marx and Freud, his brooding passions break through the barriers of poverty and alienation, and transcend conditions that are local and historical. — Oberlin College Press

Justice, Donald. *New and Selected Poems.* 176p. pap. $16.00 (0-679-76598-0). New York, NY: Knopf, Alfred A., Fall 1995; Spring 1997 (paper). Using fully the complexities of his language, Justice has always demonstrated that the highest purpose of literature is to illuminate those things which are hard, disturbing, painful, moving, and repeat themselves — not to obscure them. —John Irving. Justice, is, among other things, the supreme heir of Wallace Stevens. His brilliance is never at the service of merely flash and display; it is always subservient to experienced truth, to accuracy, to Justice, the ancient virtue as well as the personal signature. He is one of our finest poets. — Anthony Hecht

Kacian, Jim. *Six Directions: Haiku & Field Notes.* 88p. pap. $10.00 (0-9631909-4-6). Albuquerque, NM: La Alameda Press, Spring 1998.

The cycling seasons and the very elements themselves speak to us in these meditative haiku and haibun. Like Thoreau at Walden Pond, Kacian celebrates in the rhythms of Six Directions those of the planet itself. — Penny Harter

Kacian, Jim, ed. *The Red Moon Anthology, 1996.* 146p. pap. $13.95 (0-9657818-0-1). Winchester, VA: Red Moon Press, Spring 1997. A compendium of the finest haiku, senryu, haibun, renku, sequences and theoretical articles published around the world in English in 1996. — Red Moon Press. An excellent volume that is a recommended addition to any personal or institutional library. — Modern Haiku

Kacian, Jim, ed. *The Red Moon Anthology, 1997.* 150p. pap. $13.95 (0-9657818-5-2). Winchester, VA: Red Moon Press, Fall 1998. Two hundred and twelve haiku, senryu, haibun, sequences, linked forms, and essays, culled from hundreds of books, magazines and newspapers from around the world by eleven internationally prominent editors — the best of 1997. —Red Moon Press. This outstanding anthology fills an important void in contemporary haiku literature.

—Lee Gurga, Haiku Society of America

Kamenetz, Rodger. *Stuck: Poems Midlife.* 67p. pap. $12.50 (1-56809-033-1). St. Louis, MO: Time Being Books, Fall 1997. These are grim and meaty poems, carefully crafted and tight. The experiences dealt with are those that break people, but these poems are far from broken. For a slender volume, it is remarkably substantial. —Marge Piercy

Kang Dean, Debra. *News of Home.* 95p. pap. $12.50 (1-880238-66-7). Rochester, NY: BOA Editions, Fall 1998. Daughter of Korean and Okinawan parents in Hawai'i, Kang Dean explores the juxtaposed territories of the outsider by virtue of ancestry and the insider by virtue of birth. —BOA Editions. Kang Dean thinks big, sharing a sense of her life as it arcs from O'ahu across the Pacific to the mainland United States. A poet reconciling words, doing honor to the language, telling us what it means to be alive "free to look in both directions, behind us and ahead," she makes a memorable and exciting debut in this first book. —Colette Inez

Kaplan, Carol Genyea. *An Ordinary Heart.* 58p. pap.

$12.00 (1-56439-069-1). Detroit, MI: Ridgeway Press, Fall 1997. Kaplan['s] poems are as passionate as they are precise, the combination of deep feeling and concrete image show a remarkable fusion of a biologist's specificity and a poet's startling turns of emotion. —Daniel Hughes. Kaplan brings her fine knowledge of science to bear on a poetry that is, not withstanding, never dry, or cold. Quite the opposite. A caring conscience and emotional intensity are the hallmarks of this poets' deeply involving work. —Mitzi Alvin, The Bridge

Kaplan, Janet. *The Groundnote.* 79p. pap. $11.95 (1-882295-19-6). Farmington, ME: Alice James Books, Fall 1998. Passion and intelligence, the hallmarks of Kaplan's poetry, rank her among the leading poets of the newest generation of American writers. Miraculously, luminously, she places her gut-wrenching personal history in the wider contexts of myth, class, and geography. Not only is it unusual, it is downright thrilling to read a first book of such stature, plucky grace, and range. —Molly Peacock

Kaplan, Janet. *The Solid Ground.* 10p. pap. $3.00.

Saunderstown, RI: Premiere Poets Chapbook Series, Fall 1996.

Karageorge, Penelope Sevaste. *Red Lipstick and the Wine-dark Sea.* 87p. pap. $10.00 (0-918618-67-3). New York, NY: Pella Publishing, Fall 1997. In a series of vivid and haunting images, Karageorge embraces both a geographic landscape and a terrain of the heart. Whether writing of the silence of a Greek island or of the clatter of a New York street, of fleeting love or the shackles and joys of family life, she captivates and enriches her readers. —Harry Mark Petrakis. As if to imitate her Homeric namesake, Karageorge has woven her American identity by day and unwoven it at night to honor her Greek identity, and thus she's been true to her homesick heart — neither 'here" nor "there" but alive and at home in her restless, brave imagination. —William Matthews

Karos, George. *Biorhythm Dais.* 24p. pap. $4.00 (0-9637704-8-9). Alexandria, VA: Red Dragon Press, Spring 1997. Filled with images revealed as modern archetypes, Karos's poetry marks personal parallels between the cycles of physiological bio-rhythm and the functional transformations of the intellect, seemingly out of control and constantly changing with the external environment. — Red Dragon Press

Karr, Mary. *Viper Rum.* 78p. $19.95 (0-8112-1382-X). New York, NY: New Directions, Spring 1998. Hardboiled, hardedged, hardbitten — these are consummately American adjectives, and peculiarly American literary postures. Karr's bracing, tightlipped poems bring these terms to mind, but it's a credit to her probity and her prickly intelligence that one stops short of defining her by them. Avowedly unsentimental, Karr doesn't overcompensate by striking exaggerated poses of disabused wisdom or affecting mandarin disdain for the muddle of human relations. But, like the late laureate of desolation Philip Larkin, Karr evidently holds that "suffering is exact." —Poetry. Like Larkin and Heaney, Karr intends poetry of the plain style and the truth of the unmistakably situated self, but is taught also, by desire, to expect that among the deliquescent ruins of the final body there will be found, as she says, "illumined, my soul at last uncaged from ribs, rising." —Allen Grossman

Kasdorf, Julia. *Eve's Striptease.* 86p. $25.00 (0-8229-4064-7). pap. $12.95 (0-8229-5668-3). Pittsburgh, PA: University of Pittsburgh Press, Spring 1998. "You are embraced this instant," says Kasdorf in one of these poems, and in another, "hanging on. . . is our only home." Such plainspoken gestures reveal not only the robust particularity of her imagination, but also its sexual nerve and essentially affirmative nature. Crosshatched by body, spirit, and the relation between them; animated by bright instinctive exchanges between carnal and religious zone of experience; driven by an honest, explicitly female consciousness of what "animal" and "soul" might mean, the poems in Eve's Striptease keep pace with a considered life in its search for some consoling "homeliness" in the world. —Eamon Grennan

Kashner, Sam. *Don Quixote in America.* 80p. $20.00 (1-882413-39-3). pap. $12.00 (1-882413-38-5). Brooklyn, NY: Hanging Loose Press, Spring 1997. Astonishing, unnervingly friendly poems. True American originals. —Agha Shahid Ali. Kashner has a way of stopping, abruptly, and making us take not a second look, but a longer first look, in fact a look so long we are flat-on nose to nose with the object of our attentions. Snatched forward and planted with such force we find ourselves in a breathless moment of Zen astonishment. And yet who can take us by the hand and lead us over the edge more subtly than Kashner, interweaving the real and the surreal so flawlessly readers are feeling right at home before even noticing that the furniture they are sitting on is really quite strange. — Maureen Owen

Kasischke, Laura. *Fire and Flower.* 66p. $1-882295-21-8.00. (11.95). Farmington, ME: Alice James Books, Fall 1998. [Kasischke's world] is a world in which grace and horror, beauty and carnage, tragedy and hilarity commingle. —Harvard Review. Kasischke peels back the blander sufaces of the quotidian as if to find the unconscious realm just beneath the Formica. —James Harms. Sex, death and a weird spirituality are wired together here in loose animistic narratives which have both wit and morbid drama. I recommend Kasischke to readers and writers in need of energy, recklessness and style. —Tony Hoagland

Katrovas, Richard.
Dithyrambs: Choral Lyrics.
102p. $20.95 (0-88748-252-X). pap. $11.95 (0-88748-253-8). Pittsburgh, PA: Carnegie Mellon University Press, Spring 1998. Katrovas revives the choral lyric form and bravely explores the form's possibilities for late twentieth century verse. These vehement, ecstatic, gnomic choral voices most resemble the exuberance of the raucous, participatory audiences of contemporary "talk television," ingeniously interspersed with dramatic monologues addressed to the imaginary world of television land. His parodies rise to high camp, while somehow never quite forsaking the pathos of genuine desire. —Carolyn Forché. Originality of this kind is rare. . . large and ambitious. Katrovas's dithyrambs — and they really are a modern version of that ancient rhapsodic form — make for a bold and fascinating experiment. —Donald Justice

Katz, Eliot. *Unlocking the Exits.* 144p. pap. $13.95 (1-56689-079-9). Minneapolis, MN: Coffee House Press, Fall 1998. Another classic New Jersey bard! Katz has created his own original poetics for personal observation, animated discourse, critical insight, fantasy, and communal vision. His verses bespeak the colloquial heart of world tragedy and hope from his haunts, New Brunswick U.S.A. — Allen Ginsberg. For years, Katz has been an exuberant heir of Walt Whitman, William Carlos Williams, and Allen Ginsberg. He has been oracular, comic, furiously compassionate, explosively and winsomely political, madly inventive, acutely vernacular. To read or hear him is to become energized by his contagious humanity. And now Katz has become a major poet of witness. —Alicia Ostriker

Kaufman, Alan. *Who Are We?.* 94p. pap. $9.95 (1-881822-01-X). San Francisco, CA: Davka: Jewish Cultural Revolution, Fall 1997. A new young Kerouac. Kaufman's poetry has the bebop sound of the best Beat poetry. —Ruthe Stein, San Francisco Chronicle. [Kaufman is] a great young poet. His verbal chords are big crashing blues chords and boogie-woogie chords and loud thrash poundings. Under that verbal rocking is the heart of Walt Whitman. —San Francisco Weekly

Keelan, Claudia. *The Secularist.* 85p. pap. $15.95 (0-8203-1802-7). Athens, GA: University of Georgia Press, Spring 1997. In this collection of "coming of age" poems, Keelan tests the limits of influence [of] literature, family and organized religion on her notions of self and God. —American Poet. The urgent intensity of Keelan's poetry is driven, it seems to me, by a peculiarly American desire: to inscribe the place of spirit, the positive site of belief, without embodying a specific religious faith. In these poems, there is a persistent haunting, a lament, a blues, an elegy. Her work is eloquent, unironic, and persuasive. —Ann Lauterbach

Keller, Lynn. *Forms of Expansion: Recent Long Poems by Women.* pap. $18.95 (0226429717). Chicago, IL: University of Chicago Press, 1997. Expanding the boundaries of both genre and gender, contemporary American women are writing long poems in a variety of forms that repossess history, reconceive female subjectivity, and revitalize poetry itself. In the first book devoted to long poems by women, Keller explores this rich and evolving body of work. —University of Chicago Press

Kelley, Harriet Stovall. *The ArctAngel and Other Cold Poems.* 28p. pap. $7.00. Dallas, TX: HaSk, Fall 1996.

Kelly, Robert. *The Time of Voice: Poems 1994-1996.* 188p. $27.50 (1-57423-080-8). pap. $15.00 (1-57423-079-4). Santa Rosa, CA: Black Sparrow Press, Fall 1998. Kelly's new poems are perhaps his most accessible to date, underscoring the familiar brilliance of mind and movement with a new depth of emotional understanding. This is writing that jump-starts not only the cerebrum, nerves and senses but the feeling heart: a poetry of key moments, necessary rituals, inevitable passages, recurrent beginnings and ends. —Black Sparrow Press

Kempher, Ruth Moon, ed. *Joyful Noise: Friendly Creatures 2.* 108p. pap. $12.00 (1-888832-00-2). St. Augustine, FL: Kings Estate Press, Fall 1996. Anthology of creature poems and short prose. —Kings Estate Press

Kempher, Ruth Moon, ed. *My Shameless St. Augustine Scrapbook.* 220p. pap. $18.50 (1-888832-11-8). St. Augustine, FL: Kings Estate Press, Spring 1998. Poems and short prose set in St.

Augustine, Florida. —Kings Estate Press

Kennedy, Dorothy M., ed. Illustrated by Sasha Meret. *Make Things Fly: Poems About the Wind.* 32p. $16.00 (0-689-81544-1). Simon & Schuster/Margaret K. McElderry Books, Spring 1998. Here is a rich collection of twenty-seven poems, some written specifically for children and some written for adults that children will enjoy as well. Included are poems by African-American and Asian-American writers as well as other familiar modern poets such as John Ciardi, Norma Farber, Aileen Fisher, Russell Hoban, Karla Kuskin, Myra Cohn Livingston, and Eve Merriam. Old favorites A.A. Milne, Christina Rossetti, and Robert Louis Stevenson are also represented. —Simon & Schuster

Kennedy, Jo Bowman. *Wind River Song.* 20p. pap. $3.50 (0-9625011-8-2). North Port, FL: Anabiosis Press, Spring 1998. Winner of the 1997 Anabiosis Press Chapbook Contest. The book's central metaphor is of fishing in the darkness. —Anabiosis Press

Kenyon, Jane. *Otherwise: New and Selected Poems.* 232p. $23.95 (1-55597-240-3).

pap. $16.00 (1-55597-266-7). St. Paul, MN: Graywolf Press, Spring 1996; Fall 1997 (paper). Selected for their Most Notable Book List by the American Library Association. One may also read these precise and lmpid works simply for the beauty of their expression. In a just world, Otherwise would become a bestseller. — Washington Post. Her words, with their quiet, rapt force, their pensiveness and wit, come to us from natural speech, from the Bible and hymns, from which she derived the singular psalmlike music that is hers alone. — New York Times Book Review

Kerman, Judith. *Mothering & Dream of Rain.* 65p. pap. $12.00 (1-56439-062-4). Detroit, MI: Ridgeway Press, Spring 1997. In every respect, a most exceptional book. — Robert Creeley. This is an image-rich, resonant book, rooted in the logic and sensory presence of a landscape on the borderlands of reality and dream. It cannot be paraphrased; it can be experienced: perhaps the final litmus-test of poetry. I like its coherence, its evocation of the physical world, its confrontation of the ambiguities of anger, tenderness and grief. —Marilyn Hacker

Kerner, Benjamin A. *A Petroglyph of His Own Choosing.* 82p. pap. $14.95 (0-9658945-0-9). Maple City, MI: Lin Com Press, Fall 1997. Lyric poems about the creative process, sailing, love and life on the Great Lakes. —Lin Com Press

Keys, Kerry Shawn. *Blues in Green: The Brazilian Poems.* 54p. pap. $10.00 (0-930502-20-5). Landisburg, PA: Pine Press, Fall 1996. Keys's poetry is very beautiful, tense and metaphorically rich. —Lêdo Ivo. What I love in Keys is the language, the marvelous language, and the exoticism, and the craziness, and the wonderful sane humor. —Gerald Stern

Keys, Kerry Shawn. *Narrow Passage to the Deep Light.* 72p. pap. $10.00 (0-930502-21-3). Landisburg, PA: Pine Press, Spring 1997.

Kikel, Rudy. *Period Pieces.* 100p. pap. $9.95 (1-886383-25-1). Lynnwood, WA: Pride Publications, Fall 1997. If Frank Bidart had written The Spoon River Anthology, if Rita Dove's Thomas and Beulah had been of Gottscheer stock, or if Marilyn Nelson Waniek's Magnificat had been a story of obsessive gay love, these poems might have been the result. Like any good poet Kikel talks to his ghosts but doesn't tame them. They begin to haunt us as well. —Jennifer Rose. To read [Kikel] is to gain a history lesson and an up-to-the-minute understanding of today's war bulletins from Sarajevo. Kikel's strong, clear voice carries the chronicle without a sidestep or stumble. A poet of large heart, crystalline insight and skillful technique. —Lois Ames

Kilcher, Jewel. *A Night Without Armor.* 139p. $15.00 (0-06-019198-8). New York, NY: HarperCollins Publishers, Fall 1998: Spring 1999 (new paper). In A Night Without Armor, Jewel explores the fire of first love, the fading of passion, the giving of trust, lessons of betrayal, and the healing of intimacy. Frank and honest, serious and suddenly playful, A Night Without Armor is an artist's intimate portrait of what makes us uniquely human. —HarperCollins

Kiley, Eve. *A Potpourri of Poetry.* 56p. pap. $6.00 (1-57502-682-1). Kearney, NE: Morris Publishing, Spring 1998. Her poetry socks it to you, even while it tears at your heartstrings. —Morris Publishing

Killian, Sean. *Feint by Feint.* 36p. pap. $4.00 (1-893032-01-9). Talisman House, Publishers / Jensen/Daniels, Fall 1998.

Kim, Chiha. Translated by Won-Chung Kim and James Han. *Heart's Agony: Selected Poems.* 104p. pap. $14.00 (1-877727-84-9). Buffalo, NY: White Pine Press, Spring 1998. Born in South Korea in 1941, Chiha Kim was first imprisoned in 1964 and sentenced to death in 1974. His crime: writing poetry that provoked the military government of Chunghee Park. Worldwide efforts to save him were begun in Japan, where his work had first been published. His sentence was commuted in 1980 following the assassination of Park and the downfall of his regime, a demise Kim predicted. A legendary figure in South Korea, Chiha Kim won the Lotus Prize, generally regarded as the Third World's Nobel Prize, while imprisoned in 1975. Heart's Agony gathers poetry from all phases of his career, including poems that led to his imprisonment and torture and those written from prison. —White Pine Press

Kim, Elaine H., and Lilia V. Villanueva, eds. *Making More Waves: New Writing by Asian American Women.* 308p. pap. $18.00 (0-8070-5913-7). Boston, MA: Beacon Press, Fall 1997. This inclusive new collection gathers a diverse range of poems, essays and fiction by Asian American women, established writers and new voices alike. — Beacon Press. Making More Waves is a continuum, a celebration and acknowledgment of our unique artistic visions, our differences, our often painful histories and complex experiences. An empowering collection. —Jessica Hagedorn

Kim, Myung Mi. *Dura.* 108p. pap. $11.95 (1-55713-292-5). Los Angeles, CA: Sun & Moon Press, Fall 1998. Conceived as one long poem, Dura is a whirling experimental symphony of images, forms and rhythms assembled and juxtaposed to translate the experience and gestures of the Korean immigrant woman surviving in America at the end of the twentieth century. Dura relates questions of history, gender, knowledge and power, registering tenuous yet tenacious links between cultures and languages that necessitates an on-going "translation" between here / there, east /

west, singular / collective, and subjugation and liberation. Dura is already on its way to being recognized as one of the most moving experimental "translations" in contemporary poetry. —Sun & Moon Press

Kim, Myung Mi. *Under Flag.* 46p. pap. $9.00 (0-932716-49-0). Berkeley, CA: Kelsey Street Press, Fall 1998. Winner of the 1991 Multicultural Publishers Book Award. Not since Oppen has the eroding presence of war on the wholeness of human existence been so vividly located. But the construction of perspective that has shifted from male to female, occupier to occupied. Kim's language is pure and commanding and brings us to a place of grieving we have needed to acknowledge. —Kathleen Fraser. [Kim's] work manifests the fact of poetry's undeniably ancient force as chronicle and political document. In Kim's work somewhere else is always here, as witness to a poetics which resists being neutralized or categorized. —Ammiel Alcalay

Kimball, Jack. *Quite Vacation.* 27p. pap. $6.00 (0-937013-83-8). Elmwood, CT: Potes & Poets Press, Fall 1998.

Kimbrell, James. *The Gatehouse Heaven.* 64p. $20.95 (1-889330-13-2). pap. $12.95 (1-889330-14-0). Louisville, KY: Sarabande Books, Spring 1998. Winner of the 1997 Kathryn A. Morton Prize in Poetry. Kimbrell sings a serious song. The poems are deft and sure, there is a sense of vision in them, and I have the feeling that this is the start of something significant. And if, as Flaubert said, language is like a cracked kettle on which we beat out tunes for bears to dance to, while all the time we long to move the stars to pity, then the stars have prime seating for these songs. —Charles Wright

Kimes, Marion. *Crows' Eyes: Of Multiplication and Light.* 34p. pap. $6.00. Winston, OR: nine muses books, Fall 1997.

Kincaid, Joan Payne. *Skinny-Dipping.* 24p. pap. $8.95. Arlington, VA: Bogg Publications, Fall 1998. A collection of formal and innovative poems focusing loosely on the conceit of skinny-dipping. —Small Press Review. A volume of white magic. —Maurice T. Watson

Kincaid, Joan Payne. *Understanding the Water.* 53p. pap. $12.95 (1-888832-03-7).

St. Augustine, FL: Kings Estate Press, Spring 1997. Poems centered in Long Island. From free verse to pantoum, to nineteenth century calligramme. . . sophisticated poetry. —Sandra Schofield

King, Willie James. *At the Forest Edge.* 42p. pap. $5.95 (0-9622815-7-3). Montgomery, AL: Black Belt Press, 1992.

Kinzie, Mary. *Ghost Ship.* 86p. $21.00 (0-679-44645-1). pap. $13.00 (0-679-76604-9). New York, NY: Knopf, Alfred A., Spring 1996; Fall 1997 (paper). Ghost Ship is Shakespearean in its verbal energy, its lavishness, its metaphorical richness, its harvesting of echoes. [Kinzie can] do anything with apparent ease. —Jonathan Holden, Prairie Schooner. With Ghost Ship [Kinzie] has secured a place among those poets who have been recording our lives as well as their own. Ghost Ship has the heft of a thoroughly composed volume, structured like a performance that builds up to and falls away from climaxes. It also shines with a deeply felt sense of shared humanity. — Willard Spiegelman, Boston Review

Kirchwey, Karl. *The Engrafted Word.* $22.00 (0-8050-5606-8). pap. $13.00 (0-8050-5607-6). New York, NY: Holt, Henry, and Company, Spring 1998. Like the golden bough on the dark oak, here are Kirchwey's "engrafted words" that graft the present onto antiquity, substance onto shadow, fresh life onto perennial memory. A restorative collection of poems, as meticulously made as they are moving. —Robert Fagles. Kirchwey's outstanding new book broadens the scope of his two fine previous books without any grotesque and willed generic shifts; he has become even more profoundly the elegiac poet of places and sited moments, more than merely skillful and interpretively adroit. —John Hollander

Kirschner, Elizabeth. *Postal Routes.* 57p. pap. $11.95 (0-88748-262-7). Pittsburgh, PA: Carnegie Mellon University Press, Spring 1998. Kirschner offers a splendid chronicle of exiles and reprieves, a chronicle in which vision operates at the extremes of materiality, upon the flesh of everything. —Donald Revell,The Ohio Review. Kirschner explores the relationships between wild things in the woods and the mysteries in our own minds and hearts. She plays culture and wilderness against one another in poems that resist current stylistic labels of poetry and surprise our humdrum expectations. These mediations on the human in the natural world open a singular existence to a multitudinous vision. —Elizabeth Oakes, Willow Springs

Kistler, William. *Notes Drawn From the River of Ecstasy.* 92p. pap. $12.00 (1-57178-068-8). Tulsa, OK: Council Oak Books, Spring 1998. An Oklahoma Book Award winner for The Elizabeth Sequence. Kistler has written poems of vision and experience rising up from the riverflow of the timeless. —Council Oak Books

Kizer, Carolyn, ed. *100 Great Poems by Women: A Golden Ecco Anthology.* 186p. $22.00 (0-88001-422-9). pap. $15.00 (0-88001-581-0). Hopewell, NJ: Ecco Press, Fall 1995; Fall 1998 (new paper). Kizer begins with a woman writing anonymously in the fifteenth century and takes us up to the present with such contemporary authors as Marianne Moore, Adrienne Rich, Margaret Atwood, Sharon Olds, Louise Glück, Jorie Graham, and Thylias Moss. This extraordinary anthology also contains such major poets as Emily Dickinson, Sylvia Plath, and Gertrude Stein. — Ecco Press. This is a splendid collection. Five centuries of women's verse speak here with breadth and freshness and consistent strength. —Richard Wilbur

Klein, Magdalena. Translated by Susan Simpson Geroe. *Pearls and Lace.* 64p. pap. $9.00 (1-56474-190-7). Santa Barbara, CA: Fithian Press, Spring 1997. This is the poetic journal of a young Jewish Roumanian woman, Magda Klein (1920-1946), kept through the years of the rise of fascism and the ultimate deportation of her family to Auschwitz-Berkenau. Edited and translated by her niece, these poems are a testament to the human spirit that transcends even the most horrific events of history. —Fithian Press

Klein, Michael, and Richard McCann, eds. *Things Shaped in Passing: More Writing From the AIDS Pandemic.* 212p. pap. $13.95 (0-89255-217-4). New York, NY: Persea Books, Spring 1997. This important and passionate collection presents the work of forty-two American poets whose vision and language bear the impress of the AIDS pandemic, now almost in its third decade. It complements Poets for Life, the classic anthology of poetry on AIDS, and is also an update, presenting a poetry different from what has gone before, in which the elegist leaves the bedside to look at the whole fractured world, the world as it is, with AIDS in it. — Persea Books

Kleinzahler, August. *Green Sees Things in Waves.* 80p. $22.00 (0-374-16672-2). New York, NY: Farrar, Straus and Giroux, Spring 1998. Kleinzahler is that rare bird, an unashamed experimentalist with the vision and confident skill to make American poetry new. —Clive Wilmer, The Times (London). Kleinzahler's best poems seem improvisatory, even jotted, at first, but they deepen on rereading, revealing a secret seriousness. His sometimes friendly, sometimes confrontational tones, winning vigor and idiosyncratic speech rhythms give these ambitious oddities grace and lasting appeal. —Publishers Weekly. Kleinzahler's means of delight are his light-handedness with language, his willingness to strike up a dance or a tune, his offbeat structures, and his revelling in the comic grotesque. [He uses] the medium to its fullest, not only in weaving the fascinating tex-

tures of his verse but also in getting the maximum out of the minimum. —Helen Vendler, The New Yorker

Klenburg, Jana Liba. *Timeless Resonance: A Poetic Adventure to Higher Consciousness.* 106p. pap. $14.00. New York, NY: Lone Pine Press/Global Book Productions, Fall 1996. Klenburg's poems sound a deep cord of spiritual wisdom, lyricism, beauty and magic. The work surprises us with its ability to touch upon both sensual passion and higher truths. —Brenda Sh. Lukeman

Kloefkorn, William. *Treehouse: New and Selected Poems.* 224p. pap. $15.00 (1-877727-65-2). Buffalo, NY: White Pine Press, Fall 1997. The State Poet of Nebraska, Kloefkorn is consistently accessible and restrained, practicing art without artifice. —Publishers Weekly

Knight, Brenda, ed. *Women of the Beat Generation: The Writers, Artists, and Muses at the Heart of a Revolution.* 366p. $19.95 (1-57324-061-3). pap. $14.95 (1-57324-138-5). Berkeley, CA: Conari Press, Fall 1996; Spring 1998 (new paper). A one-of-a-kind biographical anthology of 40 writers, artists, and muses who broke with convention during the rigidly conformist fifties to help forge one of the most fascinating chapters of American literary history. —Conari Press. A fantastic collection of Outrider women. . . amazing research. —Anne Waldman. Long overdue. . . an excellent colloquium of some of the finest poets in the English language. —Michael McClure. Thorough and well-researched. . . an unprecedented look at a group of women whose works were largely ignored until now. — Publishers Weekly

Knott, Bill. *Death and the Mountain.* 36p. Boston, MA: Knott, Bill, Spring 1997. Knott's poems are the poems Beckett's Gogo would write if he were among us. —Sharon Dunn, Massachusetts Review (1990)

Knott, Bill. *Homages.* 45p. Boston, MA: Knott, Bill, Fall 1998; Spring 1999 (new edition). Bill Knott is a genius. —Tom Andrews, Ohio Review. It is no accident that the major British and American poets of the 19th and 20th centuries were outsiders. The most original poet of my generation, Bill Knott, is also the greatest outsider. — Stephen Dobyns, AWP Chronicle

Knott, Bill. *Laugh at the End of the World: Collected Comic Poems 1965-1995.* 54p. Boston, MA: Knott, Bill, Spring 1997. Knott is the secret hero of a lot of poets. [P]oets who differ radically from Knott look to his work for the shock of recognizing themselves. —David Kirby, American Book Review (1991)

Knott, Bill. *One Hundred Quatorzains.* 68p. Boston, MA: Knott, Bill, Spring 1998. Bill Knott is a genius. —Tom Andrews, Ohio Review (1997)

Knott, Bill. *Other Strangers Than Our Own: Selected Love Poems.* 50p. Boston, MA: Knott, Bill, Spring 1997. It is no accident that the major British and American poets of the 19th and 20th century were outsiders. The most original poet of my generation, Bill Knott, is also the greatest outsider. —Stephen Dobyns, AWP Chronicle (1995)

Knott, Bill. *Other Strangers Than Our Own: Selected Love Poems 1963-1998.* 49p. Boston, MA: Knott, Bill, Fall 1998 (new edition). Knott is the secret hero of a lot of poets. Poets who differ radically from Knott look to his work for the shock of recognizing themselves. —David

Kirby, American Book Review. Few people can create a world so completely and concisely as Knott does time and time again. —Kevin Hart, Overland

Knott, Bill. *Plaza de Loco.* 70p. Boston, MA: Knott, Bill, Spring 1997 (new edition). Among people who know his work, Knott is regarded as one of the most original voices in American poetry. —Charles Simic, blurb for Poems 1963-1988 (1989)

Knott, Bill. *Plaza de Loco: New Poems 1998.* 55p. Boston, MA: Knott, Bill, Fall 1998. Knott is no parlor poet. His work is the most sharply original of any poet in his generation. —Jim Elledge, Booklist. Knott sets up principles far outside most of those we know, and he always writes up to and beyond those standards. —Sandra McPherson

Knott, Bill. *Selected Short Poems (1963-1996).* 32p. Boston, MA: Knott, Bill, Spring 1997. Knott is an American original. No one else could have imagined what James Wright once referred to as Bill Knott's "indespensible poems." —Stuart Dischell, Harvard Book Review (1989)

Knott, Bill. *Selected Short Poems 1966-1996.* 28p. Boston, MA: Knott, Bill, Fall 1998 (new edition). I think Bill Knott is the best poet in America right now. —Thomas Lux, Emerson Review. Among people who know his work, Knott is regarded as one of the most original voices in American poetry. —Charles Simic

Ko Un. Translated by Young-Moo Kim and Brother Anthony. *Beyond Self: 108 Korean Zen Poems.* 50p. pap. $12.00 (0-938077-99-6). Albany, CA: Parallax Press, Fall 1997. Ko Un is a magnificent poet, combination of Buddhist cognoscente, passionate political libertarian, and naturalist historian. This little book of Son (Zen) poems gives a glimpse of the severe humorous discipline beneath the prolific variety of his forms & subjects. These excellent translations are models useful to inspire American Contemplative poets. —Allen Ginsberg. These tiny, irreverent, compassionate, often humorous vignettes open to vast fields of understanding. Ko Un's poems live amid the democracy of all being, looking directly and with great pleasure at this very moment's bright-leaping essence. — Jane Hirshfield

Koch, Kenneth. *Straits.* 89p. $22.00 (0-375-40136-9). New York, NY: Knopf, Alfred A., Fall 1998. Koch continues to expand the range of what it is possible to do in poetry. His title poem is a stirring collection of disconnected and connected sentences on such themes as love, politics, and the exploration of sub-polar seas. "Vous etes plus beaux que vous ne pensiez" is a series of bright, rapid sketches of the lives of ten artists and writers. Writing in a variant of the style of the 18th century poet James Thomson, Koch revives an old genre — praise of the seasons — with his own characteristic mixture of clarity and sensuous excitement. A group of 25 poems called "Songs from the Plays" creates a new genre: songs written for plays that don't exist but from which plays might be imagined or constructed. "My Olivetti Speaks" is perhaps Koch's clearest and wittiest meditation on the nature of poetry itself. The themes of time and change in individual lives are given an unusual look in "Study of Time" and the Villon-like "Ballade." — Alfred A. Knopf

Koch, Kenneth, ed. *Making Your Own Days: The Pleasures of Reading and Writing Poetry.* 317p. $27.50 (0-684-83992-X). New York, NY: Simon & Schuster/Scribner, Spring 1998. This book makes the somewhat mysterious subject of poetry clear for those who read it and for those who write it — and for those who would like to read it and write it better. —Simon & Schuster. A person in love is torn between needing to keep his enthusiasm secret and wanting to share it with the world. Koch in his new book strikes the ideal compromise. How generous he is with his patient intelligence, and how original with his crucial perception! Like all real artists, he show us what we did not know we knew. He is that rare phenomenon, the poet who can write prose — prose that is necessary and lucid. In this book, he offers a new and healthy dimension to the life of virtually everyone. —Ned Rorem

Koestenbaum, Phyllis. *Criminal Sonnets.* 70p. pap. $12.00 (1-884516-03-3). Jacaranda Press/Writer's Center Editions, Fall 1998. Criminal Sonnets reflects an out-of-control world of lawlessness and paranoia. Horrible, yet grimly funny, these poems connect our century's greatest crimes with the calamity of the poet's personal history. —Jacaranda Press.

This is a wonderful book — fierce, bold, comic, and immensely skilled. The "criminal" in these poems is immediately accessible as an intelligence; a woman of a certain age taking the measure of her world's violence. Waiting at the supermarket checkout stand, your eyes have avoided the stories she tells in these sonnets, but you know what they are, and she has made sense of them, made art of them. —Diane Wood Middlebrook. Koestenbaum has lion-tamed raw feeling into sonnets. These poems are gritty, obsessional and addicting. —Maxine Kumin

Koethe, John. *Falling Water.* 71p. pap. $12.00 (0-06-095257-1). HarperCollins/HarperPerennial, Spring 1997. The poems of [Koethe's] new book are like no one else's. In them, even the most extreme exertions of consciousness are transformed into the luminous measures of beautiful speech. —Mark Strand. This is a poetry of magnificent undertow, all proximity of thought, singularity of contemplation, protest, pretext, reflection — all disenchantment and then, suddenly, blazing re-enchantment, with the newly, lovingly, seen-through real. —Jorie Graham

Kofler, Silvia. *Butterflies.* 15p. pap. $5.00. TL Press, Spring 1998.

Komunyakaa, Yusef. *Thieves of Paradise.* 136p. $19.95 (0-8195-6330-7). Hanover, NH: University Press of New England/Wesleyan University Press, Spring 1998. Komunyakaa delivers a powerful meditation on American, and particularly African American life in the wake of Vietnam. In poems overflowing with language, memories of childhood are tinged with memories of war. The collection centers on the disorienting experiences of the returning soldier. Drawing on multiple traditions, Komunyakaa's poetry is potent, live, and, like the strains of jazz running through it, an erudite and soulful music. —University Press of New England/Wesleyan University Press

Koon Woon. *The Truth in Rented Rooms.* 97p. pap. $8.95 (1-885030-25-8). New York, NY: Kaya, Fall 1998. Koon Woon, like Bob Kaufman, is a writer of solitudes. But like Walt Whitman, his solitudes contain multitudes. —Steve Cannon. A unique kind of blues that reverberates all the way from little village Canton to the homeless alleys of Seattle. The

soup of this poet produces a
bitter but satisfying warmth
that needs to be experienced.
—Alan Chong Lau.
Miraculously, Koon Woon has
written THE TRUTH. You
read it! —Bob Holman. These
poems set a thousand horses
galloping in the Asian diaspo-
ra in which so many are
caught. —Lawrence
Ferlinghetti

Kosmicki, Greg. *How Things
Happen.* 60p. pap. $35.00.
Omaha, NE: Bradypress, Fall
1997. Letterpress edition with
wood engravings by Eric May.
Fifteen poems — playful,
ironic, hopeful reflections of a
common (not ordinary) man
on the wonders of family, the
drudgery of work, and the
small details of life. —
Bradypress

Kovacik, Karen. *Nixon and I.*
18p. (0-87338-592-6). Kent,
OH: Kent State University
Press, Fall 1998. Kovacik's
poems are strong, distinctive,
and thoroughly wonderful
works. Her Richard Nixon
persona poems are stunning,
brave, and original. American
poetry, and American writing
in general, tends to be sadly
ahistorical, and the way these
poems take on one of history's
most loved and hated figures,
giving him voice and making
him human, is truly impres-

sive. Nixon and I is an amazing debut. —Jesse Lee
Kercheval

Kowit, Steve. *Epic Journeys,
Unbelievable Escapes.* 28p.
pap. $7.00. Brockport, NY:
State Street Press, Spring
1998. From Greenwich Village
to Mexico to California,
Kowit's poems reach beyond
landscape into the geography
of emotion. With generosity
and power, he wakens us with
the exuberant music of memory. —Judith Kitchen

Kowit, Steve. *For My
Birthday.* 4p. pap. $5.00. San
Diego, CA: Caernarvon Press,
Fall 1997. For My Birthday is
a long rhapsodic poem in a
limited edition of 360 copies.
—Caernarvon Press. I loved
the poem. —Tom Lux.
Strong, touching, funny. —
Bin Ramke

Kraeft, Norman. *Scholaster:
His Life and Times, A
Sequence of Poems.* 28p. pap.
$6.00. Brooklyn, NY: Somers
Rocks Press, Fall 1998.
Readers who still delight in
poems that rhyme and scan
(count me among them) will
welcome this new collection
by Kraeft. His Scholaster
poems are a double tour de
force: they not only add up to
a wise and witty character
study (or, one suspects, a self-

portrait), but also supply a concise handbook (with models) for poets who care to write in traditional form. — X.J. Kennedy. Kraeft has a craftsman's hand, a perfect ear, and observant and ironic eye. —J.D. McClatchy

Krajeck, Elizabeth A. *Trigger.* 48p. pap. $3.95 (1-880649-32-2). Indianapolis, IN: Writers' Center Press, Fall 1994. Winner of the Third Indiana Chapbook Contest. This collection meets the test of the best poetry: it invites repeated readings and at each reading gives up new pleasures and illuminations. — Leonard Trawick

Kramer, Larry. *Brilliant Windows.* 92p. pap. $11.95 (1-881163-23-7). Oxford, OH: Miami University Press, Spring 1998. I've been a fervent admirer of Kramer's poems for years, as his is a voice capable of irony without condescension, of tenderness without sentimentality — a rare poetic intelligence whose surfaces and depth continually surprise and delight his readers. This is a remarkable and moving book. —Lynne McMahon. Lyrically charged, passionately conceived, completely free of the moribund trappings of literary fashion, the music of these poems rises

to the pitch of their grandly secular vision. This is a book that — like a talisman for the twenty-first century — one could, in all faith, slip into the hands of one's children or one's children's children. — Sherod Santos

Krampf, Thomas. *Shadow Poems.* 66p. pap. $12.00 (0-9616797-2-7). St. Bonaventure, NY: Ischua Books, Fall 1997. I think this new book is a wonder: it does just what you'd hope it would — leads confidently into a new dimension. —Robert Lax. Delicately interconnected, these poems open us to the music of a sharply-observed life. —Colette Inez

Krapf, Norbert. *Blue-Eyed Grass: Poems of Germany.* 125p. pap. $12.50 (1-56809-035-8). St. Louis, MO: Time Being Books, Fall 1997. Krapf is today's strongest poetic voice in search of German heritage. —German Life. The mix of sunny and dark images places the poet in a Frostian tradition as well as a Whitmanian one; Krapf's poems reverberate with the mystery of human character at the core of his family roots. —Confrontation

Kraus, Sharon. *Generation.* 80p. pap. $9.95 (1-882295-14-5). Farmington, ME: Alice James Books, Fall 1997. Sensual, passionate, earthly and unearthly together, Kraus's work brings a fierce grief up into the sane daylight of her words. The most heartbreaking poems in Generation are the childhood poems, but the others reflect that childhood's fire: the book is 'homemade,' and it has a rare necessity about it, and gallantry. —Jean Valentine. Kraus unflinchingly documents the eros of abuse. Traveling backward through a violent past, Kraus methodically remembers the specifics so that she can analyze, evaluate and, finally, allow herself to feel. —Publishers Weekly

Kriesel, Michael. *Long Dark.* 52p. Kriesel, Michael, Fall 1996. Long Dark originally appeared as a 40-page chapbook published in December 1993 by Zerx Press. Parts of it have since appeared in Psychedelic Wasteland, Rusty Scupper, Silent Skies, WISdom, and Wooden Head Review. —Michael Kriesel

Krüger, Michael. Translated by Richard Dove. *At Night, Beneath Trees: Selected Poems.* 100p. pap. $12.50 (0-8076-1431-9). New York, NY: Braziller, George, Spring 1998. Krüger's second volume of poetry to appear in English, drawn from his 1993 and 1996 collections, marks an important shift in his work; moving away from the deeply philosophical dialogues of his earlier work, Krüger engages here in reflective, lyrical musings on the meaning of existence. —George Braziller

Krumholz, Márgalo Eden. *A Force of Tides: Poems of the Natural World and Beyond.* 64p. pap. $8.00 (0-9663410-0-7). Anchor Thorn Publishing, Fall 1998. Beyond the sometimes haunting, sometimes humorous scenes she evokes of flora and fauna, [Krumholz's] poems explore relationships between nature, people and God, creation and the poet. They reflect a deep concern for the natural world and its conservation. —Anchor Thorn Publishing

Krysl, Marilyn. *Soulskin.* 105p. pap. $12.95 (0-88737-675-4). New York, NY: National League for Nursing Press, 1996. Krysl's new book is made of words that are clear and strong and naked. These poems journey out of the many empty spaces of America into flesh and pulse. She is a woman on a journey that is both poetic and carries mortal weight. —Linda Hogan. The first time I read her poetry, my breath was taken away by the clarity of her insights into those who suffer so, as well as into the knowledge that we are all in some way that matters, even when devastated, complete in soul. Krysl is a fine, fine poet, the kind that is both rare and blessed. —Clarissa Pinkola Estés. In these poems of revelation and beauty, Krysl steps into the skin of the compassionate mystic. She makes songs for the healer and the one to be healed, who are often one and the same. —Joy Harjo

Krysl, Marilyn. *Warscape With Lovers.* 71p. $22.50 (1-880834-29-4). pap. $12.00 (1-880834-28-6). Cleveland, OH: Cleveland State University Poetry Center, Fall 1997. Krysl has found balance in places shaken by deprivation and injury. This is a beautiful book of poetry, not because it is lyrical (though it is), but because it treats suffering with love. —Marvin Bell. Krysl's poetry is funny, funky, tragic, brave, lyrical, humane, political, and full of surprises. She is still writing the liveliest sestinas in America. —Alicia Ostriker

Kuhl, Nancy. *In the Arbor.* 34p. pap. $4.75 (0-87338-570-5). Kent, OH: Kent State University Press, Spring 1997. The movement at the center of so many of these poems is that of air, fire, water, night — of what cannot be seen, even as the speaker moves ever inward to face her own dreams, her demons and her desires. —Judith Kitchen. The sources of these poems are sometimes harrowing, sometimes serene; in every case [Kuhl] alchemizes them into distilled energy. This is the first collection of a poet to watch in the future, yes, but also to read right now. —Tom Andrews

Kumin, Maxine. *Connecting the Dots.* 86p. $18.95 (0-393-03962-5). pap. $11.00 (0-393-31695-5). New York, NY: Norton, W.W., and Company, Spring 1996; Fall 1997 (paper). [Kumin] commands the nuances and music of rhyme and slant-rhyme as powerfully as any living poet. The entire book is studded with linguistic brilliance and formal excellence. —George Weld, Poetry. [Kumin] just gets better and better. These are the kind of poems one wants to share with family and friends, to savor again and again. Every poem in this collection is a treasure. — Library Journal

Kumin, Maxine. *Selected Poems: 1960-1990.* 294p. $27.50 (0-393-04073-9). pap. $17.95 (0-393-31836-2). New York, NY: Norton, W.W., and Company, Fall 1997; Fall 1998 (new paper). A New York Times Notable Book of the Year. Thirty years of honest work by a versatile poet who adheres to no particular school and whose poems tell family stories and seek to preserve family history. —New York Times Book Review. A pastoral poet, Kumin is quite simply one of the best poets writing today. This collection represents a lifetime (until now) of Kumin's work and includes works from all her published volumes. —Library Journal. [A] perceptive, distinctive voice. The evolution and inherent integrity of Kumin's poetry, wise, generous, and passionate, is deftly captured in this forceful selection. —Publishers Weekly

Kunitz, Stanley. *Passing Through.* pap. $12.00 (0-393-31615-7). New York, NY: Norton, W.W., and Company, Fall 1995; Spring 1997 (paper). Winner of the 1995 National Book Award. Kunitz, one of the masters of contemporary poetry, presents his ninth collection, which includes a rich selection of new poems and nearly all the poems of Kunitz's later years, beginning with The Testing Tree (1971). Most of the poems in Passing Through are unavailable in any other edition. —W.W. Norton. One of America's great poets. Most poets dry up at 50. For him to be writing poems at 90 is just incredible. —Mark Strand. Perhaps the closest American poetry has come in our time to achieving an urgency and aura that deserves — even demands — to be called visionary. Passing Through is, above all, a book of revelations. — David Barber, Atlantic Monthly

Kunitz, Stanley. Translated by Adam Szyper. *Passing Through.* 87p. (0-89304-077-0). (0-89304-078-9). Merrick, NY: Cross-Cultural Communications, Fall 1998. The first English/Polish edition of Passing Through, which won the 1995 National Book Award.

Kutchins, Laurie. *The Night Path.* 87p. $20.00 (1-880238-48-9). pap. $12.50 (1-880238-49-7). Rochester, NY: BOA Editions, Fall 1997. Kutchins writes about pregnancy and birth in poems that are concrete and lyrical, factual and wildly speculative. —Maxine Kumin. In a time of increasing concern for the survival of the planet and the power of memory to avert oblivion, Kutchins contributes to our understanding of nature in visionary poems of quiet integrity. —Colette Inez

Kuzma, Greg. *What Poetry Is All About.* 248p. pap. $15.00 (0-937179-12-4). Pocatello, ID: Blue Scarab Press, Fall 1998. This collection is not about how to write, read, publish or promote poetry. It is simply what poetry is all about. As Kuzma says, I wanted to write a book in praise of what I knew, what I had learned from those who had been willing to expose themselves to ridicule, who had been kind and yet cruel, whose loyalties were first to words, and some truth higher than the expedient which sells shoes. But such a book has been written, is written more or less every time a poet writes a book of poems. And so I wanted to write a different book altogether. —Blue Scarab Press

Kyser, Eric. *Before You Wake: Good Dreams and Healing Thoughts.* 80p. pap. $6.95 (0-9641606-7-6). Cupertino, CA: Easy Break, First Time Publishing, Spring 1998. These poems speak from the voice of the Inner Child, translating word and image into a carousel. —Easy Break, First Time Publishing

La Fontaine, Jean de. Translated by Norman Shapiro. *Fifty More Fables of La Fontaine.* 192p. $39.95 (0-252-02346-3). pap. $24.95 (0-252-06650-2). Champaign, IL: University of Illinois Press, Spring 1998. It is a pleasure to open a book as sure and sly as these translations. [Shapiro] gets the tune right and the tone right and manages to echo both the folk wisdom and the poker-faced formality of the originals. —Seamus Heaney

La France, Danielle, ed. *Berkeley! A Literary Tribute.* 240p. pap. $14.95 (0-930588-94-0). Berkeley, CA: Heyday Books, Fall 1997. Whether portraying the traditional academic ideals that founded a great university, the creative ferment of the Beat Generation, or the turmoil of the Free Speech Movement, Berkeley! A Literary Tribute offers a fresh, passionate, and often slyly ironic view of a unique American city. Includes work by Jack Kerouac, Maxine Hong Kingston, Ishmael Reed, Allen Ginsberg and many others. —Heyday Books

LaFemina, Gerry. *A Print of Wildflowers: Love Poems.*

32p. pap. $8.00 (1-56439-065-9). Detroit, MI: Ridgeway Press, Spring 1997. I love Gerry LaFemina's poems — for their urgency, their life. He understands that "all our lives we love/looking to be whole." If there's a better poet under 30 in America, I haven't read him or her. —Thomas Lux

Lamantia, Philip. *Bed of Sphinxes: New and Selected Poems 1943-1993.* 141p. pap. $12.95 (0-87286-320-4). San Francisco, CA: City Lights Books, Spring 1997. Bed of Sphinxes offers a selection of poems representing five decades of impressive poetic achievement, from [Lamantia's] early years of association with surrealists-in-exile through the Beat Generation era to the present. The poems range from visionary apocalypse to a lyrical fusion with nature. By turns nightmarish, erotic, hermetic, they create an astonishing world charged by Lamantia's energy and erudition. —City Lights Books. A man in command of a wild imagination. . . with a particular place in the ranks of the most important moderns. —Library Journal

Lammon, Martin. *News From Where I Live.* 72p. $20.00 (1-55728-507-1). pap. $12.00 (1-55728-508-X).

Fayetteville, AR: University of Arkansas Press, Spring 1998. The authenticity of feeling, the feelings themselves and the subjects from which they arise, the honesty with which [Lammon] confronts the pain of existence and the consequences of our mortal damage and liability, the evanescence of what we love, our implications in the losses we live through, and the chord of mixed feelings that is the bass accompaniment of our survival are all there, and constantly there in his work. — W.S. Merwin. News From Where I Live contains many love poems, tender moments of remembrance and innocence. What I like about Lammon's work is its feel, the softness of lines that also hold firm. I like the hidden presence of God. This new collection of poems is a reason for celebration. —E. Ethelbert Miller

Lamson, Suzy. *A Rose Between Her Teeth.* 73p. pap. $10.00 (1-887012-15-X). Newtown, CT: Hanover Press, Fall 1998.

Lander, Tim. *The Myth of Adam and Eve: An Operatic Dialog for Three Voices.* 16p. pap. $5.00. Port Townsend, WA: Sagittarius Press, Fall 1995; Spring 1998 (new edition). A semi-comical plea for the environment with serious undertones. —Sagittarius Press

Lansky, Bruce, ed. *Lighten Up!: 100 Funny Little Poems.* 111p. pap. $5.95 (0-88166-320-4). Minnetonka, MN: Meadowbrook Press, Fall 1998. A collection of the funniest light verse ever written, by world-class humorists such as Ogden Nash, Dorothy Parker, Jack Prelutsky, Dorothy Sayers, Alexander Pope, and many more. —Meadowbrook Press

Larkin, Joan. *Cold River.* 48p. pap. $12.00 (0-96515585-4). New York, NY: Painted Leaf Press, Fall 1997. In Cold River Larkin's poems move deeper than ever into grief and tenderness and praise, her own wild and quiet voice the embodiment of desire. —Jean Valentine. I return to Larkin's poems again and again because I love their clarity, their revelatory strength, their allegiance to something like history and their great and surprising humor. But there is more.

The poems in this little book that face AIDS are certainly some of the bravest and most eloquent ones on the subject. To put it simply, they floor me. —Michael Klein

Larsen, Lance. *Erasable Walls.* 64p. $22.00 (0-932826-59-8). pap. $12.00 (0-932826-60-1). Kalamazoo, MI: New Issues Press, Spring 1998. A series of elegant personal meditations on the always-evolving self. These beautifully crafted poems show a degree of mastery that's rare in a first book. Though quiet and subtle, Larsen's voice is also nervy and truth-telling, with considerable cumulative power. —Chase Twichell. I have been waiting for Larsen's first collection for years, knowing it would be an event. It's here, and there has rarely been so assured an introduction, nor one so clearly of our time and yet firmly in the tradition. The poems are all strong, the best of the superb. —Leslie Norris

LaRue, Debrah. *Dance With the Dark Poet.* 54p. pap. $5.95 (0-9641606-3-3). Cupertino, CA: Easy Break, First Time Publishing, Fall 1996. Dance With the Dark Poet is a personal dealing with the struggle of a woman in a state of transition and documenting the end of a relationship and the

quest for self discovery. —
Easy Break, First Time
Publishing

Lasdun, James. *Woman
Police Officer in Elevator.*
80p. $19.00 (0-393-04043-7).
pap. $11.00 (0-393-31838-9).
New York, NY: Norton, W.W.,
and Company, Spring 1997;
Fall 1998 (new paper). Mixing
the classical and the cosmopolitan, these poems concern themselves with transformations, dislocations, and
metamorphoses, as vividly
rendered landscapes from
Tuscany to New Jersey evolve
into meditations on love,
myth, and sexual and social
politics. —W.W. Norton.
American readers who want to
see rejuvenated form in
untroubled action, giving brisk
shape to contemporary and
classical events, will find it in
Lasdun. —Helen Vendler,
New York Review of Books.
Brilliant. These newest poems
by Lasdun are full of linguistic
panache, uncommon depths of
feeling, fine ironies, and taut
drama. He seems to me certainly among the most gifted,
vivid, and deft poets now writing in English, and far better
than many who are more
famous. His capacities are
solidly established; his
promise is nearly infinite. —
Anthony Hecht

Lasko, G.P. *Impressions of
Paris in Red: A Narrative
Poem.* 48p. pap. $3.65.
Albany, NY: Armadillo Books,
Spring 1995. A narrative poem
set at the time of the Paris
Commune of 1871. With
painter Gustave Courbet as its
central figure, the poem
explores the social milieu in
which Impressionism was
born. —Armadillo Books

Lassell, Michael. *A Flame for
the Touch That Matters.* 113p.
pap. $12.00 (0-9651558-9-7).
New York, NY: Painted Leaf
Press, Spring 1998. A Flame
for the Touch That Matters is a
remarkable achievement. I
know of no other poet since
Cavafy who has written so
insistently and so elegantly
about homosexual desire.
Lassell's voice is far-reaching,
generous, filled with yearning
and heartbreak. This is a poet
who sings the pleasures of the
body but also reveals the mysteries of the human heart. —
Jaime Manrique. Passion and
precision, spontaneity and
candor, fright and despair,
delight in sex, reverence for
beauty: Lassell's A Flame for
the Touch That Matters is an
irrepressible, irreverent, irresistible collection of memories
and reflections on lost friends,
surviving family, lips touching
lips (and other erogenous
zones), the joy and pain of life

with and without the "touch that matters." —Richard Labonté

Lauchlan, Michael. *Sudden Parade.* 40p. pap. $8.00 (1-56439-057-8). Detroit, MI: Ridgeway Press, Spring 1997. I have admired the gritty, huge-hearted and intense urban poems of Michael Lauchlan for many years. As he says of the subject of a poem called "Oncology Nurse," "You pour the voice of mercy"— so do these poems. This is a beautiful and stunning collection. — Thomas Lux

Laughlin, James. Edited by Hayden Carruth. *A Commonplace Book of Pentastichs.* 94p. $19.95 (0-8112-1386-2). New York, NY: New Directions, Fall 1998. A Common Place Book of Pentastichs is the last book of his own that Laughlin, the founding publisher of New Directions, helped to prepare in his lifetime. A 'pentastich' refers simply to a poem of five lines, without regard to metrics. The present selection consists of 249 short-line compositions in a natural voice cadence, many of them marginal jottings and paraphrases of common place book notations. —New Directions. For the reader it is a survey of lit-

erature that will never be found in a classroom — praise whatever gods may be — but indubitably will be found in loving and long-standing proximity on many a bedside table. —Hayden Carruth.

Laughlin, James. *Poems New and Selected.* 293p. pap. $12.95 (0-8112-1375-7). New York, NY: New Directions, Fall 1998. In these poems, Laughlin reveals himself as a master of concision, of the well-placed word that penetrates the human heart. The 225 poems included here show his technical brilliance as well. —New Directions. Not an ounce of surplus fat, all beautifully spry and clean-limbed. Just the sort of testament one owes to life and nothing wanting. —Charles Tomlinson

Laughlin, James. *The Love Poems of James Laughlin.* 64p. $14.95 (0-8112-1360-9). pap. $6.95 (0-8112-1387-0). New York, NY: New Directions, Fall 1997; Fall 1998 (new paper). Who else today writes such bittersweet, ironic, rueful, erotic, tough-minded witty love poems, poems that run the gamut from ecstasy to loss. —Marjorie Perloff. I think what most delights is the insistently human scale, the old-time

Roman clarity of terms. But there is also that timeless intelligence of love's musing reflection, in whatever language impinges, or makes possible such ultimately human speech. —Robert Creeley

Laughlin, James. *The Secret Room.* 184p. $22.95 (0-8112-1343-9). pap. $14.95 (0-8112-1344-7). New York, NY: New Directions, 1993; Spring 1997 (reissue). Four paths of a lifetime's learning converge in these poems: Eroticism, from the Sanskrit; Satire, from the Latin; Plain Speech, from the American; and, above all, from the Greek, Perfection. —Eliot Weinberger. The Secret Room continues Laughlin's program of shaping his long life into poem after poem of clearest crystal and richly human feeling. Witty, elegiac, sexy, satiric, naughty, poignant, wise, they amount to a personal anthropology of our world as fetchingly readable as those of the old masters in Greece and China. —Guy Davenport

Laurence, Mary Sanford, ed. *More Treasured Poems That Touch the Heart: Cherished Poems and Favorite Poets.* 256p. $14.00 (0-88486-171-6). New York, NY: Bristol Park Books, 1997. The poems were chosen for their ability to express the incredible, the joyous, and the heartbreaking. Poets included are: Byron, Blake, Longfellow, Wordsworth, Browning, Shakespeare, Donne, Keats, Emerson, and Dickinson. —Bristol Park Books

Lauterbach, Ann. *On a Stair.* 85p. pap. $14.95 (0-14-058793-4). New York, NY: Penguin Books/Viking Penguin, Fall 1997. Lauterbach's fifth collection, On a Stair, takes its title from Emerson's great essay, Experience: "Where do we find ourselves?" he asks. Lauterbach's search for an answer veers precariously between a desire for spiritual vitality and a sense of the overwhelming materiality of our world. Lauterbach brings us, with a dazzling range of formal and imagistic resources, to a new understanding of the relationship between self-knowledge and cultural meaning. —Penguin Books/Viking Penguin

Lawless, Gary. *Caribouddhism.* 88p. pap. $9.95 (0-9423968-0-4). Nobleboro, ME: Blackberry Books, Fall 1998.

Lawrence, David. *Steel Toe Boots.* 80p. pap. $9.50 (1-56474-188-5). Santa Barbara, CA: Fithian Press, Fall 1996. Lawrence turns prison bars sideways into five-line staves and types his remarkable songs "that sing on paper": defiant, intimate, startling and provocative. These poems deliver a knockout punch to the American prison system. —Chiz Schultz. Steel Toe Boots is a unique and powerful book. The poems are bitter, funny, fierce, lucid, and deeply human. Lawrence is the genuine article. —Thomas Lux

Laws, Kyle, and Tony Moffeit. *Tango.* 72p. pap. $14.95 (1-888832-05-3). St. Augustine, FL: Kings Estate Press, Fall 1997. Laws and Moffeit combine their separate musics. Laws's Frida Kahlo poems, and Moffeit's Billy the Kid poems move together to create a whole that dazzles with emotion and movement. —Kings Estate Press. The tango has always been a dance of great sexual energy and that, also, is the kind of excitement these poems generate. — Todd Moore

Lawson, Denise Liddell. *Even the Smallest Act.* 16p. pap. $15.00 (1-889589-02-0). Mill Valley, CA: Em Press, Fall 1998. Lawson's luminous fourteen poem sequence is a sensual articulation of spiritual incandescence. The sense of the suspended persists throughout this poem series, with its lyrically colliding voices and echoes of the sonnet form. —Em Press

Lax, Robert. Edited by Paul Spaeth. *A Thing That Is: New Poems.* 75p. $19.95 (0-87951-699-2). New York, NY: Overlook Press, Spring 1997. The first volume of all new poems to be published in the US since the 1960's by "the last unacknowledged major poet of his post-60's generation." —New York Times. This new book of Lax's poems proves yet again that the gift to be simple is the gift to be strong, that less is more, and that least may sometimes be most. —John Ashbery. These narrow-lined poems seem to tremble with energy. They are like high energy stanchions or pylons driven into the hillsides of the rocky Greek Islands, such as Patmos, where Lax has lived for so many years. —Ed Sanders

Lax, Robert. Edited by James J. Uebbing. *Love Had a Compass: Journals and Poetry.* 253p. $22.00 (0-8021-1587-X). New York, NY: Grove Press, Fall 1996. The works in Love Had a Compass represent every stage of Lax's development as a poet, from his early years in the 1940's as a staff writer for the New Yorker to his present life on the Greek island of Patmos. —Grove Press. Among America's greatest poets, a true minimalist who can weave awesome poems from remarkably few words. Lax remains the last unacknowledged major poet of his post-60's generation. —The New York Times Book Review

Lazer, Hank. *3 of 10.* 157p. pap. $14.00 (0-925904-18-X). Tucson, AZ: Chax Press, Fall 1996. "Throughout all history and despite all academics," wrote Ezra Pound in 1940, "living language has been inclusive and not exclusive." Lazer's 3 of 10 is a deliberate movement towards such freedom. The excitement of this writing is its ability to track the course of a drive towards freedom. Lazer asserts that poets are "portals multiply open." It is a formulation that is deeply involved with a perception about mythology, for to think mythologically is to think chordally, in clusters of simultaneously-sounded "tones." That is the kind of thinking—and writing—we "hear" in this deeply con-

scious, deeply self-conscious work. —Jack Foley

Le Guin, Ursula K. *Lao Tzu: Tao Te Ching: A Book About the Way and the Power of the Way.* 125p. $20.00 (1-57062-333-3). Boston, MA: Shambhala Publications, Fall 1997. This is a completely fresh and poetic version of the twenty-five-hundred-year-old Chinese spiritual classic, by one of America's most thought-provoking writers. Le Guin's version captures all the brilliance of Lao Tzu's poetry while conveying with immediacy and clarity the astonishing depth of his spiritual insights. It also corrects many of the distorted views of Lao Tzu's philosophy, freeing it from gender-bias and revealing its universal relevance. — Shambhala Publications

Le Guin, Ursula K., and Diana Bellessi. *The Twins, The Dream: Two Voices/Las Gemelas, El Sueño: Dos Voces.* 225p. $16.95 (1-55885-170-4). pap. $8.95 (1-55885-179-8). Houston, TX: Arte Público Press, 1997. In The Twins, The Dream/Las Gemelas, El Sueño, two distinguished literary voices of the Americas offer a heartfelt meditation on language, love, personal identity, and the transforming power of friendship. The two authors have translated each other's work as a means of bridging geographical distances and fostering cross-cultural dialog. —Arte Público Press

Leader, Mary. *Red Signature.* 72p. pap. $12.95 (1-55597-255-1). St. Paul, MN: Graywolf Press, Spring 1997. Winner of the National Poetry Series. [Red Signature] impresses with its originality and its variety of forms and music. —Publishers Weekly. The best poems in this book are like looking at a great John Ford film: something elemental within American experience, something born in deprivation but capable of possessing grandeur, has found classical expression. —Frank Bidart

Lease, Joseph. *Human Rights.* 63p. pap. $13.00 (0-944072-85-2). Cambridge, MA: Zoland Books, Spring 1998. Human Rights is a remarkable accomplishment, telling a complex story of human rites and their often painful authority with a range of resources any poet would be blessed to command. This singular book marks the beginning of what promises to be in all senses a brilliant career. —Robert Creeley. You don't read his poems. There is a shimmer into which you are pulled as under the lit surface of a dark water. Lease is writing extraordinary poems, poems as poignant, lush, and disturbing as experience, thoroughly felt. Human Rights is a stunning book. —Forrest Gander

LeBlanc, Diane. *Hope in Zone Four.* 40p. pap. $4.00. Talent, OR: Talent House Press, Fall 1998.

Lederer, Katy. *Music, No Staves.* 22p. pap. $6.00 (0-937013-80-3). Elmwood, CT: Potes & Poets Press, Fall 1998.

Ledesma, Alberto. *(Not) a Machine.* 13p. Berkeley, CA: Chicano Chapbook Series, Spring 1998. The Chicano Chapbook Series, edited by Gary Soto, issued twelve title in the late 1970's and early 1980's, including works by Sandra Cisneros, Alberto Ríos, Jimmy Santiago Baca and others. The chapbooks are distributed free of charge to selected libraries with Chicano collections. (Not) a Machine is #17.

Leftwich, Jim. *Improvisations Transformations.* 45p. pap. $7.00 (0-937013-76-5). Elmwood, CT: Potes & Poets Press, Fall 1998.

Leftwich, Jim. *Sample EXample: Visual Lyrics.* 27p. pap. $7.00 (1-8922-8001-9). Columbus, OH: Luna Bisonte Prods, Fall 1998. Visual poems using a variety of conceptual, graphological, typographical, and computer-driven techniques. —Luna Bisonte Prods

Leithauser, Brad. *The Odd Last Thing She Did.* 83p. $22.00 (0-375-40141-5). New York, NY: Knopf, Alfred A., Fall 1998; Spring 2000 (new paper). Once again [Leithauser's] poems evince a profound love of nature and a mastery of poetic forms. But they also reflect a deepening interest in storytelling, as Leithauser, who has also published four novels, here brings the narrative drive that propels his fiction into the domain of verse. —Alfred A. Knopf. A rhyming family man, amateur cosmologist, and addict of intricate stanzas, Leithauser warms the past and present with his lovingly intense scrutiny and powerfully compressed phrases. —John Updike. A solid reputation for mastery is sustained and reconfirmed in this brilliant cluster of dazzling, touching, witty and deeply felt poems. Borne confidently on the strength of an unfailing talent, we are conveyed through drunken arithmetic, along nimble caperings of the mind, to exotic margins of a world both delicate and adamantine, where it is revealed to us how perilously delight or heartbreak teeters on the pinpoint of a word. —Anthony Hecht

Leonard, John C. *Poetry Soup.* 53p. pap. $9.95 (1-56315-127-8). Pittsburgh, PA: Sterling House, Fall 1998. Contemporary free verse and experimental poetry designed to affect the world in a positive way. Leonard has put together a collection of short poems with one goal in mind — to get people to understand that each and every person has the potential to become truly peaceful within themselves. — Sterling House

Leonhardt, Kenneth, and Wayne Hogan. *Lightwise.* 20p. pap. $6.00. Cookeville, TN: Little Books Press, Fall 1996. This is a fulsomely illustrated book of short poems that takes a swipe at virtually everybody and everything. —Little Books Press

Lerner, Linda. *New & Selected Poems.* 88p. pap. $12.00 (1-889289-24-8). New Haven, CT: Ye Olde Font Shoppe, Spring 1998. As a city dweller in the latter 20th century, with bridges burning behind her, Lerner observes the war wounded, the capsized, the hidden victims of internal and perpetual murder and refuses to be burnt out. —Janine Pommy Vega

Lesser, Rika. *Growing Back: Poems 1972-1992.* 90p. $15.95 (1-57003-232-7). pap. $9.95 (1-57003-233-5). Columbia, SC: University of South Carolina Press, Fall 1997. Lesser finds herself creating a personal and literary archaeology. Steely-eyed and soft-hearted, [she] makes her way back to her esthetic and emotional origins, then grows up through them in this unusual book spanning twenty years of musing, grousing, focusing, veering, and transcending. — Molly Peacock. Recuperative, Janus-headed, Growing Back is a book bridging more than two decades for this poet in whom autobiography and learning are so intimately blended. As the title poems asserts, "the bridges we think we have burned behind / are more secure than any destination." In the face of gulfs psychic, linguistic, temporal, and geographical, these are poems of courage, resilience, and humor. —Karl Kirchwey

Levchev, Lyubomir. Translated by Chtiliana Halatcheva-Rousseva. *Sky*

Break. 112p. pap. $12.00 (1-57889-034-9). Pueblo, CO: Passeggiata Press, Spring 1997. Levchev is one of Bulgaria's most prolific poets. This collection, a kind of love letter to America, is a brilliant rumination on the six months he spent in the states. — Passeggiata Press. Like Gulliver, [Levchev] is able to see the landscape with the fresh eyes of a foreigner, explaining us to ourselves. — Richard Harteis

Levering, Donald. *Mister Ubiquity.* 30p. pap. $6.95 (0-944754-087). Johnstown, OH: Pudding House Publications, Spring 1997.

Levertov, Denise. *The Life Around Us: Selected Poems on Nature.* 77p. $19.95 (0-8112-1351-X). pap. $8.95 (0-8112-1352-8). New York, NY: New Directions, Spring 1997. Book by book, I have read [Levertov's] poems for their subtle music, for their deep compassionate intelligence, for their imagination, for the author's dignity and integrity and grace; and, most of all, for the indomitable and humble spirit that hungers there. I have savored them like salt, like honey. —Sam Hamill. Here [Levertov] relocates her quiet ecstatic meditation of blessing and burden, gift and given, to a Pacific Northwest coast and range landscape of magisterial, consoling beauty. —San Francisco Examiner-Chronicle

Levertov, Denise. *The Stream & the Sapphire: Selected Poems on Religious Themes.* 88p. $19.95 (0-8112-1353-6). pap. $8++.95 (0-8112-1354-4). New York, NY: New Directions, Spring 1997. Levertov writes finely honed, intensely accurate descriptions in the conviction that all things — writer, reader, and world — constitute one over-arching manifestation of the presence of God. Levertov's poetry reveals the almost infinite power of metaphor. Because she calls us to stop, to consider, to see, she necessarily calls us to meditate, to contemplate, and to pray. — Harold Isbell, Commonweal

Levin, Harriet. *The Christmas Show.* 84p. pap. $12.00 (0-8070-6837-3). Boston, MA: Beacon Press, Fall 1997. Winner of the 1996 Barnard New Women Poets Prize. If poetry is that which makes your hair stand on end as you read it, then Levin's The Christmas Show is poetry. Her poems call to something deep within us. In truth they haunt us with their very human witness. —Paul

Mariani. Levin is a wonderfully courageous and exacting poet. [Her] poems will attract many readers. —Eavan Boland

Levin, Phillis. *The Afterimage.* 64p. pap. $9.95 (0-914278-67-3). Providence, RI: Copper Beech Press, Fall 1995. The poems of Levin's second collection embrace loss and rapture. Meticulously observant, she captures the paradox of our connection with and distance from others. . . Levin speaks powerfully from a place "Between detachment and wonder." — Publishers Weekly. In elegant formulations. . . Levin explores the gaps and forges the links between language, thought, and matter. She is an "alchemist of the vernacular" whose clarities are hard-won and whose mindfulness is lit by a passionate flame. She has written a glowing book. —Edward Hirsch. Levin reaches beyond form and beyond occasion to draw in a deep, light mystery: the world we know and yet do not know, until we meet it here in her mercurial poems. —Jean Valentine

Levine, Laurence. Compiled by Claire Levine; Edited by C. Yates Hafner. *The Bud That Stays: Poetry, Prose and*

Drawings. 220p. pap. $15.00 (1-56439-070-5). Detroit, MI: Ridgeway Press, Fall 1998. There are few writers in this world who are both articulate scientists and sensitive poets. Levine was a unique scholar-artist who, through his essays and poetry, made reason romantic. —Rabbi Sherwin Wine. What a pleasure to read [Levine's] essays and poems. They convey his excitement over the drama of evolution, his joy at the beauty of nature, and his devotion to the cause of preserving this beauty and advancing the well-being of all humanity. —Morris Goodman

Levine, Philip. *Unselected Poems.* 112p. pap. $13.95 (0-9655239-0-X). Santa Cruz, CA: Greenhouse Review Press, Spring 1998. For over 30 years now readers of contemporary poetry have known Levine's work for its elegiac narrative, its forceful rhythms and rhetoric, and its Vivas praising the dignity of the human spirit. With Unselected Poems he rescues many of his best earlier poems and offers a selection of stunning new and uncollected work. —Christopher Buckley. His poems are about endurance in all its senses, and that is their affirmation. They are about the kind of courage people have when courage fails. In short, they are such poems as possess, beyond their technical strength and emotional urgency, a kind of necessity: whatever it is the truth must exist — for all our sakes. —Hayden Carruth, Bookletter

Levis, Larry. Edited by Philip Levine. *Elegy.* 75p. $25.00 (0-8229-4043-4). pap. $12.95 (0-8229-5648-9). Pittsburgh, PA: University of Pittsburgh Press, Fall 1997. Elegy was written by one of our essential poets at the very height of his powers. His early death is a staggering loss for our poetry, but what he left is a major achievement that will enrich our lives. —Philip Levine

Levitsky, Rachel. *2 [1X1] Portraits.* 18p. pap. $5.00 (1-887997-10-5). boulder, CO: Baksun Books, Fall 1998.

Levitz, Linda C. *The Dark Face of Planting.* 96p. pap. $9.95 (1-56474-205-9). Santa Barbara, CA: Fithian Press, Spring 1997. Levitz's poems create a mysterious, sensual world enriched by memory and fantasy. With lean language and a direct voice that seems at times to spring from her body, Levitz gives personal and particular meaning to the natural world, illustrating

that "everything can be used."
—Natalie Safir

Levy, Andrew. *Continuous Discontinuous: Curve 2.* 136p. pap. $13.50 (0-937013-68-4). Elmwood, CT: Potes & Poets Press, Fall 1997. Levy's wonderful new book can be read, in part, as a meditation within and upon its title, Continuous Discontinuous. That it, it raises the question, what is or isn't discontinuous with what. The question pertains both to phrases of language and to moments of experience; it pertains, that is, both to meaning (those fragile junctures) and to identity (potential continuities of the self). The four forceful, lovely works collected here, though very different from each other, all represent profound and yet quickly changing encounters with sense and sensation. All are swiftly impressionistic and rigorously thoughtful. —Lyn Hejinian

Levy, Andrew. *Elephant Surveillance to Thought.* 32p. pap. $6.00. Buffalo, NY: Meow Press, Fall 1998.

Levy, Robert J. *Chefs at Twilight.* 28p. pap. $5.00 (0-9637849-8-6). Bristolville, OH: Bacchae Press, Fall 1996.

Lewis, Lisa. *Silent Treatment.* 79p. pap. $14.95 (0-14-

058902-3). New York, NY: Penguin Books/Viking Penguin, Fall 1998. Winner of the National Poetry Series. The large meditating presences [of these poems] live within a great still space, within a passionate need to speak and a palpable fear of not being heard. It is as if [Lewis] were trying to write her way into silence as well as finding her way from silence, and this is that poetry. —Stanley Plumly. This is a wonderful book — severe, dark, uncompromising. The poetry is dense with sorrow and saturated with irony. There is a marvelous tension between the weighty cadences of these poems and their bristling, expansive portrayals of American culture. Silent Treatment is filled with the marvelous and the indecorous, the romantic and the unruly, and with the panoramic details of daily life. —Lynn Emanuel

Ley, Jennifer. *The Astrophysicist's Tango Partner Speaks.* 24p. pap. $7.00. Ley, Jennifer, Fall 1996.

Lieberman, Laurence. *Compass of the Dying.* 130p. $22.00 (1-55728-509-8). pap. $16.00 (1-55728-510-1). Fayetteville, AR: University of Arkansas Press, Fall 1998. Prose reportage should be this good! —Ray Olson, ALA Booklist.. There aren't many American poets of any age who can synchronize elegance with spontaneity half so well as he. There is such a fullness to his art that our reading becomes an adventure — breathless, invigorating, enlightening. —Publishers Weekly. There's a remarkable sensibility guiding these poems, an inquisitiveness, a strong sense of humor and compassion. His subjects, his style and syntax, his syllabic lines and cascading stanzas — are all impossible to imitate or mistake for anyone else's. — Thomas Swiss

Lieberman, Michael. *Sojourn at Elmhurst.* 96p. pap. $14.95 (0-89823-189-2). Minneapolis, MN: New Rivers Press, Spring 1998. Lieberman's Frank Goldin is, by his own judgment, insane. He's a bio-chemist by profession, a hus-band, now a hospital patient, an entertainer of visions. He is visionary, in fact, one might say holy, as only one of God's fools can be. —New Rivers Press. Science and art teach us to love the questions, as Rilke noted. Lieberman's Goldin asks and asks in a lan-guage we love, rich as his name. —Hilda Raz

Liebler, M.L., ed. *Brooding the Heartlands: Poets of the Midwest.* 147p. pap. $9.95 (0-933087-50-0). Huron, OH: Bottom Dog Press, Fall 1998. Features the work of Jim Daniels, Sean Thomas Dougherty, W.D. Ehrhart, Aurora Harris, Faye Kicknosway, M.L. Leibler, Ed Sanders, Larry Smith, and Tyrone Williams. —Bottom Dog Press

Lifshin, Lyn. *Cold Comfort: Selected Poems 1970-1996.* 278p. $25.00 (1-57423-041-7). pap. $14.00 (1-57423-040-9). Santa Rosa, CA: Black Sparrow Press, Fall 1997. Lifshin writes with energy, fire and truth of the common world of experience. Like images of battle on a shield, these poems carry the history of the mind and body as enduring tokens of what it is to be alive. —Black Sparrow Press

Light, Kate. *The Laws of Falling Bodies.* 73p. pap. $11.00 (1-885266-55-3). Ashland, OR: Story Line Press, Fall 1997. If you have been wondering what hap-pened to enchantment in con-temporary poetry, open up Light's magical debut collec-tion, The Laws of Falling Bodies. These diaphanous poems seem more conjured

than written! Effortless, sylph-
like, but jauntily embodied,
Light's love sonnets and
poems about art and learning
the art of living dare to
beguile you with their truths
and music. Unabashedly metaphysical, they speak to the
utterly contemporary dilem-
mas of falling in and out of
love. With her combination of
wit and whimsy, Light proves
herself to be among our finest
new poets. —Molly Peacock

Light, Lisa. *The Pavement
Laughing: Map of an
Unfinished Road.* 80p. pap.
$7.00. New York, NY: Big Fat
Press, Fall 1997. Whether on
foot, on freeway, or through
deepest sense memory, the
journey itself provides the
metronome under this rich,
rhythmic language. —Big Fat
Press

Lim, Shirley Geok-lin. *What
the Fortune Teller Didn't Say.*
82p. pap. $8.95 (0-931122-91-
0). Albuquerque, NM: West
End Press, Fall 1998. With
tenderness, precision, and
verve, acceptance and defiance, Lim sings a rich song of
exile. Here are the lines of
loss — of family, country, self
— yet what is lost is also what
is found, and these poems
probe a woman's many and
changing truths. —Alicia
Ostriker. Sharp-edged, sensu-

ous, and acute. —Meena
Alexander

Lima, Frank. Edited by
David Shapiro. *Inventory:
New and Selected Poems.*
208p. pap. $12.95 (1-889097-
10-1). West Stockbridge, MA:
Hard Press, Fall 1997. It is
breathtaking to re-encounter
the exemplary, tender, incandescent, incendiary, utterly
authentic poems of Frank
Lima. Reading them now,
thirty years later, is like stum-
bling on the essential work of
a lost American master — the
missing piece of suffering and
art that redeems the whole.
What makes that discovery all
the more startling is the more
recent poetry, which shows
Lima has been with us all
along, continuing to write lyrical, imaginative poemas
humános. He has kept the
faith; it is now our job to take
in his accomplishment. —
Phillip Lopate

Lind, Michael. *The Alamo:
An Epic.* 351p. $25.00 (0-395-
82758-2). Boston, MA:
Houghton Mifflin Company,
Spring 1997. For generations,
we Texans have boasted that
the battle at the Alamo was an
epic. Finally, Lind has had the
guts and the gifts to take that
boast seriously. Lind writes
with feeling, wit, and clarity
about a defining conflict in the

life of the Americas. The Alamo advances the tradition of the greatest poetic narratives, from Homer and Virgil forward: this is a major literary achievement, even by Texas standards. —Dan Rather. Lind has done an amazing thing — he has reinvented the American epic poem — not as a modernist grab bag á la Pound or Merrill but in its original sense of a heroic poem embodying history. Compellingly retelling one of the great mythic moments of our past, The Alamo is that rare book that can be read satisfyingly both as poetry and history. —Dana Gioia

Lindsay, Sarah. *Primate Behavior.* 104p. $20.00 (0-8021-1619-1). pap. $11.00 (0-8021-3557-9). New York, NY: Grove Press, Fall 1997. Finalist for the National Book Award. Named a 1997 Notable Book by the American Library Association. Lindsay's dark-edged, sometimes creepy poems are also imbued with a buoying sense of respect — for the different, the unexpected and the challenging. —Publishers Weekly. As a poet, Lindsay is fearless. Subjects others would find unpromising or intimidating she forms into poems of eerie, spectral beauty. Primate

Behavior is a must read. — Fred Chappell

Lindskoog, Kathryn. *Light Showers.* 34p. pap. $5.00 (0-940895-28-6). Chicago, IL: Cornerstone Press Chicago, Fall 1996. Lindskoog travels from early childhood to the crossing of the threshold between time and eternity. Light Showers reveals her literary prowess and her sense of humor. —Cornerstone Press Chicago

Lisick, Beth. *Monkey Girl: Swingin' Tales.* 122p. pap. $11.95 (0-916397-49-1). San Francisco, CA: Manic D Press, 1997. Lisick machetes her way through an overgrown tangle of strip malls, junkfood habits, smarmy resorts, 12-step programs, and yuppie pick-up joints. —Manic D Press. Lisick is an engagingly off-hand, personable performer. . . rich in wryly observed instances. —San Francisco Examiner

Liu, Timothy. *Say Goodnight.* 100p. pap. $14.00 (1-55659-085-7). Port Townsend, WA: Copper Canyon Press, Spring 1998. Ruefully beautiful and fearless, Say Goodnight adds to Liu's already considerable renown as a poet of galvanizing sexual frankness and surprising spiritual grace. It's clear that the musk of tenderness, the poise Liu so often achieves is always precious, fought-for, imperiled. Wide-ranging, provocative, accomplished, packed with trenchant detail, Say Goodnight confirms Liu is a true and expansive talent. —Cyrus Cassells. Liu's poems are vicious, beautiful, over the top and deceptively well-mannered. I like the way they surprise with their utter lack of innocence. Or clutter. Like life, they simply stop. Both seething and commanding: Say Goodnight. —Eileen Myles

Livingston, Myra Cohn. Illustrations by Kees de Kiefte. *Cricket Never Does: A Collection of Haiku and Tanka.* 42p. $15.00 (0-689-81123-3). Simon & Schuster/Margaret K. McElderry Books, Spring 1997. Sensitive and evocative, these verses entice the reader on from page to page. They will also tempt young readers to begin to put down their own thoughts and feelings. This is a book to return to again and again. —Simon & Schuster

Locke, Edward. *Names for the Self.* 76p. pap. $7.00 (0-9646587-5-5). Canton, MA: Harlequinade Press, Fall 1997.

Locke, Edward. *Swimming in the Gene Pool.* 74p. pap. $7.00 (0-9646587-4-7). Canton, MA: Harlequinade Press, Spring 1997.

Locke, Edward. *To the Lighter House.* 78p. pap. $7.00 (0-9646587-7-1). Canton, MA: Harlequinade Press, Fall 1998. [The poems] are serious, distinguished, and very much about subjects one cares about. I read them with pleasure. —Stephen Spender

Locke, Edward. *What Time Is it?.* 66p. pap. $7.00 (0-9646587-6-3). Canton, MA: Harlequinade Press, Spring 1998. Locke drives deep, fearlessly takes risks, and approaches reality from surprising angles. His best poems are, I think, absolutely first-rate. —X.J. Kennedy

Locke, Edward. *Where We Park.* 78p. pap. $7.00 (0-9646587-2-0). Canton, MA: Harlequinade Press, Fall 1996.

Locklin, Gerald. *Art Farmer Suite.* 20p. pap. $4.00. Albuquerque, NM: Zerx Press, Spring 1997.

Locklin, Gerald. *The Hospital Poems.* 92p. pap. $13.00 (1-888832-06-1). St. Augustine, FL: Kings Estate Press, Fall 1998.

Loden, Rachel. *The Last Campaign.* 32p. Sleepy Hollow, NY: Slapering Hol Press, Fall 1998. Winner of the 1998 Slapering Hol Press Chapbook Competition. The Last Campaign 's poems are witty, assured in their craft, and wide in their range. There's an edge to these poems, a sly, sardonic edge that lays bare the tricky changes of a world filled with campaign slogans and dissembling politicians. —Allison Joseph

Logan, William. *Vain Empires.* 77p. pap. $14.95 (0-14-058894-9). New York, NY: Penguin Books/Viking Penguin, Spring 1998. [Logan is] among a handful of contemporaries able to command attention with their pure command of technique. —G.E. Murray, Chicago Tribune Book World. An accomplished and original poet. — Richard Tillinghast, The New York Times Book Review. He is like the eel in the well — a purifying agent. —Sven Birkerts, Boston Review

Logghe, Joan, and Miriam Sagan, eds. *Another Desert: Jewish Poetry of New Mexico.* 174p. pap. $15.00 (0-9644196-9-6). Santa Fe, NM: Sherman Asher Publishing, Fall 1998. MPBA Regional Book Award finalist. Sagan and Logghe create a mosaic of poems filled with the color of shabbos candles against vthe turquise sky, the sounds of the shofar along the Rio Grande, and the tastes of chiles, apples, and blintzes. —Sherman Asher Publishing

Logue, Mary. *Settling.* 63p. pap. $11.00 (0-922811-33-4). Minneapolis, MN: Mid-List Press, Fall 1997. A gifted storyteller, Logue's attention is often focused on the lessons abiding within ambiguity. In her second collection of poems, she investigates the world close to home—the relationships between sister and sister, parent and child, lover and beloved. —Mid-List Press. Mary Logue is a poet's poet. Her insight, clarity and simplicity of language, and unshakable calm set the standard for other poets to follow. —Calyx

Lohmann, Jeanne. *Granite Under Water.* 80p. pap. $8.95 (1-56474-180-X). Santa Barbara, CA: Fithian Press, Fall 1996. Lohmann's eye is clear and her voice is strong. Her poems celebrate the world she has experienced as lover, wife, and mother, and they mourn what she has lost to illness and to death. Her commitment to what is beautiful is as strong as the love she celebrates, and it makes these poems a powerful monument to what endures after loss has been reckoned. —Stephen Arkin

Lombardo, Gian. *Sky Open Again.* 80p. pap. $10.00 (0-940475-92-8). Baltimore, MD: Dolphin-Moon Press, Spring 1997. [Lombardo's] pieces are enigmatic and quietly surrealistic, walking a very fine high wire stretched between the everyday and a dryly sardonic personal folklore. A harmless-looking little reality-bomb set to implode quietly in the imagination. —John Strausbaugh, New York Press. They delight and they distress. From Baudelaire to Edson: they know their history and are not crushed by it. Lombardo's masterful prose poems are a significant contribution to the genre. —Askold Melnyczuk, Agni

loncar, m. *66 galaxie.* 59p. (0-87451-878-4). University Press of New England/Middlebury College Press, Fall 1998. Winner of the Katherine Bakeless Nason Prize in Poetry. A car-culture quest-romance told in playful visual and prosodic rondos, jump-cut images in collision with poignant sentiments. In 66 galaxie, Quentin Tarantino meets e.e. cummings in the first American epic haiku noir. —Garrett Hongo. loncar's 66 galaxie does not even remotely resemble anyone else's poetry. Rapid, hypodermic, it is always a scream — in both senses of the word. That is, loncar's comic faculty never disappoints, and simultaneously his poetry screams in the same way that the best of Allen Ginsberg's poetry howls. As 66 galaxie glides past, its chrome flashing disconcertingly, one instantly recognizes it as a classic. — Richard Tillinghast

Long, Ardell J. *Woman to Woman: In the Mind of a Mindful Addict in Recovery.* 36p. pap. $4.00 (0-929688-36-8). Eureka Springs, AR: Bear House Publishing, Fall 1997.

Long, Robert Hill. *The Effigies.* 95p. pap. $12.00 (1-887628-05-3). West Hartford, CT: Plinth Books, Fall 1998. Long's poems have the feel of land and history seen in moments of personal definition, seen through the lens of a family. His voice speaks in long and fluent lines with both freedom and formal assurance, of the experience of war, and of the war and peace of human affection. It is a voice that praises the voluptuous body of earth, and incorporates the sad flotsam of a family, of mortality. At times wickedly funny, at others haunted by the legend and landscape of America, his poems are always politically informed and alert. —Robert Morgan

Long, Robert Hill. *The Work of the Bow.* 90p. $17.50 (1-880834-23-5). pap. $10.00 (1-880834-22-7). Cleveland, OH: Cleveland State University Poetry Center, Spring 1997. Winner of the 1995 Cleveland State University Poetry Center Prize. 'The name of the bow is life," Heraclitus said, "but its work is death." In these powerful poems, at once lyrical and concrete, Long attains a profound realization of life by looking into the eye of death. — Cleveland State University Poetry Center.The Work of the Bow is intense, edgy, but at the same time serene; it builds and moves like a river. There are poems here that are so human and alive they will break your heart and end up leaving it better. This is a beautiful book. —Thomas Lux

Longenbach, James. *Threshold.* 70p. $26.00 (0-226-49245-1). pap. $12.00 (0-226-49247-8). Chicago, IL: University of Chicago Press, Fall 1998. Meditative and often somber, Longenbach's measured verse explores the boundaries between human and spiritual existence, between man and nature, between parent and child, and between the everyday and the transcendent. An impressive debut. —Kirkus Reviews. Threshold stands out among first books of poetry for its intelligence and thematic coherence: this is a book about fear, particularly the fear that outside of a charmed circle of normality disaster waits. The subject is treated without melodrama on one side or complacency on the other. This is an admirable and splendidly promising book. — Robert Pinsky

Longo, Perie. *The Privacy of Wind.* 79p. pap. $10.00 (1-880284-23-5). Santa Barbara, CA: Daniel, John, and Company, Fall 1997. Everything that seems to me the essence of really good poetry is here in Longo's work: precision, economy, lyrical beauty, wit, deep feelings and the gift of conveying those feelings to the reader with heartbreaking power. — Charles Champlin

Loomis, Jon. *Vanitas Motel.* 70p. pap. $12.95 (0-932440-81-9). Oberlin, OH: Oberlin College Press, Spring 1998. The first time I read one of

Loomis's poems, I knew I had encountered a poet whose work I would want to watch for. His poems are clean and clear-eyed, remarkably distilled, often ferociously understated or matter-of-fact about pain and loss. They dart quickly, shading through tenderness and hilarity, aching with wit and exhilarating insights. Vanitas Motel has more purpose and control than we usually encounter in first collections. Loomis has arrived in our midst, fully formed as a poetic voice, and he will bear watching. — David Young

Loomis, Sabra. *Travelling on Blue.* 26p. pap. $7.00. New York, NY: Firm Ground Press, Spring 1998.

Lorca, Federico García. Edited by Christopher Maurer. *In Search of Duende.* 112p. pap. $7.00 (0-8112-1376-5). New York, NY: New Directions, Spring 1998. A brand new collection of essays and poetry including three newly translated never-before-published works. —New Directions. Lorca's works, which combine elements of Andalusian folklore with sophisticated and often surrealistic poetic techniques, cut across all social and educational barriers. Spain's great

poet and playwright is being rediscovered. —The New York Times

Lorca, Federico García, and Juan Ramón Jiménez. Translated by Robert Bly. *Lorca and Jiménez: Selected Poems.* 193p. pap. $10.00 (0-8070-6213-8). Boston, MA: Beacon Press, Fall 1997. A unique gathering of poems by two great twentieth-century poets, both in the original Spanish and in powerful English translations. In a new preface to this edition, editor and translator Robert Bly explores what the poems reveal today—about the spirit, politics, and the purpose of art. —Beacon Press

Lorde, Audre. *The Collected Poems of Audre Lorde.* 489p. $35.00 (0-393-04090-9). New York, NY: Norton, W.W., and Company, Spring 1997; Spring 2000 (new paper). Collected here for the first time are more than three hundred poems from one of this country's most influential poets. —W.W. Norton. Lorde wrote as a Black woman, a mother, a daughter, a lesbian, a visionary; poems of elemental wildness and healing, nightmare and lucidity. Lorde's is a poetry which extends beyond white Western politics, beyond the anger and wisdom of Black America. These are poems which blaze and pulse on the page. — Adrienne Rich

Lossy, Rella. *Time Pieces: A Collection of Poetry 1944-1996.* 152p. $24.95 (1-57143-059-8). pap. $13.95 (1-57143-060-1). Berkeley, CA: Reflections Press / RDR Books, Fall 1996. Time Pieces' three sections span four decades of Lossy's life. The portion entitled "Metronomes" includes thirty powerful and sometimes humorous poems based on her experience with metastatic breast cancer. She succumbed to that disease seven days after sending Time Pieces to the printer. —Reflections Press. In a time when American poetry is mainly isolated in a subjective mode, Lossy's poems are marked by a rare, objective, descriptive ability. In "Metronomes" she measures her struggle with cancer in a powerful group of poems that illuminate the human condition with wit and compassion. —Jim Schevill

Louis, Adrian C. *Ceremonies of the Damned.* 71p. pap. $10.00 (0-87417-302-7). Reno, NV: University of Nevada Press, Fall 1997. In these new poems, Louis writes the purest kind of elegy. In a voice that ranges from curse to prayer, often in the same breath, he mourns the ghosts he walks among: his own past selves, and the multitudes lost to death, love, drink, and the virulent sad politics of America. Among these are the most tough-minded and moving poems on Alzheimer's that I've ever read. As always, Louis is bent on stripping away whatever is not the truth, be it personal or political, so that the present can be fully understood. —Chase Twichell. Louis channels the energy of anger into poetry with as much incendiary power as any poet writing in this country today. —Martín Espada

Lourie, Dick. *Ghost Radio.* 117p. pap. $12.00 (1-882413-48-2). Brooklyn, NY: Hanging Loose Press, Spring 1998. This volume, [Lourie's] first in a long time, includes elegies and love poems. It's good to hear his voice again after a lapse of some years — a voice he found early, and which speaks with a unique and convincing eloquence. —Denise Levertov. Poetry promises to hold so much: love and death, friendship and anger, history and politics, music and humor. Lourie's poems not only deliver on the promise, they suffuse each of these things with all the others, so that we are soon reading (among other things) a comic history of the politics of music, as refined by rage and polished by friendship. Ghost Radio is a delicious blend. — Lewis Hyde

Lovric, Michelle, and Nikiforos Doxiadis Mardas, trans. *The Sweetness of Honey and the Sting of Bees: A Book of Love From the Ancient Mediterranean.* 97p. $14.95 (1-55670-680-4). New York, NY: Stewart, Tabori & Chang, Fall 1997. Ezra Pound once described translations of archaic authors as "blood brought to ghosts." This strikingly beautiful book breathes warm life into the poems and letters of both the great and unknown vanished lovers of the ancient Mediterranean. Their 2000-year-old words are as fresh, passionate, and sometimes as irreverent as today's raw song lyrics. Illustrated by the Fayum Portraits. — Stewart, Tabori & Chang

Lowenfels, Walter. Edited by Joel Lewis. *Reality Prime: Selected Poems.* 113p. pap. $12.95 (1-883689-71-6). Jersey City, NJ: Talisman House, Publishers, Fall 1998. This is the most comprehensive collection of Lowenfal's poetry available. Its cornerstone is the three "Death

Elegies." Crucial texts for the avant-garde during Lowenfel's Paris years, they appear together for the first time. — Talisman House, Publishers. Way before the sixties, Lowenfels perceived the lopsided canon of our poetry; he did a great deal to change the climate. —Armand Schwerner

Loy, Mina. Edited by Roger L. Conover. *The Lost Lunar Baedeker.* 236p. pap. $13.00 (0-374-52507-2). Farrar, Straus and Giroux/Noonday, Spring 1996; April 1997 (paper). In recent years, the neglected Loy has been rediscovered by a new generation of readers. The Lost Lunar Baedeker rescues Loy's key works from the pages of the forgotten publications in which they first appeared. The volume includes all of her Futurist and feminist satires, poems from her Paris and New York periods, and the complete cycle of "Love Songs," as well as previously unknown texts and detailed notes. —Farrar, Straus and Giroux. Loy has finally been admitted into "the company of poets," the canon. As if she cared. —Thom Gunn, The Times Literary Supplement

Lubin, Ruth. *Living This Moment.* 28p. pap. $5.00. Lubin, Ruth, Spring 1997.

Lucina, Mary. *Guardians of Air.* 64p. pap. $8.50 (1-880286-27-0). Canton, CT: Singular Speech Press, Fall 1997. Lucina's poems invite the reader into spaces both of light and darkness, seeing and not seeing, the spaces where discovery is possible. — Singular Speech Press

Ludvigson, Susan. *Trinity.* 63p. $19.95 (0-8071-2115-0). Baton Rouge, LA: Louisiana State University Press, Fall 1996. Trinity is a three-poem meditation on the inexplicable mysteries of flesh and spirit in which Ludvigson shows a remarkable grace braided with the steeliest of wills to see. In these poems God answers Emily Dickinson, and Mary Magdalene tells the Jesus story in a voice that is as erotic as it is plaintive and charming. Ludvigson proves herself a poet as adept at mythic scope as she has proved compelling in her earlier work. — Dave Smith. Ludvigson achieves what all great poets achieve: compression of time and language and, at the same time, spiritual, emotional, and aesthetic expansiveness. The collection is at once daring (it may approach blasphemy in

some circles) and compelling. —Andrea Hollander Budy

Ludwig, Laura Lonshein. *What Do You Think, You're Smart or Something?.* 16p. pap. $5.00. Brooklyn, NY: Diamond Hitch Press, Fall 1996.

Luna, James G. *Youth of the 80's.* 128p. pap. $10.95 (0-9641606-0-9). Cupertino, CA: Easy Break, First Time Publishing, ©1994. These poems document a young man's life from age 15, as he enters into manhood and his perception of the real world is awakened. —Easy Break, First Time Publishing

Luoma, Bill. *Works & Days.* 144p. pap. $15.00 (1-889097-28-4). Hard Press/The Figures, Fall 1998. An astonishingly readable prose-poetry road trip through the U.S. which takes in the often overlooked sights and sounds of everyday life, including baseball and literature, with their implicit quirkiness, humor and desperation. —Hard Press/The Figures

Luttrell, Steve. *Home Movies.* 61p. pap. $10.95 (1-878471-05-8). Pacifica, CA: Big Bridge Press, Fall 1998.

Lutz, Jeanne. *Just the Right Rock.* 20p. pap. $5.00. Port Townsend, WA: Sagittarius Press, Spring 1998. Poems about child abuse. — Sagittarius Press

Lux, Thomas. *New and Selected Poems 1975-1995.* 174p. $23.00 (0-395-85832-1). pap. $14.00 (0-395-92488-X). Boston, MA: Houghton Mifflin Company, Spring 1997; Spring 1999 (new paper). Reading the poetry of Thomas Lux is an experience unlike any other. Who else would write a poem about an unopened jar of maraschino cherries in a refrigerator, or feel himself able to speak for today's commercial leech farmer? In one poetic voice Lux comments on the absurd, the pathetic, and the common-place in our culture, writing with compassion as well as satire. —Houghton Mifflin. A world torn open, by origi-nality of language and vision, to release intense feeling. . . . [Lux] rescues something in the human psyche and turns it into poetry. —Citation of the Poetry Society of America's Alice Fay di Castagnola Award. Lux may be one of the poets on whom the future of the genre depends. He has the stuff to win readers back from their unhappy places of

exile. —Sven Birkerts, Wigwag

Luzzaro, Susan. *Complicity.* 36p. pap. $7.00 (0-932264-17-4). Portland, OR: Trask House Books, 1996. Luzzaro has the voice of a deeply intelligent friend, a woman you can trust. She writes as though our lives depended upon these poems. Reading them one cannot help but share her desire for justice, for a more tender engagement with the physical world. — Sandra Alcosser

Luzzaro, Susan. *The Flesh Envelope.* 64p. pap. $8.95 (0-931122-88-0). Albuquerque, NM: West End Press, Spring 1998. [In Luzzaro's poems] Eros curls beside logos, and they whisper together in the dark. [Luzzaro] has the voice of a deeply intelligent friend, a woman you can trust. She writes as though our lives depended upon these poems, and reading them one cannot help but share her desire for justice, for a more tender engagement with the physical world. —Sandra Alcosser

Lykes, Dorothy Raitt. *Cobalt Blue.* 64p. $20.00 (0-933313-24-1). pap. $12.95 (0-933313-25-X). Tucson, AZ: SUN/gem-ini Press, 1995. There is a story here of love, reminis-cence, widowhood, devastation, love and the independence of resilience. Cobalt Blue is a journey within language for the eye and heart, a splendid gift I'm grateful for. —Pamela Stuart

Lynch, Thomas. *Still Life in Milford.* 139p. $21.00 (0-393-04659-1). New York, NY: Norton, W.W., and Company, Fall 1998; Fall 1999 (new paper). In Still Life in Milford, he brings to hand a book that reads like a life's work and the work of a life that has at once fulfilled its promise and promises to go on telling "the news of the world" for the length of the journey. — Michael Heffernan. Through its sonic elegance and wry wisdom, Still Life in Milford testifies to the durable music of the otherworldly within the everyday. —Alice Fulton. The poems in Still Life in Milford sing many wonderful tunes with great verve. Lynch loves the sounds of the human voice, his own and others, and takes such joy in the singing that the pleasure must be illicit. Must be — because it's so good. —Andrew Hudgins

Mac Cormack, Karen. *The Tongue Moves Talk.* 57p. pap. $11.00 (0-925904-12-0). Chax Press/West House Books, 1997. Sense is made and remade word for word in Mac Cormack's The Tongue Moves Talk. Exquisitely refractory, incessantly modulating, sumptuously uttering, these poems attain a state of aesthetic grace without recourse to hooks or props. —Charles Bernstein.The Tongue Moves Talk is ablaze with boisterous verbal precision. There's no end to her range, her textual mobility. She is meticulous, compelling, incessant, unexpected. Just clap. —Maggie O'Sullivan

Macaluso, Peter. *American Pharoah: The Poetry of Peter Macaluso 1988-1996.* 142p. Flushing, NY: Copperjacket Concepts, Fall 1996.

Macaluso, Peter. *Bolt Complex.* 45p. Macaluso, Peter M., Spring 1998. Sometimes shocking, lyrical poetry with a rock n'roll feel. — Peter M. Macaluso

Macdonald, Cynthia. *I Can't Remember.* 79p. $21.00 (0-679-45457-8). New York, NY: Knopf, Alfred A., Fall 1997. Macdonald's poems are quite extraordinary in their range and daring. She is brilliantly versatile in adopting the views, attitudes, or moods of fictive or actual persons different from herself, and she does so with a delicate empathy. She can be remarkably witty, as well as deeply moving, and sometimes even ruthless in her insights, which are more like X rays than snapshots. She is a poet of many skills and formidable dexterity. —Anthony Hecht

Macer-Story, Eugenia. *Crossing Jungle River.* 72p. pap. $6.00 (1-879980-11-8). Yankee Oracle Press, Fall 1998.

Maciel, Olivia, ed. *Shards of Light / Astillas de Luz.* 136p. pap. $12.95 (1-882688-18-X). Chicago, IL: Tia Chucha Press, Fall 1998. This bilingual anthology presents the work of twenty-one poets in Chicago whose cultural and linguistic heritages are rooted in Latin America and Spain. Among the contributors are Ana Castillo, Carlos Cumpián, Ray González, Luis Rodriguez and Diana Solís. —Tia Chucha Press

Macioci, R. Nikolas. *Why Dance?.* 72p. pap. $8.50 (1-880286-22-X). Canton, CT: Singular Speech Press, Fall 1996. Macioci has said, "Wherever I find destruction, I want to build," and he believes, with Kafka, that "A book is an axe to break the frozen sea within us." These poems demonstrate the power of that belief. Here is Macioci,

building. —Singular Speech Press. Intensity pervades [Macioci's] poetry. His creative images provide telling surprises. —Byline

Mackey, Nathaniel. *Whatsaid Serif.* 112p. pap. $12.95 (0-87286-341-7). San Francisco, CA: City Lights Books, Fall 1998. Whatsaid Serif is comprised of installments 16 through 35 of Song of the Andoumboulou, an ongoing serial work named after a Dogon funeral song. —City Lights Books. Mackey's poem is a brilliant renewal of and experiment with the language of our spiritual condition and a measure of what poetry gives in trust — "heart's / meat" and the rush of language to bear it. —Robin Blaser. Mackey's raspy rebus-like cultural resurfacings are both beautiful to read and worthy of repeated efforts at comprehension. — Publishers Weekly

Madhubuti, Haki R. *Ground Work: New and Selected Poems of Don L. Lee (Haki R. Madhubuti) From 1966-1996.* 329p. $29.95 (0-88378-172-7). pap. $19.95 (0-88378-173-5). Chicago, IL: Third World Press, Fall 1996. More than any other Black poet who became influential in the last sixties [Madhubuti] remained actively loyal to the richness of his faith in and love for Black people. —Gwendolyn Brooks. The poems reflect both the disturbing changes in American society in the last thirty years and Madhubuti's persistent determination to unmask the illusion of progress. —Dr. Joyce A. Joyce

Madhubuti, Haki R. *HeartLove: Wedding and Love Poems.* 87p. $16.95 (0-88378-202-2). Chicago, IL: Third World Press, Spring 1998. Madhubuti has created warm, elegant poems that give honor to his long life of community work and poetry. Some of the finest human poems in English are in this book. —Robert Bly. What is more needed than these poems celebtrating our traditional selves, our long history of loving and being loved? Who better than Madhubuti to continue writing them? A necessary book. — Lucille Clifton

Madsen, Michael. *Burning in Paradise.* 157p. pap. $14.00 (1-888277--06-8). San Diego, CA: Incommunicado Press, Spring 1998. Actor and writer Madsen's poetry explores the intense and gritty experiences of a man living life on the edge. Chronicling episodes of loneliness, infidelity, depression, drugs and sex, Madsen exposes his weaknesses as

well as his disappointments amidst the false pretenses of our so-called civilized world. —Incommunicado Press. A natural menace. —Rolling Stone. I like him better than Kerouac. Raunchier, more poignant. He's got street language. Images I can relate to. He blows my mind with his drifts of gut-wrenching riffs. —Dennis Hopper

Magner, James, Jr. *Only the Shadow of the Great Fool.* 182p. pap. $10.00. Cleveland, OH: Blue Flamingo Productions, Fall 1996.

Magowan, Robin. *Lilac Cigarette in a Wish Cathedral.* 74p. $15.95 (1-5700-3269-6). pap. $9.95 (1-5700-3270-X). Columbia, SC: University of South Carolina Press, Fall 1998. Magowan has explored the frontiers of the senses, the borders of the spirit, and returned with poems that seem to speak in tongues of what can and cannot be seen, can and cannot be understood. The result is a rare illumination. — J.D. McClatchy

Mahon, Derek. *The Yellow Book.* 57p. $17.95 (0-916390-82-9). pap. $11.95 (0-916390-82-9). Winston-Salem, NC: Wake Forest University Press, Spring 1998. In The Yellow Book, the home-seeking traveler finds lodgings in our fierce fin de siécle under the roof of his Dublin attic flat. Amid echoes from dead writers, "clouds of unknowing" and ghosts from his own life, the poet muses wisely and wittily on our wound-down decade and expiring double millennium. —Wake Forest University Press. A magnificently playful book, intricately designed and executed, a worthy addition to the Mahon canon. —David Mason, The Hudson Review

Mahon, Jeanne. *The Wolf in the Wood.* 66p. pap. $8.00 (0-9626406-1-1). Youngstown, OH: Pangborn Books, Fall 1996. Clearly written and sensuous in its particulars, grounded in the natural world, Mahon's poetry takes a path that leads us from childhood journeys to an adult realm where compassion and music prevail. She is a lithe story teller, inviting us in to share her feast of memory and insight. This is an accomplished book that deserves a large audience. —Colette Inez. Mahon's work is poetically sure both in the great value it places on the ordinary things and experience of our lives and in its steadfast, rhythmical voice. —Len Roberts

Mahony, Phillip, ed. *From Both Sides Now: The Poetry of the Vietnam War and Its Aftermath.* 314p. $30.00 (0-684-84946-1). pap. $16.00. New York, NY: Simon & Schuster/Scribner, Fall 1998. No conflict has given rise to more deadly stereotypes than the war in Vietnam. Mahoney's moving anthology helps to counteract such stereotypes while deepening our understanding of the single most divisive series of events in recent American history. —David Lehman

Major, Clarence. *Configurations: New and Selected Poems 1958-1998.* 323p. pap. $17.00 (1-55659-090-3). Port Townsend, WA: Copper Canyon Press, Fall 1998. In Configurations, Major adds a substantial body of new poems to work culled from eight previous volumes to present a clear assessment of his forty-year career. Driven by a music as inspired by blues and jazz as it is by the Cantos of Ezra Pound, Major's poems are both visual and lyrical. —Copper Canyon Press. Major is a master of everyday language and textual fine-turning. This ninth collection should render this prolific novelist, poet, and anthologist eminently readable and teachable. —Publishers Weekly. It's refreshing to come across the spank and sparkle that jumps up on every page. There's not a breath that's predictable. Every time we turn a page of Major's poetry we find our- selves on a delicious new roller coaster of vigor and vit- riol. —Rocky Mountain News. Major writes poetry with the resistant, angular sur- face of tumbled brick, as if the poem has been literally smashed. An improvisational, jazz-like quality. Some tough, sharp observations. —Kirkus Reviews

Makkai, Adam, ed. *In Quest of the 'Miracle Stag": The Poetry of Hungary.* 964p. $89.95 (0-9642094-0-3). pap. $39.95 (0-9642094-1-1). Champaign, IL: University of Illinois Press, Spring 1997. A comprehensive anthology that brings 800 years of great Hungarian poetry, from its shaman roots to the present, to English-speaking readers. This collection offers a rare and penetrating look into the heart and soul of a nation. — University of Illinois Press. This anthology belongs in all public and academic libraries as well as in the homes of lovers of world literature. — Roger Williams Wescott

Makofske, Mary. *Eating Nasturtiums.* 28p. pap. $7.00

(1-886226-04-0). Chico, CA: Flume Press, Spring 1998. Winner of the 1997 Flume Press Manuscript Competition.

Makuck, Peter. *Against Distance.* 95p. $20.00 (1-880238-44-6). pap. $12.95 (1-880238-45-4). Rochester, NY: BOA Editions, Spring 1997. Makuck's poetry does for the coastal waters of North Carolina what Wallace Stevens did for the Florida Keys, and Robinson Jeffers for Big Sur. He revives in language the very look, feel, and smell of beach and wetlands, and gives a human measure to the com- plex imbrication of shore, sky and sea. —Emily Grosholz. What sets these poems apart is their ethos, their attentiveness to the world outside the self and their capacity to love: people, creatures, landscape. Makuck's poetry shows us not only how to see, but how to live. —Jonathan Holden

Mallarmé, Stéphane. Translated by Henry Weinfield. *Collected Poems.* 282p. pap. $18.95 (0-520-20711-4). Berkeley, CA: University of California Press, Fall 1994. The gaping empty space on the shelf has now been filled, handsomely, almost miraculously, by Weinfield's magnificent ver- sion of Mallarmé's Collected

Poems. —Arthur Goldhammer, Washington Post Book World. Weinfield's versions are superb — true miracles, I believe — and give us the flavor of Mallarmé's work for the first time. —Paul Auster. Throughout, the poet's creative process imitates nature as it ripens into the fresh fruits of his poetry. Essential for all libraries that collect poetry in English translation. —Judy Clarence, Library Journal

Mallory, Lawrence. *Ned and the Monster Poems.* 22p. pap. $7.95 (1-891219-04-9). Siasconset, MA: Linear Arts, 1997.

Malone, Hank. *New Mexico Haiku.* 100p. pap. $6.95 (1-888923-05-9). Westland, MI: Poetic License Press, Spring 1998 (revised edition). Malone is a lovely poet, full of piss and vinegar, along with some milk of human kindness. Read him. —Carolyn Kizer. Malone's poetry is continuously incisive, funny, and fueled with passion. Armed with a sharp wit and an ample supply of irony, he cuts through the contradictions and absurdities of the human condition. — David Silver

Maltz, Wendy, ed. **Passionate Hearts: The*

Poetry of Sexual Love. 212p. $16.00 (1-57731-007-1). Novato, CA: New World Library, Fall 1996; Fall 1999 (new paper). Culled from classic works of poetry, literary and erotica journals, and unpublished poetry, Passionate Hearts celebrates the joys of sexual expression. —New World Library. An essential addition to any sexuality library. —Patricia Love

Mandel, Charlotte. *Sight Lines.* 100p. pap. $12.00 (1-877675-27-X). New York, NY: Midmarch Arts Press, Spring 1998. Mandel presses down "on the holding pedal of memory," preserving for us a World War II childhood, the events of a long marriage, and domestic and foreign scenes that combine the commonplace and the bizarre in crisp and lucid language. —Maxine Kumin. A book of immaculate precision, every word an exact cup. —Cynthia Ozick

Mandel, Tom. *Prospect of Release.* 58p. pap. $12.95 (0-925904-11-2). Tucson, AZ: Chax Press, Fall 1996. These 50 poems, 700 lines confront self, other, identity, loss, history, language and meaning through the most concrete instance we have of what the poststructuralists call "an absent presence" — the death of a parent. These are the most intensely felt poems I have ever read. —Ron Silliman

Mandel, Tom, and Daniel Davidson. *Absence Sensorium: A Poem.* 132p. pap. $14.00 (0-937013-64-1). Elmwood, CT: Potes & Poets Press, 1997. In an e-mail ether Absence Sensorium passed between its 3000-mile-apart-progenitors. Its renaissance silvas, 7-line stanzas whose lines are 7 or 11 syllables, enjamb a quantitative imperfect paradise of attention, deeply traditional but wearing the indelible emblem of the damaged human present. From the authors' distance and from the silent range of the medium, the poem gained its scope. —David Thomas Son-El. Two enormous poetic talents and two richly imaginative perspectives combine to make a single magnificent poem, one that "holds the night between two pale fingers." —George Lakoff

Mangan, Pat. *The Harness.* 52p. pap. $12.95 (1-884800-15-7). Marshfield, MA: Four Way Books, Spring 1998. Intelligent, laconic, sparely written, these poems trace the unsettling links between our gestures of affection and the often unwitting cruelties we inflict on those we love.

Mangan's quiet objectivity effectively dramatizes the scene while making fine moral discriminations that never preach or oversimplify. His ability, in Yeats' phrase, to hold reality and justice in a single thought, marks this book as a mature work of art. —Tom Sleigh

Mangold, Sarah. *Blood Substitutes.* 45p. pap. $7.00 (0-937013-77-3). Elmwood, CT: Potes & Poets Press, Fall 1998.

Manrique, Jaime. Translated by Edith Grossman and Eugene Richie. *My Night With / Mi Noche con Federico García Lorca.* 125p. pap. $12.00 (0-9651558-3-8). New York, NY: Painted Leaf Press, Spring 1997. Throughout Manrique's poetry a faint overtone of humor runs, permanent and subtle as the scent of saffron in the air of a kitchen in Barranquilla, the town in Colombia where he grew up. Humor as elegy, elegy as humor — which is it? Hard to say, but our luck is to have been allowed to sit next to him in the little movie house of his memories. —Alfred Corn. A stunning book. Like Neruda, he has a careful affinity to the atmosphere and climate of the poem, it's light, exposure, latitude, and heat. These poems are breathtaking and vulnerable. —The James White Review

Marcello, Leo Luke. *Nothing Grows in One Place Forever: Poems of a Sicilian American.* 119p. pap. $14.50 (1-56809-037-4). St. Louis, MO: Time Being Books, Fall 1998. Marcello is one of those rare poets who knows how to peel back and examine the delicate layers of the past. Often these poems find occasion for celebration, but just as often for lamentation. Always, though, they are the hard-won affirmations of an honest and searching heart. —David Bottoms

Marcus, Morton. *When People Could Fly.* 128p. $21.00 (1-882413-45-8). pap. $13.00 (1-882413-44-X). Brooklyn, NY: Hanging Loose Press, Fall 1997. Marcus is the kind of priest-poet who, like Peguy or Jacob, gets to the Light by tearing up the universe in ecstatic dance. — Andrei Codrescu. These eloquent prose poems journey over a vast landscape of human experience, myth, folk tale, and family history. Larger than life, spinning through time and space with imaginative pyrotechnics and acute perception, the poems are entertaining, sobering, and

above all, wise. —Shirley Kaufman

Mariani, Paul. *The Great Wheel.* $18.95 (0-393-03921-8). pap. $11.00 (0-393-31702-1). New York, NY: Norton, W.W., and Company, Spring 1996; Fall 1997 (paper). Mariani has availed himself of the medieval concept of the Great Wheel of Fortune [to dramatize] the vital issues in people's lives. [The Great Wheel] is the most skillful and compelling of his poetry to date. —David Ignatow. The poems in The Great Wheel have nothing at all to do with theories of what poetry ought to be but are — surprise! — about real life, raw and credible; and very powerful, very dramatic they are, too. After this book the reader should be able to spot a Mariani poem anywhere without checking for the signature. —Donald Justice

Marlatt, David. *A Hog Slaughtering Woman.* 50p. pap. $12.00 (0-932826-49-0). Kalamazoo, MI: New Issues Press, Fall 1996. A sister kicked by a horse, a stray hog run down by a Flacon sedan, a glimpse of a grandmother's hair undone, a man killing blue-gill with a spoon — these and other incarnations achieve, in Marlatt's testimony, the grim and wondrous power of icons and relics. These are poems that disturb and endear us to the species we recognize — not always with gladness — as our own. In A Hog Slaughtering Woman, the blood offerings, sacrifices, gospels and gossip, love and losses that we call "family" are, as in the ancient liturgies, witnessed, celebrated, sung outright. Marlatt's is a welcome debut. —Thomas Lynch

Marlis, Stefanie. *Rife.* 64p. $20.95 (1-889330-11-6). pap. $12.95 (1-889330-12-4). Louisville, KY: Sarabande Books, Spring 1998. Marlis's poetry is indeed "rife," abundant with clarity, compassion, wisdom, forgiveness. Hers is a world of departures and returns, losses and recoveries, where wry indirection, nuance and detail, a bell-like delicacy, prevail. Her mode of peripheral vision reveals a special quality of light and lightness. She's a marvel. No other poet is quite like her. —Ronald Wallace. Rife is a book of scope, compassionate heart, and invention; of vision and surprise. In these splendid poems, prose poems, and "definitions," Marlis offers the reader the nourishment and joy — at times chastened — of life acknowledged in all its complexity, all its rich range. —Jane Hirshfield

Marlowe, Christopher. Edited by E.D. Pendry. *Complete Plays and Poems.* 543p. pap. $9.95 (0-460-87043-2). Boston, MA: Tuttle, Charles E./Everyman, 1996. A comprehensive paperback edition with introduction, glossary, bibliography and chronology of Marlowe's life. The text of this complete edition reveals Marlowe as a highly gifted but disturbed young man, more disillusioned than idealistic, who produced works of great strength and complexity. —Tuttle, Charles E./Everyman

Martin, Carl R. *Genii Over Salzburg.* 104p. pap. $10.95 (1-56478-186-0). Normal, IL: Dalkey Archive Press, Spring 1998. In a work which resists classification, Martin's use of the permutations and gradations of meaning, the nuance created in artistic space by the tension inherent in the relation of thought and image, defies literal interpretation. His words mimic his technique. —Dalkey Archive Press. Martin reminds me of certain great "outsider" poets of the past like Gérard de Nerval or Robert Walser — writers whose work one seizes on greedily at moments when one

feels like drowning in poetry.
This is the right stuff. —John
Ashbery

Martin, Jack. *Weekend
Sentences: When Truth
Begins.* 15p. pap. $6.95 (0-
614-24054-9). Johnstown,
OH: Pudding House
Publications, Fall 1997. [A]
series of dramatic monologues
in the voice[s] of men and
women "involved" with the
Workenders Program of the
Larimer County Detention
Center. —Pudding House
Publications

Martin, Richard.
Modulations. 112p. pap.
$12.00 (1-878580-67-1).
Paradise, CA: Asylum Arts
Publishing, Fall 1998.
[Martin] is the chronicler of
the empty dynamism of this
culture, but he knows its joys
too. In the fast-paced world of
his verse there beats a fierce
and oddly tonic heart. —
Andrei Codrescu. I, personal-
ly, take solace and hope from
these poems, amiable a-bombs
to consciousness. Crack this
book, Reader, and see things
as they are. —Bob Holman.
It's not often there's a poet so
simply a pleasure and so
secure in what he as to offer.
Martin knows what he's doing
and has that dependable
virtue. —Robert Creeley

**Martinez, Carla; John
Sousa, and Toni Wynn.** *Color
Voices Place.* 120p. pap.
$12.95 (0-9638843-9-5). Santa
Margarita, CA: Mille Grazie
Press/SeaMoon Press, Spring
1997. Color Voices Place
brings together the distinctive
and lively voices of three sea-
soned poets. [It] speaks honestly, clearly and without compromise to our
mind/body/spirit
delight/dilemma in a choir of
distinguished voices. —Santa
Barbara News-Press

Martínez, Demetria.
Breathing Between the Lines.
61p. $24.95 (0-8165-1796-7).
pap. $12.95 (0-8165-1798-3).
Tucson, AZ: University of
Arizona Press, Spring 1997.
Many of the poems in this
book touch on the themes
from Mother Tongue,
Martínez's novel about an
American activist who falls in
love with a Salvadoran political refugee. Weaving together
threads of love and family,
social conviction and activism,
loss and renewal, Breathing
Between the Lines carries the
reader deep inside the head
and heart of a talented
Chicana writer. —University
of Arizona Press. Martínez has
been noted mostly for her very
political fiction and
reportage/political prose. She
is first and foremost, however,

a poet, and she demonstrates in these works that the personal and the spiritual are truly the most political works we can write. —Luis Alberto Urrea

Martínez, Dionisio D. *Bad Alchemy.* $17.95 (0-393-03733-9). pap. $12.00 (0-393-31531-2). New York, NY: Norton, W.W., and Company, Spring 1995; Fall 1996 (paper). [Martínez's] exuberance is a very winning quality. It is decidedly American, but it is also — and to me the most movingly — an expression of the immigrant's sense of America, suggestive of sadness no less than innocence. Martínez's poems reflect poignantly on the poet's status as a Cuban exile destined to a perennial sense of dislocation. Nostalgia combined with ardor results in good chemistry — or Bad Alchemy. —David Lehman. Martínez is one of the most exciting new voices in American poetry. His poems are mysterious and intellectually provocative. They are the poems of a survivor. —Stephen Dunn

Martz, Sandra, ed. *The Tie That Binds: A Collection of Writings About Fathers & Daughters, Mothers & Sons.* 192p. $18.00 (0-918949-20-3).

(0-918949-19-X). Watsonville, CA: Papier-Mache Press, 1992. The poetry, fiction and photos in this emotionally charged collection, highlight the unique relationships between parents and their children at different stages of life, and invite a close, intimate exploration of the parent / child relationship. —Midwest Book Review Newsletter

Martz, Sandra Haldeman, ed. *At Our Core: Women Writing About Power.* 216p. pap. $11.00 (1-57601-007-4). Watsonville, CA: Papier-Mache Press, Spring 1998. These stories, poems, and photographs show women in control of their own lives. Breathtakingly honest and courageous, these voices honor and validate women's uniquely personal definitions of power. —Papier-Mache Press. A book that needs reading and rereading, and that should prompt women of all ages to think and talk with one another. —San Francisco Bay Guardian

Martz, Sandra Haldeman, ed. *There's No Place Like Home for the Holidays.* 160p. pap. $9.95 (1-57601-053-8). Watsonville, CA: Papier-Mache Press, Fall 1997. A charming selection of stories, poems and anecdotes relating to the traditional holidays of Christmas, Passover and Thanksgiving. —Publishers Weekly. Delightful. — Independent Publisher

Martz, Sandra Haldeman, ed. *When I Am an Old Woman I Shall Wear Purple (Abridged Version).* 64p. $6.95 (1-57601-052-X). Watsonville, CA: Papier-Mache Press, Fall 1997. Continues the universal message that aging is a natural gift of life. —Papier-Mache Press. The intimacy and humor of these writings should touch readers old and young. —Booklist

Marvell, Andrew. Edited by Paul Negri. *"To His Coy Mistress" and Other Poems.* 64p. pap. $1.00 (0-486-29544-3). Mineola, NY: Dover Publications, Spring 1997. One of the greatest of the Metaphysical poets, Marvell (1621-1678) was also among the most eclectic, writing love poems, satires, religious and political verse that can be savored for their complexity and intellectual rigor and for their beauty. —Dover Publications

Marzán, Julio. *Puerta de tierra.* 67p. (0-8477-0315-0). San Juan, Puerto Rico: University of Puerto Rico Press, Fall 1998.

Masterson, Dan. *All Things, Seen and Unseen, Poems: New and Selected, 1967-1997.* 123p. $20.00 (1-55728-485-7). pap. $12.00 (1-55728-486-5). Fayetteville, AR: University of Arkansas Press, Fall 1997. Selected from thirty years of work, the poems in this volume have collected accolades from some of the best-loved poets of our times. Anne Sexton wrote, "Legacy by Water surpasses what most of us have done by many a lap. It is an inspiration to me to read a poem so moving, so well plotted, so intensely tactile." James Wright wrote, "On Earth As It Is is genuinely disturbing because its technical mastery illuminates from beginning to end so many complex and moving themes. I have read it over and over again, and I've carried it about with me as I've done with precious few books in recent years. I think the book carries absolute artistic conviction. It is a wonderful achievement." William Stafford wrote, "When you start World Without End, you are in for a trip. The road, the path, the track, will take you into places you haven't seen before. It's a find, this book, solid as a well-built cabin, chinked and pinned and ready for winter." —University of Arkansas Press

Matar, Muhammad Afifi.
Translated by Ferial Ghazoul
and John Verlenden. *Quartet
of Joy.* 72p. $16.00 (1-55728-
487-3). pap. $10.00 (1-55728-
488-1). Fayetteville, AR:
University of Arkansas Press,
Fall 1997. The rich poetic
world of Matar has the ecstatic
expansiveness of St. John
Perse's oceanic vision and the
mythical intelligence of
Octavio Paz's remaking of
meso-America. Yet Matar's
work springs fully from an
ancient Islamic tradition. The
translators have rendered the
complexities of Matar's work
with remarkable sensitivity,
making them, in effect, works
in English. A remarkable feat.
—Andrei Codrescu

Mathis, Cleopatra. *Guardian.*
105p. $19.95 (1-878818-49-
X). pap. $12.95 (1-878818-58-
9). Riverdale-on-Hudson, NY:
Sheep Meadow Press, Fall
1995; Spring 1997 (paper).
Mathis's poetry discovers,
then just before she seems to
say finally "This is true," she
strikes us with the opposite.
She gives us the heaven and
hell of it — or does she show
us the pin in the butterfly of
the poem? Giving birth and
the Creation are among the
subjects of Guardian. They
seem inevitably hers, with
their exquisite pain and pleasure. —Sheep Meadow Press.

As long as we have Mathis's
clarity of imagination, the
intricacy and breadth of her
engagement with the world,
and the depth of her meeting
of others, we'll have the
warmth to help us deal with
our own centers of cold. —
A.R. Ammons. Mathis's poetry "enthralls without throwing
the reader off a cliff. And all
the while she brandishes the
gifts of a talented poet who
has hit her stride." —The
New York Times Book
Review

Matias, David. *Fifth Season.*
135p. $35.00 (0-944854-38-9).
pap. $10.00 (0-944854-37-0).
Provincetown, MA:
Provincetown Arts Press, Fall
1998. Matias has the great gift
or art of a beguiling, disarm-
ingly intimate, sweet trans-
parency of voice. As poem
builds upon poem, one comes
to love the soul that has made
this book. The struggle to survive and the search to find
manifestation on the page here
are one: new, tender, quick.
Despite roughnesses (mysteriously, partly perhaps because
of them) this is a great book.
—Frank Bidart. In his "fifth
season," a young poet, David
Matias, turned his eye with
growing empathy, appreciation
and wisdom, to the journey of
his illness. These heartbreaking, radiant poems delineate

the transcendent soul-making of a life, telling of a great heart's mortal progress toward understanding and acceptance. —Gail Mazur. This is a rich, deeply intelligent book, a triumph of art and feeling. — Robert Pinsky

Matthews, William. *After All: Last Poems.* 64p. $20.00 (0-395-91340-3). Boston, MA: Houghton Mifflin Company, Fall 1998; Spring 2000 (new paper). After All , completed shortly before Matthews's death, is the last word from one of the most pensive and delicious of all our poets. — Houghton Mifflin. Reading Matthews is like driving at night with a slightly mad but compassionate, and, above all, lucky companion who always seems to find the map to the unsayable in the nick of time. —Library Journal. The wisest poet of his generation. —Peter Stitt, Georgia Review. There is no one like Matthews in America today. He doesn't spare us the heavy burden of clarity and lucidity. He's an extraordinarily important American poet. —Gerald Stern

Matthews, William. *Night Life.* 54p. (0-916375-28-5). Lewisburg, PA: Press of Appletree Alley, 1997. Letterpress limited edition.

Matthias, John. *Beltane at Aphelion: Longer Poems.* 203p. $28.95 (0-8040-0983-X). Athens, OH: Ohio University Press/Swallow Press, 1995. Beltane at Aphelion collects all of Matthias's longer poems. It includes his exuberant experiments from the 1960's, his comedic diptych from the 1970's set on a Polish and a Russian ocean liner, and his meditation on history and language set in Scotland. It concludes with the three long poems which explore ancient paths and river routes in the East Anglian region of Britain and the American Midwest, and, in the most ambitious poem he has yet written, the famous pilgrim trails to Santiago de Composela in Spain. —Ohio University Press / Swallow Press

Matthias, John. *Swimming at Midnight: Selected Shorter Poems.* 157p. $28.95 (0-8040-0948-8). Athens, OH: Ohio University Press/Swallow Press, 1995. Swimming at Midnight collects the short and middle-length poems from Matthias's earlier books together with twenty poems that have previously appeared only in magazines. It is published simultaneously with Beltane at Aphelion, which includes all of Matthias's longer poems. The two books together represent some thirty years of his work. —Ohio University Press / Swallow Press

Mauer, Susan. *By the Blue Light of the Morning Glory.* 32p. pap. $7.95 (1-891219-03-0). Siasconset, MA: Linear Arts, Spring 1997. A poetic journal, a pillow and paper book, By the Blue Light of the Morning Glory re-tells the story of an illicit love-triangle whose members slowly morph into archetypal rescensions of the text: reader, writer, critic forming the tryst whose untangling will be the poem itself. —Linear Arts. This is a very good beginning. —Sam Hamill

Maurer, Susan, and Bill Kushner. *Pawdy-do Sank-ee oon-Twah.* 8p. pap. $4.00. Quarter Horse Press, Spring 1998. Letterpress Limited Edition.

Maxwell, Noemie. *Thrum.* 24p. Buffalo, NY: Meow Press, Fall 1998.

Maybe, Ellyn. *The Cowardice of Amnesia.* 132p. pap. $10.00 (1-880985-58-6). Los Angeles, CA: 2.13.61 Publications, Spring 1998. Maybe's work is raw and unpretentious. —LA

Weekly. Maybe is the best poet on her side of the country. —Eileen Myles. A magnificent pathos is the power that drives Maybe, placing her among the finest voices to emerge from the pre-millennium west. —Wanda Coleman

Mayer, Bernadette. *Another Smashed Pinecone.* 83p. (0-935992-20-0). Brooklyn, NY: United Artists Books, Fall 1998. Mayer is the ultimate visionary of the mechanics of animal language. She is the secret agent of urban, rural, and extraterrestrial anarchy. She is the great knower of the ways of men, women, and children. She has been, is, and always will be the genius of the beautiful syntactical moment of truth. —Lisa Jarnot. Like a homeopathic dose of blue liquid, Mayer's poems kick you into a higher dimension every day. —Lee Ann Brown

Mayröcker, Friederike. Translated by Rosmarie Waldrop and Harriett Watts. *with each clouded peak.* 88p. pap. $10.95 (1-55713-277-1). Los Angeles, CA: Sun & Moon Press, Fall 1998. Beginning with personal remembrances, experiences, and feelings, Mayrocker adds linguistic material collected from a variety of sources to create a grand collage in which is subject to the permutations, repetitions, and rediscoveries of everyday life. The result is a magnificent text that does not easily fit into any genre, as it straddles autobiography, essay, fiction, and poetry. —Sun & Moon Press

McAlpine, Katherine, and Gail White, eds. *The Muse Strikes Back: A Poetic Response by Women to Men.* pap. $15.95 (1-885266-49-9). Ashland, OR: Story Line Press, Spring 1998. Atwood to Homer; Bogan to Swift; Kizer to Lowell; Sexton to Snodgrass: the women poets in The Muse Strikes Back are anything but silent. This lively anthology of spirited backtalk introduces the "reply poem" — a form in which the female subject of a male poet tells her side of the story. These poems are addressed to every level of the male-dominated poetry canon — from the Bible to Bukowski — and range in tone from wryly amused to fiercely outraged. —Story Line Press

McCann, Janet. *Looking for Buddha in the Barbed-Wire Garden.* 62p. pap. $10.00 (1-888105-08-9). Greensboro, NC: Avisson Press, 1996.

McClatchy, J.D. *Ten Commandments.* 104p. $22.00 (0-375-40137-7). New York, NY: Knopf, Alfred A., Spring 1998; Spring 2000 (new paper). A masterful sequence of intimate, classical, ironic poems, both a cabinet of moral curiosities and a tour through the underworld of desire. —Alfred A. Knopf. The year's best book of poems. —Walter Kirn, Time Magazine. The complexities and lucid articulation of feeling, the intent awareness, the informed play of language, have distinguished each of [McClatchy's] books, and the assurance and directness of Ten Commandments move to new ground with authority. These poems are a mature disclosure of a particular life in our age, glimpsed, projected, refracted, recognized "as if at last defined," in speech that proves to be a celebration. — W.S. Merwin. McClatchy's new book is a work of brilliance, clarity, and song. In its oblique and provocative contemplations of Moses's great supposes it is gorgeous and witty; here heaven meets earth and is smitten. Ten Commandments comprises the most stunning poems yet from one of our great poets. — Lorrie Moore

McCombs, Judith.
Territories, Here & Elsewhere.
26p. pap. $6.00 (0-932412-10-
6). Saginaw, MI: Mayapple
Press, 1996. This is poetry full
of living detail, and within the
detail is an ongoing motif of
adventure, risk and survival.
McCombs is a pleasure. —
Alicia Ostriker. The poetry is
pared down and muscular.
Many are like photographs
that catch a slice of time, so
exactly that what is left out
makes what is caught even
more vivid and memorable.
—Lyn Lifshin

McDaniel, Jeffrey. *The
Forgiveness Parade.* 80p. pap.
$11.95 (0-916397-55-6). San
Francisco, CA: Manic D
Press, Fall 1998. In these wonderful new poems by
McDaniel, it is hard to separate the humor from the pain.
Both qualities are omnipresent
and are presented in fresh and
original ways. This book is
heartbreaking and hilarious
simultaneously. And
McDaniel's love of language
is everywhere evident, making
images you won't soon forget.
—James Tate. It takes genius
to transcend the boring fac-
tionalism of U.S. poetry and
that's what McDaniel's got:
his affiliation is to the imagination. Fresh, provocative,
non-doctrinaire, his poems are
the kind I want to write when

I grow up. —Bill Knott. These
poems are everything poems
should be: wild, fierce, irreverent, full of praise and
lament, and deeply, intensely
human. —Thomas Lux

McDaniel, Wilma Elizabeth.
Sleeping in a Truck. 38p. pap.
$5.00 (1-890887-03-X). Santa
Barbara, CA: Mille Grazie
Press, Spring 1998. McDaniel
demonstrates her unmatched
skill to probe the extraordinary
lives of ordinary people, that
has made her the unrivaled
chronicler of the working class
experience in California's
great Central Valley. Her stories are so compelling and her
characters so immediately recognizable, that it isn't until
after we look up from the page
that we discover we have been
in the hands of a master poet
as well. —Mille Grazie Press

McDonald, Country Joe.
Navy Poems. 18p. pap. $7.00
(1-56439-073-X). Detroit, MI:
Ridgeway Press, Fall 1998.
Famous rock musician and
well-known '60s cultural icon
relates his hilarious, bizarre,
and thoughtful stories of his
Vietnam War era military service as an Air Traffic
Controller for the U.S. Navy
and later for Trans-Love
Airlines. —Ridgeway Press

McDonald, Karen. *"And It Was Good".* 68p. pap. $9.95 (1-880451-22-0). Baden, PA: Rainbow's End, Fall 1997. Through her poems, McDonald seeks to provide a dramatic glimpse of God. Her work is passionate, exciting, and important. —Rainbow's End

McDonald, Paul. *Write of Passage: 13 Poems.* 37p. pap. $7.00. Louisville, KY: Apocrypha/Gris-Gris Press, Fall 1997. Write of Passage is a riot. McDonald pokes his pen at his own paranoia and neuroses in [verses that mix] together the heroic and mundane, showing just how silly and profound humans can be. He is a poet who can take a punch [at his own poems] when they get too serious for their own good. —The Louisville Eccentric Observer

McDonald, Walt. *Blessings the Body Gave.* 109p. $25.00 (0-8142-0804-5). pap. $14.00 (0-8142-5004-1). Columbus, OH: Ohio State University Press, Fall 1998. Winner of the Ohio State University Press / The Journal Award in Poetry. These poems deal with the loss of McDonald's father in World War II as well as with his own experiences in Vietnam. They tell of living with the memories of war, of celebrating and coping with the fact of survival, in the context of love of one's family in a place at once harsh and beautiful. —Ohio State University Press. McDonald once again looks keenly, as only he can, at all four horizons of his seemingly limitless Texas landscape. Poem by poem we share this poet's acute sense of place. This is the American West, and McDonald is a realist who sites his poems in a moral landscape amid the steers and hawks and barbed-wire fences and Stetsons. —David Citino

McElroy, Colleen J. *Travelling Music.* 88p. pap. $13.95 (1-885266-65-0). Ashland, OR: Story Line Press, Fall 1998. Keenly observant, McElroy explores foreign travel, taking in contradictions, ironies, and displacements. Richly narrative, these poems take us across borders that transcend geography. —Maxine Kumin. In this brilliant collection, McElroy writes of travel in the broadest sense: the migrations of sleep, mortality, time, and imagination. The result is a poetry of kickass similes and mentioned unmentionables. In an age of well-behaved poetics, such an uncompromising stand is as necessary as it is refreshing. —Alice Fulton

McEntyre, Marilyn Chandler, ed. *Where Icarus Falls.* 139p. pap. $12.95 (0-9655497-3-9). Summerland, CA: Santa Barbara Review Publications, Fall 1998. To invite you to meditate on elemental things, the poems in this collection are grouped under four headings that represent the first Periodic Table of Elements — Earth, Air, Water, and Fire. The ancients believed that all things were made of these, and the larger truth of that belief lies in meditation on the subtleties and complexities of each, both in their physical properties and in their symbolic richness. — Marilyn Chandler McEntyre

McFadden, Mary Ann. *Eye of the Blackbird.* 63p. pap. $12.95 (1-884800-12-2). Marshfield, MA: Four Way Books, Spring 1997. Winner of the 1995 Four Way Books Series Competition. In its first few lines, Eye of the Blackbird declares itself to be a book with rare authority. Its obsessions are pursued with a passion that's reckless but also meticulously careful with the truth. This is a large work of intelligence and imagination, an inquiry into the formation of self that takes us on an adventure in which language, emotion, and the thinking mind seem made of the same substance. It's also wonderfully free of the usual authorial presence — autobiography still tethered to "what happened." However much fact it may drag in its undertows, this voice is pure invention.Eye of the Blackbird is a genuinely ambitious book, a book with big wings. —Chase Twichell

McGarry, Terry. *Imprinting.* 34p. pap. $5.95. Palo Alto, CA: Anamnesis Press, Spring 1998. Winner of the 1997 Anamnesis Poetry Chapbook Award.

McGee, Lynn. *Bonanza.* 36p. pap. $8.00 (0-9624178-6-6). Sleepy Hollow, NY: Slapering Hol Press, Fall 1996. Bonanza is a collection of poems which lives up to its title—a rich vein mined by an observer-poet as intelligent as she is watchful. Forming an explicit narrative, the poems offer richly textured observations, canny uses of the free verse line, and a clear poetic voice traveling through time, geography, and the families we choose as well as those we inherit. Here disguises, gender roles and identifications, shifting victims and sacrifices are all motifs in the complex mix of what erodes, what stays. These poems stay. —Carole Simmons Oles

McGrath, Campbell. *Spring Comes to Chicago.* 88p. pap. $12.95 (0-88001-484-9). Hopewell, NJ: Ecco Press, Fall 1996. An acrobatic, exuberant poet, part Whitman, part Tom Waits, enthralled by America's natural landscapes and its artificial mallscapes alike, obsessed with "the nation's extravagant beauty and materialistic soul." Accessible and relevant, these poems show McGrath to be a writer who could help save poetry from academia and get the rest of us reading it again. —Outside

McGrath, Thomas. *Letter to an Imaginary Friend.* 414p. $35.00 (1-55659-077-6). pap. $20.00 (1-55659-078-6). Port Townsend, WA: Copper Canyon Press, Spring 1998. For thirty years McGrath labored over this epic poem, publishing part one in 1963 and part four in 1985. Now, working from McGrath's archival notes, his longtime friend and colleague Dale Jacobson has prepared an authoritative text of the whole poem, making available for the first time in a single volume the greatest epic of our time. —Copper Canyon Press. I hope I can someday give this country or the few poetry lovers of this country something as large, soulful, honest, and beautiful as McGrath's great and still unappreciated epic of our mad and lyric century, . . . a book from which we can draw hope and sustenance for as long as we last. —Philip Levine. A tremendous odyssey of sense and spirit. —Library Journal. By turns fierce, somber, rollicking, and outrageous. — The Nation

McGuckian, Medbh. *Selected Poems 1978-1994.* 96p. $17.95 (0-916390-78-0). pap. $11.95 (0-916390-77-2). Winston-Salem, NC: Wake Forest University Press, Fall 1997. Generous selections from each of McGuckian's five books. The sensual, rhapsodic implications of her early work and the engagement of more recent poems with the politics of her native province represent a convincing vision. Selected Poems marries intellectual and emotional courage with vital language, startling but appropriate images, and beguiling art. —Wake Forest University Press. Her language is like the inner lining of consciousness, the inner lining of English itself, and it moves amphibiously between the dreamlife and her actual domestic and historical experience as a woman in late-twentieth-century Ireland. — Seamus Heaney

McGuckian, Medbh.
Shelmalier. 120p. $17.95 (0-916390-87-X). pap. $11.95 (0-916390-86-1). Winston-Salem, NC: Wake Forest University Press, Fall 1998. Taking her title from the Wexford fishermen who became gunmen in the Irish rising of 1798, McGuckian transforms the rebels' "still unused voices" into "soon-to-be-living words" that may yet resonate in an island where hope itself remains difficult two centuries later. —Wake Forest University Press

McGuigan, Christine.
Imbalance: An Experimental Collection of Micro Stories and Poetry. 64p. pap. $9.95 (1-891571-00-1). Cupertino, CA: Easy Break, First Time Publishing, Spring 1998. Traditionally structured haiku and senryu poems coupled with stories. —Easy Break, First Time Publishing

Mcilroy, Leslie Anne. *Gravel.* 44p. pap. $6.00. Niagara Falls, NY: Slipstream Publications, Spring 1997. Winner of Slipstream's Tenth Annual Poetry Chapbook Contest. Mcilroy's work is brutally and refreshingly honest in its portrayal of the events in her life. Sometimes her work is not easy to read, yet one cannot look away from the page. — Pittsburgh Tribune

McIrvin, Michael. *Dog.* 66p. pap. $9.95 (0-944550-43-6). Albion, CA: Pygmy Forest Press, Fall 1997. Chosen Best Book of Poetry 1997 by Cedar Hill Review. Dog may be the best book of poetry I've read this year. It is bleak, deep, and heartbreaking. —Douglas Spangle, Anodyne

McIrvin, Michael. *The Book of Allegory.* 74p. pap. $10.00 (1-891812-03-3). Mena, AR: Cedar Hill Publications, Fall 1998.

McMichael, James. *The World at Large: New and Selected Poems, 1971-1996.* 204p. $29.95 (0-226-56104-6). pap. $12.95 (0-226-56105-4). Chicago, IL: University of Chicago Press, Fall 1996. The collection allows the reader to see not only the incredible variety of modes and idioms McMichael has mastered over the course of his distinguished career, but the thematic unity from poem to poem, book to book. —Reference and Research Book News. It is difficult to write something concise about a book that is so important. The World at Large examines and celebrates the essential chink in the order, the flaw that caused any one of us to be. With brilliance and precision, McMichael [attends] thoroughly to what is of the world, [giving] the underlying and unspeakable power of mystery its rightful place. —Killarney Clary

McMorris, Mark. *The Black Reeds.* pap. $14.95 (0-8203-1873-6). Athens, GA: University of Georgia Press, Fall 1996. The Black Reeds takes up poetry as an intersection of the history of the individual with a history and geography of migrations understood in multiple senses, as the movement of lyric poetry through the changing syntax, rhythms, inflections, and vocabulary of English, as the movement of peoples both actual and imagined across territory and in time, and as the movement of readers among the expeditions of a book into experimental and unfamiliar terrain. — University of Georgia Press. The Black Reeds fuses blood, sea, flame, and sun to create a "zone that has no mooring," a poetry of dense particularity and free-ranging meditation. —Village Voice

McNair, Wesley. *Talking in the Dark.* 69p. pap. $13.95 (1-56792-094-2). Boston, MA: Godine, David R., Publisher, Fall 1998. In his fifth collec-

tion, one of New England's most respected poets brings us the inhabitants of his region as they struggle to contend with life's darknesses. How McNair's characters talk about their difficulties — or why they can't — is central to this volume, as are meditations in which the poet speaks directly to the reader about the trials and affirmations of human experience. These poems demonstrate McNair's ability to tell a life in a line and to disclose the knowledge of the heart. —David R. Godine. Because he is a true poet, [McNair's] New England is unlimited. Whole lives fill small lines, real to this poet and real to us. —Donald Hall, Harvard Book Review

McNair, Wesley. *The Town of No & My Brother Running.* 176p. pap. $15.95 (1-56792-056-X). Boston, MA: Godine, David R., Publisher, Spring 1997. Collects McNair's two most celebrated books into one volume. [McNair] has a gorgeous ear for the rubbing-together of adjacent words. He is a New England poet, preserving the speech and character of a region intimately known. Because he is a true poet, his New England is unlimited. Whole lives fill small lines, real to this poet and real to us. —Donald Hall, Harvard Book Review

McReynolds, Ronald W. *Telling of Bees and Other Poems.* 95p. pap. $10.00 (0-910479-05-4). Warrensburg, MO: Mid-America Press, Fall 1998. Poems by a teacher, world traveler, gardener, jewelry craftsman, husband and father, and bee-keeper in rural Johnson County, Missouri. —Mid-America Press

McShea, William P. *From Under a Broken Umbrella.* 53p. Pittsburgh, PA: Caliban Book Shop, Fall 1998.

Medina, Tony. *Sermons From the Smell of a Carcass Condemned to Begging.* 128p. pap. $10.00 (0-9654738-2-1). Hoboken, NJ: Long Shot Productions, Spring 1998. The power of Medina's third volume of poetry lies in its simplicity of purpose. Delivered as a running dialogue between a homeless man and the people he encounters every day on the streets of New York, Medina's lines in fact carry the weight of a world in heavy self-denial. — Long Shot Productions

Meek, Jay. *Headlands: New and Selected Poems.* 120p. $20.95 (0-88748-234-1). pap. $11.95 (0-88748-235-X).

Pittsburgh, PA: Carnegie Mellon University Press, Spring 1997.

Mehmedinovic, Semezdin. Translated by Ammiel Alcalay. *Sarajevo Blues.* 122p. pap. $12.95 (087286345X). San Francisco, CA: City Lights Books, Fall 1998. From one of Bosnia's most prominent poets and writers: spare and haunting stories and poems written under the horrific circumstances of the recent war in Bosnia-Hercegovina. —City Lights Books. A battle report and a philosophical investigation. Mehmedinovic charts the collapse of a world with heartbreaking clarity and precision. —Paul Auster. Mehmedinovic's slender book forcefully conveys a sense of the utter helplessness of his characters. The final selection — a fascinating interview between Mehmedinovic and Ammiel Alcalay — is a thoughtful, moving analysis of his life as a writer, both in Bosnia and in exile. —The New York Times Book Review. Sarajevo Blues is widely considered to be the best piece of writing to emerge from this besieged capital since Bosnia's war erupted. —The Washington Post

Melhem, D.H. *Country: An Organic Poem.* 128p. $25.00 (0-89304-222-6). pap. $15.00 (0-89304-223-4). Merrick, NY: Cross-Cultural Communications, Spring 1998. What a geography of the mind and heart this new work of Melhem's is, a hymn to humanity's shifting gears of behavior and activity, contradiction and constancy. — Martin Tucker. Melhem is one of our brilliant contemporary talents. As a writer she is serious, fervent, meticulous. She possesses one of the most remarkable minds of our time. —Gwendolyn Brooks

Memmott, David. *Within the Walls of Jericho.* 26p. pap. $5.00. Portland, OR: 26 Books , Fall 1998. Memmott focuses linguistic and perceptual energy on matters of memory and daily life. Poems about the musical dynamics of love and family. —26 Books

Mendenhall, Kitty McCord. *Parade.* 70p. pap. $9.95 (1-884754-29-5). Prairie Village, KS: Potpourri Publications, Fall 1997. In these poems, the parade of friends, pets and famous people, of moments and memories, glitters like sudden fireflies or halts to "kneel upon silence." Along the way the poet celebrates — with inner dance and casual rhyme — her community in this world. —Judy Ray

Meng Chiao. Translated by David Hinton. *The Late Poems of Meng Chiao.* 87p. pap. $14.95 (0-691-01236-9). Princeton, NJ: Princeton University Press, Fall 1996. Late in life Meng Chiao developed an experimental poetry of virtuosic beauty, a poetry that anticipated landmark developments in the modern Western tradition by a millennium. With the T'ang Dynasty crumbling, Meng employed surrealist and symbolist techniques as he turned to a deep introspection. This is truly major work, work that may be the most radical in the Chinese tradition. And though written more than a thousand years ago, it is remarkably fresh and contemporary. This is the first volume of [Meng's] poetry to appear in English. — Princeton University Press

Meredith, William. *Effort at Speech: New and Selected Poems.* 231p. $39.95 (0-8101-5070-0). pap. $17.95 (0-8101-5071-9). Northwestern University Press/TriQuarterly Books, Spring 1997. From his early, deeply personal poems to the later poems concerned with tolerance, civility, and shared values, Meredith's craft is marked by an unusual thoughtfulness. He is the master of the poem that seems colloquial at first glance, but is in fact deliberately voiced, measured out, and shaped. His is a voice of unequaled honesty and clarity. — Northwestern University Press. Meredith's work suggests that we can recognize the hardest truths about ourselves and still live in the world. —The New York Times Book Review

Merwin, W.S. *Flower & Hand: Poems 1977-1983.* 172p. pap. $15.00 (1-55659-119-5). Port Townsend, WA: Copper Canyon Press, Spring 1997. This volume collects all of Merwin's poetry from The Compass Flower, Feathers From the Hill, and Opening the Hand, returning to print a large body of work by a poet who, over half a century, has redefined American poetry. —Copper Canyon Press. Merwin has attained a wonderful streamlined diction that unerringly separates and recombines like quicksilver scattered upon a shifting plane, but which remains as faithful to the warms and cools of the human heart as that same mercury in the pan-pipe of a thermometer. — James Merrill

Merwin, W.S. *The Folding Cliffs: A Narrative.* 331p. $25.00 (0-375-40148-2). New York, NY: Knopf, Alfred A., Fall 1998. An epic historical narrative in verse, told from mythic and personal perspectives, of the events of the 19th century that led the Hawaiian islands to lose their independence. —Alfred A. Knopf. At one masterstroke, Merwin here restores to American poetry the narrative grandeur, mythic resonance, and sweeping moral scrutiny of an earlier age's epics. His book is an astonishment that will quicken and enlarge the spirit. —J.D. McClatchy. A bold and stunning chronicle of Hawaii, beautifully fashioned in a rare epic poetry which is also a kind of transcendent prose. A classic. —Peter Matthiessen. The Folding Cliffs is a masterpiece — a truly original masterpiece, on a very big scale. I read it with a mixture of amazement and admiration that went on growing to the last page. —Ted Hughes

Merwin, W.S. *The Vixen.* 76p. $21.00 (0-679-44477-7). pap. $14.00 (0-679-76601-4). New York, NY: Knopf, Alfred A., Spring 1996; Spring 1997 (paper). Merwin has always been a contemplative poet, drawn to the lessons of the natural world and the rigors of unmediated vision. He has also been a romantic poet, heroic in his quest for the depths and intensities, the powers and possibilities of consciousness. Best of all, he has been a surprising poet, continually slipping the bonds of anyone's easy admiration. —J.D. McClatchy, The New Yorker

Merwin, W.S., trans. *East Window: The Asian Translations.* 352p. pap. $16.00 (1-55659-091-1). Port Townsend, WA: Copper Canyon Press, Fall 1998. That any of W.S. Merwin's poetry and translations ever slipped out of print is a tragedy; that Coppery Canyon Press has reintroduced his work is, as Harvard Review notes, "cause for celebration." East Window gathers hundreds of poems and aphorisms from four out-of-print books, as well as several previously uncollected works. [It includes] translations and versions of poems from Asian languages as varied as Urdu, Chinese, Sanskrit, Japanese, Persian, and Vietnamese, and works by some of the world's greatest writers, such as Rumi, Tu Fu, Li Po, and Muso Soseki. — Copper Canyon Press. One of our most important poets. — Library Journal

Messerli, Douglas. *After.* 133p. pap. $10.95 (1-55713-347-6). Los Angeles, CA: Sun & Moon Press, Fall 1998. Beginning in the late 1970s poet, dramatist, and fiction writer Messerli began casually "translating" poems that he had difficulty comprehending in other translations. Describing these sometimes loosely translated works as poems "after" the originals, he began experimenting in his own poetry with some of the poetic techniques and themes he had worked with in the poems of other languages. In 1993 he began pairing the poems he had written with the poems "after" other writers. In the process, the writing of After called into question the whole endeavor of translations and the interrelationships of differing cultures. —Sun & Moon Press

Messerli, Douglas, ed. *Mr. Knife, Miss Fork, No. 1: An Anthology of International Poetry.* 179p. pap. $10.95 (1-55713-345-X). Los Angeles, CA: Sun & Moon Press, Fall 1998. Despite the increasing popularity of poetry and the greater number of translations currently published, there is a dearth of good journals and serial anthologies publishing international poetry. With this in mind, Sun & Moon began this new series of international poetry anthologies, Mr. Knife, Miss Fork. Each volume will contain new poetry by international poets of the 20th century, both younger poets and established figures, living and dead; commentary by three or four poets, and reviews of new books of poetry in translation and as they appear in their original languages. Most of the poets included will be printed bilingually. —Sun & Moon Press

Mesyats, Vadim. *A Guest in the Homeland: Selected Writings.* 84p. pap. $10.50 (1-883689-45-7). Jersey City, NJ: Talisman House, Publishers, Fall 1997. I find these poems fascinating like very few things I have liked in my life. These poems make me envious. . . because of the inner life behind them. —Joseph Brodsky. [Mesyats] is poet and prose writer who seemingly confuses two genres, but in reality attempts to overcome the loss of direction surrounding us today. —Ivan Zhdanov

Metcalf, Paul. *Collected Works: Volume I, 1956-1976.* 591p. $35.00 (1-56689-050-0). Minneapolis, MN: Coffee House Press, Fall 1996. The comprehensive three-volume collection will bring together all of Metcalf's major work, most of it originally published in limited editions by small idealistic presses and now long out-of-print. Volume I includes the complete texts of his early, formative novel, Will West; his monumental breakthrough, Genoa; the quirky Patagoni; the lyrical Apalache; and perhaps his darkest book, The Middle Passage. —Coffee House Press. My excitement and pleasure is such that I would like to emphasize here my very great respect for Paul Metcalf's writing and the unique significance of its publication. Much like his great-grandfather, Herman Melville, Metcalf brings an extraordinary diversity of materials into the complex patterns of analogy and metaphor, to affect a common term altogether brilliant in its imagination. —Robert Creeley. Perhaps it is the fate of voices in advance of their time to be lost in their own. Such is the case with Metcalf. He has a style all his own, constantly and relentlessly renewing itself, utilizing primary source material, poetry, musical notation, and straight narrative. His seems a writing career that needed a certain obscurity in order to remain so boldly adventurous. —Publishers Weekly

Metcalf, Paul. *Collected Works: Volume II, 1976-1986.* 600p. $35.00 (1-56689-056-X). Minneapolis, MN: Coffee House Press, Fall 1997. Second of three volumes. This volume is comprised of the complete texts of I-57, Zip Odes, Willie's Throw, U.S. Dept. of the Interior, Both, The Island, and Waters of Potowmack. —Coffee House Press. Metcalf maps an invaluable literary landscape, unrestrained by any form or geography. At last, it is open to the general public. — Publishers Weekly. Metcalf's project has been solitary and glacial in its undertaking, but readers would be at a serious deficit without it. —Library Journal

Metcalf, Paul. *Collected Works: Volume III, 1987-1997.* 524p. $35.00 (1-56689-062-4). Minneapolis, MN: Coffee House Press, Fall 1997. Third of three volumes. Of particular note to Metcalf collectors is the debut of his latest two significant works—Huascarán, a magnificent poetic tribute to the Indians of Peru and The Wonderful White Whale of Kansas, a brilliant essay encompassing a thoughtful look at Melville, The Wizard of Oz, and the concept of home, available exclusively in this edition. Also included are Louis the Torch, Firebird, Golden Delicious, ". . . and nobody objected," Araminta and the Coyotes, Mountaineers Are Always Free!, Where Do You Put the Horse?, and Three Plays. — Coffee House Press

Metras, Gary. *Today's Lesson.* 32p. pap. $8.00. Jamaica, VT: Bull Thistle Press, Fall 1997. A letterpress chapbook of 14 poems on education and teaching in a regional high school in Western Massachusetts by a teacher of 25 years. —Bull Thistle Press

Meyers, Susan. *Lessons in Leaving.* 26p. (1-879009-33-1). Whispering Pines, NC: Persephone Press, Fall 1998. Winner of the 1998 Persephone Press Book Award. [Meyers's] particular gift is taking the fine gradations of light and shadow that make up everyday existence, and proving once and for all how important these things are in our lives, how they are, in fact, what constitute our lives. Behind her quiet poetic voice the reader finds a startling complexity that confronts essential issues with an almost mythopoetic force. —S. Paul Rice

Michaels, Kevin, ed.
Remembering Allen Ginsberg Online:// Email, Poetry & Prose (A Tribute From the Electronic World). 30p. pap. $10.00. Hicksville, NY: S.A. Books, Spring 1998. An anthology of poems and prose from the internet, in celebration of the work of Allen Ginsberg. —S.A. Books

Michelangelo. Translated by John Frederick Nims. *The Complete Poems of Michelangelo.* 185p. $25.00 (0-226-08033-1). Chicago, IL: University of Chicago Press, Spring 1998. Michelangelo used poetry to express what was too personal to display in sculpture or painting; what he dared not say directly, he gave voice to in the harmonies and discords of verse. Nims, an eminent poet in his own right, has translated the entire body of Michelangelo's poetry, from the artist's ardent twenties to his anguished and turbulent eighties. Nims brings to his translations a unique sensitivity and grasp of both Michelangelo's language and his poetic temperament. He realizes in our language all the pathos, complexity, and ardor of Michelangelo's verse. — University of Chicago Press

Michener, James A. *A Century of Sonnets.* 117p.

$24.00 (1-880510-50-2). Austin, TX: State House Press, Fall 1997. Published in honor of his 90th birthday, this volume of Michener's collected poems, almost all of them previously unpublished, will both astound and delight Michener fans. Through his poetry he discusses aspects of his life with a soul-searching intensity and frankness that he has never before expressed in his writings. His poems are more autobiographical than even his autobiography. — State House Press

Mihalas, Dimitri. *The World Is My Witness.* 43p. pap. $5.00 (1-881900-01-0). Champaigne, IL: Hawk Productions, Fall 1997. This work addresses harmful collective human behavior such as war, racism, weapons development, and the future of mankind. —Hawk Productions

Miller, E. Ethelbert.
Whispers, Secrets and Promises. 116p. pap. $10.95 (1-57478-011-5). Baltimore, MD: Black Classic Press, Spring 1998. Poems marked with exuberance, energy and affection. —Reetika Vazirani

Miller, Errol. *Downward Glide.* 92p. pap. $10.50 (0-9663047-0-5). Northhampton, MA: BGB Press, Fall 1998. A native son of the South, Miller mines the region's indelible history: a milieu of culture, myth and hopeless failings, hope and a triumphant will to proceed with the business of living. —Vincent Bator, The Pannus Index. When Miller begins a poem, his destination is unknown. He is fueled by a subterranean energy that investigates everything in its path. —Alan Britt

Miller, Errol. *From the Engine Room.* 52p. pap. $10,95.00. Lawrence, KS: Broken Boulder Press, Fall 1998.

Miller, Errol. *Star City Concerto.* 45p. pap. $5.00. Sagamore Beach, MA: Encircle Publications, Spring 1998.

Miller, Errol. *The Writer's Ancestral Sense of Place.* 28p. pap. $4.00. San Jose, CA: French Bread Publications, Fall 1998. This is why I like Miller's poetry. Not for the clever subtleness of word choice or the insightful, mordant commentary on contemporary art, or the beauty of the line, or the way he elevates the ordinary to the extraordinary. It's more visceral than that. It's the niggling thoughts left lingering after the words are gone. It's the vaporous, amorphous land mass that now exists in your mind because this figure chose to put down in writing what cannot be written down. —French Bread Publications

Miller, Errol. *This Side of Chicago.* 39p. pap. $5.00. Sagamore Beach, MA: Encircle Publications, Fall 1998.

Miller, Greg. *Iron Wheel.* 104p. $21.00 (0-226-52797-2). pap. $11.00 (0-226-52798-0). Chicago, IL: University of Chicago Press, Spring 1998. In Miller's poems, redemption has more to do with a truthful accounting of the world than with transcending it into a sacred reality. That he writes in rhyme and meter and in a taut, free verse that keeps harking back to meter, subtly expresses how his mind perceives relations between the human and the divine. He's one of the best poets in his generation. —Tom Sleigh. I particularly like Miller's combination of the awkward and unfinished in feeling and tone with the "finish" of his language and versification. It's a difficult balance to achieve, but he manages it magnificently. —Thom Gunn

Miller, Jim Wayne. *The Brier Poems.* 154p. pap. $14.50 (0-917788-62-1). Frankfort, KY: Gnomon Press, Spring 1997. Miller is a poet of a particular geographical place, yet he sings, he preaches, and just plain talks in a language from the earth. Oddly, this kind of poetry is not in fashion these days, but I think it will outlive most of what is. —Edward Field. Brier is a shrewd, well informed, fearlessly outspoken figure. He is like Yeats' Crazy Jane, who offers in terms of folk speech a wisdom that is more than folk wisdom. — Fred Chappell

Miller, Leslie Adrienne. *Yesterday Had a Man in it.* 88p. $20.95 (0-88748-269-4). pap. $11.95 (0-88748-271-6). Pittsburgh, PA: Carnegie Mellon University Press, Spring 1998. Miller's unflinching new book, her best yet, shows her to be a poet of rich abandon, of sensuous longing and headlong desire for the Other turned back against the self, with regret, with fury. I am moved by these poems of independence infused with a dark self-knowledge, with a wry wisdom and tough vulnerability, with a hopefulness she cannot forget, will not forego.

These poems enlarge experience and engage life. — Edward Hirsch

Miller, Stephen M. *Jessica.* 26p. pap. $6.95 (0-614-24057). Johnstown, OH: Pudding House Publications, Fall 1997.

Milligan, Bryce; Mary Guerrero Milligan and, and Angela De Hoyos, eds. *Floricanto Sí!: A Collection of Latina Poetry.* 310p. pap. $14.95 (0-14-058893-0). New York, NY: Penguin Books/Viking Penguin, Spring 1998. Throughout the United States, from the pens of new talents and major figures alike, a Latina poetic sensibility is emerging.These pages shimmer with the sensual imagery and vibrancy of poetry that interprets American identity, womanhood, love, and art in new ways. —Penguin Books/Viking Penguin

Mills, Ralph J. Jr. *In Wind's Edge.* 95p. pap. $12.95 (1-55921-187-3). Wakefield, RI: Asphodel Press/Moyer Bell, Fall 1997. In his twelfth collection, Mills again shows himself a master of the spare, finely-tuned poem. Brief, yet visually compelling, each poem observes the natural world with intensity, the line fragments evoking the particu-

lars of our existence. —
Asphodel Press. These are
poems of pure sensation. They
are visually artful poems about
vision and the numinousness
of wholly attended seeing.
They are as restorative as
prayer. —Booklist. Mills has
brought to the classic tratition
of Objectivism a remarkable
ear for word sounds, single or
grouped, and a percipient eye
— he can actually make words
dance on the page in number-
less different patterns. —
James Laughlin

Milne, Teddy. *Flight: Views
of Earth From Sky.* 27p. pap.
$4.50 (0-938875-40-X).
Northampton, MA:
Pittenbruach Press, Spring
1998. Poems by a frequent
flyer about viewing Earth
from 30,000 feet. —
Pittenbruach Press

Milne, Teddy, ed. *A Scent of
Apple: An Anthology of Poetry
on Family Relationships.* 53p.
pap. $9.95 (0-938875-37-X).
Northampton, MA:
Pittenbruach Press, Fall 1997.
The result of Pittenbruach's
tenth anniversary poetry contest series, these poems focus
on family relationships. They
are as varied as the families
they reflect: painful, poignant,
sane, tentatively blissful,
unsettling. —Pittenbruach
Press

Milne, Teddy, ed.
*Circumference of Days: An
Anthology of Poems on
Endings and Beginnings.* 84p.
pap. $11.50 (0-938875-38-8).
Northampton, MA:
Pittenbruach Press, Fall 1997.

Milosz, Czeslaw. Translated
by Czeslaw Milosz and Robert
Hass. *Road-side Dog.* 208p.
$22.00 (0-374-25129-0). New
York, NY: Farrar, Straus and
Giroux, Fall 1998. Milosz
makes a wise, wryly human
fin de siècle companion.
Publishers Weekly. The book,
brief and pithy, is a pleasure.
Milosz turns his agile mind to
whatever crosses its path. The
upshot is a wealth of insights
on a variety of topics. Though
a modest and understated
work, the poet's generosity of
spirit is is unmistakable. —
Kirkus Reviews. In a note-
book of the soul, Milosz's
hard-won, prayerlike meditation soars. His work has
enriched civilization with an
unwavering allegiance to sani-
ty and truth. —Library
Journal. Milosz's greatness as
a writer has something to do
with his gift for going straight
to the heart of a question —
be it moral, artistic, political,
autobiographical — and
answering it directly with singular personal force. —
Seamus Heaney. Milosz's
genius is for the very small

and the very large — the intensely sensual detail and the bleak interstellar spaces. — Helen Vendler

Milosz, Czeslaw, ed. *A Book of Luminous Things: An International Anthology of Poetry.* 320p. pap. $14.00 (0-15-600574-3). San Diego, CA: Harcourt Brace/Harvest Books, Spring 1996; Spring 1998 (paper). Milosz's personal selection of the world's greatest poetry ranges among 300 of the finest poems written through the ages and around the world. The works selected are memorable for their language, their imagery, and their ability to move the reader. A testament to the stunning varieties of human experience, this unique international anthology is both instructional and inspirational, and vividly reminds us of the singular importance of poetry to our minds and souls. — Harcourt Brace

Mitchell, Joni. *The Complete Poems and Lyrics.* 321p. $27.50 (0-609-60008-7). New York, NY: Crown Publishers, Fall 1997. This is the first collection of Mitchell's poetic lyrics. The book is annotated with commentary from the artist and includes a selection of her line drawings. This remarkable collection offers a new perspective on Mitchell's ability to tell her own generation's story with rare beauty and perception. —Crown Publishers

Mitchell, Nora. *Proofreading the Histories.* 72p. pap. $9.95 (1-882295-10-2). Farmington, ME: Alice James Books, Fall 1996. In a wide-ranging collection of poems—from lyric, to chant, to elegy, to song — Mitchell surprises and sometimes stuns the reader with the force of her lines and her vision. —Ron Schreiber. Mitchell's poems swing the soul in a sensory vortex whose syllables are berries on a forest floor of artifact and rubble yet whose vines draw struggle and image from a water purified by memory and the sheer ethics of sensation in relentless bombardment. —Olga Broumas

Mitchell, Roger. *Braid.* 64p. pap. $10.00 (0-935724-90-7). Great Barrington, MA: Figures, The, Fall 1997. Mitchell's poems are full of revelatory observations on nature, culture, and language. Breezy, skeptical, and elegiac by turn, Mitchell intertwines what's most elusive with what's closest at hand, and we come away from his work having seen very much indeed. —Elaine Equi

Mitchell, Roger. *The Word for Everything.* 54p. pap. $10.95 (1-886157-06-5). Kansas City, MO: BkMk Press of the University of Missouri-Kansas City, Fall 1996. Many poets write about memory, but few manage to track the actual motions of the mind as it roams across the past. Mitchell delineates that fine line between the thing remembered and the mechanics of remembering. The poems are poignant and intimate, but they're also wonderfully brainy. Their self-scrutiny keeps them tough and lean. —Chase Twitchell. Half dream, half wry, hard bitten quite ordinary fact, it's the unsentimental goodness in the work that most moves me. And how each poem turns and turns again, making its way by slow surprise. This is a book to treasure. —Marianne Boruch

Mitsui, James Masao. *From a Three-Cornered World: New and Selected Poems.* 98p. pap. $12.95 (0-295-97598-9). Seattle, WA: University of Washington Press, Spring 1997. Mitsui's poems are memorable, finely honed — combining imagistically startling vignettes, witty and melancholy ars poetica, and moving personal reminiscence. Yet the many poetic memorials to Japanese American history are this poet's finest accomplishment. —Garrett Hongo. Again and again the little significant parts of experience shape themselves into patterns, so that what comes at us in life as separate touches from the world become in Mitsui's poems pieces of realization. —William Stafford

Miura, Yuzuru, ed. *Classic Haiku: A Master's Selection.* 119p. pap. $12.95 (0-8048-1682-4). Tuttle, Charles E., Fall 1997 (reprint). Miura has selected and translated poems by past masters like Basho and Buson, as well as haiku by contemporary poets. Fireflies, pheasants, a summer shower, winter snow, camellias – all the favorite haiku subjects are included among the one hundred poems of this impressive new anthology. —Charles E. Tuttle

Moffeit, Tony. *Midnight Knocking at the Door.* 40p. pap. $5.00 (1-889289-50-7). New Haven, CT: Ye Olde Font Shoppe, Spring 1998. Poems from the blues-shouting, conga-pounding poet. —Ye Olde Font Shoppe

Moldaw, Carol. *Chalkmarks on Stone.* 120p. pap. $12.00 (1-888809-07-8). Albuquerque, NM: La Alameda Press, Spring 1998. Moldaw's poems unite tact, delicacy, keenness of sight, and daring. A butterfly, its thorax, legs, eyes, and circumflex-marked wings minutely studied, alights on the poet's hand and there taps "out a secret code, / the secret names of God." That is the scope of this remarkable and elegant volume, in which "carafe" rhymes with "cenotaph," and the modest objects and acts of daily life glow, along with tragic facts, in the blessing of the poet's attention. Moldaw has a sure hand, a light touch, a subtle ear, and a strong and compassionate heart. — Rosanna Warren. Moldaw has written a book of adult knowledge, of adult griefs and joys. Hers are poems of intelligent consideration and a deft and heart-born music. —Jane Hirshfield

Monroe, Melissa. *Machine Language.* 48p. pap. $12.00 (1-882509-05-6). New York, NY: Alef Books, Spring 1998. In Monroe's remarkable first book of poems, the technical, apparently unpoetic information and language associated with a variety of practical and scientific pursuits—among

them botany, robotics, metallurgy, and body-snatching— occasion a series of subtle and surprising lyric and narrative inventions. —Alef Books. Monroe has discovered terrae incognitae of postmodern consciousness that are all her own, and her discoveries are what make these poems both mysterious and memorable. —Lloyd Van Brunt, n.b.

Monsour, Leslie. *Earth's Beauty, Desire, & Loss.* 24p. $25.00. pap. $7.50. Edgewood, KY: Barth, Robert L. (R.L.B.), Spring 1998. Monsour has the gift of recognizing the large significances that often dwell in small moments. Her technical grace gives weight to the epiphanies of these fine poems. — Timothy Steele

Montale, Eugenio. Translated by Jonathan Galassi. *Collected Poems 1920-1954.* 625p. $40.00 (0-374-12554-6). New York, NY: Farrar, Straus and Giroux, Fall 1998. Montale, who won the 1975 Nobel Prize in Literature, brought the tradition of Italian lyric poetry that begins with Dante into the twentieth century with unrivaled power and brilliance. Galassi's versions of Montale's major work are the clearest, most accurate, most convincing yet made. They are accompanied by an interpretive essay and by extensive notes that elucidate the extremely rich context of Montale's often dense and allusive poetry. — Farrar, Straus and Giroux. Galassi's marriage of creative literary research and inspired poetic scholarship helps make Montale accessible to English-speaking readers. Highly recommended for all major poetry collections. —Library Journal. One of the century's great poets in a magnificent new translation. —Charles Simic. Galassi's translations capture with uncanny precision the nervous, ironic, lyrical, and obsessive rhythms of one of the great poets of the twentieth century, a poet who deserves to be much better known in the English-speaking world. This edition of Montale's major work is quite simply a triumph. —Marjorie Perloff

Montale, Eugenio. Translated by William Arrowsmith; Edited by Rosanna Warren. *Satura: 1962-1970.* 220p. $29.95 (0-393-04647-8). New York, NY: Norton, W.W., and Company, Spring 1998; Fall 1999 (new paper). First published in Italy in 1971, Satura is the fourth collection of poems by the Nobel Prize winner Eugenio Montale. In Satura, the poet experimented with dialogue, journalistic notation, commentary, aphorism, and half-strangled song, and pressed Italian literary language into terrain it had never touched before. These are poems whose reductions and sacrifices define a new lyric art. —W.W. Norton. We are privileged and lucky to have this latest collection of Montale poems in Arrowsmith's brilliant translations. The poems abound with mystery, vigor, and energy. And always with tight-lipped honesty. They constitute a complicated farewell, and reading them induces its own beautiful anguish. —Anthony Hecht. Montale's world of enlightened but disenchanted spirit is beautifully served by Arrowsmith's fluent, colloquial translation. No other translator captures with such nuance the radical disaffection of Montale's mind. —Tom Sleigh

Montgomery, Wardell, Jr. *Politics, Religion, Sex.* pap. $10.00 (0-9652092-02). Sharp Tongue Press, 1996.

Moody, Rodger. *Unbending Intent.* 26p. pap. $5.00. Portland, OR: 26 Books, Spring 1997. Moody covers three decades, one war, several loves and two children with terse, heart-felt lyricism.

Unbending Intent is another of 26 Chapbooks in a new series of poetry from the Pacific Northwest —26 Books

Moore, Gerald, and Ulli Beier, eds. *The Penguin Book of Modern African Poetry.* 449p. pap. $15.95 (0-14-118100-1). New York, NY: Penguin Books/Viking Penguin, Spring 1998. This fourth edition has been substantially revised and expanded with a new introduction. Wonderfully comprehensive, the anthology now contains the poetry of ninety-nine poets, thirty-one of them included for the first time, from twenty-seven countries. Equally wide-ranging is the content of the poetry itself: war songs, satires and political protests as well as poems about human love, African nature and the surprises that life offers. —Penguin Books. No reader to whom this collection is his or her first taste of African verse is going to be in any doubt that, as the editors claim, Africa is producing some of the most original and exciting poetry now being written anywhere in the world. —Edward Blishen

Moore, Julia A. Edited by Thomas J. Riedlinger. *Mortal Refrains: The Complete Collected Poetry, Prose, and Songs of Julia A. Moore, The Sweet Singer of Michigan.* 310p. pap. $24.95 (0-87013-449-3). Michigan State University Press, Spring 1998. In the late 1870's, Moore had a national following as a gifted writer of hilarious, "bad" verse. Mark Twain attributed the "deep charm" of Moore's poems to her innocent habit of making the "intentionally humorous, pathetic, and the intentionally pathetic, funny." Mortal Refrains is the first complete collection of Moore's work. —Michigan State University Press

Moore, Lilian. Illustrations by Tad Hills. *Poems Have Roots: New Poems.* 44p. $15.00 (0-689-80029-0). Simon & Schuster/Atheneum, Fall 1997. Poems Have Roots and Moore does, too — deep taproots that go down into the rich soil of poetry. How does she keep flowering year after year? With a clear poetic eye, the deceptive simplicity of line, and the casual insights that shock young readers (and old!) into awareness. —Jane Yolen

Moore, Marijo. *Spirit Voices of Bones.* 96p. pap. $12.95 (0-9654921-2-5). Renegade Planets Publishing, Spring 1997. In the context of our violent and often despairing times, Moore evokes the marrow of ancestral bones — the regenerative powers of blood memory, of spirit voices that spur and heal. She calls us to remember that "we all create each other." —Marilou Awiakta

Moore, Mary. *The Book of Snow.* 64p. pap. $8.00 (1-880834-36-7). Cleveland, OH: Cleveland State University Poetry Center, Spring 1998. With a coast-to-coast American vision, the sensibility of pioneering botanists and painters, Moore makes discoveries that are not infrequently frightening. Her poems are full of light and motion. To read Moore's poems is to ride them. They are completely exhilarating. —Sandra McPherson. The reach and range of Moore's aesthetic ambition are breathtaking, sometimes heart-stopping. [The collections] alternates sonnets of dazzling magnitude, brief meticulous incantations, and mellifluously extended meditations. — Sandra Gilbert

Moore, Richard. *Pygmies and Pyramids.* 79p. pap. $12.95 (0-914061-71-2). Alexandria, VA: Orchises Press, Spring 1998. [Moore's poetry is] alive with refreshing sinuosities. —Richard Eberhart

Moose, Ruth. *Smith Grove.* 28p. pap. $9.00 (1-885912-15-3). Abingdon, VA: Sow's Ear Press, Fall 1997. Twelve poems about farm life and farm buildings. —Sow's Ear Press

Mora, Pat. *Aunt Carmen's Book of Practical Saints.* 128p. $20.00 (0-8070-7206-0). Boston, MA: Beacon Press, Fall 1997; Fall 1999 (new paper). The northern New Mexico tradition of saint carving began in the 1700's as an expression of individual devotion among faithful Catholics in isolated villages. Here Mora, who The New Mexican has called "one of the most significant Chicana poets of our time," extends the tradition in words rather than wood, tin, and cloth. Using traditional forms in Spanish and English from lullabies to sonnets, Mora gives voice to Aunt Carmen's private devotion. In doing so, Mora gives us access to the bridge between our own stories and the sacred in ourselves. — Beacon Press

Morgan, Elizabeth Seydel. *On Long Mountain.* 58p. $19.95 (0-8071-2252-1). pap. $11.95 (0-8071-2253-X).

Baton Rouge, LA: Louisiana State University Press, Spring 1998. I don't know any contemporary poetry that's more to the point of what we're all about than Morgan's. Her gift for language is as astonishing as her powers of observation. The poems on the pages of On Long Mountain are thrillingly alive. — Louis D. Rubin, Jr. With a characteristically burly delicacy, Morgan achieves a remarkable accuracy of perception which is the occasion, again and again, for her display of a fearless honesty of intellect and spirit. She can also be wry and sly and very funny. "Come on, come in,/ knock me out," she says in "Enthusiasm," and she does, too, in poem after poem. — David R. Slavitt. Vivid wordplay, a clear singing, knockout endings — Morgan is grand with all of these and more. The natural ease with which these poems pull the reader into the poet's warm confidence is deceptive, because again and again she surprises us not with the revelation but with the secret, the one the world will keep. —Betty Adcock

Morgan, Robert. *Wild Peavines.* 29p. $35.00 (0-917788-65-6). pap. $10.00 (0-917788-63-X). Frankfort, KY: Gnomon Press, Fall 1997.

Moriarty, Laura. *The Case.* 124p. pap. $11.50 (1-882022-36-X). O Books, Fall 1998. Deceptively quiet and contemplative in tone, The Case is searing, lush, austere, tender, loving and terrifying not by turns, but all at once, all the way through and all the time. Moriarty has for years been one of our finest poets and now she takes us to a new level. —Ron Silliman. Experience is encountered, not described, the present is what it's like when it's happening even if it's pain. Though The Case is a private domain it isn't exclusive: the poet is alone thinking, yet others feel nearby in their warmth. The Case is appropriately muted, but not reticent. Its colors seem wisely chosen. The subject of the book isn't all darkness, it's the peculiarly lit and peculiarly gracious space in which rituals of loss take place. —Alice Notley

Morin, Edward. *Labor Day at Walden Pond.* 65p. pap. $12.00 (1-56439-056-X). Detroit, MI: Ridgeway Press, Spring 1997. Morin writes of daily, white collar, and middle-class experiences that are often overlooked in American poetry. "It's a living," he says, as indeed it it, sort of. Labor Day at Walden Pond enters a poetic realm very much worth

tending to, worth attending.
—Edward Hirsch. I was continually delighted by the freshly observed details and casual eloquence of these intelligent, musical poems. A brilliant sequence explores the exigencies of earning a living and the frustration and absurdity of downsized workplaces. These [are] wisely subtle poems by a charmingly acute observer. — Alice Fulton

Morland, Margaret Ward.
Gift of Jade. 102p. pap. $12.95 (0-938572-21-0). Hedgesville, WV: Bunny and the Crocodile Press/Forest Woods Media Productions, Fall 1998. For years I have admired Morland's ability to say gracefully in a poem that she loves the world, not only for its generous way with breathtaking moments, both beautiful and ominous, but also for its breakages, its losses, the pain that gives meaning to courage and to love. — Henry Taylor. In their lyric perfection, the poems in Gift of Jade stretch across borders and generations not only with exquisite language and womanly wisdom, but with great heart and compassion. — Judith Minty

Morley, Hilda. *The Turning.* 194p. $24.95 (1-55921-202-0). Wakefield, RI: Asphodel

Press/Moyer Bell, Spring 1998. Published just after Morley's death, these final poems are the observations of a keenly intelligent "poet's poet" as she maps both outer and inner landscapes. — Asphodel Press/Moyer Bell. Whether mining images "to know the fullness of / the weight of time" or searching her past and honoring friends, the poems form a diary-in-verse of a meditative mind's graceful turns. —Publishers Weekly. These poems bring to us the necessary, vivid art of Hilda Morley. Here is a world seen and relished in angles of syntax, abrupt swerves of cadence. Here is the vision of the painter in the hands of the poet: the ability to render a lost friend, a woman at a grocery counter, a half-ripe apricot with such accuracy that suddenly there it is: a world rinsed off in light and language. —Eavan Boland. The poems in The Turning are radiant with details that show us how what we see turns into song; how passing instants turn into dwellings for the soul; how what we thought was lost returns in the intricate patterns of narrative retrieval; how life turns into art. —Ann Lauterbach

Morphew, Melissa. *The Garden Where All Loves End.* 77p. pap. $10.00 (0-931721-13-X). La Jolla, CA: La Jolla Poets Press, Fall 1996. Morphew's striking poems, sometimes grim but always lovely, persistently seek that realm where the ordinary need not be settled for merely because it is in fact what we have, where loss and failure rightly perceived — and rightly spoken — become beautiful, lasting triumph. — Stephen Corey

Morra, Isabella. Edited and Translated by Irene Musillo Mitchell. *Canzoniere.* 64p. pap. $9.00 (1-884419-18-6). West Lafayette, IN: Bordighera, Fall 1998. This bilingual edition of Isabella di Morra's poems introduces an English-speaking public to one of the unjustly forgotten women poets of the Italian Renaissance. Mitchell renders Isabella's ten sonnets and three canzoni in an English idiom that captures the palpable restiveness and the fragile grace of Isabella's Italian. The translator's introduction invites the reader to consider Isabella as a poetic voice grounded in geographical and historical realities of Southern Italy in the sixteenth century. The volume is a valuable resource for all of us who seek to enhance our knowledge of the diversity of Italian Renaissance culture. — Marilyn Migiel

Morrill, Donald. *At the Bottom of the Sky.* 96p. pap. $11.00 (0-922811-36-9). Minneapolis, MN: Mid-List Press, Spring 1998. Morrill's writing searches for meaning in the universal while giving careful insight into the particular. Morrill is a writer of life; he is a poet the literary community will be hearing much more of. —GW Review. The poems in At the Bottom of the Sky are deeply reflective and intelligent and more: they are robust and generous, the product of both mind and heart. The sentences are rich and complex, breaking perfectly across lines that are measured with a deft authority. This is a powerful, distinguished collection, and Morrill deserves our attention and praise. —Frank X. Gaspar. Candid and self-aware, the speaker in At the Bottom of the Sky creates astonishing intimacies of thought, feeling, and perception between himself and his readers. Morrill is a wonderful poet, brave enough both to speak his mind and to answer to his heart. —Kelly Cherry

Morris, Tracie. *Intermission.* 81p. pap. $11.00 (1-887128-

30-1). New York, NY: Soft Skull Press, Fall 1998. Morris has held Championship Titles in both the Nuyorican Grand Slam and the National Haiku Slam. This print debut of her lauded live style pulls the reader to where the stage can not. The streetwise sass and boombastic Brooklynese are all here, but Morris also displays prowess and verve with riskier, lyric work. —Soft Skull Press. If you are a fan of Morris, as I am, then you know she writes the real deal; that these poems will have that magnificent blend of music, wit, and daring power that caught your breath the first time you saw her take stage. If Intermission is the stage between acts, then Morris's work promises that there is a lot to look forward to. —Cornelius Eady. Morris is a step into the next century, the verse of the new millennium in sight. —Miguel Algarin

Morrison, R.H. *The Voice of the Hands.* 56p. pap. $7.50 (1-880286-35-1). Canton, CT: Singular Speech Press, Fall 1997. Real, radiant poems [that have an] unusual freshness and luminosity. — Temenos

Morse, Elizabeth. *True Crimes and False Accusations.*

36p. pap. $4.00. Talent, OR: Talent House Press, Fall 1998.

Mortimer, Curtiss. *Chicago in Adagio.* 36p. pap. $5.00 (0-940895-30-7). Chicago, IL: Cornerstone Press Chicago, Fall 1996.

Morton, R. Meir. *Behold a Star!.* 52p. pap. $15.00. Louisville, KY: Summitt Poetry Publishing, Fall 1998. Unlike breakers crashing against the rocks, Morton's poetry resembles a gentle incoming tide. In it we find words that flow, carrying us toward a world of ethereal ideas. —Herman Landau. A passionate volume infused with the intense love of life, lore, land and people of Israel. —Marshall A. Portnoy

Morton, R. Meir. *Music: Variations on a Theme.* 52p. pap. $7.50. Louisville, KY: Summitt Poetry Publishing, Fall 1997. Morton's poetry is rarely predictable. The elusive, the ethereal, the ineffableness of music is hard to put into words. As a musician, I found them to be quite amazing in the overall quality, variety of subjects within the subject, the excellent style choices in the writing. Many poems caught me off guard and "lump-in-the-throat" memories came rushing back! —Samuel A. Hodges

Morton, R. Meir. *Stone for a Pillow.* 52p. pap. $7.50. Louisville, KY: Summitt Poetry Publishing, Spring 1998. Morton's vibrant collection of poems are haunting, beautifully crafted, featuring a vocabulary that is both terse and shining. She embraces people, speaking of things the rest of us are beginning to see. —Jane Stuart

Moss, Stanley. *Asleep in the Garden: New and Selected Poems.* 159p. $20.00 (1-888363-63-0). New York, NY: Seven Stories Press, Fall 1997. It is time to celebrate the singular beauty and power of Moss's poetry. He is a citizen of the world, both past and present, one who seems to have been everywhere and missed nothing. These are poems, out of the fullness of life, that impress me as being all at once deep, strange, loving, bountiful, and a joy to read. The damp genius of mortality presides. —Stanley Kunitz. In many voices, in lines rugged yet eloquent, Moss sings us songs of his unbelievable belief, his unlovable love — songs of anguish, songs any of us would sing if we could. I find them disconcerting and extraordinarily moving. —Hayden Carruth. Moss addresses the God of the Jews, of the Christians, and of the Moslems with awe and familiarity, and chants to lesser gods of his own invention, such as the "God of paper and writing," with jocosity and gratitude. All forms of being grab his ardent attention; he writes a letter to the butterflies, and tells the stories of bears, birds, dogs, and centaurs. In every surprising poem, every song to life, beautiful life, Moss, by turns giddy and sorrowful, expresses a sacred sensuality and an earthly holiness. —Booklist

Moss, Thylias. *Last Chance for the Tarzan Holler.* 117p. $24.00 (0-89255-229-8). New York, NY: Persea Books, Spring 1998; Spring 1999 (new paper). Moss already is a permanent American poet, canonical in the old, authentic sense. Her Last Chance for the Tarzan Holler is a profound and disturbing volume. Its difficulties are necessary and rewarding, and enrich me. —Harold Bloom. Last Chance for the Tarzan Holler reaffirms the reputation of Moss as a poet of fierce intelligence and radiant intensity. Complex, original, inventive, even daring, this is poetry that demands — and deserves — our riveted attention. We should celebrate the power in these poems. —Martín Espada

Moulds, Julie. *The Woman With a Cubed Head.* 73p. pap. $12.00 (0-932826-66-0). Kalamazoo, MI: New Issues Press, Fall 1998. Moulds has battled non-Hodgkin's lymphoma for five years, through remissions, recurrences, and a bone marrow transplant. In The Woman With a Cubed Head, Moulds summons up an exotic band of kindred spirits to accompany her as she engages the forces of darkness. In poems of wit and attitude; in language that is sensual, fresh, and unabashed, Moulds goes forth, tilting with real windmills. —New Issues Press. Moulds's poems are unflinching, funny, and wise. In her first book, she explores the horror and brilliance of transformed bodies, especially those changed by illness. Moulds is a 21st century Gretel — singed by smoke from the witch's oven, she escapes, urgent to tell us all about it. —Denise Duhamel

Mowrey, Joseph. *Winter Moon.* 104p. pap. $14.00 (0-933553-12-9). Santa Fe, NM: Mariposa Printing and Publishing, Fall 1998. Accessible yet intricate in their simplicity, these are well-crafted poems about important subjects. Winter Moon is an engaging blend of lyric and narrative voices intended to satisfy the spirit as well as the senses. —Mariposa Printing and Publishing. A promising new collection of poems by Mowrey, whose talent both deserves and rewards our most attentive reading. —Lucille Adler. Mowrey marries his impressive printer's craft with an equally strong poet's heart. He brings us poems that explore terror and terrific beauty. —Joan Logghe

Moxley, Jennifer. *Imagination Verses.* 96p. pap. $8.95 (0-927920-07-7). New York, NY: Tender Buttons Press, Fall 1996. A Publisher's Weekly starred selection. A serious intellectual engagement with hope in the political, the emotional, and the artistic spheres of human life. Though threaded through by elegy, Moxley's poems still manage to detect the heart's power, alive in the tenuous loves we practice amidst the dying dream of a meaningful civic life. —Tender Buttons Press

Mueller, Lisel. *Alive Together: New and Selected Poems.* 223p. $24.95 (0-8071-2127-4). pap. $17.95 (0-8071-2128-2). Baton Rouge, LA:

Louisiana State University Press, Fall 1996. Winner of the 1997 Pulitzer Prize. In a collection that represents over thirty-five years of [Mueller's] writing life, this distinguished poet explores a wide range of subjects, which include her cultural and family history and reflect her fascination with music and the discoveries offered by language. Her book is a testament to the miraculous power of language to interpret and transform our world. —Louisiana State University Press

Mueller, Melinda. *Apocrypha.* 34p. pap. $10.00 (0-9652272-4-3). Sedro Woolley, WA: Grey Spider Press, Spring 1998. Letterpress Edition

Muldoon, Paul. *Hay.* 131p. $22.00 (0-374-16831-8). New York, NY: Farrar, Straus and Giroux, Fall 1998. If Northern Irish poets are expected to write Wordsworthian lyric verse about their rural childhoods, Muldoon instead composes allusively postmodern, cosmopolitan poetry. As much at home in mainstream pop culture as in the obscure corners of the literary tradition, sharp-witted Muldoon both parodies and honors with panache. He's the Cassius Clay of poetic craft. —

Publishers Weekly. Muldoon's mischievous wit punctures the self-seriousness of poetry as it punctures our false expectations of ourselves. A poet of such energy necessarily throws off countless sparks. Muldoon, who has always had a remarkable ability to make hay from the ordinary grass of experience, consistently turns Hay into the fire of poetry. — The Boston Phoenix

Mulkey, Rick. *Before the Age of Reason.* 69p. (1-877603-60-0). San Antonio, TX: Pecan Grove Press, Fall 1998. Certainly Mulkey can turn a wonderful phrase. And certainly his choice of subjects is engagingly wide. But I've followed Rick's work ever since he was a student of mine, and am pleased with how avidly he's always a student of life; and even more exacting than turn of phrase or subject matter is his willingness to explore the inarticulatable questions, "why we exist / as we do," and to enter that unchartable terrain, "the wounds we live in." —Albert Goldbarth. With poems that are generously imagined, Before the Age of Reason lets us see the extremities of our nature. [These poems] are magic lanterns by which we illuminate the featureless and unknown, and affirm the imagination as an agent for giving, selfless and reasoning. —Jay Meek

Mulrooney, C. *Apostrophe.* 28p. pap. $2.75. Los Angeles, CA: LOS, Fall 1998.

Munger, Kel. *The Fragile Peace You Keep.* 80p. pap. $12.95 (0-89823-186-8). Minneapolis, MN: New Rivers Press, Fall 1998. Forged in the impulses of memory and the need to bear witness, Munger's poetry creates a dialogue between the poet and her experience as a police woman. —New Rivers. Munger blasts gender and parades her protean poetics throughout history, the American work place, right into your local precinct. There is absolutely nothing fragile about these hard-hitting poems nor the peace-keeper's heart within. —Maureen Seaton. In edgy poems often centered in traditional forms and through traditional subjects set free on the blown landscape, Munger develops a powerful paradox: wherever we stand is both the center and the edge. Balanced in our separate lives, we have in common a fragile peace we keep. —Neal Bowers

Murawski, Elisabeth. *Troubled by an Angel.* 32p. pap. $6.00 (1-880834-37-5).

Cleveland, OH: Cleveland State University Poetry Center, Fall 1997. These poems are brave, both in the honesty of their pain, and in the new images chosen to represent it. —Linda Pastan. Murawski's work probes the wounds at the interstices of knowledge and experience. From the sadness of domestic love and tragedy, to the exaltations of consciously being in history, to the most subdued cry of disappointment towards a God, there's a rigor and a spirit in her poems both moving and gratifying. —C.K. Williams

Murphy, Michelle. *Jackknife & Light.* 92p. pap. $10.00 (1-880713-11-X). Penngrove, CA: Avec Books, Fall 1998. In *Jackknife & Light's* insistently meditative prose poems, Murphy brightlines human intimacies with a remarkable formal inventiveness. "If I had just one story," she writes, "I'd rather starve than have to live by it." Fortunately, she has enough imagination, strangeness, and verve to nourish us all. —Forrest Gander. Murphy's writing carries its own weight. Hers is an astute, penetrating voice that jars a reader out of the ordinary through surprise and fearlessness. When you least expect it, you'll be dragged away to be devoured by beauty and intelligence. —George Evans

Murphy, Sheila E. *Falling in Love Falling in Love With You Syntax: Selected and New Poems.* 209p. pap. $16.50 (0-937013-66-8). Elmwood, CT: Potes & Poets Press, Fall 1997. Welcome indeed is this major selection. Murphy combines an extraordinary level of literary experimentation, daring, and playfulness with an absolute honesty, clarity of vision, intimacy, and comprehensiveness in one of the strongest, clearest, and most distinctive voices writing in English today. Murphy is a poet who can use some of the most daring techniques around and show the feeling and consciousness they imply. —John M. Bennett

Murphy, Sheila E. *Leaflets.* 26p. pap. $4.00. Saratoga, ca: Instress, Fall 1998.

Murphy, Timothy. *The Deed of Gift.* 112p. pap. $12.95 (1-885266-62-6). Ashland, OR: Story Line Press, Fall 1998. The poems of Murphy's fine first collection come from the plains of Dakota. They are mostly short-lined quatrains and other regular forms that Murphy makes crackle and shine with sharp rhymes and crisp meters. Their distinctions are clear images, rueful wisdom, wry wit and — what may surprise some — the manly expression of gay love. —Booklist. A master of the short lyric, Murphy has created a compressed, expressive, almost emblematic style. What an unexpected voice to emerge from the Dakotas. —Dana Gioia

Murray, Dan. *None of This Is on the Map.* 77p. pap. $10.00 (0-935252-51-7). Sound Beach, NY: Street Press, Spring 1998. [Murray's is] a poetry of uncharted and austere beauty. —William Heyen

Murray, Les. *Subhuman Redneck Poems.* 104p. $18.00 (0-374-27155-0). pap. $12.00 (0-374-52538-2). Farrar, Straus and Giroux/Noonday, Spring 1997; Spring 1998 (new paper). Winner of the T.S. Eliot Prize in the U.K. Australia's best-known and most widely exported poet has picked up his compatriots' habit of cosmopolitanism. These poems tour an array of tonal prospects, like satire, song, and invective, which we don't often hear in our literary republic. Few poets have Murray's gift for marrying the musical and the political. Subhuman redneck he is not. —The New Yorker. As a calculated risk, Subhuman Redneck Poems has both balls, and, well, grace. It's the best introduction to this man, this poetry. Murray writes fat poetry in lean times, and there's no more instructive poet writing today. —Tom D'Evelyn, The Boston Book Review

Muske, Carol. *An Octave Above Thunder: New and Selected Poems.* 200p. pap. $16.95 (0-14-058794-2). New York, NY: Penguin Books/Viking Penguin, Fall 1997. Muske is a beautiful, ambitious poet who has not rested on her gifts for language and cadence. She has chosen instead to let a musical light become the infinitely more testing light of disaster and interrogation. —Eavan Boland. Muske is one of the best poets of her generation. Her poetry is emotionally rich without being sentimental or exhibitionist or indulgent; it is psychologically complicated without being neurotic or showing signs of repression; it is aware and alert to the present world without being polemical. —Donald Justice

Myers, Gary. *Lifetime Possessions.* 36p. pap. $5.00 (1-890044-07-5). Scottsdale, AZ: Riverstone Press, Fall 1997. Winner of the 1997 Riverstone Poetry Chapbook Award.

Myers, M., ed. *Elizabeth Stoddard: An Anthology in Memoriam (1823-1902).* 105p. pap. $15.95 (1-879183-38-2). Bristol, IN: Bristol Banner Books, Fall 1998.

Myers, M., ed. *Memorable Poetry 1998: People, Animals, and Events To Be Remembered in Our Hearts.* 118p. pap. $15.95 (1-879183-37-4). Bristol, IN: Bristol Banner Books, Fall 1998.

Myers, M., ed. *Sara Jane Clarke Lippincott: An Anthology in Memoriam (1823-1904).* 108p. pap. $15.95 (1-879183-36-6). Bristol, IN: Bristol Banner Books, Spring 1998. Poems that pay tribute to Lippincott, one of the earliest women in the United States to become a regular newspaper correspondent. —Bristol Banner Books

Myles, Eileen. *School of Fish.* 197p. $25.00 (1-57423-032-8). pap. $14.00 (1-57423-031-X). Santa Rosa, CA: Black Sparrow Press, Spring 1997. Myles hooks our attention and reels it in with a pulsing, sinuous rush of images seized from urban life's experimental flow. Illuminating these densely and intensely alive new poems is an eloquent and revealing prose essay, "The Lesbian Poet," wherein Myles addresses the source of her art, paying homage to her favorite living poets and early influences, and spelling out her own vitalist/proprioceptive aesthetic. —Black Sparrow Press

Nason, Richard W. *Horace, Home in Time for the Year 2000: Epistles From Providence, Rhode Island I, II and III.* 55p. pap. $11.95 (0-9659715-0-3). Providence, RI: Spitfire Press, Fall 1997.

Nathanson, Tenney. *One Block Over.* 30p. pap. $8.00. Tucson, AZ: Chax Press, Spring 1998. Letterpress Edition.

Nauen, Elinor. *American Guys.* 103p. $20.00 (1-882413-41-5). pap. $12.00 (1-882413-40-7). Brooklyn, NY: Hanging Loose Press, Spring 1997. [Nauen's] work is boyish girlish. Though it's not trans-gender, it's trans-William Carlos Williams. Kind of a female anthem to male dumbness. Her poetry has no existential dilemma, no interrogated "I." The self simply goes away in a state of chuckling awe. It's a first book with many long innings and a love

of tight pants. In American Guys, all parts of the reader get satisfied, even ones she didn't know she had. —Eileen Myles

Navansky, Bruno, ed. *Sixty Years of American Poetry: Celebrating the Anniversary of the Academy of American Poets.* 384p. $35.00 (0-8109-4464-2). New York, NY: Abrams, Harry N., Fall 1996. In 1984, Fifty Years of American Poetry was released to commemorate the fiftieth anniversary of the Academy of American Poets, with poems from each of the Academy's Chancellors, Fellows, and prizewinners. Sixty Years of American Poetry, the expanded edition, increases the roster to more than 200 poems and poets, representing a cross-section of six decades of the best in American poetry. —Harry N. Abrams

Navansky, Bruno, trans. *Festival in My Heart: Poems by Japanese Children.* 120p. $29.95 (0-8109-3314-4). New York, NY: Abrams, Harry N., 1993. A collection of poetry written by Japanese elementary school children originally printed as a daily feature in Japan's leading newspaper, Yomiuri Shimbun. Here are more than one hundred poems accompanied by seventy-seven illustrations representing the scope of Japanese art. Together, the poems and illustrations provide a compelling portrait of Japanese culture. —Harry N. Abrams

Needell, Claire. *Migrations.* 35p. pap. $4.00 (1-893032-03-5). Talisman House, Publishers / Jensen/Daniels, Fall 1998.

Negri, Paul, ed. *Civil War Poetry: An Anthology.* 128p. pap. $1.50 (0-486-29883-3). Mineola, NY: Dover Publications, Fall 1997. This inexpensive anthology brings together a superb selection of poems from both North and South, comprising the best and most representative poetry of those turbulent times. Ranging from boisterous calls to arms to poignant memorials for the slain, these poems reflect the heroism, horror, exaltation and anguish of the bloodiest and most crucial conflict in the nation's history. —Dover Publications

Neider, Mark. *First Person Plural.* 94p. pap. $12.95. Hopewell, NJ: Bedloe Books, Fall 1996.

Neiss, Jon. *dream — fog and sweet.* 8p. pap. $1.00. West Orange, NJ: Neiss, Jonathan, Spring 1997.

Nelson, Cynthia. *The Kentucky Rules.* pap. $10.00 (1-887-128-26-3). New York, NY: Soft Skull Press, Spring 1998. Indie-rock poetry with recollections of childhood and observances of everyday life. —Soft Skull Press

Nelson, Howard. *Bone Music.* 30p. pap. $7.95 (1-879205-72-6). Troy, ME: Nightshade Press, 1997.

Nelson, Marilyn. *The Fields of Praise: New and Selected Poems.* 209p. $24.95 (0-8071-2174-6). pap. $16.95 (0-8071-2175-4). Baton Rouge, LA: Louisiana State University Press, Spring 1997. 1997 National Book Award Finalist. Rooted in the basic soil of redemptive imagination, the voices in Nelson's poems seek a lyrical foothold in our daily lives. Her words teach us how to praise ourselves by praising each other. —Yusef Komunyakaa. [Nelson's] wisdom is to understand that our stubborn, deeply human longings for one another are also the grounds of spiritual life. Nelson's bold and sure poems long for heaven and — happily for us — continue a lifelong affair with the occasions of earth. —Mark Doty

Nelson, Stanley. *Immigrant, Book IV: The Conclusion.* 96p. pap. $13.00 (0-913559-42-3). Delhi, NY: Birch Brook Press, Spring 1998. Letterpress Edition. Immigrant is a powerful, insightful book-length poem of epic sweep across the Brooklyn of the imagination, of history, and of human potential. —Birch Brook Press. One of the most important books of the second half of the twentieth century. — Hugh Fox. Here we see one of the most complex and original poets of our time grappling with issues that underlie the framework of our culture. — Jared Smith, Small Press Review. Immigrant may be the richest, and most diversely focused, most personal and liturgical, of any American poem dealing with a limited American territory. —Donald Phelps

Neruda Pablo. Translated by George Schade. *Fifty Odes.* 363p. $35.00 (0-924027-13-5). (0-924027-14-3). Austin, TX: Host Publications, 1996.

Neruda, Pablo. Translated by Stephen Mitchell. *Full Woman, Fleshly Apple, Hot Moon.* 269p. $26.00 (0-06-018285-7). New York, NY: HarperCollins Publishers, Spring 1997. Mitchell has selected 49 poems and brought them to life for a whole new generation of readers. [He] focuses on the poetry of Neruda's ripeness, from the first book of Elemental Odes, published when he was fifty, to Full Powers, published when he was fifty-eight, eleven years before his death.Full Woman, Fleshly Apple, Hot Moon is a bilingual edition, with the English translation facing Neruda's original Spanish text. — HarperCollins Publishers

Neruda, Pablo. Edited by Dennis Maloney; Translated by Maria Jacketti, Dennis Maloney, and Clark Zlotchew. *Neruda at Isla Negra.* 128p. pap. $15.00 (1-877727-83-0). Buffalo, NY: White Pine Press, Spring 1998. In this collection of poems we see the poet in the company of his muse, walking alongside the source of his most lyrical inspiration: the sea. Gazing from his house on the shores of Isla Negra, Neruda discovered a new way of seeing, as the ocean became a living metaphor for the infinite riches of the world, gleaming in his poetry. I am grateful to White Pine Press that now I can share these poems (in Spanish or English) with my students, the community of poets, or anyone who would appreciate Neruda's passion for existence. —Martín Espada

Ness, Pamela Miller. *Driveway From Childhood.* 24p. pap. $5.00. Concord, CA: Small Poetry Press, Spring 1997. Reminiscences of childhood in the form of haiku and senryu. Signed and numbered limited edition. —Small Poetry Press

Ness, Pamela Miller. *Pink Light, Sleeping.* 32p. pap. $6.00. Concord, CA: Small Poetry Press, Spring 1998.

Neville, Tam Lin. *Journey Cake.* 75p. pap. $11.95 (1-886157-13-8). Kansas City, MO: BkMk Press of the University of Missouri-Kansas City, Spring 1998. [Neville] draws from folk literature a particular love of the humble, the singular, the lonely, as if they speak most accurately of the soul. Her poems span time and culture, taking in ancient and modern China and pioneer America. But in whatever setting, her characters, and especially her women, quietly insist on their dignity and independence. The poems in Journey Cake are profoundly original in their way of being moral, mysterious and intimate all at once. —Betsy Sholl. What I'm drawn to in Neville's work is

how curiously solitary it is, deeply meditative but never self-absorbed. These poems disturb and comfort. The mix is surprising and lovely. — Marianne Boruch

Newman, Denise. *Of Later Things Yet to Happen.* 32p. Buffalo, NY: Meow Press, Fall 1998.

Newman, Lesléa. *Still Life With Buddy: A Novel Told in Fifty Poems.* 100p. pap. $9.95 (1-886383-27-8). Lynnwood, WA: Pride Publications, Fall 1997. Still Life With Buddy, a novel told in fifty poems, explores the passionate friendship between a woman and a gay man who dies of AIDS. Both deeply personal and undeniably universal, the narrator tells her story with rage, humor, sadness, and most of all, undying love. —Pride Publications. Newman is as fine a writer as we (women, lesbians, Americans, humans — pick one or more) have. Her poetry is extraordinary. —Bay Area Reporter

Ngai, Sianne. *Criteria.* 78p. pap. $10.00 (1-882022-33-5). O Books, Fall 1998. Relationships of science, language, and the body are part and parcel to the patterned movements of [Ngai's] texts, which please this reader above all because of their lucid sensibility, skepticism, and wit. —Carla Harryman. In her first collection, Ngai deftly deploys the language of capital to phenomenalize the betrayals and failures of both words and commodities. As the lines in these poems repeat and fold back on themselves, a narrative of loss & groundlessness accrues. This heady yet plaintive verse alternately builds and demolishes its own rhetorical architectures to emerge with a new "criteria" for poetic entitlement. —Peter Gizzi

Ngai, Sianne. *Discredit.* 36p. pap. $8.00 (1-886224-25-0). Providence, RI: Burning Deck, Fall 1997. The logics of ownership and possession are used in the world not only to authorize my bank account and rental agreement, but my authority to speak or write. (It is said that the mad have "lost possession" of themselves.) This is what the poem disavows and resists. Hence "discredit:" lack of credit in the financial sense, and lack of creditability, authorial authority, the "personal voice." — Burning Deck

Nguyen Quang Thieu. Translated by Martha Collins and Njuyen Quang Thieu with Nguyen Ba Chung. *The Women Carry River Water.*

125p. $27.50 (1-55849-086-8). pap. $13.95 (1-55849-087-6). Amherst, MA: University of Massachusetts Press, Fall 1997. This book is the first English translation of a collection of poems by a Vietnamese writer of the post-1975 generation. Whether recalling the village of his childhood or exploring the rural and urban complexities of his adult life, Thieu roots his poems in a Vietnamese tradition that honors place. His respect for the passage of time is traditional, but he moves fluidly through landscapes of the past, present, and future with distinctly contemporary juxtapositions and metaphors. While few of the poems mention the war directly, its effects are both felt and transcended in these sometimes sad but always strikingly beautiful pieces. —University of Massachusetts Press

Nick, Dagmar. Translated by Jim Barnes. *Numbered Days.* 134p. $22.00 (0-943549-53-1). pap. $15.00 (0-943549-54-X). Kirksville, MO: Thomas Jefferson University Press/New Odyssey Press, Fall 1998. Through Barnes' good offices we can experience this prolific German writer's angry and compassionate poems. Her world which Barnes translates for us here has no parallel on the American scene today. —John Knoepfle. Nick has found, in fellow poet Barnes, the best possible translator for her work. —Lucien Stryk

Nickson, Richard. *Stones: A Book of Epigrams.* 84p. (0-9663720-0-X). Chicago, IL: Lithic Press, Fall 1998. [In Nickson's poems] the lyrical and the acerb often jostle each other in a waltz of wit. —Lithic Press

Niedecker, Lorine. Edited by Cid Corman. *The Granite Pail: Selected Poems.* 136p. pap. $14.50 (0-917788-61-3). Frankfort, KY: Gnomon Press, Fall 1996. One's first impulse, after awe, on reading The Granite Pail is a double dose of shame: shame at not being more familiar with her work: shame at ever having complained of the narrowness of one's life. —Carolyn Kizer

Nielsen, A.L. *Stepping Razor.* 62p. pap. $10.00 (0-9619097-9-X). Edge Books/Upper Limit, 1997. What Bogart was to crime-flicks, Nielsen is to postmodern poetry — a conscience and a court-jester by turns. Rueful comedy, at once spacey and rigorous, very funny. Read this book if it's the first thing you do. —David Bromige

Nisbet, Jim. *Across the Tasman Sea.* 64p. pap. $10.00 (1-879457-54-7). San Francisco, CA: Thumbscrew Press, Spring 1997. One of the best books of poetry of the past decade, smart, sincere, playful. It should win an award. —Barry Gifford

Nobles, Edward. *Through One Tear.* 87p. $22.00 (0-89255-227-1). New York, NY: Persea Books, Fall 1997. Nobles's poetry is distinguished by its astonishing precision, its careful concentration of the eye on the object, and the tautness of its rhythms. Nobles refuses easy solution; the hallmark of his poetry is what Williams called "rigor of quest." —Marjorie Perloff. Nobles is a strange poet — I mean this as a compliment. His work is not like other work being written in America today. It somehow combines the madness of Eliot with the wild associations of Lorca. His poems feel as if they are flung to all parts of the universe; they are wide-ranging, unrestrained and full of thought. —Liz Rosenberg

Noel, Susan. *Autobiography in Words.* 32p. pap. $5.95 (0-9666328-1-8). New York, NY: CUZ Editions, Fall 1998. Autobiography in Words shifts the terrain of philosophical inquiry from purity and "high culture" to the impersonal subjective and a sort of shattered self-reference. —CUZ Editions

Noguchi, Rick. *The Ocean Inside Kenji Takezp.* 96p. $24.95 (0-8229-3959-2). pap. $10.95 (0-8229-5613-6). Pittsburgh, PA: University of Pittsburgh Press, Fall 1996. Winner of the 1995 Associated Writing Programs' Award Series in Poetry. These spare, demotic lyrics ride with innocence, humility, humor, and doggedness. The Ancient, the Little, the constant Mariner: the human soul, as bare among the cultural wreckage as it always was, surfer of the primordial. —Olga Broumas

Noll, Mark A. *Seasons of Grace.* 95p. pap. $10.99 (0-8010-5777-9). Grand Rapids, MI: Baker Books, Fall 1997. Noll's poems belong to the noble tradition of meditative lyrics on the Christian life. Refusing to acknowledge any division between the sacred and the everyday, Noll's poetic reflections traverse seen and unseen worlds. —Baker Books

Noriega Bernuy, Julio, ed. Translated by Maureen Ahern. *Pichka Harawikuna: Five Quechua Poets.* 91p. pap.

$14.95 (0-935480-98-6). Pittsburgh, PA: Latin American Literary Review Press, Fall 1998. A collection of work by contemporary Peruvian poets Dida Aguirre, Lily Flores, William Hurtado, Eduardo Ninamango, and Porfirio Meneses. Presenting poems in Quechua along with their Spanish and English translations, this publication celebrates the rich indigenous heritage of Peru and provides rare insight into a culture that remains largely unknown. — Latin American Literary Review Press

Norlen, Sherron. *Entomologist's Dreambook.* 48p. pap. $10.00 (0-9665810-1-6). San Francisco, CA: Protean Press, Fall 1998. Fine press edition, $95, ISBN 0-9665810-0-8. Insects emerge in Entomologist's Dreambook as mythic messengers from the natural world: from carrion beetles sculpting bone's true form to the praying mantis's fierce habits to a scarab's capture and flight. —Protean Press. Each poem is finely crafted, surprising and interesting. Some, appropriately small, are little firecrackers or jewels; others are more extended meditations. This is a book to enjoy both for the poems and for the art of the book, the fine press edition being one of the most beautiful books I've ever seen. — Paul Merchant

North, Rusty. *Christmas Past.* 12p. pap. $5.00. Port Townsend, WA: Sagittarius Press, Fall 1998. An unblushing tribute to Christmas before the time of Barbie dolls, written for the author's grandchildren. —Sagittarius Press

North, Rusty. *Little Old Lady in Tennis Shoes.* 20p. pap. $5.00. Port Townsend, WA: Sagittarius Press, Spring 1996 (reissue); Spring 1998 (new edition). Poems about life as an older woman in our culture. —Sagittarius Press

North, Rusty, ed. *Uppety Women.* 20p. pap. $5.00. Port Townsend, WA: Sagittarius Press, Fall 1998. A collection of poetry by women with an attitude. —Sagittarius Press

northSun, nila. *A Snake in Her Mouth: Poems 1974-96.* 80p. pap. $8.95 (0-931122-87-2). Albuquerque, NM: West End Press, Fall 1997. Although easy to read, [northSun's] poems are often as deep as the roots of the Nevada mountains. Quirky and lyrical, by turns gentle and harsh, the many notes she sounds all make strong music. Although it has been too long

coming, this first major volume of northSun's work has been worth the wait. — Joseph Bruchac

Notley, Alice. *Mysteries of Small Houses.* 139p. pap. $14.95 (0-14-058896-5). New York, NY: Penguin Books/Viking Penguin, Fall 1998. In this new collection, Notley searches for the nature of the self, vividly reconstructing the journey from young girl to young woman to accomplished artist. In their knife-edged, intelligent renderings of moments both precise and ephemeral, Notley's poems manage to mirror and transcend the times they evoke. —Penguin Books. The most challenging and engaging of our contemporary radical female poets. —San Francisco Chronicle

Nóto, John. *Psycho-Motor Breathscapes.* 68p. pap. $7.95 (0-9654877-0-9). Vatic Hum Press, 1997. Nóto's language erupts in Shelleyesque furor, firestorms of anger and delight. Amazing! The poems move in total conviction, insisting that nothing be unchanged in their wake. — Ed Foster, Talisman

Nurkse, Dennis, ed. *This Beautiful Name Is Mine: Collection of Poetry From the*

Writing With Rhythm Young Adult Workshops. 99p. (1-891001-00-0). Brooklyn, NY: Brooklyn Public Library, Fall 1997. The poets whose works are included in this collection participated in the "Writing with Rhythm" program at the Brooklyn Public Library [intended to] guide and encourage teenagers from throughout Brooklyn to explore and express their poetic talents. —Howard Golden, Brooklyn Borough President. These keen and widely divergent voices are forged in the openness and complexity of city — triumphant and astonishingly vulnerable, sophisticated and awed. The reader is struck by the immediacy and depth of the poets' concerns, by the courage, by the will to create something lasting, something "seen for the first time," out of the welter of daily life in a huge and constantly changing city. — Dennis Nurkse

Nye, Naomi Shihab. *Fuel.* 136p. pap. $12.50 (1-880238-63-2). Rochester, NY: BOA Editions, Spring 1998. Nye values the innocence of the young; her poems exult in simple things and possibilities, for "Nothing is impossible," she shouts. —Kirkus Reviews

Nye, Naomi Shihab, ed. *The Space Between Our Footsteps: Poems and Paintings From the Middle East.* 144p. $19.95 (0-689-81233-7). Simon & Schuster Books for Young Readers, Spring 1998. More than a hundred poets and artists from nineteen Middle Eastern countries come together in a collection by acclaimed anthologist Nye. Poems by writers such as Palestine's Mahmud Darwish and Hanan Mikha'il 'Ashrawi, Egypt's Naguib Mahfouz, Lebanon's Fuad Rifka, and Israel's Yehuda Amichai and Moshe Dor are paired with glorious full-color paintings to make an anthology that is by turns exquisite, startling, heartbreaking, humorous, and joyful. — Simon & Schuster

O'Brien, Geoffrey. *Floating City: Selected Poems 1978-1995.* 114p. pap. $10.50 (1-883689-38-4). Jersey City, NJ: Talisman House, Publishers, Fall 1996. O'Brien is a poet of tremendous gifts and astounding, all-embracing erudition. —John Ashbery. O'Brien writes with the eye of an historian and the ear of a cellist. All too volatile, myth, memorabilia, event find residence, sonorous grounding, in O'Brien's finely crafted measures. Here, where "bushes creak with language," the conveyor, once again, comes to the rescue of the conveyed. Music prevails. —Gustaf Sobin

O'Hehir, Diana. *Spells for Not Dying Again.* 80p. $26.00 (0-910055-30-0). pap. $14.00 (0-910055-31-9). Cheney, WA: Eastern Washington University Press, Spring 1997. Winner of 1997 Prix d'Assisi from the Arts International Workshop. Patterned after the mysterious enchantments in the Egyptian Book of the Dead, O'Hehir's poetry examines daunting, age-old themes — loss, reconciliation, and regeneration. —Eastern Washington University Press. No one else combines worldly wryness with the eerie, spacey overtones of human feeling — represented, here, by the grotesque yet haunting imagery of the ancient Egyptian afterlife — in quite her inimitable way. —Alan Williamson. The poems speak with unsettling candor, awe and terror; miraculously they are also full of compassion and a wry, mordant humor. The rhythms of deeply felt mystery are here, stunned into words. —Dabney Stuart

O'Melveny, Regina. *Blue Wolves: Poems and Assemblages.* 82p. pap. $12.00 (0-9646844-7-0). Treadwell,

NY: Bright Hill Press, Spring 1998. Winner of the Bright Hill Press Poetry Book Award. Writing about hair thieves in Rio or a mouse toe bone or a silk chemise, [O'Melveny] offers an intensely focused vision and a lush, evocative soundscape. Astonishingly mature for a first collection, Blue Wolves announces the arrival of an important poet. —Michael Waters. O'Melveny's] poems are rooted in a world where nature's mystery makes itself palpable and known; a world of intuition and divination that glows with a sexual phosphorescence, a yearning to be cracked wild and dancing, to be released, as she has written, like "fire / in the stones that ache to be born." —Peter Levitt

O'Shea-Noonan, Mary-Beth. *Hungry Grass.* 48p. pap. $12.95 (0-941895-14-9). Amherst, MA: Amherst Writers & Artists Press, Fall 1998. O'Shea-Noonan writes poetry of exceptional depth and passion. Her richly-textured images, clean phrasing, and gift for metaphor combine in poems that resonate in the reader's experience long after the reading. This is a true poetry. —Paul Smyth. Each word, each image resonates with both fierceness and tenderness. The poems are full of passion and a vibrant life-force. They speak of a physical time and place yet are connected to the rich inner landscape of dream and imagination. Each poem is a heartsong. These are the canticles of a soul returned home. —P.J. Curtis

Oder, Phyllis. *The Clerihews - One Hundred - of Phyllis Oder.* 111p. pap. $11.95 (0-933243-08-1). Laurel Publications, Fall 1996. Phyllis Oder offers an extraordinary collection of wit and wisdom. —Aaron Kramer

Oeur, U Sam. Translated by Ken McCollough and U Sam Oeur. *Sacred Vows.* 226p. pap. $15.00 (1-56689-069-1). Minneapolis, MN: Coffee House Press, Spring 1998. Sacred Vows retells the recent terror of Cambodia and the beauty of its culture. A survivor of the Pol Pot regime, Oeur inspires young Cambodians to reacquaint themselves with their heritage and make it once again vibrant. Using myths, stories, prophecies, history, and tradition as ironic counterpoint to Cambodia's present-day situation, Oeur foretells freedom's imminent return. Sacred Vows is a mesmerizing call to freedom. —Coffee House Press.

Like the beautiful lily that has its roots in mud, the poetry in Sacred Vows is the voice of an anguished heart emerging from the blood and gore of violence. A book all peace makers must read. —Arun Gandhi

Ogden, John D. *Nature Plays for Keeps.* 124p. pap. $9.50 (1-56474-166-4). Santa Barbara, CA: Fithian Press, Fall 1996. In these lovely poems the wisdom of experience complicates itself with humor, irony, anger, grief — the life of all ages of life. — A.R. Ammons. In their understatement, in their irony and even in their wit, these poems are as wise as they are moving. —James McConkey

Okantah, Mwatabu S. *Cheikh Anta Diop: Poem for the Living.* 232p. pap. $24.95. Philadelphia, PA: Black History Museum, UMUM/LOH Press, Fall 1997. Cheikh Anta Diop: Poem for the Living is the first poem to be published in English, French and Wolof (a West African language) in the U.S., and is the first modern epic of its kind written by an African American. —Black History Museum. In sheer existential horror and poetic surreality, Okantah takes us through the history of Black consciousness and delivers us to ourselves intact. It is a journey through which the self is transmuted and made whole. —Philadelphia Tribune

Older, Julia. *Higher Latitudes.* 64p. pap. $8.00 (0-9627162-3-5). Hancock, NH: Appledore Books, Fall 1995. This broad spectrum of well-crafted poems explores the quiet drama of upcountry New England. —Appledore Books. Older writes non-trendy poems, literate without affectation, ironic, audacious, compassionate. —Sonya Dorman, The Puckerbrush Review

Oliver, Douglas. *Selected Poems.* 136p. pap. $10.50 (1-883689-34-1). Jersey City, NJ: Talisman House, Publishers, Fall 1996. What was the shock of reading . . . The Waste Land when it was published in 1922? I think I know. I've just read Oliver's epoch-making long poem, Penniless Politics. I never thought I would ever read anything like it in the 1990's. Penniless Politics sets the agenda for the next 20 years. —Howard Brenton, The Guardian. After years of headbanging rhetoric about uniting the personal and the political, why not see how a visionary poet does it? — Boyd Tonkin, City Limits

Oliver, Mary. *West Wind: Poems and Prose Poems.* 63p. $21.00 (0-395-85082-7). pap. $13.00 (0-395-85085-1). Houghton Mifflin Company/Mariner Books, Spring 1997; Spring 1998 (paper). In this stunning collection of forty poems, [Oliver] writes of nature and love, of the way they transform over time. And the way they remain constant. — Houghton Mifflin. From the chaos of the world, her poems distill what it means to be human and what is worthwhile about life. —Library Journal. Her poems do indeed make us "shiver with praise." — Booklist

Ollivier, L.L. *Albert Einstein in Las Vegas.* 32p. Baltimore, MD: Maryland Poetry Review, 1997. I delighted in the skillful use of sound rhythm and line in these poems, not to mention the beauty of the imagery. The thoughts in these poems seem to rise out of the landscapes. It's a pleasure to read a poet who uses free verse so skillfully and with such depth of thought — a very rare thing. —Michael Fallon

Oppenheimer, Joel. Edited by Robert J. Bertholf; Drawings by John Dobbs. *Collected Later Poems of Joel*

Oppenheimer. 506p. (0-922668-15-9). (0-922668-16-7). Buffalo, NY: SUNY University Libraries, The Poetry/Rare Books Collection, Spring 1997. Profoundly a poet of place, in this beautiful later work Oppenheimer transcends his homeplaces: Black Mountain College, Greenwich Village, Rural New Hampshire. [Oppenheimer] was a paterfamiliar anarchist poet whose radically simple poems field irony when necessary, but risk stealing basic care, always. —Lyman Gilmore

Orbán, Ottó. Translated by Bruce Berlind. *The Journey of Barbarus.* 91p. pap. $10.00 (1-57889-054-3). Pueblo, CO: Passeggiata Press, Spring 1997. [These are] poems written during [Orban's] stay in Iowa in 1976 and during his visiting professorship in Minnesota in 1987. [Orban's] America is full of visual and emotional adventure. Exploring America, however provides no relaxation. He is tense and alert, buoyant and scathing all the time, styling himself as "Barbarus," a sophisticated Barbarian observing the center of the Roman Empire. —World Literature Today

Orlen, Steve. *Kisses.* 73p. pap. $11.95 (1-881163-23-7). Oxford, OH: Miami University Press, 1997. Orlen is a wonderful poet and one of the best practitioners of free verse writing today. The sounds of his poems bang and glide. Most fine poetry strikes the mind and heart. This is true of Orlen as well, but his poems also strike the ear. They feel good in the mouth. —Stephen Dobyns

Ormsby, Eric. *For a Modest God: New and Selected Poems.* 139p. $20.00 (0-8021-1607-8). New York, NY: Grove Press, Spring 1997. A most excellent poet, resonant and delicately exact with words and objects. Ormsby's reverent attention to things as they are lights up his every page with a glow. —John Updike. The present work identifies him as a master of the poetry of sheer observation. His method demonstrates the delight and potency of pure description, which, with Ormsby, unfailingly exposes the unexpected extraordinary in the ordinary subjects it addresses. This volume deserves a prominent place in all poetry collections. Highly recommended. —Library Journal

Orr, Priscilla. *Jugglers and Tides.* 92p. $21.95 (1-889262-02-1). Stamford, CT: Hannacroix Creek Books, Fall 1997. Orr's poems have been wrestled from the body — visceral, physical pierces lured, then, through the mind and to the page. Her strength is her powerful certainty, her belief in the body, that the body is the being salted by the mind. Nothing here is half-hearted, nothing could be: such a heart is firmly lodged at a profound center and no drawing upon it will weaken its ability to get its story out. —Renee Ashley, Salt

Ortiz Cofer, Judith. Translated by Elena Olazagasti-Segovia. *Bailando en silencio: Escemas de una niñez puertorriqueña.* 159p. pap. $11.95 (1-55885-205-0). Arte Público Press/Piñata Books, 1997. The long awaited Spanish translation of Ortiz Cofer's award-winning collection. Themes of female conditioning and female roles, culture shock and immigrations texture this moving collection which includes poems that lyrically elaborate the narrative essays. The English language edition was the recipient of a PEN citation and a Martha Albrand Award, was included in the 1991 Best American Essays, and selected as one of The New York Public Library's Books for the Teen Age. —Arte Público Press/Piñata Books

Osbey, Brenda Marie. *All Saints: New and Selected Poems.* 128p. $22.95 (0-8071-2197-5). pap. $15.95 (0-8071-2198-3). Baton Rouge, LA: Louisiana State University Press, Fall 1997. Like the feast day recalled in its title, this collection of twenty narrative poems venerates the dead. Osbey invokes, impersonates, and converses with her Afro-New Orleans forbears — both blood ancestors and spiritual predecessors — weaving in hypnotic cadence a spell as potent as the religious and magical mysteries of her native culture. —Louisiana State University Press. Osbey's book is as rich as any cuisine coming out of New Orleans. When she writes about Nina Simone or Luis Congo, you want the world to hush and pay attention. —E. Ethelbert Miller

Osherow, Jacqueline. *With a Moon in Transit.* 83p. $20.00 (0-8021-1599-3). New York, NY: Grove Press, Fall 1996. Marked by an inimitable anecdotal expansiveness and uncompromising control, Osherow's poems are among the most ambitious being written. I am always deeply absorbed when I read Osherow's work, and I never fail to be exhilarated by its scope, its narrative ease, its good-natured and probing intelligence. —Mark Strand. Abundant in whimsy, philosophical speculation, and earthly affections, Osherow's poems inhabit their forms with insouciance and wit. She chats with the moon in terza rima, summons up the refrigerator's late-night hum in a villanelle, and tosses off sonnets to the heavenly bodies. Whether in mourning or celebration, hers is a voice of dazzling confidence and humane and generous wisdom. —Rosanna Warren

Ostriker, Alicia Suskin. *The Little Space: Poems Selected and New, 1968-1998.* 231p. (0-8229-5680-2). Pittsburgh, PA: University of Pittsburgh Press, Fall 1998. One of the most intelligent and lyric of American poets. —Iowa Review. Ostriker has become one of those brilliantly provocative and imaginatively gifted contemporaries whose iconoclastic expression, whether in prose or poetry, is essential to understanding our American selves. —Joyce Carol Oates. Ostriker explores the eroticism implicit in all relationships. Her poems read

like passionate letters to a familiar you, utterly specific, yet tantalizingly mysterious. —Village Voice. Stunning, unforgettable poems. —San Francisco Chronicle

Ouzoonian, Amy. *Inkubaiting Estrogin.* 33p. pap. $5.00. New York, NY: Fly by Night Press/A Gathering of the Tribes, Spring 1998. This book is bad! And rocks! — Steve Cannon

Owen, Maureen. *American Rush: Selected Poems.* 157p. pap. $15.95 (1-883689-69-4). Jersey City, NJ: Talisman House, Publishers, Fall 1998. Owen has brought the stuff of everyday North American life into outlandish surrealism. — American Book Review. Maureen Owen is one of those American originals whose work could never be mistaken for anyone else's: her rushing phrasal line, her architectonic wit, her conjunction of elegance and down-to-earthness, the intelligence and edge of her sensibility. —Alice Notley

Owen, Stephen, ed. *An Anthology of Chinese Literature: Beginnings to 1911.* 1212p. (0-393-97106-6). New York, NY: Norton, W.W., and Company, Spring 1996. Hailed as a groundbreaking text in Chinese

Studies, An Anthology of Chinese Literature brings together representative works from the first millennium B.C. to the end of the imperial system in 1911. Including a range of forms — songs, letters, anecdotes, stories, plays, political oratory, traditional literary theory, and more — the anthology's innovative structure provides a previously unavailable view of the interplay among Chinese literature, culture, and history and alerts the non-Chinese reader to what a premodern Chinese reader would have noticed instinctively. —W.W. Norton. Outstrips every previous anthology in its scope and in the variety of texts and forms represented. —Eugene Eoyang

Owens, James. *Loan of the Quick.* 40p. pap. $7.00 (1-885912-18-8). Abingdon, VA: Sow's Ear Press, Fall 1998. The first chapbook of a promising new poet, a finalist for the 1998 Amy Lowell Fellowship, and a Pushcart nominee. —The Sow's Ear Press

Owens, Rochelle. *New and Selected Poems 1961-1996.* 189p. pap. $20.00 (1-881523-06-3). San Diego, CA: Junction Press, 1997. Sharp & visual, Owens combines a

landscape with a poetics, the domestic with the mythic, machines with the organic living world — from which arises a construct & a fused vision: poetry & life. — Jerome Rothenberg. In its uncompromising savagery, its passionate rejection of sentimentality, Owens' lyric voice is unique among contemporary poets. An astonishing body of work. —Marjorie Perloff

Pacheco, José Emilio. Translated by Cynthia Steele and David Lauer. *City of Memory and Other Poems.* 193p. pap. $10.95 (0-87286-324-7). San Francisco, CA: City Lights Books, Spring 1997. This volume brings two of this celebrated Mexican poet's most respected collections of poetry into English translation for the first time. [Pacheco's] poems strain mightily to reconcile the forces of creation and destruction, to understand how beauty and death can coexist in history and the natural world. — Publishers Weekly

Pahmeier, Gailmarie. *The House on Breakaheart Road.* 57p. pap. $10.00 (0-87417-313-2). Reno, NV: University of Nevada Press, Spring 1998. Pahmeier's is a purely American poetry, a tough female vision that includes the language of baseball and bread baking, well-tuned transmissions and hard-packed snow, truckstops and "wound-red lipstick." —Dorianne Laux. The House on Breakaheart Road allows us to consider the beauty as well as the agony of our deepest and most heart-felt binding human characteristics. —David Lee

Paino, Frankie. *Out of Eden.* 90p. pap. $12.00 (1-880834-33-2). Cleveland, OH: Cleveland State University Poetry Center, Fall 1997. Whether transporting the reader back to an early nineteenth-century autopsy or jack-hammering the most harrowing anti-occasional poem I've ever encountered out of her childhood, Paino possesses a riveting narrative gift and a hell-bent, unprecedented, gattling-gun ear. Out of Eden is elegiac, erotic, and brilliantly imagined. No matter what corner of human history she illuminates, she transforms it into an almost unbearable beauty. —Roger Weingarten

Palen, John. *Staying Intact.* 24p. pap. $6.00 (0-932412-11-4). Saginaw, MI: Mayapple Press, Fall 1997. Palen's quiet Midwestern voice communicates the deeper unease that lies beneath both rural and small-city surfaces. — Mayapple Press

Palma, Michael. *Antibodies.* 20p. pap. $8.95 (0-9657045-5-6). Brooklyn, NY: Somers Rocks Press, 1997. Deftly, with a detail, "small occasions / lunch in empty restaurants / eyes on the door," Palma brings us into the heart of a secret love affair. Fine shades of feeling are matched by the supple phrasing and subtle ear that have made him and award-winning translator of Italian poetry. Here the inventive language is all his own. In a variety of forms that gives pace and rhythm to the sequence, he chronicles the full heart dealt half a hand. — Suzanne Noguere

Palmer, Michael. *The Lion Bridge: Selected Poems 1972-1995.* 260p. pap. $18.95 (0-8112-1383-8). New York, NY: New Directions, Fall 1998. The Lion Bridge offers for the first time a comprehensive view of Palmer's extraordinary poetry. Dense and haunting, analytic and lyrical, classical and profoundly innovative, Palmer's work possesses a singular beauty. Rescuing from limbo much material that has gone out of print, this generous chronological selection includes individual poems, selections from serial poems, a sequence for his daughter, and two complete serial poems. — New Directions. Palmer has been one of the most influential writers in recent years, perhaps because he fuses contemporary concerns about syntax and meaning production with some very ancient poetic pleasures. —The Village Voice

Palmer, Michael; Régis Bonvicino, and Nelson Ascher, eds. *Nothing the Sun Could Not Explain: Contemporary Brazilian Poets.* 312p. pap. $15.95 (1-55713-366-2). Los Angeles, CA: Sun & Moon Press, 1997. Containing the works of twenty contemporary poets from Brazil, this anthology reveals the immense influence of and reaction to the Modernist and experimental traditions from Brazilian literature, and demonstrates a marvelous complexity of thought and commitment to the landscape. Published bilingually in Portuguese (spoken worldwide by over 200 million people) and English, this new anthology hopefully will help Americans better to understand some of the dynamic forces in contemporary Brazilian culture. —Sun & Moon Press

Pankey, Eric. *Heartwood.* 72p. pap. $12.95 (0-914061-

78-X). Alexandria, VA: Orchises Press, Fall 1998.

Pankey, Eric. *The Late Romances.* 76p. $21.00 (0-679-45454-3). pap. $13.00 (0-679-76605-7). New York, NY: Knopf, Alfred A., Spring 1997; Spring 1999 (new paper). Eros presides over the operatic spectacle of these poems, and Melancholia over their ravenous clarity. The poems themselves are pilgrimages back and forth between Eden and this green world. — Alfred A. Knopf. [Pankey] is outstanding among an emerging generation of talented and accomplsihed poets. —David Baker, The Kenyon Review. The clarity, intellectual heft, structure, poise, formal dexterity, and music of the poems in The Late Romances make it one of the most engrossing and accomplished collections published in the past several years. Pankey has become a poet of formidable skill and achievement. —Brian Henry

Paola, Suzanne. *Bardo.* 82p. (0-299-16014-9). Madison, WI: University of Wisconsin Press, Fall 1998. Winner of the 1998 Brittingham Prize in Poetry. A terrific collection of poems. Paola, freestyling snappily down the line between scholarship and sass, combines Tibetan Buddhism with the drugged-out rocked-up boomer American landscape, and brings the full bravura energy of her vision (part classical Rome, part glitzy Caesar's Palace) to bear upon all of our invaluable, fractured lives. —Albert Goldbarth. In Bardo, a god-haunted poet scrabbles for the sublime in the debris of language, the rubbish of visions. Paola's poems glimmer with verbal inventiveness but accept the discipline of clear sight and human boundaries. A flamboyant and searching book. —Rosanna Warren

Parini, Jay. *House of Days.* $22.00 (0-8050-5713-7). pap. $13.00 (0-8050-5714-5). New York, NY: Holt, Henry, and Company, Spring 1998. Parini's House of Days is a truly satisfying fourth book of poems — keen-eyed, thoughtful, artful yet unaffected. I am struck by the honesty of the poet's desires and ignorances — his forthright longing for transcendence, his forthright fear that it may not happen. —Richard Wilbur. In these poems, at once lyrical and reticent, Parini has given us a restrained yet deeply felt set of meditations on nature and time. The world of the book (the literary scholar's writing and reading life) is in House of Days everywhere interfaced

with the book of the world — the ever-changing scene, beautifully and unsentimentally evoked here, of rural New England, its seasons and turns, its rhythms and reminders. — Rachel Hadas

Parker, Alan Michael. *Days Like Prose.* 48p. pap. $12.00 (1-882509-04-8). New York, NY: Alef Books, Spring 1997. The deft, formal quality of these poems coupled with Parker's eye for the telling detail make this a book of stirring, quiet beauty. — Publishers Weekly. Parker has written a poetry of living music and sonic complexities, whose textures modulate from the circumspect to the resplendent. Whether meditating on the Sears catalogue or narrating a widow's recent grief, these poems intimate rather than explicate; they bespeak the reticence in the folds of the world. —Alice Fulton

Parker, Carolyn, ed. *The Poetry of Roses.* 64p. $19.95 (0-8109-3736-0). New York, NY: Abrams, Harry N., Fall 1995. Exquisite photographs taken by Parker complement poetry from all places and times: Sappho joins Rumi in speaking of the soul's joy in the rose. Haiku master Basho takes a petal shower beneath mountain roses. Native

Americans sing of the colors of roses in love charms, while contemporary Brazilian author Jorge Luis Borges unfolds an invisible rose and reveals its erotic center. —Harry N. Abrams

Parker, Doris. *A Poetry Collection.* 56p. pap. $3.00 (1-57502-243-5). Kearney, NE: Morris Publishing, Fall 1996.

Parmiani, Floria. *Imagery and Reality.* 103p. pap. $13.00 (0-9653783-1-4). Sunnyvale, CA: Floria Publications, Fall 1998. Sensitive and self-revealing, these reflective poems about nature, love and personal interaction change our paradigms and create lyrical imagery in a truth-telling exercise. —Bookman News. These are moving, daring, and irreverent portraits of the human soul; yet they are necessary to expose the truth as a means of survival. —Midwest Book Review

Parnell, Anthony D. *Mind Games.* 88p. pap. $10.95 (0-9644205-1-1). Altadena, CA: Dreams & Visions Publishing, Spring 1997. Mind Games is a self-help book in poetry, exploring ways to transcend the challenges of emotional passivity and self-delusion. —Dreams & Visions Publishing

Parsons, Linda. *Home Fires.* 72p. $22.00 (1-885912-14-5). pap. $12.00 (1-885912-12-9). Abingdon, VA: Sow's Ear Press, Spring 1997. If there is any use left for that time-worn word, prosody, perhaps it is to help us describe the cardiovascular system of a poem as it delivers life-saving oxygen out to the edges of silence. Once might hastily describe Parsons's beautiful and touching poems as free verse, and by so doing relegate them to the current fashion, but to do so would be to overlook the tremendous energy they develop as this poet's richly observed life pulses out into the masterfully designed and infinitely various capillaries of her art. This is as fine a collection of poems as I have seen in a very long time. —Ted Kooser

Pascale, Isabelle. *Her Lullaby for Your Soul.* 56p. pap. $10.00. New York, NY: Liquid Light Publishing, Spring 1997.

Pastan, Linda. *Carnival Evening: New and Selected Poems 1968-1998.* 289p. $27.50 (0-393-04631-1). New York, NY: Norton, W.W., and Company, Spring 1998. [Pastan] is a cultural philanthropist. We are lucky to have her work and her presence in our lives. —William Stafford.

Some critics point to Emily Dickinson when citing Pastan's lapidary style and metaphysical wit, a comparison that does justice to either poet when Pastan is at her best. —Floyd Collins, Gettysburg Review. Her gift of poetry, of insight, her illumination of the mysteries of beauty and terror result in work of metaphysical power, a poetry that offers sustenance. —Chelsea Review

Payack, Peter. *Blanket Knowledge.* 128p. pap. $11.95 (0-944072-83-6). Cambridge, MA: Zoland Books, Fall 1997. This collection is Payack at his witty, pithy, and perceptive top form, and is one of his most fanciful flights. —Tama Janowitz. Payack's genuine concern for the place of humankind in the cosmos is intermixed with much high wit. Uniquely amusing and entertaining. —Michael Benedikt

Paz, Octavio. *A Tale of Two Gardens: Poems From India 1952-1995.* 111p. pap. $8.00 (0-8112-1349-8). New York, NY: New Directions, Spring 1997. A Tale of Two Gardens collects the poetry from over 40 years of Paz's many and various commitments to India — as Mexican ambassador, student of Indian philosophy,

and, above all, as poet. Despite having written many acclaimed prose books on the region, he has always considered those to be footnotes to the poems. From the long work "Mutra," written in 1952, to his recent adaptations from the classical Sanskrit, Paz scripts his India with a mixture of deft sensualism and hands-on politics. —New Directions. Paz's poetry is a seismograph of our century's turbulence, a crossroads where East meets West. — Publishers Weekly

Pearlberg, Gerry Gomez, ed. *Queer Dog: Homo Pup Poetry.* 144p. pap. $12.95 (1-57344-071-X). San Francisco, CA: Cleis Press, Spring 1997. Dogs run through every one of these poems, just as the very essence of poetry runs through dogs. Poetry and dogs share a number of qualities—they're both immediate, temporal, social creatures; they are souls laid bare for all the world to see, yet full of hidden implication. In any good poem, there's an invisible shade of energy, thought and emotion that lies beyond the grasp of language. I like to think of that as the same realm where dogs come by their unique powers, their sense of thrill and hunt and humor, their gentle devotion. —Gerry Gomez Pearlberg

Pearse, Richard. *Come Back Vanishing.* 78p. pap. $9.95 (1-891219-58-8). Siasconset, MA: Linear Arts, Fall 1998. At times elegant, at times colloquial, in a voice sometimes dressed for dinner, or brawling with intelligence, this is writing that runs or spars, dodges or lurches, flies or waltzes briskly among the urban terra firma, concocting illusion and managing truth. —Linear Arts

Péloquin, Claude. Translated by Lucie Ranger. *Pellucid Waters: Selected Poems.* 62p. pap. $10.00 (1-55071-066-4). Guernica Editions, Fall 1998.

Penfold, Nita. *The Woman With the Wild Grown Hair.* 32p. pap. $7.95. Johnstown, OH: Pudding House Publications, Spring 1998.

Perkins, Wil. *!Scat: The Scat Poetry of Wil Perkins.* 93p. pap. $9.95 (1-884773-04-4). Los Angeles, CA: Heat Press, Fall 1997. Extends the African American traditions of orality and music in ways that are idiosyncratic and masterful. An experience in visual and sound poetry, a phenomenal performance of words on the page. —Heat Press

Perkoff, Stuart Z. Edited by Gerald T. Perkoff. *Voices of the Lady: Collected Poems.* 486p. (0-943373-48-4). Orono, ME: National Poetry Foundation, Fall 1998. This volume makes available in its entirety for the first time one of the great lost masterworks of twentieth century American poetry. In common with poets like Pound, Olson, Blackburn, and Creeley, Perkoff saw everything that he wrote as part of a continuous poem. From time to time he published bits and pieces of this endless poem, in magazines and a few small collections. This full collection reveals him to be a great poet not only in his capacity to describe his own tragic life-history, but also in his affirmation of the bonds that draw human beings together, and in his deeply religious sense that human life is a dialogue with "he who must remain unnamed." — National Poetry Foundation. [Perkoff was] the quintessential Beat poet. —Paul Vangelisti

Perlman, Jim; Ed Folsom and Dan Campion, eds. *Walt Whitman: The Measure of His Song.* pap. $20.00 (0-930100-78-6). Duluth, MN: Holy Cow! Press, Fall 1998. First published to wide critical acclaim in 1981, this revised and expanded anthology charts the ongoing American and international response to Whitman's legacy. This new edition contains over 100 responses from Henry David Thoreau, Ezra Pound, D.H. Lawrence, Pablo Neruda, Allen Ginsberg, Adrienne Rich, Sherman Alexie, and Gary Snyder, among others. —Holy Cow! Press. The selections are varied, strong, and often surprising and offer overwhelming proof of Whitman's triumphant achievement. —Justin Kaplan

Perrin, Arnold. *Window.* 28p. pap. $4.00. Talent, OR: Talent House Press, Fall 1998.

Pessoa, Fernando. Translated by Richard Zenith. *Fernando Pessoa & Co.: Selected Poems.* 304p. $25.00 (0-8021-1628-0). pap. $14.00 (0-8021-3627-3). New York, NY: Grove Press, Spring 1998; Spring 1999 (new paper). Winner of the 1998 Pen Award for Poetry in Translation. Zenith has taken three of Pessoa's major "heteronyms" (the poet's term for his numerous literary alter egos), as well as the poetry Pessoa wrote "as himself," and created a volume of extraordinary emotional depth and poetic precision. His verse is as searing as that of Rilke or Mandelstam. —

The New York Times Book Review. A beautiful one-volume course in the soul of the twentieth century. —Booklist. Remarkable. Rife with kindred moments of surprising and paradoxical self-reflection, [this is] an arresting body of work, punctuated with compact, discomfiting epiphanies. It is impossible to do justice to the power and range of the poems. —Newsday

Pessoa, Fernando. Translated and Edited by Edwin Honig and Susan M. Brown. *Poems of Fernando Pessoa.* 240p. pap. $15.95 (0-87286-342-5). San Francisco, CA: City Lights Books, Fall 1998. [Pessoa] wrote under several identities, which he called heteronyms; each of his "voices" is completely different in subject, temperament, and style. This volume brings back into print the comprehensive collection of his work published by Ecco in 1986. —City Lights Books. One of the fascinating figures of all literature, with his manifold identities, his amazing audacities, his brilliance and his shyness. He is, in some ways, the poet of modernism, the only one willing to fracture himself into the parcels of action, anguish and nostalgia that are the ground of our actual situation. —C.K. Williams. Pessoa is one of the great originals of the European poetry of the first part of this century. — W.S. Merwin. In Honig's and Brown's superb translations, Pessoa and his "others" live with miraculous style and vitality. —Mark Strand

Pessoa, Fernando. Translated by Richard Zenith. *The Book of Disquietude.* 323p. pap. $17.95 (1-878818-65-1). Riverdale-on-Hudson, NY: Sheep Meadow Press, Fall 1996. The Book of Disquietude is the "factless autobiography" of "Bernardo Soares," one of the 72 literary personae with which Portugal's greatest poet Fernando Pessoa created the theater of himself. Conceived in 1916, "Soares" is, Pessoa declares, "a mutilation" of his own personality. This is the first, and only complete, English edition. —Sheep Meadow Press. Anglomaniac, myopic, courteous, evasive, dressed darkly, reticent and agreeable, a cosmopolitan who preaches nationalism, "solemn investigator of futile things," humorist who never smiles but chills our blood, inventor of other poets and destroyer of himself, author of paradoxes as clear as water and, as water, dizzying: "to pretend is to know yourself," mysterious man who does not cultivate

mystery, mysterious as the mid-day moon, taciturn phantom of the Portuguese midday — who is Pessoa? —Octavio Paz

Peternel, Joan. *Howl and Hosanna.* 103p. pap. $7.95 (0-9649718-1-6). Southhampton, NY: Whelks Walk Press, Fall 1997. I salute Peternel's lively Howl and Hosanna, with its "gardens and gardens" of vivid verse. —Sandra Gilbert. This is what a poetry textbook ought to be: definition and demonstration. Each selection of the sequence begins with an introductory essay which is followed by the exemplary poetry. —Len Fulton

Petras, Kathryn, and Ross Petras, eds. *Very Bad Poetry.* 126p. pap. $10.00 (0-679-77622-2). Vintage Books, Spring 1997. The 131 poems collected in this first-of-its-kind anthology are so glaringly awful that they embody a kind of genius. From Fred Emerson Brooks's "The Stuttering Lover" to Matthew Green's "The Spleen" to Georgia Bailey Parrington's misguided "An Elegy to a Dissected Puppy," they mangle meter, run rampant over rhyme, and bludgeon us into insensibility with their grandiosity, anticlimax and malapropism. —Vintage Books

Petrouske, Rosalie Sanara. *The Geisha Box.* 35p. pap. $6.00 (1-882983-32-7). Greensboro, NC: March Street Press, Spring 1997. The emotional jolt of these plain-spoken, intensely intimate poems is considerable and lasting. What I'm most impressed by is Petrouske's courage and grace as she confronts our human limitations — those failed desires, losses, and sadnesses — while allowing the spirit to soar. This is the way the heart articulates when it speaks honestly, always daring its deepest secrets and truths. —Jack Driscoll

Pflum, Richard. *A Strange Juxtaposition of Parts.* 80p. pap. $8.95 (1-880649-33-0). Indianapolis, IN: Writers' Center Press, 1995. [Pflum] has a quiet passion, in ordinary speech, that floats into fantasy and pathos, and by the time you are through [reading], you have been beguiled. —Willis Barnstone. It is a sign of the confusion of our time that the poems of Pflum are unknown. Cloaking himself in a "ragged costume of legends" and a comic paranoid surrealism, this book, Pflum's "newest escape" from the asylum, will be welcomed by all

his fellow inmates. —Roger Mitchell

Philbrick, Stephen. *Up to the Elbow.* 23p. pap. $8.00 (0-938566-76-8). Easthampton, MA: Adastra Press, Spring 1997. Poems from a sheep farmer, husband, lover and Protestant minister. Handset, handsewn letterpress limited edition. —Adastra Press

Phillips, Carl. *From the Devotions.* 84p. pap. $12.95 (1-55597-263-2). St. Paul, MN: Graywolf Press, Fall 1998. Finalist for the National Book Award. Phillips's poems are acts of attention; their exquisite observations render the world a space for epiphanic encounter. —Chicago Tribune. In his extraordinary new book of poems, by far his best, Phillips has [plotted] the romantic landscape of desire. Myths are unsheathed and glisten. History is held and pondered. Violence shimmers, desires are silhouetted against the light of love and death. His tone is at once erotic and mystical, hushed and compelling. The book is a blessing, a ravishing, a haunting. I urge you to read it — to succumb to it. —J.D. McClatchy

Phillips, Rodney, with Susan Benesch, Kenneth Benson, and Barbara Bergeron.

Essays by Dana Gioia. *The Hand of the Poet: Poems and Papers in Manuscript.* 265p. $40.00 (0-8478-1958-2). New York, NY: Rizzoli/Universe Publishing, Spring 1997. Based on an enormously successful exhibition at The New York Public Library, The Hand of the Poet draws the reader into the real world of the poet — ink spots, tobacco stains, and all — by presenting a wide range of working drafts, letters, diary entries, photographs, and memorabilia. One hundred writers from the seventeenth century to the present day are represented. — Rizzoli Publications. Deletion and erasure — once a sort of revolutionary attack of the afterthought on the fore-thought — now is, like any attack on mass culture, absorbed and exploited by the primary text without leaving a trace of bloodshed. So the beauty or interest of the manuscripts reproduced in this volume is that they remind us of the author as being of two minds and more; of being able to think and think again; of having a violent approach to the words that he or she inscribed in the first place. — Fanny Howe

Phillips, Timothy R. *Between the Fog and the Freight Train.* 85p. pap. $9.25 (0-9660055-2-X). Lakewood, CA: Twaanévie Poetry House, Spring 1998.

Philpot, Tracy. *Incorrect Distances.* 104p. pap. $15.95 (0-8203-1957-0). Athens, GA: University of Georgia Press, Fall 1997. [Philpot's] poetry is filled with evidence of the damages accruing from various misuses of power — in father-child relationships, in the imbalance between teachers and students, in various affairs of the mind and body, of family and culture. These poems are always beautiful in their honesty, and sometimes brutal in their necessary anger. —University of Georgia Press

Piercy, Marge. *What Are Big Girls Made Of?.* 159p. $25.00 (0-679-45065-3). pap. $15.00 (0-679-76594-8). New York, NY: Knopf, Alfred A., Fall 1997. ALA Notable Book of 1998. This major new collection by one of our best-known poets opens with a powerful cycle of elegies for her charming half-brother. It goes on to include both funny and serious poems about women — women allowing themselves to be caught in the painful dilemma of being "retooled, refitted and redesigned" to match the style of every decade. — Alfred A. Knopf. Piercy is my idea of the very model of a modern major feminist. There is sheer, toe-curling pleasure to be gained from reading this robust, protean and hilarious woman's poems. — Washington Post Book World.

Pilibosian, Helene. *At Quarter Past Reality: New and Selected Poems.* 96p. pap. $11.50. Watertown, MA: Ohan Press, Fall 1998. This collection of largely autobiographical work contains narrative poems about Armenian-American Pilibosian's childhood and five generations of her family. —Ohan Press

Pilkington, Kevin. *Getting By.* 40p. pap. $5.00. Jamaica, NY: Ledge Press, Fall 1997. Often playful but always poignant, the poems in this collection reveal a remarkable wit and metropolitan sensibility. Tersely eloquent and utterly authentic, Pilkington is a promising poet whose work will be worth following. — Ledge Press. Pilkington's narratives of daily life are tender and melancholy, lightened with a gentle surreal humor and a steadfast affection for the people and the city he is kin to. —Jean Valentine

Pilkington, Kevin. *Spare Change.* 105p. pap. $10.00 (0-931721-14-8). La Jolla, CA: La Jolla Poets Press, Fall 1997. I have been reading and admiring the tough, quirky and lucid poems of Kevin Pilkington for over a decade. Mostly urban, they are plain spoken, but jazzy, even sometimes jittery in their rhythms. This is a poet unafraid of being understood, who will not hide behind decorativeness or the oblique. Read these poems aloud and you will hear an authentic and quintessentially American voice not only writing but also speaking to you. —Thomas Lux

Pinckney, Diana. *White Linen.* 50p. pap. $9.95 (1-879205-75-0). Troy, ME: Nightshade Press, Fall 1998. A moving portrait of southern family life, with its warm, sunny days as well as its dark and shady places. — Nightshade Press

Pinsky, Robert. *History of My Heart.* 51p. pap. $12.00 (0-374-52530-7). Farrar, Straus and Giroux/Noonday, Spring 1998 (new paper). Awarded the William Carlos Williams Prize. First published in 1984, Pinsky's History includes parents and boyhood neighbors, Fats Waller warming the Christmas crowd at Macy's, Holocaust victims and inspired derelicts. Pinsky has a rare gift for action, character, and atmosphere clearly and buoyantly proportioned. —Roland Flint, The New York Times Book Review. "The Figured Wheel" is a mad, brilliant vortex that draws into itself gods, men, art, rags and bones, atoms and dust. Simply reading the poem is breathtaking; it starts its uninterruptible progression, gradually gaining speed and power, and ends in a violent giant step over self and art. It is in every sense a stunning and dangerous poem. —Joan Todden Keefe, San Francisco Chronicle

Pinsky, Robert. *The Figured Wheel: New and Collected Poems 1966-1996.* 308p. pap. $15.00 (0-374-52506-4). Farrar, Straus and Giroux/Noonday, April 1997. The volume includes Pinsky's four acclaimed books of poetry — Sadness and Happiness, An Explanation of America, History of My Heart, and The Want Bone — as well as a dozen new poems and a section of Pinsky's highly regarded translations, notably the last canto from his award-winning translation of Dante's Inferno. —Farrar, Straus and Giroux. Pinsky's extraordinarily accomplished and beautiful volume of collected poems will remind readers that here is a poet who, without forming a mini-movement or setting himself loudly at odds with

the dominant tendencies of American poetry, has brought into it something new. —Katha Pollitt, The New York Times Book Review

Planz, Allen. *Dune Heath: Selected Poems.* 118p. pap. $15.00 (1-886435-06-5). Sag Harbor, NY: Canio's Editions, Fall 1998. I have always loved Planz's wonderful sea poems. They invigorate the grit and feel of the waters and bring to life the shapes and silhouettes of the wild things flying beneath the sparkling surface as well as over it. —Peter Matthiessen

Plumly, Stanley. *The Marriage in the Trees.* 79p. $22.00 (0-88001-487-3). pap. $14.00 (0-88001-546-2). Hopewell, NJ: Ecco Press, Spring 1997; Fall 1998 (new paper). Reading Plumly is like having someone whisper unceasingly in your ear, humming of light, trees, sleep, snow. —New York Times Book Review. Plumly's sense of an abiding and mysterious spiritual essence lends a depth to his work that is rarely found anywhere. And this vision is itself reflected within the very texture of the poetry — in image, in language, in rhythm, Plumly manages to communicate the same surprising and magical quality. —Peter Stitt, American Poetry Review

Plumpp, Sterling. *Ornate With Smoke.* 103p. $22.95 (0-88378-193-X). pap. $12.95 (0-88378-198-0). Chicago, IL: Third World Press, Spring 1998. Riffing through the canon of jazz greats from Charlie Parker and John Coltrane to Ornette Coleman, Plumpp's Ornate With Smoke comes the closest to a saxophone solo-in-verse as you're likely to read. —Publishers Weekly. A tribute to the creativity and emotional power of a jazz master, Ornate With Smoke also exemplifies a poet's restless questioning of America and himself. Plumpp creates as free, as inventive, as surprising, as masterful a passage through our language as Coltrane did through scales and changes. This is a beautiful, astonishing book. —Reginald Gibbons

Polansky, Paul. *Living Through it Twice: Poems of the Romany Holocaust (1940-1997).* 125p. (80-86103-11-0?). Merrick, NY: Cross-Cultural Communications, Fall 1998. This collection of poems represents the long-awaited publication of Polansky's research into the treatment of Czech Roma (Gypsies) during World War II. In the plain lan-

guage of a journalist-poet, Polansky uses these poems as amplifiers for the voices of the concentration camp survivors whose oral histories he has been collecting for years. These poems can and should be read as much for their historical value as for their emotional impact. —Gwendolyn Albert. Ladies and gentlemen, hold onto your hats, this ride'll freeze you to the bone. —Ivan M. Jirous. Polansky's spare, stark renderings of Romany survivors' voices have the hardness of memorial stone. But in reading them, the stone dissolves and something infinitely tender and unspeakable takes its place. The restraint and hardness hold in the tears — just barely. — Andrei Codrescu

Pollack, Frederick. *Happiness: A Novel in Verse.* 160p. pap. $12.95 (1-885266-58-8). Ashland, OR: Story Line Press, Fall 1998. Happiness dwells in that realm of telegraphic metaphor that science fiction and poetry share with each other. Pollack creates a dystopia in which the Left inherits the earth and is as free to dispense rewards and punishments as Dante himself. The result is a Death Wish revenge fantasy for the politically correct — at once a stern judgement and a guilty pleasure. —Thomas M. Disch. The novel in verse is up-and-coming nowadays. [And now here is] Pollack's take, in free-verse quatrains, on a classic sf setup, the utopia. —Ray Olson, Booklist

Polo, Su. *Turning Stones: A Collection of Poems and Stories.* 20p. pap. $5.00. Polowichak, Su, Spring 1998.

Pompei, Jessica; Holaday Mason, and Sarah Maclay, eds. *Echo 681.* 147p. pap. $8.00 (1-892184-04-4). Venice, CA: Beyond Baroque Books, Spring 1998. This anthology collects the work of the Beyond Baroque Wednesday Night Poetry Workshop. —Beyond Baroque Books

Ponsot, Marie. *The Bird Catcher.* 91p. $22.00 (0-375-40135-0). New York, NY: Knopf, Alfred A., Spring 1998; Spring 2000 (new paper). Ponsot's new book is a major achievement. It fully confirms the praise that has been bestowed on her by critics and peers. —Alfred A. Knopf

Porter, David. *Phases of the Moon: Flowers From the Garden of Hel.* 64p. pap. $5.95 (0-9641606-9-2). Cupertino, CA: Easy Break,

First Time Publishing, Spring 1998.

Porter, William, trans. *A Hundred Verses From Old Japan: A Translation of the Hyaku-nin-isshiu.* 100p. pap. $12.95 (0-8048-1256-X). Tuttle, Charles E., Fall 1997 (reprint). One of the most popular anthologies of Japanese classical poetry, this collection comprises love poems and "picture poems" describing scenes from nature in tanka form. . . . This book is ideal for readers making their first acquaintance with this celebrated anthology and those who appreciate writing of truly engaging quality. — Charles E. Tuttle

Powell, D.A. *Tea.* 71p. $17.95 (0-8195-6334-X). University Press of New England/Wesleyan University Press, Spring 1998. Powell's Tea is on the move, it reads like a handheld camera. It's writing that's willing to be as strange as it needs to be to get at experience, and the effect is both disturbing and exhilarating. —Robert Hass. In his debut volume, Tea, the ceremony of innocence takes to the mortal road and goes the distance. Tea is a book of immediate importance and truth. —Donald Revell

Powell, Shirley. *Other Rooms.* 110p. Poet's Press/Grim Reaper Books, 1997. Lyrical, supernatural, narrative, and deft in portrayal of characters, Powell's poems startle many with their freshness, and their sense of being narrated by a timeless voice. She is a prairie twister of a poet. —Poet's Press/Grim Reaper Books

Prado, Holly. *Esperanza: Poems for Orpheus.* 83p. pap. $12.00 (0-9649240-5-6). Los Angeles, CA: Cahuenga Press, Fall 1998. These poems hold a sweet ripeness, a vast dark promise: poetry will heal us, heal our world. —Diane DiPrima

Preston, Georgette. *Air Wedded to Light: Poems of the Aegean.* 70p. pap. $10.00. Islip, NY: Live Poets Society, Spring 1998. Air wedded to Light is a poet-daughter's book dedicated to her painter father born in Greece; it should accompany the seeking traveler to that land of light and myth. This is the thoughtful, joyous poetry [Preston] dedicates to her audience. — Barbara Guest. With my elated heart and delighted ear, I recommend to the reader Air Wedded to Light., swept along as I am by its musicality, its ecstatic re-creation of the heavenly blue of the Aegean,

and of the glory of the spirit that is eternally Greece. — Diana Chang. Air Wedded to Light is full of grace. These poems are prayers: supple, melodic, and honest. — Edward Boccia

Prevallet, Kristin. *Perturbation, My Sister.* 75p. pap. $10.00 (1-889960-02-0). Lawrence, KS: First Intensity Press, Spring 1997. Proceeding from the collages of Max Ernst, Prevallet has created her own convulsive beauty, a parallel narrative of instantaneous adventure in a torrent of unexpected forms. Here the enigmatic is revealed as aesthetic potency, the gravitational field of memory, and, above all as absolute necessity. —Rikki Ducornet. Transfigurations of the divine & perfunctory, a radical vision of Ernst's dramatic & exquisite corpse. Brava! —Anne Waldman

Price, Michael. *Doombook.* 68p. pap. $10.00 (0-935724-94-X). Great Barrington, MA: Figures, The, Fall 1998. For this extraordinary young poet — to my mind one of the most arresting and promising voices of his emerging generation — the weight of the past is a burden that alternately puzzles, crushes and redeems. Coming to terms with genealogical and sociological facts of origins, Price creates a poetic fictional world where the generations of his family are permitted to take place in an atmosphere of filial respect and tender for-giveness, but also of hard-eyed acknowledgment and recognition. These are com-ing-to-manhood poems equipped with unexpected maturity: adroitly deploying a wry self-deprecating humor, an engaging openness and a delicate impulse to play. — Tom Clark

Price, Michael; Dale Smith, and Kevin Opstedal. *Fuck You, La Jolla.* 32p. Mike & Dale's Press/GAS Editions, Fall 1998.

Price, Reynolds. *The Collected Poems.* 471p. $37.50 (0-684-83203-8). New York, NY: Simon & Schuster/Scribner, Fall 1997. Price's poems are full of his own personality — his own divine mischief, his ordina-tions, over many years, into the societies of deepest friend-ship, love, work, physical pain and faith. Price is a writer (and a man) to be cherished by those who honor the elegance of literature, and the fortitude and clear-eyed investigations of the spirit. He is as erotic as Auden, as life-loving as Keats, as religious as Hopkins. As the

first poem in this book moves on its somber cadences, through its dazzling details, the reader senses that here is the true country of poetry — not merely poignant, but ecstatic, unbearable, and reve-latory. —Mary Oliver

Price, V.B. *7 Deadly Sins.* 25p. pap. $8.00 (1-888809-03-5). Albuquerque, NM: La Alameda Press, Fall 1997. Price's Seven Deadly Sins dis-sects the vices with a steady hand, showing the mechanism — lures, hooks, poison sacs — by which we debase our-selves. Beautiful and damn-ing, they remind us that our most intimate failings are uni-versal after all. —Daniel Abraham

Prout, Quintin. *Nobe's Kitchen.* 64p. pap. $10.00 (0-914278-75-4). Providence, RI: Copper Beech Press, Fall 1998. Steeped in particulars and fiercely personal, [Nobe's Kitchen] pays homage to [Prout's] Cape Verdean her-itage and evokes as a sense of community. This book cele-brates the saving grace of African-American culture even as it testifies to the power of poetry to save a life. —Copper Beech Press. Strong in clarity and spirit, fluent and supple, rich with fresh breath, tender truth, and more than one kind of music, these are delicious words to sing. A landmark volume of precious reminders. —Naomi Shihab Nye

Prudentius, Aurelius (Clemens). Translated by David R. Slavitt. *Hymns of Prudentius: The Cathermerinon; or, The Daily Round.* 61p. (0-8018-5412-1). Baltimore, MD: Johns Hopkins University Press, Fall 1996. A pioneer in the creation of a Christian literature, Prudentius is generally regarded as the greatest of the Christian Latin poets, [whose] legacy informed the work of future poets, among them Herbert and Donne. The Cathemerinon Liber is a collection of twelve hymns, in English called "TheDaily Round." Essentially literary in nature, the hymns replaced mythology with stories from the Scriptures. For centuries they were an immensely popular part of the liturgy of the church. —Johns Hopkins University Press

Prufer, Kevin. *Strange Wood.* 64p. $12.00 (0807123501). Winthrop University Poetry Series, Fall 1998.

Pruitt, Patricia. *Sessions: I-IV.* 32p. pap. $4.00 (1-893032-02-7). Talisman House,

Publishers / Jensen/Daniels, Fall 1998.

Prynne, J.H. *Red D Gypsum.* 19p. pap. $4.95. Barque Books, Fall 1998.

Pupello, Anthony J. *The Sax Man's Case.* 64p. pap. $10.00 (0-9657818-6-0). Winchester, VA: Red Moon Press, Fall 1998. To say that Pupello vividly depicts the energy and grit of life in the big city is to underestimate his work. What distinguishes him from other haiku poets writing in this context is his depth of perception — an alliance of realism and lyricism that addresses the human condition and, quite simply, rings true. —Dee Evetts

Pushkin, Alexander. Translated by Babette Deutsch; Edited by Avrahm Yarmolinsky. *Eugene Onegin: A Novel in Verse.* 192p. pap. $8.95 (0-486-40423-4). Mineola, NY: Dover Publications, Fall 1998. This translation of Pushkin's most acclaimed work, the source of Tchaikovsky's popular opera, recounts a tale of post-Napoleonic society in which a jaded young aristocrat rejects the love of a country maiden. Sparkling with satirical humor tinged by gentle melancholy, the tale unfolds in the polished and elegant verse for which Pushkin is well known. Evocative lithographs appear at the start of each chapter, and extensive supplements include an introduction, notes, and an appendix consistenting of the extant fragment of Chapter Ten. —Dover Publications

Quignard, Pascal. Translated by Keith Waldrop. *Sarx.* 40p. pap. $5.00 (1-886224-20-X). Providence, RI: Burning Deck, Fall 1997. Sarx moves across an existential landscape suggested by Herodotus' account of Scythians, a landscape of flesh (sarx) and of flesh bitten into (sarcasm). Sarcasm is language in a state of nature, negating its own message in favor of body, of surface rather than depth, of clarity rather than import. Quignard's Sarx is a postmodern Waste Land — no King, no Grail, no Question. —Burning Deck

Quiñonez, Naomi. *The Smoking Mirror.* 69p. pap. $8.95 (0-931122-89-9). Albuquerque, NM: West End Press, Spring 1998. This is poetry that questions and finds no facile answers. It asks us to look into ourselves. It is unforgiving and it is lovely. — Tey Diana Rebolledo. As a warrior of language, Quiñonez aims to rupture silence and fill

it with a new vitality. Her poems are part and parcel of a confident storyteller who indulges in a given subject with exuberance and profundity. Highly lyrical, sensitive and evocative poetry. — Francisco Lomeli

Quisenberry, Dan. *On Days Like This.* 89p. pap. $12.95 (1-884235-24-7). Kansas City, MO: Helicon Nine Editions, Fall 1998. The first collection of poems by one of America's favorite baseball pitchers takes us from the fast, boisterous world of baseball to the private world of family and faith. [Quisenberry] was like nobody else. These poems will delight you with their honesty, humor, excitement, and good will. — Helicon Nine Editions. Like his pitches, Quisenberry's poems come at you unexpectedly, rising from a different part of the field, clear and unthreatening in their intentions, and then startling you with a late swoop or slant: What was that? As always, the satisfaction you get from Quiz's stuff takes in the thoughtfulness and ingenuity of its originator. —Roger Angell

R, Joe. *Do Yu Know. What Distortion. Sowndz Like.: An Urban Legend.* 198p. pap. $16.00 (1-891408-07-0). NEW

YORK, NY: Green Bean Press, Fall 1998. Plow through the author's intentionally butchered spelling and punctuation, then the strange pleasures of an odd treasure await. —Colin Bane, Washington City Paper. Joe R is a vibrant, incandescent voice, who owes little to tradition or literary convention. —Robert L. Penick, Chance Magazine

Rabinowitz, Anna. *At the Site of Inside Out.* 75p. $20.00 (1-55849-092-2). pap. $10.95 (1-55849-093-0). Amherst, MA: University of Massachusetts Press, Spring 1997. Winner of the 1996 Juniper Prize for Poetry. This is what every writer longs for: a debut of intense invention, with language at a height and experience at a depth that the whole art suddenly appears as a plinth on the plain of American letters. Rabinowitz brings us to the fulcrum of human change: memory as it is born, the body as it ages, vision as it limits time. Her voice is so bright that it explodes traditional ways of understanding, making us wiser and more playful, and as full of discovery as she is. — Molly Peacock. Rabinowitz brings to bear an astonishing display of formal resources, both traditional and invented, through which she explores

boundaries of the human spirit. Attuned to the graphic particularities of individual and historical survival, at the heart of these poems is a deep regard for the mundane veracity and ferocity of life, which includes, at every turn, the life of language. —Ann Lauterbach

Radavich, David. *By the Way: Poems Over the Years.* 104p. (0-9658045-1-8). (0-9658045-0-X). Champaign, IL: ButtonWood Press, Spring 1998. Through the undulating grasses of Kansas, audience questions on The Phil Donohue Show, and shimmering colors of the exotic Middle East, Radavich takes us exploring and experiencing: a poetic world of variety, rhythm, and lyrical power. — Buttonwood Press

Rafaela, Judith, and Nancy Fay, eds. *The Practice of Peace.* 208p. pap. $15.00 (0-9644196-7-X). Santa Fe, NM: Sherman Asher Publishing, Fall 1998. Beautifully designed. A book to treasure. —Bloomsbury Review. Sparks a spiritual flame in readers. — New Mexico Magazine. A conflagration of spirit and flesh. —Taos News. These poems guide us toward our own tenderness, wisdom and grace, and the lasting treasure of knowing and practicing peace. —Jerry Jampolsky

Rafaela, Judith, and Nancy Fay, eds. *XY Files: Poems on the Male Experience.* 224p. pap. $15.00 (0-9644196-6-1). Santa Fe, NM: Sherman Asher Publishing, Spring 1997. Here are almost two-hundred poems full of the music of male-ness, of multitudes of voices concerned with the growing and changing lives of men, and the women who can also speak to the male experience of our century. —David Keller. As I read these moving poems, I found myself coming face to face with myself and other men I know. This is truly a book for Everyman (and for anyone who wants a peek at what makes him tick). —Paul B. Janeczko

Raffel, Burton, trans. Edited by Alexandra H. Olsen and Burton Raffel. *Poems and Prose From the Old English.* 228p. $32.50 (0-300-06994-4). pap. $15.00 (0-300-06995-2). New Haven, CT: Yale University Press, Spring 1998. This is a splendid work to introduce students to the culture of the Anglo-Saxons. Raffel's translations of the Old English poems become poems in modern English. But we have always known that he can work such wonders. What

is new is his supple handling of the often very unsupple Old English prose. —University of Massachusetts, Amherst

Raffeld, David. *Into the World of Men.* 42p. $40.00 (0-938566-74-1). pap. $10.00 (0-938566-75-X). Easthampton, MA: Adastra Press, Spring 1997. A Small Press Review "Pick of the Month" May 1997. Raffeld mines the dark, quiet corners of existence. — The Berkshire Eagle

Ragain, Maj. *Burley One Dark Sucker Fired: Collected Poems.* 80p. pap. $9.95 (0-933087-45-4). Huron, OH: Bottom Dog Press, Spring 1998. The poetry of Maj Ragain is satisfying — poem after poem. This man knows Ohio, the Midwest, himself, and everyplace he finds himself in. —Jennifer Bosveld, Pudding Magazine. A poet who knows the vernacular and dances with the soul of the honest working man, the midwesterner with hayseed in hair or machine oil on hands, the man who has lost and lost again in love, Ragain is one of Cleveland's favorite poets. — Amy Bracken Sparks, Cleveland Free Times

Ragan, James. *Lusions.* 85p. $20.00 (0-8021-1603-5). New York, NY: Grove Press, Spring

1997. Ragan's poems are full of arresting collocations and striking phrases. Sometimes the latter are mysterious, and sometimes (as in "the mimosa breathing the wind's still spirit") they take a fresh look at some aspect of the world. — Richard Wilbur. In present-day poetry, few things are more anticipated than this book by a poet who dominates the art of image, the art of poetic line, and the art of poetic narration to the level where the poems form a permanent stream of revelations. — Miroslav Holub

Ragan, James. *The Hunger Wall.* 112p. $17.00 (0-8021-1576-4). New York, NY: Grove Press, 1995. Ragan's poetry lights the passage to the larger world of global citizenship. —William Matthews. Ragan's poetry is splendidly candid, original, energized, connected to the real world, honed, human, connected to a series of finely articulated voices, full of nuances, of music, of idioms he's heard and invented. —Michael S. Harper

Ramsdell, Heather. *Lost Wax.* 80p. pap. $11.95 (0-252-06706-1). Champaign, IL: University of Illinois Press, Spring 1998. Selected by James Tate as one of five vol-

umes published in 1998 in the National Poetry Series. These poems map a metaphysical treasure hunt, here a stick, there a door, a closet, a shirt. As the book unfolds, the accretion of their ascetic values forms an ever more human shape in a symphony of poems that is original and profoundly full of wonder. —James Tate. The poems in Ramsdell's stunning first collection are poised between the unsayable and the already said, an aporia only the most inventive language can address. —Anne Lauterbach. Perhaps it is only in such an extreme poetry of skewed personalities that we can discover, after all, a kind of divinity erupting in the everyday. —David Shapiro

Ramsey, Martha. *Blood Stories.* 75p. pap. $10.00 (1-880834-19-7). Cleveland, OH: Cleveland State University Poetry Center, Fall 1996. [Ramsey] transforms autobiography into a larger inquiry by telling it from both inside and out, always tearing at its edges, where the lies of retrospect can creep in. This is a poet who is simultaneously steely and tender, bent on telling the truth in its full complexity. She has written a book that documents the evolution of a self with grace and dignity. —Chase Twichell

Randall, Margaret. *Hunger's Table: Women, Food & Politics.* 109p. pap. $10.00 (1-57601-000-7). Watsonville, CA: Papier-Mache Press, Spring 1997. Randall takes us from the front lines to the kitchen in this new collection of poems. We, her readers, find that there is politics in the making of pretzels or Antonio's plain white rice and nourishment in our revolutionary-poet-chef's savory words. —Julia Alvarez. Randall is always a unique provider, and here the feast is altogether generous. Her bedrock sensibility, her tenacious caring for our common word, her relieving laughter, and her insistently sensuous delight, all are here in abundance. Enjoy! — Robert Creeley

Randolph, Karin, ed. *Mind the Gap: New York/London.* 39p. pap. $3.00. Brooklyn, NY: Mind the Gap, Fall 1998.

Rankin, Paula. *Your Rightful Childhood: New and Selected Poems 1970-1995.* 120p. $20.95 (0-88748-245-7). pap. $11.95 (0-88748-246-5). Pittsburgh, PA: Carnegie Mellon University Press, Spring 1997. Rankin has the Jamesian grasp of poetry: it remembers us and with it we remember, and that rejoining with the lost parts of our expe-rience is deeply compelling. . . Her gift for specific detail and the mosaic of scene is so intense as to deny time's passage, for she will plunge us into moments of love and harm as quickly as recall the contents of a dead neighbor's refrigerator. Rankin is both a pastoralist of the unbeautiful and a maker of memorials, but you could tour her town with the information her poems hold. . . Her poems are so compelling and passionate they invite any life to live with them, to re-join. —Dave Smith

Rankine, Claudia. *The End of the Alphabet.* 100p. $20.00 (1-80211-634-5). New York, NY: Grove Press, Fall 1998. Despair and loss of meaning in The End of the Alphabet are palpably realized by Rankine. This is a long look into the enervating dark of a postmodern soul fissured by loss. But this is not so much a depressing celebration of darkness as it is an attempt at healing. — Ploughshares. In the amazing subtlety of even everyday contexts lie extraordinary intensities, and it is these that Rankine has discovered. In her writing, dailiness has the eloquence of the diurnal. —Lyn Hejinian. Rankine is a powerfully impressive poet. The End of the Alphabet gives pleasure from initial A to ultimate omega. —David Lehman

Ransom, Jane. *Scene of the Crime.* 50p. pap. $11.00 (1-885266-56-9). Ashland, OR: Story Line Press, Fall 1997. Reading Ransom's poetry is like being in the cage with the lion tamer. It's thrilling and impressive to be so close to such mastery — but you never stop being terrified. The whip and chair impose a mind-bending order while the pant and roar keep your eyes wide open and your feet ready to sprint. The heart quickens in an intricate dance with something huge and untamable. — Jan Richman

Rao, Velcheru Narayana, and David Shulman, trans. *A Poem at the Right Moment: Remembered Verses From Premodern South India.* 211p. (0-520-20849-8). Berkeley, CA: University of California Press, Fall 1998. A Poem at the Right Moment collects and preserves poems that have circulated orally for centuries in South India. The poems are remarkable for their wit and precision, their lyrical insight into the commonplace, their fascination with sensual experience, and their exploration of the connection between language and desire. Each poem is presented in its contemporary English translation along with the Indian-language original. —University of California Press. Thought-provoking and entertaining. A Poem at the Right Moment harbors a radical revision of Indian poetics. —Stuart Blackburn

raphael, dan. *Trees Through the Road.* 36p. pap. $5.00 (1-878888-23-4). Winston, OR: nine muses books, Fall 1997.

Ras, Barbara. *Bite Every Sorrow.* 78p. (0-8071-2263-7). Baton Rouge, LA: Louisiana State University Press, Fall 1998. Winner of the 1997 Walt Whitman Award of the Academy of American Poets. Ras's poems are informed by a metaphysically erudite and whimsical exuberance. Ras structures poems with a zaniness and an unpredictable cunning, and her verbal expertise and lucidity are as bright and surprising as her knowledge of the world is profound. This is a splendid book, morally serious, poetically authentic, spiritually discerning. —C.K. Williams. These poems luxuriate in a daylight world of honeybees and earrings and tongue sandwiches, yet they constantly obey the miner's admonition Go farther, Go deeper. What is astonishing about them, given their restlessness, is their unruffled embrace of everything human. I don't know when I've read poems that turn so daringly and achingly and hopefully from one mood to another, or poems whose language is so wildly alive. —Paul Jenkins. In lyrics full to the bursting point, Ras accurately captures the tug of war between the quotidian and the miraculous — how the two keep mystifying, inciting and delighting us by trading places. —Amy Gerstler

Rash, Ron. *Eureka Mill.* 63p. pap. $12.95 (0-930769-13-9). Corvallis, OR: Bench Press, Fall 1998. Eureka Mill pulls 42 of Rash's poems into a tight sequence that depicts life in a mill village. —Bench Press. He leads us into a saga of child labor and union deaths, the temporary panacea of moonshine and revivals, lungs filling irrevocably with dust and lint, and the chronic longing for the feel, again, of earth. —Cathy Smith Bowers. Rash is a brave new voice in American poetry. —Robert Morgan

Rasnake, Sam. *Necessary Motions.* 68p. pap. $12.00 (1-885912-10-2). Abingdon, VA: Sow's Ear Press, Spring 1998. These poems, set in two landscapes, seashore and moun-

tains, and varied in form, are unified by the themes of family and music — blues, jazz, country, and classical. —The Sow's Ear Press

Rasnake, Sam. *Religions of the Blood.* 27p. pap. $7.95. Johnstown, OH: Pudding House Publications, Spring 1998.

Ratcliffe, Stephen. *Mallarmé: Poem in Prose.* 100p. pap. $12.95 (0-9655497-1-2). Summerland, CA: Santa Barbara Review Publications, Fall 1998. [Ratcliffe's poems] are rinsed with a surprising glow in the valiant process of relieving the Mallarméan tension, while maintaining his own arena of sensitivity. — Barbara Guest. In this endeavor to catch primal innocence, Ratcliffe finds himself in a room full of objects and words, and a window which fuses with roses, people and memories, all contributing to a kind of desperation which propels poetic lines onto the page. —Etel Adnan

Ratcliffe, Stephen. *Sculpture.* 112p. pap. $10.95 (1-55713-297-6). Los Angeles, CA: Littoral Books, Fall 1997. Using the linguistic sculptor's tools of image, juxtaposition, repetition, fragment, melody, rhythm, and the word,

Ratcliffe builds, unbuilds, and rebuilds a poetic world where the physical and the conceptual are resituated at various radii around the center of emotion on the verge of becoming itself. In its four evenly measured sections, the meanings of Sculpture accumulate like the verdigris of weather on sculptural work, leaving the work itself altered by the very matter of which it is made. —Littoral Books

Rattiner, Susan L., ed. *Great Poems by American Women.* 256p. pap. $2.00 (0-486-40164-2). Mineola, NY: Dover Publications, Spring 1998. From the colonial-era poets to such 20th-century writers as Marianne Moore and Sylvia Plath, this inspiring anthology offers a retrospective of more than three centuries of poems by American women. —Dover Publications

Ratzlaff, Keith. *Man Under a Pear Tree.* 70p. $18.95 (0-93078-51-8). pap. $10.00 (0-93078-50-X). Tallahassee, FL: Anhinga Press, Spring 1997. Winner of the Anhinga Prize for Poetry. Reading Ratzlaff's poems is like watching Charlie Chaplin on a ten-speed bike or listening to Mozart in fast forward. There's a pell-mell quality to these poems, a wittiness, a joy that sharpens sor-row, and yes, even a recklessness that American poetry desperately needs right now. — Robert Dana. Ratzlaff's is the sort of debut collection which we all hope for, but which is sadly rare. He is less a surrealist than a kind of hyper-realist, able in poem after poem to make lively associative leaps which derive from his astute (and quirky) observations of the world around him and within him. . . Ratzlaff is a stunning writer. —Stephen Dunn

Rawlins, C.L. *In Gravity National Park.* 80p. pap. $11.00 (0-87417-322-1). Reno, NV: University of Nevada Press, Fall 1998. For Rawlins, poetry is a kind of low-tech Global Positioning System — an instrument tempered by heart, head, and senses that tells him his place on the rugged, wild Earth. And it is a place from which he never loses sight of the elemental amazement to find himself in a body and to find that body alive in a world of staggering beauty and grief. He is an anti-romantic Romantic whose poems sing the hard-won pleasures of consciousness coming into awareness and form. — Alison Hawthorne Deming

Rawson, Joanna. *Quarry.* 75p. $25.00 (0-8229-4081-7).

pap. $12.95 (0-8229-5681-0). Pittsburgh, PA: University of Pittsburgh Press, Fall 1998. Winner of the 1997 Associated Writing Programs' Award Series in Poetry. Rawson will not let us turn away from the violence of our time and of our making—forcing us to experience both the ecstasy and the exhaustion of being alive in contemporary America. —University.of Pittsburgh Press. The individuality and power of Rawson's first book come from its blend of existential issues and daily life. It thinks and it sings at the same time. It is for all careful readers as well as poets. —Arthur Vogelsang

Ray, David, and Judy Ray, eds. *Fathers: A Collection of Poems.* 254p. $16.95 (0-312-15527-1). New York, NY: St. Martin's Press, Fall 1997. Whether writing of fathers who were heroes or anti-heroes, defenders or pacifists, those who went away suddenly or those who reappeared after a long period of time, the poets here cast the net wide to harvest the infinite variety of the father-and-child relationship — a relationship that can be simultaneously unique and universal. The result is this moving anthology, which runs the gamut of emotions, presenting powerful poems full of

humor, heartbreak, tragedy, and forgiveness. —St. Martins Press

Raz, Hilda. *Divine Honors.* 117p. $25.00 (0-8195-2248-1). pap. $11.95 (0-8195-2249-X). University Press of New England/Wesleyan University Press, Fall 1997. Raz offers up a collection of lyrical, graceful, and challenging poems that speak of life's gifts, its "bruises," and its capricious nature. —Bette-Lee Fox, Library Journal. Transgressive and transcendent, Raz's new poems are intimately involved with the physical, corporeal world, and constantly making the leap of faith necessary to its re-embodiment in words. These poems push the boundaries of what language can do to enunciate perception. Their beauty, their clarity, their mystery equally compel. — Marilyn Hacker

Reavey, Kate. *Through the East Window.* 16p. pap. $5.00. Port Townsend, WA: Sagittarius Press, Fall 1998. A dynamic balancing of death and new beginnings. — Sagittarius Press

Reed, Eve. *Letter To Earth.* 32p. ET, Fall 1998. This evocative science fiction poetry is sure to stimulate the reader's passion, while at the same time intellectually chal-lenging one's ideas about man's past, present, and future. —ET

Reed, Tennessee. *Airborne: Poems (1990-1996).* 98p. pap. $12.00 (0-913666-69). Raven's Bones Press, Fall 1996. Reed's poems concern themselves with a range of concerns, from global travel and the stunning achievements of black aviation pioneer Bessie Coleman, to global warfare, the misuse of hi-tech-nology, and the process of aging. This young, gifted poet writes with clarity, wit and wonder, and with an open-hearted passion that disarms, refreshes, and delights. —Al Young

Reese, Steven. *Enough Light to Steer By.* 45p. pap. $8.00 (1-880834-34-0). Cleveland, OH: Cleveland State University Poetry Center, Fall 1997. Reese explores a wide range of quotidian mysteries in language that puts on such a performance — vigorous and surprising, punctuated by leaps like a dancer's — the poems never settle down or settle for less: they keep mov-ing and pushing. The mode here is what I'd call High Palaver, the tongue both at play and deadly serious. — Philip Dacey

Reichhold, Jane, and Werner Reichhold. *In the Presence: Tanka.* 128p. pap. $10.00 (0-944676-22-7). Gualala, CA: AHA Books, Spring 1998. Printed in response to an invitation to attend the Imperial New Year's Poetry Party at the Palace in Japan, and to present their tanka to the Imperial Family, In the Presence contains the complete poems of Jane Reichhold's A Gift of Tanka, and the complete tanka in Bowls I Buy--Drama for Seven Voices. The second half of the book contains 18 of Werner Reichhold's tanka sequences. —AHA Books

Reichhold, Jane, and Werner Reichhold. *Invitation.* 72p. pap. $12.00. Gualala, CA: AHA Books, Spring 1998. In 1998 Jane and Werner Reichhold were invit-ed by the Emperor of Japan to attend the Imperial New Year's Day Poetry Recital at the palace in Tokyo. This is a record of that journey, with color photos. A free download of the book is available at http://ahapoetry.com. —AHA Books

Reichhold, Jane, ed. *Tanka Splendor 1997.* 40p. pap. $7.00 (0-944676-64-2). Gualala, CA: AHA Books, Fall 1997. A chapbook anthology of award-winning tanka from the 1997 competition sponsored by AHA books and judged by George Swede. — AHA Books

Reichhold, Jane, ed. *Tanka Splendor 1998.* 48p. pap. $7.00 (0-944676-65-0). Gualala, CA: AHA Books, Fall 1998. Thirty-one poems chosen from the annual AHA Tanka Contest, judged this year by Hatsue Kawamura. — AHA Books

Reiner, Chrisopher. *Ogling Anchor.* 68p. pap. $10.00 (1-880713-14-4). Penngrove, CA: Avec Books, Fall 1998.

Renaud, Jeanne. *Still No Sign of Them.* 96p. pap. $10.95 (1-888996-08-0). Palmdale, CA: Red Hen Press, Fall 1998. Renaud's poems are wholly remarkable pieces — they have rich, complex, undiluted and insecticide-free lives. They touch us quickly and constantly, and always in unexpected places. — Frederick Barthelme. These poems record a post-post-modern California of illusions gone dry. Renaud addresses a diminished world with saving accuracy: her book, stern and tragi-comic, is a delight. — Angela Ball

Renker, Skip. *Sifting the Visible.* 36p. pap. $6.50 (0-932412-13-0). Saginaw, MI: Mayapple Press, Fall 1998. Renker's poems distill a profound and mysterious silence from the sensory experience of everyday life: luminous, sometimes humorous, mundane, and at the same time much more. —Mayapple Press

Revell, Donald. *There Are Three.* 49p. pap. $12.00 (0-8195-2247-3). University Press of New England/Wesleyan University Press, Fall 1998. Revell's new poems seek moments of harmony between language and silence. The death of the poet's father and almost concurrent birth of his son form the emotional underpinnings of this meditation on faith. These spare and elegant poems speak of a conversion in which a new city is founded in the heart of silence, and grace is a refinement of grammar. —University Press of New England. The impossible, unanswerable question of grace, redemption, reprieve drives Revell's poems toward a pitch, and a grace, not often attained in our time. The urgency of their appeal lingers in the mind long after the page has been turned. —Michael Palmer

Revere, Michael Rigsby. *Fire and Rain.* 82p. pap. $12.50 (1-887905-08-1). Boone, NC: Parkway Publishers, Fall 1998. Revere's poetry reflects a skewed but vital vision of life in an altered state, then bounds out the other side to embrace redemption through love and nurturing. Precise, detailed natural landscapes sometimes contrast and other times parallel the landscape of the mind to expose both the complex and simple facets of human nature. —Toni D. Knott. The poems in this collection, when read chronologically, form a narrative of one man's harrowing journey from the edge of madness to the verge of redemption. —Chris Cox

Rexroth, Kenneth. Edited by Sam Hamill and Elaine Laura Kleiner. *Sacramental Acts: The Love Poems of Kenneth Rexroth.* 132p. pap. $15.00 (1-55659-080-6). Port Townsend, WA: Copper Canyon Press, Fall 1997. The most original synthesis of transcendant metaphysical and erotic verse ever written by an American poet. —Sam Hamill and Elaine Laura Kleiner. Rexroth's work has a classic stance and a majestic tread in its vigor and solidity, its inclusive range and specific utterance. . . the flavor of a Roman poet and the attitude of a Chinese sage —The San Francisco Chronicle. I believe it is [Rexroth's] love poetry that matters most in the end. He is a great love poet during the most loveless time imaginable. —James Wright, Parnassus

Reynolds, N. Scott. *Black Roses.* 18p. pap. $4.00. Nashville, TN: Hirst, Pamela, Fall 1997.

Reynolds, Rebecca. *Daughter of the Hangnail.* 60p. $22.00 (0-932826-56-3). pap. $12.00 (0-932826-57-1). Kalamazoo, MI: New Issues Press, Fall 1997. Reynold's poems are leavened by a good strangeness; they infuse the everyday with wonder and music. Whether she writes of perception or relationships, Reynolds maps the singular emotional terrain that comprises the self. Her work — more ontology than confession — exists where Rilke's glowing harmonics meet the raw edge of the millennium. Her exquisitely elliptical lyrics are founded on an intelligence as shimmering as it is convincing. —Alice Fulton

Ricapito, Joseph V.
Florentine Streets and Other Poems. 58p. pap. $9.00 (1-884419-08-9). West Lafayette, IN: Bordighera, Spring 1997. Ricapito's poems are rich and clear, crowded with the life of the street of Europe, reverberating with echoes of an Italian-American boyhood in Brooklyn during the war. Take him at his word: "I shall not bury myself in history"— No, he resurrects history, his own and that of the world he grew up in. —Charles De Gravelles, New Orleans Poetry Journal Press

Rice, Howard L., and Lamar Williamson, Jr., eds. *A Book of Reformed Prayers.* 256p. pap. $15.00 (0-664-25701-1). Louisville, KY: Westminster John Knox Press, Fall 1997. Rice and Williamson have done a remarkable job of sifting through five centuries of the recorded prayers by Reformed Christians to produce this collection. —The Presbyterian Outlook

Rice, Patty. *Manmade Heartbreak.* 48p. pap. $5.00 (1-889289-33-7). New Haven, CT: Ye Olde Font Shoppe, Fall 1998.

Rice, Stan. *Fear Itself.* 93p. $20.00 (0-679-44441-6). pap. $14.00 (0-679-76600-6). New York, NY: Knopf, Alfred A., Fall 1995; Spring 1997 (paper). In his new collection of poetry, Rice is an expert practitioner of the paranoiac-surreal. His true subject is the uneasy equation between horror and beauty, the "liquification of flame" and the "liquid of order." He is often capable of delivering the instructive surprises of the best poetry. — Graham Christian, Library Journal

Richards, Derek. *Lost in Dogtown.* 31p. pap. $4.95. Beverly, MA: This Poets Press, Fall 1998.

Richards, Tad. *The Gravel Business.* 32p. pap. $4.00 (1-88928-02-7). New Haven, CT: Ye Olde Font Shoppe, Fall 1996.

Richards, Tad. *The Map of the Bear.* 32p. pap. $4.00 (1-889289-03-5). New Haven, CT: Ye Olde Font Shoppe, Fall 1996.

Richie, Eugene. *Island Light.* 108p. pap. $12.00 (0-9651558-8-9). New York, NY: Painted Leaf Press, Spring 1998. Richie's poems negotiate the sum of what is lost and what is found. They are hopeful in the face of myriad threats. And graceful in a world where grace is often not prized. —James Tate. These subtle, deft poems are like an intimate conversation: full of an uncanny delight in the companionship of a world whose details are as ordinary as they are miraculous. "What directions do we follow, what puzzles can we solve?" Richie knows how to ask the right questions, and to answer them "in a language we call home." —Ann Lauterbach

Richman, Paula. *Extraordinary Child: Poems From a South Indian Devotional Genre.* 297p. pap. $36.00 (0-8248-1063-5). Honolulu, HI: University of Hawai'i Press, Fall 1997. For hundreds of years Tamil poets have been composing devotional texts in which they adopt the voice of a mother and address praises to an extraordinary child. The poems, called pillaittamil form a major genre of Tamil literature. In recent times pillaittamils have been dedicated to the Prophet Muhammad, the Virgin Mary, and Baby Jesus, as well as notable political figures and moviestars. Extraordinary Child provides a sampler of translations from, and analysis of, seven pillaittamils of particular religious, aesthetic, or political significance. —University of Hawai'i Press. The sweep of this book, both in terms of centuries covered and in terms of religious communities represented is wonderful. This is a lean book, and the quick progression from chapter to chapter is sometimes quite breathtaking. —John Stratton Hawley

Richman, Robert. *Voice on the Wind.* 59p. pap. $10.00 (0-914278-72-X). Providence, RI: Copper Beech Press, Spring 1997. [If you want] poems based on honest observation and intent on getting at something like the truth, Voice on the Wind is most definitely for you. —Donald Justice. Richman writes with poise, grace, and wide-eyed clarity about the emotional complexity of adult life. He is quietly celebratory about what must sustain us: family, place, and vocation. Emily Dickinson once wrote, "I find ecstasy in living — the mere sense of living is joy enough." Richman is a poet who would agree. —Elizabeth Spires

Rickard, Jack. *Staining the Grass Red.* 32p. pap. $7.95. Johnstown, OH: Pudding House Publications, Fall 1997. Poems by this renowned Arizona painter about his Sioux blood brother and The Sundance for which Rickard travels to the Dakotas annually. —Pudding House Publications

Riding, Laura. Edited by Robert Nye. *A Selection of the Poems of Laura Riding.* 163p. pap. $12.95 (0-89255-221-2). New York, NY: Persea Books, Fall 1996. This selection draws from the full range of Riding's poetic work, and includes eighteen poems from the last-published volume, First Awakenings: The Early Poems of Laura Riding. — Persea Books. When the true history of twentieth-century poetry in the English language comes to be written, I believe that the poems of Laura Riding — and the story that goes with them — will be seen to be as important as anything in it. —Robert Nye

Rilke, Rainer Maria. Translated by Edward Snow. *Uncollected Poems.* 266p. pap. $13.00 (0-86547-513-X). Farrar, Straus and Giroux/North Point Press, Spring 1996; April 1997 (paper). It is wonderful to have a whole new (and sizable) volume of Rilke poems given us by Snow, who is far and away Rilke's best contemporary translator — one who never imposes his own personality or idiosyncrasies of style between us and the original, but gives to it that respect which proves him worthy of the task. —Denise Levertov. Snow translation of Rilke's neglected later poems is worth of Snow's versions of the two books of New Poems. Something of the non-vatic Rilke, poet of perception and sensation, is best conveyed in English by Snow's mediations. —Harold Bloom

Rilling, Helen E. *A Fer Piece.* 80p. pap. $7.00 (0-929688-97-X). Eureka Springs, AR: Bear House Publishing, Spring 1998. A poet looks at life as it was a few decades ago and what it is today; what's been lost and what's been gained. —Bear House Publishing

Rillo. *Public Enemy of North America: A Beguiling Route Through a Picaresque Novel.* 42p. pap. $9.00 (1-880516-21-7). Barrytown, NY: Left Hand Books, Fall 1996. The Pueblo Indians and other Southwest tribes believe that the coyote can occur as a multiple of himself. Public Enemy stages this belief as a model for writing new texts from existing ones. A narrative-collage, Public Enemy frames the primordial myth of the cattle theft committed by the trickster-god Hermes within the 16th century Spanish picaresque novel Lazarillo de Tormes. As it jumps from archaic to modern frames of reference, it appropriates The Public Enemy, the 1930 Warner Brothers film directed by William Wellman. The synergy between the different texts generates a cartoon-like, polyphonic effect. —Left Hand Books

Rimer, Thomas, and Jonathan Chaves, trans. *Japanese and Chinese Poems to Sing: The Wakan roei shu.* 329p. $39.50 (0-231-10702-1). Irvington, NY: Columbia University Press, Fall 1997. For centuries, The Wakan roei shu, compiled by the poet Fujiwara no Kinto around 1013 A.D., was sung and revered by Japanese courtiers, and for nearly a millennium it served as an inspiration and source of materials for Japanese calligraphers, poets and artists. —Columbia University Press. The Wakan roei shu has played a major role in the shaping of the Japanese literary tradition. Through this new translation, the first of its kind, readers of English can now appreciate the true cultural significance of the work and at the same time savor the many fine poems it includes. —Burton Watson

Rivard, David. *Wise Poison.* 72p. pap. $12.95 (1-55597-

247-0). St. Paul, MN: Graywolf Press, Fall 1996. Winner of the 1996 James Laughlin Award of the Academy of American Poets. Finalist for the Los Angeles Times Book Prize. These poems pursue the contemporary and existential, pursue memory, invent new, surprising, idiosyncratic directions both thematic and syntactic. These poems take risks and leaps. —Harvard Review. The poems in Rivard's compelling and delicious new book do not smother you with grandiosity nor come creeping towards you bowed down in self-effacement. These are poems of a human scale; they are complicated, muscled with irony, and their wonderful voice is startling in its power to move, interest, delight. —Lynn Emanuel

Rivas, Victoria. *Small Victories.* 28p. pap. $4.00 (1-889289-01-9). New Haven, CT: Ye Olde Font Shoppe, Fall 1996.

Rivas, Victoria, ed. *Generation Next: Poetry From Teens on the Internet.* 44p. pap. $5.00 (1-889289-14-0). New Haven, CT: Ye Olde Font Shoppe, Fall 1996.

Rizzuto, Phil. Edited by Tom Peyer and Hart Seely. *O Holy*

Cow!: The Selected Verse of Phil Rizzuto. 107p. pap. $10.00 (0-88001-533-0). Hopewell, NJ: Ecco Press, ©1993. Rizzuto played short-stop for the New York Yankees from 1941 until 1956. He began broadcasting Yankee games for radio and television in the early 1960's. This col-lection gathers his funniest and most inspiring verses — from comments on Maris get-ting booed to explications of how the Red Sox control the weather. Game stats follow each poem. O Holy Cow! is a must for baseball fans. — Ecco Press

Robb, Laura, ed. *Music and Drum: Voices of War and Peace, Hope and Dreams.* 32p. $16.95 (0-399-22024-0). New York, NY: Philomel Books, Spring 1997. Music and Drum brings together powerful voices in poems that span the world — and the world's wars — written by children, survivors, and such poets as Lucille Clifton, Carl Sandburg, and Langston Hughes. Here are poems that speak of fighting, of running, of loss, of war and survival — poems that speak of the yearn-ing for a peaceful tomorrow. —Philomel Books

Roberson, Ed. *Just In: Word of Navigation Challenges,*

New and Selected Work. 144p. pap. $14.95 (1-883689-79-1). Jersey City, NJ: Talisman House, Publishers, Fall 1998. Ed Roberson offers us the nerve-edge of poetic speech, sequences of the unanticipat-ed, as poetry of real signifi-cance is meant to do. This selection graphs the develop-ment of a poet committed to the articulation of a resistant, multi-faceted identity. — Michael Palmer. Roberson is among the very best of all. — American Book Review

Roberts, James P., ed. *Haunted Voices: Selected Poetry & Art From Lituanus.* 86p. pap. $8.00 (0-9636544-4-6). Madison, WI: White Hawk Press, Fall 1996.

Roberts, Judith Towse. *Chrysanthemums I Once Thought Sweet.* 77p. pap. $10.00 (0-910479-02-X). Warrensburg, MO: Mid-America Press, Fall 1998. Roberts is a writer whose voice deserves to be heard for its power and insight. — Stanley E. Banks. Roberts has earned, through experience, the strength of these poems. The power of her words comes from the direct and honest details that take courage to reveal. Roberts shows us a woman who has known the edge and survived.

This book is her liberation. — Maryfrances Wagner

Roberts, Katrina. *How Late Desire Looks.* 80p. pap. $9.95 (0-87905-815-3). Layton, UT: Smith, Gibbs, Publishers/Peregrine Smith Books, Fall 1997. Roberts's How Late Desire Looks is a breathtaking collection. These poems reveal an extraordinary new talent whose kaleidoscopic imagination, operatic vision, and dazzling verbal virtuosity propel us along the often twisting currents of experience. —David St. John. Discarding Modernist principles of economy, Roberts puts everything in, ransacking the dictionaries, the etymologies, the storehouses of formal variation. The result is a big, fresh poetry, smart and painterly and passionate. —Mark Doty

Roberts, Len. *The Trouble-Making Finch.* 128p. pap. $14.95 (0-252-06693-6). Champaign, IL: University of Illinois Press, Spring 1998. Roberts is a poet of unwavering truthfulness and unwavering mercy — somehow the mercy always equal to the truth. —Sharon Olds. Roberts's poems are parables of suffering and redemption. He is a great presence, a great moral presence: and one of the most trustworthy and gracious

poets writing today. —Gerald Stern. There is always in Roberts's poems a gentle sensibility, a probing intelligence and an acute attentiveness to what is urgent in our lives that tempers the poems, and that situates them in that precious space between poet and reader which is our common bond and common exaltation. — C.K. Williams

Roberts, Stephen R. *Small Fire Speaking in the Rain.* 28p. pap. $4.00. Talent, OR: Talent House Press, Fall 1998. Grand Prize Winner of the Fifth Annual Talent House Press Chapbook Contest. Small Fire Speaking in the Rain is a collection of earth poems, an attempt to relate to the natural world despite technology. —Stephen R. Roberts

Robertson, Robin. *A Painted Field.* 89p. $22.00 (0-15-100366-1). San Diego, CA: Harcourt Brace/Harvest Books, Fall 1997: Spring 1999 (new paper). Robertson is instantly recognizable as a poet of vivid authority, commanding a surprised, accurate language of his own. The evocative truth and the crystalline ring of his words, line by line, make a kind of hope in themselves. This is a first book of extraordinary gifts and assured maturity. —W.S. Merwin

Robiner, Linda Goodman. *Reverse Fairy Tale.* 34p. pap. $7.95. Johnstown, OH: Pudding House Publications, Spring 1997. These poems redefine [the] "divorce poem" as [a] spiritual journey and simultaneously cast [it] into the realm of fine contemporary poetry. These aren't sob stories, these are revelations. —Pudding House Publications

Robinson, Elizabeth. *Other Veins, Absent Roots.* 28p. pap. $4.00. Saratoga, ca: Instress, Fall 1998.

Robles, Al. *Rappin' With Ten Thousand Carabaos in the Dark.* 123p. pap. $16.95 (0-934052-25-5). Los Angeles, CA: UCLA Asian American Studies Center, Fall 1996. At last! This long overdue collection by poet, shaman, and storyteller Robles is finally with us. His soulful, earthy and loving poems give voice and vibrant music to the rich language, bittersweet dreams, and difficult lives of the manongs of Pilipino America. — Jessica Hagedorn. There is a geography-crunching aspect to Pilipino American writing, which is becoming a sizable American contribution to a world literature now in the

making. Robles is one of the pioneers. —N.V.M. Gonzalez

Robles, Jaime. *Unseen Stream.* 16p. pap. $15.00 (1-889589-01-2). Mill Valley, CA: Em Press, Fall 1998. Robles's poem traces elemental fluencies as two lovers follow the hidden stream that flows beneath their city. Drawings and a watercolor by Adam Broner. —Em Press

Rodgers, Carolyn M. *We're Only Human.* 23p. pap. $6.50. Chicago, IL: Eden Press, Fall 1996. Explores the miraculous durability and fallibility of the human spirit. —Eden Press

Rodia, Becky. *Another Fire.* 19p. pap. $7.00 (0-938566-78-4). Easthampton, MA: Adastra Press, Fall 1997. A first collection on the themes of growth to adulthood. Handset, handsewn, letterpress limited edition. —Adastra Press

Rodríguez, Luis J. *Trochemoche.* 92p. pap. $12.95 (1-880684-50-0). Willimantic, CT: Curbstone Press, Fall 1998. Rodriguez writes powerfully and passionately about urban youth, family, and the plight of neglected communities, while exploring the rich cultural roots of his Chicano ancestry. Trochemoche explores recovery and personal growth, ways of knowledge, revolution, and the power of poetry. — Curbstone Press. [Rodriguez's poetry] is of the barrio yet stubbornly refuses to be confined in it — [his] perceptive gaze and storyteller's gift transport his world across neighborhood boundaries. — Publishers Weekly

Rogers, Bertha, ed. *Out of the Catskills and Just Beyond: Literary and Visual Works by Catskill Writers and Artists.* 380p. pap. $24.95 (0-9646844-6-2). Treadwell, NY: Bright Hill Press, Fall 1997. Literary and visual artists have been drawn to the Catskill Mountains since the early 1800's, many finding the blue "land in the clouds" the perfect place to reside. The ground-breaking Out of the Catskills and Just Beyond presents the works of almost 200 writers and artists, including more than 50 Catskill high-school writers and artists, in all their rich diversity. — Bright Hill Press

Rogers, Pattiann. *Eating Bread and Honey.* 95p. pap. $13.95 (1-57131-406-7). Minneapolis, MN: Milkweed Editions, Fall 1997. Reading the work of Rogers — if one can call such beauty "work" — a reader invariably loses

his or her grip on firm ground and is without fail swept wonderfully up from bedrock and into the stars and fire-mist, or is transported some ancient distance back down into and beneath one's bedrock. —Rick Bass. What a keen eye Rogers has! And what insight accompanies her vision. Read Book Two of this collection (Animals and People) and come to know who you are. —Maxine Kumin

Rollings, Alane. *The Logic of Opposites.* 79p. $35.00 (0-8101-5081-6). pap. $14.95 (0-8101-5082-4). Northwestern University Press/TriQuarterly Books, Fall 1998. This is a unique collection: written by a poet who has suffered from bipolar illness, these paired poems represent opposites in both mood and perspective: they are confessional without being autobiographical in detail; intimate and accessible while maintaining a curious detachment; utterly serious, yet often seductively casual in tone. These poems are an exploration of the nature of contradiction, and as such they are entirely, and convincingly, self-consistent. — Northwestern University Press

Romero, Danny. *P/V.* 16p. Berkeley, CA: Chicano Chapbook Series, Spring

1997. The Chicano Chapbook Series, edited by Gary Soto, issued twelve title in the late 1970's and early 1980's, including works by Sandra Cisneros, Alberto Ríos, Jimmy Santiago Baca and others. The chapbooks are distributed free of charge to selected libraries with Chicano collections. P/V is #13. P/V is an abbreviation in graffiti for por vida, or "For Life."

Romero, Levi. *In the Gathering of Silence.* 48p. pap. $7.95 (0-931122-84-8). Albuquerque, NM: West End Press, Fall 1996. [Romero's poems] make me shake my head, laugh, cry, say "Well, yes." —Sandra Cisneros. Romero is destined to become an important New Mexican voice. His poems speak to the blending of languages and to the honored place that the land occupies in our lives. Levi's words are familiar yet astounding in their recall of minute and crucial detail. — Luci Tapahonso

Ronk, Martha. *Eyetrouble.* 96p. pap. $14.95 (0-8203-1992-9). Athens, GA: University of Georgia Press, Spring 1998. These poems remind us that things are not always what they appear to be. In Eyetrouble, things that ought to be there, including expected syntax and transitions, are not, and what seems clear at first glance fades in and out of focus. — University of Georgia Press. Subtly nuanced. Beautifully effusive. —Publishers Weekly

Rose, Samé. *Hits Called Love: A Collection of Intense and Sensitive Perceptions About Domestic Violence.* 61p. pap. $9.95 (1-56315-099-9). Pittsburgh, PA: Sterling House, Fall 1998. A shocking, gut-wrenching explosion of verse exploring the chilling reality of spousal abuse and the struggle for survival that battered women must face. Rose explores the daily struggles women face as they attempt to exist in a world of never ending degradation. Through the irony of her words, the poet reveals the stark reality of the interpersonal conflicts that lead to the cycle of abuse. —Sterling House

Rosen, Michael J. *Telling Things.* 85p. $22.00 (0-15-100240-1). San Diego, CA: Harcourt Brace/Harvest Books, Fall 1997. Rosen has achieved a sustained account of contemporary domestic life that may well stand with Auden's About the House from the 1950's. Rosen's mature, sane, witty, elliptical, and wise voice — measured as it often is into subtly audible pentameter lines — rises to moments, even to whole poems, of a Horatian dignity. —Reynolds Price. Rosen examines the domestic life with an exacting lens because he knows that home is where meaning is to be found. Hard-won, alive with formal and emotional intelligence, the humanity of Telling Things is matched only by its grace. —Mark Doty

Rosen, Michael J. *Traveling in Notions: The Stories of Gordon Penn.* 103p. $15.95 (1-57003-156-8). pap. $9.95 (1-57003-157-6). Columbia, SC: University of South Carolina Press, Fall 1996. With this fine book Rosen forces us to reexamine our "notions" of what poetry can and should do. An unusual and worthy achievement. — Jacqueline Osherow. Traveling in Notions chronicles the triumphs and despairs of an everyman — businessman, father, husband, grandfather, senior citizen, and lover. These are poems whose textures mirror the deritus of our days: phone-in talk shows and Velcro, platinum credit cards and remodeled high-rises. Circumscribed and uplifted by mortality, the poems bear testimony to the blessedness of

outreach to others. —Robert Phillips

Rosenberg, Liz, ed. *Earth-Shattering Poems.* 126p. $15.95 (0-8050-4821-9). New York, NY: Holt, Henry, and Company, Spring 1998. From the aching beauty of Margaret Menges' "A Love Poem" to the agony of Sylvia Plath's "Lady Lazarus," here is an international collection of language distilled to its emotional essence. —Henry Holt and Company

Rosenzweig, Geri. *Half the Story.* 43p. pap. $6.00 (1-882983-34-3). Greensboro, NC: March Street Press, Fall 1997. Radiant in their fresh play of color and tone, their engagement with nature, Rosenzweig's poems give us whole-hearted evocations of an Irish childhood remembered and revisited, of family sorrows and losses set in a world whose every hedge, fern, bird song, and starry constellation is lovingly recorded. This is the work of a moving and generous poet; it deserves wide praise. —Colette Inez

Rossini, Clare. *Winter Morning With Crow.* 77p. $24.95 (1-884836-30-5). pap. $12.95 (1-884836-31-3). Akron, OH: University of Akron Press, Fall 1997.

Winter Morning With Crow, Rossini's painterly title for this impressive debut collection, suggests how much more pleasure it gives the poet to look than to know. Her intelligence thrives by a wary distrust of itself. Her brain and heart share, rather than contend for, the feast her eye provides for them. —William Matthews. It is Rossini's consciousness – attentive, prescient, inspired – that makes her miraculous art, makes a poetry so pure and spare, so free of artifice or contrivance, that it seems to reinvent the page. This is poetry that restores us to something we have lost. It returns beauty, and faith in beauty, then reminds us (as the great painters remind us) that we are not meant to possess it – or the objects of our love. Rossini is, with this extraordinary first book, already a master. —Carol Muske

Roth, Paul B. *Nothing Out There.* 99p. pap. $9.95 (0-9632547-6-6). Glyndon, MD: Vida Publishing, Fall 1996. Roth creates a poetic language through the incarnation of the divine in the real. —Duane Locke

Rothenberg, Jerome and Pierre Joris, eds. *Poems for the Millenium, Volume Two.* 902p. $65.00 (0-520-20863-3). pap. $24.95 (0-520-20864-1). Berkeley, CA: University of California Press, Spring 1998. Rothenberg and Joris have performed a heroic service to poets and poetry. This second volume bears out the assertion that the works gathered here constitute, not a "minority poetics" but rather an ocean, a manifold, a non-linear habitat where we meet and remeet an extraordinary range of poetic life forms. For the reader of poetry, here is both archive and visionary adventure. For poets (and would-be poets), here is a mine of legacies and incitement to the scope and possibilities of our own task. For students of history and culture, here is a world pulse. Though such a collection can never be definitive, this one is admirable in its generosity of spirit. —Adrienne Rich

Rothenberg, Jerome, ed. *Revolution of the Word: A New Gathering of American Avant-Garde Poetry, 1914-1945.* 259p. pap. $15.95 (1-878972-24-3). Boston, MA: Exact Change, Fall 1998.

Rothenberg, Joyce Andrea. *Seasons of Change.* 20p. pap. $5.00. Wyzard, Jim, Publisher, Spring 1998.

Rubin, Steven J., ed. *Telling and Remembering: A Century*

of American Jewish Poetry.
499p. $27.50 (0-8070-6838-1).
pap. $20.00 (08070-6839-X).
Boston, MA: Beacon Press,
Fall 1997; Fall 1998 (new
paper). The first comprehen-
sive collection of its kind,
Telling and Remembering
gathers together more than
two hundred poems by
American Jewish poets on
Jewish subjects and themes.
Its contributors include seven
winners of the Pulitzer Prize
for poetry (Louise Glück,
Anthony Hecht, Maxine
Kumin, Stanley Kunitz, Philip
Levine, Howard Nemerov, and
Karl Shapiro) and many other
poets of exceptional achieve-
ment (Allen Ginsberg, Grace
Paley, Marge Piercy, Robert
Pinsky, Adrienne Rich, Gerald
Stern and C.K. Williams
among them). —Beacon
Press. A brilliant spectrum of
poetic voices. —Booklist. An
important collection. —
Library Journal

Rubinstein, Raphael. *The
Basement of the Cafe Rilke.*
79p. pap. $10.00 (1-889097-
07-1). West Stockbridge, MA:
Hard Press, Fall 1996.
Rubinstein reconciles beautifully the everyday with the
ellipses necessary for his
negations. With an obsessive-
ly self-lacerating elegance, the
poet gives us panoramas of a
very expansive happiness.

This concise and self-conscious style seems as flat as a
blueprint and as accurate.
These unconfused cavalier
poems are witty as new ruins
should be. —David Shapiro

Rumi, Jelaluddin. Translated
by Jonathan Star. *Rumi: In the
Arms of the Beloved.* 209p.
$21.95 (0-87477-894-8). New
York, NY: Tarcher, Jeremy P.
/Putnam, Fall 1997. This is a
breathtakingly gorgeous pre-
sentation of the beyond belief
joy of liberated vision. —
Sylvia Boorstein. Each poem
in this timeless anthology of
Rumi's inspired verse is a
jewel. The choice of poems
and the subtle magnificence
through which Star renders the
metaphoric language of spirit
left me in a profound state of
grace. —Joan Borysenko

Rumi, Jelaluddin. Translated
by Deepak Chopra and
Fereydoun Kia. *The Love
Poems of Rumi.* 62p. $12.00
(0-609-602430-8). New York,
NY: Crown
Publishers/Harmony Books,
Spring 1998. This volume
consists of new translations by
Farsi scholar Fereydoun Kia,
edited by Deepak Chopra to
evoke the rich mood and
music of Rumi's love poems.
Exalted yearning, ravishing
ecstasy, and consuming desire
emerge from these poems as

powerfully today as they did on their creation more than 700 years ago. —Crown Publishers

Russell, Timothy. *In Lacrimae.* 24p. pap. $5.00. Fox River Grove, IL: White Eagle Coffee Store Press, Spring 1997. Despite the pervasive decay and industrial blight [in these poems], objects and people exhibit their own luminous integrity. Russell's poems redeem the threats of poverty and death with a doomed, stunning beauty that leaves us in lacrimis, in tears. —Peter Blair

Rutherford, Brett. *Anniversarium: The Autumn Poems.* 98p. pap. $11.95. New York, NY: Poet's Press, Fall 1996 (expanded and revised). [Rutherford writes about nature with] a special validity and integrity, and clearly from first-hand experience and observation. —John Burnett Payne, Poets Fortnightly

Rutkowski, Thaddeus. *Basic Training.* 39p. pap. $6.00 (1-882983-29-7). Greensboro, NC: March Street Press, Spring 1997. Minimalism is alive and well in the work of Rutkowski, who can say more about America and family life in a paragraph than most writ-

ers can say in fifty pages. — Alison Lurie

Rutkowski, Thaddeus. *Journey to the Center of My Id.* 69p. Siasconset, MA: Linear Arts, 1997.

Rux, Carl Hancock. *Pagan Operetta.* 149p. pap. $14.95 (0-9639585-8-5). New York, NY: Fly by Night Press/A Gathering of the Tribes, Spring 1999. Dense, funny, lyrical and profane — Rux's Pagan Operetta is an urban brew that absolutely lives up to its name. —Jessica Hagedorn. Pagan Operetta is a brilliant and provocative debut collection. —Sapphire, Rux's poems revel in our lives and the sweet dreams we make out of them. They are paeans to lust, sin, shame and reckless abandonment. Prayers for the dying, love for the damned, the different and unrepentantly beautiful. — Greg Tate

Ryan, G.B. *Poems 1-11.* 114p. New York, NY: Elkhound Publications, Spring 1998.

Ryan, N. Jesse. *Junebug Prophecy.* 23p. pap. $6.00 (1-877801-31-3). Galloway, NJ: Still Waters Press, Fall 1997. Ryan's poetry is a testimony to how art can survive and thrive through adversity. With breathtaking simplicity, her poems take us back to her childhood. Her work allows us to see life through the eyes of the girl who was taking notes for the future. It sings out in honesty and stunning clarity. —Claire Braz-Valentine

Rybicki, John. *Traveling at High Speeds.* 50p. pap. $12.00 (0-932826-45-8). Kalamazoo, MI: New Issues Press, Fall 1996. Rybicki ignites the page. His vital, urgent poems celebrate pleasures some would call — mistakenly — small. Or, as in "Asthma," brilliant metaphor underscores the visceral fear of being trapped in one's own body. I have copied out lines from his poems and kept them on my desk for years; I needed them that close by. —Amy Hempel. Rybicki has a hurricane-heart, a hammer-heart, that is just waiting to be unleashed upon this perhaps-undeserving world. —Rick Bass

Saba, Umberto. Translated by Stephen Sartarelli. *History and Chronicle of the Songbook.* 264p. pap. $13.95 (1-878818-39-2). Riverdale-on-Hudson, NY: Sheep Meadow Press, Fall 1998. History and Chronicle of the Songbook is a unique book of memoir, self-criticism, and criticism. Here

we have Saba writing about the art of poetry, the birth and meaning of his own poems [comprising] the Songbook. —Sheep Meadow Press

Sacks, Peter. *Natal Command.* 80p. $30.00 (0-226-73342-4). pap. $12.95 (0-226-73343-2). Chicago, IL: University of Chicago Press, Fall 1997. In this stunning third collection, South African émigré Sacks confronts the ghosts of two continents, finding them both vicious and vengeful. Whether writing in long lines or [in] the minimalist style of poets such as Cid Corman, Sacks displays [a] rare combination of skill and subject matter. —Library Journal. The poems are informed not only by complex relations of power and race, but also by a larger sense of the conflicted desires regarding the very notion of a homeland. At once personal and historical — responding to the work of mourning with an intensely embodied desire for redress — the poems take up the challenge of cultural repair against collective rage and grief. Sacks's new book gathers unmatched music to far-reaching work of compassion, beauty and power. —Jorie Graham

Sadoff, Ira. *Grazing.* 88p. pap. $12.95 (0-252-06737-1). Champaign, IL: University of Illinois Press, Fall 1998. Celebration abounds but never gives way to sentamentalism in this sixth volume by Sadoff. Often spare in his descriptions, Sadoff allows objects and observations to suggest their stories rather than overstate them. —Chicago Tribune. How heartening to find an already accomplished poet inventing a new voice, with a new richness of experience and insight, and a denser, more intricate music. Reality itself, the reality of the world, and of the soul, seems intensified and renewed in Grazing: a splendid book. —C.K. Williams

Saenz, Gil, and Jacqueline Rae Rawlson Sanchez. *Lavender & Lace.* 33p. pap. $5.00 (0-910863-17-2). Detroit, MI: Sounds of Poetry, Fall 1998.

Saidenberg, Jocelyn. *Mortal City.* 79p. pap. $8.00 (1-879342-14-6). San Diego, CA: Parentheses Writing Series, Fall 1998.

Saijo, Albert. *Outspeaks a Rhapsody.* 200p. pap. $12.00 (0-910043-50-7). Honolulu, HI: Bamboo Ridge Press, Fall 1997. Winner of a Pushcart Prize. Here's what happens when you really speak from the heart. Comic, serious, proposing a poetics of immanence and a call for language "that all animals understand" [Saijo] looks both ways and then goes straight ahead. These poems expand outward toward their limits even has you read them. Saijo's poem is a great life's strong song. Here's a wild man who's totally refined. —Gary Snyder

Saiko, Ema. Translated by Hiroaki Sato. *Breeze Through Bamboo: Kanshi of Ema Saiko.* 245p. pap. $15.50 (0-231-11065-0). Irvington, NY: Columbia University Press, Spring 1998. Saiko (1787-1861) was a remarkably evocative Japanese poet, one of the few known women writers of kanshi — poems written in classical Chinese. —Columbia University Press. It is delightful to know such a woman existed in Tokugawa Japan. Here is a poet-painter who was able to consort on an equal footing with the male scholars and poets of her day. Her poetic voice is refreshingly direct and honest. Many readers will find a kindred spirit here. —Sonja Arntzen

Saint, Assotto. *Spells of a Voodoo Doll.* 405p. pap. $12.95 (1-56333-393-7).

Masquerade Books/A Richard Kasak Book, Fall 1996. A fierce, spellbinding collection of the poetry, lyrics, essays and performance texts of Assotto Saint — one of the most important voices in the renaissance of black gay writing. —Masquerade Books. A powerful, courageous and impressive poet. —David Trinidad. Saint's equanimity is startling, and he has an almost Zen-like approach to the painful realities of racism, homophobia, and AIDS-phobia. —Victoria A. Brownworth

Saito, Fumi. Translated by Hatsue Kawamura and Jane Reichhold. *White Letter Poems.* 115p. pap. $10.00 (0-944676-23-5). Gualala, CA: AHA Books, Fall 1998. Selected poems from the Poet Laureate of Japan, the first of her tanka to be translated into English. —AHA Books

saíz, próspero. *Chants of Nezahualcoyotl & Obsidian Glyph.* 88p. $23.00 (0-941160-15-7). pap. $17.00 (0-941160-13-0). Madison, WI: Ghost Pony Press, Fall 1996. The long poem Chants of Nezahualcoyotl explores the role and meaning of poetry in Aztec Mexico by focusing on the greatest of Nahuatl poets, Fasting Coyote. Obsidian

Glyph is a collection of lyric meditations on the sacred rites and poetic practices of the Aztecs in the time of the 5th Sun. —Ghost Pony Press. próspero saíz is the poet-laureate of the pre-Columbian. He goes beyond lamenting about lost pre-Columbian glories into the center of pre-Columbian existentialism itself, the basic, fundamental sense of total ephemeralness. He is one of the most challenging writers to appear on the literary scene within recent memory. —Hugh Fox

saíz, próspero. *Horse.* 24p. $16.00 (0-941160-14-9). pap. $12.50 (0-941160-12-2). Madison, WI: Ghost Pony Press, Fall 1996. saíz pierces, with haunting precision, the veil of the ancient, fateful connection of the horse and mankind, and meditates on the sacred role of the horse as a wellspring of dread and art. [He] explores the role of the horse in the destruction of the Peoples of the Great Plains, the Spanish conquest, the incursion into the American Southwest, and the fascist bombing of the Basque town of Guernica as presented by Picasso. Now hallucinatory, now dream-like — rooted in the poet's beloved Southwest, this exquisite collection demonstrates the remarkable range of saíz's brilliant style. —Ghost Pony Press

Sakaki, Nanao. *Let's Eat Stars.* 145p. pap. $11.95 (0-942396-76-6). Nobleboro, ME: Blackberry Books, Fall 1997. A collection of new poems, three plays, and exper-imental prose pieces from the 1960's by the wandering Japanese poet. —Blackberry Books

Salaam, Kalamu ya, ed. With Kwame Alexander. *360°: A Revolution of Black Poets.* 208p. (1-888018-14-3). Black Words/Runagate Press, Fall 1998.

Salamun, Tomaz. Edited by Christopher Merrill. *The Four Questions of Melancholy: New and Selected Poems.* 265p. pap. $15.00 (1-877727-57-1). Buffalo, NY: White Pine Press, Spring 1997. Playful and brooding, meditative and declamatory, these poems affirm Salamun's status as a major Central European poet. —The New Yorker. What a joy — a large, wonderfully selected, collection of Salamun's poems — one of Europe's great philosophical wonders. Finally seeing so much of the work in one sequence makes clear how brilliantly and stubbornly — and uniquely — he has

explored the nature of the real, how many avenues of percep-tion he has coursed down. Realism, surrealism, song, aphorism, lyric, anti-lyric — everything from Apollinaire's physical wonder to Rilke's the-ological fear swirl through these beautiful, scary and deeply original poems. — Jorie Graham. This is that rare thing, a necessary volume of poetry. —David St. John

Salas, Floyd. *Color of My Living Heart.* 80p. pap. $8.00 (1-55885-171-2). Houston, TX: Arte Público Press, Fall 1996. Here, the seasoned boxer, street dude, ex-hippy and ex-pachuco bares his heart in poems about love in all its agony, deception, disillusion-ment, glory and sexual eupho-ria. —Arte Público Press. Salas has a fierce feel for his world and his language. — Boston Globe. Remarkably sparse and stirring —The New York Times Book Review. Piercing and eloquent. Beautifully written, gritty, and deeply human. —Kirkus Reviews

Salerno, Joe. *Dream Paintings From the Heaven of Obscurity.* 53p. pap. $5.00 (1-886841-03-9). Andover, NJ: Skylands Writers & Artists Association/Ars Poetica, Fall 1997. When Joe Salerno died of lung cancer at the age of 48, his friends Joe Weil and Sander Zulauf vowed they would bring his poems into print. Salerno believed that poetry was to be found in the realm of the ordinary. He had published poems in journals like Wormwood Review, but supported his family by writing dry technical manuals on things like integrated circuit checkers. When Zulauf and Weil began to assemble a comprehensive collection of his poems to be called Only Here, they learned from a scholar of Japanese culture about an unusual series of poems Salerno had sent him based on an alter ego, a failed Chinese painter who, because he lacked the talent to paint the beauty around him, painted word pictures, poems, instead. These are those poems. The publication of Dream Paintings and Only Here both were made possible by the contributions of more thatn 100 people. —Skylands Writers & Artists Association

Salerno, Joe. *Only Here: Selected Poems.* 75p. pap. $10.00 (1-886841-07-1). Andover, NJ: Skylands Writers & Artists Association/Ars Poetica, Fall 1998. The greatest characteristic of Salerno's poetry is love for the world of things, of flesh, and of language. His sensibility is amative and erotic. Joe has left behind a triumphant, sweet, and astounding book. —Donald Hall

Salinas, Luis Omar. *Sometimes Mysteriously.* 64p. pap. $10.00 (1-887573-03-8). Chugiak, AK: Salmon Run Press, Spring 1997. To be sure, the Salinas hallmark of brilliant and arresting imagery is evident throughout this book, poems that assail the entire emotional spectrum. But there is more in these fresh and mature poems — there is compassion and a tough understanding, a wisdom that has scraped a little light from a recalcitrant world and left it on the page. — Christopher Buckley

Samuels, Lisa. *The Seven Voices.* 88p. pap. $10.00 (1-882022-32-7). O Books, Fall 1998. There is nothing procedural in this writing. It is necessity, forced and yielding a suspended judgment in the made relations of language, an available truth. —Barrett Watten. "Ordinary grace" becomes ineluctably sufficient in Samuels's first collection of poems, as if each of its seven voiced veils opened into rippling, then melting perceptions — language emblazoning itself. —Charles Bernstein

Sanchez, Carol Lee. *from spirit to matter: new and selected poems 1969-1996.* 269p. pap. $14.95 (0-931552-09-5). San Francisco, CA: Taurean Horn Press, Spring 1997. [Sanchez's] poetry combines satiric wit, irony and sheer fun with profound humanistic reflection and insight. It arises from a complex context of Native and European cultures, interweaving physical and metaphysical dimensions of matter, mind, heart and spirit. —Mara Lynn Keller

Sanchez, Neomi. *What's Not Forgotten.* 9p. Berkeley, CA: Chicano Chapbook Series, Spring 1998. The Chicano Chapbook Series, edited by Gary Soto, issued twelve title in the late 1970's and early 1980's, including works by Sandra Cisneros, Alberto Ríos, Jimmy Santiago Baca and others. The chapbooks are distributed free of charge to selected libraries with Chicano collections. What's Not Forgotten is #18.

Sánchez, Ricardo. *The Loves of Ricardo.* 160p. $22.95 (1-882688-13-9). pap. $12.95 (1-882688-14-7). Chicago, IL: Tia Chucha Press, Spring 1997. Sánchez was one of the creators of la poesía chicana and his voice was the concentrate of many silent voices. His written poetry was ambassador of the non-written sufferings of so many chicanos, whose bare feet were in the USA, but whose barefoot soul was endlessly walking sobre la tierra seca mexicana, muriendo de la sed. —Yevgeny Yevtushenko

Sanchez, Sonia. *Does Your House Have Lions?.* 70p. (0-8070-6830-6). pap. $10.00 (0-8070-6831-4). Boston, MA: Beacon Press, Fall 1997. An epic poem on kin estranged, the death of a brother from AIDS, and the possibility of reconciliation and love in the face of loss. —Beacon Press. Sanchez is a lion in literature's forest. When she writes, she roars, and when she sleeps other creatures walk gingerly. —Maya Angelou. Sanchez's powers of empathy shine with rare luminosity. —The Philadelphia Enquirer

Sanchez, Sonia. *Like the Singing Coming Off the Drums: Love Poems.* 144p. $15.00 (0-8070-6842-X). pap. $12.50 (0-8070-6843-8). Boston, MA: Beacon Press, Spring 1998; Spring 1999 (new paper). Sanchez's new and selected love poems have been gathered together here for the first time. In her own style of haiku, tanka, and sensual blues, Sanchez writes as no one else can of the many forms love takes. —Beacon Press. In a collection that matches bodily desire with social exigency, Sanchez hits with percussive force. — Publishers Weekly. Sanchez's poetry asks the reader to risk dizziness, to attempt to catapult the body beyond book covers, to be ready for more of what's out there. —Kimiko Hahn, Philadelphia Inquirer

Sanders, Edward. *1968: A History in Verse.* 260p. $25.00 (1-57423-038-7). pap. $14.00 (1-57423-037-9). Santa Rosa, CA: Black Sparrow Press, Spring 1997. Sanders is distinguished among the poets of his generation by his engagement with history. Here, in a masterwork of poetic history, he shadows the Time Ghost in retrospect back toward that generation's vital and tragic sources, reconstructing the decisive year 1968 in a unique commingling of personal and political recounting. —Black Sparrow Press

Sandhu, Harbeer, and Antonio DiPietro. *A Pocketful of Poesy (and Pictures).* 36p. Sandhu, Harbeer, and Antonio DiPietro, 1997.

Sandy, Stephen. *The Thread: New and Selected Poems.*

205p. (0-8071-2257-2). (0-8071-225-0). Baton Rouge, LA: Louisiana State University Press, Fall 1998. Sandy is extraordinarily versatile in approach, mode, and form, and his poems — truthful and frequently poignant — keep discovering the depth and difference of everyday events, and the live words for conveying such findings. — Richard Wilbur. This engaging book's thread is the impressive gathering of a life's experience in all senses, from the daily news to the family in its own fact, its places, times, and people. [Sandy] is a poet confident of his craft's resources and his heart's determined fidelity to what it knows and loves. —Robert Creeley

Sanelli, Mary Lou. *Close At Hand.* 71p. pap. $12.95 (0-93-127147-9). Glendo, WY: High Plains Press, Fall 1998. Sanelli's playful, compassionate, and, at times, wonderfully gritty sense of relationship permeates this collection. It's a pleasure. —Christianne Balk. These poems bring us close, close enough to know "the taste of salt in the mouth, to negotiate the business at hand." Sanelli's poems make way for sun. Close at Hand brings light "with enough will to change everything." — Kevin Miller

Sappho. Translated by Willis Barnstone. *Sappho: Poems, A New Version.* 143p. pap. $10.95 (1-55713-358-1). Los Angeles, CA: Sun & Moon Press, Spring 1998. This edition reintroduces Sappho to the modern reader, providing a vivid, contemporary translation, which captures the spareness and intensity of Sappho's line. In Barnstone's brilliant translations, Sappho's work is presented in its darkly antiromantic idiom that rejects sentimentality and "prettiness." — Sun & Moon Press

Saroyan, Aram. *Day and Night: Bolinas Poems.* 226p. $27.50 (1-57423-086-7). pap. $15.00 (1-57423-085-9). Santa Rosa, CA: Black Sparrow Press, Fall 1998. An unashamedly youthful book, starry-eyed in its approach to family-starting and community-founding, innocently celebrative of the simple wonders of a life lived close to nature. Glancing back at a glamorous but troubled childhood spent among the bright lights of Manhattan and the luxuriant palms of Beverly Hills, the young Saroyan experiences this new world with a Blakean freshness of vision. —Black Sparrow Press

Sarton, May. *Coming Into Eighty.* 71p. pap. $10.00 (0-393-31623-8). New York, NY: Norton, W.W., and Company, Fall 1994; Spring 1997 (paper). For as long as I have been alive, Sarton has been bravely writing poems that are more than mere bright moments in our shoddy culture. In her finest poems, she enlarges the way we feel and the way we think, challenging the best in us to come forward. —George Garrett. Sarton is a Survivor, spiritually as well as physically. Her poetry, too, will survive, attesting to the fact that a woman of magnificent radiance — a Truth-teller!! — was and is Here. —Gwendolyn Brooks

Sarton, May. *Letters From Maine.* 62p. pap. $10.00 (0-393-31716-1). New York, NY: Norton, W.W., and Company, Fall 1997 (reissue). In Letters From Maine Sarton's inspiration was a new, brief, and passionate love affair. The book celebrates that time, marks its passing, and opens up the poetic vision it left behind. The poems speak of the permanence of the memory of love and of the flowering it brings. They also draw on the rich, sometimes harsh, beauty of nature and its solace. — W.W. Norton

Sassi, Maria. *Rooted in Stars.* 41p. pap. $7.00 (1-880286-45-9). Canton, CT: Singular Speech Press, Fall 1998. Sassi's poems have surprising words. . . and a felicity that can speak. —Richard Wilbur. Sassi's work has the depth, the range, and the power of unique imagery we look for in a new collection of poems. Frequently drawing on paintings and music, she fuses art forms with dazzling results. Through her poetry, we see, hear, and feel what we would have missed without her vision. —Stephen Minot. Although Sassi writes in both controlled and free forms, much of her work reveals a fantastic imagination and some of it is Surrealist. Her poetry is challenging, enigmatic, and evocative. —Alfred Dorn

Sassi, Maria. *What I See: A Folio of Poems From Art.* 18p. pap. $4.00 (1-887012-08-7). Newtown, CT: Hanover Press, 1997. Poems on two Surrealist masterpieces, Dali's "Apparition of Face and Fruit Dish on a Beach" and "The Lovers" by Magritte. The poems cast an astonishing light upon those cryptic canvases without diminishing their mystery and magic. By deftly juxtaposing incongruous images, the poet has matched the mind-teasing inventiveness of Dali and Magritte. Startling, challenging, enigmatic, and evocative, the poems are full of lightning that will jolt the complacent reader. —Alfred Dorn

Savant, John. *Brendan's Voyage and Other Poems.* 96p. pap. $10.00 (0-912449-53-5). Cedarville, CA: Floating Island Publications, Fall 1997. Always musical, sometimes humorous, the poems are, almost casually, weighted with profundity. Best of all, they involve us in the suspense of being human. —Rosalie Moore

Savitt, Lynne. *The Burial of Longing Beneath the Blue Neon Moon.* 56p. pap. $5.00 (1-889289-34-5). New Haven, CT: Ye Olde Font Shoppe, Fall 1998. Savitt is the Janis Joplin of poetry. I read everything she puts out. Immediately. —Charles Plymell. No one writes lust and life and our secrets like this. If you are breathing, Savitt's poems are a must. —Leo Connellan

Scalapino, Leslie. *Green and Black: Selected Writings.* 100p. pap. $10.50 (1-883689-36-8). Jersey City, NJ: Talisman House, Publishers, Fall 1996. One of the most unique and powerful writers at the forefront of American literature. —Library Journal. Scalapino's way seeks to restore the intensive duration of temporal flux to the dead and deadening shelf of habitual life. —Sulfur

Scalapino, Leslie. *The Return of Painting, The Pearl, and Onion: A Trilogy.* 230p. pap. $16.95 (1-883689-57-0). Jersey City, NJ: Talisman House, Publishers, 1997. There is a hallucinatory exactitude in her presentation of sentences, an intense encapsulating of the moment with no latitude for the illusions and comforts of reflection and detachment. The book's great virtue is claritas, the intensity of the experience itself. — Multicultural Review. What makes this writing go is an incredible ease. A sense of a text that is capable of breathing. —Village Voice

Scarecrow. *Three From Scarecrow.* 4p. pap. $10.00. Maple City, MI: Smiling Dog Press, Spring 1997. Three of Scarecrow's poems. Handset letterpress edition with graphics from linoleum and wood blocks and bindings that utilize cattail reeds and beachgrass roots. —Smiling Dog Press

Schaefer, Judy. *Harvesting the Dew: A Literary Nurse Bearing Witness to Pain.* 101p. pap. $12.95 (1-880254-46-8). Long Branch, NJ: Vista Publishing, Spring 1997. These poems discover the voice of a nurse whose goal is connection — not only with her patients, but also with the great forces of healing. [Schaefer] leads us to the brink of illness and death, and by this journey delivers us into the realm of recovery. We could have no better guide. —Cortney Davis. Schaefer has the eyesight of a nurse and the insight of a poet — a notable and unique case of double vision. —John Stone

Schaffner, M.A. *The Good Opinion of Squirrels.* 76p. pap. $10.00 (0-915380-34-X). Word Works/Writer's Center Editions, Fall 1996. Winner of the 1997 Columbia Book Award. The subject of these savagely smart, moving poems is who now lives in America's parks, cities, and exurbs, and Schaffner's recurring squirrels are not in fact anthropomorphic at all — quite the opposite. In their vivid and deflected landscapes, it's the nation's human inhabitants who tend to go animal, subtly or unmistakably. —Elizabeth Macklin

Scharper, Diane, ed. *Thy Mother's Glass: Poems for Mothers and Daughters.* 48p. pap. $8.95 (0-944806-11-2). Baltimore, MD: Icarus Books, Spring 1998. The poems in this chapbook offer an accurate and deeply-felt expression of the relationship between mothers and daughters. — Icarus Books

Schelling, Andrew. *The Road to Ocosingo.* 61p. pap. $6.00 (0-9658877-3-1). Erie, CO: Smokeproof Press, Fall 1998.

Schelling, Andrew, trans. Translated by Andrew Schelling. *The Cane Groves of Narmada River: Erotic Poems From Old India.* 90p. pap. $9.95 (0-87286-346-8). San Francisco, CA: City Lights Books, Fall 1998. Of all the world's ancient poetry, that of classical India was the most vividly erotic — uninhibited, tender, sad and joyous by turns. The poems sound as if they might have been written yesterday, although the period they cover ranges from roughly 200 CE until about the eleventh century. In old India, human love was intricately entwined with the natural world, and these short poems make a claim not only for sexual freedom but preservation of the wild. —City Lights Books. A brilliant selection of

refined, provocative, shivery-lovely poems. It has a generous bibliography and an astute introduction that illuminates both poetics and scholarship with its insights into the wealth of nature imagery, the implicit watershed consciousness, and a sense of the Wild as Tryst. What a gem of a book! It's the best gathering of Indian short poems yet. — Gary Snyder

Schmidt, Paul. *Night Life.* 81p. pap. $10.00 (0-9651558-0-3). New York, NY: Painted Leaf Press, Fall 1996. Night Life is a single utterance, for all its diversifications and masquerades, the seven or so next-to-last words: "I'm afraid. Find me, Daddy. Make me grow". The passion of a life spent, spilt, spoiled, and ultimately, by the poem itself, spared. —Richard Howard

Schmidt, Paul. *Winter Solstice.* 44p. pap. $10.00 (0-9651558-2-X). New York, NY: Painted Leaf Press, Fall 1996. In the streaming body of this prose poem Schmidt suggests "it says much for creation that language came last." Here it (language) bursts through holes, through pinpoints of light, an amazing poetic work of despair, glee, camaraderie & fetching brilliance—a short important work finally avail-

able, lately shed, maybe even
excreted from a very mad and
worth it American life —
Eileen Myles

Schneider, Ada Jill. *Fine
Lines and Other Wrinkles.*
72p. pap. $10.00 (0-9636068-
0-8). Dighton, MA: Grautlau
Press, 1995. These poems are
deeply felt, quietly private,
clearly crafted, and sculptured
with image and diction. They
never leave you off the hook.
—Mike Fink, Rhode Island
Jewish Herald

Schneider, Ada Jill. *The
Museum of My Mother.* 69p.
pap. $10.00 (0-963068-1-6).
Dighton, MA: Grautlau Press,
Fall 1996. Like pebbles left at
a graveside, Schneider's
poems, fiercely honest and
stubbornly unsentimental, give
testimony to a daughter's love,
and say for us all, "Mother, I
have been here." —Faye
Moskowitz

Schoenberger, Nancy. *Long
Like a River.* 81p. $25.00 (0-
8147-8105-5). pap. $12.95 (0-
8147-8104-7). New York, NY:
New York University Press,
Fall 1998. Winner of the 1997
NYU Press Prize for Poetry.
The deep sense of how our
world is one with the world
before history, the world of
myth, imbues Long Like a
River with the visionary rich-

ness we long for in poetry. —
Andrew Hudgins. Divinely
original Nancy Schoenberger!
Aesthetically daring and emotionally bold, she is all I look
for in a poet. At the same time
that Long Like a River
delights us with wordplay so
zesty it teases our tastebuds, it
pierces us with its ideas, memories, and locale. As readers
we are blessed by this voice
that never goes on too long or
cuts us off before full knowledge. Audaciously observed,
with non-stop eloquence,
Schoenberger employs her
thinking woman's lyricism to
present us with a world we
can fully enter — shimmering,
surprising, and profound. —
Molly Peacock. One wonders
why her name is not better
known and her poems not
more widely read. Among the
many poets whose recognition
is incommensurate with the
quality of their literary output,
Schoenberger surely ranks
highly. —Harvard Review

Scholnick, Michael. Edited
by Gary Lenhart, Steve
Levine, Greg Masters, and
Bob Rosenthal. *Clinch:
Selected Poems.* 95p. pap.
$12.95 (1-56689-070-5).
Minneapolis, MN: Coffee
House Press, Spring 1998. I
have long been an admirer of
Scholnick's poetry, both for
the twist and dash and bash of

its language and for its largeness of mind and bigness of heart. —Ron Padgett. Scholnick's lines surprise by giving pleasures one hadn't known one wanted and that turn out to be better than those one had expected. His poetry is the real thing. —Kenneth Koch

Schorb, E.M. *Murderer's Day.* 112p. pap. $12.95 (1-55753-120-X). West Lafayette, IN: Purdue University Press, Spring 1998. Winner of the Verna Emery Poetry Prize. Schorb's poems shine calmly even as they buzz with energy; are connaissant with world and yet transcend it; make something deeply funny and yet highly sad — given a world and a time and a good mind's eye. This is the work of a mature intelligence, its ironies unadulterated by cynicism, and its swells informed by understatement. A feisty book, a confident book, and in its own way, a furiously festive one. — Heather McHugh

Schreiner, Steven. *Too Soon To leave.* 72p. pap. $10.00 (1-56439-063-2). Detroit, MI: Ridgeway Press, Spring 1997. A beautiful voice is singing here, a song of mourning, a song of praise. Schreiner renders the difficulty of an individual life through adamant lyric clarity and finds consolation in the stark realm of the urban landscape and the wide expanse of the American wilderness. —Eric Pankey. Schreiner's poetry is infused with a lyric dignity of form and emotional intelligence. The feeling-tone of these poems is sustained again and again by a careful notation of mood and gesture. He is a scrupulous poet who never overstates: the pleasures and sorrows in these poems come to us clothed in language that suits them perfectly. Too Soon to Leave is a wonderful book. —Charles Baxter

Schug, Larry. *Obsessed With Mud.* 28p. pap. $4.95 (1-886895-10-4). Duluth, MN: Poetry Harbor, Fall 1997. Winner of the 1997 Poetry Harbor Chapbook Competition, these are poems about life in Central Minnesota. —Poetry Harbor

Schultz, Susan M. *Addenda.* 28p. Buffalo, NY: Meow Press, Fall 1998.

Schulz, Lawrence. *Say It Strong: Motion in Poetry.* 42p. pap. $6.00 (1-885021-05-4). Long Beach, CA: Orange Ocean Press, Spring 1997. This is poetry about life in Los Angeles and Orange County, written in an aggressive stand-up style. —Orange Ocean Press. Say It Strong is a story told through poems. To get the story, read these poems loud and fast! —G. Murray Thomas

Schwartz, Leonard. *Words Before the Articulate: New and Selected Poems.* 114p. pap. $10.50 (1-883689-53-8). Jersey City, NJ: Talisman House, Publishers, 1997. I can't imagine any problems more worth solving than the ones Schwartz has set himself here. Analytic under his daily knife, his days don't stop their thinking. I want to follow these thoughts as far as he takes them, because they lead so often and so kindly to my favorite place: pure contradiction. —Fanny Howe. Schwartz labors marvelously in a tradition that demands of its practitioners concision of expression, complexity of thought, and a voice that in the high lyric mode bespeaks the need for a transcendent and light-filled world to hold up against the delimiting immediacy of the senses. — American Book Review

Scott, E. Ray. *Empiric and Esthetic Thoughts.* 54p. pap. $8.95. Scott, E. Ray, Fall 1998.

Scott, Steve. *The St. Petersburg Fragments.* 30p. pap. $5.00 (0-940895-11-0). Chicago, IL: Cornerstone Press Chicago, Fall 1996.

Seay, James. *Open Field, Understory: New and Selected Poems.* 182p. $24.95 (0-8071-2129-0). Baton Rouge, LA: Louisiana State University Press, Spring 1997. Though southern to the core, Seay is also very much a part of the modern world we commonly know. He can decode its scrambled signals — from Russia to the Midi, Caribbean island to bayou fishing, Elvis to commissar. We go with him readily to place his world alongside our own and hear a voice speaking which is always honest, both complex and clear. —Elizabeth Spencer. [Seay's] rich meditations take a hard look at things as they are even as they burn through the darkness to fresh understanding. Clear, startling, luminous. —Edward Hirsch

Seid, Christopher. *Prayers to the Other Life.* 62p. pap. $9.95 (1-884235-20-4). Kansas City, MO: Helicon Nine Editions, Fall 1997. Winner of the 1997 Marianne Moore Poetry Prize. [This] book is much more than the sum total of its passions, impressively framed with unobtrusive discipline, and an appealing poetic line. This poet is clearly entering a new phase. —David Ray

Seidel, Frederick. *Going Fast.* 99p. $22.00 (0-374-16488-6). New York, NY: Farrar, Straus and Giroux, Spring 1998; Spring 2000 (new paper). Seidel spins paradoxes like tops, captures the jitteriness of city streets, the peculiar menace of nighttime interiors, the drama of a simple gesture, the terror of space, the sickening, whirling suck of violence. These poems are beautiful, but each is like a well-made glove covering a fist of iron: the soft and lambent veneer does nothing to soften the blow. —Booklist. In American poetry today there is no one with Seidel's sheer ambition, comprehensive sense of our times, sophistication, nerve, and skill. His unique embodiment of clashes between social and poetic truths makes him one of the most vital and important poets we have, wielding poems almost like daggers, but in blessing. —Lawrence Joseph, The Nation. [Seidel] grips the twentieth century between his teeth like a blade as he speaks. —Calvin Bedient, Poetry

Seifert, Jaroslav. Translated by Dana Loewy. *The Early Poetry of Jaroslav Seifert.*

221p. $25.00 (0-8101-1383-X). Northwestern University Press/Hydra Books, Fall 1997. Seifert's poetry is strongly situated within the Czech literary tradition of Poetism, which evolved into a playful, lighthearted refuge from world history while maintaining an edge of social consciousness. The playfulness of Seifert's early poetry expresses itself in anecdotes and witty aphorisms, and relies on such sound patterns as alliteration, assonance, and euphony. Beyond its obvious aesthetic interest, Seifert's early poetry also has a specific historical value as a manifestation of the avant-garde in the Europe of the 1920's and 1930's. —Northwestern University Press

Seifert, Jaroslav. Translated by Ewald Osers; Edited with prose translations by George Gibian. *The Poetry of Jaroslav Seifert.* 255p. pap. $14.95 (0-945774-39-7). Catbird Press/A Garrigue Book, Fall 1998. Poems by the first Czech to win the Nobel Prize for Literature. Although Seifert lived through the many historic turns of his homeland, his was not a political poetry, except in its constant expression of love for his homeland, its beauties and its values. His work was unpretentious, lyrical yet irreverent, earthy, charming. Seifert was known for the simplicity of his verse, yet his poems are full of surprises, never what they seem at first. They are marked by imagery that is beautiful or comical, by good, deep values, and by love in all its forms. — Catbird Press

Seiler, Barry. *Black Leaf.* 86p. $24.95 (1-884836-32-1). pap. $12.95 (1-884836-33-X). Akron, OH: University of Akron Press, Fall 1997. From the genuine horror of Sam Peckinpah to the tragic lyricism of Sam Cooke, Seiler's Black Leaf explores Americana with a poetic that announces to the reader that the mantra of what we know ourselves to be is all there is. Seiler takes Auden's origin of poetry in language and makes the subject happen. Black Leaf is exquisite poetry of subtle and ironic commitment, steeped in a love and respect for language. —Afaa M. Weaver

Selby, Spencer. *The Big R.* 90p. pap. $11.00 (0-9623806-7-9). Brooklyn, NY: Angle Press, Fall 1998.

Selwyn, David, ed. *The Poetry of Jane Austen and the Austen Family.* 106p. pap. $12.95 (0-87745-580-5). Iowa City, IA: University of Iowa Press, Spring 1997. Skilled and witty, these poems give pleasure to general readers and provide scholars with insight into a largely neglected, essentially private aspect of Austen's writing. — University of Iowa Press

Semansky, Chris. *Blindsided.* 26p. pap. $4.00. Portland, OR: 26 Books, Spring 1998.

Sepúlveda-Pulvirenti, Emma. Translated by Shaun T. Griffin. *Death to Silence: Muerte al silencio.* 100p. pap. $8.95 (1-55885-203-4). Houston, TX: Arte Público Press, Fall 1997. The terror and beauty that color this collection of powerfully spare and evocative poetry bear witness to the disquieting circumstances that inspired the poet, who fled Chile when the military junta led by Augusto Pinochet came to power in 1973. —Arte Publico Press. Sepúlveda's voice is ardent and passionate, whether mourning the brutal dictatorship of her native Chile, or in the open sensuality of her personal poems. She is a poet greatly daring and wonderfully passionate. —Carolyn Kizer

Serin, Judith. *Hiding in the World.* 98p. pap. $10.00 (0-9661671-0-4). San Francisco, CA: Eidolon Editions, Fall 1998. One of the open souls of poetry is swirled into these poems, and it is not so hidden. In fact, it is open-eyed and open-hearted. These words move with delicacy at the edge of consciousness. — Michael McClure. Serin's dreamlike poems move in crescendos from the personal to the archetypal. This is an unexpected and lyrical collection. —Diana O'Hehir

Seuss-Brakeman, Diane. *It Blows You Hollow.* 64p. pap. $12.00 (0-932826-65-2). Kalamazoo, MI: New Issues Press, Fall 1998. Full of beauty and violence in equal parts, relentless and incantatory, these poems confront whatever it is that guides us in a life that is sensuous, yet exacting in its terrible cost. —New Issues Press. These sensual and irreverent poems erupt with unexpected turns of language at once elegant and fierce. Reading them made the back hairs of my neck bristle in recognition that real poetry is going on here. Hers is a gift of metaphoric daring and wit that dazzles and consoles with elan, vital and probing truth. —Colette Inez

Seven American Poets. *A New Pléiade: Selected Poems.* 233p. $39.95 (0-8071-2329-3). pap. $18.95 (0-8071-2330-7). Baton Rouge, LA: Louisiana State University Press, Fall 1998. A celebration of close literary friendships among seven eminent American poets — Fred Chappell, Kelly Cherry, R.H.W. Dillard, Brendan Galvin, George Garrett, David R. Slavitt, and Henry Taylor. —Louisiana State University Press. A New Pléiade is a splendid idea, consisting as it does of a constellation of first-magnitude poets, all of them blessedly readable. —Richard Wilbur. Playfully comparing themselves to the seven 16th-century French poets Ronsard called La Pléiade, a community of seven distinguished American poets have at century's end made a selection of their poems that offers a prophecy of the continuing vitality of American poetry in the new millennium. —Lewis P. Simpson

Sewell, Lisa. *The Way Out.* 60p. pap. $9.95 (1-882295-17-X). Farmington, ME: Alice James Books, Spring 1998. Sewell's poetry brings to mind Keats' phrase, "thinking through the heart." More than any young poet writing today, her work frames an urgency shot through with history as she builds a model of consciousness, original, strange. These poems enact a lyric muscle that explodes narrative, throws it wonderfully off track into new regions of feeling, thought, experience. — Deborah Digges. "We are hopelessly enclosed by the measure of our skins," Sewell writes. The argument at the heart of this book is whether the body is a source of hopelessness or of hope. "I put my faith in the physical," Sewell tells us, but she understands how belief necessitates doubt. Focused and accomplished, this fine debut collection is a fierce and engaging quarrel with the fact of flesh. —Mark Doty

Sexton, Tom. *Leaving For a Year.* 20p. pap. $8.00 (0-938566-79-2). Easthampton, MA: Adastra Press, Fall 1998. Fourteen poems by Alaska's Poet Laureate about returning to his native New England. — Adastra Press

Seyburn, Patty. *Diasporadic.* 94p. pap. $9.95 (1-884235-26-3). Kansas City, MO: Helicon Nine Editions, Fall 1998. Winner of the 1997 Marianne Moore Poetry Prize. What distinguishes Seyburn's first volume of poetry is her magic habit of managing disparate

but simultaneous perspectives. Almost yoga-like, she seems able to train her focus at once on big subjects and small details as if she had a different capacity for perspective than the rest of us. Her poems are created from an alluring willingness not to know all the answers, and thus to be able to interpret the world for us flexibly, in all its excitement and mystification. —Molly Peacock. For Seyburn, presence of mind means being mindful of the past; it is without the consolation of forgetting that she opens that presence, that mind — open at both ends, therefore, a perspective of transit. What capacities for movement she registers, what conundrums for meaning she resolves! — Richard Howard

Shabtai, Aharon. Translated by Peter Cole. *Love and Selected Poems.* 222p. $24.95 (1-878818-53-8). Riverdale-on-Hudson, NY: Sheep Meadow Press, Fall 1997. In his fusions of the sensual and the spiritual, the ordinary and the exalted, the sexual in the suffering psyche and the intelligent consciousness searching and spinning through history, myth and layers of language, Shabtai is one of the most exciting poets writing anywhere, and certainly the most audacious. The poems have a wonderful almost vertiginous energy, an enormous erudition, and a startling, finally inspiring candor. A splendid book, brilliantly translated by Peter Cole. —C.K. Williams

Shaffer, Gregory. Illustrations by Ewa Kuryluk. *Forest.* 28p. Artemis Art Gallery, Spring 1998. Shaffer's poetry is a delight. Carefully observant, Shaffer looks at nature and the human condition with exquisite precision. Deeply lyrical, these heartfelt poems are breathtaking. —Kathleen Spivack

Shange, Ntozake. *For Colored Girls Who Have Considered Suicide/When the Rainbow Is Enuf: A Choreopoem.* 64p. pap. $8.00 (0-684-84326-9). New York, NY: Simon & Schuster/Scribner, Fall 1997. Remember when poetry used to give you chills, make you tremble? Shange writes that kind of rousing poetry. It has the power to move a body to tears, to rage, and to an ultimate rush of love. —Marilyn Stasio, Cue. Shange celebrates the capacity to master pain and betrayal with wit, sister-sharing, reckless daring, and flight and forgetfulness if necessary. She celebrates most of all women's loyalties to

women. —Toni Cade Bambara, Ms.

Shapiro, Harvey. *Selected Poems.* 104p. pap. $12.95 (0-8195-2252-X). University Press of New England/Wesleyan University Press, Fall 1997. Shapiro's voice is unmistakably of the city yet by virtue of the intensity of his reaction to the city, in his seeking, holding, loving and longing and bitterness, he distinguishes himself from the chaos often with lyrical poignancy, elsewhere with sardonic wit. —David Ignatow. Shapiro writes in sardonic reverence. [His poetry] is modest, usually simple, but precise, courageous, and unflinching in its sadness. —Hayden Carruth, The Nation. Working within the conventions of alienation and isolation, [Shapiro] develops a quietly distinctive and forceful idiom. —Samuel French Morse, New York Times Book Review

Shapiro, Karl. Edited by Stanley Kunitz and David Ignatow. *The Wild Card: Selected Poems, Early and Late.* 224p. $26.95 (0-252-02389-7). pap. $18.95 (0-252-06689-8). Champaign, IL: University of Illinois Press, Fall 1998. Shapiro is an American poetic treasure and an acknowledged master of lyrical poetry whose subjects have ranged from commonplace objects and occurences to biting political commentary to open celebrations of the necessary contradictions in humanity's moral nature. — University of Illinois Press. This selection reminds us that Shapiro has for decades thought and felt honestly about poetry, history, society and family, and is a rewarding sampling of the work that thought has produced. — Publisher's Weekly

Shapiro, Norman R., trans. *The Comedy of Eros: Medieval French Guides to the Art of Love, 2nd Edition.* 160p. pap. $14.95 (0-252-06581-6). Champaign, IL: University of Illinois Press, Spring 1997. The Comedy of Eros, a high-spirited collection of medieval French love poetry in modern translation, takes delightful advantage of the preoccupation of writers of that time and place with love and sex. Decidedly sexist by today's standards, it offers the modern reader translations from seven texts, among them Ovid's Ars armatoria, one of the earliest "practical" love guides—a satirical treatise chockablock with shrewd tips for seducers and lovers. — University of Illinois Press.

Shapiro, Susan. *Internal Medicine.* 64p. pap. $10.00 (0-9654651-1-X). Takoma Park, MD: IM Press, Fal 1997. [Shapiro] knows that "unborn souls choose their mothers" and that poets are chosen by their poems. Her voice is passionate and honest. Of course she is a witch, it goes with the territory. —Erica Jong. The paintings of Chagall, stories of Sholem Aleichem, music of klezmer bands — all contained in a debut collection of poignant, hilarious monologues and meta-vignettes. Whether describing family, friends, or coming of age as a "young woman of ambition" in New York, Shapiro plays doctor with memory and desire. Internal Medicine does not sugar-coat the pill, but its bittersweet pizzazz promises a cure for fin-du-millénaire pallor in American poetry. —James Reiss

Sharp, Tom. *Spectacles: A Sampler of Poems and Prose.* 83p. pap. $10.95 (0-931552-10-9). San Francisco, CA: Taurean Horn Press, Spring 1998. These poems are in the Imagist line and acknowledge their models, especially Williams and Creeley and Eigner. They are language poetry before it became too mannered in its self-regard. —Albert Gelpi

Sheck, Laurie. *The Willow Grove.* 70p. $21.00 (0-679-44714-8). pap. $13.00 (0-679-76603-0). New York, NY: Knopf, Alfred A., Spring 1996; Fall 1997 (paper). [Sheck's] lines are fluid and seductive, the images powerful and arresting, and the voice insistent. This is a poet who sees beauty and danger as parallel forces, and senses with some dread the fragility of our human arrangements. —Suzanne Matson, Harvard Review. The poems interconnect so deeply that the book is nearly one poem. A common spirit rises so directly from these poems' source that it is nearly invisible on its first reading. But it is essential, and rises through them as water through trees. The language is confident and accurate, its images tracking reality with utmost care. —Pamela Alexander, The Boston Book Review

Sheehan, John. *Leaving Gary.* 64p. pap. $10.95 (1-882688-16-3). Chicago, IL: Tia Chucha Press, Fall 1997. Rooted in the social activism of Vatican II and the sixties, Sheehan's work confronts issues of race and class, religion and landscape, memory and media, chronicling places which have changed and places we wish we could change. —Tia Chucha Press. Luminous, life affirming and radiant. —Tony Fitzpatrick. Sheehan is one of the few poets I know to combine politics and spirituality and irony and truth in a single poem that can work in a powerfully moving way. Here is a sensitive, forthright poet who reminds us again and again of the challenge and complexity of human life. In his hand, almost every poem speaks with the voice of authentic humanism. —Charles Tinkham

Sheehan, Marc. *Greatest Hits.* 67p. pap. $12.00 (0-932826-63-6). Kalamazoo, MI: New Issues Press, Fall 1998. Sheehan tells the story of the dispossessed better than anyone since Raymond Carver. In a voice that is gentle yet honest, he is able to lay bare our most desperate moments and to leave in the stillness a redemption offered up by something as simple and beautiful as a blue snake gliding over stones at the edge of a grassy quarry. —New Issues Press. These are such well-made poems. Manifest is the sharp edge of self-editing and a careful ear. Sheehan understands the traffic between myth and biography, the space between utterance and quiet. Greatest Hits is a powerful

and welcome debut. —
Thomas Lynch

Shepard, Neil. *I'm Here Because I Lost My Way.* 120p. pap. $12.00 (0-922811-38-5). Minneapolis, MN: Mid-List Press, Fall 1998. In Shepard's moving and delicate new collection, nature's quietly shimmering veil resonates with those few moments of true human grace any of us are allowed. These poems are filled with the same passion and deft humor we've come to expect from all of Shepard's marvelous work. —David St. John. Shepard writes essential, elegant poems. As much about recovery as loss of any kind, this work is rich with evocations and layers, a stunning interplay of language and scenes. —Naomi Shihab Nye. From the bitter stuff of history, the filmy stuff of memory, Shepard makes phoenix poems of resurrection and second chances seized. His work bears brilliant witness in a language free of polemics and rich with the sustenance of art. Few poets understand — or restore — so much. —Alice Fulton

Shepherd, Reginald. *Angel, Interrupted.* 96p. $24.95 (0-8229-3960-6). pap. $10.95 (0-8229-5614-4). Pittsburgh, PA: University of Pittsburgh Press, Fall 1996. *Angel, Interrupted* is written on water. Fluid, bright, and moving, fully aware of the fleeting beauty of the things of this world, these poems catch the light between lyric and myth. —Susan Stewart. This is a book of unabashed lyricism and in-your-face contemporaneity, bristling with intelligence, challenging the reader to envision at once the panhandlers of Chicago and the princes of Troy, the iconic beauty of Narcissus or Antinoüs superimposed upon numinous black and white American bodies in warily passionate embrace. — Marilyn Hacker

Sherman, Bill. *From the South Seas: A Small Selection of Recent Poems.* 20p. pap. $15.00 (0-9615784-7-5). Margate, NJ: Branch Redd Books, Spring 1997. Romantic, yet innovative non-formalist poetry. —Branch Redd Books

Sherman, Joan R., ed. *African-American Poetry: An Anthology, 1773-1927.* 96p. pap. $1.00 (0-486-29604-0). Mineola, NY: Dover Publications, Spring 1997. This anthology offers a rich selection of 74 poems ranging form the religious and moral verse of Phillis Wheatley Peters to the 20th century work of Countee Cullen and Langston Hughes. —Dover Publications

Shiedermayer, David L., M.D. *House Calls, Rounds, and Healings: A Poetry Casebook.* 190p. pap. $12.95 (1-883620-17-1). Tucson, AZ: Galen Press, Fall 1996. Each poem is a case-study of a patient or colleague who has stirred the author's thoughts. Written by a practicing internist, these verses lower the physician's mask to reveal the human vulnerabilities within and capture feelings that many physicians experience, but cannot express. — Galen Press. If every medical student in the country received a gift of this book, I have no doubt that the next generation of physicians would be more perceptive and more sensitive. They would also more fully enjoy the practice of medicine and their patients as people, and society would begin to respect doctors the way it once did. —C. Everett Koop, M.D., Sc.D., Surgeon General

Shields, Bill. *Lifetaker.* 120p. pap. $11.00 (1-880985-30-6). Los Angeles, CA: 2.13.61 Publications, 1995. The third installment of Shields' unique American nightmare, Lifetaker resonates with the shattered memories that remain arcwelded to his soul. An uncompromising collection of poetry, Lifetaker drags his memories kicking and screaming into the present, and spares no one, including the author himself, from the horrors of the Vietnam War. — 2.13.61 Publications

Shiki, Masaoka. Translated by Burton Watson. *Selected Poems.* 117p. $45.00 (0-231-11090-1). pap. $16.50 (0-231-11091-X). Irvington, NY: Columbia University Press, Fall 1997. Here are graceful and timeless poems by one of Japan's greatest modern writers, rendered by a master translator. Shiki is credited with modernizing Japan's two traditional verse forms, haiku and tanka. He freed them from outdated conventions, made them viable for artistic expression in modern Japan, and paved the way for the haiku to become one of his nation's most influential cultural exports. These poems — more than a hundred haiku, several tanka and three kanshi— are arranged chronologically within in each genre, revealing the development of Shiki's art and the seamless way in which he wove his life into his poetry. —Columbia University Press

Shirley, Aleda. *Long Distance.* 77p. pap. $11.95 (1-881163-17-2). Oxford, OH: Miami University Press, Fall 1996. Shirley pays close attention to craft, and her language resonates with an honesty and openness to experience that is both seductive and refreshing. —Library Journal. Her work is remarkably touching. — Alice Fulton, Poetry

Sholl, Betsy. *Don't Explain.* 65p. $17.95 (0-299-15720-2). pap. $10.95 (0-299-15724-5). Madison, WI: University of Wisconsin Press, Fall 1997. Winner of the 1997 Felix Pollak Prize in Poetry. Don't Explain accomplishes that most difficult of tasks: the weaving together of seemingly unrelated events so that revelation unfolds effortlessly. These poems are what narrative can aspire to — namely, the grace and ease of the lyric rhapsody. And yet the charm of the anecdotes, Sholl's facility with line and image, never take precedence over the hard facts of our daily living. — Rita Dove. Sholl's poems insist that there is no separation between self and world, and that the moral duty of poetry is to carry the world with the same delicacy and grace with which their speaker bears herself. Don't Explain is

an urgent and prophetic book. —David Wojahn

Shomer, Enid. *Black Drum.* 88p. $22.00 (1-55728-494-6). pap. $14.00 (1-55728-497-0). Fayetteville, AR: University of Arkansas Press, Fall 1997. Shomer gets better and better. This is mature, engaging work, taking "only one tomorrow at a time." Shomer uses form with extraordinary grace and seems almost effortlessly to achieve a level of passion rare in today's poetry. — Maxine Kumin. Each of these poems has truths that are shocked into language and shine with the new brightness of their minting. This is a strong, serious book by a writer who has mastered her art. —Harvey Shapiro

Shore, Jane. *Music Minus One.* 107p. $20.00 (0-312-14686-8). pap. $10.00 (0-312-16944-2). New York, NY: Picador USA, Fall 1996. Finalist for the National Book Critics Circle Award. Music Minus One is resolutely autobiographical, reaching from [Shore's] 1950's New Jersey childhood, through her adolescence and sexual awakening to her acknowledgment of maturity, occassioned by her daughter's birth and her parents' death. This impressive sequence imparts a sense of deepening consciousness, of shifts in perspective over time. The poems [form] a seamless arc of personal history, both artful and accessible. — Gardner McFall, The New York Times Book Review

Shotetsu. Translated by Steven D. Carter. *Unforgotten Dreams: Poems by the Zen Monk Shótetsu.* 232p. pap. $17.50 (0-231-10577-0). Irvington, NY: Columbia University Press, Spring 1997. The Zen monk Shotetsu (1381-1459) is widely considered to be the last great poet of the classical waka tradition. Though his more than 11,000 poems comprise the single largest body of work in the Japanese canon, this is the first major collection of it in English. —Columbia University Press. The work of Shotetsu is the great undiscovered country of medieval waka. Rich in fantasy, by turns earthly and pitilessly stark, it has found a modern master whose own experimental technique sets the standard for contemporary translation. — Edwin A. Cranston

Shugrue, Jim. *Icewater.* 34p. pap. $7.00 (0-932264-20-4). Portland, OR: Trask House Books, 1997.

Shuntarô, Tanikawa. Translated by Harold Wright. *Map of Days.* 107p. pap. $12.95 (0-942668-50-2). University of Hawai'i Press/Katydid Books, Fall 1996. Shuntarô is contemporary Japan's most widely read poet and its most adventurous. —Kitagawa Toru

Sia, Beau. *A Night Without Armor II: The Revenge.* 128p. pap. $10.00 (0-966204-29-8). Mouth Almighty Books, Fall 1998. A funny spoof of pop sensation Jewel's bestselling poetry collection. —Publishers Weekly. Hers is flowery and sensitive. His is wry and absurd. —USA Today

Siamanto. Translated by Peter Balakian and Nevart Yaghlian. *Bloody News From My Friend.* 80p. pap. $12.95 (0-8143-2640-4). Detroit, MI: Wayne State University Press, Fall 1996. Siamanto (1878-1915), one of the most important Armenian poets of the twentieth-century, was among the Armenian intellectuals executed by the Turkish government at the onset of the genocide during the first decade of the century. Available for the first time in English translation, his Bloody News From My Friend depicts the atrocities committed by the Ottoman Turkish government against its Armenian population. The cycle of twelve poems bears the imprint of genocide in a language that is raw and blunt; it often eschews metaphor and symbol for more stark representation. Siamanto confronts pain, destruction, sadism, and torture as few modern poets have. —Wayne State University Press

Sidney, Philip. Edited by Elizabeth Porges Watson. *Defence of Poesie, Astrophil and Stella and Other Writings.* 208p. pap. $8.95 (0-460-87659-7). Boston, MA: Tuttle, Charles E./Everyman, Fall 1997. The most comprehensive select edition available, with introduction, notes and chronology of Sidney's life and times. —Charles E. Tuttle/Everyman

Siegel, Amie. *The Waking Life.* 90p. pap. $11.95 (1-55643-297-6). Berkeley, CA: North Atlantic Books, Fall 1998. There is a freshness here, a lucid non-linear discourse we have not heard before. What excites is the sensuous complexity of thought spoken clear and spacious. Siegel doesn't sound like anybody else — all the old tunelessnesses give way to real writing: she makes the page talk. —Robert Kelly. Her

language is always firm, yet unexpected and searching. An impressive volume, by an impressive young poet. — Elizabeth Frank

Sikelianos, Eleni. *The Book of Tendons.* 40p. pap. $7.00 (0-942996-29-1). Sausalito, CA: Post-Apollo Press, Fall 1997. These taut beautiful poems are full of curious resonances. The past and future run through the body of this work like streams flowing mysteriously through words or rivers "slipping between atoms." In the process the ungovernable darkness of language pours through. —Peter Gizzi

Silk, Dennis. *William the Wonder-Kid: Plays, Puppet Plays and Theater Writings.* 251p. pap. $13.95 (1-878818-50-3). Riverdale-on-Hudson, NY: Sheep Meadow Press, Fall 1996. Silk is a delicious poet. Utterly natural, entirely himself, he works by a curious method. What he does, in his easy way, is to surround the inexpressible, which is charmed by his siege and surrenders. It's all very simple. —Saul Bellow

Silver, Alice Moolten. *Climbing the Acropolis.* 63p. pap. $9.95 (1-886094-48-9). Louisville, KY: Chicago Spectrum Press, Fall 1996.

The reflections of a woman experiencing the modern world. The book contains selected new and previously published poems and a tribute to an unusual marriage. — Chicago Spectrum Press

Silverthorne, Marty. *Pot Liquor Promises.* 30p. (1-879009-26-9). Whispering Pines, NC: Persephone Press, Fall 1997. I admire the strength and clarity of [Silverthorne's] poems. — Maxine Kumin. Gutsy, intuitive and tender in person and in his poetry. The Muse could not ask a truer attendant. — Ron Bayes

Simpson, Louis, ed. *Modern Poets of France.* 468p. pap. $16.95 (1-885266-44-8). Ashland, OR: Story Line Press, Fall 1996. In this bilingual anthology, editor and translator Simpson selects those masterpieces of French poetry that formed the taste of generations of readers throughout the world. Here are the "moderns" of 1848, the Symbolist poets of the turn of the century, the Dadaists, and the Surrealists who flourished in the 1930's. Also included are biographies of the poets and descriptions of main literary movements. —Story Line Press

Sirowitz, Hal. *My Therapist Said.* 143p. $15.00 (0-609-60130-x). New York, NY: Crown Publishers, Spring 1998. By putting his therapist's advice into poetry, [Sirowitz] conjures up some of his funniest work yet. [His] most intimate experiences are pasted onto the page with that deadpan humor that has become [Sirowitz's] trademark. —Crown Publishers. Deadpan Sirowitz has found a niche as the performance-poet cousin of those Jewish comedians and fictioneers who channel their angst into art. —Publishers Weekly

Skellings, Edmund. *Collected Poems 1958-1998.* 291p. $29.95 (0-8130-1606-1). Gainesville, FL: University Press of Florida, Fall 1998. This collection presents the most compelling work of Skellings, Poet Laureate of Florida. It gathers together poems from five books and includes a reading on compact disk of fifty of them. A foreword by critic Donald L. Kaufmann discusses Skellings's major themes and purposes and places him in the tradition of contemporary American letters. —University Press of Florida. At their best, [his poems] shine like silver in the sun. —Norman Mailer. Racy gifts. They hardly hold

themselves down to earth. —
Richard Eberhart

Skoyles, John. *Definition of the Soul.* 61p. $20.95 (0-88748-260-0). pap. $11.95 (0-88748-261-9). Pittsburgh, PA: Carnegie Mellon University Press, Spring 1998. [Skoyles] lyric, compassionate and observant poems project simultaneously a dignity and a modesty which is not quite like any other contemporary poet. —Puerto del Sol. Poems written with a receptive ear for music, a visceral sense of rhythm, and a penetrating vision through the ordinary. —The American Book Review.

Slavitt, David R. *Epic and Epigram: Two Elizabethan Entertainments.* 64p. $19.95 (0-8071-2151-7). pap. $11.95 (0-8071-2152-5). Baton Rouge, LA: Louisiana State University Press, Spring 1997. Rendering Latin's pointed brevity into English is never easy, but Slavitt's agile versions of John Owen's once famous verses manage smartly. His amusing epigrams seem surprisingly comfortable next to meditations on The Faerie Queen by a narrator who is sometimes that epic's sharp-eyed and dirty tongued villainess and sometimes, more or less, the poet himself

as he associates the often dim witted hero's adventures with later European history and the story of Slavitt's own family. —Louisiana State University Press. Steeped in the great Roman satirists, Slavitt speaks as confidently as they did of the heart's resistance to human folly and human wisdom, both. The collation of Spenser and the current English royal family in the epic section of this book — smart, funny, but not, thank Jupiter, "wise" — would make Alexander Pope's ghost giggle. —William Matthews

Slavitt, David R. *PS3569.L3.* 88p. $19.95 (0-8071-2300-5). pap. $12.95 (0-8071-2301-3). Baton Rouge, LA: Louisiana State University Press, Fall 1998. What a treat it is to come upon another collection of Slavitt's poetry, to witness once again his incomparable combination of erudition and irreverence. It's like watching Harlequin strolling on a high wire from felicity to wit, from wry self-mockery to unflinching sympathy, alternately evoking gasps and belly-laughter. This is definitely a collection to relish and treasure. —Donald Finkel. PS3569.L3 confirms Slavitt's reputation and virtuosity and stands as his most elegantly constructed book of poems thus far, opening doors that have been closed too long to much contemporary poetry. This is a book to cherish and admire. —George Garrett. Equal parts elegy, Wisdom Literature, and satire, PS3569.L3 is bound to move, delight, and enrage the poetry audience. In Slavitt's masterful new poems we find the child's burning curiosity and playfulness tempered by the sage's cold wit. —Daniel Mark Epstein

Sloan, Mary Margaret. *Moving Borders: Three Decades of Innovative Writing by Women.* 744p. pap. $36.00 (1-883689-47-3). Jersey City, NJ: Talisman House, Publishers, Spring 1998. A major anthology, providing an essential source for the best writing of our time. It is the specificity of each author's art that is most rewarding here: the exhilarating originality of each poetic project and the deep reflection with which these poets explore not just poetry but the possibilities of meaning through language. —Charles Bernstein. In its range, breadth, discrimination, and selectivity, as well as its profound knowledge of the "state of the art," Moving Borders bears witness to the very real revolution that has occurred in the poetry of

North American women over the past three decades. Sloan's Borders are indeed Moving: from the lyric to visual text, from prose poem to documentary collage, and from the poems themselves to the astonishingly varied poetics that animate them. For anyone who still believes that the poetry of our time is "marginalized" or in decline, Sloan has provided an ideal port of entry. —Marjorie Perloff

Sloman, Joel. *Stops.* 128p. $19.95 (0-944072-82-8). Cambridge, MA: Zoland Books, Spring 1998. Sloman can evoke sensory impressions with thrilling, hallucinatory precision; among them his anxious questions vanish and reappear like pilgrims wandering in an immense but enticing forest. —Denise Levertov. Sloman's poetries seem in a lineage with the postmodern strum of discursive rhythm and language play — shiny at the surface, deep at the center. The poems reflect an ongoing keen relationship with a still conceivable natural world. — Anne Waldman

Sloss, Henry. *The Threshold of the New.* 95p. $15.95 (1-57003-234-3). pap. $9.95 (1-57003-235-1). Columbia, SC: University of South Carolina Press, Fall 1997. The

Threshold of the New is an odyssey of pure wonder. Sloss writes of a new beginning in Italy with fresh insights and with depth. "Until a world that would not have occurred / To us becomes both real and heaven sent." He is engaging, passionate, and delightful. — Grace Schulman

Smart, Ninian. *Smart Verse: The Owl Flies Amid the Wood Wind Hooting.* 128p. pap. $9.50 (1-56474-171-0). Santa Barbara, CA: Fithian Press, Fall 1996. Poems about theology, current events, geography and the quirks that make us human, written by one whom Publishers Weekly dubbed "one of the grandfathers of the study of the history of religion. —Fithian Press

Smith, Charlie. *Before and After.* $21.00 (0-393-03775-4). New York, NY: Norton, W.W., and Company, Spring 1995; Spring 1997 (paper). In some family narratives, the romance fades with the accelerated disappearance of stars at dawn. In Smith's new collection, the constellation of the family reverberates with loss, and from these sketches of the poet's mother and father there emerges, drawn inevitably with the bluntest of gestures, his own self-portrait. Though the songs of the son may

often, in the end, grow hollow and spare in their sadness, the poems of Before and After remain resilient, faithful and brave. —David St. John. Of his generation in America, [Smith] is one of the most prodigiously gifted. —Robert Phillips. [Smith] shows us his power without seeming to try — one mark of a major poet. —Publishers Weekly

Smith, Daniel; Edwina Pendarvis, and Philip St. Clair. *Human Landscapes: Three Books of Poems.* 184p. pap. $10.95 (0-933087-42-X). Huron, OH: Bottom Dog Press, Spring 1997. These Midwest poets speak their people and place—Illinois, Ohio, West Virginia. Three collections of poetry by Edwina Pendarvis, Daniel Smith, and Philip St. Clair. — Bottom Dog Press

Smith, Joan Jobe. *Bukowski Boulevard.* 48p. pap. $10.00 (1-888219-10-6). Long Beach, CA: Pearl Editions, Fall 1998. Although Smith's poems reflect Bukowski's raunch, she is never submerged by him. She blends humor with poignancy [and] go-go dances always to her own beat. — Robert Peters, Chiron Review

Smith, Larry, and Mei Hui Huang, trans. *Chinese Zen*

Poems: What Hold Has This Mountain?. 112p. pap. $8.95 (0-933087-49-7). Huron, OH: Bottom Dog Press, Fall 1998. A fresh bilingual collection of more than 100 poems from China, selected and translated for their Zen spirit. Drawn from twenty centuries of writing, the book includes poems by such favorites as Han Shan, Wang Wei, Li Po, and Tu Fu. —Bottom Dog Press

Smith, Laura, ed. *Nature: Pocket Poems #2.* 36p. pap. $2.00 (0-933087-46-2). Huron, OH: Bottom Dog Press, Fall 1997. A collection of 20 Midwestern poets celebrating nature. These poems evoke a remembrance that, beneath the asphalt pathway, under the sprawl of industry, there remains a low constant hum of water /sky/ earth, its creatures and greens. —Laura Smith

Smith, Patti. *The Coral Sea.* 272p. pap. $12.00 (0-393-31626-2). New York, NY: Norton, W.W., and Company, Spring 1996; Fall 1997 (paper). In elegant and lyrical prose, Smith honors Robert Mapplethorpe (1946-1989). In linked pieces, she tells the story of a man on a journey to see the Southern Cross, who is reflecting on his life and fighting the illness that is consum-

ing him. Metaphoric and dreamy, this tale of transformation arises from Smith's knowledge of Mapplethorpe as a young man and as a mature artist, his years surviving AIDS, and his ascent into death. Set against photographs by Mapplethorpe, the work emerges as a hymn, a prayer, a fable wishing him Godspeed on his latest journey. —W.W. Norton. Through these poems, a singular, glowing vision of Robert Mapplethorpe emerges. In The Coral Sea, Smith (in the words of Tennessee Williams) "rings the bell of pure poetry." — William S. Burroughs

Smith, W. Loran. *Night Train.* 71p. $24.00 (1-887628-00-2). pap. $12.00 (1-887628-01-0). West Hartford, CT: Plinth Books, Spring 1997. If you're planning to sip tea while reading this, you might consider changing into something asbestos. Smith's poetry is not of the effete European Culture Tour genre; it's a night train, as it says, a bruising rocket-of-a-ride with one of the lords of the local netherworld where the only scenic wonder you're likely to encounter is beauty smoking up from random head-on collisions of otherwise anonymous lives. In the tradition of Levine, Ginsberg, Corso, and

Burroughs, Smith has lived this hard-bitten stuff. He's one of us. —Jack Myers. *Night Train* makes for a reading experience as compelling as any novel. It is as dark, mysterious, and rooted in our collective fantasies and dreams as its title suggest. —Richard Tillinghast

Smith, William Jay. *The World Below the Window: Poems 1937-1997.* 240p. $29.95 (0-8018-5859-3). Baltimore, MD: Johns Hopkins University Press, Spring 1998. Grace, a highly personal and responsible relation to form, and effortless and natural imagination combine in Smith's poems to create an atmosphere which is a valuable, liveable space. When wit is added, as it often is, his art becomes inimitable indeed. No one should miss these poems. —James Dickey. A most gifted and original poet. One of the very few who cannot be confused with anybody else. —Richard Wilbur. Smith has given us many of the truest and purest poems an American has written: the most resonantly musical, the most magical. —X.J. Kennedy

Smock, Frederick, ed. *The American Voice Anthology of Poetry.* 130p. (0-8131-0956-6). University Press of Kentucky, Fall 1998. This fifteenth anniversary anthology collects eighty poems from some of the most original and daring writers of our time; [it] brings together some of the best selections from an award-winning journal, making clear why Small Press dubbed The American Voice one of the "most impressive journals in the country." —University Press of Kentucky

Sneed, Pamela. *Imagine Being More Afraid of Freedom Than Slavery.* 80p. $22.00 (0-8050-5473-1). pap. $12.00 (0-8050-5474-X). New York, NY: Holt, Henry, and Company, Spring 1998. Imagine Being More Afraid of Freedom Than Slavery is lyrical and provocative, humorous and potent as it tackles both personal and contemporary issues of enslavement, sexuality, psychological trauma, and physical abuse. From beginning to end, these poems chart the journey that is life and one woman's cycle of dependency as she recovers her lost identity. —Henry Holt and Company. If a sledgehammer could whisper, its name would be Pamela Sneed. —Boston Globe

Snively, Susan. *The Undertow.* 76p. $19.95 (0-8130-1568-5). pap. $10.95 (0-8130-1569-3). Gainesville,

FL: University Press of Florida, Spring 1998. Clean-cut, fluent, witty, direct, full of personality and surprise. Snively can also be deeply meditative, grave and affecting, uproarious. In all her work, which varies expertly in form as well as mood, her words have a delectable texture. —Richard Wilbur. Reading Snively's poems is like sitting next to a great talker at a dinner party. Full of stories, jokes, digressions, and wicked little asides, they seduce and entertain. But beneath the protective coloration of their wry and witty surfaces, something else is happening. The poems' real work is to strip away whatever obscures the heart's true story, and to look long and hard at the history of damages done over the years. In The Undertow, grief and joy dance together, inseparable. —Chase Twichell

Snodgrass, W. D., trans. *Selected Translations.* 156p. pap. $13.50 (1-880238-60-8). Rochester, NY: BOA Editions, Spring 1998. This collection includes little-known Eastern European poets as well as celebrated poets, troubadours and composers. It offers us the imaginative power and the playful wisdom of poems, folk songs, fables, street songs,

drinking lyrics, ballads and art songs gleaned from more than five-hundred years of Western tradition. —BOA Editions

Snow, Carol. *Bowl.* 16p. pap. $15.00 (1-889589-03-9). Mill Valley, CA: Em Press, Fall 1998. With a clear and generous precision, Snow transcribes her acute scrutiny of the pitch and cadence of the thinking mind. —Em Press. Snow is cunning, subtle, and she can write. —Robert Hass

Snydal, James. *Living in America.* 36p. pap. $4.95 (0-9648133-7-8). Tulsa, OK: New Thought Journal Press, Spring 1997. A panorama of American history in verse telling stories about Walt Whitman, Edward Hopper, Robert Oppenheimer, the death of John Lennon, Vietnam demonstrations and the author's own battle with cancer. —New Thought Journal Press

Snyder, Gary. *Mountains and Rivers Without End.* 166p. $20.00 (1-887178-20-1). Washington, DC: Counterpoint, Fall 1996. Snyder's ardent fans have waited patiently through the past forty years for the completion of Mountains and Rivers Without End. The entire work appears for the

first time in this volume. It is
an epic of geology, prehistory,
and planetary mythologies, a
poem about land and its
processes, a book about wisdom, compassion and myth,
and a narrative work that is
not quite like anything else. It
will stand as a masterpiece for
the long poem in English. —
Counterpoint

Sobin, Gustaf. *Articles of
Light & Elation.* 46p. (0-
932274-53-6). Tiburon-
Belvedere, CA: Cadmus
Editions, Fall 1998.

Sobin, Gustaf. *Towards the
Blanched Alphabets.* 123p.
(1-883689-67-8). Jersey City,
NJ: Talisman House,
Publishers, Fall 1998. Cast
against the tenuous landscapes
of human history, Sobin's latest collection of poems celebrates the redemptive power
of language in its encounter
with that history. Voice arises
out of vestige; sound, out of
shattered artifact. Sobin creates, out of so many meticulously measured components,
a poetry — as much lyric as
reflective — of luminous disclosure. —Talisman House. A
consummate poet. —Robert
Creeley. Sobin's is a music of
the spoken which bears witness to the struggle of word
and world to overcome the
distances. It is a music we've

never heard before, and it is
very old. —Michael Palmer

Solan, Miriam. *A Woman
Combing.* 118p. pap. $10.00
(1-889097-11-X). West
Stockbridge, MA: Hard Press,
Fall 1997. Solan's lively,
inventive poems are a tonic
reminder that the world need
not be excluded from the language it generates. This is a
terrific book, brimming with
much needed fresh air. —
Charles North. A true language lover, entangling and
disentangling fun and grief.
—Grace Paley

Solensten, John.
Curmudgeon. 32p. pap. $4.00.
Talent, OR: Talent House
Press, Fall 1998.

Sommer, Jason. *Other
People's Troubles.* 68p. $26.00
(0-226-76815-5). pap. $12.95
(0-226-76816-3). Chicago, IL:
University of Chicago Press,
Fall 1997. Sommer writes of
troubles that unfold at the
intersection of self and other,
of wakefulness and sleep. Son
of a Holocaust survivor, he
lives in a Post-Holocaust
world, and the poetic voice in
this book emerges from that
calamity, telling the stories of
those who have finally begun
to speak to him, and now
through him. As a survivor's
child, Sommer must consider

how to live in the wake of history, among those who are indelibly marked by it. Moved by their pain and survival, he seeks the stories that they cannot tell, hoping to compensate their losses in words. This book will interest not only teachers and students of poetry and creative writing, but all those affected by the Holocaust. —University of Chicago Press. [An] evocative, funny, sad, and damn near perfect new book. —H.L. Hix, Ploughshares. These poems honed from the past and present are heartfelt epistles to the future. All the hard topics are tackled with grace and care. —Yusef Komunyakaa

Somoza, Joseph. *Sojourner, So to Speak.* 98p. pap. $12.00 (1-888809-04-3). Albuquerque, NM: La Alameda Press, Fall 1997. Somoza's sharp, quirky, luminescent poems have an Asturian bite. [They] live at the intersection between the ephemeral and the eternal. —Arthur Sze. From quietness like Somoza's the real sound emerges. It curls along, close to the page. You can read it like a fox reads fields. Somoza's poems proceed with slyness and elegance down-to-earth down the white page, like fox-tracks in the snow. —Jack Collom

Sonnenfeld, Mark. *Park Slope NY.* 2p. (1-887379-17-7). Marymark Press, Fall 1998.

Sor Juana Inés de la Cruz. Translated by Jaime Manrique and Joan Larkin. *Sor Juana's Love Poems/Poemas de Amor.* 86p. pap. $12.00 (0-9651558-6-2). New York, NY: Painted Leaf Press, Fall 1997. For the first time ever, here is an exquisite sampling of love poems, some of them clearly addressed to women, by the visionary and passionate genius of Mexican letters, the 17th century nun Sor Juana Inéz de la Cruz. The poems included in this selection have been culled from Sor Juana's extensive body of poetry on the many kinds of love. Some of them are rooted in Renaissance courtly conventions; others are startlingly ahead of their time, seemingly modern in the naked power of the complex sexual feelings they address. —Painted Leaf Press

Sorby, Angela. *Distance Learning.* 64p. $22.00 (0-932826-61-X). pap. $12.00 (0-932826-62-8). Kalamazoo, MI: New Issues Press, Spring 1998. I was knocked out by Distance Learning. Sorby is a truly fresh, vital, and powerful poet, a talent who will be with us for a long time. —Alane Rollings. Wry, always engaging, and quietly compassionate poems which ground themselves in the essential surreality of American life. It's a landscape we may all know, but Sorby's flair and command of particulars makes us see it anew — and in all of its bittersweet complexity. Sorby is a sly and graceful poet, and Distance Learning is a book of unusual promise. —David Wojahn

Soto, Gary. *Junior College.* 83p. pap. $12.95 (0-8118-1543-9). San Francisco, CA: Chronicle Books, Spring 1997. Soto displays a rare understanding of how the ordinary and the transcendent meet in the fleeting pain and pleasures of everyday life. —Chronicle Books. Soto's poems are fast, funny, heartrending, and achingly believable, like Polaroid love letters, or snatches of music heard out of a passing car; patches of beauty like patches of sunlight; the very pulse of a life. —Joyce Carol Oates

Soular, James. *The Thousand-Yard Stare.* 88p. pap. $9.50 (1-880286-28-9). Canton, CT: Singular Speech Press, Spring 1997. Against the nightmare panorama of a landscape full of blackness. Soular here memorializes — often at the moment of their violent deaths — the lost friends he fought with and can never forget. But familiar as these must be to all Vietnam veterans, in Soular's hands these Bosch-like confrontations with horror at its ugliest worst are suffused by the agonizing tenderness of real poetry. This is poetry that lives at the edge of a universe of terror, where "the thousand-yard stare" belongs to men who blindly reach. . . "toward a distant, confusing light / that may be you, Lord." —Patricia Goedicke

Soulé, Anne Bacon. *The Fat Lady Sings: Fifty Poems.* 52p. pap. $8.00 (0-9653587-4-7). San Francisco, CA: Meridien PressWorks, Fall 1997. Anne Bacon Soule was born 70 years ago in San Francisco which may be the reason for her weird outlook on life, or it may not. It has, however, been subject matter for verse, which she has been writing since the age of 6. She is the author of more than 1,000 poems, most of which wound up in the round file, but those that did not were published. Regarding all of this, her summation is sage: "People can say I couldn't write, but no one can say I didn't write." — Meridien PressWorks

Sparrow. *Republican Like Me: A Diary of My Presidential Campaign.* 90p. pap. $7.00 (1-887128-22-0). New York, NY: Soft Skull Press, Fall 1998. A hilarious document of the vociferous and impassioned campaign trail of a socialist poet. —Soft Skull Press. One of the funniest men in Manhattan, over and above everything else, Sparrow offers something to believe in. —Village Voice

Spaziani, Maria Luisa. Translated by Laura Stortoni. *Sentry Towers.* pap. $13.00 (0-9641003-1-2). Berkeley, CA: Hesperia Press, Fall 1995. Sentry Towers is a welcome addition to the growing body of English translations of Spaziani's poetry. Rich and sensuous in language and imagery, this poetry is a strong celebration of desire and memory, and articulates a powerful woman's voice within the symbolist and hermetic tradition. —Gian-Paolo Biasin

Spence, Michael. *Adam Chooses.* 96p. pap. $9.95 (0-9651210-4-6). Seattle, WA: Rose Alley Press, Spring 1998. These spare, understated poems have the elegant design

and the formal ease we've come to expect of Spence's work. The stance is reminiscent of James Wright's Green Wall poems in their escape from "that vacant Paradise" to the celebration of the here and now. —Madeline DeFrees. Spence's poems, often cunning experiments in traditional form, dramatize the way experience leads to knowledge. We should be grateful for them. —Mark Jarman

Spenser, Edmund. Edited by Douglas Brooks-Davies. *The Fairy Queen: A Modernized Selection.* 633p. pap. $10.50 (0-460-87572-8). Boston, MA: Tuttle, Charles E./Everyman, Fall 1996. The only paperback edition available in modern English, with introduction, notes, lexical glosses, bibliography and chronology of Spenser's life and times. — Charles E. Tuttle/Everyman

Spiegel, Rich. *Defining Boundaries.* 12p. pap. $7.00. Staten Island, NY: Bard Press, Spring 1998.

Spiegel, Richard, and Barbara Fisher, Co-Directors. *Fear and Trembling (Book One): Bibliomania 8.* 48p. Waterways Project/NYPL, Spring 1998.

Spiegel, Richard, and Barbara Fisher, Co-Directors. *Fear and Trembling (Book Two): Bibliomania 8.* 48p. Waterways Project/NYPL, Spring 1998.

Spires, Elizabeth. *Worldling.* 63p. $18.95 (0-393-03855-6). pap. $10.00 (0-393-31628-9). New York, NY: Norton, W.W., and Company, Fall 1995; Spring 1997 (paper). With not one wrong move, not one word off-key or trivial, this collection lets us at times see the struggle behind the refined sensibility. Spires asks the big questions with such competence and polish that we admire her sweating, our metaphysical gladiator, guarantor of our considerable pleasure. —Nancy Nahra, Philadelphia Inquirer. Spires's fourth collection of poetry is radiant, suffused with a sense of, or perhaps a desire for, the sacred. Her often tricky reasoning and firm command of language do challenge us as we thrill to the beauty and intelligence of her poems. — Donna Seaman, Booklist

Spurgeon, Michael. *Valente's Delicate Wrist.* 36p. pap. $4.00. Talent, OR: Talent House Press, Fall 1998. Second Place Winner of the Fifth Annual Talent House

Press Chapbook Contest. Spurgeon righteously distrusts the authority of the self and so his poems take playful and spirited delight in a world of imagined scenarios and characters. His work comes to reveal how a single life may be composed of many missing lives, and how poems may serve as a means to call them back together. —Alison Hawthorne Deming

Squires, Suzanne Marks. *AIR.* 32p. pap. $45.00 (1-889589-00-4). Mill Valley, CA: Em Press, Fall 1998. The measure of the 21 poems in this first book is barometric, a vertical exertion, the rising or falling of air pressure or breath. This is a poetry of reflections and reversals. The clarity imposed by its pairings is mirror or lake-like. —Em Press

Stablein, Marilyn. *Vermin: A Bestiary.* 40p. pap. $5.00 (0-9608920-3-6). Kingston, NY: Reservoir Press, Fall 1997. I laughed like hell, and so did the audience at a local reading Stabein gave of Vermin.. Hers is a subversively deadpan humor. It's outstanding characteristic is unblinking compassion. —Michael Perkins, Woodstock Times

Stafford, William. *The Way It Is: New & Selected Poems.* 290p. $24.95 (1-55597-269-1). St. Paul, MN: Graywolf Press, Spring 1998. Stafford's quiet presence in the landscape of American poetry in my lifetime has been a kind of continuing reassurance whose value always seemed to me beyond question. Even those of us who have read him for years are almost certain to be surprised now, I think, and repeatedly surprised, at the range and freshness of his gift, its responsiveness to the small, the plain, the apparently usual. I think his work as a whole will go on surprising us, growing as we recognize it, bearing witness in plain language to the holiness of the heart's affections which he seemed never to doubt. A treasure that he has left us. —W.S. Merwin

Stanton, Joseph, ed. *A Hawai'i Anthology: A Collection of Works by Recipients of the Hawai'i Award for Literature, 1974-1996.* 279p. pap. $36.00 (0-8248-1977-2). Honolulu, HI: University of Hawai'i Press, Fall 1997. Since its inception in 1974, the Hawai'i Award for Literature has recognized the work of writers who have captured important dimensions of the story of Hawai'i and of the many groups of people who have made Hawai'i their home. Historians, linguists, folklorists, and practitioners of other disciplines of cultural study, as well as poets, novelists, and playwrights, are among the contributors to this extensive anthology celebrating more than two decades of the best writing in the Islands. —University of Hawai'i Press

Stanton, Maura. *Life Among the Trolls.* 86p. $20.95 (0-88748-266-X). pap. $11.95 (0-88748-267-8). Pittsburgh, PA: Carnegie Mellon University Press, Fall 1997. [Reading Stanton] my ultimate impression is of a poet of snow and flame, one who conveys a sense of burning reality, of the strange fire within and without, crackling with spirit and invention. —Stanley Kunitz. [In these poems] imagination and reality intersect, lending weight to the fantasies and a numinous dimension to ordinary lives. Imagination becomes a tool of compassion and a vehicle of social conscience. —Ben Howard, Poetry. Stanton makes a believable claim to being one of America's most authoritative poetic voices. —Booklist.

Steeves, Dean. *Visions of Tomorrow: The War Against the Power of Fear.* 133p. pap. $16.95 (0-9657073-1-8). Del

Mar, CA: 3-D Marketing LLC, Fall 1996.

Stefans, Brian Kim. *Free Space Comix.* 86p. pap. $9.95 (0-937-804-74-6). New York, NY: Roof Books, Spring 1998. Stefans's work is smart, wise-cracking, sweet, energetic, brand new, and thoroughly brilliant. Pay attention! — Stacy Doris. "Total=loco." Read on! An insouciant taffy-pull of generational originality, this lingo fracas moves outside that "Hello! broken" personality of "Aging American Poetry." Reason-bewitching contraptions sparkle, a "mercurial hit parade" of images ransomed at the heartthrob butchershop. A voracious eroticism of style, in both "descalped truth's" neon prose and dizzying syntactic eloquence. —Bruce Andrews

Stephenson, Shelby. *Poor People.* 40p. pap. $9.95 (1-879205-72-6). Troy, ME: Nightshade Press, Fall 1998. A full-length collection of lyric poems tells the story of Blacks and Whites together growing up poor in the South of mid-twentieth century America — a definitive statement from this beloved bard and songster. —Nightshade Press

Steptoe, Lamont B. *In the Kitchens of the Masters.* 57p.

pap. $10.00 (1-877968-14-5). Manasquan, NJ: Iniquity Press/Vendetta Books, 1997.

Stern, Gerald. *Odd Mercy.* 112p. pap. $11.00 (0-393-31630-0). New York, NY: Norton, W.W., and Company, Fall 1995; Spring 1997 (paper). Stern is one of those rare poetic souls who makes it almost impossible to remember what our world was like before his poetry came to exalt it. —C.K. Williams. I turn to Stern's poetry because he's so wholehearted in his embrace of the paradoxical nature of life, because of the ebullient way his poems praise the foolishness and grace of our mortal dance. What's so liberating about Stern's poems is the lyrical restlessness, the zany jigs, the yearning, that are inseparable from the lifetime he declares he's spent "grieving and arguing." —Gail Mazur, Boston Sunday Globe

Stern, Gerald. *This Time: New and Selected Poems.* 288p. $27.50 (0-393-04640-0). New York, NY: Norton, W.W., and Company, Spring 1998 ; Fall 1999 (new paper). Winner of the National Book Award. The poems in this substantial volume, the majority of which are no longer available in other editions, have been selected from seven previous collections (1972-1995). — W.W. Norton. For over two decades, no one has equaled Stern's compassionate, surreal parables about the burden of and the exaltation of being alive. —Library Journal

Stevens, Wallace. *Wallace Stevens: Collected Poetry and Prose.* 632p. $35.00 (1-883011-45-0). New York, NY: Library of America, Fall 1997. Here are all of Stevens' published books of poetry, as well as over one hundred poems uncollected by Stevens, and the most comprehensive selection of his prose writings available, some previously unpublished: reviews, speeches, short stories, criticism, philosophical writings, aphorisms, plays, poetic notebooks, and responses to the work of Eliot, Moore, Williams, and other poets. Rounding out the volume is a fifty-year span of journal entries and letters — newly edited from manuscript — providing fascinating glimpses of Stevens' thoughts on poetry and the creative process. —Library of America

Stever, Margo. *Reading the Night Sky.* 36p. pap. $5.00 (1-890044-06-7). Scottsdale, AZ: Riverstone Press, Fall 1996. Winner of the 1996 Riverstone Poetry Chapbook Award.

Stever, Margo, ed. With Photographs by Lynn Butler. *Imperiled Landscapes, Endangered Legends.* 104p. $35.00 (0-916857-10-7). New York, NY: Rizzoli/Universe Publishing, Fall 1997. Butler shot the photographs while in motion, on horseback in such visually stunning locations as the Hudson Valley, The Camargue in Provence, the Maine coast and The Esselen Tribal Community in Big Sur, California. She selected these areas because each faces the threat of commercial development that could permanently alter these environmentally sensitive sites. Poems on horses and nature by Ted Hughes, Galway Kinnell, Gwendolyn Brooks, Maxine Kumin, James Dickey and other literary voices enhance the photographs and celebrate Butler's twin passions: nature and preservation. — Rizzoli/Universe Publishing. Like the French Impressionist paintings that her photographs are often compared with, Butler's work is more than a series of pretty pictures. [You] don't see the landscape as much as feel it. —The New York Times

Stewart, Frank, and Arthur Sze, eds. *The Zigzag Way: New Writing From the America, the Pacific, and*

Asia. 208p. pap. $16.00 (0824820576). University of Hawai'i Press/Manoa Books, Spring 1998.

Stewart, Frank, and Charlene Gilmore, eds. *Inland Shores: New Writing From America, the Pacific, and Asia.* 232p. pap. $16.00 (0824821432). University of Hawai'i Press/Manoa Books, Fall 1998.

Stewart, Pamela. *The Red Window.* 73p. pap. $14.95 (0-8203-1894-9). Athens, GA: University of Georgia Press, Spring 1997. These poems are deceptively simple at first glance, but clearly they are wondrously refined in the way they amplify the forum of the self. After reading them I feel like I've just played chess with myself and, unknowingly, replayed a championship match. —Ricardo Pau-Llosa

Stone, John. *Where Water Begins: New Poems and Prose.* 89p. $22.95 (0-8071-2326-9). pap. $12.95 (0-8071-2327-7). Baton Rouge, LA: Louisiana State University Press, Fall 1998. Stone's singular gift is to allow us to see the sacred in the ordinary, to give voice to thoughts and sentiments we recognize in ourselves but never thought there were words for. To finish reading Where Water Begins is to be inspired and transformed; one puts down the book believing we can now begin to see the world with the same wonder, wisdom, humor and generosity with which he views it. And should we fail, should our passion diminish, it is only necessary to go back to his text and once again hear his robust, reflective and musical voice to find the cure. —Abraham Verghese. Stone is not only a valuable physician, but a poet who is able to get his outstanding qualities of imagination and formal technique into a relationship that produces poems of great human value. —James Dickey

Stone, Sandra. *Cocktails With Brueghel at the Museum Cafe.* 100p. $22.50 (1-880834-26-X). pap. $10.00 (1-880834-25-1). Cleveland, OH: Cleveland State University Poetry Center, Fall 1997. Here is a real discovery — the secret book like the secret room one dreams about. Stone's is that rare original voice which seems to come from an awareness so unusual it can't help but be true to itself, its only real model. Brought to light out of a mother lode of language, Stone's poems create impressions, never merely receive them. This is gener-

ous and vibrant poetry. —
Sandra McPherson

Stortoni, Laura. *The Moon and the Island.* 100p. pap. $13.00 (0-9641003-3-9). Berkeley, CA: Hesperia Press, Fall 1997. In Stortoni's poems there is the slightly crusty taste of salt, the sea wind on our lips. There is Mediterranean light and the long spaces of ancient days close as our skin. Laura's work makes bridges. Her world extends from primordial time to the present moment, as her life has literally spanned the old world and the new; it is all palpable and in focus. —Diane di Prima

Stortoni, Laura Anna, and Mary Prentice Lillie, trans. Edited by Laura Anna Stortoni. *Women Poets of the Italian Renaissance: Courtly Ladies and Courtesans.* 300p. pap. $20.00 (0-934977-43-7). New York, NY: Italica Press, Spring 1997. Here for the first time in English translation is the women's poetry of the Italian Renaissance: from the love lyrics of famous courtly ladies of Venice and Rome to the deeply moral and spiritual poets of the age. —Italica Press. A comprehensive anthology. [These poets] react with a kind of instinctive feminism to the Petrarchan model, which they shift so as to redress the balance of power between the sexes. —Times Literary Supplement

Strand, Mark. *Blizzard of One.* 55p. $21.00 (0-375-40139-3). New York, NY: Knopf, Alfred A., Fall 1998; Spring 2000 (new paper). Winner of the 1999 Pulitzer Prize for Poetry. Standing between abstraction and the sensuous particulars of experience, these poems, both stoic and often unexpectedly funny, move with unerring ease between the commonplace and the sublime. Blizzard of One is an extraordinary book — the summation of the work of a lifetime by one of our very few true masters of the art of poetry. —Alfred A. Knopf. His apparently simple lines have the eerie, seductive ring of the inevitable. —Deborah Garrison, The New York Times Book Review

Striar, Marguerite M., ed. *Beyond Lament: Poets of the World Bearing Witness to the Holocaust.* 565p. (0-8101-1555-7). pap. $19.95 (0-8101-1556-5). Evanston, IL: Northwestern University Press, Fall 1998. Beyond Lament is a rich and varied anthology consisting of new and previously published poems about the Holocaust, including works by well-known poets such as Paul Celan, Nelly Sachs, Czeslaw Milosz, Dannie Abse, and Robert Pinsky, as well as by many lesser-known or unknown poets. — Northwestern University Press

Strickland, Stephanie. *True North.* 85p. $19.95 (1-884511-36-8). pap. $12.00 (0-268-01899-5). Notre Dame, IN: University of Notre Dame Press, Fall 1997. Winner of the 1997 Ernest Sandeen Poetry Prize and the Alice Fay Di Castagnola Award from the Poetry Society of America. It's no wonder Strickland's remarkable book is twice a prize winner. With a voice and, more importantly, a way of writing that sweeps text into hypertext, Strickland tumbles her cornucopia of ideas and ideals out into what we might giddily call cyberpoetry — though she herself is calm, piercingly intelligent, and clear-eyed. Here comes our poetry for the twenty-first century — and a brilliant poet who appears at just the right moment to be our guide. — Molly Peacock. Strickland is the fanatical heir of tiny and enormous languages: earthtalk, cybertalk, Mother Goose, witchcraft, science, Cuneiform, direction, isolation, mathematics, privilege,

history and that grand old elusive: truth. —Maureen Seaton

Stroud, Joseph. *Below Cold Mountain.* 115p. pap. $14.00 (1-55659-084-9). Port Townsend, WA: Copper Canyon Press, Spring 1998. There is range and amplitude here found among only the very best. There aren't a few high points but dozens. We don't have here a few isolated mountains but a whole range, a cordillera. Like all of the best poets, Stroud makes the earth again consolable. —Jim Harrison. Stroud offers us an honest and unflinching witness to what he calls "the everyday wreckage of the world." Odd to think that praise and lamentation sometimes rise off the same breath, but out of our human wreckage Stroud salvages and polishes the moments of joy we all live for. These extraordinary poems will make you believe again in the possibility of beauty and consequence in our lives. — David Bottoms

Stryk, Lucien. *And Still Birds Sing: New and Collected Poems.* 305p. $39.95 (0-8040-1004-8). pap. $19.95 (0-8040-1005-6). Athens, OH: Ohio University Press/Swallow Press, Spring 1998. Drawing together his previously collected poems as well as the three books published since then, a sampling of his renowned translations of haiku, and a generous number of previously unpublished new poems, this collection is Stryk's most important book. And Still Birds Sing is the masterwork of a major voice in American poetry. —Ohio University Press/Swallow Press. His poems are spirit events, the finest of their kind, and anyone can live in their company. —Choice. One of our best poets working in American today. —Library Journal

Stuart, Dabney. *Long Gone.* 62p. $19.95 (0-8071-2120-7). Baton Rouge, LA: Louisiana State University Press, Fall 1996. From its haunted opening to the complex affirmation of its final lines, this profound collection presents a palimpsest of the spirit in the modern age. With jagged syncopations, lyrical stop-time, and a kind of elegiac swing, these poems spiral through multiple dimensions of time, memory, and emotion, evoking perspectives of the psyche as brooding and cryptic as the Antarctic. —Louisiana State University Press

Stuart, Jane. *Journeys: Outward/Inward/Home.* 54p. pap. $10.00. Louisville, KY: Summit Poetry Publishing,

Spring 1998. It is good to see a serious poet of the '90's giving attention to form, and doing so without compromising emotional or intellectual content. This is a work of merit from a mature, facile mind. —Jim Bush

Students From Inside Out. *Stop Motion.* 39p. pap. $8.95. Detroit, MI: Broadside Press, Fall 1998. The poems and photos in Stop Motion are the result of an experiment: to have Detroit teens use both photography and poetry to explore their city and themselves. Whether in the voice of an imagined character, a statue or a flag, their words inhabit and speak for the scenes they have chosen. These pages show that our young people are not only image makers, but meaning makers. —Terry Blackhawk

Su, Adrienne. *Middle Kingdom.* 72p. pap. $9.95 (1-882295-15-3). Farmington, ME: Alice James Books, Fall 1997. Su's Middle Kingdom is the slippery, hard-to-read territory between languages, cultures, identities—a fluid, confusing boundary zone which is both enriching and embattled. Suburban, Asian-American, at home and exiled in places and tongues, Su negotiates the mercurial new world of cultural commingling in witty, formally assured poems. —Mark Doty. Su is so unusual, such a good poet, and has so much to say, that she's addictive: once you start reading her poems you want to go on forever in the Middle Kingdom. Also, she is such a good rhymer that you don't know she's rhyming: you find out, as you read along, that you have been rhymed deeply. —Alan Dugan

Suárez, Virgil. *You Come Singing.* 103p. pap. $10.95 (1-882688-19-8). Chicago, IL: Tia Chucha Press, Fall 1998. In his first full collection of poetry, Suarez speaks with intimacy and urgency of a life filled with the dislocation and alienation born of exile. —Tia Chucha Press. Listen well, reader; his is a beautiful song, rich in tradition yet unmistakably new. —David Kirby

Summers, Rita. *An Unsorted Drawer.* 36p. pap. $4.00 (1-889289-06-X). New Haven, CT: Ye Olde Font Shoppe, Fall 1996.

Sung-Il Lee, trans. *The Moonlit Pond: Korean Classical Poems in Chinese.* 153p. pap. $17.00 (1-55659-076-8). Port Townsend, WA: Copper Canyon Press, Spring 1998. This major anthology,

the first of its kind in English, presents more than two hundred poems drawn from a tradition spanning a thousand years of Korean poets writing in the classical Chinese style. These poems explore a unique cultural phenomenon, expressing a Korean perspective on the transitoriness of life and the ephemerality of kingdoms and beauty, and the joy and longing of the eternal present. —Copper Canyon Press

Sutherland, David Hunter. *Between Absolutes.* 48p. pap. $9.95 (0-9655915-0-6). Alexandria, VA: Menace Publishing, Spring 1997. Lithe yet structured verse that transcends both current convention and worn tradition with a vibrancy and deftness wholly uncommon. —Menace Publishing

Sutherland, Keston. *At the Motel Partial Opportunity.* 14p. pap. $4.95. Barque Books, Fall 1998.

Sutton, Eve. *Breaking.* 26p. pap. $6.00. Palo Alto, CA: Perma Press Books, Fall 1997.

Sutton, Eve. *The Pixels of My Letter to You: And Other Poems to Fill Up the Book.* 26p. pap. $6.00. Palo Alto, CA: Perma Press Books, Fall 1997.

Svenvold, Mark. *Soul Data.* 80p. pap. $12.95 (1-57441-046-6). Denton, TX: University of North Texas Press, Spring 1998. Winner of the Vassar Miller Prize in Poetry. Svenvold writes with the top down, and his sleek late-model imagination in fifth gear. Honk if you love first books that can cruise or race with full-throated eloquence. Here's one! —J.D. McClatchy. Soul Data is rarely compounded — of wit and music, surface elegance and intellectual depth, quirk and quandary. Its sensual intelligence is on high alert, and the sheer unsheerness of its language — all its densities and textures is a linguiphiliacal delight. A fine rhetorical savvy, in a mind inclined to the chillier depths: among poetic gifts these days it's an uncommon conjunction, a gift of mysteries, like the sight (across a night pond's surface) of bright-blue shooting star: one hopes the other humans get to see it. —Heather McHugh

Swander, Mary. *Driving the Body Back.* 96p. pap. $12.95 (0-87745-652-6). Iowa City, IA: University of Iowa Press, Fall 1998 (reprint). A marvelous collection of folk humor, wild ways and down-home storytelling. Driving the Body Back is a sometimes harsh but always deeply compassionate narrative, and so well constructed that the reader occasionally forgets, as one does with Arabian Nights, who is doing the telling and why. And one doesn't care. It is enough to let Swander's characters enthrall and teach with the stories of their lives. — New York Times Book Review

Swander, Mary, ed. *Bloom & Blossom: The Reader's Guide to Gardening.* 275p. $25.00 (0-88001-473-3). Hopewell, NJ: Ecco Press, Spring 1997. Swander juxtaposes excerpts from early American settlers with nineteenth century classics and the work of prominent twentieth century writers to offer new perspectives on the seductive pleasure of coaxing flowers, fruits, and vegetables from the earth. —Ecco Press

Sweet, Denise. *Songs for Discharming.* 54p. pap. $12.95 (0-912678-95-X). Greenfield Center, NY: Greenfield Review Press, Fall 1997. Winner of the 1996 North American Native Authors First Book Award for Poetry. Sweet is an Anishinabe, enrolled at White Earth Reservation. Her poems are filled with sadness and anger, protest and celebration. — Greenfield Review Press. Power and surprise are the essential ingredients in every one of her poems. —Geary Hobson

Swensen, Cole. *Noon.* 113p. pap. $10.95 (1-55713-287-9). Los Angeles, CA: Sun & Moon Press, Spring 1998. Winner of the 1995 New American Poetry Competition, selected by Rae Armantrout. A stunning meditative mix of lyrical and prosaic poetry in constant motion. Swensen turns and returns images from our external world while exploring a spiritual landscape marked by separation and the desire for reunion. —Sun & Moon Press

Swift, Joan. *Intricate Moves: Poems About Rape.* 52p. pap. $10.00 (1-887344-02-0). Goshen, CT: Chicory Blue Press, Spring 1997. Swift's poems bring the transforming power of the imagination to a subject matter that is rarely addressed in poetry. Intricate Moves tells a complex story that started twenty-five years ago with a brutal rape. It is #9 in the Crimson Edge Chapbook Series, which seeks to support and encourage older women writers and to increase their publishing opportunities. —Chicory Blue Press

Swiss, Thomas. *Rough Cut.* 69p. pap. $12.95 (0-252-06615-4). Champaign, IL: University of Illinois Press, Spring 1997. Swiss has crafted a quietly ferocious poetry of deep psychological insight and great vernacular clarity, where characters wake to find their lives gone suddenly and mysteriously awry, their ordinary existences made extraordinary through the plain abjection of their sorrow. Swiss is a master of blunt demotic narrative, and he treats his characters with a kind of dignity and stubborn tenderness that makes the best of these poems nothing short of remarkable. He is a wise and rueful writer. —David Wojahn

Swist, Wally. *The New Life.* 77p. pap. $12.00 (1-887628-06-1). West Hartford, CT: Plinth Books, Fall 1998. Swist's poems are lean and clean to the bone. Meditations on nature, love, sanity and evil are limned with grace and clarity. Finally, though, this book is a celebration, the way one man coming face to face with a fox is a kind of celebration. —James Tate. These poems are reports from the world of their subjects, but — in contrast to reportage — Swist's lyrical use of detail and image lifts these "reports" to the level of emotional memory: poems. —Joseph Langland

Swope, Helen Perry. *The Butterfly League.* 125p. pap. $12.00 (0-9639938-0-1). Hydesville, CA: Lodestar Press, 1994. Addressing such polarities as male & female, rural & urban, pleasure & pain, youth & age, and reason & imagination, Swope embraces the human condition unflinchingly. —David R. Rollins

Sylvester, Janet. *The Mark of Flesh.* 94p. $19.00 (0-393-04094-1). New York, NY: Norton, W.W., and Company, Spring 1997; Fall 1999 (new paper). Sylvester's brilliantly time-layered poems take life on her own intricate and original terms. Jefferson and Lafayette go to bed drunk on reason's dream, and a late twentieth-century poet wakes up with a hangover, and a hard case of awareness. Bracing, heartbreaking, mind-engaging poems — this book speaks eloquently to our current perplexity, and our perennial desire. —Eleanor Wilner. Sylvester has written a knock-out collection of poems. [She] blends epigrammatic punch with the sweep and grace of an architect in blank verse. The Mark of Flesh is restless,

savvy poetry. I admire it! — Dave Smith

Sze, Arthur. *The Redshifting Web: Poems 1970-1998.* 272p. pap. $17.00 (1-55659-088-1). Port Townsend, WA: Copper Canyon Press, Spring 1998. The Redshifting Web spans more than a quarter-century of published work and makes available for the first time the full range of Sze's poetry. It includes selections from five previous books as well as a generous selection of new poems. —Copper Canyon Press. Sze is the kind of poet I have hoped for all my life: he possesses the gravity of the great Chinese poets of the T'ang, the levity of a Japanese Zen master, along with a voice that is wholly contemporary. He is a master of description of the natural world. With typical modesty, he can refer to his many travels and his absorption of many cultures in a totally unaffected way. This book is a landmark and a signpost. —Carolyn Kizer. Sze composes an elegant, quietly intense, very human, beautiful poetry, one that is remarkable for its commitment to metaphor and musical language. I consider him to be one of the foremost poets of his generation. He is wise, intelligent, a joy to be with and to read. —Quincy Troupe

Szporluk, Larissa. *Dark Sky Question.* 73p. pap. $12.00 (08070-6845-4). Boston, MA: Beacon Press, Fall 1998. Winner of the 1997 Barnard New Women Poets Prize. Her effects are breathtaking. — Daniel L. Guillory, Library Journal. Szporluk weaves magic out of indeterminacy. —Samuel Jay Keyser, Harvard Review. [She] creates an animate new universe out of cryptic original speech. — Brenda Hillman. If those two strange, haunted beings, Emily Dickinson and Georg Trakl, wedded, these poems might well be the offspring. — Gregory Orr

Szymborska, Wislawa. *Poems New and Collected 1957-1997.* 273p. $27.00 (0-15-100353-X). San Diego, CA: Harcourt Brace/Harvest Books, Spring 1998. Szymborska is unquestionably one of the great living European poets. She's accessible and deeply human and a joy — though it is a dark kind of joy. A poet to live with. — Robert Hass. Szymborska captures the nightmarish contingency of human survival, and the human callousness toward nature, with an ironic elegance miraculously free of bitterness. —The New Yorker

Tabios, Eileen, ed. *Black Lightning: Poetry-in-Progress.* 450p. $54.95 (1-889876-06-2). pap. $19.95 (1-889876-03-8). New York, NY: Asian American Writers' Workshop, Spring 1998. Tabios presents drafts of poems from early stages through numerous alterations, which makes for engrossing revelations and ultimately rewarding insights into the birth of a poem. — Library Journal. By illuminating the creative process of fourteen poets, Black Lightning widens and deepens our understanding of what it means to be an Asian American writer today. In doing so, Black Lightning makes an important contribution to contemporary American poetry and poetics. —Arthur Sze. Black Lightning is groundbreaking, not only in its contribution to the teaching of creative writing, but in its expansion of the boundaries of "Asian American" literature, allowing it to move beyond a focus solely on ethnic subject matter. —Sunaina Maira. I know of no other book that shows as clearly how the lightning flash of inspiration is born of many painful drafts and long hours of hard work. —Marianne Villanueva

Tádjèck, Sandor (Kurt Brown. *A Voice in the Garden.* 30p. pap. $5.00 (1-892184-13-3). Venice, CA: Beyond Baroque Books, Spring 1998.

Taggart, Phil. *Opium Wars.* 31p. pap. $5.00 (1-890887-01-3). Santa Barbara, CA: Mille Grazie Press, Fall 1997. Nothing is arbitrary or left to chance as [Taggart] carefully guides the reader into a world of exact sonics, astute portraits, and pointed social observations. Yet his is also a poetry of engagement, inviting his audience to become co-creators by attaching their own personal associations to the linguistic matrix he skillfully designs. —Mille Grazie Press

Tagliabue, John. *New and Selected Poems: 1942-1997.* 388p. $49.95 (0-943373-44-1). pap. $19.95 (0-943373-45-X). Orono, ME: National Poetry Foundation, Spring 1998. Tagliabue writes out of a deeply sacramental sense of nature and history. He is, moreover, that rare person to whom poetry appears to come as naturally as breathing. It comes to this reader, poem by poem, as a Franciscan act of courtesy and praise. —Amy Clampitt. Tagliabue eats noodles with the Emperor's brother, at least in his often aston-

ishing poems. His real toads in imaginary gardens have a glint of oriental light in their eyes and their skin textures are almost frighteningly convincing. One of the most imaginative, diverse, universal yet personal American poets, his work is always accomplished and insinuatingly profound. —Willis Barnstone

Tagore, Rabindranath. Introduction by W.B. Yeats. *Gitanjali.* 127p. pap. $8.00 (0-684-83934-2). New York, NY: Simon & Schuster/Scribner, Fall 1997. The publication of the English edition of Gitanjali in 1911 earned Tagore the Nobel Prize in literature. A collection of over one hundred inspirational poems, Gitanjali covers the breadth of life's experiences, from the quiet pleasure of observing children at play to a man's struggle with his god. These are poems that transcend time and place. —Simon & Schuster/Scribner

Talcott, William. *Benita's Book.* 59p. pap. $10.00 (1-879457-53-9). San Francisco, CA: Thumbscrew Press, Fall 1997. Benita has a way of lighting up a stanza, illuminating some unusual juxtaposition of fantasy and fact, then walking off with that sense of her own sensuosity that is proof she has practiced walking away until the pure sashay of it will madden a man — or drive a poet to write frantically, wonderfully — who must watch her go. That she never quite leaves, entirely, well, that's the genius of the collection. —G.E. Coggshall. Even without the narrative power that holds it together, some of the images and passages are enough to justify reading and remembering it as an example of how to sketch in a few words — not with the transience of haiku, but the precision and power of a laser. — Jerry H. Jenkins

Tam, Reuben. *The Wind-Honed Islands Rise: Selected Poems.* 102p. pap. $12.95 (0-8248-1932-2). University of Hawai'i Press/Manoa Books, Fall 1996. [Tam's] poems always showed, over the long years of his poetic work, the artist/scientist's determination to get right the precise features of the external world. And, simultaneously, his poems always showed his love of the more human, natural world of wordplay and verbal carefulness. His poems are as finely crafted as any you can find west of Monhegan Island. — Tony Quagliano

Tapahonso, Luci. *Blue Horses Rush In: Poems and Stories.* 120p. $22.95 (0-8165-

1727-4). pap. $12.95 (0-8165-1728-2). Tucson, AZ: University of Arizona Press, Fall 1997. Winner of the Mountains and Plains Bookseller's Association Regional Book Award fro Poetry. Blue Horses Rush In is a major accomplishment on the same level as Leslie Silko's Storyteller or Scott Momaday's The Names. It's the kind of work that comes about with an accumulation of wisdom and insight gained after living and writing for more than a few years, when one is nearly equidistant between death and birth. — Joy Harjo

Tasso, Torquato. Translated by Maria Pastore Passaro. *King Torrismondo.* 332p. $35.00 (0-8232-1633-0). pap. $19.95 (0-8232-1634-0). Bronx, NY: Fordham University Press, Spring 1997. This translation, the first to be made directly from the Italian to English, provides readers with a wider range of the Italian tragedy as a genre; it also allows readers to acquire a deeper awareness of the entire spectrum of the Italian Renaissance in its final brilliance. —Fordham University Press

Tate, James. *Shroud of the Gnome.* 72p. $23.00 (0-88001-561-6). Hopewell, NJ: Ecco Press, Fall 1997; Spring 1999 (new paper). A bravura performance in Tate's signature style: playful, wicked, deliriously sober, charming and dazzling. One of America's most masterful poets celebrates the inexplicable in his own strange tongue. —Ecco Press. Tate never ceases to astonish, dismay, delight, confuse, tickle and generally improve the quality of our lives. —John Ashbery

Taus, Roger. *If You Ask Me Where I've Been.* 104p. pap. $10.00 (0-9627891-9-4). Bedford, NH: Igneus Press, Fall 1998.

Taylor, Henry. *Understanding Fiction: Poems, 1986-1996.* 64p. $19.95 (0-8071-2110-X). pap. $11.95 (0-8071-2061-8). Baton Rouge, LA: Louisiana State University Press, Fall 1996. In his first collection since winning the Pulitzer Prize, Taylor often uses the craft of writing as a metaphor for the examined life, exploring with wry wisdom our slow-dawning awareness of evanescence. —Louisiana State University Press. As its double-take title indicates, Understanding Fiction is spiked with irony, but it is also

overflowing with feeling. Taylor is a master of the anecdotal form and the easy pentameter gait; and he reminds us that the most fundamental responsibility of poetry is to give pleasure. —Billy Collins

Taylor, Thomas Lowe. *The Texts of Anabasis (1968-69).* 26p. Portland, OR: 26 Books, Spring 1998.

Taylor, Velande. *Homilies in the Marketplace: Parables for Our Time.* 64p. pap. $12.00 (0-9649947-0-4). Seattle, WA: WordCraft Books, Fall 1996. A collection of poetry and prose poetry reflective of the author's broad spectrum of experiences in the US and overseas. Upbeat, serious, yet balanced with touches of wry humor. —WordCraft Books

Tayson, Richard. *The Apprentice of Fever.* 72p. $22.00 (0-87338-614-0). pap. $12.00 (0-87338-615-9). Kent, OH: Kent State University Press, Fall 1998. Winner of the 1997 Stan and Tom Wick Poetry Prize. A brilliantly corporeal first book. . . rooted in the day-to-day life of a man implicated in the AIDS epidemic, living on the edge, crossing, transforming and transgressing boundaries, always, always paying an extreme and active attention. Tayson's voice is unmistakable: direct, witty, passionate and desperate, in poems with the crucial acid to etch themselves into the reader's consciousness. — Marilyn Hacker. The meat and blood of Tayson's poetic universe is wildly beautiful, exact and honest to the bone. Read [these poems] and take a breath of intimate real life. — Tim Miller

Templeton, Fiona. *Cells of Release.* 120p. pap. $13.95 (0-937804-69-X). New York, NY: Roof Books, 1997. A document of the poetry installation at the abandoned panopticon Eastern State Penetentiary written on continuous paper over six weeks at the site with photos and descriptive materi-al. —Roof Books

Terris, Susan. *Curved Space.* 102p. pap. $10.00 (0-931721-15-6). La Jolla, CA: La Jolla Poets Press, Spring 1998. Terris is an exquisite poet. Her work is filled with an unerring dramatic poise and subtle lyric calm. She guides us through the oscillations of the complicated human family we all share, and the grace of her narratives is matched only by her compassion and her wisdom. This is a book we can all hold close against our own silences. —David St. John

Tham, Hilary. *Lane With No Name: Memoirs and Poems of a Malaysian-Chinese Girlhood.* 211p. $32.00 (0-89410-830-1). pap. $16.95 (0-89410-831-X). Boulder, CO: Rienner, Lynne, Publishers/Three Continents Press, Spring 1997. Tham's memoirs reveal the many images, cultures, myths, and memories out of which her poetry has emerged. Poems interspersed in the text and family album photographs enrich this narrative of a life in which poetry, passion, warmth, stubbornness, community, and clarity of thought all play leading roles. — Lynne Rienner, Publishers/Three Continents Press

Thaxter, Celia. Edited by Julia Older. *Selected Writings.* 312p. Hancock, NH: Appledore Books, 1997.

The American Poetry & Literacy Project, ed. *101 Great American Poems.* 128p. pap. $1.00 (0-486-40158-8). Mineola, NY: Dover Publications, Spring 1998. Focusing on popular verse from the 19th and 20th centuries, this treasury of great American poems invites poetry lovers to savor a taste of the nation's rich poetic legacy. Selected for both popularity and literary quality, 101 time-honored poems in this entertaining volume include work by Whitman, Frost, Hughes, Dickinson, Pound, Eliot, Stevens, Moore and many others. —Dover Publications

Thilleman, Tod. *The Corybantes: A Book of Strophaics.* 74p. pap. $10.00 (1-881471-19-5). New York, NY: Spuyten Duyvil, Fall 1997. Thilleman has achieved a perfect fusion between poetry and philosophy in this unusual work. —David Rothenberg

Thilleman, Tod. *The New Frequency & The Music of Annihilation.* 70p. pap. $12.00 (0-966-1242-00). Princeton, NJ: Ma'arri, Fall 1998. The waverings, flurries, gaps and gusts of phrases, by turns recondite and plain, harsh and eloquent, compose a deeply credible kind of spiritual music, appropriately broken, but alive with despair and exaltation. —Joseph Donahue

Thomas, David E. *Buck's Last Wreck: Selected Poems.* 83p. pap. $7.95 (0-9649009-0-4). Missoula, MT: Wild Variety Books/Olsen's Publishing, Fall 1996. [Thomas's poetry] marks him as the last and best of the hippie, working class, street smart poets. —James Crumley. [Thomas's] presence and his poems, his good grace and humor, remind us that these times, sweet and sometimes bitter, all day long, inescapably, are what we get to have, and while they won't last forever, they can indeed be enough. —William Kittredge

Thomas, David J. *Only the Trying.* 52p. pap. $12.50 (1-55618-169-8). Lawrenceville, VA: Brunswick Publishing, Spring 1998. In language veined with humor and dense with Hopkinsesque metaphor, Thomas muses on love, time's transhifting, and life's quirky anarchy. A fine first book! —Ruel E. Foster. Thomas's collection of verse compellingly observes the complexities of intimacy, the grittiness of city life, and the mass appeal of popular culture. I highly recommend this volume. —Walter Wieloh

Thomas, Gail. *Finding the Bear.* 87p. pap. $10.00 (0-9660459-0-4). Shutesbury, MA: Perugia Press, 1997. The visual precision of Thomas's language is matched by the stunning honesty of her emotional terrain. Finding the Bear is a moving and beautifully presented collection. —Perugia Press. These are poems of deep caring and clear observation of the natural and political world. — Almitra David

Thompson, Daniel. *Even the Broken Letters of the Heart Spell Earth.* 90p. pap. $18.95 (0-933087-47-0). Huron, OH: Bottom Dog Press, Fall 1998. Thompson delivers the news with poems that drive home the necessity for keeping open the eyes and heart. —Bottom Dog Press. Thompson's poems show us how a poet keeps his songs, is kept by his songs. His poems spell our hearts. — Maj Ragain

Thomson, Jeffrey. *The Halo Brace.* 64p. pap. $13.50 (0-913559-51-2). Delhi, NY: Birch Brook Press, Fall 1998. A cycle of poetry on the lingering vibrations of love's effects, of the "lush spice" of sex, and of life after love. — Birch Brook Press

Thornton, R.K.R., and Marion Thain. *Poetry of the 1890's.* 326p. pap. $14.95 (0-14-043639-1). New York, NY: Penguin Books/Viking Penguin, Fall 1997. Fascinated alike by artifice, religious ritual and the chance encounters of the London streets, a generation of writers demanded a new freedom to look at perverse and morbid kinds of

love and expressed themselves in lyric outbursts, vigorously colloquial pieces, ballads such a Wilde's from Reading gaol, and even versions of Baudelaire, Verlaine and Mallarmé. The anthology includes works by Housman, Henley and Hardy, Beardsley and Dowson, Kipling, Symons and Yeats. Reissued for our own fin de siécle, it now features many more contributions by women poets, who forged the ideal of the New Woman (female equivalent of the dandy), battled with the conventions of the masuline literary tradition and looked forward, often with hope rather than languid despair, to the dawn of the twentieth century. —Penguin Books/Viking Penguin

Tipton, James. *Letters From a Stranger.* 82p. pap. $12.00 (0-9657159-3-0). Crested Butte, CO: Conundrum Press, Fall 1998. Truly a pure and beautiful voice, a light. What a beautiful poet Tipton is, what new ways he shows the soul. I carry these poems with me. — Grace Cavalieri. Tipton's poems are a celebration — lovely and lush. —Conrad Hilberry

Titche, Leon. *Reflections From a Desert Pond.* 69p. pap. $15.95 (0-9659417-1-X).

Thomaston, ME: Century Press, Fall 1998.

Tobin, Juanita Brown. *Ransom Street Quartet Poems and Stories.* 164p. pap. $14.95 (0-9635752-8-7). Boone, NC: Parkway Publishers, 1995. Nothing about Juanita Tobin is separate. What she writes is what she is. She is a square-rigged sailing ship that goes right into the wind. —Irene Cosmo

Tomlinson, Charles. *Selected Poems: 1955-1997.* 226p. pap. $13.95 (0-8112-1369-2). New York, NY: New Directions, Fall 1997. This edition of Tomlinson's poems provides perfect entry into the work of one of England's contemporary masters. —New Directions. He is fascinated — with his eyes open: a lucid fascination — at the universal busyness, the continuous generation and degeneration of things. —Octavio Paz. A master of his craft, his poems have the finality of form which you find only among the first rate. —Donald Hall

Topp, Mike. *Six Short Stories & Seven Short Poems.* 16p. pap. $5.00 (0-9605626-6-4). Long Island City, NY: Low-Tech Press, Spring 1997.

Torreson, Rodney. *The Ripening of Pinstripes: Called Shots on the New York Yankees.* 129p. pap. $10.00 (1-885266-37-5). Ashland, OR: Story Line Press, Spring 1998. Walt Whitman wrote: "I see great things in Baseball." The New York Yankees are what Torreson sees. From Babe Ruth's called shot to Don Mattingly's ailing back, The Ripening of Pinstripes teems with baseball's legends, gamers, scrubs and scape-goats. —Story Line Press. Like Sandburg's ballplayers, Torreson knows what it's like to have "fought in the dust for a song." He's got the desire, the moves, the language, and the timing, and he stands in — tough as Berra— until he finds the poetry of baseball that was always there but needed a real poet to release it. The book's a home run with the bases loaded. —David Allan Evans

Townsend, Ann. *Dime Store Erotics.* 76p. pap. $12.00 (1-878851-11-X). Eugene, OR: Silverfish Review Press, Spring 1998. Townsend writes the romance of "everyday" life in Dime Store Erotics, but the exquisite act of her attention makes every minute a precipice, every detail an opening door — not into the dime store but out into the spinning original dimensions of her lyric consciousness. She is an intoxicating poet. —Carol Muske. Townsend's first book marks the arrival of a poised and powerful young poet on the American literary scene. These are poems which, with precision and chilling beauty, subtly reveal the abyss below the surface of daily gestures, the motions of "anarchic Eros" subverting domestic routine, the danger waiting just beyond the periphery of vision. And they are poems which, in acknowledging precarity, danger, the violent underside of human exchanges, celebrate the diverse acts of creation, the intelligence of love, the order we make in full sight of the void. —Marilyn Hacker

Trachtenberg, Jordan, and Amy Trachtenberg, eds. *Verses That Hurt: Pleasure and Pain From the Poemfone Poets.* 212p. pap. $14.95 (0-312-15191-8). New York, NY: St. Martin's Press, Spring 1997. With unabashed fervor the Poemfone poets are redefining poetry as we know it. Archaic literary rules that have never been bent have suddenly been broken, and Verses That Hurt chronicles this poetic phenomenon. This is a revolutionary gathering of disparate and brash talent that

is not to be missed. —St. Martin's Press

Trakl, Georg. Translated by Daniel Simko. *Autumn Sonata: Selected Poems.* 160p. pap. $13.95 (1-55921-251-9). Wakefield, RI: Asphodel Press/Moyer Bell, Fall 1998. Haunted by the "cold radiance" of death, Trakl's poems and two prose pieces collected in this bilingual volume create a romantically heightened interior world of suffering and hoped-for transcendence. — Publishers Weekly. In this generous bilingual edition, Daniel Simko's eloquently sensitive translations rediscover for a new generation of readers Trakl's dark and haunted imagination. — Stanley Kunitz. These are brilliant translations of stunning poems. Simko has deftly found the overtones and the undertow and Trakl's genius is alive — again. —Jorie Graham

Tran, Barbara; Monique T.D. Truong and Luu Truong Khoi, eds. *Watermark: Vietnamese American Poetry and Prose.* 227p. (1-889876-05-4). pap. $19.95 (1-889876-04-6). New York, NY: Asian American Writers' Workshop, Spring 1998. Watermark is a fresh and compelling addition to the literatures of Asian America. Forged in the crucible of a painful diaspora, these literary landscapes are haunted by the Vietnam War, imparting to the collection complex and often exhilarating dimensions. Immersed in immediacy as well as steeped in a sense of loss, of difference and mordant humor, these writers show how the space between cultures has irrevocably become the new frontier. Quirky, vibrant, worldly and meditative at the same time, these are voices America very much needs to hear. —Luis H. Francia

Tremblay, Gail. *Indian Singing.* 82p. $23.95 (0-934971-65-X). pap. $11.95 (0-934971-64-1). Corvallis, OR: Calyx Books, Fall 1998 (revised edition). This revised edition includes new poems, new artwork, and an introduction by Joy Harjo. Indian Singing is not a quiet book; the musical poetry of Gail Tremblay demands to be read, sung, out loud. Her poetry is a visionary quest, a work of hope. —Calyx Books. In her lyrical, rhythmic text, Tremblay sings the stories we must tell in order to survive. —Belles Lettres. Tremblay is a singer of eminent power and grace. And we are compelled

to listen, to sing with her. —Joy Harjo

Triplett, Pimone. *Ruining the Picture.* 96p. $39.95 (0-8101-5086-7). pap. $14.95 (0-8101-5087-5). Northwestern University Press/TriQuarterly Books, Fall 1998. In their unique blend of linguistic energy and stunning emotional conviction, Triplett's poems weave the strands of myth, culture, and history into a personal landscape of the imagination. —Northwestern University Press

Tritica, John. *How Rain Records Its Alphabet.* 105p. pap. $12.00 (1-888809-09-4). Albuquerque, NM: La Alameda Press, Fall 1998. Recalling at times the densely textured orchestrations of Hart Crane, Robert Duncan, or Clark Coolidge, Tritica's poetry ultimately stakes out its own territory, adding something of high value to the 20th century tradition of experimental lyricism. —Stephen-Paul Martin. Tritica is fluent in miracles often unnoticed. . . This work finds nourishment by juxtaposing human habit and its sister industry of bees, branches, rain, evolving into spirit toward "Stillness, an intense act." —Sheila E. Murphy

Truitt, Sam. *Anamorphosis Eisenhower.* 71p. pap. $12.00 (0-918786-48-7). Barrington, RI: Lost Roads Publishers, Spring 1998. Truitt gives mouth to mouth resuscitation to the ancient quest poem as he writes "to voyage is to become / Hysterical." In the maximal narrative loop of this book, Marilyn Monroe's skirt is perpetually going "whoosh" in an Einsteinian vacuum where "the displacement of the figure is the form." — Peter Gizzi. Truitt has assembled here a gorgeous trembling maximalism invested with erudition, tenderness, with a shimmering full deck, wild card and all. —Ann Lauterbach

Trungpa, Chögyam. *Timely Rain: Selected Poetry.* 240p. pap. $15.00 (1-57062-174-8). Boston, MA: Shambhala Publications, Spring 1998. Poems by the renowned Tibetan Buddhist monk and cofounder of the Naropa Institute, these poems and songs combine a background in classical Tibetan poetry with Trungpa's intuitive insight into the spirit of America, evoked in his use of colloquial metaphor and contemporary imagery. — Shambhala Publications

Truscott, Danielle. *Anthems of an Uncut Field.* 96p. pap. $9.95 (1-883197-15-5). Cullowhee, NC: New Native Press, Fall 1997. Truscott ranges widely in this first collection across mental and physical landscapes detailed as firmly and delicately by the minuteae of the earth as by the delineation of psychological states of being. Whether the utterance is bardic, rhapsodic and surrealistic, or colloquial, offhanded and slangy, the poems always seem to be inhabiting their forms with a perfect fit. —Tony Connor

Tsvetaeva, Marina. Translated by Nina Kossman with Andrew Newcomb. *Poem of the End: Selected Narrative and Lyrical Poetry.* 190p. $35.00 (0-87501-112-8). Ardis Publishers, Fall 1998. Hailed by Nabakov as "a poet of genius," Tsvetaeva is acknowledged today as one of the twentieth-century's greatest poets. This bi-lingual collection contains six of her acclaimed narrative poems, as well as a selection of lyrics, most translated into English for the first time. —Ardis Publishers. My impression of Tsvetaeva was that she was absolutely natural, and fantastically self-willed. When I read her poetry and letters now, I realize that what she always needed was to experience every emotion to the maximum, seeking ecstasy not only in love, but in abandonment, loneliness and disaster as well. —Nadezhda Mandelstam. There has been no more passionate voice in twentieth-century Russian poetry. —Joseph Brodsky

Tucker, Martin. *Attention Spans.* 60p. pap. $9.95 (1-884754-25-2). Prairie Village, KS: Potpourri Publications, Spring 1997. Like William Carlos Williams, Tucker is a poet of elegant simplicity, a dead-serious poet who is often slyly funny. —Philip Appleman. Tucker's poems make you think of the birth of blazing peacocks rupturing their shells: his images always take you by surprise. Tucker's pressure-gathering lines show how quietude can burst into fierce seeing. —Cynthia Ozick. Tucker has arranged the three sections of the book, "Living," "Dying," and "Living Again," in symbolic order. It speaks significantly to the reader of the wheel of existence to which we are all subject, and Tucker does it with sensitivity and care — a book to read in appreciation of its decency and compassion. —David Ignatow

Tucker, Memye Curtis. *Admit One.* 28p. pap. $7.00. Brockport, NY: State Street Press, Spring 1998. Winner of the 1998 State Street Press Prize. Tucker explores the fine line between music and poetry, art and politics. —Judith Kitchen

Tucker, Memye Curtis. *Storm Line.* pap. $5.00 (1-891508-C2-4). Aiken, SC: Palanquin Press, Spring 1998. Winner of the 1997 Palanquin Press Prize. Storm Line is a book of difficult weathers — shark and saber-tooth, fire and Bardo journey, rapture and return. —Palanquin Press

Tucker, Memye Curtis. *The Watchers.* 72p. $24.95 (0-8214-1252-3). pap. $12.95 (0-8214-1253-1). Ohio University Press, Fall 1998. Winner of the 1998 Hollis Summers Poetry Prize. The writing is elegant in the sense engineers use, the forms and style being fitted to their purpose. I was not able to predict what this highly intelligent writer would turn to next, and found that whatever it was would be a pleasure to read. —Louis Simpson. Tucker is "drawn by a fierceness," as she states in one of her poems, and that passionate drive marks her poetry as a quest for knowledge. As she says in yet another of her many fine and quotable poems, when we read her work, we can't help but say, "Yes, the world." —Mark Jarman

Tudor, Stephen. *Haul-Out.* 159p. pap. $18.95 (0-8143-2659-5). Wayne State University Press/Great Lakes Books, Fall 1996. Tudor shares a life absorbed by the power of the sea with the reader, evoking a powerful internal voyage, one of insight and devotion. It is a must-read for anyone who loves poetry, sailing, living life to the fullest, and searching for the true sense of spirit and self. —Wayne State University Press/Great Lakes Books. [These poems] blossom into . . . a vision of the dark end of all journeying. —Robert Dana

Turco, Lewis. Joseph Alessia. *A Book of Fears.* 57p. pap. $9.00 (1-884419-20-8). West Lafayette, IN: Bordighera, Fall 1998. These canny, haunting poems, imaginatively conceived and finely crafted, by telling us hard, mortal truths about the inner and outer spaces of our days, grant us permission to be human. — David Citino. Turco is one of the most original and diversely talented Italian American poets. What a pleasure to read him in two languages at once

— his own zesty English and an Italian translation. —Dana Gioia

Turcotte, Mark. *The Feathered Heart.* 65p. pap. $10.95 (0-87013-482-5). East Lansing, MI: Michigan State University Press/Lotus Poetry Series, Fall 1998. Turcotte's poetry is sound-vision stirring echoes of an Earth-based relationship in urban places, and offering the hope of a deeper human future. —Louise Erdrich. Brisk, but neither hard nor cold. Exciting energy and venturesomeness. — Gwendolyn Brooks. An honor song of bright energy and searing honesty — a lament, a celebration, a powerful blend of old dreams and new realities. —Susan Power

Tuthill, Stacy Johnson, ed. *Laurels: Eight Women Poets.* 190p. $20.00 (0-930526-23-6). Scop Publications, Spring 1998. Although this country is rich with women poets, only eight have been assigned to serve as Poet Laureate. Laurels deals with the tenure of these women at the Library of Congress through short essays, interviews, a listing of publications and honors, and samples of poetry. —Scop Publications

Twichell, Chase. *The Ghost of Eden.* 72p. $17.95 (0-86538-083-X). Ontario Review Press, 1995. "Please tell me what to feel / when everything I love. . . / blisters in the sudden radium of fear," Twichell writes in her fierce new book. Although she accuses herself of the "sin of despair," Twichell's compassion arouses the reader to identify and connect in poem after poem with the human element inside our imperiled environment. This is a must-read book. — Maxine Kumin. Twichell has written with utter honesty, and grave splendor, about the overriding fact of our brief moment on earth — the sudden erosion of the real, the natural, the baseline actual that has grounded our lives since we came to consciousness as a species. These are necessary poems. —Bill McKibben

Tyler, Mike. *From Colorado To Georgia.* 482p. pap. $39.95 (0-9655055-0-2). New York, NY: Carlton Arms Hotel, 1997. Ezra Pound out of Beavis and Butthead. — London Sunday Times. Language always invigorating, carefully deranged and almost magical. —Santa Barbara Independent. Pulses with the same euphoric heartbeat that made Rimbaud the proto punk-rock hero. —The Village Voice

Ueda, Makoto, trans. *Modern Japanese Tanka.* 265p. pap. $16.50 (0-231-10433-2). Irvington, NY: Columbia University Press, Spring 1997. Includes four hundred poems by twenty Japanese poets who have made major contributions to the history of tanka in the late nineteenth and early twentieth centuries. Ueda captures the distinct voices of these individual poets, providing biographical sketches of each as well as transliterating Japanese text below each poem. Modern Japanese Tanka elegantly conveys an authentic sense of Japanese lyric to a Western audience. — Columbia University Press

Ullman, Leslie. *Slow Work Through Sand.* 90p. pap. $10.95 (0-87745-615-1). Iowa City, IA: University of Iowa Press, Spring 1998. Winner of the 1997 Iowa Poetry Prize. Ullman has the ability to spin illuminating spells through and around the matter of earth and life. Her vision penetrates with an attention as careful and as transforming as day through clear water, as moonlight on stone. She is an artisan with words, and the results are poems embodying the intricacy and beauty of the subjects they honor. — Pattiann Rogers

Um, Sylvia Sohn. *The Rooted Heart.* 40p. pap. $18.00 (1-888553-07-3). Tucson, AZ: Kore Press, Spring 1998. [Um's] voice is uncompromising, sure, ruptured and finally, joyful: "the shape of canaries set free / to breathe and beat on their own." —Barbara Cully

Unbearables. *Crimes of the Beats.* 223p. pap. $18.95 (1-57027-069-4). Brooklyn, NY: Autonomedia, Spring 1998.

Unbearables. Edited by Ron Kolm. *Unbearables Portfolio Two.* 40p. pap. $125.00. Brooklyn, NY: Ackerman Loft Gallery, Spring 1997. Poems from the Unbearables printed letterpress on individual sheets. —Ackerman Loft Gallery

Urrea, Luis Alberto. *Ghost Sickness.* 95p. pap. $11.95 (0-938317-30-X). El Paso, TX: Cinco Puntos Press, Fall 1997. Named by the Bloomsbury Review as one of ten picks for Young Writers to Watch. Selected by Adrienne Rich for The Best American Poetry, 1997. Ghost Sickness is a powerful and moving testimony of living moments. Urrea

has captured the grief of a parent's passage in death, multiplied ten-fold by violence. And yet there is respite, grace and peace in this harsh, all too real landscape. Each word in this collection delights, haunts, and touches bedrock. — Denise Chávez

Utley, Steven. *This Impatient Ape.* 44p. pap. $5.95. Palo Alto, CA: Anamnesis Press, Spring 1998. Science fiction and fantasy poetry by the well-known science fiction author. —Anamnesis Press

Uyematsu, Amy. *Nights of Fire, Nights of Rain.* 104p. pap. $12.00 (1-885266-52-9). Ashland, OR: Story Line Press, Spring 1998. Uyematsu measures the cadences of her inner life against the cataclysmic throb of the public world, and in so doing, raises the stakes for any poet who hopes to deal honestly with the overwhelming complexity of contemporary urban life. — Eloise Klein Healy. Uyematsu's poetry is wise and rare. Her eye is so sure, her touch so subtle, that there is a palpable thread of utter stillness in these poems that dreams the healing flesh and blood of our common ancestors back into our world. — Peter Levitt

Valdés, Gina. Translated by Katherine King and Gina Valdés. *Puentes y fronteras/Bridges and Borders.* 82p. pap. $9.00 (0-927534-62-2). Tempe, AZ: Bilingual Press, Fall 1996. Valdés uses the copla, a Spanish verse form that harks back to the Middle Ages and arises from the popular oral tradition, to explore barriers between people and countries. Valdés uses the copla both in protest against elite poetic forms and as a mechanism of social protest. —Bilingual Press

Valdez, Catherine. *A Woman in Bloom.* 66p. (1-890254-09-6). pap. $8.95 (1-890254-11-8). Scottsdale, AZ: Rythm Books/Innovative Publishing Concepts, 1997. Excellently written, highly inspirational. Poems which motivate readers to consider their own lives and make positive changes. — Kelley Pitts

Valente, Peter. *Forge of Words a Forest.* 36p. pap. $4.00 (1-893032-04-3). Talisman House, Publishers / Jensen/Daniels, Fall 1998. Valente's poems don't describe the world so much as explore its hidden intent: "sigils / of the heart's parallel knowledge." Vectorial by nature, they lead us — with great con-viction — through. —Gustaf Sobin

Valentine, Jean. *Growing Darkness, Growing Light.* 65p. $20.95 (0-88748-241-4). pap. $11.95 (0-88748-242-2). Pittsburgh, PA: Carnegie Mellon University Press, Spring 1997.

Valéry, Paul. Translated by Ralph Manheim. *Sea Shells.* 96p. $18.00 (08070-6430-0). Boston, MA: Beacon Press, Fall 1998. A beautifully illustrated gift book for literary nature lovers by the French poet-philosopher; an engaging mediation on the aesthetics of the seashell. Wondering at the enormous variety of shells, Valery compares the "making" of human beings with that slow, continuous formation that is the "making" of nature. Foreward by Mary Oliver. — Beacon Press

Van Alstine, Ruth. *Fairies and Fantasies.* 40p. pap. $3.00. Van Alstine, Ruth, Fall 1996.

Van Wert, William. *Don Quickshot.* 102p. $19.95 (0-942979-31-1). pap. $9.95 (0-942979-32-X). Livingston, AL: Livingston Press, Fall 1996. In this mad picaresque journey through Latin America, the original Don is joined by Gulliver's figures, myth, literary theory and other B movies, as well as the shade of Lewis Carroll, memories of Vietnam, Egypt, and time travel. Most of all Don Quickshot is a celebration of language, in couplets through a novel. Van Wert's joyful nuttiness is without parallel. —Toby Olson

Van Wert, William F. *Proper Myth.* 64p. pap. $12.95 (0-914061-67-4). Alexandria, VA: Orchises Press, Spring 1998. From the painful force of Dido's long meditation through the author's own consciousness of myth's meaning, Van Wert examines the history of the race, women with men foremost, from a feminist perspective properly and often, in these poems' humor, improperly as well. Once again, his heady poetry seems infinitely various in its tones and complexities. Once again, Van Wert is as rich as his sources. —Toby Olson

Van Winckel, Nance. *After a Spell.* 78p. (1-881163-24-5). pap. $11.95 (1-881163-25-3). Oxford, OH: Miami University Press, Fall 1998. Van Winckel's angels are those of experience, of a life lived in a world populated by the strange and sordid, the supremely fictional and the shockingly real. —High Plains

Literary Review. [The] slide into and away from violence energizes her work. Like Rilke, she is a poet trying to leave the cerebral behind her in order to move into a more spiritual realm via the senses. —The Indiana Review. Like all successful spell casters, Van Winckel knows just what to offer, just what to withhold. And through these assured, finely crafted poems, we follow her brilliant summons into all the worlds of "after-ing": desire, pursuit, the shaping of time. —Linda Bierds

Vasconcellos, Cherry Jean. *Before Our Very Eyes.* 44p. pap. $6.00 (1-888219-06-8). Long Beach, CA: Pearl Editions, Spring 1997. Vasconcellos weaves poems [that] create a vision of the world as a place of longing and desire. —Denise Duhamel, Chiron Review

Vaultonburg, Thomas L. *Detached Retinas.* 70p. pap. $10.00 (0-9670191-0-9). Byron, IL: Zombie Logic Press, Spring 1997. Extremely original and daring poems by one of the most talented young poets in America. —Zombie Logic Press

Veinstein, Alain. Translated by Robert Kocik and Rosmarie Waldrop. *Even a*

Child. 64p. pap. $10.00 (1-886224-28-5). Providence, RI: Burning Deck, Fall 1997. Veinstein's haunting elegies and meditations try to encircle the impossible space between not yet and already no more, between having to talk and not being able to speak. His very language burrows into the earth, tries, literally and obsessively, to come to grips with birth and death, with the all too fragile, vulnerable body. —Burning Deck

Velásquez, Gloria. *I Used To Be a Superwoman.* 127p. pap. $8.95 (1-55885-191-7). Houston, TX: Arte Público Press, Spring 1997. The Chicana movement lives on, fierce and passionate, in the voice of Velásquez. Challenging our complacency, her resonant cries for justice "refuse to be silent/to be buried in obscurity." A consummate oral performer and speaker, Velásquez has been uniquely successful in transferring onto the printed page the drama of reciting poetry on barrio streets. These pages burn with the fire of action and commitment. —Arte Publico Press

Venclova, Tomas. Translated by Diana Senechal. *Winter Dialogue.* 148p. $22.50 (0-8101-1491-7). Northwestern

University Press/Hydra Books, Spring 1997. This collection of thirty poems may be compared to the critical essays that have made Venclova famous: they are as distinctive and insightful as they are finely and intelligently crafted. Featuring an introduction by the late Joseph Brodsky, this edition also includes an exchange between Venclova and Nobel laureate Czeslaw Milosz, about the city of their respective youths and its profound influence on their work. —Northwestern University Press. Venclova is not only the best living poet of the Lithuanian language, but also the best poet that Lithuania has ever had. —Stanislaw Baranczak

Vest, Jennifer Lisa. *Names.* 63p. El Cerrito, CA: Indigenous Speak, 1997.

Vicinanza, Faith E. *In the Thick of It.* 21p. pap. $5.00 (1-887012-03-6). Newtown, CT: Hanover Press, 1996. Vicinanza has given us a book of poetry which leads us into oncoming traffic. Perhaps there should be a sign on the front cover — "You must stand this high — before readig this book" — or — "Those with weak hearts. . . " It's probably best for all of us that Vicinanza is a gifted poet,

not a taxi cab driver! —
Elizabeth Thomas. Vicinanza's
poetry has the ability to startle, to seethe with emotion,
and to move you with its
intensity and vivid imagery.
—Joe Ramirez

Vicuña, Cecilia. Translated by
Esther Allen; Edited by M.
Catherine de Zegher. *Quipoem
/ The Precarious: The Art and
Poetry of Cecilia Vicuña.*
250p. $30.00 (0-8195-6324-2).
University Press of New
England/Wesleyan University
Press, Spring 1998. Vicuña
combines Andean vernacular
with other languages to form
highly condensed metaphors,
puns, and anagrams, thus
inventing language looms on
which meaning is woven. —
University Press of New
England / Wesleyan
University Press. For the
Inkas, everything in the world
existed to end up in a quipu.
Vicuña 's quipoem is a 30-year
count of the threads, an
account of her dangling work
as poet, sculptor, installation
artist, performance artist, and
filmmaker. —Eliot
Weinberger

Vicuña, Cecilia, ed.
Translated by John Bierhorst.
*Ül: Four Mapuche Poets: An
Anthology.* 150p. pap. $15.95
(0-935480-99-4). Pittsburgh,
PA: Latin American Literary

Review Press, Spring 1998. A
collection of work by contemporary Chilean poets Elicura
Chihuailaf, Leonel Lienlaf,
Jaime Luis Huenún, and
Graciela Huinao. Written in
the poets' native Mapudungun
and Spanish, and appearing
with English translations,
these extraordinary poems celebrate the rich indigenous heritage of Chile. —Latin
American Literary Review
Press

Villani, Luisa. *On the Eve of
Everything.* 24p. pap. $5.95.
Fox River Grove, IL: White
Eagle Coffee Store Press,
Spring 1998. Villani's poems
reverberate with a dark and
charming pulse of spiritual
expectancy. What can happen
On the Eve of Everything? As
the title suggest, these poems
are [filled with a longing for
life] to, at last, merge with the
luminosity of its under-life
reflection, and reveal itself in
a wild reverent vision. —
Scott Lumbard

Villanueva, Alma Luz.
Desire. 171p. pap. $12.00 (0-
927534-76-2). Tempe, AZ:
Bilingual Press, Fall 1998. In
poems that are lyrical, humorous, and gritty, Villanueva
embraces all of life's experiences — the bittersweet experience of motherhood, affection for people and animals,

ritual, death, grief, and exaltation. Her poems fuse the personal and the political, anchoring the abstract in the sensual world and revealing a belief in the power of language to connect us to the world, to each other, and to ourselves. — Bilingual Press. Her transformational journey becomes my journey. She speaks from the heart and reaches the heart. — Burleigh Muten

Villanueva, Tino. *Shaking Off the Dark.* 101p. pap. $9.00 (0-927534-73-8). Tempe, AZ: Bilingual Press, Spring 1998. Villanueva was among the Chicano poets who emerged between the late 1960's and the early 1980's to write in both English and Spanish, often switching between the two languages in the same poem, thereby stressing the tension as well as the richness of living within two different languages. Shaking Off the Dark journeys between the world of the self and the world of social conflict, moving easily from lyrical to playful to prophetic. First published in 1984, Shaking Off the Dark has established itself as one of the classics of Chicano literature. This new edition features a section of haiku and tanka not included in the first edition. —Bilingual Press

Villatoro, Marcos McPeek. *They Say That I Am Two.* 87p. pap. $8.95 (1-55885-196-8). Houston, TX: Arte Público Press, Spring 1997. Villatoro explores life in the Latino world, both in Central America and in the United States. From the vision of a beautiful Nicaraguan woman guarding the Honduran border during wartime to a raucous, heretical reflection upon organized religion, They Say That I Am Two is poignant, comic and planted deep in the rich soil of many languages and voices. —Arte Público Press. If you hunger for poetry that itself hungers, that kisses the earth and counts the bones, rejoice. Villatoro writes it. Here is the power of life freshly clarified by the imagination. Above all, here is the vision and compassion of a poet with something to say and the language in which to say it. — Marvin Bell

Villella, Charlene. *White Silk.* 91p. Concord, CA: Small Poetry Press, 1994.

Vlasopolos, Anca. *Through the Straits, At Large.* 36p. pap. $8.00 (1-56439-053-5). Detroit, MI: Ridgeway Press, Spring 1997. Detroit poet Vlasopolos takes a journey through the dire straits of life and death in post-industrial America. —Ridgeway Press

Volkman, Karen. *Crash's Law.* 64p. $18.95 (0-393-03956-0). pap. $11.00 (0-393-31722-6). New York, NY: Norton, W.W., and Company, Spring 1996; Fall 1997 (paper). With a jumpy, jazzy feel for language, this poet's spirit doesn't put on angel airs. Volkman can make an evanescence out of a carnivorousness; thus she's an analyst of love. From its very first words, Crash's Law bespeaks a mind attuned no less to the accidents than to the orders of a sensual life. —Heather McHugh. Volkman's poems are quintessentially lyric — blood raw, soul-stinging, torqued by their forcefulness. A riveting, fresh collection. —Booklist

Vollmer, Judith. *Black Butterfly.* 22p. pap. $45.00. New York, NY: Center for Book Arts, Fall 1997. Letterpress edition. Winner of the 1997 Center for Book Arts Poetry Chapbook Contest, judged by Sharon Dolin and Mark Doty.

Vollmer, Judith. *The Door Open to the Fire.* 70p. pap. $12.00 (1-880834-41-3). Cleveland, OH: Cleveland State University Poetry Center, Fall 1998. Winner of the 1997 Cleveland State University Poetry Center Prize. Vollmer is a poet of righteous rages and bad moods, hilarity and tender griefs. She has done for the city of Pittsburgh what William Carlos Williams sought to do for Paterson, what O'Hara did for New York, and Baudelaire for Paris. —Liz Rosenberg. Vollmer's embrace is so wide, her enthusiasm for participation in the streaming variations of life so evident, that these poems sweep us up in their energies, their flesh-and-blood longings, their deeply human sense of helplessness and hope. This is a citizen's testament, as passionate and complicated as a great city demands. —Mark Doty. What is amazing is the book's exemplary originality. The Door Open to the Fire is a book about the city as an idea, about the city as a body. The writing is stern and gorgeous, wry and mournful. —Lynn Emanuel

Vroman, Leo. *Flight 800/Vlucht 800.* 48p. pap. $50.00 (0-89304-188-2). Merrick, NY: Cross-Cultural Communications, Fall 1997. Limited Letterpress edition.

Wade, Sidney. *Green.* 75p. $15.95 (1-5700-3267-X). pap.

$9.95 (1-5700-3268-8).
Columbia, SC: University of
South Carolina Press, Fall
1998. The landscape of these
poems ranges from the shores
of the Orient to a uniquely
metaphysical American
Midwest, as well as the classical underworld, Romanesque
basilicas, the often rocky terrain of the territory of marriage, and the more intimate
geographies of the kitchen, the
cupboard, the bed, and the
body. The book begins in bliss
and ends on the brink, in a
journey that charts the intrica-
cies of the all-too-human,
bewildered heart. —University
of South Carolina Press

Wagner, Thomas. *The
Diffident Beast, The Amiable
Lord, The Lorn Amorist.* 82p.
$10.95 (1-887750-03-7).
Bethel, CT: Rutledge Books,
Fall 1996. The infectious pleasure of Wagner's poems recalls
a time when such playful
invention had useful authority,
and one could speak one's
mind in all the ways one could
muster. Dear thanks to him
for reminding us it can be fun!
—Robert Creeley

Wakoski, Diane. *Argonaut
Rose.* 184p. $27.50 (1-57423-
047-6). pap. $14.00 (1-57423-
046-8). Santa Rosa, CA: Black
Sparrow Press, Spring 1998.
An epic journey of search and
discovery. Here, sexuality
remains the constant ground of
deception. Desire and betrayal, the gold of youth and the
silver of age, intuition and
wisdom intermingle in a rich
thematic weave. —Black
Sparrow Press

Walcott, Derek. *The Bounty.*
78p. $18.00 (0-374-11556-7).
pap. $12.00 (0-374-52537-4).
New York, NY: Farrar, Straus
and Giroux, Spring 1997;
Spring 1998 (new paper).
Walcott has moved with gradually deepening confidence to
found his own poetic domain,
independent of the tradition he
inherited yet not altogether
orphaned from it. The Walcott
line is still sponsored by
Shakespeare and the Bible,
happy to surprise by fine
excess. It can be incantatory
and self-entrancing. It can be
athletic and demotic. It can
can compel us with the almost
hydraulic drag of its words.
—Seamus Heaney. For
almost 40 years his throbbing
and relentless lines kept arriv-
ing in the English language
like tidal waves, coagulating
into an archipelago of poems
without which the map of
modern literature would effectively match wallpaper. He
gives us more than himself or
"a world"; he gives us a sense
of infinity embodied in the
language. —Joseph Brodsky

Waldman, Anne. *Iovis: All Is Full of Jove, Book II.* 312p. pap. $15.95 (1-56689-053-5). Minneapolis, MN: Coffee House Press, Fall 1997. In this second volume, Waldman pursues the duty she charged herself with at the close of her previous volume — "to blunt the knife." Male war making and aggression, old stubborn patriarchal social forms, and the damages of industrial and military expansionism raise the poet into a rage of spiritual compassion. This is epic poetry that goes beyond the old injunction "to include history"— its effort is to change history. —Coffee House Press. Waldman has embarked on a fearless cultural intervention. The second volume continues this bardic exploration by turning to the female and feminine materials of our culture. Waldman manifests an avid female intelligence in her poetry of human joy. —Rachel Blau DuPlessis

Waldman, Anne; Eleni Sikelianos, and Laird Hunt. *Au Lit Holy or Transgressions of the Maghreb.* 30p. pap. $4.50 (0-9658877-2-3). Erie, CO: Smokeproof Press, Fall 1998.

Waldner, Liz. *Homing Devices.* 86p. pap. $9.00 (1-882022-31-9). O Books, Spring 1998. More of a small wiry museum than a book, Robert Walser-like, a cute girl chewing a pencil, God it's my dream of literature, this kind of writing, shapeless and surprising, then not. Stern and quite alert. Waldner's Homing Devices awakened me to how often I'm unused when I read, here I'm occupied, confused, satisfied. The book is enough. She's great. —Eileen Miles. So much of what has been wonderful in American poetry continues and blossoms entirely afresh in Homing Devices that I am delighted and a little awed to discover it. Here I find the beautiful salutations of James Schuyler in dew voice. Here I witness the tender experiment of Gertrude Stein practised with new acuity this very moment. Best of all, I find an original companion voice for the end of the century, one with whom to "walk with a step like milk." Homing Devices is superb. — Donald Revell

Waldrop, Keith. *Analogies of Escape.* 80p. pap. $10.00 (1-886224-29-3). Providence, RI: Burning Deck, Fall 1997. Waldrop is among the most important writers, translators and publishers of avant-garde literature in our time. His general subject — memory, the mother of the muses — is classical, while the form, mixing poetry and prose fragments, is more experimental. The result is a highly engaging and eclectic exploration of the follies of memory. Waldrop's light touch and understated humor cast a sustained spell. We are privileged to listen in. —Publishers Weekly

Waldrop, Keith. *The Silhouette of the Bridge (Memory Stand-Ins).* 76p. pap. $8.95 (1-880713-08-X). Penngrove, CA: Avec Books, 1997. A beautifully spare and inventive work of reflection on the elusive nature of memory, perception and experience, it is suffused with a particular humanity and an appreciation for the absurd, even the grotesque in daily life. With his quietly precise sense of modulation and his unerring gaze, Waldrop remains one of the vital and requisite, semi-secret presences in American letters. —Michael Palmer. Writing with his usual consummate clarity, Waldrop has given us a meditation with the intimate thrall of a bedtime story —Ann Lauterbach

Waldrop, Rosmarie. *Another Language: Selected Poems.* 118p. pap. $10.50 (1-883689-51-1). Jersey City, NJ: Talisman House, Publishers, Fall 1997. A thinker and a

poet is an extraordinary combination. Waldrop is both. —World Literature Today.

Waldrop, Rosmarie. *Blindsight.* 28p. pap. $4.00. Saratoga, ca: Instress, Fall 1998.

Waldrop, Rosmarie. *In a Flash.* 17p. pap. $4.00. Saratoga, ca: Instress, Spring 1998.

Waldrop, Rosmarie. *Split Infinites.* 112p. pap. $14.00 (0-935162-17-8). Philadelphia, PA: Singing Horse Press, Fall 1998. This influential avant-garde doyenne handily manages the paradox of the lucid enigma. Although her poems — with their casual abstractions and philosophical tints — wear their French influences on their sleeve, she maintains a distinctly American voice — quick-witted, conversational, and visually concrete. [Her's is] a poetry that pleases no less than it puzzles. —Voice Literary Supplement

Waldrop, Rosmarie, and Keith Waldrop. *Well Well Reality: Collaborations.* 92p. pap. $14.00 (0-942996-30-5). Sausalito, CA: Post-Apollo Press, Spring 1998. These are collaborations between Rosmarie and Keith Waldrop, each of whom has authored more than a dozen books of poetry. —Post Apollo Press. When Rosmarie and Keith [Waldrop] write poems together, whose poems are those poems? They are the poems of a third poet, whose name and gender and origin and language we do not know. — Jacques Roubaud

Walke, Roger. *The Beach and Other Poems.* 56p. pap. $5.95 (0-936015-77-2). Blacksburg, VA: Pocahontas Press, Fall 1997. Walke embraces life like a lover who is repeatedly rebuffed but never gives up — knowing that while she will never fully accept him, life will never entirely reject him either. —Pocahontas Press

Walker, Jeanne Murray. *Gaining Time.* 80p. pap. $12.95 (0-914278-73-8). Providence, RI: Copper Beech Press, Fall 1997. Walker's Gaining Time is alight with her love of life. She has richly and profoundly imagined the history of her Minnesota village, and has given us a paean to the continuity of experience. Hers is a poetry of lyricism, intelligence, clarity, and wit. —Daniel Hoffman. Walker flies high — also low and close when necessary — over her mighty subject, the inventing of

America. Chronicling it with the accurate extravagance it deserves, she discovers the fabulous in the daily and the wayward as a way of life. — Theodore Weiss

Walker, Michele. *Trainkickers.* 42p. pap. $7.00. Chicago, IL: Inertia Press, Fall 1997.

Wallace, Ronald. *The Uses of Adversity.* 114p. $25.00 (0-8229-4067-1). pap. $12.95 (0-8229-5671-3). Pittsburgh, PA: University of Pittsburgh Press, Fall 1998.

Wallach, Yona. Translated by Linda Zisquit. *Wild Light.* 74p. pap. $12.95 (1-8878818-54-6). Riverdale-on-Hudson, NY: Sheep Meadow Press, Fall 1997. Wallach's mystical "wild light," which bestows "understanding of the doubleness within her," is a light that takes darkness into account. The illness is therefore that necessary night, without which it is impossible to arrive at "the hidden inner light." This is the way down which is the way up; this is Yona's way. —Aharon Shabtai

Wallenstein, Barry, Coordinator. *Poetry in Performance 26: Annual Spring Poetry Festival, May*

15, 1998. 173p. City College of New York, Spring 1998.

Walsh, James. *Foundations.* 125p. pap. $15.00 (1-880516-18-7). Barrytown, NY: Left Hand Books, Fall 1997. Foundations documents James Walsh's wall-hung and site/non-site specific sculptures executed in mud, leaves, chalk, bricks and stones. These rectangular forms evoke building foundations and what Robert Smithson termed "ruins in reverse." Walsh's text is itself a map, siting his foundations both within his personal history and the history of culture. Walsh links his work to both ancient and modern contexts, revealing how his minimalist work connects to the Nazca lines and 20th century land art. —Left Hand Books

Wanek, Connie. *Bonfire.* 95p. pap. $12.95 (0-89823-178-7). Minneapolis, MN: New Rivers Press, Fall 1997. Wanek's poems seem quiet and unassuming, and they are, but they are not so benign as they may superficially appear. Wanek never allows us to get too comfortable in this world. Her poems take the moment, turn it upside down, open it, examine it. They give us a view from the dragonfly's eye, they show us the beauty, the

humor, the danger we might have missed. —Louis Jenkins

Wang Ping. *Of Flesh and Spirit.* 102p. pap. $12.95 (1-56689-068-3). Minneapolis, MN: Coffee House Press, Spring 1998. Wang Ping is a cultural treasure, an heroic person, and the first great poet of the new millennium. —Lewis Warsh. Riveting, confessional, fierce poetry. Wang Ping makes her singular way with passion and vigor. She explodes the safe boundaries of culture, gender, and female sexuality. These meditations reveal the incongruities between Byzantine bureaucracy and the needs of a free spirit. —Anne Waldman. Wang Ping's poems are notable for their incisive images and psychological acuity. Of Flesh and Spirit journeys from China to America and weaves passion and memoir into a shining loop. —Arthur Sze

Ward, B. J. *17 Love Poems With No Despair.* 41p. pap. $6.50 (1-55643-243-7). Berkeley, CA: North Atlantic Books, Spring 1997. 17 Love Poems With No Despair resounds with the voice of a clear, powerful speaker. Ward does not naively deny despair but rather refuses it, making a case to the reader that proffers love as an antidote. This book is an offering of passion wrought with charm and poignancy. —N.F. Ingram. A book, this book, made a difference in my life. [These are] 17 of the most beautiful poems I ever read. —B. Vouglas, Hunterdon Democrat

Ward, Candace, ed. *World War One British Poets: Brooke, Wen, Sassoon, Rosenberg and Others.* 64p. pap. $1.00 (0-486-29568-0). Mineola, NY: Dover Publications, Spring 1997. Moving and powerful, this carefully chosen collection offers today's readers an excellent overview of the broad range of verse produced as poets responded to the carnage on the fields of Belgium and France. Includes work by Robert Graves, Thomas Hardy, Siegfried Sassoon, Wilfred Owen and many others. —Dover Publications

Ward, Edward R. *Where Memory Gathers: Baseball and Poetry.* 91p. pap. $9.95 (0-945213-33-6). San Francisco, CA: Forum Press/Rudi Publishing, Spring 1998. In a unique and inviting work, Ward blends poetry and the American national pastime — baseball. His poems and insights combine the basic moves of poetry with the action found on a baseball dia-

mond. Baseball enthusiasts will appreciate the extensive list of additional reading on the quintessential American sport. —Forum Press

Waring, Belle. *Dark Blonde.* 88p. $20.95 (1-889330-07-8). pap. $12.95 (1-889330-08-6). Louisville, KY: Sarabande Books, Fall 1997. Dark Blonde is graceful and streetwise. Here's a collection that traverses multiple worlds, and yet it demands our feet tread solid earth. Wherever Waring takes us, whether it's among the pages of a prison nurse's diary or into the dark heart of a crow's mysterious language, we are delighted to follow because we can trust the craft in Dark Blonde to transport us to a clear-sighted summit. — Yusef Komunyakaa. Waring exhibits the street-smart ear and unflinching eye that made her first collection, Refuge one of Publishers Weekly's Best Books of 1990. The images and headlong rhythms of these new poems exert a wide-ranging, often irresistible pull. —Publishers Weekly.

Warren, Robert Penn. Edited by John Burt. *The Collected Poems of Robert Penn Warren.* 830p. $39.95 (0-8071-2333-1). Baton Rouge, LA: Louisiana State University Press, Fall 1998. A central figure in twentieth-century American literature, Robert Penn Warren wrote enduring fiction as well as influential works of literary criticism and theory. Yet, as this variorum edition of his published poems suggests, it is his poetry — spanning sixty years, sixteen volumes of verse, and a wide range of styles — that places Warren among America's foremost men of letters. In this indispensable volume, John Burt, Warren's literary executor, has gathered together every poem Warren ever published (with the exception of Brother to Dragons). A record of Burt's comprehensive analysis is found in this edition's textual notes, list of emendations, and explanatory notes. — Louisiana State University Press

Warsh, Lewis. *Private Agenda.* 48p. pap. $9.00. Hornswoggle Press, Fall 1996.

Washburn, Katharine; John S. Major, and Clifton Fadiman, eds. *World Poetry: From Antiquity to Our Time.* 1338p. $45.00 (0-393-04130-1). New York, NY: Norton, W.W., and Company, Fall 1997. This long-awaited, indispensable volume contains more than 1600 poems drawn from dozens of languages and cultures, and spans a period of more than 4000 years from ancient Sumer and Egypt to the late twentieth century. This is no mere sampler: in choosing only works of the highest intrinsic quality, the editors have created a book that will surprise knowledgeable readers and lead newcomers to an understanding of the glories of world poetry that is our common heritage. —W.W. Norton

Washington, Peter, ed. *Love Songs and Sonnets.* 256p. $12.50 (0-679-45465-9). Knopf/Everyman's Library Pocket Poets, Fall 1997. Here are songs, sonnets, and lyric poems that focus on love in the widest sense, encompassing relationships of all kinds. The volume includes Ronsard, Yeats, Lowell, Elizabeth Barrett Browning, and Burns, whose comparison of his love to a red, red rose is in amusing contrast to Heine's comparison of his beloved Gertrude to a beautiful pig. —Knopf

Washington, Peter, ed. *The Roman Poets.* 256p. $12.50 (0-375-40071-0). Knopf/Everyman's Library Pocket Poets, Fall 1997. Odes, elegies, and epigrams; humor, passion, wit, scathing satire, and touching lyricism: the best of the great Roman poets presented here in translations by poets such as Christopher

Marlowe, Alexander Pope, Alfred, Lord Tennyson, and Rudyard Kipling. —Knopf

Waters, Mary Ann. *The Names of Time.* 76p. $20.00 (1-881090-29-9). Lewiston, ID: Confluence Press, Spring 1998. [Waters's] poems combine, with power and grace, the elements of both her poetic vocation and her profession as teacher. In every poem of this posthumous collection is the sense of her delight in the craft, her reticence, her love and care for her people and her world. —James J. McAuley

Waters, Michael. *Green Ash, Red Maple, Black Gum.* 80p. $20.00 (1-880238-42-X). pap. $12.50 (1-880238-43-8). Rochester, NY: BOA Editions, Spring 1997. Waters' poems challenge us to abide one another and embrace humanity's imperfections. Viewing curiosities in a medical museum, Waters asks: "How then can I forget / these jars stuffed with the invisible / masses who touch us in our dreams, who steep / our yearnings in their milky waters?" —BOA Editions. Waters' varied and adroit applications of rhyme often lend synoptic clarity to a profusion of sensory detail. Moreover, he manages to emboss his lines with images

and metaphors that evade the inherent pitfalls of voluptuousness. I cannot call to mind anyone of Waters' generation who is currently writing better poetry. —Floyd Collins, The Gettysburg Review

Watson, Ellen Doré. *We Live in Bodies.* 80p. pap. $9.95 (1-882295-12-9). Farmington, ME: Alice James Books, Spring 1997. Watson is an eloquent, passionate poet; generosity of imagination distinguishes both her gift for language and her emotional sympathy: interrogative, tender, wildly inventive, with the wonder of childhood and a grown woman's comic sense. And her work has the quality of movement. Watson's poetry is the real thing. —Robert Pinsky. You will close this book exhilarated by its quirky, passionate poems and grateful for its huge heart fired and fed by a prodigious imagination. This is brilliant, urgent work. —Thomas Lux. These poems reveal the strange and hidden beauty of the body, and show us how, as both landscape and vehicle, it can drive us deep into our truest selves. — Dorianne Laux

Watson, Jr., Maurice T. *The Gloria Cycle.* pap. $10.00 (1-888832-09-6). St. Augustine,

FL: Kings Estate Press, Fall 1998.

Watten, Barrett. *Bad History.* 152p. pap. $12.95 (1-891190-02-4). Berkely, CA: Atelos, Fall 1998. In a famous modern definition an epic is a poem including history. In Bad History, history includes the poem. Begun to mark the first anniversary of the Gulf War, the poem looks back on the decades previous and forward toward a duration of events, which, because the poem is in history, do not cease to occur. The poem, too, becomes the event of its own recording. — Atelos

Watten, Barrett. *Frame (1971-1990).* 325p. pap. $13.95 (1-55713-239-9). Los Angeles, CA: Sun & Moon Press, Fall 1997. Watten crosses shifting cultural terrains by means of deliberate engagements in language. His thought, embodied with visionary clarity, passes forcefully between differing modes of experience. His innovative techniques recall the poetics of André Breton's points sublimes. —Sun & Moon Press. I would be hard pressed to think of an art writing which is more engaged with the relation of poetic method and contemporary political and cultur-al materials than Watten's. — Ron Day

Weaver, Afaa M. *Talisman.* 95p. pap. $10.95 (1-882688-17-1). Chicago, IL: Tia Chucha Press, Spring 1998. Descriptive and endearing poems capture five of the women in the poet's life. The poems are a bit like the relationships — engaging and alive, but with a kick and a surprise at the end. —Akiba Sullivan Harper

Webb, Charles Harper. *Dr. Invisible and Mr. Hide.* 40p. pap. $6.00 (1-888219-09-2). Long Beach, CA: Pearl Editions, Spring 1998. A collection on topics as diverse as fishing and introspection dazed by regret, written with emotion that cartwheels through love and derision, optimism and realism, comedy and error. —Tim Grobaty, Long Beach Press-Telegram

Webb, Charles Harper. *Reading the Water.* 85p. pap. $10.95 (1-55553-325-6). Boston, MA: Northeastern University Press, Fall 1997. Webb has a wild inventive energy, a quirky, at times even manic wit, and a deep sense of wonder at the world. His poems are filled with curiosities, with odd facts and details, with unlikely anecdotes — all of which he takes personally. As a poet, he's a wiseacre, a troublemaker — part stand-up comic, part anthropologist, part visionary. He is funny and can be withering about contemporary life; his irony gives him no rest. And yet he is a romantic despite himself: a singer of tales, a poet of praise. —Edward Hirsch

Webb, Don. Edited by Bobbi Sinha. *Anubis on Guard: The Selected Poetry of Don Webb.* 34p. pap. $4.95. Concord, CA: Dark Regions Press, Fall 1998. Planet visits: dream of cool on Venus, blood Moon, Jupiter's "wonderful scale," sunlight rumor on Pluto. Space tour segues to hearty mytho-gram prose, otherworld wise sonnets, sci-fi fantasy paradigm hi-tides and revital magic verse. —Dragon's Breath

Weber, Mark. *February Is the Crookedest Month.* 32p. $16.00. pap. $8.00. Cape Porpoise, ME: Clamp Down Press, Fall 1998. [Weber has been an] incomparable, major voice in the American small press for more than ten years. —Joan Jobe Smith

Weber, Mark. *I'll Be Go To Hell.* 20p. pap. $4.00. Albuquerque, NM: Zerx Press, Spring 1997.

Weber, Mark. *Libretto to Compact Disk: O Shenandoah Be Not Telling Me This.* 26p. pap. $4.00. Albuquerque, NM: Zerx Press, Fall 1997. [Weber] brings to contemporary poetry a wry sense of humor, a jaundiced observation and an instinct for the absurd. —Kirk Silsbee

Weber, Mark. *Pleasure Time.* 10p. Maple City, MI: Smiling Dog Press, Fall 1996. Handset letterpress edition with lineoleum carvings. —Smiling Dog Press

Weber, Mark. *Some Sort of Easy Life.* 46p. pap. $4.95. Cold River Press/ Mt. Aukum Press, Fall 1997. Personal history. California Okies. Junkie & jail stories. Poems. True. —Cold River Press/Mt. Aukum Press

Weber, Mark. *Vehicle Vortex Vertigo.* 24p. pap. $4.00. Albuquerque, NM: Zerx Press, Fall 1998. Halucinatory poetry about cars and driving. —Zerx Press

Webster, Catherine, ed. *Over This Soil: An Anthology of World Farm Poems.* 166p. $24.95 (0-87745-616-X). pap. $12.95 (0-87745-617-8). Iowa City, IA: University of Iowa Press, Spring 1998. The poems in Over This Soil are a poignant reminder of the critical bond between the amazing renewable natural resources of our farms and who we are as people. As goodwill ambassadors, these poems are timeless and humbling. They should be on every shelf for quick reference when the soul needs replenishing. —Ralph Grossi

Weems, Mary E. *White.* 36p. pap. $4.75 (0-87338-571-3). Kent, OH: Kent State University Press, Spring 1997. Energy, dynamic energy emanates from Weems's careful observing eyes into her language. These poems offer immediacy, intelligent response, and rich repartee with the difficult urban world of a gentle warrior. —Diane Wakoski

Weil, Joe. *In Praise We Enter: Poems 1972-1997.* 71p. pap. $10.00 (1-877968-18-8). Cranford, NJ: Rain Bucket Press, Spring 1998. Weil shapes an urban landscape that is clear to us all, with a threadbare beauty and a cast of characters who maintain their dignity against all odds. —Maria Mazziotti Gillan. Our Whitman. . . real, simple in the sweet sense, imagistically gifted and energetic. One of the very best poets in

America today. —Emanuel di Pasquale. A genuine artist. — Ruth Stone

Weinberger, Florence. *Breathing Like a Jew.* 46p. pap. $10.00 (1-887344-04-7). Goshen, CT: Chicory Blue Press, Fall 1997. Weinberger's poems [are] rooted in details of personal and family life and their connection to this century's history. She raises, out of pleasure and horror, out of mysticism and skepticism, on long breaths and almost incantatory music, a moving affirmation of being in the world. Breathing Like a Jew is #11 in the Crimson Edge Chapbook Series, which seeks to support and encourage older women writers and to increase their publishing opportunities. — Chicory Blue Press

Weinberger, Florence. *The Invisible Telling Its Shape.* 96p. pap. $10.00 (1-56474-195-8). Santa Barbara, CA: Fithian Press, Spring 1997. Weinberger's project is to limn the outlines of the invisible world so that we may become aware of it. Although her specific subjects are autobiographical, Weinberger's technique is like magical realism, transforming the world to better reveal it. —Booklist. What intrigues me about these poems is how they combine directness with mystery. Though their surface is straightforward, they don't give themselves away. The storyteller's impulse is strong even in poems that are not narrative. —Lisel Mueller

Weiner, Hannah. *We Speak Silent.* 70p. pap. $9.95 (0-937804-68-1). New York, NY: Roof Books, Fall 1996. We Speak Silent is an opus of the quirky relationships between people and their words. In it, Weiner becomes a vessel for the emotional spectrum of the human comedy. It confirms hers as one of the most unique and fascinating of oeuvres, a continuing adventure in language. —Roof Books

Weingarten, Roger. *Ghost Wrestling.* 86p. $19.95 (1-56792-039-X). Boston, MA: Godine, David R., Publisher, Spring 1997. In a polite age, Weingarten's poems are resolutely impolite; they allow for the snarl and the howl, for rancor and jealousy, lust and resentment and regret laced with dark laughter. His edgy voice [is] an unmistakable presence in contemporary poetry. —Mark Doty. Musical, funny, terrifying poems of relationship in which the domestic is linked to the feral, the demotic to the fantastic. Weingarten writes like no other. —Alice Fulton. These poems come and getcha like a carny barker at a raree show, who promises high-octane energy — and delivers. You can put in your thumb at random and be sure of retrieving the one true plum that satisfies. —Albert Goldbarth

Weiss, Mark. *Fieldnotes.* 96p. pap. $11.00 (1-88152-304-7). San Diego, CA: Junction Press, 1995.

Weiss, T. and R. Weiss, eds. *Quarterly Review of Literature, Volume 36.* pap. $12.00 (1-888545-03-8). Princeton, NJ: Quarterly Review of Literature, Spring 1997. The five full length collections included here are works by Yannis Patilis, Camel of Darkness: Selected Poems (1970-1990), translated from the Greek by Stathis Gourgouris; Warren Carrier, An Ordinary Man; Christopher Bursk, The One True Religion; Joseph Powell, Getting Here; and Fadhil Al -Azzawi, In Every Well a Joseph Weeping, translated from the Arabic by Khaled Mattawa. —Quarterly Review of Literature

Welch, Don. *A Brief History of Feathers.* 53p. pap. $9.95 (0-9635559-6-0). Lincoln, NE: Slow Tempo Press, Spring 1997.

Wendell, Julia. *Wheeler Lane.* 83p. pap. $9.95 (1-891272-00-4). Bedford, NH: Igneus Press, Spring 1998. Strong, direct, personal and passionate, Wendell's poems gain their power not from the painful loss they explore but from the difficult knowledge they admit their readers to examine. Wheeler Lane is Wendell's highest achievement yet as a poet. —Michael Collier. This is a gorgeous book. The poems do what poems should — link small or temporal bits of reality to the big things that endure. — Jenny Keith, Baltimore's City Paper

Werner, Marshall. *Thawing the Mermaid.* 28p. pap. $9.00. Werner, Marshall, Fall 1998.

Wesley, Patricia Jabbeh. *Before the Palm Could Bloom: Poems of Africa.* 84p. pap. $12.00 (0-932826-64-4). Kalamazoo, MI: New Issues Press, Fall 1998. In Before the Palm Could Bloom, Wesley writes poems of the Liberian civil war and the devastation it has wrought; in poems of village life and customs, the city life of Monrovia, the rites of childhood and adolescence, Wesley records for the reader a world that has been forever changed. [Her] poems incorporate many African voices, and range in tone from sorrow and longing, to humor and ironic wit. —New Issues Press. Liberian emigre Wesley brings us frontline poetic reportage. Many of the voices in these poems speak only here. —Publishers Weekly

West, Charles M. *Moods of Life: A Collection of Christian Poetry Centering Around Real Life Issues.* 51p. pap. $9.95 (1-56315-117-0). Pittsburgh, PA: Sterling House, Fall 1998. [West] shares with us sentiments often thought but seldom spoken. He demonstrates great power and insight and beautifully expresses his passion for God in a book that people of any faith will want to read. —Sterling House. A unique collection that reflects the world view of a man who takes God, family, friends and life seriously. —Dr. Tony Evans

Wetzsteon, Rachel. *Home and Away.* 94p. pap. $14.95 (0-14-058892-2). New York, NY: Penguin Books/Viking Penguin, Fall 1998. Wetzsteon has been hailed by John Hollander as the writer of "the most impressive verse I have seen by anyone of her generation" and by Richard Howard as "the most variously gifted of our new poets." Home and Away is her second collection.

—Penguin Books. Wetzsteon's effortless lyricism gives her moralized landscapes and urban pastorals a fluent grace. But her poems also sparkle with mischief. Often mordantly, they trace complex, paradoxical geographies of mind and heart, knowledge and need. —Rachel Hadas

Whalen, Philip. Selected by Miriam Sagan and Robert Winson. *Canoeing Up Cabarga Creek: Buddhist Poems 1955-1986.* 68p. pap. $12.00 (0-938077-79-1). Albany, CA: Parallax Press, Fall 1996. Whalen must be the most celebratory poet writing in American English. These poems are filled with great wisdom, boundless good humor, compassion and eternal delight. —Sam Hamill. Whalen's poems are packed with that strict wild Zen humor, enough to make the buddhas of old slap their thighs. —Andrew Schelling, Tricycle. Whalen's poems are nothing less, nothing more, than Zen Master Dogen's definition of enlightenment: intimacy with all things. —Jane Hirshfield

Wheeler, Susan. *Smokes.* 59p. pap. $12.95 (1-884800-19-X). Marshfield, MA: Four Way Books, Spring 1998. Smokes is a book that sets itself the

task of continuous invention and surprise. It's like listening to the still chancy and experimental transmission of the postmodern vehicle gleefully downshifting into the breezy updrafts of the traditional musics of English verse, and then lurching into the future again. Smokes contains elegies, poems of urban and domestic angst, laments, invectives, cakewalks, struts. Its confident, rueful, and playful grasp of its tradition is eye-opening and, sardonic as it is, boisterous fun. —Robert Hass

White, Claire Nicolas. *News From Home.* 43p. pap. $8.95 (1-878173-16-2). NORTH-PORT, NY: Birnham Wood Graphics, Fall 1998. These are poems infused with adroit and often poignant depictions of the space between the maleable and the enduring. It is a collection in devout attendance to the realization of mortality and intergenerational place-taking, with all its sense-laden richness. — George Wallace. Grounded in her close, painterly observations of the material world, you barely feel the liftoff when [White's] wit and intelligence take the poems to higher realms of discovery and revelation. But what is most moving, finally, is the keen sense of time's mysterious motion as it quietly negotiates between the now and then of this new, welcome collection. —Ron Overton

White, Kim. *Scratching for Something.* 68p. pap. $10.95 (0-9659890-0-3). New York, NY: Columbia University Creative Writing Center/Quarto Books, Spring 1998. [These interlocking prose poems] work both singly and as a whole with wonderful ease, combining a rich surface with a variety of undercurrents that ebb and flow, thematically and stylistically. This is a fine and rewarding debut. — Nicholas Christopher

White, Michael. *Palma Cathedral.* 90p. pap. $12.95 (0-87081-516-4). University Press of Colorado/Center for Literary Publishing, Fall 1998. Winner of the 1998 Colorado Prize for Poetry. There is a Wordsworthian grandeur about White's poems, a rhetorical and emotional fullness that is breathtaking. His attention to the shifting complexity of the natural world, his precise diction, his finely tuned cadences carry with them an unusual power, an immense gravity. Reading him, one feels the irresistible pull of belief in the retrievals of poetry, and in the imagination as the central and most persuasive means by

which we say Yes to the world. —Mark Strand

White, Sharon. *Bone House.* 76p. pap. $10.00 (0-932616-65-8). Towson, MD: Brickhouse Books, Fall 1998.

Whitman, Walt. Chosen by the The New York Public Library. *Leaves of Grass: Selected Poems and Prose.* 447p. $18.50 (0-385-48727-4). New York, NY: Doubleday/Anchor Books, 1997. Presents a selection of Whitman's greatest and most beautiful lyrics. Also included are four of [his] superbly poetic essays, among them the landmark preface to the first edition of Leaves of Grass. Enhanced by treasures from the archives of the New York Public Library, including handwritten poems and letters and a stunning array of portraits and illustrations, this Collector's Edition allows readers a rare opportunity to experience the poet and his world. —Doubleday/Anchor Books. Certain writers belong not only to the history of literature but to History itself, and Whitman is one of them. — Howard Moss.

Wickwire, Chester. *Longs Peak.* 80p. pap. $10.00 (0-932616-66-6). Brickhouse Books/Chestnut Hills Press,

Fall 1998. After years as an activist, Wickwire, in his 80s, turns to poetry to look back with a modest, wise, at times rueful, and always affectionate eye at his own history. — Eleanor Wilner. Longs Peak is about the work of a daring lifetime; it is also the work of a lifetime. Wickwire is, in turn, guide, provocateur, balm, bard and witness. —Lia Purpura

Wieners, John. *The Journal of John Wieners Is To Be Called 707 Scott Street for Billie Holiday, 1959.* 126p. pap. $12.95 (1-55713-252-6). Los Angeles, CA: Sun & Moon Press, Fall 1996. 707 Scott Street represents the poet at the height of his powers, and in this important work he alternates between the personal and the general, between prose observations and diaristic entries ("Sur-real is the only way to endure the real we find heaped up in our cities.") and some of the very best of his poetic lyrics. In fact, 707 Scott Street might be best described as a series of poems in the form of a journal, which, givem Wieners's belief in living as a form of poetry itself, should come as no surprise to his readers. —Sun & Moon Press

Wilde, Oscar. Edited by Anthony Fothergill. *Plays, Prose Writings and Poems.* 599p. pap. $8.95 (0-460-87655-4). Boston, MA: Tuttle, Charles E./Everyman, Fall 1996. A unique selection, with introduction, notes, selected criticism and chronology of Wilde's life and times. — Charles E. Tuttle/Everyman

Wilkins, W.R. *Strip Search.* 79p. pap. $10.00 (1-56474-216-4). Santa Barbara, CA: Fithian Press, Fall 1997. Wilkins bases his lines on the lure of the familiar. On the surface his poetry is about everyday things and experiences. Here we find the shock of the new in the familiar. — Statesman Journal. He's at his best when he remembers the hard times of his boyhood — cold bean sandwiches and third in line on the hand-me-down clothes. A fine trip through a good man's life. — Charles Champlin

Wilkinson, Claude. *Reading the Earth.* 75p. pap. $12.95 (0-87013-481-7). East Lansing, MI: Michigan State University Press/Lotus Poetry Series, Spring 1998. Winner of the 1998 Naomi Long Madgett Poetry Award. This collection demonstrates a rare sensitivity to the natural world and its significance to human lives.

Observer of the most mundane aspects of nature, Wilkinson immerses the reader in full participation in his Eden. — Michigan State University Press

Willey, Rosemary. *Intended Place.* 72p. $21.00 (0-87338-581-0). pap. $11.00 (0-87338-584-5). Kent, OH: Kent State University Press, Fall 1997. From the very first few pages, we realize that this voice embodies empathy and a to-the-point inquiry. Willey cannot keep her mind off the real things of this world, touching life where it feels good and where it pains, always snapping the chanced wishbone, and we are more blessed and richer for her daring talent. — Yusef Komunyakaa. In Willey's poems people are traveling and longing for home, or else they're at home longing to travel. If they have an intended place, where is it? What keeps us from drifting off like abandoned balloons is family life, though all too often we wish we could drift away from it. Her eye is alert, her intelligence wry, her heart wary but generous, and her poems are all of these. — William Matthews

Williams, Bruce. *Holistic Dressing: Clothes Poems and Other Obsessions.* 22p. pap.

$6.95. Johnstown, OH: Pudding House Publications, Spring 1998.

Williams, C.K. *The Vigil.* 78p. $18.00 (0-374-22653-9). pap. $12.00 (0-374-52554-4). Farrar, Straus and Giroux/Noonday, Spring 1997; Fall 1998 (new paper). Nominated for The National Book Critics Circle Award. Williams has been called one of the finest of living American poets. An original, in style and in content, he transforms inherited traditions, reweaving Whitman's long lines and Robert Lowell's intellectual energy into a self-probing, morally charged narrative-of-the-mind belonging only to himself. His work brims with the edgy dramas of what people do to, with, and for each other. —Poetry Flash. A matchless explorer of the burdens of consciousness, Williams has always written brilliantly about human pain, that which we inflict upon others and upon ourselves, and that which we experience in dreading what we're fated for. In The Vigil, Williams affirms the uncanny resiliency of love as solace for pain. It is a mystery he has probed before, but never with quite such sympathy and candor. —Jonathan Aaron, The Boston Globe

Williams, John A. *Safari West.* 78p. pap. $10.95 (0-9699349-2-0). Cross-Cultural Communications/Hochelaga Press, Fall 1998. Williams's poems are variously passionate meditations, sensitive philosophical explorations of ideas, or history. The reader thinks deeply about these poems on family, the slave trade, freedom, racism and love. This volume will add a new rich dimension to Williams's already distinguished, multidimensional career. —Clarence Major. A stunning achievement — gorgeously crafted, terribly moving, and meticulously graceful in its evocation of loss and exile, bondage and freedom. —Jay Neugeboren. [Williams is] a talent that promises to enrich American literature for a long time to come. —Arnold Rampersad

Williams, Lisa. *The Hammered Dulcimer.* 75p. $15.95 (0-87421-249-9). Utah State University Press, Spring 1998. Winner of the 1998 May Swenson Poetry Award. Williams's poems manifest a fine ear not only for the rhythms of verse in English, but for those of the argument that makes them. They extend a line of powerfully and actively contemplative poetry that marks some of the finest American verse of the twentieth century. This is not only a more than promising first book, but an original way of looking at the world — and of looking at that looking itself. It is a pleasure to greet it. —John Hollander. Williams's poems are remarkably promising variations upon her prime precursors, Wallace Stevens and Elizabeth Bishop. Williams will merit, and reward, the attention of discerning readers. —Harold Bloom

Williams, Miller. *The Ways We Touch.* 68p. $16.95 (0-252-02362-5). Champaign, IL: University of Illinois Press, Spring 1997. Williams [is] a poet of the American idiom. That his language is most often colloquial, however, is not to say the poems are non-lyrical. Williams has the practiced ability to continually rediscover what is vital and musical in the language Americans speak and imagine by. —Choice. Most contemporary poets might well go to him for lessons in the art of speaking plainly in disciplined lines alive with emotional energy. —X.J. Kennedy. Serious, droll, expansive, gnomic, religious and heretic by turns, Williams crafts poems that bite. —Dave Smith

Williams, S.L. *Poetic Prophecy: Life Cycles Within the Circle of Life, Inspirational Poems.* 114p. pap. $9.95 (0-9657842-2-3). Brooklyn, NY: Triangle Press, Fall 1997. Williams writes poetry for all occasions. — Irwin Gonshak

Williams, Sandra. *Detours.* 28p. pap. $7.00 (0-932264-09-3). Portland, OR: Trask House Books, 1995. Detours charts a steady course and delivers the poetry we need — passionate, accurate, and human poems which are rich with the freshness of quiet invention. Ranging from the elegaic to the comic, these poems are a pleasure to read — and that ultimate test — to reread. — Vern Rutsala

Williams, Tracey Lee. *Hillbilly Psycho: A View From Within.* 93p. pap. $12.00. Los Angeles, CA: Goddessdead Publications, Spring 1997. Williams has used her art as a sort of. . . exorcism: releasing those shadowy and self-destructive demons that dwell in most. —Small Press Review

Williamson, Alan. *Res Publica.* 73p. $26.00 (0-226-89934-9). pap. $12.00 (0-226-89935-7). Chicago, IL: University of Chicago Press, Fall 1998. Williamson's chronicles of historical events and personalities are at their best when the poet grafts snatches of other modes like pop song, Blakean ontology and biography onto otherwise spare tales. —Publishers Weekly. Williamson is the unequaled detective of the mythic reverberations behind the psyche's complex inner weather. In Res Publica he expands his meditative analysis from the introspection to the troubled psyche of Vietnam-age America. —Peter Dale Scott. Through Williamson's thoughtful re-imaginings, [the Sixties] achieve the lustre of things experienced in our youth and early manhood, when we brought to new experiences the full charge of our passion, intellect, and bewilderment. — Richard Tillinghast

Williamson, Ann Louise. *Too Hot, Too Cold, Just Right.* 81p. pap. $12.95 (0-911051-77-5). Austin, TX: Plain View Press, 1994. With stories of angels who are cats, who are grandmothers, and who are real women in America, Williamson's finely crafted poems startle with truth and heart. Hers is the clear voice of one who sees between the molecules, notices when "soup

bones leap in the soup." —
Margo LaGattuta

Wilner, Eleanor. *Reversing the Spell: New & Selected Poems.* 341p. pap. $16.00 (1-55659-082-2). Port Townsend, WA: Copper Canyon Press, Spring 1998. Aptly titled for a book summarizing a career that continues to rewrite our myths of life and art, Reversing the Spell is a perfect introduction into the work and world of Eleanor Wilner. The MacArthur Award-winning poet and activist writes with the courage of her convictions, and the delicacy to remind us how "Dreaming we turn the gods into such shapes / as lead us on" —Publishers Weekly. [Wilner] is attempting to rewrite Western myth and biblical tradition and drives straight into the oncoming highlights. Her sudden flights of lyricism are disarming and dazzling. —The New York Times Book Review

Wilson, Roy D., ed. *The Circle of Equilibrium: Poems of Conscience and Leadership by Native, Latino, African and Asian American Youth..* 51p. (0-9656868-0-9). Seattle, WA: Institute for Community Leadership, Fall 1997. It would be a sin to dismiss these vibrant, accessible, tender and important voices as the voices of "children." These are the voices of all of us, whispering when delicacy is called for, screaming when necessary, slapping us awake to a world too few take time to really see. These are not children; these are griots, leading us into a widening circle of light. We would do well to listen, and follow. —Patricia Smith. These children need to be honored. To be read again and again. They tell us what we know in our bones but have forgotten. —Luis Rodriguez

Wilson, Thomas Zvi. *Deliberate and Accidental Acts.* 64p. pap. $9.95 (1-886157-10-3). Kansas City, MO: BkMk Press of the University of Missouri-Kansas City, Fall 1997. Wilson wandered out of his art studio to explore in poetry the geography of suffering, the maze of ethnicity, the intricacies of form, the history of self. His poems neither deny subject matter in the name of style, nor abandon style in pursuit of experience. Here is a poet of ideas, of performance, of emotional power, in pursuit of the poem that will stick in the gut rather than slickly satisfy the momentarily fashionable. — Dan Jaffe

Wiman, Christian. *The Long Home.* 80p. pap. $12.95 (1-885266-67-7). Ashland, OR: Story Line Press, Fall 1998. Winner of the 11th Annual Nicholas Roerich Poetry Prize. What these poems offer is an original and powerful re-statement of the oldest connections in life and art: the tie between place and story. Land and shadow and Texas speech and unwholesome seasons enrich this book. Wiman's deft narratives and graceful cadences reach right into the lives and losses of his speakers, subjects and readers. This is a beautiful, authoritative first book. — Eavan Boland

Winans, A.D. *America.* 31p. pap. $5.00 (0-932593-22-4). Croydon, PA: Black Bear Publications, Spring 1998. Winans is one of the best poets writing in the U.S. today. His work is powerful, human and humane. —Hugh Fox

Winters, Yvor. Edited by R.L. Barth. *The Uncollected Poems of Yvor Winters 1919-1928.* 36p. pap. $7.50. Edgewood, KY: Barth, Robert L. (R.L.B.), Fall 1997.

Winters, Yvor. Edited by R.L. Barth. *The Uncollected Poems of Yvor Winters 1929-1957.* 24p. pap. $7.50. Edgewood,

KY: Barth, Robert L. (R.L.B.), Spring 1997.

Woessner, Warren. *Iris Rising.* 24p. pap. $6.00 (1-886157-09-X). Kansas City, MO: BkMk Press of the University of Missouri-Kansas City, Fall 1998. The founder of Abraxas and a biotechnology patient attorney, Woessner uses themes of nature to examine various facets of life, including conflicts between the natural and man-made worlds. —BkMk Press

Wojahn, David. *The Falling Hour.* 80p. $25.00 (0-8229-3995-9). pap. $12.95 (0-8229-5642-X). Pittsburgh, PA: University of Pittsburgh Press, Spring 1997. A polyphonic dirge for love lost, for estrangement, for communal breakdown, that is also at the same time a heart wrenching celebration of love, connection, and all the perishable bonds that join us to each other, The Falling Hour finds in every song of grief a song of praise. This is a great book by one of our very finest poets. —Alan Shapiro. I would not have thought that a poetry of conscience could be this hypnotic or lulling in its long passage — these vivid, intelligent, and sad poems compensate for the late century's loss of someone true, such

as Rukeyser or Auden. —
Norman Dubie

Wolf, Michele. *Conversations During Sleep.* 75p. $18.95 (0-938078-55-0). pap. $10.95 (0-938078-56-9). Tallahassee, FL: Anhinga Press, Spring 1998. Winner of the 1997 Anhinga Prize for Poetry. Conversations During Sleep feels like a logbook of gutsy revelations, transporting us to a territory both ethereal and earthy. We care about the lives that nudge us awake in this dark luminosity, a heartfelt journey we don't want to miss. —Yusef Komunyakaa

Wong, Nellie. *Stolen Moments.* 44p. pap. $10.00 (1-887344-03-9). Goshen, CT: Chicory Blue Press, Fall 1997. Wong's exuberant poems reveal the working life of a woman, the pleasure she takes in food, music, movies, her roots in Chinese-American culture and her deep commitment to justice everywhere. They move energetically and unselfconsciously between the personal and the political. Stolen Moments is #10 in the Crimson Edge Chapbook Series, which seeks to support and encourage older women writers and to increase their publishing opportunities. — Chicory Blue Press

Wood, Eve. *Paper Frankenstein.* 33p. pap. $5.00 (1-892184-00-1). Venice, CA: Beyond Baroque Books, Spring 1998.

Wood, John. *The Gates of the Elect Kingdom.* 94p. pap. $10.95 (0-87745-581-3). Iowa City, IA: University of Iowa Press, Spring 1997. Winner of the 1996 Iowa Poets Prize. The four parts of this highly accomplished collection showcase the varied facets and wide breadth of Wood's poetic talent. Displayed here are his skills at sustaining a sequence, his adeptness with lyricism and the short form, and his sensuous feeling for this life and the life of the past. — University of Iowa Press. Wood is a poet of well-known and accomplished grace; now he demonstrates his considerable ability as a chronicler of our American prairie past. — Robert Coles

Woodd, Leslie. *In My Garden of Passion and Hate.* 56p. pap. $7.95 (0-932693-10-5). San Fransisco, CA: Jukebox Press, 1997. Woodd is a fine new poet. The wind races through her poems. A Joan of Arc hearing voices in the night. A rare treasure in this modern age. —Jack Micheline

Wormser, Baron. *When.*
104p. $20.95 (1-889330-03-5).
pap. $12.95 (1-889330-04-3).
Louisville, KY: Sarabande
Books, Fall 1997. Winner of
the 1996 Kathryn A. Morton
Prize in Poetry. Graced with
humor, lust, and bracing narrative momentum, Wormser's
poetry presents a menagerie of
wonderfully familiar strangers.
—Publishers Weekly.
Wormser's poems are not fashion victims. His work is per-
meated by a linguistic singularity that amounts to style; an
ongoing poetic engagement
untouched by poetic trends.
An unabashedly American
poet, Wormser has a sense of
place which extends beyond
suburbia to missile silos, Las
Vegas, housing projects, and
traffic on the beltways. —
Alice Fulton

Wright, C.D. *Deepstep Come
Shining.* 111p. pap. $14.00 (1-
55659-092-X). Port
Townsend, WA: Copper
Canyon Press, Fall 1998.
Merging the mysteries of formal and linguistic experiment
with traditional narrative,
Wright creates a cinematic
odyssey through the rural
South. —Copper Canyon
Press. Expertly elliptical
phrasings, and an uncounter-
feitable, generous feel for real
people, bodies and places,
have made Wright one of

America's oddest, best, and
most appealing poets.
Deepstep teems with wry, rich
sentences no one else could
have written and leaps exhiler-
atingly among verbal registers.
—Publishers Weekly. This
book-length poem, punctuated
by snippets of song lyrics, literary puns, and local color,
moves by association of sound
and image through parts of
Georgia and South Carolina.
Wright is intelligent and witty.
—Library Journal. Wright is
entirely her own poet, a true
original. —The Gettysburg
Review

Wright, Charles. *Appalachia.*
67p. $20.00 (0-374-10571-5).
New York, NY: Farrar, Straus
and Giroux, Fall 1998. Almost
thirty years ago, Wright began
a poetic project of Dantean
scope — a trilogy of trilogies.
With Appalachia, Wright has
now brought to completion the
third trilogy in the series. The
final book in this great work
shows us a master poet's con-
frontation with his own mortality and his stunning ability
to discover transcendence in
the most beautifully ordinary
of landscapes. —Farrar, Straus
and Giroux. Wright is a
philosopher-poet with a gift
for gloriously whimsical
imagery and a keen sense of
the ephemeral. —Booklist.
These attractive new poems

retain the style, ambitions and concerns of Wright's work over the last two decades. Gleams of wisdom and linguistic gems throughout. — Publishers Weekly. Has any other American poet been writing as beautifully and daringly over the past twenty-five years as Wright? Possibly. But I cannot imagine who it would be. —Philip Levine

Wright, Charles. *Black Zodiac.* 85p. $19.00 (0-374-11410-2). pap. $12.00 (0-374-52536-6). Farrar, Straus and Giroux/Noonday, Spring 1997; Fall 1998 (new paper). Winner of the 1998 Pulitzer Prize and the National Book Critics Circle Award. This haunted, elegiac book could not have been more beautiful. —James Longenbach, The Nation. In an age of casual faithlessness, Wright successfully reconstitutes the provocative tension between belief and materialism. —Albert Mobillo, The Village Voice. Black Zodiac concentrates Wright's considerable poetic endowment into a new poignance that has to be termed religious. Some of the poems achieve an authentic gnosis in a rapt mode of negative transcendence. —Harold Bloom

Wright, Franz. *Ill Lit: Selected and New Poems.*

186p. $28.95 (0-932440-82-7). pap. $16.95 (0-932440-83-5). Oberlin, OH: Oberlin College Press, Fall 1998. Ill Lit brings together a substantial selection of poems from earlier volumes, some of them significantly revised by the author, and a group of twenty-one new poems, along with a selection of translations. A courageous writer who has, in his words, committed himself to the task of "giving a voice to conditions or states of mind normally associated with speechlessness," Wright demonstrates here, again and again, his ability to make poems that are haunting, somber, and luminous. — Oberlin College Press. No contemporary American poet has explored the wretchedness of broken connections more unrelentingly, and with more startling results, than Franz Wright. —Brett Ralph, Rain Taxi. This is a terrific book by a terrific poet. Never has any poet, anywhere, been so dark-minded and at the same time so almost playful, so childlike about it all. A unique and major talent. —Donald Justice

Wright, Leilani, and James Cervantes, eds. *Fever Dreams: Contemporary Arizona Poetry.* 231p. $35.00 (0-8165-1588-3). pap. $16.95 (0-8165-1589-1). Tucson, AZ:

University of Arizona Press, Spring 1997. If one cannot keep vigil in a canyon, then one can be humbled by the expanse and learn something of the Sonoran Desert's power by reading these poems, which sojourn in the future as well as the deep past, in dream-time that resembles the aboriginal, a fever dream of fire-clouds, chamizo, loaded guns and uranium. —Carolyn Forché

Wright, Richard. Edited by Yoshinobu Hakutani and Robert L. Tener. *Haiku: This Other World.* 320p. $23.50 (1-55970-445-4). New York, NY: Arcade Publishing, Fall 1998. [These haiku were] written during Wright's French exile, almost forty years ago, throughout the last eighteen months or so of his life. [Writing them] not only helped him to place the volcanic experience of mourning under the self-control of closely counted syllables, but also enabled him to come to terms with the difficult beauty of the earth. . . . They are Wright's poetry of loss and retrieval, of temperate joy and wistful humor, of exile and fragments of a dreamed return. They lie somewhere in that transitional twilight area between the loss for words and the few charmed syllables that can heal the loss. —Julia Wright.

It is astonishing to think that it has taken nearly 40 years to make Wright's poetry available. Wright is indisputably one of the giants of American letters. He belongs among our best poets, and Haiku: This Other World belongs in everyone's library beside Native Son and Black Boy. — Seattle Weekly. A major literary event [from] one of our all-time great writers. —Publishers Weekly

Wyndham, Harald. *The Christmas Sonnets.* 60p. (0-937179-11-6). Pocatello, ID: Blue Scarab Press, 1996. The Christmas Sonnets were composed as Christmas cards beginning in 1971 when Wyndham moved from Ohio to Idaho and continuing through 1995—a period of 25 years. The poems are accompanied by linoleum block prints by Linda Wolfe. The prints and the poems represent two bodies of work on a single theme, a co-operative enterprise by two artists, each responding to the Christmas season in a personal way. — Blue Scarab Press

Wynne, Robert. *Patterns of Breathing.* 31p. pap. $5.00 (1-890887-02-1). Santa Barbara, CA: Mille Grazie Press, Fall 1997. At the heart of Wynne's poetry lies a sharp and sensitive perception which on the surface affirms the basic optimism found in popular images of contemporary life, but slowly and carefully peels back those surfaces to reveal the sediments of hurt and disappointment beneath. —Mille Grazie Press

Xark, Bob. *Lip Thinker: A Poetry in the Vernacular.* 88p. pap. $8.95. New York, NY: Bomb Sniffing Dog Records, Fall 1996. From the bowels of New York City, a place of carhorns, pollution, and ugly buildings, comes this wildly original "renaissance man," a webmeister, DJ-sound engineer, electo-industrial poet / guitarist and singer. His is a hard industrial, yet humorous take on 20th century urban poets like Dylan Thomas, Charles Bukowski, William Burroughs, Cameron Jefferies, and Langston Hughes. The end result may not be for everyone, but there's nothing else like it. —Bomb Sniffing Dog Records

Xavier, Emanuel. *Pier Queen.* 50p. pap. $6.99 (0-9658708-3-9). Pier Queen Productions, Fall 1997. Once in a generation, a new voice emerges that makes us see the world in a dazzling new light. Xavier is that kind of writer: exciting, vibrant, unique, a

visionary bard. —Jaime Manrique

Xue Di. Translated by Keith Waldrop with Wang Ping, Iona Crook, Janet Tan and Hil Anderson. *Heart Into Soil: Selected Poems.* 93p. pap. $10.00 (1-886224-32-3). Providence, RI: Burning Deck, Spring 1998. Poems by a Beijing native who left China after taking part in the 1989 demonstrations in Tian'anmen Square. —Burning Deck

Yañez, Rich. *Sacred Heart.* 12p. Berkeley, CA: Chicano Chapbook Series, Fall 1997. The Chicano Chapbook Series, edited by Gary Soto, issued twelve title in the late 1970's and early 1980's, including works by Sandra Cisneros, Alberto Ríos, Jimmy Santiago Baca and others. The chapbooks are distributed free of charge to selected libraries with Chicano collections. Sacred Heart is #15.

Yarbrough, Beverly Yvonne. *Words From the Soul.* 15p. pap. $5.95 (0-9656873-0-9). San Diego, CA: Beverly Yvonne Enterprise, Spring 1997. Love poems from the heart of "Sister Soul." — Beverly Yvonne Enterprise

Yasusada, Araki. Translated by Tosa Motokiyu, Ojiu

Norinaga, and Okura Kyoyin. *Doubled Flowering: From the Notebooks.* 174p. pap. $14.95 (0-937804-71-1). New York, NY: Roof Books, 1997. The materials of the Japanese poet Araki Yasusada, a survivor of Hiroshima, were published in Grand Street, Conjunctions, Abiko Quarterly, First Intensity, Stand, and The American Poetry Review. Gradually the rumor began circulating that Yasusada did not exist and that the poems were a "hoax" perpetrated by the Japanese American author Tosa Motokiyu or by his literary executor, the American poet Kent Johnson. Readers now have the chance to draw their own conclusions about Doubled Flowering . —Roof Books. This book makes the argument for anti-essentialism. That it has done it so well infuriates folks with a proprietary interest in categories. Thank you Araki Yususada. —Ron Silliman

Yau, John. *Forbidden Entries.* 200p. $25.00 (1-57423-017-4). pap. $14.00 (1-57423-016-6). Santa Rosa, CA: Black Sparrow Press, Fall 1996. Yau's Chinese American background marks him as an outsider, but he is not interested in merely recording the terms of that exclusion. His work examines ways in which lan-guage has long been used, quite often subtly, to oppress and exclude. —Black Sparrow Press

Ybarra, Ricardo Means. *A Framing Job.* 68p. pap. $9.95 (1-888996-05-6). Palmdale, CA: Red Hen Press, Fall 1997. Ybarra's salty-sweet musings on manual labor, paternal and sexual love, on friendship between men, give rise to a poetry both virile and humane. Who else could juxtapose the images of a woman brushing her hair on a porch and "the blood hot whine of a 16-penny nail / pulling away"? Here are poems handmade and heartfelt, and a language suffused in the soft and roughhewn sensations of the physical world. —Suzanne Lummis

Yeats, W.B. Edited by Richard J. Finneran. *The Collected Works of Yeats, Vol. 1: The Poems, Second Edition.* 750p. $40.00 (0-684-83935-0). New York, NY: Simon & Schuster/Scribner, Fall 1997 (second edition). This collection reveals the extraordinary breadth of Yeats's verse, ranging from skillful retellings of ancient Irish myths and legends to passionate meditations on the demands and rewards of youth and old age. The exquisite, occasionally whimsical songs of love, nature and art stand in dramatic contrast to the somber and angry poems of life in a nation torn by war and uprising. And, in the rich and recurrent imagery of the rose, the gyre and the tower, the reader can trace Yeats's quest to unite intellect and artistry in a single, compelling vision. —Simon & Schuster/Scribner

Yeats, W.B. Edited by Richard J. Finneran. *The Yeats Reader: A Portable Compendium of Poetry, Drama, and Prose.* 527p. $32.50 (0-684-83188-0). New York, NY: Simon & Schuster/Scribner, Fall 1997. The Yeats Reader is the first single volume to encompass the full range of Yeats's talents. It presents over a hundred of Yeats's best known poems, plus eight plays, a sampling of his prose tales, and excerpts from his published autobiographical and critical writings. Also included are selections from the memoirs left unpublished at his death and complete introductions written for the projected Scribner edition of his collected works. These are supplemented by unobtrusive annotation and a chronology of his life. —Simon & Schuster/Scribner

Yeats, William Butler. Edited by James Reilly. *"Easter*

1916" and Other Poems. 80p. pap. $1.00 (0-486-29771-3). Mineola, NY: Dover Publications, Fall 1997. This volume contains a rich selection of poems from Yeats' mature work, including all of the poems from The Wild Swans at Coole and Michael Robartes and the Dancer. These memorable verses, embodying subtlety and objectivity in language of stark beauty and simplicity, offer a cross-section of Yeats' multi-faceted poetic production. — Dover Publications

Yictove. *Blue Print.* 62p. pap. $10.00 (0-916620-75-1). New Orleans, LA: Portals Press, Spring 1997. Yictove has left his magical fingerprints everywhere. He writes with the resonance of a native New Orleans bluesman, the sharp eye of a New York City street poet, the rolling rhythm of a Jamaican dub-poet, and the vision of a prophet circling the modern Jericho. —James Nolan

Young, Gary. *Days.* 70p. pap. $12.00 (1-878851-08-X). Eugene, OR: Silverfish Review Press, Spring 1997. There's no word for what Young does, only for what he accomplishes — the capturing of small, daily miracles. — Dorianne Laux. I was struck by the wisdom of this work, a quiet wisdom that inheres in images so fully imagined that one can never forget them. The language has been so thoroughly purified that truth becomes, in the telling, austerely beautiful. Days is one of those rare books that I will keep beside my bed table for years to come. —Jay Parini

Young, Geoffrey. Drawings by Philip Knoll. *Admiral Fever.* 44p. pap. $10.00 (0-935724-92-3). Sailing After Lunch, Fall 1997.

Young, George. *Creating the Universe and Other Poems.* 20p. pap. $10.00 (0-912288-31). Van Nuys, CA: Perivale Press, Fall 1996. Twenty poems on nature and rock-climbing in and around Boulder, Colorado. — Perivale Press

Young, George. *Spinoza's Mouse.* 76p. pap. $10.00 (0-915380-35-8). Washington, DC: Word Works, Spring 1997. Winner of the 1996 Washington Prize. With a meticulous precision, a passionate imagination, a quirky curiosity, Young casts a physician's eye on Oliver Hardy's bones, Shelley's funeral, Hopkins's hands, Rembrandt's head, Thoreau's grave, Mozart's corpse, and finds

therein beauty, terror, grace, ecstasy, love. Young is a true original and Spinoza's Mouse is a book of wonders, a wonder of a book. —Ron Wallace

Yu Xuanji. Translated by David Young and Jiann I. Lin. *The Clouds Float North: The Complete Poems of Yu Xuanji.* 75p. $25.00 (0-8195-63439). pap. $12.95 (0-8195-6344-7). University Press of New England/Wesleyan University Press, Fall 1998. A rich human presence steps forth in these beautiful and moving poems — a sensibility both refined and precise, an intelligence both passionate and keen. This book enlarges our knowledge of the history of women's writing, and of Chinese poetry's particular and mysterious powers. —Jane Hirshfield

Yuan Mei. Translated by J.P. Seaton. *I Don't Bow to Buddhas: Selected Poems of Yuan Mei.* 109p. pap. $14.00 (1-55659-120-9). Port Townsend, WA: Copper Canyon Press, Spring 1997. This first substantial collection of Yuan Mei's poems in English is a major achievement. Seaton's translations are accurate in presenting the meaning and order of words and images from the original while revealing the true spirit of this very great poet. —Sam

Hamill. Yuan Mei has been called the last of China's great classical poets, but could equally well be called the first great modern one. The voice of these poems is personal, vivid, and idiosyncratic, and Yuan Mei's sensibility is eminently contemporary — self-questioning, humorous, modest. —Jane Hirshfield

Yuhas, Linda Claire. *A Sense of Season.* 85p. pap. $10.00 (1-887012-11-7). Newtown, CT: Hanover Press, Spring 1998. Yuhas has given us a strong collection of poetry. She has a sense of how the outer world and individual souls intersect and she has the language, skill, passion and intellect to catch that intersection in poems that are resonant, mature and winning. — John Basinger

Yuzna, Susan. *Her Slender Dress.* 73p. $24.95 (1-884836-23-2). pap. $12.95 (1-884836-24-0). Akron, OH: University of Akron Press, Fall 1996. Winner of the 1996 Poetry Society of America's Norma Farber First Book Award. There is a vibrant imagistic imagination at work in these poems that is unceasing, always moving the narrative a little further, goading it into another revelation, another version of its vision. There is

no let-up in the linguistic intensity, imagistic intensity, or narrative intensity. — Charles Wright. Yuzna's Her Slender Dress is a breathtaking and memorable debut. These are poems of such clarity, such harrowing self-reckoning, that the reader – like the poet herself – emerges bruised but triumphant. If "conscience" in poetry often seems a stark thing, Yuzna shows it can be honeycombed with the deepest of passions and most hard-earned of wisdoms. —David St. John

Zack, Michael. *Morning Glory.* 44p. pap. $7.95. Palo Alto, CA: Anamnesis Press, Spring 1998. Honorable Mention in the 1997 Anamnesis Chapbook Award competition. A collection of poems which explores the relationship between doctor and patient. —Anamnesis Press

Zagajewski, Adam. Translated by Clare Cavanagh. *Mysticism for Beginners.* 71p. $20.00 (0-374-21765-3). New York, NY: Farrar, Straus and Giroux, Spring 1998. [Zagajewski] is in some sense a pilgrim, a seeker, a celebrant in search of the divine, the unchanging, the absolute. His poems are filled with radiant moments of plenitude. They are spiritual emblems, hymns to the unknown, levers for transcendence. —Edward Hirsch, Doubletake. Zagajewski deserves the attention of readers accustomed to swerve away from poetry. And moreover, he is good: the unmistakable quality of the real thing — a sunlike force that wilts clichés and bollixes the categories of expectation — manifests itself powerfully through able translation. — Robert Pinsky, The New Republic

Zandvakili, Katayoon. *Deer Table Legs.* 82p. pap. $15.95 (0-8203-2072-2). Athens, GA: University of Georgia Press, Fall 1998. Winner of the Contemporary Poetry Series Competition. Few first books of the last decade have attempted such a delicate challenge as this one. A subtle variation on Romeo and Juliet, Deer Table Legs is multicultural in the widest, most generous use of that term. Zandvakili tells more than one kind of love story in a narrative filled with irony and tenderness. —University of Georgia Press. Filled with images [that are] powerful in their brevity, clear in their elusiveness. Each line delicate as a flower, hard as steel. —The Piedmont Post

Zanzotto, Andrea. Translated by John P. Welle and Ruth Feldman. Drawings by Federico Fellini. *Peasants Wake for Fellini's "Casanova" and Other Poems.* $39.95 (0-252-02310-2). pap. $18.95 (0-252-06610-3). Champaign, IL: University of Illinois Press, Fall 1997. Zanzotto is one of the great poets of the last fifty years, an audacious innovator whose work evokes the imaginative range and depth of Hölderlin and Leopardi. His social vision, his formal and tonal variety, are all well represented here. —Michael Palmer. A poetry that evokes the disruption of Italy's archaic peasant civilization. —Hermann W. Haller

Zaro, Mariano. *Where From/Desde Donde.* 77p. (0-9651305-0-9). Santa Monica, CA: Bay Books, Fall 1996. In these poems, originally written in two languages, are found the fiery Spanish literary tradition with which Zaro is intimately connected. Zaro writes in a kind of passionate innocence. Each of these poems is an incandescent deep song of the senses, what Garcia Lorca called "the opening of the veins." —Bay Books

Zarucchi, Roy. *Gunner's Moon.* 31p. pap. $9.95 (0-

9624912-3-3). Poland Spring, ME: Cider Press, Fall 1996.

Zeidenstein, Sondra. *A Detail in That Story.* 53p. pap. $12.95 (1-887344-05-5). Goshen, CT: Chicory Blue Press, Fall 1998. In a sequence that reads like a novel, Zeidenstein gives us a story of infidelity, of a passage in a woman's life, in the life of a marriage. What gives the book its power is her refusal to compromise in poems that are, in turn, raw, desperate, searching, and unerringly tender. —Honor Moore. A Detail in that Story is quite simply one of the best and most honest books I've read this year. These are fierce, frightening and frank poems that resonate with an eroticism that raises the collective consciousness to what life is and can be. — Sapphire

Zhdanov, Ivan. Translated by John High and Patrick Henry. *The Inconvertible Sky.* 55p. pap. $8.95 (1-883689-43-0). Jersey City, NJ: Talisman House, Publishers, 1997. Born in Siberia in 1948, Ivan Zhdanov emerged in the 1980s as one of the leading Russian poets of his generation, admired by the traditionalists and the avant-garde alike. — Talisman House. Zhdanov is the master of depicting forms that seem already to have lost their substance but regain them in memory, in times of waiting, in the depth of a mirror or the shell of a shadow. —Mikail Epstein

Zippert, Carol Prejean. *I Don't Want To Be Rich, Just Able.* 160p. $20.00 (1-881320-80-4). Montgomery, AL: Black Belt Press, Spring 1997. Writing sometimes with the hardened voice of experience, sometimes with an almost childlike awe of the world around her, Zippert has created a work of unusual depth, balance, and beauty. Some of the poems are written in a musical patois that reflects the author's early life in the Louisiana bayou country. Others draw on the civil rights experiences of rural Alabama. All of them celebrate the joys and struggles of life. —Black Belt Press

Zisquit, Linda. *Unopened Letters.* 87p. pap. $12.95 (1-878818-61-9). Riverdale-on-Hudson, NY: Sheep Meadow Press, Fall 1996. What has emerged under the pressure of her unflinching gaze is a stark and astonishingly beautiful poetry. Unlike the bland and self-serving verse so prevalent these days, it is vital reading. —Rita Dove. The ease and directness of these poems make an unexpected testament of singularly complex feeling. Zisquit's work is uniquely present, yet timeless. Its clarity has no equal. —Robert Creeley

Studies, University of Michigan

Zolynas, Al. *The Same Air: Poems of India.* 100p. pap. $12.50 (0-9640492-4-4). San Diego, CA: Intercultural Studies Forum, Fall 1997.

Zwart, Martijn, and Ethel Grene, trans. *Dutch Poetry in Translation: Kaleidoscope From Medieval Times to the Present.* 256p. $22.00 (0-9660016-1-3). pap. $14.95 (0-9660016-0-5). Wilmette, IL: Fairfield Books, Spring 1998. This collection of more than 100 Dutch poems in English translation begins with a selection from the best known medieval pieces and includes most of the major poets of the ensuing centuries. —Fairfield Books. Who said translating poetry is a compromise with the impossible? I am immensely impressed with the Zwart and Grene have translations. The view through this kaleidoscope is a delight: full of color, depth and perspective and a true insight into the rich Dutch poetry of the past, which has been kept from the English speaking world for too long. I hope this will get a wide audience. —Dr. Ton J. Broos, Director of Dutch

2.13.61 Publications
PO Box 1910
Los Angeles, CA 90078
Phone: 323-969-8791
Fax: 213-969-9451
Email: two1361@aol.com
URL:
http://www.two1361.com
Gary Ichihara, Publisher;
Heidi May, Publicity
• Maybe, Ellyn, 285
• Shields, Bill, 399

26 Books
6735 SE 78th
Portland, OR 97206
Phone: 503-777-0406
Email: raphael@aracnet.com
Dan Raphael, Publisher/Editor
• Durham, Flora, 131
• Grabel, Leanne, 171
• Memmott, David, 294
• Moody, Rodger, 306
• Semansky, Chris, 392
• Taylor, Thomas Lowe, 429

3-D Marketing LLC
3790 Via de la Valle, Suite
204
Del Mar, CA 92014
Phone: 888-809-6105
• Steeves, Dean, 415

Abbey Press
Austin, TX
• Brannon, Jack, 60

Abrams, Harry N.
100 Fifth Avenue
New York, NY 10011
Phone: 212-206-7715
Fax: 212-645-8437

Tracy Smith, Publicity
• Navansky, Bruno, ed., 319
• Navansky, Bruno, trans., 319
• Parker, Carolyn, ed., 337

Ackerman Loft Gallery
215 Willoughby Ave., 1409
Brooklyn, NY 11205
Phone: 718-399-5102
Ron Kolm, Poetry Editor
• Unbearables, 440

Adastra Press
16 Reservation Rd
Easthampton, MA 01027
Phone: 413-527-3324
Gary Metras, Publisher/Poetry
Editor
Dist. by: SPD
• Jacques, Geoffrey, 214
• Philbrick, Stephen, 343
• Raffeld, David, 354
• Rodia, Becky, 370
• Sexton, Tom, 394

Advocado Press
PO Box 145
Louisville, KY 40201
Phone: 502-899-9261
Fax: 502-899-9562
Email: edgemag@aol.com
Mary Johnson, Editor
• Fries, Kenny, 151

AHA Books
PO Box 1250
Gualala, CA 95445
Phone: 707-884-1853
Fax: 707-884-1853
Email: ahabooks@mcn.org
URL: http://ahapoetry.com
Jane Reichhold, Publisher

Dist. by: Baker & Taylor,
Barnes & Noble,
Amazon.com, Coutts
Library Service
• Eulert, Don, 138
• Reichhold, Jane, and Werner
Reichhold, 361
• Reichhold, Jane, and Werner
Reichhold, 361
• Reichhold, Jane, ed., 361
• Reichhold, Jane, ed., 362
• Saito, Fumi, 379

Alef Books
230 West 105th St, 3B
New York, NY 10025
Phone: 212-932-0198
Fax: amccord@ibm.net
Andrew McCord,
Co-Publisher
• Monroe, Melissa, 305
• Parker, Alan Michael, 337

Alhamra Publications
39159 Paseo Padre Pkwy.,
Suite 310
Fremont, CA 94538
Phone: 510-792-1957
Fax: 510-792-7806
• Baal-i-Jibreel, 25

Alice James Books
University of Maine at
Farmington, 98 Main St.
Farmington, ME 04938
Phone: 207-778-7071
Fax: 207-778-7071
Email: AJB@umf.maine.edu
URL:
http://www.umf.maine.edu/~
ajb
Peg Peoples, Program Director

Dist. by: SPD, Koen, Baker &
Taylor, Ingram
• Fairchild, B.H., 139
• Gensler, Kinereth, 159
• Gilbert, Celia, 162
• Huntington, Cynthia, 209
• Kaplan, Janet, 224
• Kasischke, Laura, 226
• Kraus, Sharon, 242
• Mitchell, Nora, 303
• Sewell, Lisa, 393
• Su, Adrienne, 421
• Watson, Ellen Doré, 454

Alki Press
2819 First Ave, Suite 240
Seattle, WA 98121
Phone: 206-441-5380
Fax: 206-443-3200
Victoria Hawker, Publisher
• Gregor, David, 175

Allen, William
204 Cayuga Road
Louisville, KY 40207
• Allen, William M., 12

Alphabeta Press
901 S Plymouth, Suite 1801
Chicago, IL 60605
Phone: (312) 922-9049
Email: alphabpres@aol.com
Gloria Klein, Poetry Editor
• Engler, Robert Klein, 135
• Engler, Robert Klein, 135

American Poetry Review
1721 Walnut Street
Philadelphia, PA 19103
Phone: 215-496-0439
Fax: 215-569-0808
Dist. by: Copper Canyon,

Consortium
• Beckman, Joshua, 36

**Amherst Writers & Artists
Press**
PO Box 1076
Amherst, MA 01004
Phone: 413-253-7764
Fax: 413-253-7764
Email: awapress@javanet.com
URL:
http://www.javanet.com/~aw
apress
Pat Schneider, Editor; Donna
Gates, Publicity
• Balter, Frances, 28
• O'Shea-Noonan, Mary-Beth,
328

Anabiosis Press
PO Box 7787
North Port, FL 34287-0787
Phone: 617-387-0491
Email: rsmyth@massed.net
Richard Smyth,
President/Editor; Richard
Brobst, Editor
• Fishman, Charles, 145
• Kennedy, Jo Bowman, 229

Anacade International
3905 State Street, Suite 7-135
Santa Barbara, CA 93105
Phone: 805-569-5689
Fax: 805-569-9908
Email: clifgord@silcom.com
president@anacade.com
URL: http://www.anacade.com
Helen Gordon, President
To Order: c/o H.H. Gordon,
3775 Modoc Rd. Apt. #135,
Santa Barbara, CA 93105-

4462
orders@anacade.com
• Gordon, Helen Heightsman,
169
• Gordon, Helen Heightsman,
169

Anamnesis Press
PO Box 51115
Palo Alto, CA 94303
Phone: 650-856-4647
Fax: 415-255-3190
Email: anamnesis@com-
puserve.com
URL: http://ourworld.com-
puserve.com/homepages/ana
mnesis/
Keith Allen Daniels,
Publisher; Toni Luna
Montealegne, Publisher
Dist. by: SPD, Baker &
Taylor, Ingram,
• Brown, Kurt, 66
• Daniels, Keith Allen, 114
• Haldeman, Joe, 180
• Jenkins, Jerry H., 217
• McGarry, Terry, 289
• Utley, Steven, 440
• Zack, Michael, 476

Anchor Thorn Publishing
2667 East 24th St
Brooklyn, NY 11235
Phone: 718-769-9876
• Krumholz, Márgalo Eden,
242

Anderie Poetry Press
PO Box 85
Easton, PA 18044-0085
Phone: 610-559-9287
Fax: 610-559-3887

Email: feelings@itw.com
URL:
   http://www.silo.com/feelings
Carole J. Heffley,
   Publisher/Editor
• Heffley, Carole J., ed., 193

Angle Press
PO Box 220027
Brooklyn, NY 11222
Dist. by: SPD
• Selby, Spencer, 392

Anhinga Press
1213 Lucy St.
Tallahassee, FL 32308
Phone: 850-521-9920
Fax: 850-442-6323
Email: info@anhinga.org
URL: http://www.anhinga.org
Rick Campbell, Director
To Order: PO Box 10595,
   Tallahassee, FL 32302
Dist. by: SPD
• Bozanic, Nick, 58
• Braggs, Earl S., 59
• Curbelo, Sylvia, 111
• Gardner, Joann, ed., 156
• Ratzlaff, Keith, 359
• Wolf, Michele, 468

Apocrypha/Gris-Gris Press
1187 E Broadway, 3
Louisville, KY 40204-1711
Phone: 502-583-8014
Email:
   paul@louisville.lob.ky.us
Paul McDonald
• McDonald, Paul, 288

Appledore Books
PO Box 174

Hancock, NH 03449-0174
Phone: 603-525-3581
Steve Sherman, Publisher
Dist. by: Koen, Baker &
   Taylor, Ingram, Maine
   Writers & Publishers
• Older, Julia, 330
• Thaxter, Celia, 430

Arcade Publishing
141 Fifth Avenue
New York, NY 10010
Phone: 212-475-2633
Fax: 212-353-8148
Email: arcadepub@aol.com
Richard Seaver, Editor;
   Phillipa Tawn, Publicity
   Manager
To Order: 800-759-0190
Dist. by: Time Warner
• Wright, Richard, 471

Archer Books
PO Box 7370
Santa Monica, CA 90406
URL: http://www.archer-
   books.com
• Bennett, Saul, 41

Arctos Press
PO Box 401
Sausalito, CA 94966
Phone: 415-331-2503
Fax: 415-386-2626
Email: runes@aol.com
C.B. Follett, Editor/Publisher
• Follett, CB, ed., 146

Ardis Publishers
24721 El Camino Capistrano
Dana Point, CA 92629
Phone: 949-248-4910

Fax: 949-248-5381
Email: publisher@ardis-
books.com
Ellendea Proffer, Publisher
To Order: 100 Newfield Ave.,
Edison, NJ 08837; 800-
877-7133
Dist. by: Ingram
• Tsvetaeva, Marina, 436

Armadillo Books
PO Box 11-481
Albany, NY 12211
Phone: 518-782-1867
George Liaskos, President
• Lasko, G.P., 248

**Arnold & Johnson,
Publishers**
PO Box 823
Wrightsville Beach, NC 28480
• Herman, William R., 196

Arte Público Press
University of Houston
4800 Calhoun 2-L
Houston, TX 77204-2090
Phone: 713-743-2841
Fax: 713-743-2847
Email: cebaker@uh.edu
URL:
http://bentley.uh.edu/arte_pu
blico
Clifford Crouch, Editor
• Le Guin, Ursula K., and
Diana Bellessi, 252
• Salas, Floyd, 380
• Sepúlveda-Pulvirenti, Emma,
392
• Velásquez, Gloria, 443
• Villatoro, Marcos McPeek,
445

**Arte Público Press/Piñata
Books**
• Ortiz Cofer, Judith, 332

Artemis Art Gallery
no address
• Shaffer, Gregory, 395

Ashland Poetry Press
Ashland University
Ashland, OH 44805
Phone: 419-289-5118
Fax: 419-289-5333
Robert McGovern, Editor
• Battin, Wendy, 33

**Asian American Writers'
Workshop**
37 St. Marks Pl
New York, NY 10003
Phone: 212-228-6718
Fax: 212-228-7718
Email: aaww@panix.com
URL:
http://www.panix.com/~aaw
w
Andrea Louie, Publications
Director
To Order: 800-447-1656
Dist. by: Temple University
Press
• Chang, Juliana, ed., 86
• Tabios, Eileen, ed., 426
• Tran, Barbara; Monique T.D.
Truong and Luu Truong
Khoi, eds., 434

Asphodel Press/Moyer Bell
Kymbolde Way
Wakefield, RI 02879
Phone: 401-789-0074
Fax: 401-789-3793

485 | DIRECTORY OF AMERICAN POETRY BOOKS

Email: sales@moyerbell.com
URL:
http://www.moyerbell.com
Jennifer Moyer, Editor; Sam
McGregor, Publicity
Dist. by: Publishers Group
West
• Gilfillan, Merrill, 163
• Mills, Ralph J. Jr., 301
• Morley, Hilda, 310
• Trakl, Georg, 434

Asylum Arts Publishing
5847 Sawmill Road
Paradise, CA 95969
Phone: 805-928-8774
Email: asyarts@sunset.net
Dist. by: SPD, Valentine
Publishing Group
• Appelbaum, Samuel, 17
• Basso, Eric, 33
• Martin, Richard, 280

Atelos
PO Box 5814
Berkely, CA 94705-0814
Dist. by: SPD
• Armantrout, Rae, 18
• Day, Jean, 118
• Watten, Barrett, 455

Autonomedia
PO Box 568 Williamsburgh
Station
Brooklyn, NY 11211-0568
Phone: 718-963-2603
Email: autonobook@aol.com
URL: http://www.autonome-
dia.org
Jim Fleming, Publisher
Dist. by: SPD
• Clausen, Andy, 93

• Hollo, Anselm; Anne
Waldman, and Jack Collom,
203
• Unbearables, 440

Avec Books
PO Box 1059
Penngrove, CA 94951
Dist. by: SPD
• Chadwick, Cydney, ed., 85
• Murphy, Michelle, 316
• Reiner, Chrisopher, 362
• Waldrop, Keith, 449

Avisson Press
3007 Taliaferro Rd
Greensboro, NC 27408
Phone: 910-288-6989
Fax: same
Martin Hester,
President/Editor
• McCann, Janet, 286

Bacchae Press
985 Hyde Shaffen Rd.
Bristolville, OH 44402
• Levy, Robert J., 258

Baker Books
PO Box 6287
Grand Rapids, MI 49516-6287
• Graham, Ruth Bell, 172
• Noll, Mark A., 325

Baksun Books
no address
Boulder, CO
Dist. by: SPD
• Levitsky, Rachel, 257

Bamboo Ridge
• Chock, Eric; James R.

Harstad, Darrell H.Y. Lum,
and Bill Teter, eds., 88

Bamboo Ridge Press
PO Box 61781
Honolulu, HI 96839-1781
Phone: 808-626-1481
URL: http://www.bambooridge.com
Lois-Ann Yamanaka,
Associate Editor
• Saijo, Albert, 378

Bard Press
393 St. Pauls Ave
Staten Island, NY 10304-2127
Phone: 718-442-7429
Fax: 718-442-4978
Email: 72713.3625@compuserve.com
URL:
http://tenpennyplayers.org
Rich Spiegel, Editor; Barbara
Fisher, Editor
• Spiegel, Rich, 413

Barque Books
no address
Cambridge, MA
Dist. by: SPD
• Davis, Jordan, 117
• Prynne, J.H., 351
• Sutherland, Keston, 422

Barracuda Press
PO Box 1730
Escondido, CA 92033-1730
Phone: 619-746-2550
• Aplon, Roger, 17

Barth, Robert L. (R.L.B.)
3122 Royal Windsor Drive

Edgewood, KY 41017-2629
Phone: 606-344-0043
Robert L. Barth, Publisher
• Disch, Tom, 125
• Hayden, Dolores, 191
• Monsour, Leslie, 305
• Winters, Yvor, 467
• Winters, Yvor, 467

Bay Books
443 Bay St., 4
Santa Monica, CA 90405
• Zaro, Mariano, 477

Beacon Press
25 Beacon Street
Boston, MA 02215
Phone: 617-742-2110
Fax: 617-723-3097
Email: kwoodcoc@beacon.org
URL: http://www.beacon.org
Kristin Woodcock, Sales
Coordinator; Colleen
Lanick, Publicity
To Order: c/o Random House,
400 Hahn Road,
Westminster MD 21157;
800-733-3000
Dist. by: Random House
• Forman, Ruth, 147
• Kim, Elaine H., and Lilia V.
Villanueva, eds., 231
• Levin, Harriet, 256
• Lorca, Federico García, and
Juan Ramón Jiménez, 266
• Mora, Pat, 308
• Rubin, Steven J., ed., 374
• Sanchez, Sonia, 382
• Sanchez, Sonia, 382
• Szporluk, Larissa, 426
• Valéry, Paul, 441

Bear House Publishing
398 Mundell Rd
Eureka Springs, AR 72631
Phone: 501-253-9351
Email: tbadger@ipa.net
URL:
    http://www.ipa.net/~tbadger
• Griffith, Geraline M., 176
• Harding, Jay, 186
• Henderson, E.A., and Ted O.
    Badger, 195
• Long, Ardell J., 264
• Rilling, Helen E., 366

Beau Rivage Press
7 East 14th St. (1112)
New York, NY 10003
Phone: 212-989-1625
• Cholst, Sheldon, 88

Beautiful Swimmer Press
20 Scott Court
Wayne, PA 19087
Email: BeautSwim@aol.com
Dist. by: SPD
• Cole, Barbara, 96
• DuPlessis, Rachel Blau, 131

Bedloe Books
36 Second Street
Hopewell, NJ 08525
Mildred Sack, Publicity
• Neider, Mark, 320

Belhue Press
2501 Palisade Ave, Suite A1
Bronx, NY 10463
Phone: 718-884-6061
Fax: 718-884-6061
Email: belhuepress@earth-
    link.net
URL:

http://www.perrybrass.com
Perry Brass, Editor
• Brass, Perry, 60

Bench Press
2410 NW Rolling Green
    Drive, Apt. 46
Corvallis, OR 97330
Phone: 541-752-3663
Dist. by: SPD
• Rash, Ron, 358

Berger, Terry Wapner
100 York St., Apt. # 5D
New Haven, CT 06511
Phone: 203-785-0720
Email: poetterry@aol.com
• Berger, Terry Wapner, 43
• Berger, Terry Wapner, 43

Berkowitz, James
4440 Ambrose Ave., #214
Los Angeles, CA 90027
Phone: 323-665-6708
• Berkowitz, James, 43

**Between Rock and a
    Reading**
459 Columbus Ave, Ste. 283
New York, NY 10024
Phone: 718-624-5660
Debby Branch
• Branch, Debby, 60

Beverly Yvonne Enterprise
1653 Pentecost Way, 6
San Diego, CA 92105
Phone: 619-264-8663
• Yarbrough, Beverly Yvonne,
    472

Beyond Baroque Books

681 Venice Blvd.
Venice, CA 90291
Phone: 310-822-3006
Fax: 310-287-7432
• Brouwer, Joel, 66
• Pompei, Jessica; Holaday
  Mason, and Sarah Maclay,
  eds., 348
• Tádjèck, Sandor (Kurt
  Brown, 427
• Wood, Eve, 468

BGB Press
158 King St.
Northhampton, MA 01060
• Miller, Errol, 299

Big Bridge Press
2000 Highway One
Pacifica, CA
• Luttrell, Steve, 269

Big Fat Press
PO Box 1168
New York, NY 10113
Email: fatliar@juno.com
Anne Elliott, Publisher/Editor
• Cabico, Regie, 74
• Castro, Guillermo, 83
• Light, Lisa, 260

Big Foot New York
57 Seafield Lane
Bay Shore, NY 11706
Phone: 516-666-8512
• Gellis, Willard, 159
• Gellis, Willard, 159

**Big Foot New York /
  Orpheophrenia Series**
• Gellis, Willard, 159

**Big Foot New York/Wild
  Strawberry Press**
• Gellis, Willard, 158

Bilingual Press
Hispanic Research Ctr,
Arizona State University,
PO Box 872702
Tempe, AZ 85281-2702
Phone: 480-965-3867
Fax: 480-965-8309
Email: akins@imap2.asu.edu
URL: http://matieas.asu.edu:
  8421/bilingual/html
Karen M. Akins, Marketing
  Mgr.; Gary D. Keller,
  Editor-in-Chief
• Valdés, Gina, 441
• Villanueva, Alma Luz, 444
• Villanueva, Tino, 445

Birch Brook Press
PO Box 81
Delhi, NY 13753
Phone: 212-353-3326
Fax: 607-746-7453
Tom Tolnay, Publisher/Editor;
  Tim Grain, Publicity
• Chace, Joel, 85
• Nelson, Stanley, 320
• Thomson, Jeffrey, 432

Birnham Wood Graphics
PO Box 114
Northport, NY 11768
George Wallace, Publisher
• White, Claire Nicolas, 460

**BkMk Press of the
  University of Missouri-
  Kansas City**
224 University House, 5101

Rockhill Rd.
Kansas City, MO 64110-2499
Phone: 816-235-2558
Fax: 816-235-2611
Email: bkmk@umkc.edu
Michelle Boisseau, Editor;
Ben Furnish, Managing
Editor
Dist. by: Baker & Taylor
• Bargen, Walter, 30
• Bauer, Bill, 34
• Buckley, Christopher, 69
• Cutler, Bruce, 112
• Friman, Alice, 151
• Mitchell, Roger, 304
• Neville, Tam Lin, 322
• Wilson, Thomas Zvi, 466
• Woessner, Warren, 467

Black Bear Publications
1916 Lincoln St
Croydon, PA 19021-8026
Email: bbreview@aol.com
• Winans, A.D., 467

Black Belt Press
PO Box 551
Montgomery, AL 36101
Phone: 334-265-6753
Fax: 334-265-8880
Email: jpayne@black-belt.com
URL: http://www.black-belt.com
Jeff Slaton, Editor; Laura
Pace, Publicity
• Blackshear, Helen F., 49
• Glaze, Andrew, 165
• King, Willie James, 233
• Zippert, Carol Prejean, 478

Black Bough

188 Grove St. #1
Somerville, NJ 08876
Phone: 908-703-1369
Fax: 908-703-1370
• Easter, Charles, 132

Black Classic Press
PO Box 13414
Baltimore, MD 21203
Phone: (410) 358-0980
Fax: (410) 358-0987
URL: http://www.blackclassic.com
Apryl Motley, Editorial
Assistant; Jovett Solomon,
Publicity
• Miller, E. Ethelbert, 299

**Black History Museum,
UMUM/LOH Press**
PO Box 15057
Philadelphia, PA 19130
• Okantah, Mwatabu S., 329

**Black Rock
Press/Rainshadow
Editions**
University of Nevada, Reno,
University Library/322
Reno, NV 89557-0044
• Hussa, Linda, 210

Black Scholar Press
PO Box 2869
Oakland, CA 94618
• Crockett-Smith, D.L., 108

Black Sparrow Press
24 Tenth Street
Santa Rosa, CA 95401
Phone: 707-579-4011
Fax: 707-579-0567

Email: books@blacksparrow-press.com
URL: http://www.blacksparrowpress.com
Michele Filshie, Editor
• Broughton, James, 65
• Bukowski, Charles, 71
• Clark, Tom, 92
• Codrescu, Andrei, 94
• Coleman, Wanda, 97
• Eshleman, Clayton, 137
• Everson, William (Brother Antoninus), 138
• Field, Edward, 143
• Kelly, Robert, 228
• Lifshin, Lyn, 259
• Myles, Eileen, 318
• Sanders, Edward, 383
• Saroyan, Aram, 384
• Wakoski, Diane, 447
• Yau, John, 473

Black Words/Runagate Press
PO Box 21
Alexandria, VA 22313
Email: blackwords@juno.com
• Salaam, Kalamu ya, ed., 380

Blackberry Books
617 East Neck Road
Nobleboro, ME 04555
Phone: 207-729-5083
Fax: 207-729-6783
Email: chimfarm@gwi.net
Gary Lawless, Editor/Publisher
• Lawless, Gary, 250
• Sakaki, Nanao, 380

Blue Begonia Press
225 S 15th Ave
Yakima, WA 98902-3821

• Derry, Alice, 122

Blue Flamingo Productions
6465 Pearl Rd
Cleveland, OH 44130
Phone: 216-884-1920
Fax: 216-884-0122
Email: yryb12a@prodigy.com
• Magner, James, Jr., 273

Blue Scarab Press
243 S. 8th Ave
Pocatello, ID 83201
Phone: 208-232-5118
Harald Wyndham, Publisher
• Kuzma, Greg, 245
• Wyndham, Harald, 471

Bluestem Press
Dept. of English, Emporia St. University, Box 4019
Emporia, KS 66801
Phone: 316-341-5216
Fax: 316-341-5547
URL:
http://www.emporia.edu/ww/w/english/bluestem.htm
Amy Sage Webb, Editor; Elly Barta-Moran
• Berger, Jacqueline, 42
• Dauer, Lesley, 115

BOA Editions
260 East Ave.
Rochester, NY 14604
Phone: 716-546-3410
Fax: 716-546-3913
Email:
boaedit@frontiernet.net
URL: http://www.boaeditions.org
Thomas Ward, Steven Huff,

Editor; Sarah Freligh,
Marketing Director
Dist. by: Consortium
• Bly, Robert, 52
• Bond, Bruce, 55
• Bosselaar, Laure-Anne, 56
• Contogenis, Constantine, and
Wolhee Choe, trans., 101
• Foerster, Richard, 146
• Hamill, Sam, 183
• Heyen, William, 196
• Hicok, Bob, 196
• Ignatow, David, 210
• Kang Dean, Debra, 224
• Kutchins, Laurie, 244
• Makuck, Peter, 275
• Nye, Naomi Shihab, 327
• Snodgrass, W. D., trans., 409
• Waters, Michael, 454

Boaz
PO Box 6582
Albany, CA 94706
Email: boazpub@earthlink.net
Dist. by: PGW
• Breedlove, Charlene, ed., 60

Bogg Publications
422 North Cleveland
Arlington, VA 22201
Phone: 703-243-6019
John Elsberg, Poetry
Editor/Publisher
• Kincaid, Joan Payne, 232

Bomb Sniffing Dog Records
PO Box 217
New York, NY 10113
Phone: 212-645-6448
• Xark, Bob, 472

Bombshelter Press

6684 Colgate Ave
Los Angeles, CA 92646
Phone: 213-651-5488
Fax: 213-651-5132
Jack Grapes, Editor; Mifanwy
Kaiser
• Grapes, Jack,ed., 172

Bookwrights Press
2255 Westover Dr
Charlottesville, VA 22901
Phone: 804-823-8223
• Hayes, Alice Ryerson, 191

Bordighera
Foreign Languages &
Literatures, Purdue
University,1359 Stanley
Coulter Hall
West Lafayette, IN 47907-
1359
Phone: 765-494-3839
Fax: 765-496-1700
Email: tamburri@pudur.edu
URL:
http://www.luc.edu/depts/mo
dern_langu/italian/bor-
dighera/
Anthony Julian Tamburri,
Director
• Morra, Isabella, 311
• Ricapito, Joseph V., 363
• Turco, Lewis, 438

Bottom Dog Press
c/o Firelands College
Huron, OH 44839
Phone: 419-433-5560
Fax: 419-433-9696
Email: lsmithdog@aol.com
URL:
http://members.aol.com:/lsm

ithdog/bottomdog
Larry Smith, Director
Dist. by: SPD
• Garrison, David Lee, and
  Terry Hermsen, eds., 157
• Liebler, M.L., ed., 259
• Ragain, Maj, 354
• Smith, Daniel; Edwina
  Pendarvis, and Philip St.
  Clair, 406
• Smith, Larry, and Mei Hui
  Huang, trans., 406
• Smith, Laura, ed., 407
• Thompson, Daniel, 432

Bradypress
5050 Pratt Street
Omaha, NE 68104
Phone: 402-554-2773
Denise Brady
• Brady, Denise, 59
• Kosmicki, Greg, 240

Branch Redd Books
9300 Atlantic Ave, 218
Margate, NJ 08402
Phone: 609-822-7050
William Sherman, Editor
• Sherman, Bill, 398

Braziller, George
171 Madison Ave.
Ste. 1103
New York, NY 10016
Phone: 212-889-0909
Fax: 212-689-5405
Mary Taveras, Editor; Julie
  DiPhilippo, Publicity
• Cairns, Scott, 75
• Krüger, Michael, 242

Brickhouse Books

541 Piccadilly Rd.
Towson, MD 21204
Phone: 410-830-2869
Fax: 410-830-3999
Email: charriss@towson.edu
Clarinda Harriss,
  Director/Editor
• White, Sharon, 461

**Brickhouse Books/Chestnut
  Hills Press**
• Wickwire, Chester, 461

Bright Hill Press
PO Box 193
Treadwell, NY 13846
Phone: 607-746-7306
Fax: 607-746-7274
Email: wordthur@catskill.net
Bertha Rogers, Director
Dist. by: B&T, North Country
  Books, SPD
• Bernard, Pam, 43
• Jolliff, William, 219
• O'Melveny, Regina, 328
• Rogers, Bertha, ed., 371

Bristol Banner Books
PO Box 1219
Bristol, IN 46507
Phone: 219-825-POEM
Fax: 219-825-7636
Email:
  bristolbannerbks@prodigy.n
  et
URL:
  http://pages.pordigy.com/bri
  stolbannerbooks
Melody Myers, Editor
• Myers, M., ed., 318
• Myers, M., ed., 318
• Myers, M., ed., 318

Bristol Park Books
386 Park Ave. South
New York, NY 10016

• Laurence, Mary Sanford, ed.,
250

Broadside Press
1301 West Lafayette, 102
Detroit, MI 48226
Phone: 313-963-8526
Fax: 313-934-1231
Donald S. Vest, Vice-
President; Willie Williams•
Students From Inside Out,
421

Broken Boulder Press
1207 W. 19th St.
Lawrence, KS 66046

• Miller, Errol, 300

Brooklyn Public Library
Brooklyn Public Library,
Marketing and
Communications, Grand
Army Plaza
Brooklyn, NY 11238

• Nurkse, Dennis, ed., 326

Brunswick Publishing
1386 Lawrenceville Plank Rd
Lawrenceville, VA 23868
Phone: 804-848-3865
Fax: 804-848-0607
Email: brunspub@jnent.com
Walter J. Raymond, Editor;
Marianne Salzmann,
Publisher
Dist. by: Washington Book

Distributors
• Thomas, David J., 431

Bull Thistle Press
PO Box 184
Jamaica, VT 05343
Phone: 802-384-0798
Greg Joly, Editor
• Metras, Gary, 298

**Bunny and the Crocodile
Press/Forest Woods Media
Productions**
PO Box 416
Hedgesville, WV 25427-0416
Phone: 304-754-8847
Fax: 304-754-8847
Email: Grace7623@aol.com
URL:
http://members.aol.com/grac
e7623/grace.htm
Cindy Comitz, Editor; Grace
Cavalieri, Editor
To Order: The Bookstore,
4925 Boonsbora Rd.,
Boonsboro Shopping
Center, Lynchburg, VA
24503; 804-384-1746
• Capitol Hill Poetry Group,
77
• Emerson, Jean, 134
• Morland, Margaret Ward,
310

Burning Deck
71 Elmgrove Ave
Providence, RI 02906
Phone: 401-351-0015
Rosmarie Waldrop, Vice-
President/Editor
Dist. by: SPD
• Albiach, Anne-Marie, 7

• Gizzi, Peter, 164
• Ngai, Sianne, 323
• Quignard, Pascal, 352
• Veinstein, Alain, 442
• Waldrop, Keith, 448
• Xue Di, 472

ButtonWood Press
PO Box 206
Champaign, IL 61824-0206
• Radavich, David, 353

By the Seat of Your Pants Press
c/o Cheryl Burke, PO Box 892
New York, NY 10009
Phone: 718-387-2326
Email: cherylb2@aol.com
• B., Cheryl, 25

Cadmus Editions
PO Box 126
Tiburon-Belvedere, CA 94920
URL: http://www.cadmus-editions.com
• Sobin, Gustaf, 410

Caernarvon Press
4665 Mississippi St, 1
San Diego, CA 92116
Phone: 619-299-1341
• Kowit, Steve, 240

Cahuenga Press
1256 N. Mariposa Ave.
Los Angeles, CA 90029
• Prado, Holly, 349

Caliban Book Shop
Pittsburgh, PA
• McShea, William P., 293
Calyx Books

216 SW Madison, Suite 14,
  PO Box B
Corvallis, OR 97339
Phone: 541-753-9384
Fax: 541-753-0515
Email: calyx@proaxis.com
Amy Callahan, Promotions
  Coordinator; Margarita
  Donnelly, Poetry Editor
Dist. by: Consortium
• Davis, Cortney, 116
• Tremblay, Gail, 435

Canio's Editions
P.O. Box 1962
Sag Harbor, NY 11963
Phone: 516-725-4926
Fax: 516-537-1825
Email: caniobks@peconic.net
Canio Pavone, Publisher
• Christo, Cyril, 89
• Planz, Allen, 346

Carlton Arms Hotel
160 E 25th St
New York, NY 10010
Phone: 212-684-8337
• Tyler, Mike, 439

Carnegie Mellon University Press
Box 30, 4902 Forbes Ave.
Pittsburgh, PA 15213
Phone: 412-268-6348
Fax: 412-268-5288
Email: it12@andrew.cmu.edu
Irma Tani, Managing Editor
• Browne, Michael Dennis, 68
• Cooley, Peter, 101
• Dodd, Wayne, 126
• Eady, Cornelius, 131
• Friedman, Jeff, 151

• Harms, James, 186
• Holmes, Elizabeth, 203
• Inez, Colette, 211
• Joseph, Allison, 222
• Katrovas, Richard, 227
• Kirschner, Elizabeth, 233
• Meek, Jay, 293
• Miller, Leslie Adrienne, 301
• Rankin, Paula, 356
• Skoyles, John, 404
• Stanton, Maura, 415
• Valentine, Jean, 441

Carolina Wren Press
120 Morris St
Durham, NC 27701
Phone: 919-560-2738
David Kellogg, Publicity
• Blaski, Steven, 50
• Green, Jaki Shelton, 173
• Green, Jaki Shelton, 173

Catbird Press/A Garrigue Book
16 Windsor Rd.
New Haven, CT 06473
Email: catbird@pipeline.com
Dist. by: IPG
• Seifert, Jaroslav, 391

Catnip Press
220 E 54th St, 9E
New York, NY 10022
Phone: 212-759-5323
Fax: 212-759-5367
Email: porchpin@aol.com
Philip Corwin
• Corwin, Phillip, 105

Cave Canem Workshop/Retreat
39 Jane St., Apt GB

New York, NY 10014
Phone: 212-522-1915
Fax: 212-522-0120
Email:
sarah_micklem@sikids.com
• Cave Canem
Workshop/Retreat, 84

Cedar Hill Publications
3722 Highway 8 West
Mena, AR 71953
• McIrvin, Michael, 291

Center for Book Arts
626 Broadway, 5th Floor
New York, NY 10012
Phone: 212-481-0295
Fax: 212-673-4635
Email:
bookarts@pipeline.com
URL:
http://www.colophon.com/g
allery/cba
Brian Hannon, Executive
Director; Sharon Dolin,
Poetry Editor
• Haug, James, 190
• Vollmer, Judith, 446

Century Press
PO Box 298
Thomaston, ME 04861
Phone: 207-354-0998
Fax: 207-354-8953
• Titche, Leon, 432

Chaet, Eric
1803 County Trunk ZZ
DePere, WI 54115-9629
Phone: 920-532-4798
• Chaet, Eric, 85

Chax Press
101 W 6th St., 6
Tucson, AZ 85701-1000
Phone: 520-620-1626
Fax: 520-620-1636
Email: chax@theriver.com
• Armantrout, Rae, 19
• Cooper, Lisa, 102
• Lazer, Hank, 252
• Mandel, Tom, 276
• Nathanson, Tenney, 319

**Chax Press/West House
Books**
• Mac Cormack, Karen, 271

CHESS Publications
232 East University Pkwy.
Baltimore, MD 21218
• Hodge-Williams, Valerie A.,
200

Chi Chi Press
PO Box 14624
San Francisco, CA 94114
Phone: 415-252-8377
• Hirshkowitz, Lois, 199

Chicago Spectrum Press
4848 Brownsboro Center
Arcade
Louisville, KY 40207
Phone: 800-594-5190
• Silver, Alice Moolten, 402

Chicano Chapbook Series
43 The Crescent
Berkeley, CA 94708
• Delgado, Juan, 120
• Jayme, Michael, 217
• Ledesma, Alberto, 253
• Romero, Danny, 371

• Sanchez, Neomi, 382
• Yañez, Rich, 472

Chicory Blue Press
795 East St North
Goshen, CT 06756
Phone: 860-491-2271
Fax: 860-491-8619
Sondra Zeidenstein, President
Dist. by: SDP
• Swift, Joan, 424
• Weinberger, Florence, 457
• Wong, Nellie, 468
• Zeidenstein, Sondra, 478

Chiron Review Press
522 East South Ave.
St. John, KS 67576-2212
Phone: 316-549-6156
Michael Hathaway, Editor;
D.C. Erdmann, Publicity
To Order: 15223 Coral Isle Ct.
Ft. Myers, FL, 33919;
941-454-6546
Dist. by: D.C. Erdmann
• Holt, Rochelle L., 204

Chronicle Books
275 5th St.
San Francisco, CA 94103
Phone: 800-722-6657
Fax: 800-858-7787
Matthew Osborn, Marketing
Asst.
• Soto, Gary, 412

Cider Press
85 Echo Cove Ln
Poland Spring, ME 04274
• Zarucchi, Roy, 477

Cincinnati Writers' Project

PO Box 29920
Cincinnati, OH 45229
• Bezner, Kevin, 46

Cinco Puntos Press
2709 Louisville
El Paso, TX 79930
Phone: 915-566-9072
Fax: 915-565-5335
Email:
cinco@cincopuntos.com
URL: http://www.cincopuntos.com
Lee Merrill Byrd, Poetry
Editor; Susie Byrd,
Publicity Director
Dist. by: Consortium
• Byrd, Bobby, 73
• Urrea, Luis Alberto, 440

City College of New York
• Wallenstein, Barry,
Coordinator, 450

City Lights Books
261 Columbus Ave.
San Francisco, CA 94133
Phone: 415-362-1901
Fax: 415-362-4921
Email: stacey@citylights.com
URL:
http://www.citylights.com
Lawrence Ferlinghetti,
Editor/Publisher; Stacy
Lewis, Publicity
Dist. by: Subterranean Co.
• Campana, Dino, 76
• Cortázar, Julio, 104
• Lamantia, Philip, 246
• Mackey, Nathaniel, 272
• Mehmedinovic, Semezdin,
293

• Pacheco, José Emilio, 334
• Pessoa, Fernando, 341
• Schelling, Andrew, trans.,
387

Cityful Press
PO Box 4477
Seattle, WA 98104-0477
• Giannini, David, 161

Clamp Down Press
PO Box 7270
Cape Porpoise, ME 04014
Phone: 207-967-2605
Joshua Bodwell
• Weber, Mark, 456

Cleis Press
PO Box 14684
San Francisco, CA 94114
Phone: 415-575-4700
Fax: 415-864-5602
Email: cleis@aol.com
Feclice Newman, Publicity
• Pearlberg, Gerry Gomez, ed.,
339

Cleveland State University Poetry Center
1983 E 24th Street, RT 1813
Cleveland, OH 44115-2440
Phone: 216-687-3986
Fax: 216-698-6943
Email: poetrycenter@popmail.csuohio.edu
Ted Lardner, Editor; Rita M.
Grabowski, Publicity
To Order: 888-278-6473
Dist. by: Ingram, Partners
• Breskin, David, 61
• Grimm, Susan, 177
• Jacobson, Bonnie, 214

Coffee House Press
27 N Fourth Street, Suite 400
Minneapolis, MN 55401
Phone: 612-338-0125
Fax: 612-338-4004
Email: jana-coffeehouse-
press@iname.com
URL: http://www.coffeehouse-
press.org
Christopher Fischbach, Editor;
Jana Robbins, Marketing
Dist. by: Consortium

Cold River Press
PO Box 483
Mt. Hukum, CA 95656
Phone: 209-245-4016
Fax: 209-245-4016
Email: bensays@bigfoot.com
URL: www2.cdepot.net/~ben-
says/
Ben Hiatt, Poetry Editor

**Cold River Press/ Mt.
Aukum Press**

Collier, John
19 Clement St.
Tiverton, RI 02878

**Columbia University
Creative Writing
Center/Quarto Books**
Creative Writing Ctr/Mail
Code4108 Lewisohn Hall,
Columbia University
New York, NY 10027
Phone: 212-854-3774
Email:
writingprogram@colum-
bia.edu

Columbia University Press
136 South Broadway
Irvington, NY 10533
Phone: 212-666-1000

• Ueda, Makoto, trans., 439

Conari Press
2550 9th St., Suite 101
Berkeley, CA 94710
Phone: (510) 649-7178
Fax: (510) 649-7190
Brenda Knight, Editor
Dist. by: PGW
• Knight, Brenda, ed., 235

Confluence Press
Lewis-Clark State College,
   500 8th Ave.
Lewiston, ID 83501-2698
Phone: 208-799-2336
Fax: 208-799-2350
Email: Conpress@lscu.edu
James R. Hepworth, Poetry
   Editor; John Wilper,
   Business Manager
• Waters, Mary Ann, 454

**Connecticut Poetry Review
   Press**
501 Crescent St.
New Haven, CT 06515
Vivian Shipley, Editor
• Chichetto, James Wm., 87

Conundrum Press
PO Box 993
Crested Butte, CO 81224
• Tipton, James, 432

Copper Beech Press
English Dept., Box 2578
   Brown University
Providence, RI 02906
Phone: 401-351-1253
Randy Blasing, Editor
• Holley, Margaret, 203

• Levin, Phillis, 256
• Prout, Quintin, 350
• Richman, Robert, 365
• Walker, Jeanne Murray, 450

Copper Canyon Press
PO Box 271
Port Townsend, WA 98368
Phone: 360-385-4925
Fax: 360-385-4985
Email: cprcanyn@olympus.net
URL: http://www.ccpress.org
Sam Hamill, Publisher/Editor;
   Mike Weigers, Managing
   Editor
Dist. by: Consortium
• Balaban, John, 27
• Bell, Marvin, 39
• Berg, Stephen, 42
• Cassells, Cyrus, 82
• Csoóri, Sándor, 109
• Ehret, Terry, 132
• Elytis, Odysseas, 134
• Galvin, James, 155
• Griffin, Susan, 176
• Haines, John, 180
• Harrison, Jim, 188
• Liu, Timothy, 261
• Major, Clarence, 274
• McGrath, Thomas, 290
• Merwin, W.S., 295
• Merwin, W.S., trans., 296
• Rexroth, Kenneth, 363
• Stroud, Joseph, 420
• Sung-Il Lee, trans., 422
• Sze, Arthur, 425
• Wilner, Eleanor, 466
• Wright, C.D., 469
• Yuan Mei, 475

Copperjacket Concepts
3506 Utopia Pkwy., #E2

Flushing, NY 11358
Phone: 718-463-4859
Fax: 516-878-0259
Email: pmacaluso@exchange.
ml.com
Peter Macaluso
• Macaluso, Peter, 271

Cornerstone Press Chicago
939 West Wilson Ave
Chicago, IL 60640
Phone: 773-561-2450
Fax: 773-989-2076
Tom Montgomery, Publicity;
Jane Hertenstein, Marketing
• Boyd, Tammy, 58
• Lindskoog, Kathryn, 261
• Mortimer, Curtiss, 312
• Scott, Steve, 390

Council Oak Books
1350 East 15th Street
Tulsa, OK 74120
Phone: 918-587-6454
Fax: 918-583-4995
Email: oakie@ionet.net
Dr. Sally Dennison, Poetry
Editor; Cindy McKee,
Publicity
• Kistler, William, 234

Counterpoint
1627 I St NW, Ste 500
Washington, DC 20006
Phone: 202-887-0363
Fax: 202-887-0567
Email: jkane@counterpoint-
press.com
Jack Shoemaker, Editor-in-
Chief; Jessica Kane,
Publicity
• Corn, Alfred, 103

• Snyder, Gary, 409

Counterpoint Publishing
6318 Craigway Road
Spring, TX 77389
Phone: 713-376-7613
Fax: 713-251-7974
Claire Ottenstein, Publisher
• Berry, Wendell, 45
• Berry, Wendell, 45

**Cross-Cultural
Communications**
239 Wynsum Avenue
Merrick, NY 11566-4725
Phone: 516-868-5635
Fax: 516-379-1901
Email: cccmia@juno.com
Stanley H. Barkan,
Publisher/Executive Editor;
Mia Barkan, Publicity
• Kunitz, Stanley, 244
• Melhem, D.H., 294
• Polansky, Paul, 347
• Vroman, Leo, 446

**Cross-Cultural
Communications/
Hochelaga Press**
• Boire, Jennifer, 54
• Williams, John A., 464

**Cross-Cultural
Communications/
Nightingale Editions**
• Catterson, Thomas M., 84
• Gilson, Saul, 164

**Cross-Cultural
Communications/ Oficyna
Konfraterni Poetów**
• Barkan, Stanley H., 30

Cross-Cultural Communications/ Ostrich Editions
• Dunn, Robert, 131

Crosstown Books
PO Box 1824 Cathedral Station
New York, NY 10025
• Brown, Dan, 66

Crown Publishers
201 East 50th Street
New York, NY 10022
Phone: 212-572-6122
Fax: 212-572-6192
Michael Denning, Poetry Editor; John Clark, Assistant Editor
• Ehrmann, Max, 132
• Jaycox, Faith, ed., 217
• Mitchell, Joni, 303
• Sirowitz, Hal, 403

Crown Publishers/Harmony Books
201 East 50th Street
New York, NY 10022
Phone: 212-572-6122
Fax: 212-572-6192
• Rumi, Jelaluddin, 375

Cummington Press
Omaha, NE 68106
Phone: 402-554-2715
• Goldensohn, Barry, and Lorrie Goldensohn, 168

Cune
PO Box 31024
Seattle, WA 98103
Phone: 206-789-7055

Fax: 206-782-1330
Email: cune@cunepress.com
URL: http://www.cunepress.com

• Bentley, Beth, 41

Curbstone Press
321 Jackson St.
Willimantic, CT 06226
Phone: 860-423-5110
Fax: 860-423-9242
Email: curbston@connix.com
URL: http://www.connix.com/ ~curbston/
Alexander Taylor, Poetry Editor; Casey A. Borch, Awards Coordinator
Dist. by: Consortium
• Alegría, Claribel, 8
• Ayala, Naomi, 24
• Bowen, Kevin, 56
• Brugnaro, Ferruccio, 68
• Dalton, Roque, 113
• De Burgos, Julia, 118
• Groves, Maketa, 178
• Rodríguez, Luis J., 370

CUZ Editions
PO Box 1599 Peter Stuyvesant Station
New York, NY 10009-1599
Email: rmeyers@interport.net
• Dubris, Maggie, 128
• Hell, Richard, 194
• Noel, Susan, 324

Cycle Press
715 Baker's Lane
Key West, FL 33040
Phone: 305-294-6979
Kirby Congdon

• Congdon, Kirby, 99
• Congdon, Kirby, 99
• Congdon, Kirby, 99
• Congdon, Kirby, 99
• Congdon, Kirby, 99

Dalkey Archive Press
ISU Campus Box 4241
Normal, IL 61790-4241
Phone: 309-438-7555
Fax: 309-438-7422
Email: aweaser@ilstu.edu
URL: http://www.dalkey
archive.com
John O'Brien, Editor; Angela
Weaser, Publicity
To Order: 401 Fairchild Hall,
Illinois State University,
Normal, IL 61761
Dist. by: University of
Chicago Distribution Center
• Giscombe, C.S., 164
• Martin, Carl R., 279

Daniel, John, and Company
PO Box 21922
Santa Barbara, CA 93121
Phone: 805-962-1780
• Longo, Perie, 265

Dark Regions Press
PO Box 6301
Concord, CA 94524
Phone: 510-254-7442
Fax: 510-254-6419
Email: isedmorey@aol.com
Bobbi Sinha-Morey, Poetry
Editor
• Grey, John, 176
• Webb, Don, 456

Dasling Publications

PO Box 856 Plane Tarium
Station
New York, NY 10024
Phone: 212-929-7608
Email: 40dasling@aol.com
• Arthur-Simons, David, 19

**Davka: Jewish Cultural
Revolution**
1126 Bush St., Suite 405
San Francisco, CA 94109
• Kaufman, Alan, 227

DDDD Publications
9715 Foster, Suite A
St. Louis, MO 63114
Phone: 314-427-3329
Fax: 314-427-3329
Email: dpart@inlink.com
URL:
http://conk.com/world/dddd
publs
Della Koster, Owner; Dee
Frances, Poetry Editor
To Order: Floriana Hall
1232 Clifton Ave
Akron OH 44310
• Cauthen, Carolyn Rebecca,
84
• Hall, Floriana, 181

Dead Tree Press
PO Box 3171
Newton, NJ 07860
Phone: 973-300-0090
• Gruswitz, Nik, 178

Delta Press
PO Box 5862
Vacaville, CA 95696-5862
Email: delta@castles.com
• Gurney, John, 178

Diamond Hitch Press
220 72nd Street
Brooklyn, NY 11209
Phone: 718-921-6689
• Ludwig, Laura Lonshein,
269

Dim Gray Bar Press
600 West 111th St.
New York, NY 10025
Phone: 212-866-4465
Email:
ordinarymind@erols.com
Barry Magid
• Doty, Mark, 126
• Doty, Mark, 126

Diminishing Books/ Green Finch Press
Golgonooza at Frog Level,
3212 Arthur Minnis Rd
Hillsborough, NC 27278
Phone: 919-967-2470
Email:
jeffbeam@email.unc.edu
• Beam, Jeffery, 35

Dolphin-Moon Press
PO Box 22262
Baltimore, MD 21203
Phone: (410) 444-7758
James Taylor, Poetry Editor
• Lombardo, Gian, 264

Doubleday/ Anchor Books
1540 Broadway, 18th Flr.
New York, NY 10036
Phone: 212-782-9390
Fax: 212-782-9261
Marly Rusoff, Publicity
• Dickinson, Emily, 124
• Divakaruni, Chitra Banerjee,

125
• González, Ray, ed., 169
• Jordan, June, 221
• Whitman, Walt, 461

Dover Publications
31 East 2nd St.
Mineola, NY 11501
Phone: 516-294-7000
Fax: 516-742-6953
Irene McCoy, Publicity
Director; Paul Negri, Editor
• Brontë, Emily, Anne, and
Charlotte, 65
• Crane, Stephen, 106
• Dunbar, Paul Laurence, 130
• Eliot, T.S., 133
• Marvell, Andrew, 282
• Negri, Paul, ed., 320
• Pushkin, Alexander, 351
• Rattiner, Susan L., ed., 359
• Sherman, Joan R., ed., 398
• The American Poetry &
Literacy Project, ed., 430
• Ward, Candace, ed., 452
• Yeats, William Butler, 474

Dr. Ducky Doolittle
PO Box 892
New York, NY 10009
Phone: 718-387-2326
Email: Cherylb2@aol.com
Cheryl Burke
• B., Cheryl, 25

Dreams & Visions Publishing
PO Box 6767
Altadena, CA 91003
Phone: 818-973-3159
• Parnell, Anthony D., 338

Dryad Press
15 Sherman Ave.
Takoma Park, MD 20912
• Goldberg Barbara, ed., 168

**Eastern Washington
University Press**
526 5th St MS 133, Eastern
Washington University
Cheney, WA 99004-2431
Phone: 800-508-9095
Fax: 509-359-4381
Email:
ewupress@mail.ewu.edu
Scott R. Poole, Editor;
Roberta Robinson, Business
Manager
• Alley, Rick, 12
• Berry, D.C., 44
• Cook-Lynn, Elizabeth, 101
• Higman, Perry, trans., 196
• Howell, Christopher, 206
• O'Hehir, Diana, 328

**Easy Break, First Time
Publishing**
22200 Cuperitno Rd
Cupertino, CA 95014
Phone: 408-777-9899
Fax: 408-777-8779
Email: ezbreak@parbell.net
James G. Luna, Publisher
• Dukes, Jonnie, 130
• Kyser, Eric, 245
• LaRue, Debrah, 247
• Luna, James G., 269
• McGuigan, Christine, 291
• Porter, David, 348

Ecco Press
100 West Broad St.
Hopewell, NJ 08525

Phone: 609-466-4748
Fax: 609-466-4706
URL:
http://www.eccopress.com
Dan Halpern, Publisher; Gail
Brussel, Director of
Publicity
• Ashbery, John, 21
• Bly, Robert, ed., 52
• Glück, Louise, 166
• Glück, Louise, 166
• Graham, Jorie, 171
• Graham, Jorie, ed., 172
• Hass, Robert, ed., 190
• Jong, Erica, 221
• Kizer, Carolyn, ed., 234
• McGrath, Campbell, 290
• Plumly, Stanley, 346
• Rizzuto, Phil, 367
• Swander, Mary, ed., 423
• Tate, James, 428

Eden Press
PO Box 804271
Chicago, IL 60680-4104
C.M. Rodgers, Editor; Beryl
Zitch, Publicity
• Rodgers, Carolyn M., 370

Edge Books
PO Box 25642
Washington, DC 20007
• Berrigan, Anselm, 44
• Fuller, Heather, 152

Edge Books/Upper Limit
• Nielsen, A.L., 324

Edgewise Press
24 Fifth Avenue, Suite 224
New York, NY 10011
Phone: (212) 982-4818

Fax: (212) 982-1364
URL:
http://www.angelfire.com/
biz/edgewisebooks
Richard Milazzo,
Editor/President
• Cagnone, Nanni, 74
• Corman, Cid, 103

Eidolon Editions
San Francisco, CA
Dist. by: SPD
• Serin, Judith, 393

Element Books
160 N. Washington St, 4th Fl.
Boston, MA 02114
Phone: 617-915-9400
Fax: 617-248-0909
Email: element@cove.com
Roberta Scimone, Editor; Jeff
Lardis, Publicity
• Jacobs, Alan, ed., 213

Elkhound Publications
PO Box 1453 Gracie Station
New York, NY 10028
• Ryan, G.B., 376

Em Press
541 Ethel Avenue
Mill Valley, CA 94941
Phone: 415-381-1243
Fax: 415-381-0110
Email: DaleGoing@aol.com
Dale Going, Publisher
• Lawson, Denise Liddell, 251
• Robles, Jaime, 370
• Snow, Carol, 409
• Squires, Suzanne Marks, 414

Emrys Press

c/o The Emrys Foundation
PO Box 8813
Greenville, SC 29604
Phone: 864-242-3652
Fax: 864-370-0111
Keller Cushing Freeman,
Editor; Jo Ann Walker,
Editor
• Inman, Sue Lile, 211

Encircle Publications
PO Box 219
Sagamore Beach, MA 02562
• Miller, Errol, 300
• Miller, Errol, 300

ESF
1 Marine Midland Plaza
Binghamton, NY 13901-3216
URL: http://tier.net/esfpub/
• Cesereanu, Ruxandra, 85

ET
no address
• Reed, Eve, 360

Exact Change
PO Box 1917
Boston, MA 02205
Phone: 617- 269-6227
• Rothenberg, Jerome, ed., 374

Fairfield Books
PO Box 8085
Wilmette, IL 60091
Phone: 708-283-9379
• Zwart, Martijn, and Ethel
Grene, trans., 479

Farrar, Straus and Giroux
19 Union Square West
New York, NY 10003

Phone: 212-741-6900
Fax: 212-206-5340
Email: cgoldstein@fsgee.com
Jonathan Galassi, Editor; Cary
  Goldstein, Publicity
• Ashbery, John, 21
• Bidart, Frank, 46
• Brodsky, Joseph, 63
• Dante, Alighieri, 115
• Ferry, David, trans., 142
• Fried, Michael, 150
• Heaney, Seamus, 191
• Homer, 204
• Hughes, Ted, 208
• Hughes, Ted, 208
• Kleinzahler, August, 235
• Milosz, Czeslaw, 302
• Montale, Eugenio, 305
• Muldoon, Paul, 315
• Seidel, Frederick, 391
• Walcott, Derek, 447
• Wright, Charles, 469
• Zagajewski, Adam, 476

**Farrar, Straus and Giroux/
  Noonday**
• Ashbery, John, 20
• Ashbery, John, 20
• Ashbery, John, 21
• García Lorca, Federico, 155
• Heaney, Seamus, 192
• Loy, Mina, 268
• Murray, Les, 317
• Pinsky, Robert, 345
• Pinsky, Robert, 346
• Williams, C.K., 463
• Wright, Charles, 470

**Farrar, Straus and Giroux/
  North Point Press**
• Rilke, Rainer Maria, 366

Figures, The
5 Castle Hill Ave.
Great Barrington, MA 01230
Phone: 413-528-2552
Fax: 413-528-2552
• Equi, Elaine, 136
• Mitchell, Roger, 303
• Price, Michael, 349

Firm Ground Press
c/o OMI Business
  Communications, 444 Park
  Ave South
New York, NY 10016
Phone: 212-683-9000 ext. 15
Fax: 212-696-9546
Victoria Hallerman, Publisher
• Hallerman, Victoria, 182
• Loomis, Sabra, 266

First Intensity Press
PO Box 665
Lawrence, KS 66044
Phone: (785) 749-1501
Email: leechapman@aol.com
Lee Chapman,
  Editor/Publisher
• Gifford, Barry, 162
• Prevallet, Kristin, 349

Fithian Press
PO Box 1525
3 W. Carrillo St, 202
Santa Barbara, CA 93102
Phone: 805-962-1780
Fax: 805-962-8835
Email: dandd@danielpublish-
  ing.com
URL: http://www.danielpub-
  lishing.com
Carolyn Fleg, Editor; John
  Daniel, Editor

Dist. by: Baker and Taylor
• Ablon, Steven Luria, 1
• Almquist, Norma, 13
• Bates, Julia, 33
• Bisso, Ray, 48
• Buckley, W.K., 70
• Fike, Francis, 143
• Green, Daniel, 173
• Johnson, Margery A., 218
• Klein, Magdalena, 234
• Lawrence, David, 250
• Levitz, Linda C., 257
• Lohmann, Jeanne, 263
• Ogden, John D., 329
• Smart, Ninian, 406
• Weinberger, Florence, 457
• Wilkins, W.R., 462

Floating Island Publications
540 Main St
Cedarville, CA 96104
Phone: 916-279-2337
Michael Sykes, Editor
• Savant, John, 385

Floria Publications
773 Limerick Ct.
Sunnyvale, CA 94098
Phone: 408-732-1588
Fax: 408-732-1588
Email: floria@floriapublications.com
• Parmiani, Floria, 338

Flower Thief Press
no address
• Hirsch, Steve, 198

Flume Press
2751 Revere Ln
Chico, CA 95973
Phone: 916-342-1583

Casey Huff, Editor
• Makofske, Mary, 275

**Fly by Night Press/ A
   Gathering of the Tribes**
PO Box 20693
Tompkins Square Station
New York, NY 10009
Phone: 212-674-3778
Fax: 212-674-5576
Email: tribes@interport.net
URL: http://www.tribes.org
• Alson, Sheila; Cheryl Boyce
   Taylor, Zephryn Conte,
   Patricia Landrum, Kathy
   Price, and Clara Sala, 13
• Boyce Taylor, Cheryl, 57
• Carter, Michael, 81
• Ouzoonian, Amy, 333
• Rux, Carl Hancock, 376

Fordham University Press
University Box L
Bronx, NY 10458
Phone: 718-817-4781
Fax: 718-817-4785
Email: cboyle@murray.fordham.edu
Margaret Van Cott; Cormac
   Boyle, Marketing Manager
Dist. by: Bookmasters
• Berrigan, Daniel, 44
• Tasso, Torquato, 428

**Forum Press/ Rudi
   Publishing**
12 Geary Street, Suite 508
San Francisco, CA 94108
• Ward, Edward R., 452

Four Step Publications
PO Box 12434

Milwaukee, WI 53212
URL: http://www.execpc.com/
  -chriftor
• Catlin, Alan, 84

Four Walls Eight Windows
39 West 14th Street, 503
New York, NY 10011
Phone: 212-206-8965
Fax: 212-209-8799
• Allen, Robert H., 12

Four Way Books
PO Box 607
Marshfield, MA 02050
Phone: (781) 837-4887
Fax: (781) 834-3896
Dzvinia Orlowsky, Founding
  Editor
• Aleshire, Joan, 8
• Berg, Stephen, 42
• Carter, Anne Babson, 81
• Jenkins, Paul, 217
• Mangan, Pat, 277
• McFadden, Mary Ann, 289
• Wheeler, Susan, 460

French Bread Publications
PO Box 23868
San Jose, CA 95153
Email: paccoastj@juno.com
• Miller, Errol, 300

Galen Press
PO Box 64400
Tucson, AZ 85728-4400
Phone: 520-577-8363
Fax: 520-529-6459
• Shiedermayer, David L.,
  M.D., 399

Garden Street Press

PO Box 1231
Truro, MA 02666-1231
Phone: 508-349-1991
Naomi Feigelson Chase,
  Publisher/Editor
• Chase, Naomi Feigelson, 86

Gateway Press
c/o S.E. Falconer
1021 Clinton St.
Philadelphia, PA 19107
Phone: 215-922-2708
• Falconer, Sandra Evans, 139

GAZ
no address
Dist. by: SPD
• Fuller, William, 153

Generator Press
3503 Virginia Ave
Cleveland, OH 44109
Phone: 216-351-9406
John Byrum, Editor/Publisher
• Hartman, Arleen, 189

Ghost Pony Press
PO Box 260113
Madison, WI 53726-0113
URL:
  http://www.geocities.com/
  Paris/4614
Ingrid Swanberg,
  Editor/Publisher
• saíz, próspero, 379
• saíz, próspero, 379

Giovacchini, Chris
no address
• Giovacchini, Chris, 164

Glover Publishing

Box 633
Canton. NY 13617
• Glover, Albert, 166

Gnomon Press
PO Box 475
Frankfort, KY 40602-0475
Phone: 502-223-1858
Fax: 502-223-1858
Email: jgnomon@aol.com
URL: http://www.quikpage.
com/g/ggnomon
Jonathan Greene, Publisher
• Greene, Jonathan, 174
• Greene, Jonathan, 174
• Miller, Jim Wayne, 301
• Morgan, Robert, 309
• Niedecker, Lorine, 324

Goats + Compasses
Brownsville, VT 05037-0524
• Foster, Edward, 147

Goddessdead Publications
PO Box 46277
Los Angeles, CA 90046
Phone: 213-850-0067
Fax: 213-850-5894
Jane Adams, Editor; Joseph
Francis, Publicity
• Williams, Tracey Lee, 465

Godine, David R., Publisher
9 Hamilton Pl
Boston, MA 02108
Phone: 617-451-9600
Fax: 617- 350-0250
Email: info@godine.com
URL: http://www.godine.com
Carl Scarbrough, Publicity
Director; Mark Polizzotti,
Editorial Director

• Bascove, ed., 32
• Goldbarth, Albert, 168
• McNair, Wesley, 292
• McNair, Wesley, 292
• Weingarten, Roger, 458

Good Poet Press
no address
• Isaksson, Kimberly, 211

Gradiva Publications
PO Box 831
Stony Brook, NY 11790
Phone: 516-632-7448/7440
Fax: 516-632-9612
Email: lfontanella@ccmail.
sunysb.edu
Luigi Fontanella, Director
• Corazzini, Sergio, 102
• Corazzini, Sergio, 103
• Di Biasio, Rodolfo, 123
• Erba, Luciano, 136

Grautlau Press
PO Box 11
Dighton, MA 02715-0011
Phone: 508-672-5989
Fax: 508-673-4648
Email:
schneider@massmed.org
A.J. Schneider
To Order: 120 Friends Cove,
Somerset, MA 02726
• Schneider, Ada Jill, 388
• Schneider, Ada Jill, 388

Graywolf Press
2402 University Ave, Ste. 203
St. Paul, MN 55114
Phone: 651-641-0077
Fax: 651-641-0036
Email:

dublinsk@graywolfpress.org
URL:
http://www.graywolfpress.org
Fiona McCrae, Poetry Editor;
   Lisa Bullard, Publicity
Dist. by: Consortium
• Aizenberg, Susan, Suzanne
   Qualls, and Mark Turpin, 6
• Alcosser, Sandra, 8
• Barber, Jennifer; Mark
   Bibbins, and Maggie
   Nelson, 29
• Grennan, Eamon, 175
• Hoagland, Tony, 200
• Howe, Fanny, 205
• Kenyon, Jane, 229
• Leader, Mary, 253
• Phillips, Carl, 343
• Rivard, David, 367
• Stafford, William, 414

Green Bean Press
PO BOX 237
New York, NY 10013
Phone: 718-302-1955
Fax: 718-302-1955
Email: gbpress@earthlink.net
URL: http://home.earthlink.net
   /~gbpress
Ian Griffin, President
Dist. by: Ingram
• Crocker, Daniel, 107
• R, Joe, 352

Greenfield Review Press
PO Box 308
Greenfield Center, NY 12833
Phone: 518-584-1728
Fax: 518-583-9741
URL: http://nativeauthors.com
Joseph Bruchac,
   Editor/Publisher

• Ballard, Charles G., 28
• Sweet, Denise, 423

Greenhouse Review Press
3965 Bonny Doon Road
Santa Cruz, CA 95060
Phone: 408-426-4355
Email: gyounggrp@aol.com
Gary Young, Editor
• Levine, Philip, 257

Grey Spider Press
37607 Cape Horn Rd
Sedro Woolley, WA 98284
Phone: 360-826-5306
Christopher Stern, Editor;
   Jules Remedios Faye, Asst.
   Editor
• Mueller, Melinda, 315

Groundwater Press
67 Edgewood Rd. 2nd Floor
Port Washington, NY 11050
Phone: 516-767-8503
Fax: 212-346-1754
Email: zannie@aol.com
Rosanne Wasserman, Editor in
   Chief; Eugene Richie,
   Publicity
• Cohen, Marc, 95
• Iino, Tomoyuki, 211

Grove Press
841 Broadway
New York, NY 10003-4793
Phone: 212-614-7850
Fax: 212-614-7886
Alexis Owen, Publicity; Joan
   Bingham, Poetry Editor
To Order: 800-788-3123
Dist. by: PGW
• Cooper, Dennis, 102

- Lax, Robert, 251
- Lindsay, Sarah, 261
- Ormsby, Eric, 331
- Osherow, Jacqueline, 332
- Pessoa, Fernando, 341
- Ragan, James, 354
- Ragan, James, 355
- Rankine, Claudia, 356

Guernica Editions
20 Sonwil Drive
Buffalo, NY 14225-5516
Dist. by: SPD
Antonio D'Alfonso, Editor
- Caccia, Fulvio, 74
- Carravetta, Peter, 78
- Péloquin, Claude, 340

H & H Press
RR 2, Box 241
Middlebury Center, PA 16935
Phone: 717-376-2821
Fax: 717-376-2674
Email: cjhoughtaling@usa.net
URL:
http:/members.spree.com/
handhpress
C.J. Houghtaling, Publisher
- Crooker, Barbara, 108

Hale Mary Press
345 Buckingham Ave.
Syracuse, NY 13210-3313
- Cofrancesco, Joan, 95

Hanging Loose Press
231 Wyckoff Street
Brooklyn, NY 11217
Phone: 212-206-8465
Fax: 212-243-7499
Email: print225@aol.com
URL: http://www.omega.cc.

umb.edu/hangloos
Robert Hershon, Publisher
Dist. by: Bookpeople, Koen,
SPD
- Alexie, Sherman, 10
- Bernstein, Carole, 43
- Jones, Hettie, 220
- Kashner, Sam, 226
- Lourie, Dick, 267
- Marcus, Morton, 278
- Nauen, Elinor, 319

Hannacroix Creek Books
1127 High Ridge Rd, 110
Stamford, CT 06905
Phone: 203-321-8674
Fax: 203-968-0193
Email: Hannacroix@aol.com
URL:
http://www.bookzone.com/
HannacroixCreek
Jennifer Ash, Poetry Editor
- Orr, Priscilla, 331

Hanover Press
PO Box 596
Newtown, CT 06470-0596
Phone: 203-426-3388
Fax: 203-426-3398
Email: faithv@aol.com
URL: http://www.hanover-
press.com
Faith Vicinanza, President
- Clocys, Ed, 94
- Connellan, Leo, 100
- Lamson, Suzy, 246
- Sassi, Maria, 385
- Vicinanza, Faith E., 443
- Yuhas, Linda Claire, 476

**Harcourt Brace/Harvest
Books**

525 B Street, Suite 1900
San Diego, CA 92101-4495
Phone: 619-231-6616
Fax: 619-699-6320
Lynne Walker, Marketing
  Associate
• Christopher, Nicholas, 89
• Eliot, T.S., 133
• Eliot, T.S., 133
• Milosz, Czeslaw, ed., 303
• Robertson, Robin, 369
• Rosen, Michael J., 372
• Szymborska, Wislawa, 426

Hard Press
PO Box 184
West Stockbridge, MA 01266
Phone: 413-232-4690
Fax: 413-232-4675
Email: editors@hardpress.com
URL:
  http://www.hardpress.com
Chad Odefey, Poetry Editor;
  Ned Depew, Publicity
• Clark, Tom, 92
• Fitzpatrick, Tony, 145
• Gizzi, Michael, 164
• Lima, Frank, 260
• Rubinstein, Raphael, 375
• Solan, Miriam, 410

Hard Press/ The Figures
• Luoma, Bill, 269

Harlequinade Press
12 Flagstaff Hill Terrace
Canton, MA 02021
Phone: 781-828-3978
Email: jlocke6@aol.com
URL:
  http://users.aol.com/jlocke6/
  harlequinade.html

• Locke, Edward, 262
• Locke, Edward, 262
• Locke, Edward, 262
• Locke, Edward, 262
• Locke, Edward, 262

HarperCollins Publishers
10 East 53rd Street
New York, NY 10022
Phone: 212-207-7000
URL: http://www.harper-
  collins.com
Paul Crichton, Poetry Editor;
  Jodi Rosoff
• Bly, Robert, 52
• Kilcher, Jewel, 230
• Neruda, Pablo, 321

**HarperCollins/
  HarperFlamingo**
• Doty, Mark, 126
• Hughes, Frieda, 207

**HarperCollins/
  HarperPerennial**
• Hirshfield, Jane, 199
• Koethe, John, 239

HaSk
4306 Bretton Bay Lane
Dallas, TX 75287
Phone: 214-250-2564
Memye Curtis Tucker, Editor
• Kelley, Harriet Stovall, 228

Hawk Productions
809 West Maple Street
Champaigne, IL 61820-2810
Phone: 217-359-5056
Dimitri Mihalis,
  President/Editor
• Mihalas, Dimitri, 299

Hawkmoon Publications
7502 E. Calle Cabo
Tucson, AZ 85750
• Beeaff, Dianne Ebertt, 37

Heat Press
PO Box 26218
Los Angeles, CA 90026
Phone: 213-482-8902
Email: artheat@aol.com
Christopher Peditto, Publisher
Dist. by: Baker & Taylor, SPD
• Perkins, Wil, 340

Heaven Bone Press
P.O. Box 486
Chester, NY 10918
Phone: 914-469-9018
Fax: 914-469-7880
Steven Hirsch, Publisher
• Axel, Brett, 24
• Dahl, David, 113

Helicon Nine Editions
3607 Pennsylvania Ave
Kansas City, MO 64111-2820
Phone: 816-753-1095
Fax: 816-753-1016
Email: twpkcmo@aol.com
Gloria Vando Hickok, Editor;
  Elizabeth Beasley, Publicity
To Order: PO Box 22412
Kansas City, MO 64113
Dist. by: B&T, Booksource,
  Ingram
• Hix, H.L., ed., 200
• Quisenberry, Dan, 352
• Seid, Christopher, 390
• Seyburn, Patty, 394

Heritage Publishing
2130 S Vermont Ave

Los Angeles, CA 90007
Phone: 213-737-2122
• Brin, Herb, 62

Hesperia Press
PO Box 9246
Berkeley, CA 94709
Phone: 510-644-8259
Fax: 510-644-2109
• Conte, Giuseppe, 101
• Spaziani, Maria Luisa, 413
• Stortoni, Laura, 419

Hey Lew Books
• Cregg, Magda, ed., 107

Heyday Books
Box 9145
Berkeley, CA 94709
Phone: 510-549-3564
Fax: 510-549-1889
Email: heyday@heyday-
  books.com
Amy Hunter, Publicity;
  Malcolm Margolin,
  Publisher
• La France, Danielle, ed., 245

Heyeck Press
25 Patrol Ct.
Woodside, CA 94062
Phone: (650) 851-7491
Fax: 650-851-5039
Email:
  books@heyeckpress.com
URL:
  http://www.heyeckpress.com
John Heyeck, Publisher;
  Robin Heyeck, Editor
• Gershenson, Bernard, 159

High Plains Press

PO Box 123, 539 Cassa Road
Glendo, WY 82213
Phone: 307-735-4370
Fax: 307-735-4590
Email: nccoyote@aol.com
Nancy Curtis, Publisher
• Buyer, Laurie Wagner, 72
• Sanelli, Mary Lou, 383

Hirst, Pamela
1016 Kipling Dr
Nashville, TN 37217
Phone: 615-366-9012
Fax: 615-366-4117
Email: beatlick@bellsouth.net
URL:
   http://www.geocities.com/
   soho/studios/9307beatlick
Pamela Hirst, Publisher
• Reynolds, N. Scott, 363

Holt, Henry, and Company
115 West 18th Street
New York, NY 10011
Phone: 212-886-9245
Fax: 212-645-5832
Email:
   susan_barry@hholt.com
Marc Aronson, Editor; Judith
   Sisko, Director of Special
   Sales
• Bierds, Linda, 47
• Carlson, Lori M., ed., 78
• Kirchwey, Karl, 233
• Parini, Jay, 337
• Rosenberg, Liz, ed., 373
• Sneed, Pamela, 408

Holy Cow! Press
P.O. Box 3170, Mount Royal
   Station
Duluth, MN 55803

Phone: 218-724-1653
Jim Pulman, Editor/Publisher
Dist. by: Consortium
• Engman, John, 135
• Hedin, Robert, 193
• Jenkins, Louis, 217
• Perlman, Jim; Ed Folsom
   and Dan Campion, eds., 340

Hornswoggle Press
no address
• Warsh, Lewis, 453

Host Publications
2717 Woolridge
Austin, TX 78703
• Grol, Regina, trans., 177
• Neruda Pablo, 321

Houghton Mifflin Company
222 Berkeley St
Boston, MA 02116
Phone: 617-351-3396
Fax: 617-351-1202
Email:
   mindy_keskinen@hmco.com
URL: http://www.hmco.com
Mindy Keskinen, Asst. Editor
• Akhmatova, Anna, 6
• Atwood, Margaret, 23
• Funkhouser, Erica, 153
• Gregerson, Linda, 174
• Hall, Donald, 181
• Hall, Donald, 181
• Hill, Geoffrey, 197
• Hill, Geoffrey, 197
• Hudgins, Andrew, 207
• Jones, Rodney, 221
• Lind, Michael, 260
• Lux, Thomas, 270
• Matthews, William, 284

**Houghton Mifflin
Company/Mariner Books**
• Oliver, Mary, 330

Hourglass Press
no address
• Arbolay, Dominick, 18

Ibex Publishers
no address
• Crowe, Thomas Rain, trans.,
108

Icarus Books
1015 Kenilworth Dr.
Baltimore, MD 21204
Phone: 410-821-7807
Fax: 410-821-7807
Email: icarus@home.com
URL: http://members.hom.net/
icarus
David Diorio, Publisher;
Thomas Dorsett, Editor
• Scharper, Diane, ed., 387

Idiom
1143 Hearst Ave.
Berkeley, CA 94702
URL: http://www.dnai.com/
~idiom
Dist. by: SPD
• Clark, Emilie, and Lytle
Shaw, 92
• Gudath, Lauren, 178

Igneus Press
310 North Amherst Road
Bedford, NH 03110
Phone: 603-472-3466
Peter Kidd, Publisher/Editor
• Taus, Roger, 429
• Wendell, Julia, 459

IM Press
PO Box 5346
Takoma Park, MD 20913-
5346
• Shapiro, Susan, 396

Incommunicado Press
PO Box 99090
San Diego, CA 92169
Phone: 619-234-9400
Fax: 619-234-9479
Email: severelit@aol.com
URL: http://www.onecity.com/
incom
Sandra Zane
Dist. by: Consortium, SPD
• Abee, Steve, 1
• Cohen, Rob, ed., 96
• Madsen, Michael, 273

Indian Mountain Press
PO Box 821
New York, NY 10024-0821
Phone: 212-873-8865
Fax: 212-496-2014
Email: ff1@columbia.edu
Franklin Feldman, Publisher
• Giannini, David, 161

Indiana University Press
601 North Morton St.
Bloomington, IN 47404-3797
Phone: 812-855-4522
Fax: 812-855-7931
Nancy Jacobus, Exhibits
Coordinator
• Cardenal, Ernesto, 77
• Feinstein, Sascha, and Yusef
Komunyakaa, eds., 141

Indigenous Speak
7240 Manila Ave.

El Cerrito, CA 94530-2444
Phone: 510-234-5684
Ashley Phillips
• Vest, Jennifer Lisa, 443

Inertia Press
4424 N Wolcott 3B
Chicago, IL 60640
Phone: 773-728-1935
Email:
  michele_walker@hmco.com
• Walker, Michele, 450

**Iniquity Press/ Vendetta
  Books**
PO Box 54
Manasquan, NJ 08736
David Roskos, Publisher
• George, Anthony, 159
• Jones, Dwyer, 220
• Steptoe, Lamont B., 416

Insight To Riot Press
2300 Pine Street, 9
Philadelphia, PA 19103
Phone: 215-546-7499
Fax: 215-545-9794
Email: coryjim@earthlink.net
James M. Cory, Managing
  Editor
• Cory, Jim, 105

**Institute for Community
  Leadership**
ICL, 2113 13th Ave South
Seattle, WA 98144
Phone: 206-720-1950
Fax: 206-325-1853
Roy D.Wilson, Editor
• Wilson, Roy D., ed., 466

Instress

PO Box 3124
Saratoga, CA 95070
Dist. by: SPD
• Brink, Leonard, 62
• Browne, Laynie, 67
• Cole, Norma, 97
• Ganick, Peter, 155
• Murphy, Sheila E., 317
• Robinson, Elizabeth, 370
• Waldrop, Rosmarie, 449
• Waldrop, Rosmarie, 449

Intercultural Studies Forum
13756 Via Tres Vistas
San Diego, CA 92129-2755
Phone: 619-484-2228
Fax: 619-484-2228
Email: Iforum@aol.com
URL: http://home.aol.com/
  iforum
Anwar Dil, Editor
• Zolynas, Al, 479

Interim Books
715 Bakers Lane
Key West, FL 33040
Kirby Congdon, Poetry Editor
• Brackenbury, Rosalind, 58
• Chapman, Matthew, 86

Ione Press
PO Box 3271
Sewanee, TN 37375
Phone: 931-598-0795
• Carpenter, Jill, ed., 78

Iranbooks
6831 Wisconsin Ave
Bethesda, MD 20815
Phone: 301-986-0079
Fax: 301-907-8707
• Hafez, 180

Iris Press
1345 Oak Ridge Turnpike,
Ste. 328
Oak Ridge, TN 37830
• Connolly, Geraldine, 100

Ischua Books
PO Box 71
St. Bonaventure, NY 14778
Phone: 716-372-5653
Fax: 716-372-5653
Email: majestic@eznet.net
Micki Layfield, Editor
• Krampf, Thomas, 241

Italica Press
595 Main St., 605
New York, NY 10044
Phone: 212-935-4230
Fax: 212-838-7812
Email: italica@idt.net;
  italica@aol.com
Eileen Gardiner, Publisher;
  Ronald J. Musto, Publicity
• Stortoni, Laura Anna, and
  Mary Prentice Lillie, trans.,
  419

**Jacaranda Press/ Writer's
Center Editions**
1963 Josephine Ave.
San Jose, CA 95124
• Koestenbaum, Phyllis, 238

JB Press
1130 N. Cabrillo
San Pedro, CA 90731
Phone: 310-832-7024
Email: cbsw70a@prodigy.com
Benedict, M.D., James S.,
  Publisher
• Benedict, James S., 40

**Jewish Women's Resource
Center**
NCJW, NY Section
9 E 69th St
New York, NY 10021
Henny Wenkart, Editor
• Jare, Karen, 215

**Johns Hopkins University
Press**
2715 North Charles St.
Baltimore, MD 21218
Phone: 410-516-6900
Fax: 410-516-6968
Margaret Galambos, Exhibits
  and Awards Coordinator;
  John Irwin, Editor
• Prudentius, Aurelius
  (Clemens), 351
• Smith, William Jay, 408

Jukebox Press
c/o Meridien PressWorks
PO Box 640024
San Fransisco, CA 94164
Phone: 415-928-8904
• Woodd, Leslie, 468

Junction Press
PO Box 40537
San Diego, CA 92164
Phone: 619-282-0371
Fax: 619-282-0297
Email: junction@earthlink.net
Mark Weiss, Publisher
Dist. by: SPD
• Brukner, Ira Beryl, 68
• Futoransky, Luisa, 153
• Owens, Rochelle, 334
• Weiss, Mark, 458

Karmichael Press

HC 3, Box 155D
Port St. Joe, FL 32456
• Carpenter, Leo, 78

Kaya
373 Broadway, Suite E2
New York, NY 10011
Phone: 212-343-9503
Fax: 212-343-8291
Email: kaya@kaya.com
URL: http://www.kaya.com
Sunyoung Lee, Assistant
Editor
Dist. by: DAP
• Koon Woon, 239

Kelsey Street Press
50 Northgate Ave.
Berkeley, CA 94708
Phone: 510-845-2260
Fax: 510-548-9185
Email: kelseyst@sirius.com
URL: http://www.sirius.com/
~kelseyst/
Patricia Dienstfrey, Editor;
Karen McKevitt, Publicity
Dist. by: SPD
• Berssenbrugge, Mei-mei, 45
• Berssenbrugge, Mei-mei, 46
• Browne, Laynie, 67
• Kim, Myung Mi, 232

Kent State University Press
P.O. Box 5190, 307 Lowry
Hall, Terrace Dr.
Kent, OH 44242-0001
Phone: 330-672-7913
Fax: 330-672-3104
Email: sbell0@kent.edu
URL:
http://www.bookmasters.com/
ksu-press/

Susan Cash, Marketing
Manager
Dist. by: Bookmasters
• Coffman, Lisa, 95
• Frech, Stephen, 149
• Hamilton, Colin, 184
• Hancock, Kate, 185
• Kovacik, Karen, 240
• Kuhl, Nancy, 243
• Tayson, Richard, 429
• Weems, Mary E., 457
• Willey, Rosemary, 463

Kim Pathways
16 Young Road
Katonah, NY 10536
Phone: 914-232-7959
Alexander Kim, Director of
Publicity
• Cypser, Cora E., 112

Kindred Spirit Press
no address
• Asner, Marie A., and
Rochelle Lynn Holt, 22

Kings Estate Press
870 Kings Estate Rd.
St. Augustine, FL 32086-5033
Phone: 800-249-7485
Ruth Moon Kempher,
Publisher/Editor
• Elsberg, John, 134
• Hogan, Wayne, 201
• Kempher, Ruth Moon, ed.,
228
• Kempher, Ruth Moon, ed.,
228
• Kincaid, Joan Payne, 232
• Laws, Kyle, and Tony
Moffeit, 251
• Locklin, Gerald, 262

• Watson, Jr., Maurice T., 454

Knopf, Alfred A.
201 East 50th Street 22-2
New York, NY 10022
Phone: 212-572-2482
Fax: 212-572-2593
Email:
jmorrison@randomhouse.com
URL:
http://www.randsomhouse.com
Jill Morrison, Publicity
Dist. by: Random House, Inc.
• Bialosky, Jill, 46
• Bowers, Edgar, 57
• Bradley, George, 58
• Brock-Broido, Lucie, 62
• Carson, Anne, 79
• Carver, Raymond, 81
• Clampitt, Amy, 91
• Cole, Henri, 96
• Davison, Peter, 117
• Digges, Deborah, 124
• Haxton, Brooks, 190
• Hecht, Anthony, 192
• Henriques, Anna Ruth, 195
• Hirsch, Edward, 198
• Justice, Donald, 223
• Kinzie, Mary, 233
• Koch, Kenneth, 238
• Leithauser, Brad, 254
• Macdonald, Cynthia, 271
• McClatchy, J.D., 286
• Merwin, W.S., 295
• Merwin, W.S., 295
• Pankey, Eric, 336
• Piercy, Marge, 344
• Ponsot, Marie, 348
• Rice, Stan, 364
• Sheck, Laurie, 397
• Strand, Mark, 419

Knopf/Everyman's Library Pocket Poets
• Coleridge, Samuel Taylor, 98
• Frost, Robert, 152
• Hollander, John, ed., 202
• Washington, Peter, ed., 453
• Washington, Peter, ed., 453

Knott, Bill
WLP Dept.
Emerson College
100 Beacon Street
Boston, MA 02116
• Knott, Bill, 236
• Knott, Bill, 236
• Knott, Bill, 236
• Knott, Bill, 236
• Knott, Bill, 236
• Knott, Bill, 236
• Knott, Bill, 237
• Knott, Bill, 237
• Knott, Bill, 237
• Knott, Bill, 237

Kore Press
503 E 9th St.
Tucson, AZ 85705
Phone: 520-882-7542
Email:
charlotterae@hotmail.com
Lisa Bowden, Editor;
Charlotte Woolard, Studio
Manager
• Um, Sylvia Sohn, 440

Kriesel, Michael
no address
• Kriesel, Michael, 242

La Alameda Press
9636 Guadalupe Trail NW
Albuquerque, NM 87114-2005

Phone: 505-897-0285
Fax: 505-897-0751
Email: jbryan9636@aol.com
J.B. Bryan, Publisher; Cirrelda
   Snider-Bryan, Publicity
To Order: 1-800-249-7737
Dist. by: University of New
   Mexico Press
• Bryan, J.B., 69
• Fox, William L., 148
• Frumkin, Gene, 152
• Goodell, Larry, 169
• Kacian, Jim, 223
• Moldaw, Carol, 305
• Price, V.B., 350
• Somoza, Joseph, 411
• Tritica, John, 435

La Caille Nous Publishing
PO Box 1004
Riverdale, MD 20738
• Cadet, Guichard, 74

La Jolla Poets Press
PO Box 8638
La Jolla, CA 92038
Phone: 619-457-1399
Kathleen Iddings, Publisher
• Morphew, Melissa, 310
• Pilkington, Kevin, 345
• Terris, Susan, 430

Last Gasp Press
777 Florida Street
San Francisco, ca 94110
Email: lastgasp@hooked.net
URL: http://www.lastgasp.com
Dist. by: SPD
• Di Prima, Diane, 123

**Latin American Literary
   Review Press**

121 Edgewood Ave.
Pittsburgh, PA 15218
Phone: 412-371-9023
Fax: 412-371-9025
Email: lalrp@aol.com
URL: http://www.lalrp.org
Kathlean M. Ballew, Assistant
   Editor; Frank Hall
• Agosín, Marjorie, 5
• Braschi, Giannina, 60
• Noriega Bernuy, Julio, ed.,
   325
• Vicuña, Cecilia, ed., 444

Laurel Publications
no address
• Oder, Phyllis, 329

Ledge Press
PO Box 310010
Jamaica, NY 11413
Timothy Monaghan, Publisher
• Pilkington, Kevin, 345

Left Hand Books
Station Hill Road
Barrytown, NY 12507
Phone: 914-758-6478
Fax: 914-758-4416
Email: lefthand@ulster.net
URL:
http://www.lefthandbooks.com
   /lhb
Bryan McHugh, Publisher
• Economou, George, 132
• Rillo, 366
• Walsh, James, 451

Ley, Jennifer
no address
• Ley, Jennifer, 258

Library of America
14 East 60th St.
New York, NY 10022
Phone: 212-308-3360
Fax: 212-750-8352
Karen Iker, Marketing
   Associate
• Stevens, Wallace, 417

Limberlost Press
17 Canyon Trail
Boise, ID 83716
Phone: 208-344-2120
Fax: 208-345-5347
Email: limlost@micron.net
Rick Ardinger, Publisher
• Aho, Margaret, 6
• Anderson, Sandy, 15
• Brewer, Kenneth W., 61
• Ferlinghetti, Lawrence, 142
• Holthaus, Gary, 204

Limelight Editions
118 E 30th St
New York, NY 10016
• Adolphe, Bruce, 4

Lin Com Press
11822 S Tower Rd
Maple City, MI 49664-9725
Phone: 616-228-7682
Fax: 616-228-7682
Email:
   Isioen@cms.cc.wayne.edu
• Kerner, Benjamin A., 230

Lindisfarne Press
RR 4, Box 94 A-1
Hudson, NY 12534
URL: http://www.taconic.net/
   dufault

• Dufault, Peter Kane, 129

Linear Arts
PO Box 758
Siasconset, MA 02564
Phone: 508-257-4029
Victor Azaro, Editor
• Beckman, Madeleine, 36
• Herman, Corie, 195
• Holman, Amy, 203
• Mallory, Lawrence, 276
• Mauer, Susan, 285
• Pearse, Richard, 340
• Rutkowski, Thaddeus, 376

Liquid Light Publishing
220 Sullivan St
New York, NY 10012
Isabelle Granet
• Pascale, Isabelle, 338

Lite Circle Books
PO Box 26162
Baltimore, MD 21210
• Burgess, Hugh, 71

Lithic Press
1001 W. Washington Blvd.
Chicago, IL 60607
Phone: 312-850-3104
Fax: 312-850-2663
Markus Greiner, Editor
• Nickson, Richard, 324

Little Books Press
c/o Wayne Hogan
PO Box 842
Cookeville, TN 38503
Phone: 931-528-1638
Fax: 931-528-6569
• Leonhardt, Kenneth, and
   Wayne Hogan, 254

Little Sky Press
c/o Peter Chelnik
575 Lexington Ave, Room 400
New York, NY 10022
• Chelnik, Peter, 87

Littoral Books
no address
Los Angeles, CA
• Albon, George, 7
• Baraka, Amiri, 29
• DiPalma, Ray, 125
• Ratcliffe, Stephen, 358

Live Poets Society
PO Box 391
Islip, NY 11751
• Chang, Diana, 86
• Preston, Georgette, 349

Liveright Publishing
500 Fifth Avenue
New York, NY 10110
Phone: 212-354-5500
Fax: 212-869-0856
• Cummings, E.E., 110
• Cummings, E. E., 110
• Cummings, E. E., 110
• Cummings, E. E., 111

Livingston Press
Station 22, University of West
  Alabama
Livingston, AL 35470
Phone: 205-652-3470
Fax: 205-652-3717
Email:
  jwt@uwamail.westal.edu
URL: http://livingstonpress.
  westal.edu
Joe Taylor, Poetry Editor
• Hammond, Ralph, 184

• Huggins, Peter, 207
• Van Wert, William, 441

Lodestar Press
PO Box 747
Hydesville, CA 95547
• Swope, Helen Perry, 425

Loft, The
Pratt Community Center
66 Malcom Ave. SE
Minneapolis, MN 55414
• Hawley, Ellen, ed., 190

Logodaedalus Press
PO Box 14193
Harrisburg, PA 17104
Phone: 717-564-1114
Paul Weidenhoff, Editor
• Frost, Celestine, 152

**Lone Pine Press/ Global
  Book Productions**
23 West 35th St
New York, NY 10001
Phone: 212-695-5703
• Klenburg, Jana Liba, 235

Long Shot Productions
PO Box 6238
Hoboken, NJ 07030
Phone: 201-752-7563
URL: http://www.longshot.org
• Medina, Tony, 293

Lorien House
PO Box 1112
Black Mountain, NC 28711
Phone: 828-669-6211
David A. Wilson, Publisher
• Beck, Al, 36

LOS
150 N. Catalina St. #2
Los Angeles, CA 90004
• Mulrooney, C., 316

Lost Coast Press
155 Cypress St.
Fort Bragg, CA 95437
Phone: 707-964-9520
Fax: 707-964-7531
Email:
    cmaden@cypresshouse.com
URL:
http://www.cypresshouse.com
Cynthia Frank, Editor; Charlie
    Maden, Publicity
• Adams, 3

Lost Roads Publishers
351 Nayatt Road
Barrington, RI 02806
Phone: 401-245-8069
Fax: 401-245-8069
URL: http://www.brown.edu/
    Departments/English/road
C. D. Wright, Editor; Forest
    Gander, Editor
• Jacobs, J.L., 214
• Truitt, Sam, 436

**Louisiana State University
    Press**
PO Box 25053
Baton Rouge, LA 70894-5053
Phone: 225-388-6666
Fax: 225-388-6461
Email: lsuprss@lsu.edu
URL: http://www.lsu.edu/
    guests/lsuprss
L.E. Phillabaum, Editor;
    Barbara Outland, Publicist
To Order: 800-861-3477;

800-305-4416 (fax)
• Andrews, Claudia Emerson,
    15
• Applewhite, James, 18
• Barrax, Gerald, 31
• Belitt, Ben, 38
• Buck, Paula Closson, 69
• Byer, Kathryn Stripling, 73
• Cherry, Kelly, 87
• Clinton, James Harmon, 93
• Clover, Joshua, 94
• Cushman, Stephen, 112
• Daniels, Kate, 114
• Deming, Alison Hawthorne,
    120
• Dobie, Ann Brewster, ed.,
    125
• Galvin, Brendan, 154
• Garrett, George, 156
• Gibbons, Reginald, 161
• Gibson, Margaret, 162
• Hankla, Cathryn, 185
• Ludvigson, Susan, 269
• Morgan, Elizabeth Seydel,
    308
• Mueller, Lisel, 314
• Nelson, Marilyn, 320
• Osbey, Brenda Marie, 332
• Ras, Barbara, 357
• Sandy, Stephen, 383
• Seay, James, 390
• Seven American Poets, 393
• Slavitt, David R., 404
• Slavitt, David R., 404
• Stone, John, 418
• Stuart, Dabney, 421
• Taylor, Henry, 429
• Warren, Robert Penn, 452

Low-Tech Press
30-73 47th St
Long Island City, NY 11103

Phone: 718-721-0946
Ron Kolm, Poetry Editor
• Topp, Mike, 433

LS Press
4662 SW 75th Ave
Miami, FL 33155
Phone: 305-262-1777
• Cepero, Nilda, 84

Lubin, Ruth
• Lubin, Ruth, 268

**Lumen Editions/ Brookline
  Books**
Brookline Books
PO Box 1047
Cambridge, MA 02238-1047
• Cramer, Steven, 106

Luna Bisonte Prods
137 Leland Avenue
Columbus, OH 43214
Phone: (614) 846-4126
John M. Bennett, Publisher
• Ackerman, Al, 1
• Argüelles, Ivan, and Jake
  Berry, 18
• Bennett, John M., 40
• Clinefelter, Jim, 93
• Ganick, Peter, 155
• Leftwich, Jim, 253

Lynx House Press
9305 SE Salmon CT
Portland, OR 97215
Christopher Howell, Editor
• Grabill, James, 171

Lyons Press
123 W 18th St., 6th Floor
New York, NY 10011

Phone: 212-620-9580
Fax: 212-929-1836
Email: janelias@aol.com
URL:
  http://www.lyonspress.com
Nick Lyons, Editor; Kristen
  Auclair, Publicity
• Engels, John, 135

M.I.P. Company
P.O. Box 27484
Minneapolis, MN 55427
Phone: 612-546-7578
Fax: 612-544-6077
Email: mp@mipco.com
URL: http://www.mipco.com
Michael Peltsman, Publisher
• Armalinsky, Mikhail, 18
• Baeyvsky, David, 26

Ma'arri
156 John St.
Princeton, NJ 08542
Phone: 609-683-7460
Email:
  ma-arri@rocketmail.com
Ziad Naji, Publisher
Dist. by: Amazon
• Thilleman, Tod, 431

Macaluso, Peter M.
no address
• Macaluso, Peter, 271

Mad River Poetry
Randolph Center, VT 05061
To Order: Maine Publishers
  and Writers, 12 Pleasant St.,
  Brunswick, ME 04011
• Coursen, H.R., 105
• Coursen, H.R., 105
• Coursen, H.R., 105

Mage Publishers
1032 29th St NW
Washington, DC 20007
Phone: 202-342-1642
Fax: 202-342-9269
Email:
mage1@access.digex.net
URL: http://www.mage.com
• Davis, Dick, trans., 117

Manchester University Press
175 Fifth Ave.
New York, NY 10010
• Ashfield, Andrew, ed., 22

Mandrake Press
PO Box 792
Larkspur, CA 94977-0792
• Adam, Cornel, 3
• Castleman, David, 83

Manic D Press
Box 410804
San Francisco, CA 94141
Phone: 415-648-8288
Email: info@manicdpress.com
URL:
http://www.manicdpress.com
Jennifer Joseph, Publisher
Dist. by: PGW
• Chin, Justin, 87
• Lisick, Beth, 261
• McDaniel, Jeffrey, 287

March Street Press
3413 Wilshire Dr.
Greensboro, NC 27408
Phone: 336-282-9754
Email: rbixby@aol.com
URL:
http://users.aol.com/marchst
Robert Bixby, Editor/Publisher

• Benedict, Elinor, 40
• Petrouske, Rosalie Sanara, 343
• Rosenzweig, Geri, 373
• Rutkowski, Thaddeus, 376

Mariposa Printing and Publishing
922 Baca St.
Santa Fe, NM 87501
Phone: 505-988-5582
Fax: 505-986-8774
Email:
jmowrey@ix.netcom.com
J. Mowrey, Editor
Dist. by: Ingram
• Mowrey, Joseph, 314

Marsilio Publishers
853 Broadway
New York, NY 10003
Phone: 212-473-5300
Fax: 212-473-7865
• Auster, Paul, trans., 23
• Baraka, Amiri, 29

Maryland Poetry Review
Drawer H
Baltimore, MD 21228
Phone: 410-744-0349
• Ollivier, L.L., 330

Marymark Press
45-08 Old Millstone Drive
East Windsor, NJ 08520
Phone: 609-443-0646
URL:
www.experimentalpoet.com
• Sonnenfeld, Mark, 411

Masquerade Books/A Richard Kasak Book

801 Second Avenue
New York, NY 10017
Phone: 212-661-7878
Fax: 212-986-7355
Email: MasqBks@aol.com
Jennifer Reit, Editor
• Califia, Pat, 76
• Saint, Assotto, 378

Mayapple Press
PO Box 5473
Saginaw, MI 48603-0473
Phone: 517-793-2801
Fax: 517-793-2801
Email: kerman@svsu.edu
URL: http://www.cris.com/
~Jkerman
Judith Kerman, Publisher
• Fox, Hugh, 147
• McCombs, Judith, 287
• Palen, John, 335
• Renker, Skip, 362

Mayhaven Publishing
PO Box 557
Mahomet, IL 61853
• Clark, William Lewis, 93

Meadowbrook Press
5451 Smetana Drive
Minnetonka, MN 55343
Phone: 612-930-1100;
800-338-2232
Fax: 612-930-1940
Joel Mondshane, Publicity;
Steve Linders, Publicity
• Lansky, Bruce, ed., 247

Mega Press
PO Box 172
New York, NY 10009
Phone: 212-560-2439

• Dépas, Albert, 121

Menace Publishing
PO Box 23151
Alexandria, VA 22304
Phone: 703-567-1068
Email: menace@ziplink.net
URL: http://www.menace.com
Casey Kane, Editor
• Sutherland, David Hunter,
422

Meow Press
PO Box 527
Buffalo, NY 14226
URL:
http://wings.buffalo.edu/epc/
presses
Dist. by: SPD
• Foust, Graham, 147
• Levy, Andrew, 258
• Maxwell, Noemie, 285
• Newman, Denise, 322
• Schultz, Susan M., 389

Mercury House
no address
San Francisco, CA
• Avena, Thomas, 24

Meridien PressWorks
PO Box 6400240
San Francisco, CA 94164
Phone: 415-928-8904
Jeanne Powell, Poetry Editor
• Easley, Craig, 132
• Soulé, Anne Bacon, 412

Miami University Press
English Dept
Miami University
Oxford, OH 45056

Phone: 513-529-5110
Fax: 513-529-1392
Email: reissja@muohio.edu
James Reiss, Editor
To Order: 800-345-6665;
603-357-2073
Dist. by: Pathway Book
Service
• Bruce, Debra, 68
• Kramer, Larry, 241
• Orlen, Steve, 331
• Shirley, Aleda, 399
• Van Winckel, Nance, 442

Michigan State University Press
1405 S Harrison Rd, Suite 25
East Lansing, MI 48823-5202
Phone: 517-355-9543
Fax: 517-432-2611
Email: msp05@msu.edu
URL: http://www.msu.edu/
unit/msupress
Julie L. Loehr, Assistant
Director
• Bednarik, Joseph, ed., 37
• Harris, Bill, 187
• Moore, Julia A., 307

Michigan State University Press/Lotus Poetry Series
1405 S Harrison Rd, Suite 25
East Lansing, MI 48823-5202
Phone: 517-355-9543
Fax: 517-432-2611
Email: msp05@msu.edu
URL:
http://www.msu.edu/unit/ms
upress
Julie L. Loehr, Assistant
Director
• Hooper, Patricia, 204

• Jacobs, Bruce A., 214
• Turcotte, Mark, 438
• Wilkinson, Claude, 462

Mid-America Press
PO Box 575
Warrensburg, MO 64093-0575
Phone: 660-747-3481
Email: rnjones@iland.net
Bob Jones, Editor
• Daldorph, Brian, 113
• Field, Greg, 143
• Franking, Cecile M., 148
• Hanley, Elizabeth Jones, 185
• McReynolds, Ronald W.,
293
• Roberts, Judith Towse, 368

Mid-List Press
4324 12th Ave South
Minneapolis, MN 55407-3218
Phone: 612-822-3733
Fax: 612-823-8387
Email: guide@midlist.org
URL: http://www.midlist.org
Lane Stiles, Senior Editor;
Marianne Nora, Associate
Publisher
Dist. by: SPD
• Behrendt, Stephen C., 38
• Ben-Lev, Dina, 39
• Logue, Mary, 263
• Morrill, Donald, 311
• Shepard, Neil, 398

Midmarch Arts Press
300 Riverside Drive
New York, NY 10025
Phone: 212-666-6990
Fax: 212-865-5510
Cynthia Navaretta, Publisher
• Mandel, Charlotte, 276

Midwest Villages and Voices
PO Box 40214
St. Paul, MN 55104
Phone: 612-822-6878
Gayla Ellis
• Fitzpatrick, Kevin, 145

Mike & Dale's Press
766 Valencia St.
San Francisco, CA 94110
Michael Price
• Herndon, John, 196

Mike & Dale's Press/GAS Editions
• Price, Michael; Dale Smith, and Kevin Opstedal, 350

Milkweed Editions
430 First Ave. North, Ste. 400
Minneapolis, MN 55401-1743
Phone: 612-332-3192
Fax: 612-332-6248
Robert Breck, Marketing Director
• Brown, Kurt,and Laure-Anne Bosselaar, eds., 66
• Brown, Kurt, ed., 66
• Goedicke, Patricia, 167
• Rogers, Pattiann, 371

Mill Creek Press
Suite 840, 50 Congress St.
Boston, MA 02109
Phone: 617-367-8622
Fax: 617-227-0079
Email:
MillCreek@thunderball.com
• Bonnell, Paula, 55

Mille Grazie Press
P.O. Box 3155

Santa Barbara, CA 93101
Phone: 805-963-8408
Fax: 805-682-2957
David Oliveira,
Publisher/Editor
• Borteck, Benjamin, 55
• McDaniel, Wilma Elizabeth, 287
• Taggart, Phil, 427
• Wynne, Robert, 471

Mille Grazie Press/SeaMoon Press
3560 Las Pilitas Rd
Santa Margarita, CA 93453
Phone: 805-438-4748
Carla Martinez, Publisher
• Martinez, Carla; John Sousa, and Toni Wynn, 280

Mind the Gap
119 N. 11th St., C-A
Brooklyn, NY 11211
Phone: 718-486-6610
Karin Randolph, Publisher
• Randolph, Karin, ed., 356

MIT Press
M.I.T
Cambridge, MA 02142
URL: http://mitpress.mit.edu
• Hejduk, John, 194

Molti Frutti Productions
1704B Llano St, Suite 121
Santa Fe, NM 87505
Phone: 505-820-0447
Email:
carigrif@roadrunner.com
URL:
http://www.moltifrutti.com
Ellen Kleiner, Editor

• Griffo, Cari, 177

Morris Publishing
3212 E. Hwy. 30
Kearney, NE 68847
Phone: 800-650-7888
Fax: 308-237-0263
• Kiley, Eve, 230
• Parker, Doris, 338

Morrow, William, and Company
1350 Avenue of the Americas
New York, NY 10019
Phone: 212-261-6844
Fax: 212-261-6595
Email: dcooper@hearst.com
URL:
http://williammorrow.com
Doris Cooper, Editor; Sharyn
Rosenblum, Publicity
• Giovanni, Nikki, 164

Mother's Hen
PO Box 695
Berkeley, CA 94701-0695
Phone: 510-549-3345
Louis Cuneo, Editor
• Day, Lucille Lang, 118

Mountain Books
PO Box 21-1104
Columbus, OH 43221
• Brown, Dale S., 66

Mouth Almighty Books
516 W 25th St, Suite 306
New York, NY 10001
Phone: 212-645-0061
Fax: 212-645-9261
Email: mouthmight@aol.com
URL:

www.mouthalmighty.com
Bill Adler, President
Dist. by: Koen, Ingram
• Sia, Beau, 401

Moving Parts Press/Chusma House Publications
10699 Empire Grade
Santa Clara, CA 95060
Phone: 831-427-2271
Fax: 831-458-2810
Email:
frice@movingparts.com
Felicia Rice, Editor/Publisher
• Arteaga, Alfred, 19

National League for Nursing Press
350 Hudson St.
New York, NY 10014
• Krysl, Marilyn, 242

National Poetry Foundation
University of Maine
5752 Neville Hall, Rm 302
Orono, ME 04469-5752
Phone: 207-581-3814
Fax: 207-581-1604
Email:
hatlen@maine.maine.edu
URL:
http://www.ume.maine.edu/
~npf/
Burton Hatlen, Director; Mark
Melnicove, Publicity
Dist. by: University Press of
New England
• Dorn, Edward, 126
• Perkoff, Stuart Z., 340
• Tagliabue, John, 427

Neiss, Jonathan

10 Mitchell St., #1
West Orange, NJ 07052
Phone: 973-731-6565
Email: jonathanneiss@usa.net
• Neiss, Jon, 320

New Directions
80 Eighth Avenue
New York, NY 10011
Phone: 212-255-0230
Fax: 212-255-0231
Email: nd@panix.com
URL: http://wwnorton.com/nd
Laurie Callahan, Publicity
  Director
• Barnstone, Willis, trans., 30
• Creeley, Robert, 106
• Creeley, Robert, 107
• Di Blasi, Debra, 123
• Duncan, Robert, 130
• Ferlinghetti, Lawrence, 142
• Gander, Forrest, 155
• H.D., 178
• Karr, Mary, 225
• Laughlin, James, 249
• Laughlin, James, 249
• Laughlin, James, 249
• Laughlin, James, 250
• Levertov, Denise, 255
• Levertov, Denise, 256
• Lorca, Federico García, 266
• Palmer, Michael, 335
• Paz, Octavio, 339
• Tomlinson, Charles, 433

New Issues Press
1201 Oliver St.
Western Michigan University
Kalamazoo, MI 49008
Phone: 616-387-2592
Fax: 616-387-2562
Email:

herbert.scott@wmich.edu
URL: http://www.wmich.edu/
  english/fac/nipps
Herbert Scott, Editor; Amy
  McInnis, Assistant Editor
Dist. by: Partners
• de la O, Marsha, 119
• Fishman, Lisa, 145
• Larsen, Lance, 247
• Marlatt, David, 278
• Moulds, Julie, 314
• Reynolds, Rebecca, 363
• Rybicki, John, 377
• Seuss-Brakeman, Diane, 393
• Sheehan, Marc, 397
• Sorby, Angela, 411
• Wesley, Patricia Jabbeh, 459

**New Myths Press/SUNY
  Binghamton**
SUNY Binghamton
Binghamton, NY 13901-6000
Bob Mooney, Publisher
• Brady, Philip, 59

New Native Press
P.O. Box 661
Cullowhee, NC 28723
Phone: 704-293-9237
Fax: 704-227-7250
Thomas Rain Crowe,
  Publisher
• Crowe, Thomas Rain, ed.,
  108
• Truscott, Danielle, 436

**New Poets Series/Chestnut
  Hills Press**
541 Piccadilly Rd.
Towson, MD 21204
Phone: 410-828-0724
Fax: 410-830-3999

• Carter, Patricia, and Nancy Adams, 81

New Poets Series/Chestnut Hills Press/Stonewall
• Fein, Richard, 141

New Rivers Press
420 N 5th Street, Suite 1180
Minneapolis, MN 55401
Phone: 612-339-7114
Fax: 612-339-9047
Email: newrivpr@mtn.org
URL: http://www.mtn.org/
~newrivpr
Bill Truesdale, Poetry Editor;
Kelly Williams, Marketing
Assistant
Dist. by: Consortium
• Alexander, Robert; Mark Vinz, and C.W. Truesdale, eds., 9
• Anderson, Jack, 15
• Anstett, Aaron, 17
• Bryant, Philip, 69
• Emmons, Jeanne, 135
• Erdrich, Heid E., 137
• Jarvenpa, Diane, 216
• Lieberman, Michael, 259
• Munger, Kel, 316
• Wanek, Connie, 451

New School Chapbook Series
c/o Jason Shinder
New School University
66 W 12 St
New York, NY 10011
Phone: 212-289-5902
• Andonov, Nicole, 15
• Cohen, Michael, 96
• Goldstein, Marion, 169

• Hill, Nick, 197

New Thought Journal Press
PO Box 700754
Tulsa, OK 74170
Phone: 918-299-7330
Fax: 918-492-6237
Ed Wincentsen,
Publisher/Editor
• Jones, Jean, 220
• Snydal, James, 409

New World Library
14 Pamaron Way
Novato, CA 94949
Phone: 415-884-2100;
800-227-3900
Fax: 415-884-2199
• Maltz, Wendy, ed., 276

New York Public Library/Granary Books
• Clay, Steven, and Rodney Phillips, 93

New York University Press
70 Washington Square South
New York, NY 10012
Phone: 212-998-2575
Fax: 212-995-3833
Email:
weisser@nyupress.nyu.edu
URL: http://nyupress.nyu.edu
Niko Pfund, Director; Rachel Weiss, Publicity
To Order: 800-996-NYUP;
212-505-9183 (fax);
orders@nyupress.nyu.edu
• Caston, Anne, 83
• Schoenberger, Nancy, 388

Nightshade Press

Ward Hill Rd. & Route 9
PO Box 76
Troy, ME 04987
Phone: 207-948-3427
Fax: 207-948-5088
Email:
 potatoeyes@uninets.net
URL: http://litline.org/html/
 potatoeyes.html
Roy Zarucchi,
 Publisher/Editor; Carolyn
 Page, Editor
• Bishop, Wendy, 48
• Chute, Robert M., 90
• Nelson, Howard, 320
• Pinckney, Diana, 345
• Stephenson, Shelby, 416

nine muses books
3541 Kent Creek Rd.
Winston, OR 97496
Phone: 541-679-6674
Email:
 mw9muses@teleport.com
Margareta Waterman,
 Publisher
• Kimes, Marion, 232
• Raphael, Dan, 357

Ninety-Six Press
Box 30891
English Dept, Furman
 University
Greenville, SC 29613
Phone: 864-294-3152;
 864-294-2224
Fax: 864-294-2224
Email: gil.allen@furman.edu
URL: http://www.furman.edu/
 ~wrogers/96press/home.htm
Gilbert Allen, Editor
• Bateman, Claire, 33

• Harris, Joseph, 187

NoNo Publications
PO Box 10235
Olympia, WA 98502
• Diamond, Red, 124

North Atlantic Books
1456 Fourth St.
Berkeley, CA 94710
Phone: 510-559-8277
Fax: 510-559-8279
Richard Grossinger, Founder;
 Emily Weinert, Editorial/
 Marketing Associate
To Order: P.O. Box 12327,
 Berkeley, CA 94712; 800-
 337-2665; orders@northat-
 lanticbooks.com
• Henderson, David, 195
• Holden, Karen, 201
• Siegel, Amie, 402
• Ward, B. J., 451

**Northeastern University
 Press**
360 Huntington Ave., 416 CP
Boston, MA 02115
Phone: 617-373-5479
Fax: 617-373-5483
Email:
 m.bakula@nunet.nev.edu
URL: http://www.nev.edu
John Weingartner, Poetry
 Editor; Jill Bahcall,
 Publicity
To Order: CUPS Services,
 Order Dept., 750 Cascadilla
 Ithaca, NY; 800-666-2211
• Greene, Jeffrey, 174
• Webb, Charles Harper, 455

Northwestern University Press
625 Colfax Street
Evanston, IL 60208-4210
Phone: 847-491-5313
Fax: 847-491-8150
Email: nupress@nwu.edu
Mary Jo Robling, Publicity Manager; Dan Koenig, Marketing Assistant
To Order: Chicago Distribution Center, 11030 S. Langley Ave., Chicago, IL 60628; 800-621-2736; 800-621-8476 (fax)
• Striar, Marguerite M., ed., 419

Northwestern University Press/Hydra Books
• Alberti, Raphael, 7
• Aygi, Gennady, 24
• Seifert, Jaroslav, 391
• Venclova, Tomas, 443

Northwestern University Press/TriQuarterly Books
• Anyidoho, Kofi, ed., 17
• Fay, Steve, 140
• Goethe, 167
• Hadas, Pamela White, 179
• Hirson, Denis, ed., 199
• Jackson, Angela, 212
• Meredith, William, 294
• Rollings, Alane, 371
• Triplett, Pimone, 435

Northwoods Press
PO Box 298
Thomaston, ME 04861
• Akmakjian, Alan P., 7

Norton, W.W., and Company
500 Fifth Avenue
New York, NY 10110
Phone: 212-790-9431
Fax: 212-869-0856
Email: egrubin@wwnorton.com
URL: http://www.wwnorton.com
Louise Brockett, Publicity; Eve Grubin, Publicity
To Order: 800-233-4830
• Ackerman, Diane, and Jeanne Mackin, eds., 2
• Ali, Agha Shahid, 10
• Ammons, A. R., 14
• Beaumont, Jeanne Marie, 36
• Biel, Steven, ed., 47
• Boland, Eavan, 54
• Boland, Eavan, 55
• Cahill, Susan, ed., 75
• Cassian, Nina, 82
• Cofer, Judith Ortiz, 95
• Dunn, Stephen, 131
• Espada, Martín, 137
• Gibb, Robert, 161
• Glazner, Greg, 166
• Harjo, Joy, and Gloria Bird, eds., 186
• Howe, Marie, 205
• Kumin, Maxine, 243
• Kumin, Maxine, 244
• Kunitz, Stanley, 244
• Lasdun, James, 248
• Lorde, Audre, 266
• Lynch, Thomas, 271
• Mariani, Paul, 278
• Martínez, Dionisio D., 281
• Montale, Eugenio, 306
• Owen, Stephen, ed., 333
• Pastan, Linda, 338
• Sarton, May, 384

- Sarton, May, 384
- Smith, Charlie, 406
- Smith, Patti, 407
- Spires, Elizabeth, 414
- Stern, Gerald, 416
- Stern, Gerald, 416
- Sylvester, Janet, 425
- Volkman, Karen, 446
- Washburn, Katharine; John S. Major, and Clifton Fadiman, eds., 453

O Books
no address
Dist. by: SPD
- Alexander, Will, 9
- Davidson, Michael, 116
- Grim, Jessica, 177
- Moriarty, Laura, 309
- Ngai, Sianne, 322
- Samuels, Lisa, 381
- Waldner, Liz, 448

Oberlin College Press
10 North Professor St.
Oberlin, OH 44074
Phone: 440-775-8408
Fax: 440-775-8124
Email: oc.press@oberlin.edu
URL: http://www.oberlin.edu/ocpress
David Young, Editor; Heather Smith, Business Manager
- Boruch, Marianne, 56
- József, Attila, 222
- Loomis, Jon, 265
- Wright, Franz, 470

Ocean Beach Boat House
Box 23
Ocean Beach, NY 11770
Ruth G. Reichbart, Publisher

- Angeleri, Carl, ed., 16

Off the Cuff Books
103B Hanna St
Carrboro, NC 27510
Phone: 919-967-1412
Email: oyster-boy@sunsite.unc.edu
- Beam, Jeffery, 35

Ohan Press
171 Maplewood St.
Watertown, MA 02472-1324
Phone: 617-926-2602
- Pilibosian, Helene, 345

Ohio State University Press
180 Pressey Hall
1070 Carmack Rd.
Columbus, OH 43210-1002
Phone: 614-292-4936
Fax: 614-292-2065
Email: ohiostatepress@osu.edu
URL: http://ohiostatepress.org
Gretchen Brandt, Marketing Assistant; Patrick Hall, Publicity
- Bergman, David, 43
- Citino, David, 90
- Citino, David, 90
- Goldbarth, Albert, 167
- Haag, John, 179
- Hall, Judith, 182
- McDonald, Walt, 288

Ohio University Press
Scott Quadrangle
Athens, OH 45701
Phone: 740-593-1158
Fax: 740-593-4536
Email: gilbert@ohiou.edu;

arnold@ohiou.edu
URL: http://www.ohiou.edu/
oupress
Richard Gilbert, Publicity;
Sharon Arnold, Marketing
Manager
To Order: University of
Chicago Distribution Center,
11030 S. Langley Ave.,
Chicago, IL 60628; 773-
568-1550; 773-660-2235
(fax)
• Carson, Meredith, 80
• Cassity, Turner, 82
• Tucker, Memye Curtis, 437

**Ohio University Press/
Swallow Press**
Scott Quadrangle
Athens, OH 45701
Phone: 740-593-1158
Fax: 740-593-4536
Email: gilbert@ohiou.edu;
arnold@ohiou.edu
URL: http://www.ohiou.edu/
oupress
Richard Gilbert, Publicity;
Sharon Arnold, Marketing
Manager
To Order: University of
Chicago Distribution Center,
11030 S. Langley Ave.,
Chicago, IL 60628; 773-
568-1550; 773-660-2235
(fax)
• Cunningham, J.V., 111
• Matthias, John, 284
• Matthias, John, 284
• Stryk, Lucien, 420

Old Wine Press
204 Cayuga Rd

Louisville, KY 40207
• Allen, William M., 12

Ontario Review Press
no address
• Twichell, Chase, 438

Orange Ocean Press
127 Bennett Ave
Long Beach, CA 90803
Phone: 562-930-0587
Fax: 562-930-0587
Email: nextmag@aol.com
G. Murray Thomas, Publisher
• Hopmans, Walt, 205
• Schulz, Lawrence, 389

Orchard Books
95 Madison Ave.
New York, NY 10016
Phone: 212-951-2600
• Johnson, Angela, 218

Orchises Press
PO Box 20602
Alexandria, VA 22320-1602
Phone: 703-683-1243
Fax: 703-993-1161
Email: rlathbur@osfl.gmu.edu
URL: http://mason.gmu.edu/
rlathbur
Roger Lathbury, Editor in
Chief
• Asekoff, L. S., 20
• Duhamel, Denise, 129
• Filkins, Peter, 144
• Houghton, Timothy, 205
• Ivry, Benjamin, 212
• Moore, Richard, 308
• Pankey, Eric, 336
• Van Wert, William F., 442

Outloudbooks
PO Box 86
Claryville, NY 12725-0086
Phone: 914-985-2998
Fax: 914-985-2998
Email:
tchewiwi@zelacom.com
• Gridley, Inez George, 176

Overlook Press
386 West Broadway
New York, NY 10012
Phone: 212-477-7162
Fax: 212-477-7525
Gene Taft, Publicity Mgr.
• Lax, Robert, 251

Owl Creek Press
2693 SW Camano Dr
Camano Island, WA 98292
Phone: 206-633-5929
• Burrows, E.G., 72

Oxford University Press
198 Madison Avenue
New York, NY 10016
Phone: 212-726-6000
Fax: 212-726-6443
URL: http://www.oup-usa.org
T. Susan Chang, Poetry
Editor; Mike Groseth,
Publicity
To Order: 2001 Evans Rd.,
Cary, NC 27513; 800-451-
7556; 919-677-2647 (fax)
• Atwan, Robert; George
Dardess, and Peggy
Rosenthal, eds., 22

Oyster River Press
20 Riverview Rd
Durham, NH 03824

Phone: 603-868-5006
Email:
wbuckley@christa.unh.edu
Cicely Buckley, Editor
• Agran, Rick, 6
• Buckley, Cicely, ed., 70
• Halperin, Amor, 183

P&Q Press
36 Commerce St.
New York, NY 10014
Phone: 212-727-0819
• Garrison, Peggy, 157
• Garrison, Peggy, and David
Quintavalle, 158

Painted Bride Quarterly
230 Vine Street
Philadelphia, PA 19106
• Barr, Tina, 31

Painted Leaf Press
308 W 40th St
New York, NY 10018
Phone: 212-594-4940
Fax: 212-594-4940
Bill Sullivan, Poetry Editor
• Black, Star, 48
• Carey, Tom, 77
• Gates, Beatrix, 158
• Larkin, Joan, 247
• Lassell, Michael, 248
• Manrique, Jaime, 277
• Richie, Eugene, 364
• Schmidt, Paul, 387
• Schmidt, Paul, 387
• Sor Juana Inés de la Cruz,
411

Palanquin Press
Dept of English, University of
South Carolina-Aiken

171 University Parkway
Aiken, SC 29801
Phone: 803-642-3992
Email: phebed@aiken.sc.edu
Phebe Davidson, Poetry Editor
• Harrod, Lois Marie, 188
• Tucker, Memye Curtis, 437

Pangborn Books
PO Box 5693
Youngstown, OH 44505
Phone: 330-746-3955
Frank Polite, Poetry Editor
• Mahon, Jeanne, 274

Pantograph Press
P.O. Box 9643
Berkeley, CA 94709
• Argüelles, Ivan, and Jack
  Foley, 18
• Berry, Jake, 44
• Cornford, Adam, 104

Papier-Mache Press
316 Walker St.
Watsonville, CA 95076
Phone: 408-763-1420
Fax: 408-763-1422
URL:
http://www.readersndex.com/
  papiermache
Molly Matava, Publicist;
  Shirley Coe, Acquisitions
  Editor
To Order: PO Box 1895,
  Watsonville, CA 95077;
  800-927-5913;
  orders.pmp.@juno.com
• Chandler, Janet Carncross,
  85
• Martz, Sandra, ed., 281
• Martz, Sandra Haldeman,

ed., 281
• Martz, Sandra Haldeman,
  ed., 281
• Martz, Sandra Haldeman,
  ed., 282
• Randall, Margaret, 356

Parallax Press
850 Talbot Ave
Albany, CA 94706
Phone: 510-525-0101
Fax: 510-525-7129
Email: parapress@aol.com
URL: http://www.parallax.org
Michelle Bernard, Editor;
  Travis Masch, Marketing
To Order: PO Box 7355,
  Berkeley, CA, 94707;
  800-863-5290
• Gach, Gary, ed., 153
• Ko Un, 237
• Whalen, Philip, 460

Parentheses Writing Series
3211 Hawthorn
San Diego, CA 92104
Phone: 619-595-1954
Fax: 619-595-1954
Pasquale Verdicchio,
  Publisher/Editor
Dist. by: SPD
• Saidenberg, Jocelyn, 378

Parkway Publishers
Box 3678
Boone, NC 28607
Phone: 828-265-3993
Fax: 828-265-3993
• Fallows, Cathey, 140
• Revere, Michael Rigsby, 363
• Tobin, Juanita Brown, 433

Passeggiata Press
PO Box 636
Pueblo, CO 81002
Phone: 719-544-1038
Fax: 719-544-7911
Email:
passeggiata@compuserve.com
Maureen Tingley, Associate
Editor; Donald Herdeck,
Editor
• Fan Chengda, 140
• Iskrenko, Nina, 211
• Levchev, Lyubomir, 255
• Orbán, Ottó, 331

Pavement Saw Press
7 James tT.
Scotia, NY 12302
Dist. by: SPD
• Brooks, David, 65

Pearl Editions
3030 E. Second Street
Long Beach, CA 90803
Phone: 310-434-4523
Email: mjohn5150@aol.com
Marilyn Johnson, Editor
• Andrews, Nin, 16
• Bradley, Jane Buel, 59
• Bradley, Jane Buel, 59
• Campbell, Carolyn Evans,
77
• Headley, Robert, and Rafael
Zepeda, 191
• Smith, Joan Jobe, 406
• Vasconcellos, Cherry Jean,
442
• Webb, Charles Harper, 455

Pecan Grove Press
Box AL
1 Camino Santa Maria

San Antonio, TX 78228-8608
• Mulkey, Rick, 315

Pella Publishing
337 W 36th St
New York, NY 10018-6401
Phone: 212-279-9586
Fax: 212-594-3602
Leandros Papathanasiou,
Editor
• Karageorge, Penelope
Sevaste, 225

**Penguin Books/Viking
Penguin**
375 Hudson St.
New York, NY 10014
Phone: 212-366-2000
Fax: 212-366-2952
Email: mrohrer@penguin.com
URL:
http://penguinputnam.com
Bernadette Burke, Publicity;
Matthew Rohrer, Publicity
To Order: PO Box 999, Dept.
17109, Bergenfield, NJ
07621; 800-253-6476
• Armitage, Simon, and Robert
Crawford, eds., 19
• Baudelaire, Charles, 34
• Carroll, Jim, 79
• Cully, Barbara, 109
• Dennis, Carl, 121
• Di Prima, Diane, 123
• Duba, Ursula, 128
• Gerstler, Amy, 160
• Hart, Melanie, and James
Loader, eds., 189
• Hunter, Robert, 209
• Jordan, Barbara, 221
• Lauterbach, Ann, 250
• Lewis, Lisa, 258

• Logan, William, 263
• Milligan, Bryce; Mary Guerrero Milligan and, and Angela De Hoyos, eds., 301
• Moore, Gerald, and Ulli Beier, eds., 307
• Muske, Carol, 318
• Notley, Alice, 326
• Thornton, R.K.R., and Marion Thain, 432
• Wetzsteon, Rachel, 459

Perivale Press
13830 Erwin St
Van Nuys, CA 91401-2914
Phone: 818-785-4671
Lawrence P. Spingarn, Publisher
• Young, George, 475

Perma Press Books
104 Ferne Avenue
Palo Alto, CA 94306
Phone: 650-493-2597
• Sutton, Eve, 422
• Sutton, Eve, 422

Persea Books
171 Madison Ave
New York, NY 10016
Phone: 212-889-0909
Fax: 212-689-5405
• Klein, Michael, and Richard McCann, eds., 234
• Moss, Thylias, 313
• Nobles, Edward, 324
• Riding, Laura, 366

Persephone Press
53 Pine Lake Drive
Whispering Pines, NC 28327-9388

Phone: 910-949-3933
MaryBelle Campbell, Poetry Editor
• Meyers, Susan, 298
• Silverthorne, Marty, 403

Perugia Press
PO Box 108
Shutesbury, MA 01027
Phone: 413-259-1216
Email: skan@valinet.com
Susan Kan, Director
• David, Almitra, 115
• Thomas, Gail, 431

Philomel Books
Putnam and Grosset Group
200 Madison Ave
New York, NY 10016
Phone: 212-951-8466
Fax: 212-532-9473
Eliza Sporn, Publicist (212-951-8470)
• Robb, Laura, ed., 368

Picador USA
175 Fifth Ave
New York, NY 10010
• Shore, Jane, 400

Pier Queen Productions
no address
• Xavier, Emanuel, 472

Pine Press
RD1 Box 530
Landisburg, PA 17040
Phone: 717-789-4466
Kerry Shawn Keys, Poetry Editor
• Keys, Kerry Shawn, 230
• Keys, Kerry Shawn, 230

Pittenbruach Press
PO Box 553, 15 Walnut St
Northampton, MA 01061
Phone: 413-584-8547
• Milne, Teddy, 302
• Milne, Teddy, ed., 302
• Milne, Teddy, ed., 302

Plain View Press
2009 Arthur Lane
Austin, TX 78704
Phone: 512-441-2452
Email: sbpvp@eden.com
URL: http://www.eden.com/
  ~sbpvp
Susan Bright, Editor
To Order: 800-878-3605
• Biderman, Stan, 47
• Bright, Susan, 62
• Bright, Susan, and Margo
  LaGattuta, eds., 62
• Bright, Susan, and Margo
  LaGattuta, eds., 62
• Ciscel, Dennis, 90
• Follett, C.B., 146
• Williamson, Ann Louise, 465

Pleasure Boat Studio
802 East Sixth
Port Angeles, WA 98362
Phone: 360-452-8686
Fax: 360-452-8686
• Driscoll, Frances, 127

Plinth Books
PO Box 271118
West Hartford, CT 06127-
  1118
Phone: 860-521-7458
Fax: 860-521-8658
Email: jforjames@aol.com
Jim Finnegan, Publisher

Dist. by: SPD
• Long, Robert Hill, 264
• Smith, W. Loran, 407
• Swist, Wally, 424

Pluma Productions
1977 Carmen Ave
Los Angeles, CA 90068
Phone: 213-463-6488
• Ibáñez, Armando P., 210

Pocahontas Press
832 Hutcheson Drive
Blacksburg, VA 24063-1020
Phone: 540-951-0467
Fax: 540-961-2847
Email: mchollim@bev.net
Dave Wallace, Editorial
  Associate; Mary C.
  Holliman, Publisher
• Gillespie, Theresa Courtney,
  163
• Walke, Roger, 450

Poet's Press
175 Fifth Avenue, Suite 2424
New York, NY 10010
• Rutherford, Brett, 376

**Poet's Press/Grim Reaper
  Books**
• Powell, Shirley, 349

Poetic License Press
PO Box 85525
Westland, MI 41885-0525
Phone: 734-326-9368
Fax: 734-326-3480
Email: Steveb1031@aol.com
URL:
http://poeticlicensepress.com
Carol A. Belding, Editor;

Steve Belding, Operations
Manager
Dist. by: Sunbelt Publications
• Malone, Hank, 276

Poetry Harbor
PO Box 103
Duluth, MN 55801-0103
Phone: 218-728-3728
Patrick McKinnon, Director
• Schug, Larry, 389

Poets Alive! Press
81 Spruce Street, Suite 4
Yonkers, NY 10701
Phone: 914-969-2119
Lisa Summer, Business
Manager; Steve Kowalski,
Editor
• Humphrey, James, 208
• Humphrey, James, 209
• Humphrey, James, 209
• Humphrey, James, 209

Polowichak, Su
no address
• Polo, Su, 348

Portals Press
4411 Fountainebleu Dr
New Orleans, LA 70125
• Bauer, Grace, 35
• Yictove, 474

Post-Apollo Press
35 Marie Street
Sausalito, CA 94965
Phone: 415-332-1458
Fax: 415-332-8045
URL: http://www.dnai.com/
~tpapress/
Simone Fattal, Editor

• Adnan, Etel, 3
• Sikelianos, Eleni, 402
• Waldrop, Rosmarie, and
Keith Waldrop, 449

Pot Shard Press
PO Box 382
Camptche, CA 95427
Phone: 707-937-0922
Jane Reichhold, Publisher;
M.L. Harrison Mackie,
Editor
• Doubiago, Sharon; Devreaux
Baker, and Susan Maeder,
eds., 127

Potes & Poets Press
181 Edgemont Avenue
Elmwood, CT 06110-1005
Phone: 860-233-2023
Email: potepoet@home.com
Peter Ganick, Publisher/Editor
Dist. by: SPD
• Berry, Jake, 45
• Cole, Barbara, 96
• DuPlessis, Rachel Blau, 131
• Etter, Carrie, 138
• Kimball, Jack, 232
• Lederer, Katy, 253
• Leftwich, Jim, 253
• Levy, Andrew, 258
• Mandel, Tom, and Daniel
Davidson, 277
• Mangold, Sarah, 277
• Murphy, Sheila E., 317

Potpourri Publications
PO Box 8278
Prairie Village, KS 66208
Phone: 913-642-1503
Fax: 913-642-2138
Email: potpourpub@aol.com

URL:
http://artnoboundaries.org/
potpouri.html
Polly W. Stafford, Editor
• Mendenhall, Kitty McCord,
294
• Tucker, Martin, 437

**Premiere Poets Chapbook
Series**
no address
Saunderstown, RI
• Kaplan, Janet, 224

Press of Appletree Alley
PO Box 608
Lewisburg, PA 17837
Phone: 717-524-7064
Barnard Taylor, Publisher
• Matthews, William, 284

Pride Publications
1811336th Ave. W, Ste J108
Lynnwood, WA 98037
Phone: 425-775-8226
Fax: same
Email: pridepblsher@aol.com
URL: http://members.aol.com/
pridepblsh/pride.html
Cris Newport, Senior Editor;
Jennifer DiMarco, Publicity
• Kikel, Rudy, 230
• Newman, Lesléa, 322

Princeton University Press
41 William St.
Princeton, NJ 08540
Phone: 609-258-4900;
609-258-5714
Fax: 609-258-6305;
609-258-1335
Email:

bill_m@pupress.princeton.edu
• HaNagid, Shmuel, 184
• Meng Chiao, 294

**Project on Cities and Urban
Knowledges International
Center for Advanced
Studies**
no address
• Bender, Thomas, Dir., 40

Protean Press
287 28th Ave.
San Francisco, CA 94121
Phone: 415-386-3044
Fax: 415-386-4980
Email: proteanpress@att.net
Terry Herrigan, Director;
Robert Weiss, Partner
• Norlen, Sherron, 325

Provincetown Arts Press
650 Commercial St.
Provincetown, MA 02657
Phone: 508-487-3167
Fax: 508-487-8634
Email:
press@capecodaccess.com
URL:
http://capecodaccess.com/
galley/arts/
Christopher Busa, Editor
Dist. by: SPD
• Cruz-Bernal, Mairym, 109
• Dudley, Ellen, 128
• Matias, David, 283

Puckerbrush Press
76 Main Street
Orono, ME 04473
Phone: 207-866-4868
Fax: 207-581-3832

Constance Hunting, Publisher
• Celan, Paul, 84
• Hunting, Constance, 209

Pudding House Publications
60 N Main St.
Johnstown, OH 43031
Phone: 740-967-6060
Email:
   pudding@johnstown.net
URL:
   http://www.puddinghouse.com
Jennifer Bosveld, Publisher
• Abbott, Steve, 1
• Alschuler, Mari, 13
• Bennett, Saul, 41
• Bosveld, Jennifer, ed., 56
• Chorlton, David, 88
• Collins, Robert, 99
• Levering, Donald, 255
• Martin, Jack, 280
• Miller, Stephen M., 301
• Penfold, Nita, 340
• Rasnake, Sam, 358
• Rickard, Jack, 365
• Robiner, Linda Goodman, 370
• Williams, Bruce, 463

Purdue University Press
1207 South Campus Cts-F
West Lafayette, IN 47907-1207
Phone: 800-933-9637
Fax: 765-496-2442
Email:
   libpup@omni.cc.purdue.edu
URL:
   http://www.lib.purdue.edu
Margaret Hunt, Poetry Editor;
   Shawn Hall, Marketing
   Associate

• Eimers, Nancy, 132
• Schorb, E.M., 389

Pushcart Press
PO Box 380
Wainscott, NY 11975
Phone: 516-324-9300
Bill Henderson, Editor
• Henderson, Bill, ed., 194

Pygmy Forest Press
PO Box 591
Albion, CA 95410
Phone: 707-937-2347
Leonard J. Cirino,
   Publisher/Editor
• McIrvin, Michael, 291

QED Press
155 Cypress St.
Fort Bragg, CA 95437
Phone: 707-964-9520
Fax: 707-964-7531
Email: qedpress@mcn.org
URL:
   http://www.cypresshouse.com
Joe Shaw, Publicist
To Order: 800-773-7782
Dist. by: B&T, Ingram,
   Mother Pickle, Partners
• de Andrade, Eugénio, 118

Quale Press
PO Box 363
132 Main St.
Haydenville, MA 01039
Phone: 413-268-3632
Fax: 413-268-3632
Email: central@quale.com
URL: http://www.quale.com
Gian Lombardo, Editor
Dist. by: SPD

• Brennan, Liz, 61
• Johnson, Peter, 218

Quarter Horse Press
no address
• Maurer, Susan, and Bill
  Kushner, 285

**Quarterly Review of
  Literature**
26 Haslet Ave.
Princeton, NJ 08540
Phone: 609-921-6976
Fax: 609-258-2230
T. Weiss, Poetry Editor
• Weiss, T. and R. Weiss, eds.,
  458

Queen of Swords Press
1329-B Arch St.
Berkeley, CA 94708
Phone: 510-540-8959
Email:
  ecqsp@worldnet.att.com
Elizabeth Claman, Editor
Dist. by: SPD
• Claman, Elizabeth, ed., 91
• Claman, Elizabeth, ed., 91

Rain Bucket Press
109 Locust Ave.
Cranford, NJ 07016
Phone: 908-931-1343
• Weil, Joe, 457

Rainbow's End
354 Golden Grove Rd
Baden, PA 15005
Phone: 800-596-RBOW
Email: btucker833@aol.com
Bettie Tucker, Editor; Glenda
  Bixler, Poetry Editor

• Duffy, Timothy J., 129
• Frisby, Cathy, 151
• McDonald, Karen, 288

Random House
201 East 50th St.
New York, NY 10022
Phone: 212-751-2600
Fax: 212-572-4949
URL:
http://www.randomhouse.com
Dan Menaker, Editor;
  Elizabeth Fogarty, Publicity
• Ackerman, Diane, 2
• Adair, Virginia Hamilton, 2
• Adair, Virginia Hamilton, 3
• Angelou, Maya, 16
• Angelou, Maya, 16
• Angelou, Maya, 16
• Anglund, Joan Walsh, 16
• Garrison, Deborah, 157

Raven's Bones Press
no address
• Reed, Tennessee, 361

Red Balloon Collective
no address
• Cohen, Michael, 96

Red Dragon Press
PO Box 19425
Alexandria, VA 22320-0425
Phone: 703-683-5877
Fax: 703-683-5877
URL:
  http://reddragonpress.com
Laura Qa, Publisher/Poetry
  Editor
• Bishop, Suzette, 48
• Cavalieri, Grace, 84
• Cole, Susan, 97

• Karos, George, 225

Red Hen Press
PO Box 902582
Palmdale, CA 93590-2582
Phone: 818-831-0649
Fax: 818-831-0649
Email: vpg@vpg.net
URL: http://www.vpg.net
Kate Gale, Editor; Amy
   Harrington, Event
   Coordinator
Dist. by: Valentine Publishing
   Group
• Bein, Sarah, 38
• Gale, Kate, 154
• Renaud, Jeanne, 362
• Ybarra, Ricardo Means, 473

Red Moon Press
PO Box 2461
Winchester, VA 22604-2461
Phone: 540-722-2156
Email: redmoon@shentel.net
Jim Kacian, Editor
Dist. by: Weatherhill Inc.
• Elsberg, John, 134
• Evetts, Dee, 139
• Kacian, Jim, ed., 223
• Kacian, Jim, ed., 223
• Pupello, Anthony J., 351

Red Wind Books
PO Box 27924
Los Angeles, CA 90027
Phone: 213-255-5223
Suzanne Lummis
• Bogen, Laurel Ann, 53

Redd Center Publications
no address
Provo, UT

• Howe, Susan Elizabeth, 206

Reflections Press/RDR
   Books
no address
Berkeley, CA
• Lossy, Rella, 267

Regent Press
6020-A Adeline
Oakland, CA 94608
Phone: 510-547-7602
Fax: 510-547-6357
Email: regent@sirius.com
URL: http://www.sirius.com/
   ~regent
Mark Weiman, Managing
   Editor
• Burch, Claire, 71

Renegade Planets Publishing
no address
• Moore, Marijo, 307

Reservoir Press
15 John St
Kingston, NY 12401
Phone: 914-339-3277
Fax: 914-331-5439
Email: alterna@ulster.net
Marilyn Stablein, Editor
• Gould, Roberta, 170
• Stablein, Marilyn, 414

Ridgeway Press
c/o The Writer's Voice of the
   YMCA of Metropolitan
   Detroit
10900 Harper Ave.
Detroit, MI 48213
Phone: 313-577-7713
Fax: 810-294-0474

Email: mlliebler@aol.com
M.L. Liebler, Publisher
To Order: P.O. Box 120,
Roseville, MI 48066
• Blackhawk, Terry, 49
• Burdine, James M., ed., 71
• Chadbourne, Eugene, 85
• Corey, Del, 103
• Foster, Linda Nemec, 147
• Hellus, Al, 194
• Kaplan, Carol Genyea, 224
• Kerman, Judith, 229
• LaFemina, Gerry, 246
• Lauchlan, Michael, 249
• Levine, Laurence, 256
• McDonald, Country Joe, 287
• Morin, Edward, 309
• Schreiner, Steven, 389
• Vlasopolos, Anca, 445

Rienner, Lynne,
Publishers/Three
Continents Press
1800 30th St., Suite 314
Boulder, CO 80301-1026
Phone: 303-444-6684
Fax: 303-444-0824
Email: mdyer@rienner.com
Donald E. Herdeck, Publisher;
Laural Bidwell, Publicity
• Tham, Hilary, 430

Rio Grande Press
4320 Canyon, Suite A12
Amarillo, TX 79109
Phone: 702-220-9082
URL:
http://www.poetpantry.com/
se_la_vie
Rosalie Avara, Editor
• Avara, Rosalie, ed., 23
• Avara, Rosalie, ed., 23

• Avara, Rosalie, ed., 23
• Avara, Rosalie, ed., 23
• Avara, Rosalie, ed., 23

Rivercross Publishing
127 E 59th St.
New York, NY 10022
Phone: 800-451-4522
Josh Furman, Editor in Chief
• Jaffe, Louise M., 214

Riverstone Press
7571 East Visao Drive
Scottsdale, AZ 85262
Phone: 610-344-4992
Email:
mholley@brynmawr.edu
Margaret Holley,
Publisher/Editor
• Barrows, Anita, 32
• Myers, Gary, 318
• Stever, Margo, 417

Rizzoli/Universe Publishing
300 Park Avenue South
New York, NY 10010
Phone: 212-387-3400
Fax: 212-387-3535
Margo Stever, Editor
• Fried, Philip, ed., 150
• Phillips, Rodney, with Susan
Benesch, Kenneth Benson,
and Barbara Bergeron.
Essays by Dana Gioia, 343
• Stever, Margo, ed., 417

Roof Books
303 East 8th St.
New York, NY 10009
Phone: 212-674-0199
Fax: 212-254-4145
James Sherry, Poetry Editor

• Grosman, Ernesto Livon, ed., 177
• Stefans, Brian Kim, 416
• Templeton, Fiona, 430
• Weiner, Hannah, 458
• Yasusada, Araki, 472

Rose Alley Press
4203 Brooklyn Ave NE, 103A
Seattle, WA 98105
Phone: 206-633-2725
Email: rosealleypress@juno.com
David D. Horowitz, Publisher
Dist. by: B&T
• Dunlop, William, 130
• Spence, Michael, 413

Runaway Spoon Press
1708 Hayworth Rd
Port Charlotte, FL 33952
Phone: 941-629-8045
Bob Grumman, Poetry Editor
• Elsberg, John, 134
• Elsberg, John, 134

Rutledge Books
Box 315, 8 F.J. Clarke Circle
Bethel, CT 06801-0315
Phone: 800-278-8533
Fax: 800-962-8345
Nina Otero, Publicity
• Wagner, Thomas, 447

Rythm Books/Innovative Publishing Concepts
PO Box 9748
Scottsdale, AZ 85252-9748
Phone: 602-970-6686
• Valdez, Catherine, 441

S.A. Books

110 Blueberry Ln
Hicksville, NY 11801
Phone: 516-939-0789
Email: pulldaisy@aol.com
Kevin Michaels, Editor; Ben Parris, Publicity
• Michaels, Kevin, ed., 299

Sagittarius Press
930 Taylor
Port Townsend, WA 98368
Phone: 360-385-0277
Rusty North, Publisher
• Canan, Janine, 77
• Fink, Sid, 144
• Lander, Tim, 246
• Lutz, Jeanne, 269
• North, Rusty, 326
• North, Rusty, 326
• North, Rusty, ed., 326
• Reavey, Kate, 360

Sailing After Lunch
no address
• Young, Geoffrey, 475

Sally Loves Sweet Baboo Press
112 Victory Dr.
Calhoun, GA 30701
• Fox, Kirsten, 148

Salmon Run Press
P.O. Box 672130
Chugiak, AK 99567
Phone: 907-688-4268
Fax: 907-688-4268
Email: jpsmelcer@aol.com
John Smelcer, Publisher
• Salinas, Luis Omar, 381

San Francisco State

University Chapbook Series
1600 Holloway Ave
San Francisco, CA 94132
• Brodsky, Nicole, 64
• Jasson-Holt, Sophie, 216

Sandhu, Harbeer, and Antonio DiPietro
no address
• Sandhu, Harbeer, and Antonio DiPietro, 383

Santa Barbara Review Publications
PO Box 808
Summerland, CA 93067
Patricia Leddy, Editor
• McEntyre, Marilyn Chandler, ed., 289
• Ratcliffe, Stephen, 358

Sarabande Books
2234 Dundee Road, Suite 200
Louisville, KY 40205
Phone: 502-458-4028
Fax: 502-458-4065
Email: SarabandeB@aol.com
URL:
  http://sarabandebooks.org
Kristin Herbert, Marketing Director; Sarah Gorham, Editor
Dist. by: Consortium
• Allen, Dick, 11
• Burkard, Michael, 71
• Clinton, Robert, 93
• Gorham, Sarah and Jeffrey Skinner, eds., 170
• Halme, Kathleen, 182
• Kimbrell, James, 232
• Marlis, Stefanie, 279

• Waring, Belle, 452
• Wormser, Baron, 469

Sasquatch Books
615 Second Ave
Seattle, WA 98104
Phone: 206-467-4300
Email:
books@sasquatchbooks.com
URL:
  http://sasquatchbooks.com
• Harris, Jana, 187

Savage Press
Box 115
Superior, WI 54880
Phone: 715-394-9513
Fax: 715-394-9513
URL:
  http://www.cp.duluth.mn.us/
  ~guest/savpress
To Order: 800-732-3867
• Bennett, Paul, 41

Scop Publications
c/o Writers Center
4508 Walsh St
Bethesda, MD 20815
Phone: 301-654-8664
Fax: 301-654-8667
Stacy Tuthill, Publisher
• Tuthill, Stacy Johnson, ed., 438

Scott, E. Ray
no address
• Scott, E. Ray, 390

Segue Books
303 East 8th Street
New York, NY 10009
Phone: 212-674-0199

• Jones, Hettie, ed., 220

Selva Editions
no address
• Ferraris, Fred, 142

Seven Stories Press
140 Watts Street
New York, NY 10013
URL:
http://www.sevenstories.com
Dist. by: Publishers Group
West
• Moss, Stanley, 313

**Sewanee Writer's Series/
Overlook Press, Co-pub-
lishers**
• Bricuth, John, 61

Shambhala Publications
Horticultural Hall
300 Massachusetts Ave.
Boston, MA 02115
Phone: 617-424-0030
Fax: 617-236-1563
Email: info@shambhala.com
URL:
http://www.shambhala.com
Peter Turner, Poetry Editor;
Jennifer Pursley, Publicity
• Akiko, Yosano, 6
• Hamill, Sam, trans., 183
• Issa, Kobayashi, 212
• Le Guin, Ursula K., 252
• Trungpa, Chögyam, 436

Sharp Tongue Press
no address
• Montgomery, Wardell, Jr.,
306

Sheep Meadow Press
PO Box 1345
Riverdale-on-Hudson, NY
10471
Phone: 718-548-5547
Fax: 718-884-0406
Email: sheepmdwpr@aol.com
Stanley Moss, Editor/
Publisher; Aimee Kwon,
Managing Editor
To Order: University Press of
New England, 23 South
Main St., Hanover, NH
03775; 800-421-1561;
603-643-1560 (fax); univer-
sitypress@dartmouth.edu
Dist. by: University Press of
New England
• Agoos, Julie, 4
• Amichai, Yehuda, 13
• Cole, Peter, 97
• Collins, Martha, 98
• Der-Hovanessian, Diana, 122
• Mathis, Cleopatra, 283
• Pessoa, Fernando, 342
• Saba, Umberto, 377
• Shabtai, Aharon, 394
• Silk, Dennis, 402
• Wallach, Yona, 450
• Zisquit, Linda, 478

Sherman Asher Publishing
PO Box 2853
Santa Fe, NM 87504
Phone: 505-984-2686
Fax: 505-820-2744
Email:
71277.2057@compuserve.com
URL:
http://www.shermanasher.com
Judith Rafaela, Editor; Nancy
Fay, Editor/Marketing

Director
Dist. by: B&T, Ingram, Koen
• Harter, Penny, 189
• Logghe, Joan, and Miriam
Sagan, eds., 263
• Rafaela, Judith, and Nancy
Fay, eds., 353
• Rafaela, Judith, and Nancy
Fay, eds., 354

Shorter College Press
315 Shorter Ave, Box 476
Rome, GA 30165
Phone: 706-232-9325
Fax: 706-235-2716
Email: drrwest@aol.com
Rose West, Publishing
Coordinator
• Hall, Thelma R., 182

Signature Books
564 West 400 North St.
Salt Lake City, UT 84116-
3411
Phone: 801-531-1483
Fax: 801-531-1488
Email: signature@thegulf.com
URL:
http://.signaturebooksine.com
Gary Bergera, Editor; Ron
Priddis, Publicity
• Caldiero, Alex, 76

Silverfish Review Press
PO Box 3541
Eugene, OR 97403
Phone: 541-344-5060
Email: SFRpress@aol.com
Roger Moody,
Editor/Publisher
Dist. by: SPD
• Caine, Shulamith Wechter,

75
• Townsend, Ann, 433
• Young, Gary, 474

**Simon & Schuster Books for
Young Readers**
1230 Avenue of the Americas
New York, NY 10020
Phone: 212-632-4947
Fax: 212-632-4957
URL:
http://www.SimonSays.com
Patricia Eisemann, Vice
President and Director of
Publicity; Giulia Melucci,
Associate Publicity Director
• Adoff, Arnold, ed., 4
• Berry, James, 45
• Nye, Naomi Shihab, ed., 327

**Simon & Schuster/Aladdin
Paperbacks**
• Fletcher, Ralph, 145

**Simon & Schuster/
Atheneum**
• Fletcher, Ralph, 145
• Janeczko, Paul B., 215
• Moore, Lilian, 307

**Simon & Schuster/Margaret
K. McElderry Books**
• Kennedy, Dorothy M., ed.,
229
• Livingston, Myra Cohn, 262

Simon & Schuster/Scribner
1230 Avenue of the Americas
New York, NY 10020
Phone: 212-632-4947
Fax: 212-632-4957
URL:

http://www.SimonSays.com
Patricia Eisemann, Vice
President and Director of
Publicity; Giulia Melucci,
Associate Publicity Director
• Algarín, Miguel, 10
• Bloom, Harold, ed., 51
• Hollander, John, with David
Lehman, eds., 202
• Koch, Kenneth, ed., 238
• Mahony, Phillip, ed., 274
• Price, Reynolds, 350
• Shange, Ntozake, 395
• Tagore, Rabindranath, 427
• Yeats, W.B., 473
• Yeats, W.B., 474

**Simon & Schuster/
Touchstone**
• Grade V Classes of the
Nightingale-Bamford
School, eds., 171

Singing Horse Press
PO Box 40034
Philadelphia, PA 19106
Phone: 215-844-7678
Fax: 215-925-7402
Email:
singinghorse@erols.com
Gil Ott, Editor/Publisher
Dist. by: SPD
• Dinh, Linh, 125
• Waldrop, Rosmarie, 449

Singular Speech Press
no address
Canton, CT
Phone: 860-693-6059
Fax: 860-693-6338
• Chace, Joel, 85
• Lucina, Mary, 269

• Macioci, R. Nikolas, 272
• Morrison, R.H., 312
• Sassi, Maria, 385
• Soular, James, 412

**Skylands Writers & Artists
Association/Ars Poetica**
PO Box 15
Andover, NJ 07821-0015
Phone: 973-786-7947
Email: daniela@garden.net
URL: http://www.garden.net/
users/swaa
Daniela Gioseffi, Editor;
Sander Zulauf, Publicity
To Order: PO Box 866, Lake
Hopatcong, NJ 07849-
0866; 973-347-1068; 973-
328-5425 (fax)
Dist. by: Ars Poetica
• Salerno, Joe, 380
• Salerno, Joe, 381

Slapering Hol Press
The Hudson Valley Writers'
Center
300 Riverside Dr
Sleepy Hollow, NY 10591
Phone: 914-332-5953
Fax: 914-332-4825
Email: hvwc@aol.com
Margo Stever, Editor; Nick
Singman, Director
• Goldsmith, Ellen, 168
• Loden, Rachel, 263
• McGee, Lynn, 289

Slipstream Publications
PO Box 2071
Niagara Falls, NY 14301
Phone: 716-282-2616
URL: http://wings.buffalo.edu/

libraries/units/pl/slipstream
Dan Sicoli, Editor
• Christopher, Renny, 89
• Mcilroy, Leslie Anne, 291

Slow Tempo Press
P.O. Box 83686
Lincoln, NE 68501-3686
Phone: 402-466-8689
David McCleery, Publisher
• Hansen, Twyla, 185
• Welch, Don, 458

Small Poetry Press
PO Box 5342
Concord, CA 94524
Phone: 510-798-1411
• Cobden, Lynda, 94
• Ness, Pamela Miller, 322
• Ness, Pamela Miller, 322
• Villella, Charlene, 445

Smiling Dog Press
9875 Fritz Road
Maple City, MI 49664
Phone: 616-334-3695
Dean Creighton,
  Publisher/Editor
• Scarecrow, 386
• Weber, Mark, 456

**Smith, Gibbs, Publishers/
  Peregrine Smith Books**
PO Box 667
1877 E Gentile St
Layton, UT 84041
Phone: 801-544-9800
Fax: 801-544-5582
Email: info@gibbs-smith.com
URL:
  http://www.gibbs-smith.com
Gail Yngve, Poetry Editor;

Monica Millward, Publicity
• Holahan, Susan, 201
• Roberts, Katrina, 369

Smokeproof Press
no address
Erie, CO
Dist. by: SPD
• Schelling, Andrew, 387
• Waldman, Anne; Eleni
  Sikelianos, and Laird Hunt,
  448

Soft Skull Press
98-100 Suffolk Street
New York, NY 10002
Phone: 212-673-2502
Fax: 212-673-0787
Email: sander@softskull.com
URL:
  http://www.softskull.com
Cat Tyc, Publicity; Sander
  Hicks, Poetry Editor
Dist. by: Consortium
• Gilroy, Tom; Anna Grace,
  Jim McKay, Douglas A.
  Martin, Grant Lee Phillips,
  Rick Roth, and Michael
  Stipe, 163
• Morris, Tracie, 311
• Nelson, Cynthia, 320
• Sparrow, 413

Somers Rocks Press
505 Court St, 4H
Brooklyn, NY 11231
Phone: 718-243-1055
Arthur Mortensen, Editor
• Kraeft, Norman, 240
• Palma, Michael, 335

Something More

Publications
Loyola Hall
Fordham University
Bronx, NY 10458
• Ivy, Evie, 212

Sounds of Poetry
2076 Vinewood
Detroit, MI 48216-5506
Phone: 313-843-2352
• Saenz, Gil, and Jacqueline
Rae Rawlson Sanchez, 378

Southern Illinois University Press
PO Box 3697
Carbondale, IL 62902-3697
• Gavronsky, Serge, trans., 158

Sow's Ear Press
19535 Pleasant View Drive
Abingdon, VA 24211-6827
Phone: 540-628-2651
Email:
richman@preferred.com
Larry K. Richman, Managing
Editor/Publisher
• Coleman, Ralph S., 97
• Crabtree, Lou V., 106
• Moose, Ruth, 308
• Owens, James, 334
• Parsons, Linda, 338
• Rasnake, Sam, 358

Spectacular Books
PO Box 250648
Columbia University Post
Office
New York, NY 10025
Email: katy@bway.net
Katherine Lederer, Editor
• Corless-Smith, Martin, 103

Spitfire Press
no address
Providence, RI 02906
• Nason, Richard W., 319

Split Shift
2461 Santa Monica Blvd, C-122
Santa Monica, CA 90404
Roger Taus, Editor
• Johnson, Eric, 218

Spuyten Duyvil
PO Box 1852 Cathedral Stat.
New York, NY 10025
Phone: 718-398-9067
Fax: 212-727-8228
Email:
spuytenduyvil@mailcity.com
URL:
http://www.freeyellow.com/
members/spuytenduyvil
Tod Thilleman, Publisher;
Katya Edwards, Publicity
Dist. by: SPD
• Thilleman, Tod, 431

St. Martin's Press
175 Fifth Avenue, Suite 200
New York, NY 10010
Phone: 212-982-3900
Fax: 212-777-6359
Email:
shaylaharris@stmartins.com
URL:
http://www.stmartins.com
Meredith Howard, Publicity;
Shayla Harris, Publicity
• Ray, David, and Judy Ray,
eds., 360
• Trachtenberg, Jordan, and
Amy Trachtenberg, eds.,

434

State House Press
no address
Austin, TX 78761
Phone: 800-421-3378
• Michener, James A., 299

State Street Press
PO Box 278
Brockport, NY 14420
Phone: 716-637-0023
Email:
  jkitchen@brockport.edu
Judith Kitchen, Editor; Stan
  Rubin, Associate Editor
• Allardt, Linda, 11
• Kowit, Steve, 240
• Tucker, Memye Curtis, 437

Steppingstone/Sugar Creek
61 Seaway Rd
Brewster, MA 02631
Phone: 508-896-7963
• Baker, Donald W., 27
• Baker, Donald W., 27

Sterling House
440 Friday Road, Dept. T-101
Pittsburgh, PA 15209
Phone: 412-821-6211
Fax: 412-821-6099
Email: leeshore1@aol.com
URL:
  http://www.olworld.com/
  olworld/sterlinghouse
Michelle Burton Brown,
  Editor
• Crist, Robert, trans., 107
• Leonard, John C., 254
• Rose, Samé, 372
• West, Charles M., 459

Stewart, Tabori & Chang
115 W 18thSt, 5th Fl
New York, NY 10011
Phone: 212-519-1201
Fax: 212-519-1210
Email: maya@stcbooks.com
Alexandra Childs, Publisher;
  Maya Lahr Gottfried,
  Publicity
• Lovric, Michelle, and
  Nikiforos Doxiadis Mardas,
  trans., 268

Still Waters Press
459 S Willow Ave
Galloway, NJ 08201-4633
Phone: 609-652-0701
Shirley Warren, Editor
• Ryan, N. Jesse, 376

Stinehour Press
80 E 11th Street
New York, NY 10011
Phone: 212-691-0670
• Behar, Diane, 37

Storm Imprints
180 Prospect Park West #6
Brooklyn, NY 11215
Phone: 718-768-1731
Email: StormImpri@aol.com
Gale Jackson, Editor
• Jackson, Gale P., 213
• Jackson, Gale P., 213

Story Line Press
Three Oaks Farm, PO Box
  1240
Ashland, OR 97520-0055
Phone: 541-512-8792
Fax: 541-512-8793
Email:

mail@storylinepress.com
URL:
http://www.storylinepress.com
Robert McDowell, Executive
Director; Deborah Elliott,
Marketing Director
Dist. by: Consortium
• Anderson, Daniel, 14
• Barr, John, 31
• Feirstein, Frederick, 141
• Finch, Annie, 144
• Haskins, Lola, 189
• Jarman, Mark, 215
• Light, Kate, 259
• McAlpine, Katherine, and
  Gail White, eds., 286
• McElroy, Colleen J., 288
• Murphy, Timothy, 317
• Pollack, Frederick, 347
• Ransom, Jane, 357
• Simpson, Louis, ed., 403
• Torreson, Rodney, 433
• Uyematsu, Amy, 440
• Wiman, Christian, 467

Street Press
PO Box 772
Sound Beach, NY 11789-0772
Phone: 516-821-0679
Email: gnash51@hotmail.com
Graham Everett, Publisher; G.
  Nash, Manager
• Duddy, Thomas, 128
• Fayth, Doc, 141
• Freed, Ray, 149
• Murray, Dan, 317

Summitt Poetry Publishing
3923 Central Ave
Louisville, KY 40218
Phone: 502-491-4441
Rebecca Renzi, Editor

• Morton, R. Meir, 312
• Morton, R. Meir, 312
• Morton, R. Meir, 313
• Stuart, Jane, 421

Sun & Moon Press
6026 Wilshire Blvd.
Los Angeles, CA 90036
Phone: 323-857-1115
Fax: 323-857-0143
URL:
http://www.sunmoon.com
Douglas Messerli, Publisher
• Ayhan, Ece, 25
• Bennett, Guy, 40
• Clark, Jeff, 92
• de Cristoforo, Violet Kazue,
  trans., 119
• Haugen, Paal-Helge, 190
• Hollander, Benjamin, 202
• Kim, Myung Mi, 231
• Mayröcker, Friederike, 285
• Messerli, Douglas, 296
• Messerli, Douglas, ed., 296
• Palmer, Michael; Régis
  Bonvicino, and Nelson
  Ascher, eds., 336
• Sappho, 384
• Swensen, Cole, 424
• Watten, Barrett, 455
• Wieners, John, 462

SUN/gemini Press
PO Box 42170
Tucson, AZ 85733
Phone: 520-299-1097
• Byrkit, Rebecca, 73
• Davis, Meg, 117
• Lykes, Dorothy Raitt, 270

SUNY University Libraries, The Poetry/Rare Books Collection
University at Buffalo
420 Capen Hall
Buffalo, NY 14260
Phone: 716-645-2917
Fax: 716-645-3714
Email:
    bertholf@acsu.buffalo.edu
URL: http://ulib.buffalo.edu/
    libraries/units/pl
Robert Bertholf, Director
• Oppenheimer, Joel, 330

Talent House Press
1306 Talent Avenue
Talent, OR 97540
Phone: 541-535-9041
Paul Hadella, Editor
• Held, George, 194
• LeBlanc, Diane, 253
• Morse, Elizabeth, 312
• Perrin, Arnold, 341
• Roberts, Stephen R., 369
• Solensten, John, 410
• Spurgeon, Michael, 414

Talisman House, Publishers
PO Box 3157
Jersey City, NJ 07303-3157
Phone: 201-938-0698
Fax: 201-938-1693
Dist. by: LPC Group/Inbook,
    SPD
• Bronk, William, 64
• Bronk, William, 64
• Bronk, William, 65
• Bronk, William, 65
• Heller, Michael, 194
• Jarnot, Lisa; Leonard
    Schwartz and Chris

Stroffolino, 215
• Lowenfels, Walter, 268
• Mesyats, Vadim, 297
• O'Brien, Geoffrey, 327
• Oliver, Douglas, 330
• Owen, Maureen, 333
• Roberson, Ed, 368
• Scalapino, Leslie, 385
• Scalapino, Leslie, 386
• Schwartz, Leonard, 390
• Sloan, Mary Margaret, 405
• Sobin, Gustaf, 410
• Waldrop, Rosmarie, 449
• Zhdanov, Ivan, 478

Talisman House, Publishers/ Jensen/Daniels
c/o Talisman House
PO Box 3157
Jersey City, NJ 07303-3157
• Barone, Dennis, 31
• Collom, Jack, 99
• Killian, Sean, 231
• Needell, Claire, 320
• Pruitt, Patricia, 351
• Valente, Peter, 441

Tarcher, Jeremy P. /Putnam
200 Madison Ave
New York, NY 10016
Phone: 212-951-8400
Fax: 212-951-8527
Email: jptarcher@aol.com;
    jptarcher@putnam.com
David Groff, Editor
• Rumi, Jelaluddin, 375

Taurean Horn Press
1355 California St, 2
San Francisco, CA 94109
Phone: 415-771-5331
Bill Vartnaw, Poetry

Editor/Publisher
• Sanchez, Carol Lee, 382
• Sharp, Tom, 396

Tebot Bach
20592 Minerva Ln
Huntington Beach, CA 92646
Phone: 714-968-0905
Email: mifanwy@ni.net
Mifanwy Kaiser, Publisher
• Jones, Richard, 220

Tender Buttons Press
PO Box 13, Cooper Station
New York, NY 10276
Phone: 212-726-8610
Email:
brown@simcl.stjohns.edu
Lee Ann Brown,
Publisher/Editor
• Moxley, Jennifer, 314

Tesseract Publications
PO Box 164
Canton, SD 57013
Phone: 605-987-5070
Fax: 605-987-5071
Janet Leih, Publisher
• Bogue, Lois, 54

**Texas Christian University
Press**
no address
Fort Worth, TX
• Colquitt, Betsy, 99

Texas Tech University Press
P.O. Box 41037
Lubbock, TX 79409-1037
Phone: 806-742-2982;
800-832-4042
Fax: 806-742-2979

Email: ttup@ttu.edu
URL: http://www.ttup.ttu.edu
Judith Keeling, Editor
• Benbow, Margaret, 39
• Bursk, Christopher, 72
• Essinger, Cathryn, 138

Third Rail Press
PO Box 350098
Brooklyn, NY 11235
Email: pinata@escape.com
• Gladstone-Gelman, Rachel,
165
• Gladstone-Gelman, Rachel,
165
• Gladstone-Gelman, Rachel,
165

Third World Press
P.O. Box 19730
7822 South Dobson Ave.
Chicago, IL 60619
Phone: 773-651-0700
Fax: 773-651-7286
Email: JamesTWP@aol.com
James Dodson, Director of
Marketing and Sales
• Madhubuti, Haki R., 272
• Madhubuti, Haki R., 273
• Plumpp, Sterling, 347

This Poets Press
PO Box 3298
Beverly, MA 01915
Email: spoke@massed.net
Neal Zagarella; Kerry
Zagarella
• Richards, Derek, 364

**Thomas Jefferson University
Press/New Odyssey Press**
MC111L, 100 E Normal

Kirksville, MO 63501-4221
Phone: 800-916-6802;
816-785-7299
Fax: 816-785-4181
Email:
newodyssey@tjup.truman.edu
URL: http://tjup.truman.edu/
newodyssey
Timothy Rolands, Poetry
Editor
• Baer, William, 26
• Espaillat, Rhina P., 138
• Nick, Dagmar, 323

Three Mile Harbor
PO Box 1335
Grand Central Station
New York, NY 10163
• Howley, Michael, 207

Thumbscrew Press
1331 26th Ave
San Francisco, CA 94122
Phone: 415-566-3367
URL: http://www.amazon.com
William Talcott, Editor
• Nisbet, Jim, 324
• Talcott, William, 427

Tia Chucha Press
c/oThe Guild Complex
PO Box 476969
Chicago, IL 60647-4120
Phone: 773-377-2496
Fax: 773-528-5452
Email:
guild@charlie.cus.iit.edu
URL:
http://nupress.nwu.edu/guild
Luis Rodriguez, Director; Kim
Masselli, Publicity
To Order: 800-621-2736

Dist. by: Northwestern
University Press
• Alexander, Elizabeth, 9
• Ali, Quraysh, ed., 11
• Duhamel, Denise, and
Maureen Seaton, 129
• Maciel, Olivia, ed., 272
• Sánchez, Ricardo, 382
• Sheehan, John, 397
• Suárez, Virgil, 422
• Weaver, Afaa M., 455

Time Being Books
10411 Clayton Rd., 201-203
St. Louis, MO 63131
Phone: 314-432-1771
Fax: 314-432-7939
Jerry Call, Editor in Chief
• Boccia, Edward, 53
• Brodsky, Louis Daniel, 63
• Brodsky, Louis Daniel, 63
• Brodsky, Louis Daniel, 64
• Brodsky, Louis Daniel, 64
• Kamenetz, Rodger, 224
• Krapf, Norbert, 241
• Marcello, Leo Luke, 278

TL Press
no address
• Kofler, Silvia, 239

Trader Books
PO Box 630
Otis, MA 01253
• Giannini, David, 161

Trask House Books
3222 NE Schuyler
Portland, OR 97212
• Bird, Gloria, 48
• Derry, Alice, 122
• Gallagher, Tess, 154

University of Arizona Press
1230 N. Park Avenue, 102
Tucson, AZ 85719-4140
Phone: 520-621-1441
Fax: 520-621-8899
Email: uapress@arizona.edu
URL:
http://uapress.arizona.edu
Joanne O'Hare, Poetry Editor;
Christopher Galvez,
Publicity
• Martínez, Demetria, 280
• Tapahonso, Luci, 428
• Wright, Leilani, and James
Cervantes, eds., 470

University of Arkansas Press
McIlroy House
201 Ozark Ave.
Fayetteville, AR 72701
Phone: 800-626-0090
Fax: 501-575-3246
Email:
uaprinfo@cavern.uark.edu
URL: http://www.uark.edu/
~uaprinfo
Elizabeth Motherwell,
Marketing Manager; Brian
King, Editor
• Aberg, William, 1
• Baker, David, 27
• Bugeja, Michael, 70
• Burns, Michael, 71
• Finkel, Donald, 144
• Lammon, Martin, 246
• Lieberman, Laurence, 258
• Masterson, Dan, 282
• Matar, Muhammad Afifi,
283
• Shomer, Enid, 400

**University of California
Press**
2120 Berkeley Way
Berkeley, CA 94720-5874
Phone: 510-643-5036
Fax: 510-643-7127
• Bahu, Sultan, 26
• Bloch, Ariel, and Chana
Bloch, trans., 51
• Gelman, Juan, 159
• Mallarmé, Stéphane, 275
• Rao, Velcheru Narayana, and
David Shulman, trans., 357
• Rothenberg, Jerome and
Pierre Joris, eds., 374

University of Chicago Press
5801 S. Ellis Ave
Chicago, IL 60637
Phone: 773-702-7740
Fax: 773-702-9756
Email:
jlg@press.uchicago.edu
URL:
http://www.press.uchicago.edu
Randy Petilos, Poetry Editor
To Order: 11030 Langley Ave.
Chicago, IL, 60628
• Baudelaire, Charles, 34
• Chitwood, Michael, 88
• Gewanter, David, 160
• Hahn, Susan, 180
• Keller, Lynn, 228
• Longenbach, James, 265
• McMichael, James, 291
• Michelangelo, 299
• Miller, Greg, 300
• Sacks, Peter, 377
• Sommer, Jason, 410
• Williamson, Alan, 465

University of Georgia Press
330 Research Dr.
Athens, GA 30602-4901
Phone: 706-369-6161
Fax: 706-369-6132
Email:
ckhome@ugapress.uga.edu
Stephanie Hansen, Exhibits
and Direct Mail Manager;
Kim Home, Sales and
Exhibits Coordinator
• Brown, Stephanie, 67
• Corless-Smith, Martin, 103
• Daniel, John, ed., 113
• Davis, Christopher, 116
• Hoover, Paul, 205
• Hummell, Austin, 208
• Keelan, Claudia, 227
• McMorris, Mark, 292
• Philpot, Tracy, 344
• Ronk, Martha, 372
• Stewart, Pamela, 418
• Zandvakili, Katayoon, 477

University of Hawai'i Press
2840 Kolowalu St.
Honolulu, HI 96822
Phone: 808-956-8255
Fax: 808-988-6052
Email: uhpmkt@hawaii.edu
URL: http://www2.hawaii.edu/
uhpress
Colins Kawai, Marketing
Manager
• Richman, Paula, 365
• Stanton, Joseph, ed., 415

**University of Hawai'i Press/
Katydid Books**
1 Balsa Road
Santa Fe, NM 87505
Phone: 505-466-9909

• Shuntarô, Tanikawa, 401

**University of Hawai'i
Press/Manoa Books**
2840 Kolowalu St.
Honolulu, HI 96822
Phone: 808-956-8255
Fax: 808-988-6052
• Stewart, Frank, and Arthur
Sze, eds., 417
• Stewart, Frank, and Charlene
Gilmore, eds., 418
• Tam, Reuben, 428

University of Illinois Press
1325 S. Oak Street
Champaign, IL 61820-6903
Phone: 217-333-0950
Fax: 217-244-8082
Email: uipress@uillinois.edu
URL:
http://www.press.uillinois.edu
Laurence Lieberman, Poetry
Editor; Susie Warren,
Marketing
To Order: P.O. Box 4856,
Hampden Post Office,
Baltimore, MD 21211
• Barnes, Jim, 30
• Christie, A.V., 89
• Hart, Henry, 189
• La Fontaine, Jean de, 245
• Makkai, Adam, ed., 275
• Ramsdell, Heather, 355
• Roberts, Len, 369
• Sadoff, Ira, 377
• Shapiro, Karl, 395
• Shapiro, Norman R., trans.,
396
• Swiss, Thomas, 424
• Williams, Miller, 464
• Zanzotto, Andrea, 477

University of Iowa Press
119 West Park Road, 100 Kuhl
House
Iowa City, IA 52242-1000
Phone: 319-335-2000
Fax: 319-335-2055
Email: sarah-walz@uiowa.edu
URL: http://www.uiowa.edu/
~uipress
Paul Zimmer, Director; Tom
Olofson, Publicity
To Order: c/o Chicago
Distribution Ctr., 11030
Langley Ave., Chicago, IL
60628; 800-621-2736; 800-
621-8476 (fax)
• Alexander, Pamela, 9
• Belli, Angela, and Jack
Coulehan, eds., 39
• Galvin, Brendan, 154
• Gildner, Gary, 163
• Gray, Janet, ed., 172
• Hedin, Robert, ed., 193
• Selwyn, David, ed., 392
• Swander, Mary, 423
• Ullman, Leslie, 439
• Webster, Catherine, ed., 456
• Wood, John, 468

**University of Massachusetts
Press**
P.O. Box 429
Amherst, MA 01004
Phone: 413-545-2217
Fax: 413-545-1226
URL: http://www.umass.edu/
umpress
Bruce Wilcox, Editor; Ralph
Kaplan, Marketing Manager
• Bowen, Kevin; Nguyen Ba
Chung, and Bruce Weigl,
eds., 57

• Espada, Martín, ed., 137
• Jacobik, Gray, 213
• Nguyen Quang Thieu, 323
• Rabinowitz, Anna, 353

**University of Massachusetts
Press/Mead Art Museum
at Amherst College**
P.O. Box 429
Amherst, MA 01004
Phone: 413-545-2217
Fax: 413-545-1226
• Danly, Susan, ed., 114

University of Missouri Press
2910 LeMone Blvd
Columbia, MO 65203
Phone: 573-882-7641
Fax: 573-884-4498
Laura J. Choukri, Publicity
and Sales
• Costanzo, Gerald, ed., 105

University of Nebraska Press
312 N 14th St
Lincoln, NE 68588-0484
Phone: 402-472-3581
• Blanchot, Maurice, 49

University of Nevada Press
Mail Stop 166
Reno, NV 89557-0076
Phone: 775-784-6573
Fax: 775-784-6200
Email: cppatt@euinox.unr.edu
Margaret Dalrymple, Editor in
Chief; Chris Patt,
Promotions Manager
To Order: 877-NVBOOKS
• Coles, Katharine, 98
• Louis, Adrian C., 267
• Pahmeier, Gailmarie, 334

• Rawlins, C.L., 359

**University of North Texas
Press**
PO Box 311336
Denton, TX 76203
Phone: 940-565-2142
Fax: 940-565-4590
Email:
gfinn@acad.admin.unt.edu
Charlotte Wright, Associate
Director
• Allen, Paul, 11
• Svenvold, Mark, 423

**University of Notre Dame
Press**
310 Flanner Hall
Notre Dame, IN 46556
Phone: 219-631-6346
Fax: 219631-8148
Email: undpress.1@nd.edu
URL:
http://www.undpress.nd.edu
Dist. by: Chicago Dist. Ctr.
• Holmes, Janet, 203
• Strickland, Stephanie, 420

**University of Pittsburgh
Press**
3347 Forbes Ave
Pittsburgh, PA 15261
Phone: 412-383-2456
Fax: 412-383-2466
Email: press@pitt.edu
URL:
http://www.pitt.edu/~press
Ed Ochester, Poetry Editor;
Colleen M. Salcius,
Publicity
Dist. by: CUP
• Blanco, Richard, 49

• Collins, Billy, 98
• Conkling, Helen, 99
• Cox, Mark, 105
• Daniels, Jim, 114
• Derricotte, Toi, 122
• Fay, Julie, 140
• Glazer, Michele, 165
• Joseph, Allison, 222
• Kasdorf, Julia, 226
• Levis, Larry, 257
• Noguchi, Rick, 325
• Ostriker, Alicia Suskin, 333
• Rawson, Joanna, 359
• Shepherd, Reginald, 398
• Wallace, Ronald, 450
• Wojahn, David, 467

**University of Puerto Rico
Press**
Vick Center
867 Muñoz Rivera Ave
San Juan, Puerto Rico 00931-
3322
Phone: 787-250-0050
Fax: 787-753-9116
Dr. José de la Torre, Poetry
Editor
• Marzán, Julio, 282

**University of South Carolina
Press**
937 Assembly St., 8th Floor
Columbia, SC 29208
Phone: 803-777-5231
Fax: 803-777-0160
Email: mdchow@sc.edu
URL:
http://www.sc.edu/uscpress/
Richard Howard, Poetry
Editor; Minna Chow,
Publicity
To Order: 718 Devine Street,

Columbia, SC 29208;
800-768-2500; 800-868-
0740 (fax)
• Bloomfield, Maureen, 52
• Cummins, James, 111
• Getty, Sarah, 160
• Lesser, Rika, 255
• Magowan, Robin, 273
• Rosen, Michael J., 373
• Sloss, Henry, 405
• Wade, Sidney, 446

**University of Washington
Press**
P.O. Box 50096
Seattle, WA 98145
Phone: 206-543-4050
• Mitsui, James Masao, 304

**University of Wisconsin
Press**
2537 Daniels St.
Madison, WI 53718-6772
Phone: 608-224-3900
Fax: 608-224-3897
Email:
uwiscpress@macc.wisc.edu
URL: http://www.wisc.edu/
wisconsinpress/
Rosalie Robertson, Editor;
Joan Strasbaugh, Publicity
To Order: Chicago
Distribution Center, 11030
So. Langley Ave, Chicago,
IL 60628; 800-621-2736;
800-621-8476 (fax)
• Bloch, Chana, 51
• Davis, Olena Kalytiak, 117
• Paola, Suzanne, 336
• Sholl, Betsy, 400

University Press of

**Colorado/Center for
Literary Publishing**
PO Box 849
Niwot, CO 80544
Phone: 800-268-6044
Fax: 303-530-5306
Email:
prattd@stripe.colorado.edu
Luther Wilson, Editor; Salem
Martin, Publicity
• Beasley, Bruce, 35
• White, Michael, 461

University Press of Florida
15 NW 15th St.
Gainesville, FL 32611-2079
Phone: 352-392-1351
Fax: 352-392-7302
Email: ml@upf.com
URL: http://www.upf.com
Deidre Bryant, Editor; Beth
Kent, Publicity
To Order: 800-226-3822
• Bates, Jennifer, 33
• Calbert, Cathleen, 76
• Skellings, Edmund, 403
• Snively, Susan, 408

**University Press of
Kentucky**
no address
• Smock, Frederick, ed., 408

**University Press of New
England/Brandeis
University Press**
23 S Main St
Hanover, NH 03755
Phone: 603-643-7100
Fax: 603-643-1540
• Agosín, Marjorie, 5

University Press of New England/Middlebury College Press
23 S Main St
Hanover, NH 03755
Phone: 603-643-7100
Fax: 603-643-1540
• Bang, Mary Jo, 29
• loncar, m., 264

University Press of New England/Wesleyan University Press
23 S Main St
Hanover, NH 03755
Phone: 603-643-7100
Fax: 603-643-1540
Email: university.press@dartmouth.edu
URL: www.dartmouth.edu/acad-indt/upne/
Suzanna Tamminen Poetry Editor; Sherry Strickland, Publicity
• Bedient, Cal, 37
• Bogen, Don, 53
• Cage, John, 74
• Dickey, James, 124
• Fraser, Kathleen, 149
• Hadas, Rachel, 179
• Hillman, Brenda, 198
• Ignatow, David, 210
• Komunyakaa, Yusef, 239
• Powell, D.A., 348
• Raz, Hilda, 360
• Revell, Donald, 362
• Shapiro, Harvey, 395
• Vicuña, Cecilia, 444
• Yu Xuanji, 475

Utah State University Press
Logan, UT 84322-7800

Phone: 801-797-1362
Fax: 801-797-0313
Michael Spooner, Poetry Editor
• Freisinger, Randall R., 149
• Williams, Lisa, 464

Van Alstine, Ruth
no address
• Van Alstine, Ruth, 441

Vatic Hum Press
no address
Dist. by: SPD
• Hill, Lindsay, 197
• Hoefer, David, 200
• Nóto, John, 326

Vida Publishing
PO Box 296
Glyndon, MD 21071-0296
• Roth, Paul B., 374

Viet Nam Generation/ Burning Cities Press
PO Box 13746
Tucson, AZ 85732
Phone: 520-790-9218
Fax: 520-790-9218
Email: kali@kavtal.com
URL: http://jefferson.village.virginia.edu/sixties/
Steven Gomes
• Jaffe, Maggie, 215

Vintage Books
c/o Random House
201 East 50th St.
New York, NY 10022
Phone: 212-751-2600
Fax: 212-572-4949

URL:
http://www.randomhouse.com
Dan Menaker, Editor;
  Elizabeth Fogarty, Publicity
• Connaroe, Joel, ed., 100
• Petras, Kathryn,and Ross
  Petras, eds., 342

Vista Publishing
422 Morris Ave., Ste. 1
Long Branch, NJ 07740
Phone: 732-229-6500
Fax: 732-229-9647
Email: info@vistapubl.com
URL: http://www.vistpubl.com
Carolyn S. Zagury, Poetry
  Editor
• Battaglia, Carol, 33
• Johnston-Rowbotham, 219
• Schaefer, Judy, 386

**Wake Forest University
  Press**
PO Box 7333
Winston-Salem, NC 27109
Phone: 336-758-5448
Fax: 336-758-4691
Email: wfupress@wfu.edu
URL:
  http://www.wfu.edu/wfu.edu
Candide Jones, Manager;
  Dillon Johnston, Director
• Bishop, Michael, trans., 48
• Carson, Ciaran, 79
• Carson, Ciaran, 80
• Carson, Ciaran, 80
• Mahon, Derek, 273
• McGuckian, Medbh, 290
• McGuckian, Medbh, 291

**Washington Writers'
  Publishing House**

PO Box 15271
Washington, DC 20003
Phone: 202-546-9865
Email: johnsond@wfs.org
Dan Johnson, Editor; Jean
  Nordhaus, Publicity
• Balbo, Ned, 28
• Carlson, Nancy Naomi, 78
• D., Ramola, 112
• Gold, Sid, 167

Waterways Project/NYPL
no address
• Spiegel, Richard, and
  Barbara Fisher, Co-
  Directors, 413
• Spiegel, Richard, and
  Barbara Fisher, Co-
  Directors, 414

**Wayne State University
  Press**
4809 Woodward Avenue
Detroit, MI 48201-1309
Phone: 313-577-2109
Fax: 313-577-6131
Email:
  sarah.a.james@wayne.edu
URL:
  http://libraries.wayne.edu/
  wsupress/index.html
Kathy Wildong, Editor
• Delp, Michael, 120
• Gouri, Haim, 170
• Siamanto, 401

**Wayne State University
  Press/Great Lakes Books**
• Tudor, Stephen, 438

Weatherhill
568 Broadway, Suite 705

New York, NY 10012
Phone: 212-966-3080
Fax: 212-966-4860
Carolyn Sevos, Marketing
  Assistant
• Addiss, Stephen, with
  Fumiko and Akira
  Yamamoto, 3

**Weatherhill/Institute for
Medieval Japanese Studies**
• Heinrich, Amy V., ed., 193

Werner, Marshall
no address
• Werner, Marshall, 459

West End Press
PO Box 27334
Albuquerque, NM 87125
Phone: 505-345-5729
Fax: 505-345-5729
John F. Crawford, Publisher
Dist. by: University of New
  Mexico Press
• Allen, Paula Gunn, 11
• Babb, Sanora, 26
• Henson, Lance, 195
• Lim, Shirley Geok-lin, 260
• Luzzaro, Susan, 270
• northSun, nila, 326
• Quiñonez, Naomi, 352
• Romero, Levi, 372

**Westminster John Knox
Press**
100 Witherspoon St.
Louisville, KY 40202-1396
Phone: 502-569-5058
Fax: 502-569-5113
Email:
  amcclure@ctr.pcusa.org

URL: http://www.pcusa.org/
  ppc/wjkcatlg/wjk.htm
Annie McClure, Publicist;
  Stephanie Egnotovich,
  Editor
• Rice, Howard L., and Lamar
  Williamson, Jr., eds., 364

Whelks Walk Press
37 Harvest Lane
Southhampton, NY 11968
Phone: 516-283-5122
Fax: 516-283-1902
Email: whelkswalk@aol.com
Joan Peternel, Editor
• Peternel, Joan, 342

**White Eagle Coffee Store
Press**
PO Box 383
Fox River Grove, IL 60021-
  0383
Phone: 847-639-9200
Email: wecspress@aol.com
URL: http://members.aol.com/
  wecpress
Frank Smith, Publisher
• Bartley, Jackie, 32
• Brown-Davidson, Terri, 67
• Harper, Linda Lee, 187
• Russell, Timothy, 376
• Villani, Luisa, 444

White Hawk Press
950 Jenifer Street
Madison, WI 53703
• Roberts, James P., ed., 368

White Pine Press
PO Box 236
Buffalo, NY 14201-0236
Phone: 716-672-5743

Fax: 716-672-4724
Email: wpine@whitepine.org
URL:
  http://www.whitepine.org
Elaine La Mattina, Director
• Agosín, Marjorie, 5
• Agosín, Marjorie, 5
• Debeljak, Ales, ed., 120
• Gorlin, Deborah, 170
• Johnson, Jacqueline, 218
• Johnson, Peter, 219
• Kim, Chiha, 231
• Kloefkorn, William, 235
• Neruda, Pablo, 321
• Salamun, Tomaz, 380

**Wild Variety Books/Olsen's
  Publishing**
1013 Faton St
Missoula, MT 59801
• Thomas, David E., 431

**Winthrop University Poetry
  Series**
no address
• Prufer, Kevin, 351

**Woman in the Moon
  Publications**
1409 The Alameda
San Jose, CA 95126
Phone: 408-27-WOMAN
Fax: 408-279-6636
Email:
womaninmoon@earthlink.net
URL: http://www.woman in
  the moon.com
Dr. SD Adamz-Bogus,
  Publisher/Editor; Jaime
  Wright, Publicity
• Bogomolny, Abby, 54

Word Works
PO Box 42164
Washington, DC 20015
Phone: 301-652-7638
Fax: 301-656-1309
URL: http://www.writer.org/
  wordwork/wordwrk1.htm
Hilary Tham, Editor; Karen A.
  Alenier, President
To Order: PO Box 416;
  Hedgesville, WV 25427-
  0416
Dist. by: Bunny and Crocodile
  Press
• Cavalieri, Grace, 84
• Jonas, Ann Rae, 219
• Young, George, 475

**Word Works/Writer's
  Center Editions**
• Schaffner, M.A., 386

WordCraft Books
910 Marion St., 1008
Seattle, WA 98104-1273
Phone: 206-621-1376
• Taylor, Velande, 429

Words & Pictures Press
1921 Sherry Lane, Apt. 87
Santa Ana, CA 92705
Phone: 714-544-7282
• Blehert, Dean, 50
• Blehert, Dean, 50

Writer's Center Editions
4508 Walsh Street
Bethesda, MD 20815
Phone: 301-654-8664
Fax: 301-654-8667
• Jason, Philip K.; Barbara
  Goldberg, Geraldine

Connolly, and Roland Flint,
eds., 216

**Writers and Readers
Publishing/Harlem River
Press**
625 Broadway, 10th Flr.
New York, NY 10012
Phone: 212-982-3158
Fax: 212-777-4924
Patricia Allen, Poetry Editor
• bandele, ashe, 28
• Cinader, Martha, 90
• Hammad, Suheir, 184

Writers & Books
740 University Ave.
Rochester, NY 14607
Phone: 716-473-2590
Fax: 716-729-0982
URL: http://www.wab.org
Joe Flaherty, Director
• Cohn, Jim, 96

Writers' Center Press
PO Box 88386
Indianapolis, IN 46208
• Krajeck, Elizabeth A., 241
• Pflum, Richard, 343

Wyzard, Jim, Publisher
no address
• Rothenberg, Joyce Andrea,
374

Xenos Books
PO Box 52152
Riverside, CA 92517-3152
Phone: 909-370-2229
• Allen, William, 12
• Azzopardi, Maria, 25
• de Palchi, Alfredo, 119

Yale University Press
PO Box 209040
New Haven, CT 06520-9040
Phone: 203-432-0956
Fax: 203-432-8485
URL:
http://www.yale.edu/yup/
Robert Flynn, Exhibits
Coordinator; Ruth.Kramer,
Exhibits Assistant
• Ansel, Talvikki, 17
• Bradley, George, ed., 58
• Raffel, Burton, trans., 354

Yankee Oracle Press
c/o Magick Mirror
Communications
511 Avenue of the Americas,
Ste 173
New York, NY 10011-8436
URL: www.yankeeoracle.org
• Macer-Story, Eugenia, 272

Ye Olde Font Shoppe
PO Box 8328
New Haven, CT 06708
Phone: 203-575-9385
Email: yeolde@webcom.com
URL:
http://www.webcom.com/
yeolde
Victoria Rivas, Publisher
• Albrizio, Eileen, 8
• Borczon, Mark, 55
• Lerner, Linda, 254
• Moffeit, Tony, 304
• Rice, Patty, 364
• Richards, Tad, 364
• Richards, Tad, 364
• Rivas, Victoria, 367
• Rivas, Victoria, ed., 367
• Savitt, Lynne, 385

• Summers, Rita, 422

Zerx Press
725 Van Buren Place SE
Albuquerque, NM 87108
Phone: 505-255-3012
Mark Weber, Publisher/Editor
• Locklin, Gerald, 262
• Weber, Mark, 456
• Weber, Mark, 456
• Weber, Mark, 456

Zohar Press
PO Box 250367, Columbia
    University Station
New York, NY 10025-1536
Phone: 212-932-1854
Danny Cohen, Publisher
• Fried, Philip, 150

Zoland Books
384 Huron Ave.
Cambridge, MA 02138
Phone: 617-864-6252
Fax: 617-661-4998
Email: azl.zoland@aol.com
Roland F. Pease, Jr.,
    Editor/Publisher; Alysia
    Linsenmayer, Publicity
• Arroyo, Rane, 19
• Cornish, Sam, 104
• Franco, Michael, 148
• Lease, Joseph, 253
• Payack, Peter, 339
• Sloman, Joel, 405

Zombie Logic Press
420 E. Third St, Box 319
Byron, IL 61010
Phone: 815-874-7265
Email: dobe1969@aol.com
• Vaultonburg, Thomas L., 442

Key to the Index
by Publisher

The Index by Publisher provides the office address, as well as phone, fax, e-mail and website informations for each of the presses whose books are represented in this volume. Ordering addresses, when they differ, follow. Then a contact person at the press is provides. The distributors and wholesalers who carry the books are given (see below for the phone numbers of those which appear most often.) Finally the authors published by the press and described in this volume are listed.

B&T	Baker and Taylor, 800-775-1100
	Bookmasters, 800-247-5663
Bpl	Bookpeople, 800-999-4650
	Consortium, 800-283-3572
	Ingram, 800-937-8000
SPD	Small Press Distribution, 510-524-1668
	Spring Arbor, 800-395-5599